MORAL KNOWLEDGE

MORAL KNOWLEDGE

Edited by

**Ellen Frankel Paul, Fred D. Miller, Jr.,
and Jeffrey Paul**

CAMBRIDGE
UNIVERSITY PRESS

CAMBRIDGE
UNIVERSITY PRESS

32 Avenue of the Americas, New York NY 10013-2473, USA

Cambridge University Press is part of the University of Cambridge.

It furthers the University's mission by disseminating knowledge in the pursuit of
education, learning and research at the highest international levels of excellence.

www.cambridge.org
Information on this title: www.cambridge.org/9780521006033

First published 2001

A catalogue record for this publication is available from the British Library

Library of Congress Cataloguing in Publication data

Moral Knowledge / edited by Ellen Frankel Paul,
Fred D. Miller, Jr., and Jeffrey Paul.   p.   cm.
Includes bibliographical references and index.
ISBN 0-521-00603-1 (pbk.)
1. Ethics.
I. Paul, Ellen Frankel.   II. Miller, Fred Dycus, 1944–
III. Paul, Jeffrey.
BJ1012 .M6325   2001
170–dc21   2001025328
                      CIP

ISBN 978-0-521-00603-3 Paperback

CONTENTS

INTRODUCTION

Philosophers since ancient times have pondered how we can know whether moral claims are true or false. Aristotle (386–322 B.C.) called attention to this concern in his *Nicomachean Ethics*: "Now fine and just actions admit of much variety and fluctuation of opinion, so that they may be thought to exist only by convention, and not by nature." The first half of the twentieth century witnessed widespread skepticism concerning the possibility of moral knowledge. Indeed, some argued that moral statements lacked cognitive content altogether, because they were not susceptible to empirical verification. The British philosopher A. J. Ayer, for example, contended in his seminal work, *Language, Truth, and Logic* (1936), that "sentences which simply express moral judgements do not say anything. They are pure expressions of feeling and as such do not come under the category of truth and falsehood. They are unverifiable for the same reason as a cry of pain or a word of command is unverifiable — because they do not express genuine propositions."

The second half of the twentieth century brought a revival of interest among philosophers in moral and political questions. Part of that revival consisted in a vigorous debate over the veracity of the earlier skepticism over the possibility of moral knowledge. Whether or not ethics can be founded upon a rational basis continues to roil the philosophical community at the dawn of the new century, with no consensus likely on these enduring questions: Can morality be founded upon facts about human nature, social agreement, volition, subjective preference, *a priori* reasoning, intuition, or some other basis? Is morality knowable in any objective sense that would make it universal and, therefore, binding on humans in all times, places, and circumstances? Or, rather, is morality inherently subjective, culture bound, or more radically still, uniquely determined by each individual for that individual? Is there an answer to Ayer's progeny who maintain that it is misguided even to think in terms of moral knowledge, on the grounds that moral utterances are expressions of feelings or attitudes rather than claims that can be known to be true or false?

The thirteen essays in this volume — written by prominent philosophers of diverse perspectives — represent the latest thinking on these questions in moral epistemology. Some authors argue for versions of moral realism and also address concerns raised by their antirealist critics. Others focus on our moral beliefs and intuitions, asking whether our reliance on them is rendered hopelessly problematic by their tenuous connection to factual matters or by the presence of moral disagreement. Several essays examine aspects of practical reason, showing how certain accounts of reason and desire can generate important consequences for other aspects of ethical theory. Still others analyze the theories of seminal thinkers in moral philosophy, assessing how they treat moral knowledge and justification.

In the volume's first essay, "Realist-Expressivism: A Neglected Option for Moral Realism," David Copp argues that elements from two seemingly opposed metaethical theories can be reconciled into a theoretically attractive position. Copp begins by explaining that moral realism holds that our moral judgments express beliefs and refer to moral properties, whereas expressivism—a position that is typically a component of antirealist theories—holds that moral judgments are expressions of attitudes or motivational states. Often thought incompatible, Copp shows that realism and expressivism can be combined into one coherent view: realist-expressivism. Though numerous realist-expressivist views are logically possible, Copp spends much of the essay elaborating upon his own preferred account. Under this account, moral judgments involve beliefs whose truth can be assessed by referring to the standards that would be involved were a society to follow the social moral code that would best meet its needs. At the same time, Copp claims, because moral terms have what Frege called "coloring," one's moral judgments also express a distinctive kind of motivational state—namely, they express one's subscription to the relevant moral standards. Respectively, these two points represent the realist and expressivist aspects of Copp's proposal. Copp concludes his essay by noting ways in which realist-expressivist views can address certain important metaethical disputes. In particular, realist-expressivism is able to account for intuitions fueling internalist accounts of the connection between moral belief and motivation, yet is itself compatible with externalism. Furthermore, realist-expressivism is also capable of accounting for various beliefs that underlie antirealism, while remaining fully realist. With these virtues, Copp says, realist-expressivism is an interesting metaethical alternative worthy of further consideration.

The volume's next pair of essays focus on aspects of our moral beliefs and intuitions. In "Thinking about Cases," Shelly Kagan begins by noting the prominent role that our intuitions about particular cases (case specific intuitions) play in our arguments about moral claims and theories. In such arguments, it seems we treat case specific intuitions as generating evidence upon which we can rely. How, Kagan asks, can we justify such reliance? The primary way such justification proceeds is by pointing to an analogy between moral intuition and empirical observation. Our observations about the world certainly seem relevant to tests of empirical theories, so this analogy goes, and our moral intuitions are likewise relevant to tests of moral theories. Kagan argues, however, that this analogy goes awry at a crucial point: whereas we have been able to construct empirical theories that largely endorse our empirical observations, we have not been able to develop an explanatorily adequate moral theory that incorporates our moral intuitions in like fashion. Thus, the evidentiary value of our moral intuitions is questionable at best. The upshot,

Kagan claims, is that with respect to our moral intuitions we must accept some form of error theory, under which many of our moral beliefs are mistaken. There is room under error theories for people to have justified moral intuitions, but which intuitions these are will depend on the specifications of whatever error theory is utilized. As Kagan shows, determining which error theory correctly reflects the reliability of our moral intuitions is difficult given factors such as widespread moral disagreement. In the end, Kagan concludes, our use of moral intuitions will inevitably continue, but their use remains problematic to the core.

George Sher's essay, "But I Could Be Wrong," also touches on the phenomenon of moral disagreement. Sher commences by noting how John Stuart Mill and John Rawls point to the contingent nature of one's moral beliefs as raising a challenge to the authority of one's moral judgments. This realization, though congenial to liberal political principles, is problematic when we engage in moral deliberation as individuals. In such deliberation, we often find that we disagree with others. If our moral judgments are based merely on contingent factors of upbringing and background, then using them to justify our actions, when others disagree, is troubling. Thus, the authority of our moral judgments is put in question both because of the contingency of our moral beliefs and the presence of moral disagreement. One might be tempted to argue that the challenge to our moral judgments rests only on one of these factors, rendering the other superfluous, but Sher shows that if we are to confront the challenge to our judgments in its strongest form, we must assume that premises of both sorts are in play. Though it is possible that the moral judgments of individuals would converge if people were to engage in rational reflection, Sher argues that this will not be enough to establish the possibility that one's own judgments are authoritative. In conclusion, he states that we may well have to reconcile ourselves to the fact that though we have rational reasons for following our own moral judgments, the truth or justifiability of these judgments may nevertheless be dubious.

Brian Leiter's "Moral Facts and Best Explanations," presses several prominent accounts of moral realism on their inability to meet the "best-explanation test." According to a popular argument supporting realist positions in the philosophies of mind and science, only those properties that fit into the best explanation of the world can qualify as real properties. The implication of this for moral realism is that it must show that moral properties fit into such an explanation. Leiter argues that this is a daunting task. He proceeds to examine two criteria by which we can evaluate explanatory accounts: consilience and simplicity. Applying these criteria to various explanatory accounts of moral judgments, he finds that moral explanations compare unfavorably with explanations provided by evolutionary psychology and psychoanalytic theory. Faced with this hurdle, the moral realist will be forced to argue for two claims: first, that moral facts are supervenient upon or identical to other, nonmoral explanatory facts; and second, that without moral facts we suffer an explanatory loss (or some similar epistemic loss) in our ability to understand the world. However, in surveying the work of prominent moral realists—Geoffrey Sayre-McCord, David Brink, and Joshua Cohen—Leiter concludes that none of their versions of moral realism truly shows that moral facts provide us with a significant explanatory gain. As a result, it seems that the best explanatory account of the world will not include moral properties, and that, therefore, such properties should not be deemed real.

Our use of terms that invoke moral properties raises an important question: where in human experience are moral terms and concepts grounded? Where in experience, that is, does the moral become salient to us? In his essay "Two Sources of Morality," Philip Pettit attempts to answer this question by providing a naturalistic genealogy of moral conceptualization. Though humans are intentional creatures who can form and act on beliefs and desires, this in itself does not establish that humans use any sort of normative concepts. As discursive creatures, however, humans engage in a practice that depends upon our giving terms common meanings. As a result, Pettit shows, expressing our thoughts through discourse demands that we follow various norms of inferential reasoning. In this way, normative concepts, though not moral concepts proper, secure a role in human conceptual thought. The emergence of moral concepts, Pettit explains, could come about in two separate ways. First, as we privilege discourse as a form of interaction, the fact that such discourse involves norms of rationality will mean that the practice itself will also involve norms concerning how interactive discourse should take place. Certain methods of expression are inconsistent with the purpose of such discourse, and terms with ethical force will arise so that we may condemn such types of expression. Alternatively, ethical concepts might emerge as we attempt to use discourse to express our sentiments in such a way as to guide others' reasons for action. These two separate sources of ethical conceptualization, Pettit notes in closing, bear connections to the important divide in contemporary ethical theory between deontology and consequentialism.

Communicating with others also plays a key role in Stephen Darwall's contribution to this volume, "'Because I Want It.'" In his essay, Darwall asks how an agent's desire or will can give him reasons for acting. In the past, many philosophers argued that all reasons for acting are based in the agent's desires, but this view is now widely rejected in favor of a vision in which desires are only in the "background" of an agent's deliberations. Some might argue that accounts of instrumental reasoning and hypothetical imperatives, or of desire's "direction of fit," could provide a way for desires to ground reasons, but Darwall shows that none of these options can really accomplish this task. What is key to the reason-giving character of one's desires is the fact that unlike one's theoretical perspective, which only gives one reasons to act to the extent that it accurately reflects the world, one's practical perspective, based in one's will, cannot be treated as though it is a mere appearance reflecting some outside phenomenon. Because of this, Darwall argues, an agent's will can have a reason-giving character rooted in one's standing as one rational agent among others. One discovers this in one's interactions with others. In making claims on another, one attempts to give the other reasons for action by engaging in "second-personal" address, which by its nature involves reciprocal recognition of one's standing as a free and rational agent. As one finds that other free and rational agents have reasons for action based in their wills, one realizes that because of one's own status as a free and rational agent, one's own will also has a reason-giving character.

The next two essays consider the interrelationship between moral realism and ethical naturalism. In "Realism, Naturalism, and Moral Semantics," David O. Brink provides an explanation and defense of the semantic commitments of those who would defend both realism and naturalism in ethics. He begins by revisiting G. E. Moore's famous attack on ethical naturalism in the "open question" argument and the recent strategy of defending ethical naturalism by appeal to the direct-reference tradition. Brink defends this strategy against arguments that direct reference implies both an antirealism form of semantic relativism and the obsolescence of moral reasoning in ascertaining the extension of moral predicates. Replies to these arguments can be made within the semantic tradition that treats the reference of moral terms as a function of the properties of people, actions, and institutions that causally regulate their use. But, Brink argues, this tradition is unable to deliver a sufficiently robust form of moral realism. A more promising line of response, he claims, appeals to the importance of referential intentions in fixing the reference of terms. On one such view, terms pick out moral properties just in case speakers have or inherit the intention to refer to properties of people, actions, and institutions that allow them to justify their conduct to others. Such an account provides a common subject matter about which adherents of rival moral codes can have a disagreement in belief, and it explains the role of moral reasoning in ascertaining the extension of moral predicates. This semantic view does not establish the truth of moral realism or ethical naturalism, but it undermines various semantic objections to combining the two.

In "Incomplete Routes to Moral Objectivity: Four Variants of Naturalism," David Sidorsky surveys four prominent accounts of ethical naturalism and discusses the problems that each faces in its attempt to establish that morality is objective. Under Aristotelian naturalism, objective moral norms are rooted in human nature and are discoverable in the same way that we can uncover norms concerning other species. There are important problems with this view, but Hume's naturalism seems to avoid many of them by linking ethics to the idea of an impartial hypothetical observer. As Sidorsky shows, though, applying Hume's theory to particular cases is difficult, throwing into doubt whether Hume's brand of naturalism is practical. In Deweyan ethical theory, competing moral hypotheses can be tested through a process of scientific inquiry in which the hypotheses are compared with respect to their consequences. However, this posited connection between ethics and scientific inquiry is questionable on several counts. The failures of these naturalistic projects and the development of various nonnaturalist theories in the early twentieth century gave rise to Sidorsky's fourth kind of ethical naturalism—linguistic naturalism. On this view, an intrinsic connection exists between the ascription or predication of moral terms and the reasons given for their use. Accordingly, such terms can be used in objectively correct or incorrect ways, depending upon the truth or falsity of the given reasons. Noting that this linguistic naturalist project hinges on whether "reason" has a fixed meaning in moral discourse, Sidorsky examines several objections to this claim and suggests that they each have telling weaknesses. Though linguistic naturalism does not provide a method of resolving moral disagreements, he concludes, it is able to ground the claim that moral judgments can be objective.

One important dispute in metaethics concerns internalism, the idea that moral claims have intrinsic motivational force. In "Explanation, Internalism, and Reasons for Action," David Sobel argues that an important contemporary argument in this debate is misguided. Bernard Williams is well known for advocating internalism, but Sobel claims that Williams's argument for the position misfires for two reasons. First, noting that Williams bases his argument for internalism on an "explanation condition," Sobel shows that various ways of interpreting this condition fail to truly support the internalist view. Sobel's second attack on Williams's position emerges from a discussion about accounts of reasons for action. Sobel is a subjectivist about reasons for action: he believes that an agent's subjective motivational set is the ultimate determinant of whether an agent has a reason to do something. Surveying various subjectivist positions, Sobel argues that the most plausible are ideal advisor accounts, according to which a person has a reason to perform some action if and only if an ideally informed version of himself would recommend that he do so. Under such accounts, however, one's own reasons for action may differ from the reasons for action held by an idealized version of oneself. As a result, we must reject both the most plausible interpretation of Williams's explanation condition and internalism itself. Sobel ends his essay by noting that the upshot of this argument is that since subjectivism and internalism are incompatible, the really interesting philosophical questions involving reasons for action may hinge not on the dispute between internalists and externalists, but rather on that between subjectivists and objectivists.

The final four essays in this volume take an historical perspective to questions in moral epistemology. In her "Moral Knowledge as Practical

Knowledge," Julia Annas compares modern views on moral epistemology with Platonic and other ancient views. J. L. Mackie, among other recent philosophers, has complained that Plato's theory of moral "Forms" is metaphysically dubious. Annas's response to Mackie is that he works under problematic assumptions representative of modern moral epistemology, and she suggests that a truer understanding of the ancients renders Mackie's complaint ill-founded. To the ancients, moral knowledge was seen as a kind of practical knowledge. Rather than involving an improved epistemic state with respect to a particular fact, "knowledge" on this model of epistemology involves acquiring an understanding of what underlies and unifies various facts that belong to a common subject matter. That practical knowledge of this sort is possible seems evident given the wide variety of practical expertise we see all around us. Skills such as speaking French or repairing computers, for example, clearly involve a sort of knowledge, one that is teachable and involves the ability to provide articulate explanations within a particular field. Annas argues that the ancients saw moral knowledge in analogous fashion, as a kind of practical expertise about how to live well and do the right thing. Seen this way, moral knowledge is hardly metaphysically puzzling. To the contrary, Annas shows that the assumptions Mackie uses to reject moral knowledge, if applied consistently, would force Mackie to reject the possibility of ordinary practical expertise of the kind we observe every day.

James Bernard Murphy's essay also compares ancient and modern views. In "Practical Reason and Moral Psychology in Aristotle and Kant," Murphy lays out Aristotle's and Kant's radically different conceptions of practical reason, and explores the implications of this difference for each scholar's ethical views. For Aristotle, "practical wisdom" involves the quest for happiness, which mainly consists in intellectual and moral excellence, while for Kant, practical reason is sharply divided between the merely prudential quest for happiness and the moral quest for virtue. These divergent views of practical reason stem from Aristotle's and Kant's differing understandings of both human nature and the moral psychology of agents. Aristotle has confidence that practical wisdom can shape our desires, passions, skills, habits, and temperament so that all of these things are internally oriented toward the good. In contrast, Kant has much less confidence that practical reason can effect such a unity. Thus, for Kant our nonmoral capacities and dispositions will always be alienated to a large degree from moral reason. Because of this, Kant liberates moral action from contingent facts of one's upbringing and abilities; he counsels that we should set these factors aside and act from rational principle alone. Aristotle suggests that we cannot achieve such radical freedom from our nature through rational thought, for he conceives of moral goodness as being inextricably linked to our natural skills and acquired habits. Though there are undoubtedly cases of individuals overcoming their character in Kantian fashion, Murphy thinks that these examples only partially obscure the deep influence that character has on agents.

Kant is the focus of our next essay as well. Thomas E. Hill, Jr.'s topic is "Hypothetical Consent in Kantian Constructivism." Broadly speaking, Kantian constructivism refers to the view that moral principles are "constructions" of certain procedures of thought or will. In his ethical writings, Kant offers numerous constructivist procedures for determining which moral principles one ought to accept; the grounding of these justificatory procedures is an important component of Kant's moral epistemology. Hill sets out to ascertain how three different forms of consent—actual, possible, and hypothetical—fit into this Kantian framework. To do this, Hill examines Kant's various formulations of the Categorical Imperative as well as Kant's idea of an original contract. On the basis of this survey, Hill argues that actual consent plays only a derivative and qualified role in determining how we ought to be treated. Kant's more basic standard is that practices are justified only if we, as rational agents, could consent to them. This seems to suggest that possible consent is of primary importance, yet Hill shows that to apply this standard, we have to make assumptions about the context of choice and the principles of rationality that determine what it is possible, in the relevant sense, for agents to will. Once this is understood, the possible-consent standard is equivalent to a hypothetical-consent standard under which practices are condemned if they are contrary to principles that any rational agent would will under specified conditions. Though there are numerous objections to particular versions of hypothetical consent, Hill probes several of these criticisms and demonstrates that Kant's theory is able to withstand them.

Our final essay, Geoffrey Sayre-McCord's "Mill's 'Proof' of the Principle of Utility: A More than Half-Hearted Defense," shifts our attention from Kant to Mill, though Kant will still make an appearance. The third paragraph of Chapter IV of Mill's *Utilitarianism* is Sayre-McCord's target; it is famous for its seemingly rampant fallacies. If the paragraph is examined in the context of the full work, Sayre-McCord claims that these "fallacies" appear only if one misinterprets Mill's aims. For example, Mill claims in this paragraph that just as the only proof that one can have that something is visible is that people see it, so it is that the only proof one can have that something is desirable is that people desire it. Numerous scholars have argued that with this move Mill embraces a "naturalistic fallacy" of thinking that evaluative concepts can be defined in naturalistic terms. In contrast, Sayre-McCord suggests that Mill is not claiming here that being desired and being desirable are equivalent, but rather that our desires are what provide us with evidence for our value judgments. In particular, the fact that people desire their own happiness suggests that they are committed to the claim that their own happiness is valuable. Next, Sayre-McCord examines another "fallacy"—Mill's apparent leap from the claim that each person values his own happiness to the claim

that each person should value the happiness of all. Sayre-McCord proposes that Mill's argument here is that acceptance of the value of one's
own happiness carries with it the implication that one must agree that
when others secure happiness, they have acquired something of value as
well. The general structure of this argument, Sayre-McCord illustrates, is
similar to that employed by Kant to show that if one values one's rational
nature as granting one standing as an end, one is committed to the proposition that other people also have standing as ends because of their own
rational natures. Thus, Mill and Kant—representatives of moral positions
usually considered antipodal—utilize a similar argumentative structure
at key points in the justification of their moral theories.

The thirteen essays in this volume span the ancients and moderns, and
represent most of the competing views in contemporary discussions of
moral epistemology.

ACKNOWLEDGMENTS

The editors wish to acknowledge several individuals at the Social Philosophy and Policy Center, Bowling Green State University, who provided invaluable assistance in the preparation of this volume. They include Mary Dilsaver, Terrie Weaver, Carrie-Ann Biondi, and Pamela Phillips.

The editors would like to extend special thanks to Publication Specialist Tamara Sharp, for attending to innumerable day-to-day details of the book's preparation; and to Managing Editor Matthew Buckley, for providing dedicated assistance throughout the editorial and production process.

CONTRIBUTORS

David Copp is Professor of Philosophy at Bowling Green State University, and a Senior Research Fellow at the Social Philosophy and Policy Center at Bowling Green State University. He taught previously at the University of California, Davis, the University of Illinois at Chicago, and Simon Fraser University. He is the author of *Morality, Normativity, and Society* (1995) and of many articles in moral and political philosophy. He is also an Associate Editor of *Ethics*.

Shelly Kagan is Henry R. Luce Professor of Social Thought and Ethics at Yale University. He is the author of *The Limits of Morality* (1989) and *Normative Ethics* (1998), and of numerous articles in ethical theory. Much of his work has focused on the debate between consequentialism and deontology; he has also written on the nature of well-being and the concept of intrinsic value. He is currently at work on a book entitled *The Geometry of Desert*.

George Sher is Herbert S. Autrey Professor of Philosophy at Rice University. He is the author of *Desert* (1987), *Beyond Neutrality: Perfectionism and Politics* (1997), and *Approximate Justice: Studies in Non-Ideal Theory* (1997). He has written widely on topics in social and political philosophy; his articles have been published in the *Journal of Philosophy*, *Philosophy and Public Affairs*, *Ethics*, *Noûs*, and numerous other journals. He is currently writing a book on blame.

Brian Leiter is Charles I. Francis Professor in the School of Law, Professor of Philosophy, and Director of the Law and Philosophy Program at the University of Texas at Austin. Coeditor of the journal *Legal Theory*, he is also editor of *Objectivity in Law and Morals* (2001) and author of *Nietzsche on Morality* (2001). He has written on various topics in legal philosophy, ethics, Continental philosophy, and philosophy of mind; his articles have appeared, among other places, in *Ethics*, the *Yale Law Journal*, the *European Journal of Philosophy*, and the *Times Literary Supplement*.

Philip Pettit is Professor of Social and Political Theory at the Research School of Social Sciences, Australian National University, and a regular Visiting Professor at Columbia University. He is the author of a number of books, including *The Common Mind: An Essay on Psychology, Society, and Politics* (1993), *Republicanism: A Theory of Freedom and Government* (1997), and *A Theory of Freedom: From Psychology to Politics* (2001). He is also coauthor of *Three Methods of Ethics* (with Marcia Baron and Michael Slote, 1997).

CONTRIBUTORS

Stephen Darwall is John Dewey Professor of Philosophy at the University of Michigan, where he has taught since 1984. His work focuses on the foundations of ethics and practical reason and on the history of fundamental moral philosophy, especially in the seventeenth and eighteenth centuries. He is the author of *Impartial Reason* (1983), *The British Moralists and the Internal 'Ought': 1640–1740* (1995), *Philosophical Ethics* (1999), and numerous articles in moral philosophy, moral psychology, and the history of ethics. He is also the coeditor of *Moral Discourse and Practice* (with Allan Gibbard and Peter Railton, 1997).

David O. Brink is Professor of Philosophy at the University of California, San Diego. His research interests are in ethical theory, political philosophy, constitutional jurisprudence, and the history of ethics. He is the author of *Moral Realism and the Foundations of Ethics* (1989) and is bringing out a new edition of T. H. Green's *Prolegomena to Ethics* through the Clarendon Press. He is currently working on issues in ethical theory and the history of ethics involving practical reason and moral demands, and on issues in constitutional jurisprudence involving judicial review and individual rights in a constitutional democracy.

David Sidorsky is Professor of Philosophy at Columbia University. He teaches moral philosophy, political philosophy, and literary theory; for a number of years, he chaired Columbia's University Seminar in General Education and the university's John M. Olin Colloquium in Political Philosophy. In addition to authoring numerous published essays, he is the editor of *The Liberal Tradition in European Thought* (1970), *John Dewey: The Essential Writings* (1977), and *Essays on Human Rights* (1979).

David Sobel is Assistant Professor of Philosophy at Bowling Green State University. He has written several articles on reasons for action and accounts of well-being; these include "Full Information Accounts of Well-Being" (*Ethics*, 1994), "On the Subjectivity of Welfare" (*Ethics*, 1997), "Well-Being as the Object of Moral Consideration" (*Economics and Philosophy*, 1998), and "Do the Desires of Rational Agents Converge?" (*Analysis*, 1999). His current research is focused on a sustained defense of subjective accounts of well-being and reasons for action.

Julia Annas is Regents Professor of Philosophy at the University of Arizona. She is the author or coauthor of ten books and numerous articles on a range of issues in ancient philosophy, with her main focus being ethics and epistemology. Her books *The Morality of Happiness* (1993) and *Platonic Ethics, Old and New* (1998) explore the structure of ethical theory in ancient philosophy. She is currently working on an introduction to a new translation of Cicero's *On Moral Ends*.

James Bernard Murphy is Associate Professor of Government at Dartmouth College. He is the author of *The Moral Economy of Labor: Aristotelian Themes in Economic Theory* (1993) and *The Normative Force of the Actual: The Morality of Positive Law,* forthcoming from Yale University Press. He has written several articles on labor, law, signs, and ethics in the Aristotelian-Thomistic tradition; these essays have appeared in, among other places, *Political Theory, The Review of Metaphysics,* and *The Thomist.*

Thomas E. Hill, Jr., is Kenan Professor of Philosophy at the University of North Carolina at Chapel Hill, where he has taught since 1984. He previously taught for sixteen years at the University of California, Los Angeles, and more briefly at Pomona College, at Johns Hopkins University, and (on visiting appointments) at Stanford University and the University of Minnesota. He is the author of *Autonomy and Self-Respect* (1991), *Dignity and Practical Reason in Kant's Moral Theory* (1992), and *Respect, Pluralism, and Justice: Kantian Perspectives* (2000).

Geoffrey Sayre-McCord is Bowman and Gordon Gray Professor of Philosophy at the University of North Carolina at Chapel Hill. He specializes in metaethics, moral theory, epistemology, and modern philosophy (especially Hume), and has written extensively in these areas. He is also the editor of *Essays on Moral Realism* (1988).

REALIST-EXPRESSIVISM: A NEGLECTED OPTION FOR MORAL REALISM*

By David Copp

I. Introduction

Moral realism and *antirealist-expressivism* are of course incompatible positions. They disagree fundamentally about the nature of moral states of mind, the existence of moral states of affairs and properties, and the nature and role of moral discourse. The central realist view is that a person who has or expresses a moral thought is thereby in, or thereby expresses, a *cognitive* state of mind; she has or expresses a *belief* that represents a moral state of affairs in a way that might be accurate or inaccurate. The view of antirealist-expressivism is that such a person is in, or expresses, a *conative* state of mind, one that consists in a certain kind of attitude or motivational stance toward something, such as an action or a person. Realism holds that moral thoughts have truth conditions and that in some cases these truth conditions are satisfied so that our moral thoughts are true.[1] Antirealist-expressivism holds, to a first approximation, that the distinctive moral content of a moral thought does not have truth conditions.

Given these contrasts between realism and antirealist-expressivism, the view I shall propose in this essay might seem surprising, for it combines moral realism with a chief positive doctrine of moral expressivism. I call the view *realist-expressivism*. It holds that our moral beliefs and judgments represent moral states of affairs and can be accurate or inaccurate to these states of affairs, which is the central realist thesis, but it *also* holds that, in making moral assertions, we express certain characteristic conative attitudes or motivational stances, which is a central positive view of expressivism.

The possibility of a view that combines realism with expressivism in this way has not been widely noticed, despite its many theoretical advantages. One explanation for this is presumably that expressivism is characteristically antirealist, so the idea of combining realism and expressivism might seem untenable. A second explanation is that the differences between realist-expressivism and certain familiar, but distinct, realist and

* I am grateful for helpful comments I received on earlier versions of this essay from Kent Bach, Justin D'Arms, Steven Davis, Janice Dowell, Don Hubin, Paul Hurley, Jeffrey C. King, Steven Rieber, David Sobel, Sigrún Svavarsdóttir, David Velleman, and the contributors to this volume.
[1] Compare Geoffrey Sayre-McCord, "The Many Moral Realisms," in Geoffrey Sayre-McCord, ed., *Essays on Moral Realism* (Ithaca, NY: Cornell University Press, 1988), 5.

1

antirealist views are rather subtle. Because of this, it can be easy to confuse realist-expressivism with other views that are quite different. There are at least two possible sources of such confusion. On the one hand, realist-expressivism might be confused with a realist version of a standard kind of *internalism*, which is a doctrine or family of doctrines that I will discuss shortly. But it is not a kind of internalism. On the other hand, realist-expressivism might be confused with a position that combines antirealist-expressivism with *deflationism* about the meaning of "true," where deflationism is another doctrine or family of doctrines that I will discuss shortly. But realist-expressivism is not any kind of antirealism; it is fully realist, and it does not presuppose deflationism. Let me try to clarify both of these areas of potential confusion here; I will return to them at the end of the essay, after I have developed my own version of realist-expressivism.

First, it is important not to confuse realist-expressivism with familiar versions of internalism. In the sense I have in mind, internalism is the doctrine that a person who believes or judges that she ought to perform some action must be motivated to some degree to do so.[2] The internalist idea is that there is a necessary connection, or an internal logical connection—even if it is a defeasible one—between the state of accepting a relevant moral claim and being motivated to act or respond appropriately. Internalism can be combined with moral realism, and the resulting view could be described in terms similar to those I used to describe realist-expressivism. That is, an internalist moral realism could be described as the view that, first, our moral beliefs represent moral states of affairs and can be accurate or inaccurate to these states of affairs, and second, our moral beliefs entail certain characteristic conative motivational states. Realist-expressivism, however, is not committed to the second half of this view.[3] The expressivism in realist-expressivism is basically the thesis that, in making a moral *assertion*, we typically *express* certain characteristic conative psychological states or motivational stances. This is a thesis about the *pragmatics* of moral assertion, a thesis that, I will argue, is explained in central cases by the *semantics* of moral terms.[4] It is

---

[2] Stephen Darwall calls this doctrine "judgment internalism" to distinguish it from other internalist doctrines. See Stephen Darwall, *Impartial Reason* (Ithaca, NY: Cornell University Press, 1983), 54–55. Philosophers sometimes propose weakened versions of internalism by specifying that, for instance, any *rational* person who believed she ought to do something would be relevantly motivated. For an example of this sort of account, see Michael Smith, *The Moral Problem* (Oxford: Blackwell, 1994), 61.

[3] Of course, it is committed to the first half. One subtlety that I need to ignore in this essay is that typical versions of antirealist-expressivism are committed to the second half of the view. Of course, no version is committed to the first (realist) half. Typical forms of antirealist-expressivism are internalist, but realist-expressivism is not (or need not be).

[4] The precise location of the line between semantics and pragmatics is controversial. The basic idea, however, is that semantics is concerned with the literal meanings of terms, expressions, sentences, and the like, insofar as their meanings can be determined independently of the contexts in which they are used. Pragmatics is concerned with properties of

not a thesis about the intrinsic nature of moral belief or thought; it does not imply that the state of accepting a moral judgment *consists* in part in a motivational state, or that it *entails* the existence of a motivational state. Hence, realist-expressivism is entirely compatible with *externalism*, which is the denial of internalism. Even so, as I will explain, it can do justice to many of the intuitions that fuel internalism.

Second, it is important not to confuse realist-expressivism with a sophisticated combination of antirealism and a deflationist account of the meaning of "true." An example of deflationism is the doctrine that to call a sentence "true" is simply to affirm it. This doctrine would permit an antirealist-expressivist to affirm, consistently with his antirealism, that, for example, it is true that capital punishment is wrong. For, according to the deflationist view, to affirm this is simply to affirm that capital punishment is wrong, which obviously is something that an antirealist-expressivist can do. In addition to this deflationist account of "true," there are also deflationist accounts of the meanings of the terms "property" and "belief." Simon Blackburn has used the central ideas of deflationism to stake out a position he calls "quasi-realism," a position that he intends to be antirealist and expressivist.[5] Deflationism permits Blackburn to combine antirealist-expressivism with the thesis that there are indeed moral "truths," moral "properties," and moral "beliefs."[6] Given that Blackburn's is an antirealist view, my own thesis that we can combine expressivism with the idea that there are moral "truths," moral "properties," and moral "beliefs" might also be viewed as antirealist. But even though realist-expressivism does justice to the expressive characteristics of moral

---

expressions and the like that are determined by their use, or by the contexts in which they are used. For example, the fact that the sentence "I promise to meet you" *can* be used to make a promise is a feature of its semantics. However, the question of whether a person *has* made a promise in uttering the sentence in a given context is a question in pragmatics. General questions about what a context must be like in order for a person to make a promise in uttering the sentence, and questions about what is required in order to use the sentence sincerely to make a promise, are also questions in pragmatics. I am grateful to Steven Davis for help with this distinction.

[5] See Simon Blackburn, "How to Be an Ethical Antirealist," *Midwest Studies in Philosophy* 12 (1988): 361–75. All subsequent references to this essay are to the version reprinted in Stephen Darwall, Allan Gibbard, and Peter Railton, eds., *Moral Discourse and Practice: Some Philosophical Approaches* (New York: Oxford University Press, 1997), 167–78. See also Simon Blackburn, *Essays in Quasi-Realism* (New York: Oxford University Press, 1993). Allan Gibbard exhibits a temptation toward quasi-realism as well; see Allan Gibbard, *Wise Choices, Apt Feelings* (Cambridge, MA: Harvard University Press, 1990). For more on Gibbard's views, see Paul Horwich, "Gibbard's Theory of Norms," *Philosophy and Public Affairs* 22, no. 1 (1993): 61–78.

[6] A deflationist about the term "property" might hold that to say there is a property of rightness is simply to affirm that some things are right. A deflationist about "belief" might hold that to say that a person believes that some things are right is simply to say that the person is disposed to affirm sentences to the effect that some things are right. On views of this kind, an antirealist-expressivist obviously can affirm, consistently, that there is a property of moral rightness and that there are beliefs about the rightness of actions; to affirm these claims would simply be to affirm that some things are right and that some people are disposed to affirm sentences to the effect that some actions are right.

discourse, it is fully realist. Any version of moral realism could, in principle, be incorporated into a version of realist-expressivism. Realist-
expressivism can be as realist as one would like.

Given the existence of deflationist positions of the kind I have described, however, the distinction between realism and antirealist-
expressivism can seem to disappear. Realism holds that moral thoughts
have truth conditions, but an antirealist-expressivist who is also a deflationist about "true" would concede that moral claims have truth conditions. It is trivial that, for example, "Capital punishment is wrong" is true
just under the condition that capital punishment is wrong. The distinction
between moral realism and antirealist-expressivism is subtle, but it is
crucial to our understanding of the cognitive status of moral discourse.
The best way to characterize the distinction, I think, is in terms of a
difference between the semantics of moral predicates and the semantics of
familiar garden-variety descriptive predicates, and in terms of a difference between the metaphysics of the "properties" referred to by predicates of these kinds.

Put in these terms, moral realism holds that moral predicates have the
same basic semantic characteristics as at least some typical nonmoral
"descriptive" predicates. Let us say, for convenience, that the central semantic role of the latter is to "refer" to "properties," but let us do so
without committing ourselves to any particular metaphysical account
either of reference or of the nature of properties. Given this manner of
speaking, we say that the predicate "perennial" refers to the property of
being a perennial. Similarly, moral realism holds, moral predicates, such
as "wrong," refer to moral "properties," such as wrongness. In the first
place, then, moral realism holds that the chief semantic role of the moral
predicates is to refer to moral properties, such as rightness, wrongness,
virtuousness, viciousness, and so on. Second, it holds that these properties have the same basic metaphysical status as ordinary nonmoral properties, whatever that is. Simply for convenience, let me speak of properties
that have this status as metaphysically "robust."[7] Third, moral realism

---

[7] As noted in the text, the problem I am addressing is how to distinguish between moral
realism and antirealist-expressivism, given a deflationist account of the meaning of "true."
Hartry Field has proposed that the distinction is best drawn in terms of the idea of an
"objectively correct" norm. See Hartry Field, "Disquotational Truth and Factually Defective
Discourse," *Philosophical Review* 103, no. 3 (1994): 440–41. I am proposing that the distinction
can be drawn in terms of the semantic role of ordinary nonmoral predicates and the idea of
a "robust property," which is in turn explained in terms of the metaphysical status of the
referents of ordinary predicate terms. The issues raised by questions about this metaphysical
status go beyond the scope of this essay. The vagueness in what I am proposing is due in
part to the fact that, as Michael Devitt has stressed, a formulation of the debate between
moral realism and antirealist-expressivism ought to be independent of general metaphysical
issues about the nature of properties. Among other things, such a formulation ought to
allow for a nominalist understanding of talk of "properties," even though a nominalist
would deny that there are any "properties" at all under some understandings of what this
would mean. This is why I speak above of "the metaphysical status of the referents of

holds that "basic" moral propositions are true, just as ordinary descriptive propositions are true, when the relevant things have the relevant properties; it adds that some basic moral propositions are in fact true.[8] Realist-expressivism accepts all three of these core realist claims.

Antirealist-expressivism, however, denies the first two of these claims. Deflationism would allow an antirealist-expressivist to agree that there are moral properties and that moral predicates refer to moral properties. It would also allow her to agree both that basic moral propositions are true when the relevant things have the relevant properties and that some basic moral propositions are true. However, an antirealist-expressivist would deny that the moral properties referred to by the so-called "thin" moral predicates, such as "wrong" and "good," are robust. That is, she would deny that moral properties have the same metaphysical status as ordinary nonmoral properties, such as the property of being a perennial. She would also deny that reference to moral properties is the chief semantic role of the moral predicates. Under antirealist-expressivism, the distinctive aspect of the meaning of moral predicates, the aspect that distinguishes *moral* predicates from other kinds of predicates, is not that they refer to a special kind of property. Their chief and distinctive semantic role, at least in their paradigmatic use in making moral judgments, is, instead, to express certain characteristic emotive or conative states of mind, such as "prescribing," "commending," or "expressing acceptance of a norm." On such an account, a person who says that something is "wrong" does not primarily assert that the action in question has the property of wrongness; instead, she expresses disapproval of the action, or some other attitude toward it. Hence, according to antirealist-expressivism, the semantics of these moral predicates is quite unlike the semantics of nonmoral descriptive predicates.

To be sure, there are "thick" moral predicates, such as "honest" and "kind," and an antirealist-expressivist would concede that these predicates refer to properties that are robust in the way that ordinary nonmoral properties are robust. She would insist, however, that this is because the properties they refer to *are* ordinary nonmoral properties—psychological properties, for example—not moral properties. Hence, she might hold that "honest" refers to a disposition to assert only what one takes to be true. Even in the case of thick moral predicates, however, she would argue that the characteristic semantic role of such predicates, at least in

---

ordinary predicate terms," and it is why, in the text, I speak of the "semantic role" of such predicate terms. I am attempting to be neutral among various accounts of these matters. See Michael Devitt, *Realism and Truth*, 2d ed. (Princeton, NJ: Princeton University Press, 1997), 302–20, esp. 316–18.

[8] A "basic" moral proposition is a proposition that entails, for some moral property M, that something instantiates M. An example is the proposition that capital punishment is wrong. Among nonbasic moral propositions are propositions such as that nothing is morally wrong and that either abortion is wrong or 2 + 2 = 4.

their paradigmatic use in making moral judgments, is to express a characteristic conative or motivational state of mind.

Antirealist-expressivists disagree about the details, of course. Nevertheless, it can be seen that antirealist-expressivism combines a negative thesis to the effect that there are no robust moral properties, and that the chief semantic role of the moral predicates is not to refer to properties, with a positive thesis to the effect that the characteristic semantic role of moral predicates is to express a distinctive conative or motivational state of mind. The negative thesis conflicts with realism, but the positive thesis is logically independent of this negative thesis. There is, therefore, room for a kind of expressivist moral realism. As a version of moral realism, this view would hold that moral predicates refer to moral properties that are metaphysically akin to ordinary nonmoral properties. As a version of expressivism, the view would hold that at least one of the semantic roles of moral predicates in their paradigmatic uses is to express a certain characteristic conative or motivational state of mind.

The availability of this sort of view is perhaps obvious, once stated. The difficulty is to develop the specifics in a plausible way. If we can do this, we can defuse many of the familiar arguments for antirealist forms of expressivism. It should already be obvious that an argument for the positive thesis of expressivism is not an argument for the negative antirealist thesis. As I will explain, realist-expressivism aims to do justice to many of the intuitions that fuel the familiar arguments for antirealist-expressivism. For example, realist-expressivism captures the intuition that to call capital punishment "wrong" is to express disapproval of it, a disapproval that does not consist simply in believing that capital punishment is wrong. Yet realist-expressivism is entirely compatible with the realist thesis that the wrongness of capital punishment would consist simply in capital punishment's having the robust property of wrongness. Once both of these things are understood, I think it will be clear that realist-expressivism is a genuinely interesting view. It can be accepted by moral realists even though it captures intuitions that can seem to ground antirealism.

In order fully to develop a version of realist-expressivism, one must develop both the realist side of it and the expressivist side. There are two chief issues on the expressivist side. First, what kind of conative or motivational state of mind is expressed in making a moral judgment? In principle, any answer to this question that is given by an antirealist-expressivist can also be given by a realist-expressivist. In the next section of this essay, I briefly discuss the views of a number of prominent antirealist-expressivists. The view that I propose later in the essay, near the end of Section VI, is similar to Allan Gibbard's, according to which, as I will explain, the relevant state of mind is a state of norm acceptance. In Sections III through V of the essay, I focus on the second chief issue: in what sense are the relevant conative or motivational states of mind "expressed"? It turns out that answering this question leads to surprising complexities. In Section VI, I propose the form of realist-expressivism that I think is most plausible, developing both the realist and the expressivist sides of the view. I specify what kind of conative state of mind is, I think, expressed in making a moral judgment. In Section VII, I provide arguments for my proposal, at least for the expressivist side of it. In Section VIII, I briefly return to the task of exhibiting the differences between realist-expressivism and both internalist moral realism, on the one hand, and the combination of deflationism with antirealist-expressivism, on the other hand. I want to stress that my main task in this essay is simply to propose a plausible formulation of realist-expressivism and to illustrate its theoretical advantages. The arguments for realist-expressivism are not conclusive, but I believe it is a position that deserves attention.

II. SOME EXPRESSIVIST DOCTRINES

In order to discuss these issues, it will be useful to adopt a uniform terminology. I will use the expression "moral judgment" to refer to the kind of speech-act we perform in making a moral claim.[9] Making a moral judgment consists in uttering a sentence with a relevant meaning with relevant intentions in a relevant context. I will use the expression "moral thought" to refer to the state of mind expressed by a person in making a moral judgment, leaving open whether such thoughts are, or involve, beliefs. For example, a person typically would be making a moral judgment in telling a man that he morally ought not to steal. But we do not need to use moral terms, such as "wrong" and "virtuous," in order to make moral judgments. I might intend to make a moral judgment, and might succeed in doing so, if I say "I would have thought twice before X-ing!" In saying this, I might succeed in expressing the thought that it was wrong to X, even though the sentence I use obviously does not mean that it was wrong to X. This example shows that a distinction needs to be drawn between what a *sentence* (literally) means or implies and what a *person* means or implies in using a sentence. In speaking of the "meaning" of *sentences*, I will talk of their "content." I will use the term "proposition" in speaking of contents that have a truth value. When the content of a sentence is (or includes) a proposition, the sentence would standardly be said to "express" the proposition, but this way of talking would invite confusion since I will be talking of assertions as "expressing" states of mind, which is a different matter. To avoid confusion, then, when the content of a sentence is (or includes) a proposition, I will say that the

---

[9] The classic sources of speech-act theory are J. L. Austin, *How to Do Things with Words* (Cambridge, MA: Harvard University Press, 1962); and John Searle, *Speech Acts* (Cambridge: Cambridge University Press, 1969). For helpful discussion, see Kent Bach and Robert M. Harnish, *Linguistic Communication and Speech Acts* (Cambridge, MA: MIT Press, 1979); and Steven Davis, *Philosophy and Language* (Indianapolis, IN: Bobbs-Merrill, 1976), 16–27.

sentence "states" the proposition. I will also speak of imperatival sentences as "stating" imperatives or commands.

Typically, when a person uses a declarative sentence with a relevant intention in a relevant context, she expresses a "belief" that takes a proposition as its object. For example, if I say that stealing is widespread, then in most contexts I would express the belief that stealing is widespread. In such cases, I will say that one makes "assertions." An assertion, then, is the use of a declarative sentence to express a belief. Since I am leaving it open whether moral thoughts are or involve beliefs, I am also leaving it open whether to make a moral judgment is to "assert" something in this technical sense.

An antirealist-expressivist can agree that some moral thoughts consist, in part, in a belief. For example, the thought that Bill Clinton is honest includes a belief attributing the property of honesty to Bill Clinton. According to the negative thesis of antirealist-expressivism, however, there are no robust moral properties. For the antirealist-expressivist, then, the property of honesty is not a robust *moral* property, and moral thoughts do not involve accepting propositions in which robust *moral* properties are attributed to things. As discussed in Section I, the positive thesis of antirealist-expressivism specifies what expressivists take to be distinctive about moral thoughts; their idea is that moral thoughts consist, at least in part, in a certain characteristic kind of conative or motivational state of mind. The positive thesis also specifies that the chief semantic role of moral predicates, in their paradigmatic use, is to express such a state. The history of expressivism contains a number of proposals about the nature of this state of mind; most notable are the proposals of Charles Stevenson, A. J. Ayer, R. M. Hare, Blackburn, and Gibbard.[10]

Stevenson, Ayer, and Hare accept the positive thesis of expressivism as I stated it. For Stevenson and Ayer, to make a moral judgment is at least in part to express a conative attitude. For Hare, to make a moral judgment is at least in part to state a command; it is to commend something, or to prescribe or enjoin the doing of something. In my terminology, all three would agree that some state of mind other than belief is involved in having a moral thought. For Stevenson and Ayer, to have a moral thought is at least in part to have a certain moral attitude. For Hare, it is to assent to or subscribe to a relevant universal command, which is in part to have an appropriate intention.[11]

[10] Charles Stevenson, "The Emotive Meaning of Ethical Terms," *Mind* 46, no. 181 (1937): 14–37 (all subsequent references to this essay are to the version reprinted in Darwall, Gibbard, and Railton, eds., *Moral Discourse and Practice*, 71–82); A. J. Ayer, *Language, Truth, and Logic*, 2d ed. (New York: Dover Publications, 1952), 108; R. M. Hare, *The Language of Morals* (Oxford: Oxford University Press, 1952), 1–5; Blackburn, "How to Be an Ethical Antirealist"; Gibbard, *Wise Choices, Apt Feelings*.

[11] Stevenson, "The Emotive Meaning of Ethical Terms," 74, 78, 79; Ayer, *Language, Truth, and Logic*, 108; Hare, *The Language of Morals*, 4, 13, 20, 168–72.

Contemporary expressivists have proposed similar doctrines. Blackburn proposes, for instance, that "the fundamental state of mind of one who has an ethical commitment" is best conceived as a "stance" rather than a belief because of the connection of ethical commitments with re-action, action, and choice, rather than information. To be sure, we do speak of "moral beliefs," but, given his deflationism, Blackburn holds that this and other features of what he calls "the important surface phenomena of ethics" are compatible with expressivism.[12] Gibbard proposes that to call something rational is not to attribute a property to it, but rather to express a certain state of mind, the state of "thinking something rational."[13] He then holds that to think something rational is, roughly, to accept norms that permit it, where a "norm" is a content that is "expressible by an imperative."[14] To "accept" a norm in the relevant sense is to have a distinctive complex of attitudes and dispositions toward the norm and the actions it calls for. Norm acceptance is thus a kind of "motivational state." Gibbard then explains moral states of mind in terms of norm acceptance. Hence, he says, to think an act wrong is, roughly, "to accept norms for guilt and resentment that, prima facie, would sanction guilt and resentment if the act were performed."[15]

Realist-expressivism accepts the key positive thesis shared by these philosophers. It agrees that, for any basic moral thought that M, there is a conative or motivational state C-M, a state of some kind similar to a desire, such that a person making the judgment that M "expresses" the state C-M. It holds, however, that a person who makes a moral judgment M expresses *both* the moral belief that M *and* a corresponding state C-M. Realist-expressivism combines the chief doctrines of moral realism with a central positive view of expressivism. As noted above, both the realist and expressivist sides of it need to be explained, as well as the relation between them. In the next section, I begin to explain the expressivist half of the view: in what sense of "express" could it be that to make a moral judgment is to express a conative state of mind?

III. Expression, Sincerity, and the Pragmatics of Assertion

The term "express" can be used to pick out several different relations between utterances and states of mind. For example, there are causal relations of the kind that obtains between a sneer and the contempt that

---

[12] Blackburn, "How to Be an Ethical Antirealist," 168–69.

[13] Gibbard, *Wise Choices, Apt Feelings*, 8.

[14] Ibid., 7, 46, 70. On norm acceptance, see ibid., 55–57.

[15] Ibid., 47. Gibbard ultimately says that normative "beliefs" are "much like any other beliefs" (ibid., 100). In his fully developed view, the state of thinking an action rational is more complex than that of accepting norms that permit it. It consists, roughly, in *ruling out* all combinations of a normative system with a possible state of the world which are such that the normative system would prohibit the action in the given state of the world.

it expresses. Perhaps the making of a moral judgment that M could be caused in a similar way by the corresponding state C-M. However, the expressivist thesis in realist-expressivism is not simply a causal thesis. It claims that there is a *linguistically* significant relation between moral assertions and relevant conative states of mind, a relation that depends in some essential way on the fact that moral assertions are speech-acts that have moral content.

Even if we restrict attention to relations of this kind, there are more than one candidate. First, there is the relation between the assertion that p and the belief that p. The assertion "expresses" the belief, and one might propose that a person making a moral assertion that M expresses the corresponding state C-M in exactly the sense of "express" as that in which she expresses the belief that M. Second, there is the relation, which I think is weaker, that obtains generally between speech-acts and their sincerity conditions. This is the sense in which promises "express" intentions and apologies "express" regret. A promise is not sincere unless the promisor intends to carry through, and an apology is not sincere unless accompanied by regret.[16] One might propose, then, that moral assertions express relevant conative states of mind in this sense of "express"; put more formally, the idea of this proposal is that the sincerity of a person making a moral judgment M depends on her being in a corresponding state C-M. I think that neither of these proposals would be adequate by itself, for even if either were true, its truth would need to be explained. If either were true, we would want to find something deeper that would explain its being true.

---

[16] Similarly, if I assert something, my sincerity depends on my believing what I say. Moore's paradox reveals that more than just this is involved in the relation between assertion and belief. To see this, consider the Moore-paradoxical sentence, "There is a smokestack in Bowling Green, but I do not believe there is a smokestack in Bowling Green." If I utter this sentence, my sincerity in saying that there is a smokestack in Bowling Green depends on my believing that there is a smokestack in Bowling Green, which I then say I do not believe. Hence, I undermine my own sincerity. But, more than this, in uttering the Moore-paradoxical sentence, I do not succeed in asserting that there is a smokestack in Bowling Green, because asserting something involves a kind of commitment to belief that I reject in the last half of the utterance. Indeed, it is not clear, other things being equal, what speech-act I perform in uttering this sentence. Compare this case with that of promising. If I promise that p, my sincerity depends on my intending that p, so it would be odd to say, "I promise to build a smokestack in Bowling Green, but I have no intention of building one." In saying this, I would undermine the sincerity of my own promise. Despite this, however, I might succeed in promising, for I might obligate myself to build a smokestack even though what I say implies that my promise is insincere. Hence, it seems, the assertion that p involves a commitment to believing that p that *cannot* be canceled without undermining the assertion. In contrast, although the promise that p involves a kind of commitment to intending that p, it appears that this commitment *can* be canceled without undermining the promise, even though canceling it does undermine the *sincerity* of the promise. See Paul Grice, *Studies in the Ways of Words* (Cambridge, MA: Harvard University Press, 1989), 42. Kent Bach and Robert Harnish provide an account of assertion that elegantly explains why it is that a person who says that p, and then adds that he does not believe that p, would fail thereby to assert that p. See Bach and Harnish, *Linguistic Communication and Speech Acts*, 15–16.

In order to forestall misunderstanding, it is important to note right away that, understood in a certain way, it cannot be denied that a person who says, for instance, "Cursing is wrong" expresses moral disapproval in exactly the sense in which she expresses her belief that cursing is wrong. This is because there is a straightforward sense in which simply to *believe* cursing is wrong *is* to morally disapprove of cursing. We can report a person's belief by saying she "disapproves" of cursing. Nothing more need be true of a person who morally disapproves of cursing than that she believes that cursing is wrong.[17] So of course a person who says "Cursing is wrong" expresses her disapproval of cursing in the sense in which she expresses her belief that cursing is wrong. However, this point does not help expressivism find a conative or motivational state distinct from belief that is expressed in moral assertion.

The thesis that is on the table, then, is that there is some conative or motivational state C-M, distinct from the belief that M, that is expressed in making the moral assertion that M. The first proposal is that this state is expressed in exactly the sense in which assertions "express" beliefs. What, though, is this sense of "express"? Fortunately, we do not need to provide a fully adequate answer to this question. This is because, if a moral assertion that M is related to a corresponding state C-M in exactly the way that the assertion is related to the belief that M, then, since the assertion's sincerity depends on whether the speaker believes that M, it follows that its sincerity must also depend on whether the speaker is in the state C-M. This, in effect, is the second proposal. That is, the first proposal entails the second, and is not adequate unless the second is adequate. We can therefore focus on the second proposal.

Gibbard invokes the distinction between the truth conditions and the sincerity conditions of an assertion to distinguish between a person's asserting that she is in a given state of mind and her expressing that state of mind. I "assert" that I am in a state of mind in saying something just in case the *truth* of what I say depends on my being in that state of mind. In contrast, I "express" a state of mind in saying something just in case *sincerity* demands that I be in that state of mind, given what I say and assuming I know the meaning of what I say.[18] Let us call expression in this sense *sincerity-expression*. Insincerity involves deceit, feigning, or pretense. For example, there is a pretense involved if I apologize for something that I do not regret. If, in saying something, I sincerity-express a certain attitude, there would be a pretense involved in my saying the thing if I do not have that attitude.

Assertions are not unique among speech-acts in having sincerity conditions. As we saw, my sincerity in apologizing for something depends on my regretting it, and my sincerity in promising to do something depends

---

[17] Compare Hare, *The Language of Morals*, 10.
[18] Gibbard, *Wise Choices, Apt Feelings*, 84.

on my intending to do it. It should be clear, however, that I can succeed in performing a speech-act of one of these kinds even if I am insincere. To say that I apologize for something I did is to apologize even if I am insincere. I can promise to do something even if I have no intention of doing it. Similarly, I can successfully assert that *p*, and thereby sincerity-express the belief that *p*, even if I do not actually believe that *p*. That is, the sincerity conditions of a speech-act are not necessarily among its success conditions.

The second proposal, then, is that the sincerity of a person making a moral judgment that M depends on her being in a corresponding state C-M. The plausibility of this idea can be illustrated with an example of Michael Smith's. Suppose you persuade me that I ought to give to famine relief, and soon thereafter I have the opportunity to make a donation. If I fail to exhibit any motivation to give, you will find my behavior puzzling. As Smith says, my behavior will "cast serious doubt on the sincerity of my claim to have been convinced that it is right to give to famine relief at all." [19] This example suggests that in making the judgment that I ought to give, I sincerity-express a motivation to give. However, the example does not *show* this. What it appears to show is merely that, as Smith says, my lack of motivation casts "serious doubt" on the sincerity of my claim to believe that I ought to give to famine relief. Perhaps, that is, my lack of motivation is *evidence* that I do not believe what I say, and therefore it is *evidence* that my assertion is insincere. But this falls short of showing that motivation is a sincerity condition of moral assertion. For it falls short of showing that my assertion that I ought to give when I am not motivated is *in itself* insincere in the way that it is *in itself* insincere to apologize when one has no regret. Consider an analogy. If a child blushes while saying something, this might be evidence that the child is speaking insincerely. However, to say something while blushing is not in itself insincere, and speaking without blushing is not a sincerity condition of assertion. Hence, I claim, even if Smith's example suggests that in making the judgment that I ought to give, I sincerity-express a motivation to give, it does not actually show this.[20]

Consider a revised version of the example. Suppose that a known amoralist agrees that he ought morally to give to famine relief; he says, "I *could* refuse to give, but it would be *wrong*." Soon thereafter he has the opportunity to make a donation, but fails to exhibit any motivation to give. If we know him to be an amoralist who is quite unmoved by moral considerations, we surely will find his behavior to be in character and not at all puzzling. Suppose he said, "I agree that it would be wrong of me to refuse to give, but of course I am not at all motivated to avoid wrong-doing. I rather like wrongdoing." We would take him to have asserted,

[19] Smith, *The Moral Problem*, 7.
[20] Janice Dowell helped me to think through Smith's example.

among other things, that it would be wrong of him to refuse to give. Moreover, I do not think that we would take him to have been insincere, for there was no apparent deceit or pretense on his part.[21] Perhaps Smith is correct that there are circumstances in which a person who said "I ought to give to famine relief" would sincerity-express a motivation to give, but an amoralist who is open about his lack of motivation is hardly speaking under the *pretense* of being motivated to give when he says he ought to give. It might be replied that he is speaking under the pretense of *believing* he ought to give, but we can stipulate that he sincerely *believes* that he believes he ought to give. It appears, then, that there need not be any insincerity on his part. If this is correct, then the sincerity of a person making a moral judgment about what he ought to do does not depend in general on his being motivated accordingly.

Hare would object here that the amoralist in my example does not use moral terms in their standard senses. In Hare's view, an amoralist who says "I ought morally to give to famine relief" but then explicitly denies that he is motivated to give to famine relief would be using the phrase "ought morally" in what Hare would call an "inverted commas" sense.[22] Hence, the amoralist would not assert, nor would he believe, that he literally *ought morally* to give to famine relief—or so Hare would respond. But Hare's response is surely implausible. It implies, for example, that the amoralist expresses a different belief in saying "I ought morally to give to famine relief" than you or I would express in saying this. This claim looks problematic if we consider cases in which we disagree with the amoralist. Suppose, for example, that we have a theory about the effects of famine-relief programs that suggests it would be wrong to give to famine relief. In such a case, it would be natural for us to deny what the amoralist says. On Hare's view, however, to deny what the amoralist says would *not* be to deny that one *ought morally* to give to famine relief. This strikes me as an untenable implication of Hare's position, and I therefore think that Hare's response is unsuccessful.[23]

There is nevertheless something important in Hare's response. If it is viewed abstractly, Hare's claim is that the fact that a person using moral terms to make a moral judgment expresses a corresponding conative state is due to the *meaning* of moral terms when they are used literally. He is also claiming that this aspect of the meaning of moral terms can be

---

[21] Steven Davis urged me, in conversation, to note cases of this kind.

[22] Hare, *The Language of Morals*, 124–26, 167 ff. See also Smith, *The Moral Problem*, 68–71.

[23] For Hare, the amoralist does not make a moral judgment. Rather, he expresses a belief about the moral judgments of other people (Hare, *The Language of Morals*, 124), or perhaps a belief about relevant local moral standards, such as the belief that local moral standards require giving to famine relief (ibid., 167). Therefore, on Hare's view, to deny what the amoralist says would be to deny something of this kind. It would not be to make a moral judgment, and hence it would not be to judge that one morally ought not give to famine relief. This is what strikes me as implausible. A full discussion of these matters is outside the scope of this essay.

canceled or eliminated by placing the terms in "inverted commas." I think that, so understood, Hare's contention is correct. As I will argue, however, this is compatible with moral realism. Indeed, it is compatible with externalist moral realism. To explain why I say this, I need to introduce my own account of the relationship between moral judgments and conative states of mind.

For present purposes, the important thing is that both the first and second proposed accounts of this relationship are about the pragmatics of moral assertion. If either of them is true, however, the explanation surely is semantic. It lies in *what* we assert when we make moral assertions. That is, if it is true in a certain context that the sincerity of a person making the moral judgment that M depends on her being in a distinctive state of mind C-M, this must be due to something distinctive about the *content* of M. Consider the sentence "Cursing is widespread," which cannot be used literally to make a moral judgment. When this sentence is used to make an assertion, the speaker's sincerity depends on her beliefs, but not on her being in any particular conative state. According to both the first and second proposals, however, when the sentence "Cursing is morally wrong" is used to make an assertion, the sincerity of the speaker depends *both* on her beliefs *and* on her being in a relevant conative state. The explanation for this alleged difference between these two sentences would surely be due to the meaning of "morally wrong."

IV. Expression, Meaning, and "Coloring"

Pejorative terms are characterized by a feature that Gottlob Frege called "coloring."[24] The coloring of a term is a characteristic of the term's meaning, at least in a wide sense of "meaning," for it is a characteristic of the linguistic conventions governing the use of the term. It is in virtue of the coloring of various familiar impolite terms for minority groups, for example, that their use standardly expresses contempt. The form of realist-expressivism that I want to propose holds that the meaning of moral terms also includes coloring. It is in virtue of their coloring, on this account, that moral terms standardly express relevant conative states of mind. To be more exact, on this view it is a matter of linguistic convention that in asserting a basic moral proposition by uttering a sentence in which a moral term is used, a speaker "expresses" a relevant conative state of

[24] Gottlob Frege, "On Sense and Meaning," in Frege, *Collected Papers on Mathematics, Logic, and Philosophy*, ed. Brian McGuinness (Oxford: Basil Blackwell, 1984), 161; Gottlob Frege, "Concept and Object," in Frege, *Collected Papers*, 185; Gottlob Frege, "Thoughts," in Frege, *Collected Papers*, 357. See also Gottlob Frege, "Separating a Thought from Its Trappings," in Frege, *Posthumous Writings*, ed. Friedrich Kambartel and Friedrich Kaulbach (Chicago: University of Chicago Press, 1979), 140–41; and Gottlob Frege, "A Brief Survey of My Logical Doctrines," in Frege, *Posthumous Writings*, 197–98. I owe these references to Janice Dowell and Kent Bach.

mind, other things being equal.[25] According to realist-expressivism, the speaker also expresses a moral belief.

Frege says in one passage that if we compare the sentences "This dog howled the whole night" and "This cur howled the whole night," we see that they state the same "thought."[26] As he says, "a different thought does not correspond to every difference in the words used." The second sentence "puts us . . . in mind of a dog with a somewhat unkempt appearance," but even if the dog is actually quite neatly groomed, it is not the case, he says, that the first sentence is true and the second false. They have the same truth value. "What distinguishes the second from the first," he says, "is of the nature of an interjection." The word "cur" implies contempt, and because of this a person might want to avoid using this word in describing a dog toward which she does not feel contempt. Despite this, Frege asks us to imagine the second sentence being "spoken by someone who does not actually feel the contempt which the word 'cur' seems to imply." Even in this case, Frege says, if the first sentence is true, "the use of the word 'cur' does not prevent us from holding that the second sentence is true as well." For, he says, "we have to make a distinction between the thoughts that are expressed and those which the speaker leads others to take as true although he does not express them." A speaker who called the howling dog a "cur" would imply that she feels contempt for the dog, but this is analogous, says Frege, to the fact that "a speaker who announces the news of a death in a sad tone of voice" creates the impression that he is sad. In such a case the speaker does not state the proposition that he is sad, or say he is sad, even though he displays sadness. "Naturally things are different," Frege writes, when a difference of the kind we are discussing is a matter of "common usage," as is presumably the case with the difference between "dog" and "cur."

Frege would deny that there is any difference in the reference or the sense of the terms "dog" and "cur." This is perhaps not true to the meaning of "cur" in English—it is defined as "mongrel dog" in at least one dictionary[27]—but we should not worry too much about the example. Let us assume that there is no difference between the references or senses of the terms "mongrel dog" and "cur." That is, let us assume that there is no difference in the properties referred to by the terms or in the concepts they express. Given this assumption, Frege would say there is no difference in the thoughts or propositions stated by the sentences "This mon-

---

[25] Recall that a basic moral proposition is a proposition that entails that something instantiates M, where M is a moral property. See note 8 above.

[26] Frege, "Separating a Thought from Its Trappings," 140–41. This paragraph and the next follow Frege's discussion.

[27] *American Heritage Dictionary of the English Language*, 3rd ed., s.v. "cur." Kent Bach and Thomas E. Hill, Jr., drew my attention, in conversation, to worries about whether the meaning of "cur" in contemporary English undermined the effectiveness of Frege's example.

grel dog howled all night" and "This cur howled all night." Yet, Frege would insist, there is a difference in the "contents" of the sentences. He holds that the proposition or thought stated by a sentence is only a "part" of its content, "the part that alone can be accepted as true or rejected as false." He says, "I call anything else that goes to make up the content of a sentence the colouring of the thought."[28] Because of differences in coloring, there is a difference between the speech-act performed in saying that a "cur" howled all night and the speech-act performed in saying that a "mongrel dog" howled all night. There is a difference in what speakers of each sentence would imply about their states of mind because there is a difference in the linguistic conventions governing the uses of the terms. Following Frege, I will speak in such cases of differences in coloring. "Cur" has a coloring such that its use standardly conveys contempt; "mongrel dog" does not have such a coloring.

The difference in coloring between "cur" and "mongrel dog" is a matter of "common usage." I want to say it is a difference in the "meaning" of the terms because the different conventions for their use affect what is *communicated* or *conveyed* by uses of the terms. I suppose that one might want to restrict the use of "meaning" for certain theoretical purposes such that coloring is not treated as a matter of meaning. For my purposes, it will be enough to acknowledge that the coloring of a term can be due to the linguistic conventions governing its use. For convenience, I will say that the expressions "cur" and "mongrel dog" have the same "core meaning" even though they have different meanings in a wide sense of the term.[29]

We now have an example of an assertion that is plausibly taken to express both a belief and a conative state. Assertions of "This cur howled all night" would express both the relevant belief and an attitude of contempt. There are numerous other familiar contemporary examples of colored terms expressing contempt. "Yankee" is used in a variety of countries to express contempt for Americans. "Canuck" is used in New England to express contempt for Canadians, particularly Francophone Canadians. Another example is the term "redneck."[30]

Inasmuch as the core meaning and coloring of a term are a function of the conventions governing its use, and since conventions can be of different kinds and can change over time, a variety of features of a term's

---

[28] Frege, "A Brief Survey of My Logical Doctrines," 197–98. I think it would be preferable to say that the coloring is a property of the sentence used to state the thought rather than a property of the thought itself.

[29] Michael Dummett would say, I think, that the relevant difference between "cur" and "mongrel dog" is to be accounted for in "the theory of force," which he takes to be part of the theory of meaning along with the theory of reference and the theory of sense. See Michael Dummett, "What Is a Theory of Meaning? (II)," in Dummett, *The Seas of Language* (Oxford: Oxford University Press, 1993), 40, 87.

[30] Compare Stevenson on the expressions "elderly spinster" and "old maid." Stevenson, "The Emotive Meaning of Ethical Terms," 77.

meaning in the wide sense can be aspects of its coloring, and the distinction between core meaning and coloring can be fuzzy. As Frege says,

> Of course borderline cases can arise because language changes. Something that was not originally employed as a means of expressing a thought may eventually come to do this because it has constantly been used in cases of the same kind. A thought which to begin with was only suggested by an expression may come to be explicitly asserted by it. And in the period in between different interpretations will be possible. But the distinction itself is not obliterated by such fluctuations in language. In the present context the only essential thing is that a different thought does not correspond to every difference in the words used, and that we have a means of deciding what is and what is not part of the thought, even though, with language constantly developing, it may at times be difficult to apply.[31]

What means do we have, then, for deciding which aspects of a term's meaning in a wide sense are aspects of its coloring?

Suppose that a person says "Your cur howled all night." As I said, Frege holds that even if the person "does not actually feel the contempt which the word 'cur' seems to imply," what she says might well be true, for the dog might well have howled all night.[32] This example illustrates one test we can use to determine which features of a term's meaning are aspects of its coloring. Let us call it the *truth test*: if the use of a term T in a given sentence suggests or implies that *p*, and if this is due to the coloring of T, then the belief expressed by a person asserting the sentence might be true even if *p* is false. For instance, the belief expressed by a person in saying "Your cur howled all night" might be true even if the person actually feels no contempt for your dog.

Despite this, however, it would be a *misuse* of a colored term to use it when the implication carried by its coloring is known or believed by the speaker to be false. This is because the coloring of a term is a feature of its meaning in a broad sense; it is a feature of the linguistic conventions governing the term's use. Accordingly, it would be *inappropriate* to use a colored term in a context in which such use conveys that *p* when the speaker knows or believes that *p* is not the case, even if doing so does not result in what the speaker says being false. Not all inappropriateness of use involves speaking falsely. A speaker who says "Your cur howled all night" might speak truly even if she lacks contempt for the dog in question, but she does nevertheless speak inappropriately. For one thing, her usage is potentially misleading. But even if she attempts to cancel the suggestion of contempt by saying "Your cur howled all night, but I do not

---

[31] Frege, "Separating a Thought from Its Trappings," 141.
[32] Ibid., 140.

mean to imply that I have contempt for your dog," she might find herself being corrected or challenged. Her use of the term "cur" calls out for explanation. It is linguistically inappropriate.

Still, it seems to me that the implications carried by coloring are *cancelable*. To be sure, they are not cancelable in the precise sense that was intended by Paul Grice, who introduced the notion that certain kinds of implication are cancelable. Grice said the implication that *p* is "explicitly cancelable" if it would be "admissible to add *but not p*, or *but I do not mean to imply that p*." It is "contextually cancelable if one can find situations in which the utterance of the form of words would simply not carry the implicature." [33] In the cur example, the person could say "Your cur howled all night, but I do not mean to imply that I have contempt for your dog." Let us call this sentence "H." It would be an odd sentence to utter, for doing so would involve a misuse of "cur" that might be challenged. In this sense it would *not* be admissible to utter H, so Grice presumably would hold that the implication of contempt is *not* cancelable in his sense. In another sense, however, it *would* be admissible to utter H. It would not be self-contradictory, and it would be fully intelligible as an assertion despite the nonstandard use of the term "cur." A person who uttered H would cancel the suggestion of contempt in the sense that the hearer would not be justified to infer on the basis of what the speaker said that the speaker has contempt for the dog in question. One might think that the use of "cur" in such a context could not be literal, but this seems incorrect, because we are imagining the term to be used with at least its standard core meaning. We might wonder why a person who knows the meaning of the word "cur" would use it to speak of a mongrel dog toward which she has no contempt. The answer might be that she does not know or cannot think of the word "mongrel." This supposition helps us to imagine a context in which a speaker says to you "Your cur howled all night" without there being any implication of contempt. Consider a situation in which you know both that the speaker likes your dog and that she does not know the word "mongrel" because she is just learning the language. In this case, the speaker could be quite sincere in saying what she says, even though she has no contempt for your dog. The implication of contempt would be contextually canceled.

Cancelability is related to a more general feature that we could call *alterability*. The usual implication of a colored term can be canceled or altered if what a speaker asserts is more complex than a simple sentence. It can be canceled or altered, for example, in cases where simple sentences involving colored terms are embedded in larger constructions. As we have seen, the usual suggestion of using the term "cur" is canceled if a

---

[33] Grice holds that "conversational implicatures" are cancelable but "conventional implicatures" are not. I am disagreeing with him, in effect, since I think coloring is an example of conventional implicature. However, I am using the term "admissible" in a less strict sense than Grice does. Grice, *Studies in the Ways of Words*, 44, 39 (emphasis in original).

person says "Your cur howled all night, but I do not mean to imply that I have contempt for your dog." In cases of this kind, the second conjunct cancels the implication, otherwise carried by the speaker's use of the term "cur," that she feels contempt for your dog. Similarly, the remark "If your dog is a cur, you ought to sell it" does not imply that the speaker has contempt for your dog, although it does seem to imply contempt for mongrels. The explanation for this lies partly in the content of the conventions governing the uses of terms, conventions in virtue of which these terms have coloring. For instance, the convention governing "Yankee" could be such that *any* use of the term expresses contempt for Americans, or it could simply be such that *calling* someone a Yankee expresses contempt for that person. Suppose someone says, "If Alice is a Yankee, she will celebrate the Fourth of July." On neither convention would the person thereby express contempt for Alice, but on the former convention, the person would thereby express contempt for Americans.[34]

Colored terms have an additional feature that was discussed by Grice, namely, that the suggestions carried by coloring should be *detachable*.[35] The implication of contempt carried by "cur" is detachable in the sense that the beliefs expressed by sentences containing the word can also be expressed by sentences that differ only by containing the phrase "mongrel dog" in place of the word "cur." In general, if a speaker's assertion of a sentence S implies that *p*, and if this implication is due to the coloring of a term T that is contained in S, then it would be possible in principle for the speaker to say or assert the same thing as is asserted by S, or to express the same belief as is expressed by means of S, without implying that *p*. In the cur example, the person could say "Your mongrel dog howled all night" instead of "Your cur howled all night." Of course, in any given case, it might turn out that there is no other term or phrase in the language that has exactly the same core meaning as the colored term T. Even in such a case, however, the relevant implication would still be detachable in principle.

We now have four rough tests for coloring: Frege's truth test, the misuse test, my test of cancelability, and Grice's test of detachability. If a speaker's assertion of a sentence S implies that *p*, and if this implication

---

[34] Kent Bach suggested to me in conversation that it might be useful to distinguish between two kinds of pejorative terms. There are (a) terms, such as "Yankee" and "cur," that are used to refer contemptuously to a class of persons or things such that their use typically expresses or implies contempt for all persons or things in that class; and (b) terms, such as "jerk," that are used to refer contemptuously to persons or things such that their use implies that the speaker has contempt for the person or thing explicitly referred to, but does not imply that she has contempt for anyone or anything else. The remark "Alice is a Yankee" implies that the speaker has contempt for Americans in general as well as for Alice, but the remark "Alice is a jerk" only implies contempt for Alice. Compare "If Alice shows up at the Fourth of July celebration, she is a jerk" with "If Alice shows up at the Fourth of July celebration, she is a Yankee."

[35] Grice uses the notion of detachability to distinguish between "conventional" and "non-conventional" implicatures. Grice, *Studies in the Ways of Words*, 39, 43–44.

is due to the coloring of a term T contained in S, then (1) the belief expressed by the person in asserting S might be true even if p is false, and the implication that p should be (2) detachable and (3) cancelable. Furthermore, (4) it would be a misuse of the term T for a speaker to assert S when she knows or believes that p is not the case.

We can apply these tests to the term "Yankee." Let us suppose that, in Bob's dialect, if Bob says "Alice is a Yankee," he thereby would standardly express contempt for Alice. Despite this, (1) the belief he expresses might be true even if he has no contempt for her, for his belief would be true if Alice were an American. (2) The implication of contempt is detachable in Grice's sense, for Bob could express his belief about Alice by saying "Alice is an American." In this way, he could avoid expressing contempt for her. Moreover, (3) he could cancel the implication that he feels contempt by saying "Alice is a Yankee, but I feel no contempt for her." Perhaps Bob lives in a community in which there is such contempt for Americans that there is no term in common use for referring to Americans except the pejorative term "Yankee." If this were so, and if it were known to be so, and if it were known that Bob is not in fact contemptuous of Americans, then he would not express contempt in calling Alice a "Yankee." The implication of contempt would be contextually canceled. Despite this, (4) the conventions governing the use of "Yankee" are such that, we supposed, when used correctly and literally, "Yankee" is used to refer contemptuously to Americans. Hence, if Bob has no contempt for Alice, it would be a misuse of the term for him to call her a "Yankee." Yet Bob could be quite sincere in saying "Alice is a Yankee," even if he feels no contempt for her. This might be so even if he knows the coloring of the term "Yankee," for perhaps he does not know any nonpejorative term that he could use in place of it.

Let us say that a speaker's use of a term *Frege-expresses* a state of mind just in case it is a matter of the term's coloring that, other things being equal, its use conveys that the speaker is in that state of mind. To be more exact, a speaker's use of a term Frege-expresses a state of mind just in case it is a matter of linguistic convention governing the use of the term that, other things being equal, if a speaker asserts a simple isolated subject-predicate sentence in which the term is used literally,[36] the fact that the speaker used the term conveys that the speaker is in the state of mind. We could call such conventions *expressive conventions.* An example might be the convention whereby calling someone a "Yankee" expresses contempt, other things being equal. An expressive convention regarding the use of a term is a convention such that speakers who use the term in contexts of a certain kind express a given conative or emotive state of mind, other things being equal. Frege-expression depends on the existence of such conventions.

---

[36] I shall not attempt to specify exactly which sentences these are.

The form of realist-expressivism that I want to explore holds that moral terms have coloring in virtue of which, other things being equal, their use in making typical moral assertions Frege-expresses a characteristic conative state of mind. To be more exact, the view is that it is a matter of linguistic convention governing the use of moral terms that, if a speaker asserts a basic moral proposition by using a sentence in which a moral term is used literally, the speaker implies, other things being equal, that she is in a relevant conative state of mind. Moral terms, on this view, are governed by expressive conventions.

It would be premature to apply our four tests for coloring to moral terms without saying something about the nature of the kind of conative state of mind that I think is expressed by a speaker in making a moral judgment. I will claim that the state of mind in question is that of subscribing to a relevant norm, but I need to explain what I mean by this. The account I will propose is that moral terms have coloring in virtue of which, roughly, their use standardly expresses the speaker's subscription to a relevant norm.

V. COLORING AND CONTENT

It might seem ad hoc and unhelpful to postulate the existence of otherwise unexpected linguistic conventions to explain the coloring of pejorative terms and the means by which they are used to Frege-express states of mind. It might seem worse than unhelpful to view moral terms as a species of pejorative term, which is perhaps how my proposal will be viewed at this point. For Frege, however, coloring is a characteristic of a great deal of our discourse, not just of pejorative discourse. Indeed, Stephen Neale has proposed that even proper names have coloring.[37] In this section of the essay, I shall place the ideas of coloring and Frege-expression in a general theoretical framework and discuss certain objections to these ideas that derive from issues in the philosophy of language.

Neale thinks that coloring "may constitute only the tip of a semantic iceburg." The iceburg in question is a phenomenon that is, he says,

> quite natural once we take into account the nature of communication. We do not seek to transmit information only about the world; communication may also involve the transmission of information about our attitudes and emotions; thus we convey information using expressions such as 'It is raining' and also sentences such as 'Damn, it's raining', 'I think it's raining', and 'Damn, I think it's raining'. That is, in many cases we use simple sentences to express a single proposi-

[37] Stephen Neale, "Coloring and Composition," in Kumiko Murasagi and Robert Stainton, eds., *Philosophy and Linguistics* (Boulder, CO: Westview Press, 1999), 72-73. I owe this reference to Kent Bach.

tion and we use modifications of those sentences to express the original proposition . . . together with a second (third, . . .) proposition.[38]

Neale's idea is that the uttering of a sentence may "express" or communicate a sequence of propositions, including a "primary" proposition as
well as one or more "secondary" propositions, where not all of the propositions communicated in this way are taken in every case to bear on the
truth of what is thereby said.[39] For example, a speaker who says "Damn,
it is raining" might communicate both the primary proposition that it is
raining and the secondary proposition that he is angry or frustrated that
it is raining. The truth value of what he thereby says would depend only
on whether it is raining, but it would be inappropriate in most contexts
for him to communicate that it is raining by saying "Damn, it is raining"
unless he were angry or frustrated. Neale has proposed that this *multiple-
propositions framework* can be used to explicate a variety of phenomena,
including coloring.

Consider the sentence "Smith's cur howled all night." Given the meaning of "cur," a speaker uttering this sentence in a typical context presumably would communicate something like the following sequence of
propositions: [primary: that Smith's mongrel dog howled all night]; [sec-
ondary: that the speaker has contempt for mongrels, or for Smith's mon-
grel]. The truth value of what the speaker says would depend only on
whether Smith's mongrel actually howled all night, but it would be semantically inappropriate for the speaker to use the sentence to state this
proposition unless he had the contempt that is expressed.

In this framework, the phenomenon that Grice called "conventional
implicature" would be treated in the same way as the phenomenon of
coloring.[40] For example, according to Grice, a person who utters "Alice is
poor, but she is honest," using the sentence literally to make an assertion,
would assert that Alice is poor and honest. Given the meaning of "but,"
however, Grice thinks that the speaker would also implicate that there is
some sort of contrast between poverty and honesty. The proposition that
there is such a contrast is implicated rather than entailed, for even if there
were no relevant contrast, what the person says would still be true if Alice
were both poor and honest. Grice calls such implicatures "conventional"
because, in Neale's words, they are due to "the linguistic conventions

[38] Ibid., 60–61.
[39] Ibid., 75 and throughout. See Kent Bach, "The Myth of Conventional Implicature,"
Linguistics and Philosophy 22, no. 4 (1999): 327–66. Bach also introduces a multiple-propositions
framework. This use of the terms "primary" and "secondary" is his. The multiple-propositions
framework is quite flexible. Neale holds that the context in which a sentence is uttered, and
the issues that are central in the conversation, can affect whether the falsity of a secondary
proposition would lead us to view a speaker's assertion as false. Neale, "Coloring and
Composition," 75.
[40] On this point, see Grice, *Studies in the Ways of Words,* 41, 46, 86; Bach, "The Myth of
Conventional Implicature"; and Neale, "Coloring and Composition," 53–61.

governing the uses of the words in question."[41] In Neale's framework, the person uttering "Alice is poor, but she is honest" would communicate the following sequence of propositions: [primary: that Alice is poor and she is honest]; [secondary: that there is some relevant contrast between poverty and honesty]. The truth value of what the speaker thereby says would depend only on the truth of the primary proposition, but it would be inappropriate for the speaker to use the sentence to state this primary proposition unless she believed that the secondary proposition was also true.

Because coloring and conventional implication are treated the same way in the multiple-propositions framework, I shall say that the secondary proposition communicated by the assertion of a sentence involving coloring is *conventionally implicated*. Hence, I shall say, a speaker who says "Alice's cur howled all night" conventionally implicates that he has contempt for Alice's dog. For my purposes, however, nothing turns on whether coloring is an example of conventional implicature or simply a phenomenon that is similar to conventional implicature.

In Neale's framework, then, realist-expressivism includes the thesis that, other things being equal, a person stating a basic moral claim M using moral terminology thereby communicates the following sequence of propositions: [primary: that M]; [secondary: that the speaker is in the corresponding state C-M]. The truth value of what the speaker thereby says would depend only on whether M is the case, but it would be inappropriate for the speaker to use the sentence to state that M unless she were in state C-M.

The multiple-propositions framework allows us to see quite clearly where there might be controversy. There are at least three significantly different views concerning the alleged communication of a secondary proposition about the speaker's motivations or conative state in the moral case. (1) On the first view, no propositions to the effect that the speaker is in state C-M are typically communicated or implied by a person in asserting a moral proposition that M. (2) On the second view, a speaker asserting a moral proposition that M does typically communicate a proposition to the effect that she is in a state C-M, and this proposition is among the truth conditions of what she says. According to this position, a person who asserts that something is wrong asserts (perhaps among other things) that she is in a corresponding state C-M. The proposition that she is in such a state is entailed by what she says or asserts, so what she says is false if she is not in such a state. This view is therefore a kind of subjectivist relativism. (3) On the third view, the realist-expressivist view, a speaker asserting a moral proposition that M typically communicates a proposition to the effect that she is in a state C-M, but this proposition is not among the truth conditions of what the speaker says.

<hr>

[41] Neale, "Coloring and Composition," 53.

On a view of this kind, the secondary proposition that the speaker is in state C-M is "implicated." It is communicated, but it is not entailed by what the speaker asserts or says in making the judgment that M.

There are at least three views of this third kind, so there are three kinds of realist-expressivism. (3a) One might hold that the speaker *conversationally implicates* that she is in state C-M. When something is conversationally implicated, the implication can be canceled without any hint of semantic or linguistic oddity and without any misuse of the terms used by the speaker. Conversational implicatures are due to pragmatic features of assertions, such as assumptions standardly made by hearers.[42] In Smith's example, for instance, I agree that I ought to give to famine relief, and it might seem that I thereby implicate that I am motivated to give. If I do implicate this, and if the implication is conversational, it relies on the hearers' assumptions about our conversation. For example, it might depend on the assumptions that we were talking about what to do and that, in saying I ought to give, I was expressing a decision. In contrast to this view, (3b) one might hold that the implication that the speaker is in state C-M is "conventional" in cases in which the speaker uses moral terms in asserting that M. That is, in such cases, the proposition that the speaker is in state C-M is communicated by the speaker in virtue of expressive conventions governing the use of moral terms, but it is not entailed by what she says in making the judgment that M. I am proposing a view of this kind. More specifically, as discussed in the previous section, I am proposing that moral terms have a coloring such that a person making a moral judgment that M using moral terms Frege-expresses a corresponding state C-M.

Finally, (3c) one might agree that a speaker making a moral judgment that M typically communicates that she is in a state C-M, but hold that this is a case neither of conversational implicature nor of conventional implicature. This position is analogous to Grice's position regarding assertion and belief. Grice holds that a speaker who asserts that *p* expresses her belief that *p* and conveys that she believes that *p*, but he denies that the latter proposition is something she conversationally implicates.[43] I will say, for convenience, that it *is* something she implicates, but the implicature here is neither conversational nor conventional. It is not conversational because it cannot be canceled without oddity, and it is not conventional because it is not detachable.[44] Similarly, one might hold, a person making a moral judgment that M implicates that she is in a cor-

---

[42] On conversational implicature, see Grice, *Studies in the Ways of Words*, 22–57. See also Bach and Harnish, *Linguistic Communication and Speech Acts*, 62–64; Bach, "The Myth of Conventional Implicature," 327; and Neale, "Coloring and Composition," 53–61.

[43] Grice, *Studies in the Ways of Words*, 42.

[44] Moore's paradox shows that we cannot successfully assert that *p* while canceling the implication that we believe that *p*. And we cannot detach the implication that we believe that *p* by carefully choosing the words we use to assert that *p*. See ibid.; on Moore's paradox, see note 16 above.

responding state C-M, but the implication is neither conversational nor conventional.

In summary, then, the alternatives are, respectively, (1) the *no C-M proposition view*, (2) the *entailment view*, (3a) the *conversational-implicature view*, (3b) the *conventional-implicature view*, and (3c) the *neither-of-the-above view*.[45] View (2), as noted above, is a version of subjectivism. It is undermined by the example of the amoralist who says he ought to give to famine relief, for we do not take the fact that the amoralist is not in a relevant conative or motivational state to *falsify* what he says about giving to famine relief. That is, we do not take his lack of motivation to show that what he says, in saying he ought to give, is *false*. I shall therefore set aside the entailment view. In Section VII of this essay, I will argue against view (1). I will argue there that a speaker does implicate a C-M proposition in making a moral judgment. For instance, I shall argue that the person in Smith's example who asserts that he ought to give to famine relief *implicates* that he is motivated to give; he does not merely give evidence that he is motivated. The example of the amoralist suggests, however, that it is possible to cancel such implications. This is because the amoralist would apparently cancel any implication that he is motivated to give to famine relief if he said, "I agree that it would be wrong of me not to give to famine relief, but do not be misled. I am not at all motivated to give." The example therefore seems to count against the neither-of-the-above view (3c), which does not make room for the possibility of canceling the implication. For these reasons, I think that the interesting controversy is between views of kinds (3a) and (3b).

In earlier work, I proposed a view of kind (3a), according to which C-M propositions are *conversationally* implicated.[46] I now think this is not generally so. As I will argue in Section VII, I now think that when a speaker uses moral terms in making a basic moral assertion, the implied C-M propositions are *conventionally* implicated. In such cases, I think that the implicature reflects the *coloring* of the moral terms.

My proposal is controversial, however, in light of two arguments found in the recent literature on conventional implicature and expressivism. One is a general argument by Kent Bach that the idea of conventional implicature is a myth.[47] The second is an argument by Frank Jackson and Philip Pettit that expressivism collapses into a crude and unacceptable

---

[45] It can be difficult to categorize a philosopher's view of these matters. Some of the things said by Jamie Dreier suggest, for example, that his version of "speaker relativism" is an entailment view. However, the better interpretation is surely that it is either a conversational-implicature view or a conventional-implicature view. It is also possible that he holds a view of kind (3c). See James Dreier, "Internalism and Speaker Relativism," *Ethics* 101, no. 1 (1990): 6–26.

[46] David Copp, *Morality, Normativity, and Society* (New York: Oxford University Press, 1995), 35.

[47] Bach, "The Myth of Conventional Implicature." Bach does not consider coloring; see ibid., 332 n. 8.

form of subjectivism, which in the present context amounts to an argument that the conventional-implicature view collapses into the entailment view.[48] If either of these arguments is sound, then realist-expressivism is only viable in the familiar guise of the conversational-implicature view. Unfortunately, a thorough discussion of the issues raised by these arguments is beyond the scope of this essay.

The root of both arguments, however, is a challenge to philosophers who think there is a distinction between conventional implicature and entailment. The challenge is to explain how it could be that a person uttering a sentence *communicates* a proposition, in virtue of linguistic conventions governing the literal use of the terms in the sentence, without thereby *asserting* that proposition such that the truth of what the person asserts or says depends on the truth of the proposition. Suppose it is a semantic error of some kind in Bob's linguistic community to call Alice a "Yankee" if one lacks contempt for Americans. How could this be so if the having of contempt is not *entailed* by what speakers say in calling people "Yankees"?

I think that the outline of the answer is clear, but I will not attempt to fill in the details. In outline, the answer is that there are different kinds of linguistic conventions. Some conventions determine what a term is to be used to refer to, when used literally. Other conventions determine that certain conative or motivational states of mind are communicated or conveyed by uses of the term in certain kinds of contexts. In Bob's dialect, the predicate "Yankee" refers to Americans, but, by convention, it is also used to express contempt for Americans. Because of this, it is a misuse to use it to refer to Americans unless one has contempt for Americans. In virtue of the convention about reference, it would be false to say of Alice that she is a Yankee unless she is an American, but in virtue of the expressive convention, it would be a linguistic gaffe, "semantic offense," or violation of "semantic proprieties" of some kind not "touching truth value" to say of Alice that she is a Yankee if one does not have contempt for Americans.[49] I think that there are both kinds of linguistic convention.

We are familiar with pragmatic conventions governing speech-acts of various kinds. According to the conventions governing promising and asserting, it is appropriate for us to promise or to assert only when (we believe) the relevant sincerity condition is fulfilled. It is clearly not the case, however, that a person making a promise reports that he intends to follow through, or that a person making an assertion reports that he has the corresponding belief. A person is taken to have promised even if she lacks the relevant intention, and a person's assertion might be true even if she does not believe that it is. Hence, there are conventions concerning

---

[48] Frank Jackson and Philip Pettit, "A Problem for Expressivism," *Analysis* 58, no. 4 (1998): 239–51. I owe this reference to Kent Bach.

[49] The quoted phrases are from Grice, *Studies in the Ways of Words*, 362, 365.

the sincerity of speech-acts that do not concern the truth conditions of what is said. The only issue is whether conventions not concerning truth conditions can be encoded in the meanings of terms, even if only in a wide sense of meaning that includes coloring. It seems to me that they can be.

VI. A Proposed Realist-Expressivism

In the previous two sections, I have been explaining the sense in which, on my proposal, a person who uses moral terms to make a basic moral assertion that M standardly "expresses" the corresponding state C-M. I propose that she Frege-expresses the state C-M; that is, other things being equal, she conventionally implicates that she is in the state C-M in virtue of the coloring of her terms. Even if a person asserts a basic moral proposition without using moral terms, I still want to say that, other things being equal, she conversationally implicates that she is in the corresponding state C-M.

In order to finish introducing my proposal, I need to explain what, in my view, the emotive or conative state is that a person expresses in making a moral judgment M. I also need to say something about the truth conditions of moral propositions in order to make clear that realist-expressivism is a form of realism as well as a form of expressivism. In this section, I will fill the most important remaining gaps on both the expressivist and realist sides of my proposal. My account will be sketchy, but I have provided more detail elsewhere.[50]

Begin with the propositions stated by moral claims. Consider the claim that cursing is wrong. It would be contradictory, I submit, to say "Cursing is morally wrong but no relevantly justified moral norm or standard prohibits it." This would be contradictory because the wrongness of cursing entails that some justified moral standard prohibits it. By a "standard" or a "norm," I mean a content that can be stated by an imperative; my usage here follows Gibbard's. To a first approximation, then, my idea is that the claim that cursing is wrong states a proposition that is true only if some relevantly justified or authoritative moral standard or norm prohibits cursing. In other words, the truth conditions of basic moral propositions are given by propositions about what is called for by relevantly justified or authoritative moral standards.[51] This idea is meant to capture

---

[50] I have elaborated on and defended the position I present in the next few paragraphs in David Copp, *Morality, Normativity, and Society.* For a brief introduction to this position, see David Copp, "Does Moral Theory Need the Concept of Society?" *Analyse et Kritik* 19 (1997): 189–212. For a reply to some objections, see David Copp, "Morality and Society—The True and the Nasty: Reply to Leist," *Analyse et Kritik* 20 (1998): 30–45.

[51] This position raises questions about the individuation of propositions and beliefs, and about the nature of philosophical analysis, that are beyond the scope of this essay. In the text, I try to finesse these issues. For discussion, see Jeffrey C. King, "What Is a Philosophical Analysis?" *Philosophical Studies* 90, no. 2 (1998): 155–79. Recall that a basic moral proposition

the normativity of moral judgment. I have called the generalization of this idea the *standard-based account* of normative judgment.

The account leaves it open what would make a moral standard relevantly authoritative. Different metaethical theories in effect make different proposals about this, and the standard-based account is amenable to various possibilities. For instance, a nonnaturalist might think that some standards simply have a "fittingness" to the moral nature of things. My own view on this underwrites a kind of naturalistic moral realism. A moral standard is relevantly justified, I suggest, just in case, roughly, its currency in the social code of the relevant society would best contribute to the society's ability to meet its needs—including its needs for physical continuity, internal harmony and cooperative interaction, and peaceful and cooperative relations with its neighbors. I call this view the *society-centered theory*. The moral standards with currency in a society form the social moral code of the society, a system of moral standards or rules. Let me use the phrase "S-ideal moral code" to speak of the moral code the currency of which in a society S would best contribute to S's ability to meet its needs. On the society-centered theory, moral claims are true or false depending on the content of the ideal moral code for the relevantly local society. The theory treats moral properties as relational: if cursing is wrong, it is wrong in relation to a society the ideal moral code of which would prohibit cursing. Wrongness—wrongness in relation to society S—is, roughly, the property of being prohibited by the S-ideal moral code.

The society-centered theory raises issues that are not raised by the standard-based account considered by itself. For example, which society is the relevant one in any given case? What, in detail, are the needs of societies? Do different societies have significantly different needs? I will have to put such questions to one side. In previous writings, I have introduced clarifications, qualifications, and amendments to the basic idea of the theory in order to deal with these and a variety of other questions and objections.[52]

Assuming that we have identified the relevantly authoritative moral standards, the standard-based account leaves it open precisely which proposition about these standards gives the truth conditions of a given moral proposition. As I said, the idea is that, to a first approximation, a basic moral proposition is true only if a corresponding moral standard or norm is relevantly justified or authoritative. For example, cursing is wrong only if (roughly) a moral standard prohibiting cursing is relevantly justified. In order to provide a complete account of the truth conditions for

---

is a proposition that entails that something instantiates M, where M is a moral property. In Copp, *Morality, Normativity, and Society,* I called basic moral propositions "paradigmatic." Something that is a standard or norm in my sense need not be embedded in the culture, nor need it be anything that people actually pay attention to in deciding how to live. A standard is the practical analogue of a proposition.

[52] See the references cited in note 50 above.

moral propositions, a great deal of detail would be required. We would need to distinguish, for instance, between the property of being morally wrong and that of being unthinkable, and between the property of being virtuous and that of being admirable. These details are not important for present purposes.

The idea that *is* important for present purposes is that a person making a moral claim expresses a moral belief, the truth conditions of which could be specified in the terms of the standard-based account and the society-centered theory. It is not a part of my view that a linguistically competent person using a given sentence to make a moral claim would know the truth conditions of the belief she expresses as they would be specified by my view. A linguistically competent person could, for instance, deny the society-centered theory without making any logical mistake. Yet I do think that a competent speaker would understand that the standard-based account is correct as far as it goes. She would realize that it would be contradictory to say, for example, "Cursing is morally wrong but no relevantly justified moral norm or standard prohibits it." In any event, the realist and naturalist side of the realist-expressivist view I am sketching in this essay is captured by the combination of the standard-based account and the society-centered theory.

The expressivist side of the view is the idea that a person making a moral judgment typically expresses a distinctive conative or motivational state of mind as well as a moral belief. What is this state of mind? This, recall, is a question I posed near the beginning of the essay and promised I would return to.

Given my view regarding the truth conditions of the beliefs expressed by persons making moral claims, it is natural to think that a person making a moral claim also expresses her acceptance of a corresponding standard. For example, if a person believes that cursing is morally wrong, her belief is true just in case cursing is a violation of an authoritative standard that prohibits cursing. In this case, my view is that, in expressing her belief, she also expresses her acceptance of a standard that prohibits cursing. Here we can make use of ideas that are found in Gibbard as well as in Hare. As noted in Section II, Gibbard writes about a state of mind he calls "norm acceptance," which he says is a distinctive kind of motivational state. Hare writes about "accepting an imperative," which he says is a matter of having relevant intentions. I myself have written about "subscription to a moral standard," which I have attempted to explain as involving a syndrome of attitudes, including an intention or policy of complying with the relevant standard.[53] Without attempting to define subscription to a standard, let me consider the idea that a person who makes a moral judgment, and thereby expresses belief in a basic moral proposition, also expresses subscription to a corresponding moral stan-

---

[53] See Copp, *Morality, Normativity, and Society,* 84.

dard. I have used the term "moral conviction" to refer to the complex state of mind that combines moral belief with subscription to a corresponding standard. The idea, then, is that a person making a moral judgment typically expresses a moral conviction.

One attractive feature of this idea is that, in Gibbard's words, it makes explicit a "kind of endorsement" that is involved in normative discourse. This characteristic kind of endorsement is not simply a matter of having a vanilla pro-attitude or con-attitude. It is a rather more complex state of mind consisting in taking something to fall within the purview of a norm that one endorses. Gibbard therefore proposes that I have endorsed an action in the relevant sense if I have said something that expresses my acceptance of a norm that requires or permits it.[54]

Another attractive feature of the idea is that it connects the state of mind of a person making a moral judgment with states that enter into her decision-making. Michael Bratman has proposed that intentions are states that constrain and guide our planning.[55] It is natural to think that a person's moral convictions likewise constrain and guide her planning. On my view, a person who makes a moral judgment expresses her subscription to a relevant standard, which is to say, among other things, that she expresses her intention or policy to conform to such a standard. On Bratman's planning theory, this is to say that a person making a moral judgment expresses a state of mind that constrains and guides her planning. Hence, if a person judges that cursing is morally wrong, she expresses a belief that is true only if cursing violates a relevantly warranted standard that prohibits cursing. On my view, she also expresses subscription to such a standard. If she actually does subscribe, she is in a state of mind that, if effective, constrains and guides her planning so that she is motivated to some degree not to curse.

VII. ARGUMENTS FOR THE EXPRESSIVISM IN REALIST-EXPRESSIVISM

In this section, I shall investigate arguments for the expressivist half of my proposed version of realist-expressivism. The distinctive part of the expressivist half of the view is that moral terms have coloring in virtue of which, other things being equal, their use in making typical moral assertions Frege-expresses a characteristic conative state of mind, namely, subscription to a relevant moral standard. That is, I claim there are linguistic conventions governing the use of moral terms which are such that if a speaker asserts a basic moral proposition by uttering a sentence in which a moral term is used literally, the speaker implies, other things being equal, that she subscribes to a relevant moral standard. The argument

---

[54] Gibbard, *Wise Choices, Apt Feelings*, 33.
[55] Michael Bratman, *Intentions, Plans, and Practical Reason* (Cambridge, MA: Harvard University Press, 1987).

proceeds in stages. First, I argue that a speaker who makes a typical moral assertion *conversationally* implicates that she subscribes to a relevant moral standard, other things being equal. The argument at this first stage depends on pragmatic considerations about moral discourse. Second, I argue that when a speaker uses moral terms to make a moral assertion, the fact that she implicates that she subscribes to a relevant moral standard does not need to be explained by assuming that there is common knowledge of such pragmatic considerations. It appears that it can be explained by reference to linguistic conventions governing the use of the terms. Third, I argue more specifically that this explanation is provided by the *coloring* of the terms. To show this, I apply the four tests for coloring to moral terms. This overall three-stage argument is not conclusive, for there are different ways of explaining the intuitions elicited by the examples that I will present at various points. I merely claim that the expressivist view I put forth deserves to be taken seriously.[56]

I take it to be common ground, for present purposes, that a person who says something with the intention to make a moral assertion that M sincerity-expresses her belief that M. The explanation for this is simple. To make an assertion is to say something with the intention that one's hearer will take one to believe what one says. Accordingly, other things being equal, to assert that M when one does not believe that M is deceptive, assuming one knows what one believes, and it is therefore insincere. The question is whether, other things being equal, a person who makes a moral assertion also expresses, in some sense, her subscription to a relevant standard.

The chief reason that we teach our children our moral values, and that we want our fellow citizens to share our moral values, is surely that we want them to govern their behavior accordingly. Our aim is not primarily that people simply agree with us in their judgments. Now, in my view, the key action-guiding moral states of mind are states of subscription to moral standards: when we act morally and act well, our behavior is guided by the moral standards to which we subscribe. Hence, I would say, the chief reason we teach our values to our children and want others to share our values is that we want them to subscribe to and endorse our moral standards, so that their behavior will be guided accordingly. Subscription to moral standards, unlike mere moral belief, is partly constituted by relevant intentions, and because of this it brings moral considerations into our planning and decisions about how to act. Indeed, the reason that the currency of a moral code can serve the needs of society is that it involves a widespread subscription to the code within the society's population, and widespread subscription to the code consists in part in a widespread tendency and policy to comply with it. From this perspective, therefore, moral belief is of secondary importance to subscrip-

---

[56] I am grateful to Justin D'Arms, Janice Dowell, Don Hubin, Steven Rieber, David Sobel, Sigrún Svavarsdóttir, and David Velleman for help with the arguments in this section.

tion to moral standards. From this perspective, the chief point of moral teaching is to bring people to have appropriate moral standards, and the point of moral discourse is in part to guide participants in the discourse to morally appropriate action-guiding states of mind—namely, states of subscription to justified standards—so that their actions will be appropriately based in a warranted moral outlook. The point of moral discourse depends, therefore, on our tending to have moral convictions in my sense, moral beliefs that are accompanied by subscription to corresponding standards.

If this account is basically correct, we can see why we would expect a person who expresses a basic moral belief to subscribe to a corresponding standard. As a result of the standard processes of moral teaching, people typically have moral convictions rather than "bare" moral beliefs. That is, if one has a moral belief, one typically also subscribes to a corresponding moral standard. A person who expresses a moral belief therefore typically has the corresponding conviction—and the point of expressing a moral belief is typically, in part, to guide others to share the corresponding conviction. Given all of this, moral conviction is the expected state of mind of a person who expresses a basic moral belief. Because of this, other things being equal, a person who makes a moral assertion conversationally implicates that she subscribes to a corresponding moral standard. This in turn means that it would be misleading of her, other things being equal, to express a basic moral belief if she did not subscribe to a corresponding standard.

This account of the pragmatics of moral assertion would explain why, in Smith's example, it would be *misleading* of me to assert that I ought to give to famine relief if I do not subscribe to a standard that requires me to give to famine relief. It does not follow, however, that I would be *insincere* to assert that I ought to give to famine relief if I do not subscribe to such a standard, for there need not be any deceit or pretense on my part. Hence, it does not follow that I sincerity-express subscription. We can, however, define a notion of *conversational-expression*. Let us say that a person conversationally-expresses a state of mind in asserting something if and only if, in asserting the thing, she implicates conversationally that she is in that state of mind. Given this definition, we can say that a person who asserts a basic moral proposition *conversationally-expresses* subscription to a corresponding standard. She implicates conversationally that she subscribes, other things being equal.

Let me use the expression "context of decision" to refer to conversational situations in which the topic at issue is what the speaker should do. The question in contexts of this kind is not merely how to classify various actions under normative properties. The conversation is instead aimed at the speaker's reaching a decision. Suppose, then, that a speaker who is in such a context says "Cursing is wrong." If she understands that the topic of conversation is whether to curse, and if she intends to be participating in the conversation and is aware that the point of moral discourse is to address and assess the moral standards subscribed to by the decision-maker and their bearing on the decision, then she must realize that she will be taken to subscribe to a standard that prohibits cursing. If she does not, then, other things being equal, it would be misleading of her to say that cursing is wrong without canceling the implication that she subscribes to a corresponding standard. It therefore appears that, other things being equal, a person who asserts a basic moral proposition in a context of decision conversationally-expresses her subscription to a corresponding moral standard.

Of course, we sometimes discuss hypothetical situations, or decisions made by other people. Even in these cases, however, the point of moral discourse retains its focus on addressing and assessing the moral standards to which we subscribe, for we could find ourselves in situations relevantly like the ones we discuss. Hence, I think, it can be misleading even in situations of this kind to make a moral judgment if one does not subscribe to a corresponding moral standard. I would seem hypocritical if, in discussing your cursing, I say "Cursing is wrong," but have no intention to avoid cursing myself and no tendency to feel negatively about myself if I curse. It thus seems plausible that, other things being equal, a person who asserts a basic moral proposition conversationally-expresses her subscription to a corresponding moral standard.

We can imagine cases in which it would not seem to be misleading to make a moral judgment without subscribing to a corresponding moral standard. Suppose that a person says "Capital punishment is wrong." Suppose also that she lives in a society that practices and strongly supports capital punishment, that she knows most people around her are strong supporters of capital punishment, and that she knows there is nothing she can do to change the situation. She is now numb to the situation; she has no intention to do anything about the fact that capital punishment is practiced in her society, and she has lost any tendency she once had to respond negatively to those who accept capital punishment. It follows that she does not subscribe—in my sense—to a standard prohibiting capital punishment. Nevertheless, if her state of mind is well understood, it would not be misleading of her to assert that capital punishment is wrong, and there need not be any insincerity in her state of mind. If this is correct, then, in saying capital punishment is wrong, she neither sincerity-expresses nor conversationally-expresses her subscription to a standard that prohibits capital punishment. In situations of this kind, it would not necessarily be insincere for me to make a moral assertion even if I do not subscribe to a relevant standard. Moreover, in situations of this kind, I do not conversationally implicate that I subscribe to such a standard.[57]

---

[57] The example I use here is similar to Michael Stocker's example of the retired politician. See Michael Stocker, "Desiring the Bad: An Essay in Moral Psychology," *Journal of Philosophy* 76, no. 12 (1979): 741.

There are also contexts of decision in which "other things" are not "equal." Consider a woman who says "Cursing is wrong," yet is known to be someone who curses like a sailor. Suppose that a priest is meeting with her and has confronted her about her cursing. The woman says, with a sneer and a chuckle, "I could continue to curse, but of course it would be wrong." She presumably understands that the issue raised by the priest is whether she should continue to curse, but it seems to me that, given what the priest knows of her, he would not take her sincerity here to depend on whether she has any intention to guide her behavior in light of the wrongness of cursing. If the priest is at all worldly, he will not be misled; the woman has not implicated that she subscribes to a standard that prohibits cursing.

I have argued that, other things being equal, a person who asserts a basic moral proposition conversationally-expresses her subscription to a relevant standard. That is, she implicates conversationally that she subscribes to a corresponding moral standard, other things being equal. The argument depends on the pragmatics of moral discourse as I see it. Given how participants in moral discourse understand what they are doing, they form certain expectations, and because of this, a person who makes a moral assertion implicates, other things being equal, that she subscribes to a corresponding standard. This explains why it can be misleading to assert a basic moral proposition if one does not subscribe to such a standard.

The argument does not turn on the use of moral terms. Suppose, for example, that Bob says to Alice, who just uttered a curse, "I would not have done that!" Bob might intend thereby to express the belief that it was morally wrong of Alice to curse, and she might realize this. If so, then given the pragmatic features of moral discourse that I have been describing, Bob might also have implicated conversationally that he subscribes to a standard that prohibits cursing. Apparently, then, one does not need to use moral terms in order to conversationally-express subscription to a moral standard.[58] In my view, the familiar moral terms are not the only terms that refer to moral properties. For example, I think that the complex expression "prohibited by the moral code the currency of which in S would best contribute to S's ability to meet its needs" refers to the property of moral wrongness. Since hardly anyone accepts the society-centered theory, it would only be in certain special contexts that we would take a person to express a moral belief if she said, "Cursing is prohibited by the moral code the currency of which in this society would best contribute to its ability to meet its needs." In these contexts, a person who said such a thing might conversationally implicate that she subscribes to a relevant moral standard.

It appears, nevertheless, that it would serve the goals of moral discourse if a convention were to develop such that a person asserting a

[58] David Sobel pointed this out in discussion.

basic moral belief by using moral terms would thereby implicate that she subscribes to a relevant moral standard. If such a convention were to develop, then the connection of moral discourse to action-guiding states of mind would be encoded in the meanings of the terms we use. Under such a convention, if a person were to assert a basic moral belief by using moral terms, we would not need to have any special knowledge of the pragmatics of moral assertion to understand the speaker to be in a state that includes subscription to a standard. As Frege suggested, conventions can develop to govern uses of a term when "it has constantly been used in cases of the same kind." [59] Hence, it would not be surprising if it were a feature of the meaning of "morally wrong" that, other things being equal, when a person says that something is "morally wrong," she thereby expresses her subscription to a relevant standard. It would not be surprising, that is, if moral terms have a coloring such that when a speaker asserts a basic moral proposition, she thereby implicates that she subscribes to a relevant standard.

To me, it seems plausible that moral terms *do* have such coloring. It would be misleading, other things being equal, for Bob to say to Alice "Cursing is morally wrong" if he does not subscribe to a standard that prohibits cursing. If Alice understands the point of moral discourse, she will take him to subscribe to such a standard. Now, I do not think that a person needs to have a sophisticated understanding of the pragmatics of moral discourse in order to understand that a person who asserts a basic moral belief in moral terms is implicating subscription to a corresponding moral standard. It seems to me that it is only necessary to understand what is said. If this is correct, then perhaps there are linguistic conventions governing the use of moral terms such that they are standardly used to express subscription to norms. Perhaps, that is, moral terms have a coloring that suits them to express subscription to norms.

To test whether the term "morally wrong" has coloring of this kind, we can apply our four tests for coloring. These are, recall, Frege's truth test, Grice's test of detachability, my test of cancelability, and the misuse test. To apply the truth test, consider an amoralist: someone who does not have any moral policies, and so does not subscribe to any moral norms. Suppose she says, "Cursing is morally wrong." Even though she does not subscribe to a norm that prohibits cursing, we certainly would not conclude on this basis that the proposition she has asserted is false. Second is the test of detachability. It seems to me that inverted commas or "scare-quotes" can be used to decolor terms that are standardly colored. I might say, for example, that such and such behavior would be "unladylike," indicating by emphasis or gesture that I put the term in scare-quotes. Alternatively, I might speak of

---

[59] Frege, "Separating a Thought from Its Trappings," 141.

"so-called unladylike behavior."[60] On this model, the amoralist could have said "Cursing is 'morally wrong'," placing "morally wrong" in inverted commas, or she could have said "Cursing is so-called morally wrong"; either method would have detached the implication that she has a policy against cursing. Third, consider the test of cancelability. An amoralist could explicitly cancel the implication that she subscribes to a standard that prohibits cursing by saying, "I agree that cursing is morally wrong, but I certainly have no policy of avoiding cursing." Finally, we come to the misuse test. It seems to me that in most contexts, the amoralist would misuse the term "morally wrong" in saying "Cursing is morally wrong," since she does not subscribe to any prohibition of cursing. Her use of the term could be challenged, just as a person's use of the term "Yankee" might be challenged if the person has no contempt for Americans. This is evidence of a misuse. Such challenges can sometimes be answered satisfactorily if the speaker was using the term in scare-quotes. For example, a person who is challenged to explain why she uses the term "Yankee" might respond that she means to use the term in scare-quotes. Similarly, if the amoralist is challenged to explain why she says that cursing is "morally wrong," she might respond that she is using the term in scare-quotes. Despite this, however, in saying "Cursing is morally wrong," the amoralist might well be expressing the belief that cursing is *morally wrong*, which is the same belief that you would express in saying "Cursing is morally wrong."[61]

Given all of this, it seems plausible to me that the term "morally wrong" has a coloring such that, other things being equal, a person who asserts

[60] I was helped with these ideas by discussions with Don Hubin, Steven Rieber, and David Velleman.
[61] There is a complication here that I do not want to address in the text. On my view, a person who uses moral terms to assert a basic moral proposition M *conventionally* implicates that she subscribes to a corresponding standard. Suppose that an individual decolors the moral terms in M by placing them in scare-quotes. On my view, she still asserts that M, for her terms still have their original core meaning. It is part of my view, however, that a person who asserts a basic moral proposition M *conversationally* implicates that she subscribes to a corresponding moral standard, other things being equal. On my view, then, it appears that the person still implicates that she subscribes to a corresponding moral standard, and that therefore she has *not* in fact managed to detach the implication by decoloring her terms. If this is correct, it threatens my thesis that moral terms are colored in the first place. The solution to this problem is that other things are not equal when one uses a decolored moral term. In decoloring a colored term, the use of which standardly implicates that p, one *both* detaches *and* cancels the implication that p. To see this, consider the term "heretical," which I take to be colored. To call a view heretical is, I suppose, to implicate conventionally one's disapproval of those who hold the view. Now suppose that I am engaged in a discussion of the conditions under which a religious view would count as heretical. The various things I say might implicate conversationally that I take heresies seriously, so that I disapprove of people who hold heretical views. My use of the term would conventionally implicate the same thing. However, if I were to decolor the term by placing it in scare-quotes, I would not only detach the conventional implication, but would also cancel the conversational implication. In similar fashion, if I called certain views "so-called heresies," I would not implicate that I disapprove of those who hold them.

that an action is "morally wrong," using the term literally in asserting a moral proposition, *conventionally* implicates that she subscribes to a standard that prohibits the action. The speaker *Frege-expresses* her subscription to such a standard. This is explained by the fact that the use of "morally wrong" is governed by expressive linguistic conventions of the kind I have described. This is the heart of the expressivist thesis of the realist-expressivist view I am proposing, as applied to the term "morally wrong." I believe it is plausible that there are similar expressive conventions governing the use of other moral terms, but I will not attempt to argue the point. The general thesis is that moral terms have coloring such that in asserting a basic moral proposition by uttering a sentence in which a moral term is used literally, a speaker conventionally implicates that she subscribes to a relevant standard. The speaker Frege-expresses her subscription.

In summary, then, I have been arguing for the plausibility of the conventional-implicature view for cases in which a speaker asserts a basic moral proposition by using moral terms. In such cases, I have been contending, the speaker conventionally implicates, other things being equal, that she subscribes to a corresponding standard. In other cases, I have said, a speaker who expresses a moral belief conversationally implicates that she subscribes to a corresponding standard, other things being equal.

VIII. The Realism in Realist-Expressivism

Near the beginning of this essay, I warned that the differences between realist-expressivism and certain other views are quite subtle. Because of this, it is easy to confuse realist-expressivism with, on the one hand, a kind of internalist moral realism, or with, on the other hand, a kind of antirealist-expressivism that exploits deflationism about the meaning of "true." I now want to underline the differences between these views and realist-expressivism.

Let me begin with the difference between realist-expressivism and familiar internalist varieties of moral realism. As I explained in Section I, internalism in this context is the doctrine that a person who believes that she ought to do something must be motivated to some degree to do it. In Smith's example, I agree after discussion that I ought to give to famine relief, but soon thereafter I fail to exhibit any motivation to give; Smith says that my behavior in this case casts "serious doubt on the sincerity of my claim to have been convinced that it is right to give to famine relief at all." As I said before, this might suggest that the sincerity of a moral assertion in a context of this kind depends on the speaker's being appropriately motivated. Even so, and even though the sincerity of a moral assertion depends on the speaker's believing what she asserts, it would be a mistake to conclude that the speaker's believing what she asserts

depends logically on her being appropriately motivated.[62] This is because
the having of the relevant belief and the having of the appropriate motivation might each be necessary to the sincerity of the speaker's assertion
without the motivation being a necessary condition of the belief.

As I showed in the previous section, the expressivist half of realist-
expressivism can explain Smith's observation in the famine-relief example. This does not mean, however, that the expressivist thesis commits
realist-expressivism to some standard form of internalism. The expressivist thesis implies simply that a person who *asserts* that she morally
ought to do something *implicates* that she is motivated to do it. It does not
follow that a person who genuinely *believes* that she morally ought to do
something must be motivated to do it.[63] Therefore, internalism does not
follow from the expressivist thesis.

Realist-expressivism does, however, support the thesis that a person
who asserts, in so many words, that she "morally ought" to do something
must also subscribe to a moral standard that calls on her to do the thing
in question—otherwise, unless she somehow cancels or detaches the implication that she subscribes to such a standard, her statement is inappropriate. In short, other things being equal, a person who says that she
"morally ought" to do something Frege-expresses her subscription to a
relevant standard; she expresses her intention or commitment to do the
thing in question. We might call this thesis *discourse internalism*. Realist-
expressivism can explain why internalism seems plausible to many moral
realists, for the correct view—realist-expressivism—supports this cousin
of internalism. Because of this, it is easy to mistake realist-expressivism
for a combination of realism with a standard form of internalism.

Let me turn now to the differences between realist-expressivism and
antirealist-expressivism. It is possible in fact to confuse realist-expressivism
with a number of different antirealist views, or at least to think that it is
not significantly different from these views. As I have already pointed
out, it might seem that realist-expressivism is merely a variant of Blackburn's quasi-realism. Realist-expressivism might also seem very similar
to the views of antirealist-expressivists, such as Hare, who agree that
there is some element of "description" in moral judgments. Finally, one
might think that realist-expressivism merely treats the "thin" moral predicates, such as "wrong," in the way that standard antirealist-expressivism
treats the "thick" moral predicates, such as "honest." I shall focus on each
of these possible confusions in turn.

Let us consider first the issue of whether there is any interesting difference between Blackburn's quasi-realism and realist-expressivism. The
central issue here is whether there is any interesting difference between

[62] Smith does not make this mistake.
[63] Similarly, a person who calls a dog a "cur" in stating a belief about the dog thereby
expresses contempt for the dog, but it does not follow that she must actually have such
contempt in order to have the belief she states.

the realist half of realist-expressivism and the quasi-realist half of Blackburn's expressivism. Given his deflationist views about the meanings of "true," "property," and "belief," Blackburn would agree with the realist that there are moral truths, moral properties, and moral beliefs. However, Blackburn does not accept the central thesis of moral realism when it is carefully formulated in the way I recommend. On my formulation, the central doctrine of moral realism is that moral predicates refer to robust moral properties; they have the same basic semantic characteristics as at least some typical nonmoral descriptive predicates. Blackburn would deny this. He says that from "inside" moral discourse, there is no discernible difference between what a quasi-realist and a moral realist would be willing to say. However, he says, when one raises "external" questions about morality, such as whether there are moral properties, the quasi-realist holds there are only the attitudes and stances of people.[64] Presumably, then, he would deny that there are moral properties in addition to these attitudes and stances, although he surely would admit that there are familiar descriptive properties, such as the property of being a perennial, in addition to the attitudes and stances of people. Blackburn therefore denies the central thesis of moral realism when it is formulated in the way I recommend. This is the most important difference between Blackburn's quasi-realism and my realist-expressivism.

Second, there are antirealist-expressivists who agree that there is an element of "description" in moral judgments. Hare says, for example, that moral terms have "descriptive meaning" as well as "evaluative meaning." In commending things, we apply standards of evaluation to them. If the standard by which a speaker is judging is well known, Hare says, we can infer that she means to attribute certain descriptive characteristics to the thing she is evaluating. Hence, he notes, "If a parson says of a girl that she is a good girl, we can form a shrewd idea, of what description she is; we may expect her to go to church, for example." This is "part of what the *parson* means" in calling the girl "good," says Hare. Hare puts this point by saying that the "descriptive meaning" of "good" is "secondary to the evaluative."[65] The realist-expressivist might reverse the order of priority, but it is not clear that this is an interesting difference between realist-expressivism and Hare's version of expressivism.

Hare ought to have said, however, that although *we* can mean something descriptive in using "good," the meaning of the *term* is not descriptive.[66] He agrees that possession of the descriptive characteristics on the basis of which we judge a person to be good is not "entailed" by what we say in calling that person good.[67] In the example of the parson, Hare

[64] Blackburn, "How to Be an Ethical Antirealist," 173. See also ibid., 168–69.
[65] Hare, *The Language of Morals*, 146. See also Stevenson, "The Emotive Meaning of Ethical Terms," 78.
[66] Hare, *The Language of Morals*, 148–49.
[67] Ibid., 145.

presumably does not think it is part of the literal meaning of the *sentence* "She is a good girl" that we may expect the girl to go to church, even though he does clearly think that this is part of what the *parson* means to say.[68] Hare's considered view, then, should be that at least the thin moral terms have only evaluative meaning. They are used to express moral states of mind, such as prescribing or commending. This brings out the fundamental disagreement between Hare's version of expressivism and the realist-expressivism that I am proposing, for according to realist-expressivism, moral terms refer to robust moral properties.[69]

Third, on any plausible version of expressivism, thick moral terms, such as "honest," have the same basic semantic characteristics as at least some nonmoral descriptive predicates. An expressivist like Hare would agree that "honest" refers to some robust nonmoral property, such as, perhaps, the property of being disposed to assert only what one believes. Of course, an expressivist would insist that the thick moral predicates are like the thin moral predicates in that they have the semantic role of expressing a characteristic conative state of mind. Nevertheless, the expressivist's view of the semantics of thick moral predicates parallels the realist-expressivist's view of the semantics of thin moral predicates such as "wrong." It might therefore seem that the only new idea in realist-expressivism is the idea that the semantics of the thin moral predicates is not importantly different from the semantics of the thick moral predicates as it has been conceived in expressivism.

This objection misses the significance of the fact that, according to familiar forms of antirealist-expressivism, the thick moral terms qualify as moral terms only in virtue of the fact that they are used to express a distinctive conative state of mind. Realist-expressivism does not agree with this. It agrees that properties such as the property of being disposed to say what is true are not moral properties. However, it holds that *if* the term "honest" is a moral term, then it does not simply refer to such a property. It refers instead to a robust *moral* property, such as, perhaps, the property of being disposed to assert only what one believes exactly to the

---

[68] Ibid., 109-10, 117-18, 118-20. In these passages, Hare appears to see that he needs to distinguish between the question "What do you mean, good?" and the question "What does 'good' mean?" The former asks about speaker's meaning, the latter about the meaning of the term.

[69] Stephen Barker has recently proposed an expressivist view according to which a person making a moral assertion that M both asserts some nonmoral empirical proposition and conventionally implicates that she has a conative or motivational state C-M. I am happy enough with the second part of Barker's proposal, but according to the first part, a person making a moral judgment does not express a moral belief—instead, she expresses an ordinary empirical belief. This strikes me as quite implausible. Barker agrees with realist-expressivism that moral terms refer to robust properties, but he has no room in his account for the existence of robust *moral* properties. For this reason, his view qualifies as a kind of antirealist-expressivism rather than a kind of realist-expressivism. See Stephen J. Barker, "Is Value Content a Component of Conventional Implicature?" *Analysis* 60, no. 3 (2000): 268-79. I owe this reference to Kent Bach.

extent that being so disposed is virtuous, or the property of being disposed to assert only what one believes exactly to the extent that being so disposed is called for by the ideal moral code of the relevant society. Of course, realist-expressivism also holds that the thin moral predicates refer to robust moral properties. This is independent of the fact that these predicates also have a coloring such that their use standardly expresses the speaker's subscription to a relevant standard.

According to the version of realist-expressivism I am proposing, the proposition that cursing is morally wrong is a moral proposition. It is a proposition that attributes to cursing the robust moral property of, roughly, being prohibited by the ideal moral code of the relevant society. If I express belief in this proposition by saying that cursing is "morally wrong," I implicate that I subscribe to a standard prohibiting cursing. This is a realist picture. It is not compatible with an antirealist version of expressivism.

IX. CONCLUSION

My goal in this essay has been to state a version of realist-expressivism, to explain the respects in which it is realist as well as expressivist, and to offer an explication and a partial defense. It seems to me that realist-expressivism has significant theoretical advantages over other views. Let me review some of its strengths.

Realist-expressivism permits moral realists in general and moral naturalists in particular to resist certain standard expressivist arguments against their views by agreeing with expressivists about the expressive quality of moral language. Gibbard claims, for example, that "the special element that makes normative thought and language normative" is that "it involves a kind of endorsement." [70] The realist-expressivist can agree that an element of endorsement is involved in normative discourse. The existence of realist-expressivism as a coherent position shows that one need not abandon "descriptivistic analyses" of moral belief in order to acknowledge the element of endorsement. Accordingly, an argument for the positive thesis of expressivism is not an argument for antirealism, because the positive thesis of expressivism can be combined with realism.

Expressivists hold that the "normativity" of moral terminology is captured by the expressive speech-act potential of sentences containing moral terminology. In Gibbard's words, as I just mentioned, the "element of endorsement" is "what makes normative thought and language normative." It is not clear what Gibbard means by "normative" in this context. But realist-expressivism acknowledges that there is a difference between the meaning of "wrong" and the meaning of any complex description in nonmoral language that could also be used to pick out the property of

---

[70] Gibbard, *Wise Choices, Apt Feelings*, 33.

wrongness. This is because the term "wrong" has a distinctive coloring in virtue of which it can be used to express subscription to a relevant moral standard. This difference could be described as a difference between the "normativity" of the term "wrong" and the "nonnormativity" of any such complex description in nonmoral language.

Realist-expressivism also acknowledges that there is a difference between the state of mind of a person who believes that, say, cursing is wrong, without subscribing to a prohibition on cursing, and the state of mind of a person who both has this belief and subscribes to such a standard. Indeed, insofar as the point of morality is to guide people's action into socially constructive channels, our goal in teaching our children about moral matters is not only to provide them with morally correct beliefs, but also to ensure that they subscribe to corresponding standards so that they will integrate moral goals into their life-planning. We want people to have appropriate moral *convictions*, in my sense of the term, and not merely to have true moral *beliefs*. Now, one could say that moral conviction, in that it involves an action-guiding subscription to a standard, is a "normative" state of mind in a way that bare moral belief is not. Realist-expressivism can thus acknowledge that there is here a real difference between moral conviction and moral belief that could justify this terminological choice. Hence, realist-expressivists can agree to a point when Gibbard says that normative thought and language derive their normativity from their connection to an "element of endorsement."

Another theoretical advantage of realist-expressivism is that it gives the realist a way of understanding open question arguments and claims about the is/ought gap, the naturalistic fallacy, and the like. According to the version of realist-expressivism I have proposed, moral terms have a coloring in virtue of which their meaning, in a wide sense, is not captured by any complex nonmoral descriptive phrase. Similarly, given the coloring of "cur," its meaning is not captured by "mongrel dog." According to my version of realist-expressivism, there are expressive linguistic conventions governing the use of moral terms that link them to relevant conative states (such as subscription to moral standards), but there are no such conventions governing the use of the complex nonmoral descriptive phrases that can also be used to refer to moral properties. This is one reason we might detect an "open question," a "gap," or a "fallacy" when a moral realist claims that wrongness is identical to some natural property, such as the property of being prohibited by the ideal moral code of a relevant society. The existence of a gap of this kind, however, is no reason to think that the realist is mistaken to identify moral properties with natural properties.

Finally, as we saw in the previous section, realist-expressivism can capture many of the intuitions that motivate internalist accounts of the connection between moral belief and motivation, and it can do this without being committed to any standard kind of internalism. Realist-expressivism does imply the view I called discourse internalism, which is the thesis that, other things being equal, a person who asserts in so many words that she "morally ought" to do something thereby Frege-expresses her subscription to a corresponding moral standard. In so doing, she expresses her intention or commitment to do the thing in question. But discourse internalism must not be confused with the standard kind of internalism that I have discussed.

In developing realist-expressivism, I have exploited a comparison between moral discourse and "cur discourse." This is perhaps unfortunate, but it is helpful. Realism holds that there are robust moral properties just as there are robust canine properties, that there are moral truths just as there are truths about canines, and that we have moral knowledge just as we have knowledge about canines. In the version I advocate, realist-expressivism adds that moral terminology gives us a way to express moral beliefs and, at the same time, to express subscription to corresponding standards. Similarly, we have the term "cur" as well as the term "mongrel dog," and because of this we have a way to express our beliefs about canines that also expresses contempt for the dogs that we refer to as "curs." Fundamentally, then, my version of realist-expressivism holds that the semantics of moral terms is similar to the semantics of terms such as "cur."

The point of moral discourse is at least in part to exploit a social means as well as an articulated means to guide people to form morally appropriate action-guiding states of mind. In order for actions to be based in a moral perspective, moral belief needs typically to be accompanied by subscription to corresponding moral standards. Subscription to moral standards, unlike mere moral belief, is partly constituted by relevant intentions, and because of this it brings moral considerations into our planning and decisions about how to act. Hence, the point of moral discourse depends on our coming to have moral convictions in my sense, not mere moral beliefs unaccompanied by subscription to corresponding standards. This point is served by the existence of conventions governing the use of our moral terms such that when we use moral terms in expressing our basic moral beliefs, we also thereby express our subscription to corresponding moral standards. I have tried to make a case in this essay that there are conventions of this kind. If I am correct, then moral discourse does not merely express bare moral beliefs; it also expresses the standards we accept and that figure in our decisions about how to act.

Philosophy, Bowling Green State University

THINKING ABOUT CASES

By Shelly Kagan

I. The Priority of Case Specific Intuitions

Anyone who reflects on the way we go about arguing for or against moral claims is likely to be struck by the central importance we give to thinking about cases. Intuitive reactions to cases—real or imagined—are carefully noted, and then appealed to as providing reason to accept (or reject) various claims. When trying on a general moral theory for size, for example, we typically get a feel for its overall plausibility by considering its implications in a range of cases. Similarly, when we try to refine the statement of a principle meant to cover a fairly specific part of morality, we guide ourselves by testing the various possible revisions against a carefully constructed set of cases (often differing only in rather subtle ways). And when arguing against a claim, we take ourselves to have shown something significant if we can find an intuitively compelling counterexample, and such counterexamples almost always take the form of a description of one or another case where the implications of the claim in question seem implausible. Even when we find ourselves faced with a case where we have no immediate and clear reaction, or where we have such a reaction, but others don't share it and we need to persuade them, in what is probably the most common way of trying to make progress we consider various analogies and disanalogies; that is to say, we appeal to still other cases, and by seeing what we want to say there, we discover (or confirm) what it is plausible to say in the original case. In these and other ways, then, the appeal to cases plays a central and ubiquitous role in our moral thinking.

Admittedly, some moral philosophers officially disavow the legitimacy of such appeals to our intuitions about particular cases. They attempt to make do without them, arguing that moral claims are better justified by appeal to something else, perhaps general principles that are themselves intuitively attractive or that can be shown to cohere well with other philosophical (or empirical) claims we find ourselves inclined to accept. But whatever the official pronouncements, I suspect that in practice the deft appeal to intuitions about cases is never actually eliminated. Like everyone else, moral philosophers—even those moral philosophers who think they know better—tend to be suspicious of moral claims that yield counterintuitive implications in particular cases. And like everyone else, moral philosophers—even those who insist that no legitimate comfort is to be had in this way—are reassured when intuitions about particular cases support the particular moral claims they are putting forward. In short, whatever it is that some of us may say, what all of us actually do is appeal to, and give considerable weight to, our intuitive judgments about cases.

This is not to say, of course, that we all take such intuitions as fixed points, judgments that must be endorsed by any adequate moral theory. Our intuitions about cases provide us with *evidence* for and against rival moral claims—and it is difficult to imagine giving them no weight whatsoever. But that is not to say that the evidence must always be taken to be decisive, overriding any considerations at all that might lead us to reject our intuitive judgment about some particular case. On the contrary, most of us are prepared to dismiss some intuitions as ill-considered, or the result of mere bias or prejudice, or perhaps even moral illusion.[1] Still, the fact of the matter is that none of us is genuinely prepared to write off all of our intuitions in this way.

What seems more open to genuine debate is the question of just how *much* weight should be given to our intuitions about particular cases. Absent compelling reason to dismiss some particular intuition, most of us are inclined to give our intuitions about cases considerable weight. We trust them to a remarkable extent, using them, as I have already indicated, as the touchstones against which our various moral claims are to be judged. We take our intuitions about cases to constitute not only evidence, but compelling evidence indeed. I think it fair to say that almost all of us trust intuitions about particular cases over general theories, so that given a conflict between a theory—even one that seems otherwise attractive—and an intuitive judgment about a particular case that conflicts with that theory, we will almost always give priority to the intuition.

It would be tempting to describe this priority by saying that we trust intuitions over theories, but that wouldn't be quite right. For the fact is that we can have intuitions about theories and general principles them-

---

[1] In ethics, then, as elsewhere, we need to distinguish between intuition and belief, since one need not believe one's intuitions. At best, intuition involves something more like a disposition to believe. But of course not all dispositions to believe are intuitions. While it would be useful to have a general characterization of intuitions, this is a complicated subject and I will have to restrict myself to two further remarks. First, intuitions are normally taken to be "immediate" or "spontaneous," and while this apparently rules out dependence upon current conscious inference or reflection, it seems to leave open the possibility that prior reflection (or current unconscious inference) may have played a role in generating the present "immediate" intuition (and so, among other things, intuitions need not be unlearned). Second, not all "immediate" and "spontaneous" dispositions to believe qualify as intuitions. There is, I think, a further characteristic quality—one that I, at least, find difficult to describe—that is required as well: roughly, its simply "appearing" to one that something is the case. (Thus, although I am immediately disposed to believe that Washington D.C. is the nation's capital, it doesn't seem to me that I have any *intuition* to this effect.) It is not clear which of these features (or others) are relevant to justifying our reliance upon intuition, in ethics or elsewhere.

selves. After all, even a general principle can strike us as intuitively plausible, and thus garner support from that very fact. And yet it seems to me that even intuitively plausible principles can come into conflict with intuitions about particular cases—thus giving us a conflict between intuition and intuition—and when this happens it remains true that we will almost always be inclined to have greater trust in the intuition about the particular case. (Of course, once again, various considerations might ultimately lead us, on reflection, to endorse the general principle rather than the particular judgment about the particular case; but insofar as we focus solely upon the evidence provided by intuition itself, we tend to trust the intuition about the case far more than the intuition about the principle.) Thus, what is striking is not only our reliance upon intuition but, more particularly, our reliance upon intuitions about particular cases.

It is not at all clear to me what to make of this fact. Perhaps our pervasive and deep-seated reliance on intuitions about particular cases—what we might call "case specific intuitions"—is misguided. It is puzzling, at any rate, for it seems to me that although the extent to which we rely upon intuitions about cases is widely recognized, we don't yet have anything like an adequate account of our practice—that is, a careful description of the various ways in which we appeal to, and give priority to, our case specific intuitions. Nor, I think, do we have anything like an adequate justification of our practice. While it is obvious that we constantly appeal to our intuitions about cases, it is far from clear what, if anything, makes it legitimate for us to give these intuitions the kind of priority we typically give them.

One ("deflationary") possibility, of course, is that our reliance upon intuitions about particular cases is simply a reflection of a more general epistemic policy of relying on *all* of our various beliefs—and inclinations to believe—to the extent that we are confident about them. On such an account, all we could say is that we just happen to be especially confident about our various case specific intuitions; and while this might be a fact that would call for some sort of explanation (perhaps along evolutionary grounds), it would need no further *justification*. But the more ambitious epistemological alternative is to think that there is indeed some special justification for our reliance on case specific moral intuitions, something that warrants our particular confidence in them and our giving them the kind of priority that we do. I take it that most of us are actually drawn to this second view, and so the question remains whether there is in fact a plausible way to defend this idea, a way to justify our particular confidence in and reliance upon case specific intuitions.

II. THE ANALOGY TO EMPIRICAL OBSERVATION

The closest we typically come, I think, to justifying this reliance on moral intuition is to appeal to a certain analogy. It is often suggested (and it is, at any rate, a natural suggestion to make) that we should think of case specific intuitions as playing a role in moral theory similar to that of *observation* in empirical theory. The suggestion, I presume, is sufficiently familiar that a bare sketch of the analogy should suffice.

Let's start with the role of observation. When arguing for or against empirical theories, we give unique weight to accommodating our observations of the world. We can simply see—immediately, and typically without further ado—that the liquid in the test tube has turned red,[2] or that the needle on the meter is pointing to 3, and an adequate empirical theory must take account of these facts. We appeal to such observations to provide support for a given theory, and we are very strongly inclined to reject any theory that runs afoul of them. Even a theory that seems otherwise attractive, and that strikes us as intuitively plausible in its own right, will be rejected if it contradicts the evidence provided by our empirical observations. To be sure, any given observation can itself be rejected (we might discover, for example, that we had unwittingly observed the test tube in red light), but for all that, no one seriously proposes that we should give no weight to our observations at all; and typically we give far greater priority to preserving the judgments of our observations than we do to maintaining our allegiance to any particular general empirical theory.

Similarly, then, when arguing for or against a moral theory we should think of our case specific intuitions as akin to observations. When thinking about particular cases we can simply see—immediately, and typically without further ado—whether, say, a given act would be right or wrong, or that it is morally relevant whether or not you have made a promise. An adequate moral theory must take account of these facts, it must accommodate these intuitions. To be sure, any given intuition can be challenged or rejected (we might, for example, realize that we made some judgment while inappropriately angry or embarrassed), but it would be quite implausible to suggest that we should give no weight to our moral intuitions at all. Indeed, even an otherwise plausible moral theory should be rejected if it contradicts the evidence provided by these intuitions; and so typically we appropriately give far greater priority to endorsing the judgments of intuition than we do to maintaining our allegiance to any particular general moral principle.

The analogy is indeed an appealing one, and it would be silly to dismiss it out of hand. But if we try to take it seriously certain points of disanalogy immediately suggest themselves. The most obvious worry— also familiar, and a natural one to think about—is this: in the case of empirical observation we have a tolerably good idea of how it is that the

---

[2] This is similar to an example of Judith Jarvis Thomson's, offered while making a similar point; see Thomson, *Rights, Restitution, and Risk* (Cambridge, MA: Harvard University Press, 1986), 257.

observations are produced. Visual observations depend upon the eyes, auditory observations depend upon the ears, and so forth. More generally, empirical observations depend upon the presence of well-functioning sense organs. In contrast, in the moral case, it is not at all obvious how it is that the corresponding "observations"—the moral intuitions—are produced. Is there a corresponding organ, a "moral sense," that is at work here? If so, it must be admitted that we know precious little about it.

Now this complaint must not be misunderstood. The main complaint about an appeal to a moral sense had better not be that we don't know how it *works*. For if that were the complaint it might not be especially worrisome. I take it, after all, that for most of human history we knew next to nothing about how the various sense organs worked either. But despite our ignorance, what was never in question was the existence of the various sense organs themselves (or that they were, indeed, sense organs). It was always fairly obvious, for example, that eyes were tied to visual observation, ears to auditory observation, and so on. In contrast, talk of a "moral sense" is nothing more than a place holder, a name for a supposed organ of moral intuition, something whose existence we may be led to infer (so as to have an account of the generation of moral intuitions), but concerning which we know virtually nothing else. And it is this, I take it, that gives us ground for skepticism, leaving us worried that there may be no such organ at all. Yet without a moral sense to correspond to the sense organs, the analogy to empirical observation is threatened.

Just how serious is the threat? Actually, this isn't at all obvious. Even if there were no moral sense, no organ generating moral intuitions, the rest of the analogy might still go through. We could still regard moral intuitions as "input" for our moral theories, in roughly the way that we let empirical observations function as input for empirical theories. Perhaps there is no single moral organ (or set of organs) corresponding to the sense organs; still, the fact of the matter is that we have the various intuitions and we can treat them as input, accommodating them and giving them priority in the way that empirical observations are accommodated and given priority.

In any event, given the undeniable fact that we do have our various moral intuitions, it is not clear what harm there is in simply going ahead and positing a moral sense in the first place. Presumably, *something* generates the intuitions—they do not arise out of thin air!—and if we want to talk of the mechanism (or mechanisms) responsible for generating them as a "moral sense" or a "moral faculty" it is not clear what objection there can be to doing so, so long as we don't thereby presuppose anything further about the structure or inner workings of that faculty.

The important question, rather, is whether we have special reason to *trust* our moral intuitions. Whether or not we posit a moral sense, the question remains whether there is good reason to take our intuitive judgments as *evidence* in anything like the way we do. Even if there is a moral sense, an organ capable of generating moral intuitions, we still need to know whether it is more or less reliable.

It is precisely at this point, of course, that the analogy to empirical observation seems to beg the crucial question. After all, we all come to the discussion already convinced of the general reliability of the sense organs. (That is, we come to *this* discussion convinced of it; skepticism about the senses is not a worry we normally embrace when doing moral philosophy.[3]) Roughly speaking, then, we take the sense organs to be generally reliable, which is to say that empirical observations are generally reliable as well: *that* is why empirical theories must accommodate them. Similarly, then, once we make the assumption that our moral intuitions are generally reliable—that our moral sense, whatever it is, is generally reliable—then of course it will follow that our moral theories must accommodate our intuitions as well. But what justifies our assumption that our moral intuitions are reliable? Insofar as the analogy to empirical observation *presupposes* the reliability of our moral intuitions, it is not obvious how it can provide us with any reason to accept the claim that they are indeed reliable.

It is possible, however, that the analogy to empirical observation might still be found helpful, even here. For it might be suggested that our reasons for trusting our moral intuitions are analogous to our reasons for trusting the evidence of our senses.

Very well, then, what exactly *is* it that justifies us in thinking our empirical observations generally reliable in the first place? This is, of course, a complicated and much contested question, but at least one attractive answer begins by emphasizing the fact that we find ourselves strongly inclined to believe these observations—immediately, and without further ado—and so in the absence of a good reason to reject them, it is reasonable to (continue to) accept them. What's more, we are able to incorporate these observations into an overall attractive theory of the empirical world, one which admittedly rejects some of the observations as erroneous, but which for the most part endorses the claims of observation as correct. These two facts—the lack of reason for wholesale skepticism concerning

---

[3] In point of fact, I don't think it altogether obvious to what extent empirical observations are indeed reliable. Consider shapes and sizes. Many people, I suppose, would be inclined to say, for example, that the stick in the water *appears* to me to be bent, even if I know better (and so believe it to be straight). But is it also the case—more controversially—that the building in the distance appears small (though I correctly infer that it is large, given its distance and apparent size), or that the penny seen from an angle appears to be oval (though I correctly infer that it is circular)? What, exactly, is it that I *observe* in such cases? What is it that I "just see," without further ado? Pursuing these questions would illuminate the nature of empirical observation, and thus might illuminate the nature of moral intuitions as well. But they seem to me quite complex—and they would certainly take us rather far afield—so I am going to put them aside, and assume in what follows that empirical observations are, indeed, generally accurate.

our senses, and our ability to construct an overall theory that in the main
endorses our observations—together go a considerable way toward justifying us in taking our senses to be reliable.

Of course, to say that our senses are reliable is to say more than that
they *happen* to be accurate, that empirical observations happen to be
true. It is to claim that this level of accuracy is nonaccidental, that there
is a connection between the truth of the relevant claims and the fact
that they are given by empirical observation. (Very roughly, the presumed connection is this: it is because of the fact that P is true that we
make the empirical observation that P; and were it not the case that P,
we would not "observe" that P.) As we normally put it, our sense
organs *respond* to the underlying empirical realities (and do so accurately, of course).[4]

This nonaccidental connection between observation and empirical reality is, obviously enough, an important part of what justifies our practice
of actually *relying* upon our observations. After all, it is not as though we
first construct a complete theory of the empirical world, and only then
decide that our observations are, in the main, accurate. Rather, we construct enough of an account of the empirical world to justify us in taking
our observations to be generally reliable, and then we use *further* observations to give us evidence concerning those aspects of the empirical
world whose character we have not yet determined (as well as providing
further confirmation for those aspects already known). We can *rely* on our
observations only because we take it to be nonaccidental that our observations are accurate; we assume, that is, that our sense organs are *responding* to the world.

But what justifies us in taking our sense organs to be not just (accidentally) accurate, but reliably responsive in this way? I suspect it is primarily the very two facts already noted: we are strongly and immediately
inclined to believe our empirical observations, and we can offer an (admittedly incomplete) overall theory of the empirical world that largely
endorses the claims of observation as correct.

Given these two facts, we are justified in believing that ultimately—
even if not initially—an account will be forthcoming which will display
the inner mechanics of the sense organs in such a way as to explain just
how this responsiveness is accomplished (that is, how it is that the nonaccidental connection between observation and fact is maintained). Of

[4] Not surprisingly, talk of "responding" to the empirical world suggests that the world
exists independently of—that is, metaphysically prior to—our empirical sensations and
observations. But I take it that even "anti-realists" (who take the world to be somehow
metaphysically constituted by our sensations or our reports of their contents) want a way to
express the thought that our empirical observations are appropriately connected to the
empirical facts, and for present purposes that is the only point at issue. Throughout this
essay—both with regard to the empirical world, and the moral domain—I make use of
familiar "realist" locutions. But I believe that roughly similar issues arise (concerning the
reliability of both moral intuition and empirical observation) for both realists and anti-realists.

course, to believe that such an account can be produced is not yet to produce it. And eventually, no doubt, that promissory note must be made good: the account must indeed be produced. But I take it that our belief in the possibility of such an account can justifiably remain a mere promissory note for a good long time, since, as I have already noted, for much of human history we couldn't actually produce even the basic outlines of the relevant accounts. Still, given that we *were* able to produce an attractive overall theory of the empirical world that largely accommodated our empirical observations, it was nonetheless reasonable to conclude (albeit provisionally) that empirical observations are, indeed, not only accurate, but reliably so.

Analogously, then, it might be argued that we are also justified in taking our moral intuitions to be reliable. We certainly find ourselves strongly inclined to believe our moral intuitions—immediately, and without further ado—and so, in the absence of good reason to reject them, it is reasonable to (continue to) accept them. And if, going beyond this, we are also able to incorporate our intuitions into an overall attractive theory of morality, one which for the most part endorses these intuitions as correct, then even if the theory rejects some of the intuitions as erroneous, we will still be justified in taking our moral intuitions to be generally reliable.

Here too, of course, we will still find ourselves with a further explanatory obligation. If we are to justify our *reliance* on moral intuition it won't suffice if moral intuitions merely happen to be accurate: there must be, instead, a nonaccidental connection between moral intuition and the underlying moral realities. Thus, we must believe that ultimately an account will be forthcoming that will display the inner mechanics of the moral sense in such a way as to reveal how it succeeds in being responsive to the moral "facts." Eventually, no doubt, we will need to make good on this promissory note, and produce the requisite account. But just as we were justified in taking sense organs to be reliably responsive, even though we lacked (for most of human history) an account of how it is that this responsiveness was accomplished, we may still be justified (for the time being) in taking our moral sense to be reliably responsive as well, even if we still lack an account of how *that* responsiveness is accomplished. In short, given the compelling nature of our immediate moral intuitions, and given the existence of an overall moral theory that largely accommodates those intuitions, we are justified in believing that the requisite account of the moral sense may yet be forthcoming. Which is to say: we are justified in taking intuition to be reliable.

If an answer along these lines is to be accepted, however, it is important to give due weight to the claim that our various moral intuitions can indeed be incorporated into an overall attractive theory of morality. For it is only if we are truly able to construct such a theory that we are entitled to take our moral intuitions to be reliable.

To see this, consider the case of empirical observation again, and imagine that we were unable to construct a theory of the empirical world which largely endorsed our empirical observations. We would then dismiss the evidence of our senses as unreliable—illusory, not to be trusted. After all, our sense organs can hardly be reliable if empirical observations are not generally accurate, but we are only justified in taking empirical observation to be accurate given our ability to construct a plausible theory of the empirical world that largely endorses the observations. Thus, if we were unable to construct such a theory, we would be forced to dismiss the evidence of our senses as inaccurate and unreliable.

The point can perhaps be put this way: the fact that we find ourselves immediately and unreflectively inclined to accept our empirical "observations" only gives us reason to accept these observations as reliable *given* that we have no reason to be skeptical of their accuracy. It provides only a presumptive argument for accepting them. But if we find that we cannot construct an overall theory of the empirical world that (in the main) endorses the observations, then this very failure provides us with good reason to be skeptical. The presumptive argument provided by the intuitive force of the observations is overcome. Similarly, then, in and of itself the mere fact that we find ourselves immediately and unreflectively inclined to accept our case specific moral intuitions provides us with only a presumptive argument for accepting them. If we were to discover that we could not actually construct an attractive overall moral theory that (in the main) endorses these intuitions, then this presumptive argument would be overcome, and we would have reason to be skeptical about our moral intuitions. So the question we must ask ourselves is this: can we indeed produce a moral theory that appropriately accommodates our moral intuitions, incorporating them into an overall theory of morality that is itself plausible and attractive?

I don't think the answer to this question is obvious, especially once we bear in mind that the requisite theory presumably must go beyond merely *organizing* the various "appearances," but must itself be sufficiently explanatory so as to provide at least the beginnings of an account of the relevant phenomena. Consider the empirical case, yet again: we are satisfied that the requisite theory of the empirical world can indeed be produced, but we would not be satisfied if all we could do was organize our various empirical observations into systematic patterns. Instead, what we want, and what we take ourselves to be able to produce, is a theory that goes below the surface and provides something of an explanation of the empirical phenomena that are the subject matter of our empirical observations. We offer, that is, a theory of objects in space and time, interacting with one another and with ourselves, a theory that begins to explain how it is that the empirical world can have the particular features reported in our observations.

Similarly, then, in looking for a moral theory that will accommodate our case specific moral intuitions, it won't suffice if all we can do is organize these intuitions into systematic patterns. Instead, what we need to find is a moral theory that goes below the surface and provides at least the beginnings of an explanation of the moral phenomena that are the subject matter of our moral intuitions. That is to say: we need a theory that offers at least the outlines of an explanation of how the moral domain can indeed have the particular features ascribed by our various intuitions. What I take to be far from obvious is whether we can in fact produce an overall moral theory that is sufficiently explanatory in this way, while still accommodating the bulk of our moral intuitions.

Of course, the difficulty of this task will depend on at least two further issues: first, the precise content of the moral intuitions we are trying to accommodate, and second, the standards we impose concerning what will constitute an explanatorily adequate moral theory. Unfortunately, pursuing either of these issues here would take us too far afield. But let me register the following skeptical note. I have argued elsewhere[5] that, in point of fact, certain widely accepted views—views central to common-sense morality and supported by the case specific intuitions of a great many individuals—cannot be provided with the kind of theoretical underpinnings we are here calling for. If I am right about this, then despite the immediate appeal of the relevant intuitions, they cannot be incorporated into an adequate overall moral theory, and in this regard, at least, our moral intuitions are unreliable.

I realize, of course, that many people would reject the particular arguments I've previously offered concerning the impossibility of providing an appealing and coherent moral theory that endorses these common moral intuitions. It is important to note, however, that in at least some cases the rejection of these arguments would simply take the form of pointing out how counterintuitive the implications of these arguments are, and in the present context, at least, such an appeal to intuition would constitute begging the question. For insofar as we are trying to establish whether our case specific moral intuitions are to be trusted or not, a simple appeal to the *force* of these intuitions shows nothing. We are only justified in trusting our intuitions if we can indeed construct a moral theory that adequately explains and incorporates them, and this, of course, is precisely what I am saying we cannot do. Thus, the mere fact that the conclusions for which I have argued are incompatible with many forceful and widely held intuitions does nothing to show that the requisite moral theory *can* be constructed. Indeed, as I have already noted, I think there are good reasons to conclude that we cannot, in fact, produce the requisite moral theory.

---

[5] See, especially, Shelly Kagan, *The Limits of Morality* (Oxford: Oxford University Press, 1989).

III. Error Theories

Let's recap. We have been taking seriously the analogy between moral intuitions and empirical observations, so as to see what might justify our practice of giving our case specific intuitions the kind of priority that we do. I have been suggesting, of course, that if we are to be justified in trusting our intuitions in this way, there must be an explanatorily adequate moral theory that endorses (not all, but most of) our case specific intuitions, just as we take ourselves to be justified in trusting our empirical observations by virtue of having an explanatorily adequate empirical theory that endorses (most of) our empirical observations. And as I have already noted, my own opinion is that once we take seriously the need to construct a general moral theory that would endorse our case specific intuitions as being for the most part accurate, we will find it difficult, indeed impossible, to produce the requisite theory. Theories that attempt to accommodate the bulk of our various case specific intuitions fail, I believe, at one or another explanatory task, and fall short in overall plausibility. What we are led to, instead, is a general moral theory according to which many of our specific moral intuitions are simply mistaken.

If I am right about this, then at a minimum we will have reason to be skeptical about these particular common moral intuitions. More generally, however, and for our current purposes more importantly, we will have reason to conclude as well that moral intuition is not, on the whole, reliable. Instead, the appropriate stance to take toward our moral intuitions will involve accepting an *error theory*, according to which at least many of our case specific moral intuitions are mistaken.[6]

Of course, there are various kinds of error theories—some more radical than others—and we've not yet addressed the question of whether our moral intuitions need to be discounted altogether. At one extreme lies just such wholesale skepticism concerning our case specific moral intuitions. But more modest versions of error theories are possible as well, and it might be that our best overall moral theory still endorses some specified range of moral intuitions, while nonetheless writing off other classes of intuitions as mistaken.

However, even such moderate error theories will seem unattractive to many. They will hold, correctly, that to accept an error theory—even a modest one—is to retreat significantly from our current practice, where appeals to intuition are generally taken across the board to be a particularly important source of evidence concerning the moral domain.

And so, despite my own skepticism, many will insist on remaining optimistic about the prospects for constructing a moral theory that actually succeeds quite generally in accommodating our case specific intu-

---

[6] Strictly, of course, everyone accepts an error theory of at least a rather *minimal* sort, since no one thinks that moral intuitions can never be mistaken. But I have in mind more ambitious theories of this type.

itions. They will want to reject any error theoretic approach to moral intuition at all. They will claim that our moral intuitions are, in point of fact, typically accurate, and that we are justified in thinking that it is nonaccidental that this is so. Thus, they will insist that we are justified in taking moral intuition to be reliable.

There are, however, still further grounds for skepticism about the overall reliability of our moral intuitions that we have not yet considered. What I have in mind is the surprising—and typically overlooked—extent to which people's intuitions actually differ with regard to specific cases. The extent of the disagreement is overlooked for the simple reason that we normally don't *look* for such disagreement. We barely entertain the possibility that others may not agree with us, and so we typically don't look around very carefully to see just how widely shared our particular intuitions actually are. And when we do stumble upon such cases of intuitive disagreement, it surprises us. Our own intuitions are sufficiently compelling and powerful that the relevant judgments strike us as virtually self-evident, and we are, accordingly, shocked if other, apparently reasonable individuals don't share them.

I do not mean to suggest, of course, that intuitive disagreements arise with regard to every case, though it does seem to me—based on years of discussing such cases with students and others—that even the most compelling examples typically fall short of garnering complete agreement. And in many cases, I think, once one probes a bit one finds that there is actually a considerable amount of disagreement. Consider, for example, "trolley problems" of the kind frequently used to determine the precise nature of the prohibition against harming others.[7] In my own classes I generally find that only about three fourths of the students share the majority intuition (say, that it is permissible to turn the trolley), while up to a fourth disagree; and even the apparent agreement of the three fourths majority dissolves when one asks further questions (for example, whether one is required, or only permitted, to turn the trolley).

To be sure, it is difficult to be confident that the opinions being reported in such informal polls truly state the immediate moral intuitions of the students in my classes. As we have already noted, we need to distinguish between the immediate pronouncements of our case specific intuitions and the various beliefs about a case one might have instead (for example, as a result of conscious reflection). In short, when students vote in such polls, are they reporting moral intuitions, or simply stating their own tentative beliefs about the cases? It might well be that despite the exis-

[7] In the basic case, a runaway trolley will hit and kill five children, unless you throw a switch which will divert the trolley onto a side track, saving the five, but killing a sixth child trapped on that side track (who would otherwise be safe). A large number of variants of this basic case have been discussed. See, e.g., Judith Jarvis Thomson, "Killing, Letting Die, and the Trolley Problem," in Thomson, *Rights, Restitution, and Risk*, 78–93; and Frances Kamm, "Harming Some to Save Others," *Philosophical Studies* 57, no. 3 (1989): 227–60.

tence of widespread disagreement in opinions about the relevant cases, there is actually far greater agreement with regard to the immediate intuitions themselves.

This is certainly a possibility, and I don't mean to suggest that I conduct my polls with sufficient care to rule it out. (It would be useful to have some careful empirical studies of these matters.) Still, it seems to me likely that intuitive disagreement is indeed a fairly widespread phenomenon.

What's more, I suspect that such disagreement is far from a random affair. It is not that any given individual almost always agrees with the majority, but sporadically finds himself faced with an idiosyncratic intuition, one as much at odds with the rest of his own intuitions (at other times, or in other cases) as it is at odds with the majority. If this were the nature of intuitive disagreement, we might well feel free to write off the occasional, quirky intuition as a mere aberration—a random misfiring in an otherwise reliable moral sense. In fact, however, it seems to me that moral disagreement is systematic and patterned. A given individual is likely to be regularly responsive to certain features that cases might display, while other individuals are routinely indifferent to the presence (or absence) of those features, or react to them in quite different ways. In short, intuitive disagreement doesn't take the form of norm and aberration. Rather, it is as though moral senses fall into distinct types, each with its own regular pattern of intuitive responses.

If I am right about this, obviously enough, it greatly complicates the position of anyone who hopes to endorse moral intuitions as largely correct. For if people actually differ considerably as to the content of those intuitions, even when thinking about the very same cases, then clearly not everyone's intuitions can be largely reliable. So what should we say?

One possibility, I suppose, would be to hold that everyone's intuition is indeed reliable, but only in those areas where there is complete agreement (assuming that such an area of complete agreement is to be found at all). But if we do say this, then we face the difficult task of explaining why intuition is indeed reliable in exactly those areas. What is it about the areas of agreement that makes intuition there function properly, and what is it about the other areas that causes intuition to break down and malfunction? Apparently, even those who hope to endorse moral intuition to this limited extent require an error theory, and an error theory of a fairly subtle sort, for they need to explain why intuition malfunctions in certain areas while working reliably in others. Absent a story about the mechanics of moral intuitions—the workings of the moral sense—any confidence that intuition is indeed to be trusted at all, even where there is agreement, may seem strained or premature.

More ambitiously still, some might hold out the hope of justifying reliance upon moral intuition even in those cases (considerable, as I believe) where there is intuitive disagreement. Clearly, however, this requires dismissing as flawed the moral senses of all those who stand in intuitive disagreement with the intuitions being endorsed. At best, the moral intuitions of only certain individuals can be held to be generally reliable. For the rest, then, we will inevitably need to embrace an error theory of a different sort: we will require an account which explains how most (or at least many) people end up with unreliable moral intuitions, while the moral sense of others nonetheless ends up functioning properly and reliably. And we will need an epistemological account as well, so as to justify us in our position concerning just whose intuition is to be trusted as reliable. (Obviously, it won't do to simply assume without further ado that it is *mine* that functions properly.)

This is not to say that these various explanatory burdens could not possibly be met. Once again, empirical observation provides a helpful analogy, for we do find ourselves, in the case of color blindness, arguing for something at least roughly comparable. Certain individuals are said to have damaged or flawed visual senses—leading to inaccurate visual observations, in at least a specifiable range of cases—while the rest of us are held to have properly functioning and reliable visual senses nonetheless. If something like this can be plausibly held to occur in the case of empirical observation, why not in the case of moral intuition as well? Is it so implausible to think that certain individuals are "morally blind"—cursed with inaccurate moral intuitions, in at least a specifiable range of cases?

The analogy to color blindness certainly suggests that something similar might arise in the case of moral intuition as well. But it is one thing to admit the mere possibility of something like this, it is quite another to make good on the claim that "moral blindness" actually occurs, and still another thing to warrant applying this label to some particular individual. In the case of color blindness, after all, we are able to demonstrate, even to the satisfaction of the color blind themselves, that their visual apparatus is indeed impaired, and that they fail to respond accurately to genuine features of the empirical world, features that the rest of us are able to detect through our own unimpaired visual senses. It is far from clear whether anything analogous can be done in the case of disagreement of moral intuitions, or even how one would go about trying to make out a comparable case. Instead, the charge of moral blindness more typically seems little more than name calling, where we blithely dismiss the intuitions of those who disagree with us, assuming without any further evidence than the mere fact of the disagreement itself that it is they who are blind, rather than us.[8]

I have been arguing that given the nature of intuitive moral disagreement, no one, not even those who hope to endorse moral intuition as

---

[8] The situation is further complicated by the fact that *each* side may fail to respond to features that the other side's intuitions mark out as morally significant. Thus, unlike the normal case of color blindness, moral disagreement may actually be closer to a situation in which many groups claim to see one or more colors that some other groups do not, and yet each group still fails to see some of the colors that other groups claim to see.

generally reliable, can escape the need to accept some kind of error theory with regard to at least many moral intuitions. And I have suggested as well that until we produce at least the beginnings of a story about the mechanics of moral intuition it is difficult to be confident that the requisite error theory can be produced. Attempts to limit the error theory—so that it impugns only a certain range of intuitions, or a certain group of moral senses—may easily fail, so that we are left with no good reason to believe our moral intuitions to be especially reliable at all.

But I do not mean to suggest that matters are particularly easier for those who hope to embrace far more radical error theories, dismissing most, or all, of our moral intuitions as suspect. For the fact is, producing a plausible error theory even of this radical sort is extremely difficult as well.

Consider, for example, the suggestion that is sometimes made that our case specific intuitions can be dismissed out of hand, as the mere historical by product of outdated religious views or neuroses about sex, or that they are merely the results of internalizing dubious moral teachings received in childhood.[9] Were this the case, there might well be little reason to give any weight at all to our case specific moral intuitions, and the wiser course of action would be to attempt to elaborate moral theories simply without appeal to them, however difficult that might prove to be.

But although accounts along these lines may well rightly cast doubt upon certain case specific intuitions (say, about sex), they seem rather inadequate as general explanations of the origins of our moral intuitions. Consider again the appeal to trolley problems as a means of determining the precise content of the prohibition against harming. Such cases are highly stylized, and unlike anything most of us have ever faced in real life, read about, or even imagined before being introduced to them for the first time as adults. Yet once the given case is described, we typically find ourselves with a moral intuition about it. I think it highly implausible, accordingly, to suggest that what happens here is that some vestige of a (perhaps forgotten) religious teaching now comes into play. No one is taught about trolley problems in childhood—nor even anything remotely similar to them—and yet we still find ourselves with intuitive reactions to the cases once they are described. Thus, whatever the actual origins of these case specific intuitions, we cannot dismiss them as artifacts of outmoded or unjustified teachings and accidental historical influences. For the simple fact of the matter is that most of our case specific intuitions cannot be plausibly explained in this way.

We may do somewhat better if we appeal, instead, to some of the primitive beliefs about physics or the nature of agency that we may well inherit as a result of our evolutionary history, as well as to certain innate

---

[9] See, for example, Peter Singer, "Sidgwick and Reflective Equilibrium," *The Monist* 58, no. 3 (1974): 516.

psychological biases in terms of how to group people and events.[10] An error theory that dismisses (many of) our case specific intuitions on the ground that they are implicitly based on inherited but dubious physical theories may well have an easier time of it explaining how we can have immediate and intuitive reactions to trolley cases, say, despite never having considered such cases previously. We may, for example, react to a given case as we do because we are innately disposed to view it in terms of mistaken concepts of causation and agency.

Here, too, such an account may rightly cast doubt upon certain of our case specific moral intuitions. But even an account of this sort seems inadequate, in large part because of the very universality of the inherited biases and beliefs that it presupposes. If our case specific intuitions are to be explained in terms of innate (though false) views about physics, say, then we would expect that people's intuitions would be fairly uniform— all reflecting the same set of inherited, though dubious, physical beliefs or psychological dispositions. In fact, however, as I have already suggested, it seems to me that we differ from one another in terms of our moral intuitions, in ways that this sort of account cannot easily accommodate. Intuitive disagreement is widespread and systematic, and it is implausible to dismiss our case specific intuitions on the ground that they are based on shared, inherited—and false!—views about the world, if in point of fact many of the relevant intuitions are not universally shared at all.

An error theory adequate to the facts about our moral intuitions would apparently have to be a rather subtle affair. It would need to accommodate the simple fact that we readily have intuitive reactions to cases quite unlike anything that we have faced or been taught about previously, and yet at the same time it would need to accommodate the fact that when we think about such cases our intuitive reactions are not all the same: people's intuitions differ, in systematic and patterned ways. It is not at all obvious what such an error theory would look like.[11]

I don't mean to suggest, however, that it will be impossible to produce an error theory adequate to the facts. Indeed, if I am right that everyone needs an error theory of some sort—both those on the whole trusting of moral intuition, and those on the whole skeptical of it—then it seems inevitable that *some* sort of error theory must be right, and I see no particular reason to assume that we cannot eventually articulate and

---

[10] See, for example, Peter Unger's discussion of protophysics and psychological grouping principles in his *Living High and Letting Die* (New York: Oxford University Press, 1996).

[11] It might seem that an emotivist or expressivist account of moral claims would have an easy time accommodating these facts, since there is nothing especially surprising in the suggestion that people's emotional (and other) attitudes vary, and that they can be readily generated in response to never before considered cases. But even accounts of this kind, it seems to me, should be troubled by the ease and force with which intuitions can be generated in response to trolley problems (and the like) since it is not at all obvious why these should so readily engage our emotions or other pro-attitudes, nor why minor changes in the cases should elicit such drastically altered reactions.

defend this theory, whatever it is. But for the time being, at any rate, it seems to me that we are rather far from having an adequate account of what this theory looks like, and so, lacking it, we are rather far from knowing to what extent our moral intuitions can be trusted.

IV. PARTICULAR CASES AND GENERAL CLAIMS

Let me close by noting one further complication. Recall the fact, previously noted, that our moral intuition is capable of responding not only to particular cases but also to general moral principles and moral theories. Consider how different this is from the case of empirical observation, where all we can directly observe are the features of particular cases. I can simply see that the meter is pointing to 3, but I cannot simply see the truth of Ohm's law or other principles of physics at all. General empirical claims must be inferred from the evidence; one cannot simply observe their truth. Apparently, our sense organs are incapable of responding directly to general empirical truths in this way.

In itself, this may be no more than a striking disanalogy between the case of moral intuition and the case of empirical observation. But it points to a deeper problem. For we have also already noted the fact that we do not give the same kind of priority to our intuitions about general moral claims. What we particularly trust, rather, are our case specific intuitions, so that given a conflict between an intuition about a particular case and an intuition about a general moral claim, we are almost always inclined to endorse the intuition about the particular case (at least, insofar as what we are attending to is the evidential force of the intuitions themselves). We give priority not to intuition in general, but, more particularly, to our case specific intuitions.

Yet how is this fact to be explained? If the situation were like that of empirical observation—with the relevant sense only capable of responding directly to particular cases rather than to general principles as well—there would, of course, be nothing further *to* explain (although, no doubt, we would ultimately want to explain just why it is that the given sense can respond only to particulars). But given that moral intuition is capable of reacting both to particular cases and to general principles, we do need a further explanation: we need to understand just why it should be the case that intuition is particularly reliable only with regard to specific cases. What makes our intuition more reliable for the one sort of object rather than the other?

Once we put the question this way, however, it may seem that the answer won't be particularly hard to come by. Even if moral intuition (unlike empirical observation) is capable of reacting both to particular cases and to general claims, there is no particular reason to assume that it will be equally adept at handling both *kinds* of objects. Although, no doubt, the details of the explanation will need to await a theory of the inner mechanics of moral sense, there is nothing particularly perplexing in the claim that intuition reacts more reliably when directed to one particular kind of object.

But this reassuring answer is itself threatened by the realization that this very distinction between two *kinds* of objects for intuition may well be misguided. For the fact of the matter, I believe, is that when we react to particular cases we are actually reacting to things of the very same type as when we react to general moral claims. It is easy to lose sight of this, given our common practice—one that I have followed in this paper as well—of saying that we are reacting to *particular* cases. But what we are actually reacting to, I think, are *types* of cases.

This is easiest to see in the situation where the kind of case we are thinking about is purely imaginary. What we are presented with, then, is only a description—and typically, all things considered, a fairly thin description at that. There is no actual, particular, concrete case that we are confronted with. So when our intuition tells us, say, that some particular act would be the right thing to do in that particular case, what we are actually intuiting, it seems, is that a certain *kind* of act would be the right thing to do in a certain *kind* of case. And this, of course, is a general moral claim.

The same thing is true, I think, even when the particular case being judged is an actual one. Again, this is easiest to see if the case, despite being real, is not one that we actually observe. We might only be *told* about the case, which means, of course, that we are again presented with a mere description. But this means, I take it, that we are not actually reacting to a particular, concrete case, but rather to a *type* of case. So here, too, when we react to the case what we are actually intuitively responding to is, it seems, something general: we are intuitively seeing that, say, this kind of act would be the right thing to do in this kind of case.

Although the point is controversial, I think the same is probably true even in those situations where we are literally faced with an actual, concrete case. Even in cases like this, I suspect that what we are actually responding to is its being a case with various salient features. By virtue of being literally faced with the case—able to observe it for ourselves—we better come to see that it has certain features, and we then intuit that the right thing to do, given a case with *these* features, is such and such. But if that is right, then here, too, we are reacting to something general: we are seeing that such and such an act is the right thing to do in this *kind* of case.

This is not to deny that being actually presented with a concrete case may elicit a different intuitive reaction than merely being presented with a description of the case. (When we literally *see* the needs of others we may intuitively see the importance of helping them, in a way that no mere description of their needs would elicit.) But even if it is true that in such cases there can be something special about intuition in the face of genuinely concrete particulars, the fact would remain that typically when we think about cases, we are only thinking about *kinds* of cases. Which is to say, typically when we think about cases we are intuitively reacting to something general.

This makes it harder to explain the priority we want to give to our intuitive reactions to "particular" cases. If all, or at least most, case specific intuitions are not actually reactions to something concrete and particular at all, then we cannot readily claim that what makes intuition more reliable here is that it is directed at a different kind of object than when we intuitively respond to a general moral claim. In both cases, it seems, what we see is something general.

Of course, there will still be differences in degrees of generality, and it might be that what we should give priority to are our intuitive reactions to the less general rather than to the more general. But this, too, calls out for explanation, and it is not clear what could be said in its defense.

For when we face the fact that typically (at least) when we think about a case, we are indeed only *thinking* about it, we are reminded of the fact that intuitive reactions are, in some suitably broad sense of the term, *a priori*. Typically, at least, we don't need to actually see the case; we only need to think about it. But it is not, as far as I can see, a general feature of the *a priori* that such thoughts are more reliable when they are directed to the less general rather than the more general. So it remains unclear why moral intuition should be thought particularly reliable in just such cases.

V. CONCLUSION

I have been arguing that our reliance upon case specific moral intuitions is problematic, and in need of a justification that we do not yet possess. Most importantly, of course, anyone who is going to rely on intuition at all—and that, I think, means all of us—needs to explain exactly why we are justified in taking intuition to be particularly reliable in the first place. This is a justificatory burden that has not, I think, been satisfactorily discharged. In particular, despite the obvious appeal of an analogy to the case of empirical observation, there are, it seems, sufficient disanalogies here, so that at a minimum considerably more needs to be said. Furthermore, if, as I think, we must all accept some sort of error theory (whether modest or radical) with regard to moral intuition, then we must face the further fact that providing an adequate error theory is itself a surprisingly difficult task. Apparently, our reliance upon intuition must be tempered; but how, or in what ways, is not yet clear.

In sum, the extent to which intuition is to be trusted—if at all—remains unsettled. Our reliance upon moral intuition remains troubling.

Still, the fact remains as well that despite these questions we are all inclined to attend to our case specific intuitions. We worry when our moral beliefs run afoul of them, and we take comfort in the extent to which our moral beliefs accord with them. It may well be, as I believe, that our moral intuition deserves considerably less respect than it is normally accorded. But it is difficult to believe that we could ever make do without it altogether. No moral argument—no claim, no theory—will ever seem compelling if it has not been subjected to the testing we provide when we think about cases.

Philosophy, Yale University

BUT I COULD BE WRONG

By George Sher

I. Introduction

My aim in this essay is to explore the implications of the fact that even our most deeply held moral beliefs have been profoundly affected by our upbringing and experience—that if any of us had had a sufficiently different upbringing and set of experiences, he almost certainly would now have a very different set of moral beliefs and very different habits of moral judgment. This fact, together with the associated proliferation of incompatible moral doctrines, is sometimes invoked in support of liberal policies of toleration and restraint, but the relevance of these considerations to individual moral deliberation has received less attention.[1] In Sections II through V, I shall argue that this combination of contingency and controversy poses a serious challenge to the authority of our moral judgments. In Section VI, I shall explore a promising way of responding to this challenge.

II. The Challenge to My Moral Judgments

In Chapter II of *On Liberty*, John Stuart Mill observes that the person who uncritically accepts the opinion of "the world"

> devolves upon his own world the responsibility of being in the right against the dissentient worlds of other people; and it never troubles him that mere accident has decided which of these numerous worlds is the object of his reliance, and that the same causes which made him a churchman in London would have made him a Buddhist or a Confucian in Peking.[2]

Along similar lines, John Rawls observes in *Political Liberalism* that the "burdens of judgment" that make moral disagreement inevitable include the fact that

---

[1] One work in which the issue is discussed did not come to my attention until after this essay was written; see Gerald Cohen, *If You're an Egalitarian, How Come You're So Rich?* (Cambridge, MA: Harvard University Press, 2000), chap. 1.

[2] John Stuart Mill, *On Liberty* (Indianapolis, IN: Hackett, 1978), 17.

to some extent (how great we cannot tell) the way we assess evidence and weight moral and political values is shaped by our total experience, our whole course of life up to now; and our total experiences must always differ.[3]

Despite their sketchiness, both passages appear to contain much truth. Moreover, the two passages are complementary in that Mill emphasizes the influence of contingent factors on the content of a person's most basic religious (and, by extension, moral and philosophical) convictions, while Rawls focuses more on the influence that contingent factors have on the inferences and judgments that a person makes *within* his basic framework. Thus, taken together, the two passages suggest that the influence of contingent factors on moral judgment is certainly extensive and may well be pervasive.

The principles that Mill and Rawls are defending in these passages are not the same: the passage from Mill appears in his famous defense of freedom of speech, while Rawls's point is that in a pluralistic society, a conception of justice must be defensible in terms accessible to all. However, each of these principles purports to provide a reason not to act in all the ways that initially appear to be called for by one's moral beliefs. This is why Mill and Rawls are both comfortable invoking a consideration — the influence of contingent factors on our moral beliefs — which, if taken seriously, is bound to undermine our confidence in the truth or rational defensibility of these moral beliefs.

But the same consideration that is so congenial to liberal principles that require us to distance ourselves from our moral beliefs in political contexts is decidedly uncongenial to our efforts to marshal these moral beliefs when we deliberate as individuals. My awareness that I would now have different moral convictions if I had had a different upbringing or different experiences may make it easier for me to put my moral beliefs out of play in the interest of allowing competing beliefs a fair hearing, or for the sake of arriving at terms of social cooperation acceptable to all. This same awareness, however, makes it correspondingly *harder* for me to act on my moral convictions when these conflict with the moral convictions of others. There is an obvious tension between my belief that my moral assessment of a situation is right while yours is wrong and my further belief that it is only an accident of fate that I assess the situation in my way rather than yours.

This tension raises questions about what I have reason to do in various practical interpersonal contexts. Perhaps most obviously, it raises such questions when I take myself to be morally justified in treating you in a way that you find morally objectionable — when, for example, I think I am not obligated to finance your dubious business venture despite our long

---

[3] John Rawls, *Political Liberalism* (New York: Columbia University Press, 1993), 56–57.

friendship, or when you demand attention that I feel I do not owe. The tension also muddies the waters when you and I disagree about something we must do together—when, for example, I want to give our failing student a retest but you worry about fairness to other students, or when we disagree about how much of our joint income we should donate to charity. It even raises doubts when I am contemplating taking some action that will not affect you at all, but of which you morally disapprove—when, for example, I am considering joining the Marines, contributing to a pro-choice candidate, or taking spectacular revenge on a hated rival, but you offer dissenting counsel.[4] In all of the aforementioned contexts, my awareness that I might well have taken a position like yours if my history had been sufficiently different will not sit well with my belief that I have more reason to act on my moral beliefs than I have to act on yours.[5]

Why, exactly, do these beliefs not sit well together? The answer, I think, is that my belief that I have more reason to act on my own moral beliefs than on yours appears to rest on a further belief that my own moral beliefs are somehow *better*—that they are truer, more defensible, more reasonable, or something similar. However, if I believe that it is only an accident of history that I hold my own moral beliefs rather than yours, then I must also believe that which of us has the better moral beliefs is also an accident of history. This of course does not mean that my belief that my own moral beliefs are better is wrong or baseless, but it does mean that I would have that same belief even if it *were* wrong or baseless. However, once I realize that I would have this belief whether or not it were true, I no longer seem entitled to use it in my practical deliberations.

III. The Challenge Not a Form of Skepticism

As just presented, the problems raised by the contingent origins of our moral beliefs bear a striking similarity to certain familiar skeptical worries. There is, in particular, an obvious affinity between the claim advanced at the end of the preceding section—that we are not in a position to tell whether we hold our moral beliefs because they are defensible or true or merely because of our upbringing—and the standard skeptical claim that we are not in a position to tell whether we hold our empirical beliefs because they represent reality accurately or merely because they have been instilled in us by an evil demon or a mad scientist stimulating

---

[4] As these examples suggest, I take morality to encompass only a set of duties that we owe to others and, by extension, a set of virtues and vices connected to these duties. As so construed, the realm of the moral excludes many forms of value.

[5] Although the cases just mentioned all involve actual disagreement, essentially the same problem appears to arise in cases in which no one actually disagrees with me, but I know there is (or could be?) someone who *would* disagree if given the chance.

a brain in a vat. Thus, isn't the current problem merely a special case of a far more general skeptical challenge—a challenge whose force we all acknowledge, but with which we long ago learned to coexist?

There is both something right and something wrong about this suggestion. What is right is its premise that the current problem has the same abstract structure as a very common form of skepticism; what is wrong is its conclusion that we can therefore live with the current problem as easily as we can live with skepticism. In fact, for three reasons, the current problem is far more vexing and urgent.

First, unlike the standard skeptical hypotheses, the claim that each person's moral beliefs were shaped by his upbringing and life experiences has an obvious basis in fact. We have no evidence at all that any of our empirical beliefs were caused by an evil demon or a mad scientist; and even the hypothesis that I am now dreaming, though somewhat more realistic, is improbable in light of the low frequency with which experiences with all the marks of wakefulness—vividness, continuity, coherence, self-consciousness, and the rest—have in the past turned out to be dreams. Thus, the most that any skeptical hypothesis can show is that all of our beliefs about the world *might* have had causes that operate independently of the truth of what we believe. In stark contrast, however, the fact that people's moral beliefs vary systematically with their backgrounds and life experiences shows considerably more, for in becoming aware of this, I acquire a positive reason to suspect that when you and I disagree about what morality demands, my taking the position I do has less to do with the superiority of my moral insight than with the nature of the causes that have operated on me.

The second reason that the current problem is harder to live with than is general skepticism is that we have significant second-order reason to be confident in our shared empirical beliefs, but no corresponding second-order reason to be confident in our controversial moral beliefs. In the case of our shared empirical beliefs, the second-order reason for confidence is provided by the various background theories that imply the reliability, within broad limits, of the processes through which these beliefs were formed—physiological theories about the mechanisms through which our sensory receptors put us in contact with the world, biological theories that imply that reliable belief-forming mechanisms have survival value, and so on. Even if appealing to these theories begs the question against global skepticism, our acceptance of them still makes such skepticism easier to ignore by reinforcing the confidence that we feel in our empirical beliefs when we are not contemplating the skeptical challenge. By contrast, my acceptance of the same background theories does not similarly reinforce my confidence that my own moral beliefs are better than yours, for because the theories imply the reliability of belief-forming mechanisms that are common to all members of our species, they provide no basis for any distinctions *among* individuals. Indeed, if anything, my awareness that a different upbringing and set of experiences would have caused me to acquire a different set of moral beliefs provides evidence that the processes through which I acquired my actual moral beliefs are probably *not* reliable.

Even by themselves, these two reasons would suggest that the current problem is much harder to live with than is general skepticism. However, a third reason makes the case even more strongly. Simply put, the most serious obstacle to our bracketing the current problem in the same way we routinely bracket skepticism is that unlike the fabrications of the skeptic, the current challenge to our moral beliefs is directly relevant to action.

For, as is often remarked, the hypotheses that all of my beliefs are being orchestrated by an evil demon or a master neuromanipulator, or that I am now dreaming, have no obvious impact either on what I *ought* to do or on what I am *inclined* to do. Even if I were able to suspend my commonsense beliefs, my awareness that various types of experience have been regularly connected in the past might well justify my "acting" as if the world were exactly as it seemed;[6] and, in any case, suspending my commonsense beliefs in practical contexts is not a live option. As Hume famously observed, even if I find skepticism convincing in the isolation of my study, I will, as soon as I emerge, "find myself absolutely and necessarily determined to live, and talk, and act like other people in the common affairs of life."[7] When it comes time to act, our robust animal realism will always dominate.

But not so our corresponding tendency to *moral* realism, for although we standardly do proceed as though our moral convictions are in some sense true, our confidence in their truth is neither anchored in our animal nature (since nonhuman animals evidently do not share it) nor invulnerable to reflective challenge. Because this confidence is relatively superficial, we cannot assume that it would survive a compelling demonstration that it cannot be defended. There is, to be sure, a real question about what it would be rational for me to do if I did lose confidence in my own moral beliefs—I would, after all, have exactly the same grounds for doubt about your moral beliefs as I would about mine—but at a minimum, this loss of confidence would reopen many questions that my own moral beliefs were previously thought to settle. Because of this, the challenge to the authority of my moral judgments seems capable of destabilizing my practical deliberation in a way that general skepticism cannot.

----

[6] The point I am making here applies only to the form of skepticism that asserts that our current experiences (or beliefs about them) might have causes that have nothing to do with their truth. Only this form of skepticism has the same abstract structure as our current problem.

[7] David Hume, *A Treatise of Human Nature*, ed. L. A. Selby-Bigge (Oxford: Clarendon Press, 1960), bk. I, sec. 7, p. 269.

IV. The Interplay of Controversy and Contingency

As just presented, the challenge to the authority of my moral judgments has a dual focus, for it appears to rest both on a premise about moral disagreement and on a premise about the contingent origins of my moral beliefs and ways of assessing evidence and weighting competing values. (For brevity, I shall henceforth refer to the combination of a person's moral beliefs and his ways of assessing evidence and weighting values as his *moral outlook*.) Respectively, these premises are as follows:

(1) I often disagree with others about what I morally ought to do.
(2) The moral outlook that supports my current judgment about what I ought to do has been shaped by my upbringing and experiences; for (just about) any alternative judgment, there is some different upbringing and set of experiences that would have caused me to acquire a moral outlook that would in turn have supported this alternative judgment.

Because these premises are logically distinct—because it could be true that you and I disagree about what one of us ought to do but false that our backgrounds have shaped our moral outlooks, or true that our backgrounds have shaped our moral outlooks but false that we disagree—it is not entirely obvious how (1) and (2) fit together. Are they both doing real work in the argument challenging the authority of my moral judgments? If so, why are they both needed? If not, which is necessary and which superfluous?

One possible answer is that the argument does *not* require both (1) and (2), but that each provides an independent route to the argument's conclusion. On this account, the version of the argument that relies exclusively on (1) is simply that

(A1) Because I am just another member of the human species (and because I am far from the smartest, the most clearheaded, or the best-informed member of that species), I have no special reason to regard my own moral judgments as being any better grounded, or any more likely to be true, than the moral judgments of any number of others who see things differently.[8]

By contrast, the version that relies exclusively on (2) asserts that

(A2) Because a different upbringing and set of experiences would have caused me to have a very different moral outlook, my

---

[8] Although this reasoning is seldom couched in singular terms, its collective counterpart appears to play a substantial role in supporting the cultural relativist's refusal to take sides when his own society's values conflict with those of other societies.

> having the moral outlook that informs my specific moral judg-
> ments is unlikely to have much to do with that outlook's jus-
> tifiability or truth.

Because these two versions of the argument have such different structures—
because (A1) turns on the fact that there is nothing special about me while
(A2) turns on the very different fact that the process through which I
acquired my moral outlook is unlikely to be reliable—we may be tempted
to conclude that each version must be evaluated separately, and hence
that the original combined appeal to (1) and (2) is a misbegotten hybrid.

But that temptation should be resisted; for by thus separating the appeals to (1) and (2), we would gravely weaken the case for the conclusion
that they both seek to establish. The reason that separating them would
have this effect is that (A1)'s appeal to (1) is vulnerable to an obvious
objection that is best blocked by introducing (2), while (A2)'s appeal to (2)
is similarly vulnerable to an obvious objection that is best blocked by
introducing (1). To bring out the underlying synergy between (1) and (2),
and thus to reconstruct the challenge to the authority of our moral judgments in its strongest form, we must look more closely at each of these
simpler arguments.

To argument (A1), which asserts that I have no special reason to favor
my own moral judgments over those of others who are no less intelligent
and well-informed, the obvious rejoinder is that the grounds for favoring
one moral judgment over another typically consist not of facts about the
persons who make the judgments, but rather of evidence or arguments
for and against the judgments themselves. There are, to be sure, some
obvious counterexamples to this claim—we may indeed be justified in
discounting someone's moral judgments if we have independent evidence that he is misinformed, confused, biased, or very stupid—but such
cases are the exception rather than the rule. In the far more standard case,
our reasoning runs just the other way: we infer that our interlocutor's
thought processes must somehow have gone awry because we believe
there are independent grounds for rejecting his conclusion. Thus, as long
as the challenge to my own moral judgments extends no further than (1)'s
claim that many others do not share them, I can resist it through the
simple expedient of reminding myself of whichever considerations I take
to make my own judgments more plausible than those of my interlocutors.

This rejoinder becomes problematic, however, as soon as we factor in
(2)'s claim that my having the moral outlook that informs my moral
judgment is itself an accident of my history; for the import of this claim
is to cast doubt not only on my judgment itself, but also on whatever
evidence or arguments I take to support it. If my upbringing and experiences had been sufficiently different, I would now share not only my
interlocutor's conviction that I ought to abandon my grand plan to humiliate the rival who has tormented me for years, but also my interlocu-

tor's disdain for the moral arguments that I currently take to underwrite that plan. However, once I agree that I have been caused to accept these arguments by factors independent of their force, I can no longer confidently base my decision on my conviction that they *have* force.

Thus, argument (A1), which appeals to (1) alone, seems unlikely to succeed unless it is supplemented by (2). Conversely, argument (A2), which appeals to (2) alone, requires supplementation by (1). Argument (A2), it will be recalled, attempts to move from (2)'s claim that a different upbringing and set of experiences would have caused me to acquire a different moral outlook to the conclusion that my having the moral outlook I do (and, by extension, my reaching the moral judgments I do) probably has little to do with its (and their) justifiability or truth. However, as it stands, this argument is a non sequitur, since even if the upbringing and experiences that caused me to acquire my current moral outlook would have had this effect on me whether or not my current moral outlook was justifiable or true, it hardly follows that the social conditions that caused me to have that upbringing and those experiences would also have existed regardless of whether or not my current moral outlook was justifiable or true. For all that has yet been said, it may have been precisely the truth or justifiability of the various elements of my current moral outlook that caused them to work their way into the culture that in turn caused me to acquire that outlook.[9] Because this possibility remains open, it does not follow from the fact that a different upbringing and set of experiences would have caused me to acquire a different moral outlook that it is unreasonable for me to continue acting on the judgments that my actual moral outlook supports.

But whatever force this rejoinder has against (A2)'s appeal to (2) alone, the rejoinder becomes problematic as soon as we factor in (1)'s claim that people's moral judgments often differ; for if my socially inculcated moral outlook has led me to reach one conclusion about what I ought to do while yours has led you to reach another, then the social determinants of at least one of our moral outlooks *cannot* be indirectly traceable to the justifiability or truth of all of its operative elements. Even if I can reasonably believe that I was caused to acquire all the operative elements of my own moral outlook by social factors that owed their existence to the justifiability or truth of those elements as long as you and I agree that I may not torture or murder my hated rival, I can no longer reasonably believe this when you go on to condemn even the less extreme plan to humiliate my rival that I consider entirely appropriate. As soon as we disagree, I am forced to conclude

---

[9] The parallel is not exact, but something roughly akin to this appears to happen whenever children are taught history or arithmetic by rote. Although the children are not given any reasons for believing what they are taught (and although they would form different beliefs if given different material to memorize), the reason they are asked to memorize precisely this material is that there in fact *are* good reasons for accepting it.

that at least one of us must have been caused to acquire some operative element of his moral outlook by some aspect of his upbringing or
experience that did *not* owe its existence to that element's truth or
justifiability; and the problem, once again, is that I have no special
reason to believe that that someone is you rather than me.

Thus, to give the challenge to the authority of my moral judgments
the strongest possible run for its money, we cannot represent it as
resting exclusively on either (1) or (2). Just as the version of the challenge that begins by appealing to (1) is unlikely to succeed without
supplementation by (2), the version that begins by appealing to (2) is
unlikely to succeed without supplementation by (1). Hence, no matter
where we start, we will end by concluding that (1) and (2) work best
when they work together.[10]

V. THE ROLE OF REFLECTION

How well, though, *does* the combined appeal to (1) and (2) work? Must
I really accept its corrosive implication that I often have no better reason
to rely on my own moral judgments than on the judgments of those with
whom I strongly disagree? Are (1) and (2) both firmly enough grounded
to support this disturbing conclusion?

There is, I think, little point in contesting (1), for its claim that I often
disagree with others about what I morally ought to do is all too obviously
true. However, when we turn to (2)'s claim that I would now view my
moral obligations differently if my upbringing and experiences had been

---

[10] As was pointed out by several contributors to this volume, the authority of my empirical beliefs faces a challenge analogous to that faced by my moral judgments. As is the
case with moral judgments, I disagree with others about various empirical matters, and for
(just about) any empirical belief that I reject but someone else accepts, there is some different
upbringing and set of experiences that would have caused me to accept that empirical belief.
Because I have taken the fact that a different background would have caused me to weigh
the evidence in a way that supports your moral judgment rather than mine to undermine
the authority of my own moral judgment, I can hardly deny that the fact that a different
background would have caused me to weigh the evidence in a way that supports your
empirical belief rather than mine is similarly subversive of the authority of my own empirical belief. However, there are several things worth noting here. First, very few of my
actual empirical beliefs *are* disputed by thoughtful, conscientious people who have simply
weighed the evidence differently. Second, when an empirical disagreement *is* of this nature —
when, for example, you and I disagree about what to make of the evidence about the causes
of a phenomenon such as intergenerational poverty — considerable diffidence on both sides
is indeed in order. It is worth noting, too, that if those with whom I disagree have not merely
assessed the shared evidence differently but either lack or are unresponsive to evidence I
have — if, for example, they are members of a prescientific society that attributes diseases to
spirits rather than microorganisms, or are creationists — then the fact that I would have their
beliefs if I had their background does *not* undermine the authority of my own beliefs. Here
I can see that, and why, my own background is the more favored. Taken together, these
considerations suggest that the combination of controversy and contingency poses far less
of a threat to the authority of my empirical beliefs than it does to the authority of my moral
judgments.

sufficiently different, the issue becomes more complicated. Briefly put, the complication is that although a person's upbringing and experiences clearly do cause him to acquire various moral beliefs and habits of judgment, these cannot be assumed to persist unaltered over time. No less than any other beliefs and habits, our moral beliefs and habits of moral judgment can be expected to evolve in response to various intellectual pressures.

We may not fully register this if we focus too exclusively on Mill's claim that "the same causes that made [someone] a churchman in London would have made him a Buddhist or a Confucian in Peking," for this claim draws attention to a single aspect of what a person believes—the particular religion he accepts—that often *is* a direct result of his background. It is obviously impossible for someone who has only been exposed to one religion to become devout in another. However, the more pertinent question is whether a person who has only been exposed to a single religion may nevertheless come to reject some or all of its teachings; and to this further question, the answer is clearly "Yes."

For because any set of claims about religion (or, by extension, morality) can be subjected to rational scrutiny, people can and often do reject even the religious and moral doctrines to which they have been most relentlessly exposed. Even when someone has at first been nonrationally caused to acquire a certain religious or moral belief, it is open to him rationally to evaluate that belief at any later point. Of course, in so doing, he will rely on various ways of assessing evidence and weighting values, and it is likely that the ways he uses will themselves have been shaped by his experiences (and, we may add, by his culture). Still, no matter how far these influences extend—and, as Rawls notes about the influence of experience, this is something we cannot know—their introduction does not alter the basic point because any resulting ways of assessing evidence and weighting values can be rationally scrutinized in turn. Thus, properly understood, the moral outlook that we have been nonrationally caused to acquire is best viewed not as a permanent fixture of our thought, but rather as a starting point that we may hope successively to improve through ongoing critical reflection.

There is, of course, no guarantee that this hope will be realized. Despite my best efforts, it remains possible that my moral outlook has from the start been hopelessly compromised by some massive error, and that my lack of access to the source of error has systematically subverted all my ameliorative endeavors. However, this hypothesis, if backed by no positive argument, is no less speculative than is the hypothesis that all my experiences are caused by a scientist stimulating a brain in a vat. Thus, as long as I have no concrete reason to believe otherwise, it may well be reasonable for me to assume that my efforts to think through the arguments for and against my fundamental moral convictions, and to correct for the distortions, biases, and false beliefs that my upbringing and earlier experiences have inevitably introduced, have on the whole made things better rather than worse.[11]

How, exactly, would the truth of this meliorist assumption bear on (2)'s claim that if I had had a sufficiently different upbringing and set of experiences, I would now judge my moral obligations differently? The answer, I think, is complicated. The truth of the meliorist assumption would not show that (2)'s claim is false, but would indeed lessen (2)'s sting. However, it would also leave intact the challenge to the authority of my moral judgments that (2) poses in conjunction with (1). Let me argue briefly for each of these three points in turn.

At first glance, the assumption that reflecting on one's moral outlook tends to improve it may indeed seem to tell against (2), for if this assumption is correct, then even two radically different moral outlooks can be expected eventually to converge if subjected to enough reflection. However, for at least two reasons, this way of arguing against (2) does not seem promising. First, even if we grant both that I would have reflected seriously on the alternative moral outlook that a given alternative history would have caused me to acquire and that I did reflect seriously on the moral outlook that my actual history caused me to acquire, there is no guarantee that the two starting points are close enough to allow anything approaching full convergence within my lifetime (or, *a fortiori*, now). In addition, at least some of the alternative histories that would have caused me to acquire a different moral outlook would also have caused me to be disinclined to engage in the kind of reflection that would be necessary to secure *any* degree of convergence. For both reasons, the assumption that reflecting on one's moral outlook generally improves it does not seem capable of supporting a refutation of (2).

Even if this is so, however, the assumption does make (2) more palatable, for as long as I can even partially overcome the nonrational origins of my moral outlook by critically reflecting on it, the fact that my moral outlook would now be different if my history had been different will not entirely undermine its credibility. Given the validating effects of critical reflection, I will, by virtue of engaging in it, at least partly transcend my moral outlook's merely contingent origins.

Yet even if *this* is so, it will hardly follow that I have any more reason to rely on my own moral judgments than on the judgments of others with whom I strongly disagree; for because these disagreements take place within a society that prizes reflection (and because, as an academic, I tend to interact with the more reflective segment of my society), I cannot as-

---

[11] Race/class/gender theory can be read as an attempt to show that all past reflection on our moral beliefs and habits of judgment *has* been subverted by a massive error—namely, our ignorance of the fact that those beliefs and habits merely rationalize the power of the privileged. However, even if this claim were true, it would not show that reflection cannot improve matters, since the aim of advancing the claim is precisely to unmask what has previously been hidden.

sume that those with whom I disagree have been any less reflective than I. Given that they, too, may well have sought to transcend the merely historical origins of their moral outlooks, an appeal to the validating effects of my reflections will not resolve my problem, but will only reraise it at a higher level. When you and I disagree about what I ought to do—when, for example, my own conscientious reflection leaves me convinced that the revenge I am planning falls well within tolerable moral limits, while yours leaves you no less convinced that I really ought to resist my ugly, vengeful urges—I cannot reasonably assume that it is I rather than you who has successfully thought his way out of his causally induced errors.

And if I am tempted to think otherwise, I need only remind myself of how often such situations arise. If I am entitled to assume that you have been less successful than me in purging your thinking of causally induced error, then I must be entitled to make the same assumption about the great majority of others with whom I disagree—about vast numbers of intelligent and sophisticated vegetarians, pacifists, postmodernists, deconstructionists, gender feminists, pro-lifers, proponents of partial-birth abortion, neutralists, advocates of hate-speech codes, fundamentalists, libertines, rigorists, and egoists, to name just a few. But although it is certainly possible that I have been more successful in avoiding error than some of these others—this is likely on statistical grounds alone—it strains credulity to suppose that I have been more successful than all, or even most, of them. It would be something of a miracle if, out of all the disputants, it was just me who got it all right.

VI. Practical Solution to These Doubts?

So what should I do? More precisely, how should I respond to the challenge to my ability to decide on rational grounds what I should do? I can see three main possibilities: first, to renew my quest for a convincing reason to believe that my own moral judgments are more likely to be true or justified than are those of the innumerable others with whom I disagree; second, to concede both that no such reason is likely to be forthcoming and that I therefore cannot rationally base my actions on my own moral judgments; and third, to acknowledge that no such reason is forthcoming but *deny* that this makes it irrational to base my actions on my own moral judgments. Unfortunately, of these three strategies, the first is pretty clearly doomed, while the second would commit me to a wholesale rejection of the moral point of view. Thus, if I am to avoid the twin pitfalls of futility and moral skepticism, I will probably have to implement some variant of the third strategy.

To do this, I will have to block the inference from "I have no good reason to believe that my own moral judgments are more likely to be justified or true than those of innumerable others who disagree with me" to "I cannot rationally base my actions on my own moral judgments." This in turn requires a demonstration that what makes it rational for me to base my actions on my own moral judgments is not simply the strength of my reasons for believing that these judgments are justified or true. More specifically, what I must show is that even when I realize that my own moral judgments are no more likely to be true or justified than are yours, it nevertheless remains rational for me to act on my own judgments simply because they *are* my own.

Can anything like this be shown? If so, it seems the argument would likely have to turn on certain features of practical reason itself. In particular, its pivotal premise seems likely to be that because no one can act rationally without basing his decisions on his *own* assessment of the reasons for and against the actions available to him, practical reason itself *requires* that I give pride of place to my own judgments. Although I can of course rationally discount any particular judgment that I take to be false or unjustified, the reason I can do this is that to discount a particular judgment is not to abdicate the task of judging; rather, it is only to allow one of my own judgments to trump another. Because acting rationally necessarily involves basing my decisions on the way *I* see things, I cannot entirely transcend my own outlook without moving decisively beyond the bounds of practical reason.

This much, I think, is clear enough. However, because not all reasons for acting are moral reasons—because, for example, I can also have reasons that are prudential, hedonistic, or aesthetic—the mere fact that practical reason requires that I base my actions on my own judgments about what I have reason to do is not sufficient to vindicate the rationality of acting on my own best *moral* judgments. To show that practical reason requires this, I must take the further step of arguing that even an attempt to transcend my own *moral* outlook would take me beyond the bounds of practical reason; and unlike the previous step, this one may seem problematic indeed.

For because my moral outlook encompasses only a small fraction of what I believe, want, and aim at, simply disregarding it would hardly leave me with nothing, or too little, upon which to base my practical decisions. Even if I were to set aside every one of my moral beliefs, I could still choose one action over another on any number of further grounds— for example, because the chosen action would be fun, because it would advance the aims of some person I care about, or because it is required for the completion of some project I have undertaken. Thus, given my awareness that my own moral judgments are no more likely to be true or justified than are the moral judgments of any number of others, isn't it indeed rational for me to set moral considerations aside and make my decisions exclusively on other grounds?

The answer, I think, is that this is *not* rational, for if I were to do it, I would merely be discounting one set of practical judgments in favor of another whose members are no less compromised by the now-familiar combination of controversy and contingency. Although a full defense of this final claim is beyond my scope, I shall end this section with a brief sketch of the argument for it.

The first thing that needs to be said is that just as the great majority of my *moral* judgments would be contested by various persons who are no less reflective than I, so too would the great majority of my *nonmoral* practical judgments. Indeed, the latter disagreements seem if anything to be even more wide-ranging, since they encompass both disagreements about which *sorts* of nonmoral considerations are relevant to the decision at hand—for example, disagreements about whether I should make the decision mainly on hedonistic, prudential, aesthetic, or affectional grounds—and disagreements about what each type of consideration gives me reason to do. Although some such disagreements obviously turn on different understandings of the facts of a given situation, many others do not. Also, while many endorse the metaprinciple that what I ought to do depends on my *own* weighting of the competing nonmoral considerations, there are also many who reject this metaprinciple. Thus, all in all, my nonmoral practical judgments are sure to be every bit as controversial as my moral judgments.

Moreover, second, my having the beliefs and habits of thought that combine to support the relevant practical judgments seems equally contingent in both the moral and nonmoral cases. Just as it is true that if I had had a sufficiently different upbringing and set of experiences, I would now hold your view rather than mine about what I *morally* ought to do, so too is it true that if I had had a sufficiently different upbringing and set of experiences, I would now hold your view rather than mine about what I have *nonmoral* reason to do. Our attitudes about the value of culture, work, friendship, planning, and much else are no less accidents of our upbringing and experiences, and are no less influential in shaping our judgments about how to live, than are our beliefs about virtue and vice and what we owe to each other.

Thus, in the end, my moral and nonmoral judgments about what I ought to do—or, better, the moral and nonmoral components of my integrated judgments about what, all things considered, I ought to do—seem likely to stand or fall together. Either it is rational for me to set both components of my own practical judgments aside or it is not rational for me to set either of them aside. If I were to set both components aside, I would indeed lack any basis upon which to make reasoned decisions about what to do. Hence, given the inescapability of my commitment to acting for reasons, my tentative conclusion is that practical rationality precludes my setting either of the components aside.

VII. CONCLUSION

My main contention in this essay has been that given the degree to which merely contingent factors appear to have shaped our moral outlooks, there is a serious question about whether I ever have good grounds for believing that I am right and you are wrong when you and I disagree about what I ought to do. However, I have also suggested that even if I never *do* have good grounds for believing this, it may nevertheless often remain rational for me to base my actions on my own moral judgments rather than yours. When they are combined, these claims have the paradoxical implication that it is often rational for me to act on the basis of moral judgments the objective likelihood of whose truth or justifiability I have good reason to regard as quite low. This implication casts (fresh) doubt on our ability to integrate our reasons for believing and for acting — that is, on our ability to square the demands of theoretical and practical reason. It also suggests that the price we pay for being clear-eyed moral agents may be a disconcerting awareness of a certain inescapable form of bad faith. Whether these are the only conclusions that the paradoxical implication warrants, or whether, in addition, it provides a platform for some further thrust by the moral skeptic, is a question I will not attempt to answer here.

Philosophy, Rice University

MORAL FACTS AND BEST EXPLANATIONS*

By Brian Leiter

I. Introduction

Do moral properties[1] figure in the best explanatory account of the world? According to a popular realist argument, if they do, then they earn their ontological rights, for only properties that figure in the best explanation of experience are *real* properties. Although this realist strategy has been widely influential—not just in metaethics, but also in philosophy of mind and philosophy of science[2]—no one has actually made the case that moral realism requires: namely, that moral facts really will figure in the best explanatory picture of the world. This issue may have been neglected in part because the influential dialectic on moral explanations between philosophers Gilbert Harman and Nicholas Sturgeon[3] has focused debate on whether moral facts figure in *relevant* explanations.[4] Yet as others have noted, explanatory relevance is *irrelevant* when it comes to realism: after all, according to the popular realist argument, it is inference to the best

---

* My thanks to Julia Annas and Allan Gibbard for comments on much earlier versions of portions of this material, to Ben Zipursky for comments on a more recent draft, to William Forbath for guidance on historical questions, to Sahotra Sarkar for guidance on evolutionary biology, and to this volume's editors and contributors for their helpful questions and comments on the penultimate version.

[1] I will use the terms "moral properties" and "moral facts" interchangeably in what follows. So, for example, one might say that inflicting gratuitous pain on a sentient creature has the property (or feature) of being morally wrong, or one might say that it is a (moral) fact that the infliction of such pain is morally wrong.

[2] See, e.g., Jerry Fodor's defense of the reality of the attitudes in Jerry Fodor, *Psychosemantics* (Cambridge, MA: MIT Press, 1987), chap. 1; and Richard Boyd's defense of scientific realism in, e.g., Richard Boyd, "Scientific Realism and Naturalistic Epistemology," in Peter D. Asquith and Ronald N. Giere, eds., *PSA 1980*, vol. 2 (East Lansing, MI: Philosophy of Science Association, 1982).

[3] Gilbert Harman, *The Nature of Morality* (New York: Oxford University Press, 1977); Nicholas Sturgeon, "Moral Explanations," reprinted in Geoffrey Sayre-McCord, ed., *Essays on Moral Realism* (Ithaca, NY: Cornell University Press, 1988); Gilbert Harman, "Moral Explanations of Natural Facts—Can Moral Claims Be Tested against Moral Reality?" *Southern Journal of Philosophy* 24, supplement (1986): 57–68; Nicholas Sturgeon, "Harman on Moral Explanations of Natural Facts," *Southern Journal of Philosophy* 24, supplement (1986): 69–78. In later work, Sturgeon has argued, with some plausibility, that "nonmoral explanations do not always appear to undermine moral ones." Nicholas Sturgeon, "Nonmoral Explanations," *Philosophical Perspectives* 6 (1992): 111–12. This point, however, even if correct, has no bearing on the argument of this essay, which supposes that the question is not whether nonmoral explanations undermine moral ones, but which explanations are *best*.

[4] See, e.g., David O. Brink, *Moral Realism and the Foundations of Ethics* (Cambridge: Cambridge University Press, 1989), 187 ff., which discusses the issue in terms of explanatory "relevance" and "irrelevance."

explanation of experience that is supposed to confer ontological rights.[5] I propose to ask, then, the relevant question about moral explanations: should we think that moral properties will figure in the best explanatory account of the world?

A preliminary word about the significance of the question is in order. Many moral realists—in particular, the so-called "Cornell realists"[6]— take explanatory potency in the above sense to be *sufficient* for realism. This position, however, no longer seems tenable in light of the powerful criticisms of inference to the best explanation (IBE) as a license for realism.[7] Instead, we should construe explanatory potency only as a necessary—but not sufficient—condition for realism. This would make the debate about explanatory potency a debate about what philosopher Geoffrey Sayre-McCord calls the "weak" version of the "Explanatory Criterion"; under this version of the criterion, "[a] hypothesis should not be believed if the hypothesis plays no role in the best explanation we have of our making the observations that we do."[8] "Real" facts— moral or scientific—must still, as philosopher Peter Railton puts it, figure "in the explanation of our experience" such that they "cannot be replaced without loss,"[9] but that they do so figure is not by itself sufficient to establish realism.

II. BEST EXPLANATIONS

Do moral properties, then, figure in the best explanatory account of the world? Of course, we cannot hope to decide here what the "best" explanatory account of the world really is, but we may at least ask whether moral properties will figure in seemingly "better" explanatory accounts. To know whether they will, however, we need to answer two questions

[5] See Geoffrey Sayre-McCord, "Moral Theory and Explanatory Impotence," in Sayre-McCord, ed., *Essays on Moral Realism*, 272–74.

[6] The "Cornell realists" are defenders of moral realism such as Richard Boyd and Nicholas Sturgeon (who teach at Cornell), as well as their students, such as David Brink.

[7] As noted above, the IBE arguments for realism claim that we are entitled to infer the real existence of those facts that figure in the best explanation of our experience. Arthur Fine has argued that as a defense of realism, IBE begs the question, which is precisely about the legitimacy of such an inference (namely, the IBE by which scientists posit unobservable entities). Bas van Fraassen, in contrast, has asked why we should think that what happens to be our best explanation should warrant an inference to truth. See Arthur Fine, "The Natural Ontological Attitude," in Jarrett Leplin, ed., *Scientific Realism* (Berkeley: University of California Press, 1984), 84–91; and Bas van Fraassen, *Laws and Symmetry* (Oxford: Oxford University Press, 1989), 142–49.

[8] Sayre-McCord, "Moral Theory and Explanatory Impotence," 267–68.

[9] Peter Railton, "Moral Realism," *Philosophical Review* 95, no. 2 (1986): 172. Note that none of this constitutes a bar to realism; Railton's realist program, for example—in both ethics and philosophy of science—eschews IBE. See also Peter Railton, "Explanation and Metaphysical Controversy," in Philip Kitcher and Wesley Salmon, eds., *Scientific Explanation* (Minneapolis: University of Minnesota Press, 1989).

that have been sadly neglected in the moral realism literature: first, what makes one explanation better than another; and second, *to what* are we comparing moral explanations?

Any account of what makes an explanation "best" or "better" is bound to be contentious, but if the realist is to defend moral facts on explanatory grounds, then he must take some stand on this question. I propose that we start with two intuitively plausible criteria for theory-choice articulated in a well-known paper by philosopher Paul Thagard: consilience and simplicity.[10] *Consilience*, according to Thagard, has to do with *"how much* a theory explains." Thus, "one theory is more consilient than another if it explains more classes of facts than the other does."[11] *Simplicity* in a theory is only a virtue when it does not come at the expense of consilience. Thus, "a simple consilient theory not only must explain a range of facts; it must explain those facts without making a host of assumptions with narrow application."[12] Notice that *ontological* or *theoretical* economy is not necessarily a virtue on this view: ontologies and theories can be complex as long as they contribute to consilience.[13] On this account, one explanation will be better than another if it explains more and does so with comparable or greater simplicity.

One might, of course, wonder why the moral realist should care about these criteria.[14] One reason is surely that they are intuitively plausible. Simplicity is, of course, a mainstay on any checklist of desiderata for theory-choice, while whole theories of explanation have been built around the idea that explanations should advance understanding by unifying disparate phenomena[15]—something that consilient theories, theories that explain different classes of phenomena in terms of some basic explanatory mechanism, would seem to do.

At least for some moral realists, however, a second reason for taking these criteria seriously seems compelling—namely, that they are, as Thagard argues, criteria operative in the history of science. Since for many moral realists—particularly those concerned to vindicate the explanatory power of moral properties—moral inquiry and moral epistemology should be continuous with scientific inquiry and scientific epistemology, it seems

---

[10] Paul Thagard, "The Best Explanation: Criteria for Theory Choice," *Journal of Philosophy* 75, no. 2 (1978): 76–92. I ignore a third criterion Thagard introduces, that of *analogy*. This is the thought that "other things being equal [i.e., without sacrificing consilience or simplicity], the explanations afforded by a theory are better explanations if the theory is familiar, that is, introduces mechanisms, entities, or concepts that are used in established explanations" (ibid., 91). This criterion is more contentious than are the other two, and is arguably more obviously inhospitable to moral explanations.

[11] Ibid., 79.

[12] Ibid., 87.

[13] The simplicity criterion is, then, a relative of Ockham's razor.

[14] This objection, especially with respect to consilience, was urged on me in conversation by Julia Annas.

[15] See Michael Friedman, "Explanation and Scientific Understanding," *Journal of Philosophy* 71, no. 1 (1974): 5–19.

fair to expect that on their accounts, moral explanations should satisfy the criteria that inform theory-choice in science.[16]

In any event, it is clear that to assess the explanatory potency of moral facts we need to have some criteria for assessing moral explanations, and Thagard's seem like reasonable candidates. Let the burden fall upon the moral realist to show why these criteria are inappropriate in the case of moral realism—and to suggest appropriate alternatives as well.

Applying Thagard's criteria yields a standard attack on the status of various putatively real facts, an attack based on what I will call *the problem of explanatory narrowness* (PEN). A property suffers from PEN if its explanatory role is too peculiar or narrow, that is, if it only explains one class of phenomena to which it seems too neatly tailored.[17] Real explanatory facts, Thagard's criteria suggest, must have some degree of extra consilience. Properties that "explain," but suffer from PEN, are not "real" properties.

Consider an example. Imagine someone called the Spirit Realist, who holds that various human actions can be explained in terms of the effects of spirits. So, for example, the Spirit Realist holds that Hitler did the evil things he did because he was possessed by evil spirits.[18] Assume further that the Spirit Realist holds that evil spirits supervene on precisely the evil-making moral properties that themselves supervene on the relevant natural properties. What's wrong, then, with "spirit facts"?

Examples like this are obviously troubling to the moral realist. However, one response that is not available here is the one philosopher David Brink offers against the defender of the explanatory power of magical facts: "What is objectionable about magical facts . . . is that they are incompatible with natural facts. Appeals to magical and natural facts provide competing explanations of the same phenomena."[19] The proposed spirit facts, however, are not magical facts in Brink's sense. The Spirit Realist, like the moral realist, assumes that his preferred facts (i.e., spirit facts) supervene on the relevant natural facts, and thus do not compete with them. Only by begging the question against the Spirit Realist could we employ a response like Brink's.

[16] That Thagard has accurately captured these criteria is nicely illustrated by this passage written by a mathematician reviewing a book by a physicist:

> The great ambition of scientists is to grasp the far from obvious nature of the physical world at ever more fundamental levels, and in doing so, to unify our understanding of phenomena that had previously appeared to be disparate. We have been enormously successful in this, demonstrating that complex objects are made from simpler components, and they in turn are made of even simpler ones. . . . [U]nderlying the immense complexity of life is a simplicity of microscopic composition.

George Ellis, "Good Vibrations," review of *The Elegant Universe,* by Brian Greene, *London Review of Books,* March 30, 2000, 14.
[17] Cf. Crispin Wright, *Truth and Objectivity* (Cambridge, MA: Harvard University Press, 1992).
[18] Cf. Sturgeon, "Moral Explanations," 245: "I do not believe that Hitler would have done all he did if he had not been morally depraved. . . ."
[19] Brink, *Moral Realism and the Foundations of Ethics,* 183.

Surely, however, we still have a good response to the Spirit Realist — namely, that spirit explanations suffer from PEN, and thus these explanations give us no reason to think that spirit properties are real properties. Spirit facts seem to do no explanatory work above and beyond that done by moral facts. The problem for the moral realist will be to show why moral properties should not meet the same fate vis-à-vis the nonmoral facts on which they supervene.

III. Naturalistic Explanations

We now know what would make one explanation better than another, but we still lack a precise comparison class for the moral explanations at issue here: we cannot decide whether moral explanations are "best" or "better" unless we know to what kinds of explanations they are to be compared. Rather than positing moral facts to explain our moral observations, Harman argues that we "need only make assumptions about the psychology or moral sensibility of the person making the moral observation." [20] In a similar vein, Freud and Nietzsche appealed to deep facts about human nature and development to explain our moral beliefs and judgments.[21] Freud's account is more detailed, and so I will focus on that account here.[22]

---

[20] Harman, *The Nature of Morality*, 6.

[21] For Nietzsche's version of these kinds of naturalistic arguments, see the discussion in Brian Leiter, "The Paradox of Fatalism and Self-Creation in Nietzsche," in Christopher Janaway, ed., *Willing and Nothingness: Schopenhauer as Nietzsche's Educator* (Oxford: Clarendon Press, 1998), esp. 230–35; and in Brian Leiter, "One Health, One Earth, One Sun: Nietzsche's Respect for Natural Science," *Times Literary Supplement*, October 2, 1998, 30–31. For a longer treatment, see Brian Leiter, *Nietzsche on Morality* (London: Routledge, 2001). Nietzsche's and Freud's approaches are compared in the book and in the *TLS* article. For Freud's naturalistic explanation of moral judgment, see especially Sigmund Freud, "The Dissection of the Psychical Personality," in Freud, *New Introductory Lectures in Psychoanalysis*, ed. and trans. James Strachey (New York: Norton, 1965).

[22] I am assuming — not uncontroversially these days — that Freud's theory is basically true, or at least that the part of the theory concerned with explaining the nature of and capacity for moral judgment and conscience is true. The standard reference point for the contrary view is Adolf Grünbaum, *The Foundations of Psychoanalysis: A Philosophical Critique* (Berkeley: University of California Press, 1984). (Strictly speaking, Grünbaum argues only that Freud's theory is not warranted by the evidence adduced, not that it is false.) Frederick Crews's shrill polemics notwithstanding, Grünbaum's critique has itself been demolished in a series of papers, of which the most important are Arthur Fine and Mickey Forbes, "Grünbaum on Freud: Three Grounds for Dissent," *Behavioral and Brain Sciences* 9, no. 2 (1986): 237–38; Jim Hopkins, "Epistemology and Depth Psychology: Critical Notes on *The Foundations of Psychoanalysis*," in Peter Clark and Crispin Wright, eds., *Mind, Psychoanalysis, and Science* (Oxford: Blackwell, 1988); David Sachs, "In Fairness to Freud: A Critical Notice of *The Foundations of Psychoanalysis* by Adolf Grünbaum," *Philosophical Review* 98, no. 3 (1989): 349–78; and Richard Wollheim, "Desire, Belief, and Professor Grünbaum's Freud," in Wollheim, *The Mind and Its Depths* (Cambridge, MA: Harvard University Press, 1993). Empirical confirmation of aspects of Freudian theory from nonclinical settings is presented, among other places, in Henry E. Adams, Lester W. Wright, Jr., and Bethany A. Lohr, "Is Homophobia Associated with Homosexual Arousal?" *Journal of Abnormal Psychology* 105, no. 3 (1996): 440–45, in which the authors report experimental evidence of the role of reaction formations in homophobia.

It seems at first that Freud's work contains two different stories of the development of moral conscience: in one, conscience arises through the internalization (or "introjection") of the parental superegos as a way of resolving the Oedipal complex;[23] in the other, conscience arises as a result of the introjection of innate aggressive drives, whose taming is a necessary precondition for the rise of civilization.[24] Philosopher John Deigh observes that the first account (the "standard account") "fits more closely into [Freud's] general theory of how one develops a personality . . . [while] the other [the "Nietzschean account"] . . . gives a more cogent explanation of how one acquires a conscience."[25] Deigh thinks the Nietzschean account marks a *change* in Freud's theory of moral development, especially in explaining the formation of conscience through repression of *aggressive* rather than *sexual* drives. It would take us too far afield into Freud interpretation to resolve this question, but let me at least suggest here that the two accounts can also be understood as complementary. This is because the superego has a dual function for Freud: the enforcement of moral standards and the maintenance of an "ego ideal" to which we may aspire. As Deigh himself notes elsewhere, "The operations of conscience [for Freud] owe their motivational force to aggressive drives; the operations of the ego ideal owe theirs to sexual drives."[26] Both accounts of the origin of the superego, then, would be needed to explain the dual functions it performs.

The crucial point, though, for our purposes is that on Freud's account, "judgments of morality and value have motivational force that is traceable to these basic [aggressive and sexual] instincts."[27] Moreover, from the standard account we know that the *content* of judgments of morality derives from the child's identification with the parental superegos that is required to resolve the Oedipal complex. Hence, both moral motivation

[23] Freud writes, "With his abandonment of the Oedipus complex a child must . . . renounce the intense object-cathexes which he has deposited with his parents, and it is as a compensation for this loss of objects that there is such a strong intensification of the identifications with his parents which have probably long been present in his ego." Freud, "The Dissection of the Psychical Personality," 57.

[24] Freud writes, "His aggressiveness is introjected, internalized; it is, in point of fact, sent back to where it came from—that is, it is directed towards his own ego. There it is taken over by a portion of the ego as super-ego, and which now, in the form of 'conscience,' is ready to put into action the ego the same harsh aggressiveness that the ego would have liked to satisfy upon other, extraneous individuals. . . . Civilization, therefore, obtains mastery over the individual's dangerous desire for aggression by weakening and disarming it and by setting up an agency within him to watch over it, like a garrison in a conquered city." Sigmund Freud, *Civilization and Its Discontents*, ed. and trans. James Strachey (New York: Norton, 1961), 78–79. This account mirrors the account Nietzsche presents in the second essay of Friedrich Nietzsche, *On the Genealogy of Morality* (1887).

[25] John Deigh, "Remarks on Some Difficulties in Freud's Theory of Moral Development," reprinted in Deigh, *The Sources of Moral Agency* (Cambridge: Cambridge University Press, 1996), 66.

[26] John Deigh, "Freud, Naturalism, and Modern Moral Philosophy," reprinted in Deigh, *The Sources of Moral Agency*, 127.

[27] Ibid.

and the content of morality receive a psychoanalytic explanation: there need be no moral facts to explain moral judgments and their force, just innate drives and standard development trajectories through which creatures like us pass.[28]

Some recent moral antirealists, such as the philosophers Simon Blackburn and Allan Gibbard, have turned not to Freud but to evolutionary theory for a naturalistic account of moral judgment.[29] Gibbard's proposal, for example, is to analyze normative judgments as expressing states of norm-acceptance and to explain the latter capacity in terms of its contribution to successful "coordination," where coordination is the "biological function" selected for by evolution.[30] I will call this *the evolutionary explanation* (EE). On this "speculative evolutionary story," supposing that

[28] Recent years have witnessed an odd marriage of Freudian insights and Kantian strictures in the work of some Anglo-American moral philosophers, including Deigh. See also Samuel Scheffler, *Human Morality* (New York: Oxford University Press, 1992), chap. 5; and J. David Velleman, "A Rational Superego," *Philosophical Review* (forthcoming). These writers believe that Freud's theory can be divested of Freud's explicitly antirationalist interpretation. Deigh, for example, complains that "the belief that [moral] judgment has motivational force solely in virtue of its being invested with instinctual force is not philosophically innocent" and that Freud simply begs the question against the rationalist who denies that premise. Deigh, "Freud, Naturalism, and Modern Moral Philosophy," 129. The difficulty, of course, is that for Freud this is an *empirical* question, not a philosophical one, and the empirical evidence favors his interpretation—or so Freud believes. (Oddly, Deigh makes the conclusory assertion that Freud did not have "evidence to support [his interpretation]" [ibid., 130], but gives no argument or discussion on this point.)

[29] Simon Blackburn, "How to Be an Ethical Antirealist," *Midwest Studies in Philosophy* 12 (1988): 361–76; Allan Gibbard, *Wise Choices, Apt Feelings: A Theory of Normative Judgment* (Cambridge, MA: Harvard University Press, 1990). See also Gilbert Harman, "Explaining Value," *Social Philosophy and Policy* 11, no. 1 (1994): 229–48, esp. 238–39. For skepticism about such evolutionary accounts, see Nicholas L. Sturgeon, "Critical Study of Gibbard's *Wise Choices, Apt Feelings*," in *Noûs* 29, no. 3 (1995): 402–24, esp. 415–18.

[30] Gibbard, *Wise Choices, Apt Feelings*, 108, 116. Among Sturgeon's more interesting objections to the speculative evolutionary story is the following: "[Gibbard] believes . . . that humans evolved biologically to have a separate motivational faculty, a 'language-infused' norm-acceptance system that emerged as we became language-users. . . . [E]valuative language thus emerged to play a special role, that of expressing the norms so accepted." Sturgeon, "Gibbard's *Wise Choices, Apt Feelings*," 407. The puzzle, then, is why "we don't now find natural languages better adapted to the function Gibbard identifies." Ibid. In other words, why didn't evolution also select for language with a noncognitive surface grammar, instead of the cognitive surface grammar that noncognitivists must work so hard to reinterpret? In the speculative evolutionary mode of thinking that this objection invites, some answers do suggest themselves. For example, it was probably advantageous in terms of facilitating successful coordination and cooperation for humans to employ a language with a uniform syntax rather than to have evolved many specialized syntaxes, especially since evolution has no reason to take sides in the debate between realism and antirealism (or cognitivism and noncognitivism). Indeed, a cognitive-looking syntax may have enhanced the value of normative talk for coordination. Only the claim that there are no moral facts—a claim on which, to repeat, evolution is utterly neutral—creates a dilemma for the philosophical interpretation of normative talk. Recall that a primary motivation for noncognitivism is the thought that *if* there are no moral facts *and* we take the syntax of normative discourse at face value, *then* it is mysterious why normative talk persists: why would a putatively fact-stating discourse that states no facts have held on for so long? Noncognitivism vindicates the point of normative talk even in the absence of normative facts.

there are "normative facts is gratuitous": we can explain our normative judgments fully without them.[31]

Admittedly, though, Gibbard's account (like Blackburn's) *is* speculative. Fortunately, research by biologists does provide some support. Many evolutionary biologists have been concerned to explain the existence of altruistic behavior, and while judgments about the value of altruism are not usually discussed, it seems reasonable to suppose that the existing evolutionary accounts could be extended in this direction: if evolution selects for altruistic behavior, surely it also selects in favor of the normative practices that support such behavior.[32] The central puzzle for evolutionary theory about altruism concerns the level on which natural selection operates. If it operates only on the level of the individual, then it is hard to see why it would favor altruistic behavior, since all such behavior would seem to detract from the reproductive success of the relevant individual. If the target of selection, however, is in some circumstances the group to which the individual belongs, then an explanation suggests itself. As Darwin, who toyed with but did not develop the idea, puts it in a famous passage:

> It must not be forgotten that although a high standard of morality gives but a slight advantage or no advantage to each individual man and his children over the other men of the same tribe . . . [t]here can be no doubt that a tribe including many members who, from possessing in a high degree the spirit of patriotism, fidelity, obedience, courage, and sympathy, were always ready to aid one another, and to sacrifice themselves for the common good, would be victorious over most other tribes; and this would be natural selection. At all times throughout the world tribes have supplanted other tribes; and as morality is one important element in their success, the standard of morality and the number of well-endowed men will thus everywhere tend to rise and increase.[33]

The treatment of *group selectionism* as an explanation for the rise of altruism (and, as we might say following Darwin, "the standard of morality") has recently received a robust defense from philosopher Elliott Sober and evolutionary biologist David Sloan Wilson,[34] but it is still far from having

---

[31] Gibbard, *Wise Choices, Apt Feelings*, 121, 108.

[32] I will assume, plausibly, that altruism is central to morality, so that we have explained a lot about morality when we have explained why we prize altruism. Altruism is, of course, central to a number of influential moral philosophies—from Schopenhauer's to Thomas Nagel's—and it enjoys pride of place in commonsense moral thinking as well.

[33] Charles Darwin, *The Descent of Man and Selection in Relation to Sex* (London: Murray, 1871), 166.

[34] Elliot Sober and David Sloan Wilson, *Unto Others: The Evolution and Psychology of Unselfish Behavior* (Cambridge, MA: Harvard University Press, 1998).

carried the day in biology.[35] Intermediate between individual- and group-selectionist accounts, and much more widely accepted by biologists, is the "kin selectionism" developed by W. D. Hamilton.[36] On this account, the target of selection is held to be larger than the individual, but smaller than the group or the tribe—the constraint is genetic similarity, that is, kinship. Rearing your sibling's kids may sometimes be a better way of passing on (some portion of) your genes than having kids of your own, and thus natural selection could prefer altruistic behavior (and attitudes) toward kin.[37] Of course, the moral value assigned to altruism is not kin-specific (at least in theory, as opposed to in practice), but we might speculate that kin-specific altruism is more robust when supported by a general moral imperative to care for the welfare of others.

Thus, psychoanalysis and evolutionary theory give us two different sorts of naturalistic accounts of moral behavior and judgment. Let us call all these accounts, which explain moral belief and judgment by appealing to the deterministic forces operative in one or more of the special sciences (psychology, physiology, biology, etc.), *naturalistic explanations* (NEs). I am going to assume in what follows that some NE actually works.[38] We can then pose the comparative question as follows: which are better explanations, moral explanations (hereinafter "MEs") or NEs? If MEs fare worse,

---

[35] See, e.g., John Maynard Smith, "The Origin of Altruism," review of Sober and Wilson's *Unto Others, Nature* 393, no. 6686 (1998): 639–40; or the polemic in Richard C. Lewontin, "Survival of the Nicest?" review of Sober and Wilson's *Unto Others, New York Review of Books,* October 22, 1998, 59–63.

[36] The theory is first sketched in W. D. Hamilton, "The Evolution of Altruistic Behavior," *American Naturalist* 97, no. 896 (1963): 354–56. It receives its classic formal expression in W. D. Hamilton, "The Genetical Evolution of Social Behavior I," *Journal of Theoretical Biology* 7 (1964): 1–16; and W. D. Hamilton, "The Genetical Evolution of Social Behavior II," *Journal of Theoretical Biology* 7 (1964): 17–52. All these papers are reprinted in W. D. Hamilton, *Narrow Roads of Gene Land* (Oxford: W. H. Freeman, 1996); future references to them will use the reprint pagination. In a 1975 paper, Hamilton himself displays some sympathy for a kind of group selectionism, though he does so on the basis of formal modeling reasons that would take us far afield. See W. D. Hamilton, "Innate Social Aptitudes of Man: An Approach from Evolutionary Genetics," reprinted in Hamilton, *Narrow Roads of Gene Land,* esp. 337.

[37] Hamilton puts the point as follows:

> [T]he ultimate criterion which determines whether [gene] G will spread is not whether the behavior is to the benefit of the behaver but whether it is to the benefit of the gene G; and this will be the case if the average net result of the behavior is to add to the gene pool a handful of genes containing G in a higher concentration than does the gene pool itself. With altruism this will happen only if the affected individual is a relative of the altruist, therefore having an increased chance of carrying the gene, and if the advantage conferred is large enough compared to the personal disadvantage to offset the regression, or 'dilution,' of the altruist's genotype in the relative in question.

Hamilton, "The Evolution of Altruistic Behavior," 7.

[38] If no NE works, then moral explanations of moral belief and judgment might seem to win by default. Even this strikes me as doubtful, however. Why should moral explanations be the default position, when they play a role only in parts of folk explanations (and the speculations of various moral realist philosophers) and have been utterly neglected by all serious empirical researchers? Psychoanalytic explanations (more controversially) and evolutionary explanations (uncontroversially) have established their explanatory credentials in many domains, even if details of their accounts of moral judgment might be disputed.

then we will have (certainly defeasible) grounds for thinking that moral properties will not make it into the best explanatory account of the world.

We can see that MEs are in fact inferior to NEs by attending again to Thagard's two criteria. Let us consider consilience first. NEs will always be more consilient than MEs; that is, NEs will always explain more than MEs do. This is because the mechanisms employed by NEs explain much more than just the class of "moral" phenomena (e.g., moral beliefs and observations), while MEs will only be able to explain the moral phenomena. This should hardly be surprising: after all, NEs were generally proffered as accounts of other phenomena first; only later did they find application in the moral cases. For example, the causal mechanisms underlying Freudian explanations work to explain not only morality, but also various neuroses as well as all the psychopathologies of everyday life. The application of EE to moral phenomena is a relatively recent and sometimes contentious matter; by contrast, evolutionary accounts of physiological characteristics, social phenomena, mental content, and other things abound, and many are now well-established.

MEs also prove inferior when we look to simplicity. MEs involve additional "assumptions with narrow application"[39]—namely, assumptions about moral facts—that are not justified by gains in consilience. By contrast, the assumptions of NEs—assumptions, for example, about unconscious psychic forces, microphysiological processes, natural selection, and so on—involve great gains in consilience, and thus (arguably) justify the increase in theoretical complexity that they entail.

Moral properties, in short, suffer from PEN: they are too neatly tailored to only one sort of explanandum—that which I am calling the moral phenomena—for us to think that moral properties are real (explanatory) properties. The comparison of MEs with NEs should make this obvious, but even without a comparison, moral facts, like our aforementioned spirit facts, seem to suffer from PEN.

IV. REJOINDER I: OPTING OUT OF THE EXPLANATORY DEBATE

How, then, should the moral realist respond to this new argument from explanatory impotence? Two general lines of response emerge in the literature. There are those who simply want to "opt out" of the debate: explanatory potency, they claim, simply does not or should not matter for moral realism. Others, however, want to respond on the explanatory merits. Let us deal with each of these approaches in turn.

Why, some philosophers have asked, should moral realists care about explanatory potency? This challenge has come in two main forms: on the one hand, there are those who think explanatory power is *irrelevant* to

---

[39] Thagard, "The Best Explanation," 87.

establishing moral realism; on the other hand, there are those who think explanatory considerations are unfair to moral realism.

Those who make the charge of "irrelevance" claim that the explanatory potency of properties simply does nothing to show whether the properties are moral; these philosophers argue that moral properties "justify" or "guide action," rather than "explain."[40] This complaint, however, misunderstands the explanatory argument. Moral realists who invoke explanatory considerations are concerned only with the *reality* of the properties, not their *morality*; thus, the claim is not (*contra* philosopher David Copp) that moral theories are "confirmable" on explanatory grounds.[41] Which properties are the "moral" properties—as opposed to the question of which properties are real—will have to be answered on other grounds. Railton, for example, suggests that we will need to draw on "our linguistic or moral intuitions" in order to pick out natural properties that "express recognizable notions of goodness and rightness."[42] The "irrelevance" complaint, then, simply misconstrues the point of the debate over moral explanations.

By contrast, the charge of "unfairness" is motivated precisely by an appreciation of the bearing that explanatory considerations are usually taken to have upon the question of realism. What motivates the charge is the thought that by making explanatory power a necessary mark of real properties, we will have unfairly prejudged the issue against moral facts. This sort of worry is expressed in philosopher Thomas Nagel's comment that "[t]o assume that only what has to be included in the best causal theory of the world is real is to assume that there are no irreducibly normative truths."[43]

This response raises complex epistemological and ontological questions, but a somewhat abbreviated reply will have to suffice here. Much of the interest of recent work on moral realism consists in the fact that it tries to show that such realism is compatible with naturalistic constraints on epistemology and ontology—constraints such as causal or explanatory potency. Values, these realists want to claim, can be real in precisely the

[40] For examples of this approach, see Sayre-McCord, "Moral Theory and Explanatory Impotence"; and David Copp, "Explanation and Justification in Ethics," *Ethics* 100, no. 2 (1990): 237–58.

[41] See Peter Railton, "Naturalism and Prescriptivity," in Ellen Frankel Paul, Fred D. Miller, Jr., and Jeffrey Paul, eds., *Foundations of Moral and Political Philosophy* (Oxford: Blackwell, 1990).

[42] Railton, "Moral Realism," 205.

[43] Thomas Nagel, *The View from Nowhere* (New York: Oxford University Press, 1986), 144. A very interesting and important critique of Nagel's metaethical views in this regard can be found in Sigrún Svavarsdóttir, "Objective Values: Does Metaethics Rest on a Mistake?" in Brian Leiter, ed., *Objectivity in Law and Morals* (New York: Cambridge University Press, 2001). Ronald Dworkin has recently objected to the "best explanation" test in terms similar to Nagel's; see Ronald Dworkin, "Objectivity and Truth: You'd Better Believe It," *Philosophy and Public Affairs* 25, no. 2 (1996): 87–139. Dworkin's views are described and criticized in detail in Brian Leiter, "Objectivity, Morality, and Adjudication," in Leiter, ed., *Objectivity in Law and Morals*.

way that everything else in the natural world is. From this perspective, one might make two responses to Nagel. First, we might want to know why we should have to make exceptions for value in our best epistemology of the world. Surely the answer cannot simply be to make room for moral realism! Second, assuming we think the naturalistic constraints are well motivated, having to make exceptions for particular properties casts doubts on those properties' ontological standing. It is still open to someone to take issue with the metaphysical picture that informs these replies, but the naturalist may be forgiven for thinking it unremarkable that moral (and perhaps many other) facts should make it into our ontology of the world once naturalistic constraints are dropped.[44]

A final, related form of objection to the explanatory-impotence argument does suggest itself at this point: namely, that these "naturalistic constraints" are *too* constraining. As philosopher Hilary Putnam puts it, the best-explanation test " 'proves too much'; for if it were right, it *would* apply to cognitive values just as much as to ethical ones!"[45] In other words, the moral realist might charge that the explanatory criterion itself cannot survive the best-explanation test, so the position of the naturalist is self-refuting. This form of argument, however, only works on the assumption that the moral antirealist must be committed to realism about epistemic norms. Why, however, should we think this? The moral skeptic should follow Quine and simply point out that the epistemic norms of our most widely accepted science include the best-explanation test, and that this test is all we have to go on when it comes to the metaphysics and epistemology of anything else. In any case, the naturalistic moral realists at issue here—unlike, say, Putnam—all accept the best-explanation test as a necessary condition for realism.

V. REJOINDER II: ARGUING THE EXPLANATORY MERITS

What then of responses on the explanatory merits? Here again, there appear to be two possible lines of reply. One invokes the possible identity or supervenience of moral properties on the explanatory properties as a way of showing that the explanatory argument for antirealism is inconclusive. The second reply argues more directly that without moral facts we do indeed suffer some explanatory or cognate epistemic loss. I will argue that in fact, the issue of explanatory loss is the decisive one for the

[44] John McDowell has built a whole realist program around a sometimes glib contempt for naturalistic constraints, and, not surprisingly, his is a promiscuous ontology, including moral, aesthetic, and comical facts, among others. The plausibility of McDowell's grounds for dismissing naturalistic constraints—grounds that are not always easy to discern— requires examination. For doubts about McDowell's program, see David Sosa, "Pathetic Ethics," in Leiter, ed., *Objectivity in Law and Morals*; and Leiter, "Objectivity, Morality, and Adjudication," pt. 4.

[45] Hilary Putnam, "Replies to Brian Leiter and Jules Coleman," *Legal Theory* 1, no. 1 (1995): 81.

whole debate about moral explanations, even for those who would try to save moral realism through appeals to claims about supervenience or identity. Let us consider, however, each reply in turn.

A. The argument from identity/supervenience

The explanatory argument, some philosophers argue, simply cannot rule out moral realism, since nothing in the explanatory argument shows that the explanatorily superior facts (e.g., the facts in NEs) are not simply the very facts with which the moral facts are identical or upon which the moral facts supervene. Think, for example, of the case of color:

[O]ur best explanations of [why we perceive roses as being red] might well make reference to certain characteristics of roses, facts about light, and facts about the psychological and perceptual apparatus of perceivers, but not the *redness* of the roses (and not to any particular feature of the roses that can be reductively identified with redness). Despite this, the availability of such explanations expands our understanding of colors; it does not show that there are not colors.[46]

In giving the scientific account of color, then, we have simply identified the facts about light and vision that constitute color facts. The moral realist might suggest here that a similar account applies to morals. For example, in giving an NE of moral phenomena, perhaps we have simply identified some of the facts that constitute moral facts. Nothing in the explanatory argument for antirealism, it seems, rules this out.

Three responses, which I will discuss in ascending order of importance, might be made to the moral realist on this score. First, the analogy with color may be the wrong place for the moral realist to look. As philosophers Paul Boghossian and David Velleman have argued, projectivism about color properties may indeed be the right response to the scientific account of color: "The projectivist account of colour experience is . . . the one that occurs naturally to anyone who learns the rudimentary facts about light and vision. It seemed obvious to Galileo, as it did to Newton and Locke."[47] Now, perhaps color and morality are relevantly different,

---

[46] Sayre-McCord, "Moral Theory and Explanatory Impotence," 274–75; for a similar point, see Brink, *Moral Realism and the Foundations of Ethics*, 193. Gibbard, it should be noted, agrees on this point, saying that "[e]ven if I am right that normative judgments have coordination as their biological function, that does not by itself show that there is no kind of fact . . . to which these judgments are adapted to correspond. One might imagine a program of 'normative realism' that proposes a kind of fact to do the job. . . . I, myself, though, have found no kind of fact that works . . ." Gibbard, *Wise Choices, Apt Feelings*, 116.

[47] Paul Boghossian and J. David Velleman, "Colour as a Secondary Quality," *Mind* 98, no. 389 (1989): 97. See also Paul Boghossian and J. David Velleman, "Physicalist Theories of Color," *Philosophical Review* 100, no. 1 (1991): 67–106. Note, of course, that Boghossian and

such that projectivism is not the "obvious" response to learning of a naturalistic explanation for moral belief. Much will turn, surely, on the sort of naturalistic explanation in the offing. In any event, the plea I should like to make here is simply for more to be said. Moral realists have been far too glib about invoking the case of color, since the "scientific" picture may plausibly "explain away" morals *and* colors. As a result, an appeal to the case of color *simpliciter* cannot help the moral realist.[48]

Second, replying to the explanatory argument by appealing to claims about identity or supervenience changes the terms of the debate about moral realism significantly. The claim under consideration is that the explanatory argument against moral realism is not conclusive because it *might* turn out that moral facts are simply constituted by the explanatory facts at issue. Note, however, that explanatory considerations will do no work in establishing this claim: we will require some independent argument for taking the moral properties to be identical with or supervenient upon the properties in the apparently better explanation. Thus, to invoke the line of response under consideration here is already to concede that explanatory considerations alone *cannot* establish moral realism. This, it seems to me, is an important point often obscured in the recent literature. It suggests that a naturalistic moral realism may still stand or fall upon the traditional obstacle: the plausibility of the posited relation between the "moral" and the "natural."

The third and most important response to the identity/supervenience argument is that it still leaves the moral realist with a simplicity problem: he must now claim that moral facts are explanatory, but only in virtue of

Velleman do not attack color realism on *explanatory* grounds, but rather on the grounds of certain epistemological and phenomenological problems that arise when we try to construe color properties as being identical with or supervenient upon the scientific facts about light and vision that explain them. For a summary of this point, see pp. 82–83 in the first article; an extended treatment appears in the second.

[48] A different route against the color analogy is suggested by Blackburn in "How to Be an Ethical Antirealist." Blackburn claims that the naturalistic picture is motivated by two elements: "(1) the fundamental identification of the commitment in question as something other than a belief; (2) the existence of a neat natural account of why the state that it is should exist" (ibid., 363). (1) is what is crucial here: Blackburn's idea is that states of mind that are not beliefs simply lend themselves to naturalistic accounts in a way that belief-states do not. "[T]he fundamental state of mind of one who has an ethical commitment makes natural sense" on the naturalistic story, he says, and this is because this "state of mind starts theoretical life as . . . a stance, or conative state or pressure on choice and action" (ibid.). Now, while Blackburn thinks there is an EE for color just as there is for moral value, thus satisfying (2) in both cases, he thinks there is a difference between the two when it comes to (1): "[T]here is no way that I can see usefully to contrast color commitments with *beliefs*. Their functional roles do not differ. So, there will be no theory of a parallel kind to develop, explaining why we have propositional attitudes of various kinds toward color talk, or why we speak of knowledge, doubt, proof, and so forth in connection with them" (ibid., 373). As a result, the naturalistic story about color will not help us make "natural sense" of the "color commitment." For this account to really undercut the color analogy, however, much more would have to be said about the first of the two elements in Blackburn's picture: immediately, it is not obvious that naturalism could not consume conative states and belief-states in its wake (think of the strong program in the sociology of knowledge).

their being identical with or supervenient upon explanatory nonmoral facts. Plainly, however, substantive theses about identity or supervenience add to the complexity of one's theory and ontology in a way that must be justified by some gain in consilience or some cognate epistemic virtue.[49] When we learn that the observable macroproperty of "being water" is identical to the unobservable microproperty of "being H_2O," we can explain features of the macroproperty (e.g., that which it describes freezes, evaporates, boils away, etc.) and in so doing can effect a certain explanatory unification of the macroproperties of water with other macrofeatures of the world (e.g., ice, steam, etc.). This unification would have been obscure without knowledge of the microproperties and the identity thesis. Thus, there is an epistemic gain (unification of phenomena) that comes from our making our theory of the world more complex by accepting the identity of "water" and H_2O, and this gain *justifies* the increased complexity.

Supervenience claims present a related issue. Consider the case of the EE: granted physicalism,[50] evolutionary facts must be identical with or, more likely, supervenient upon physical facts. Yet we make clear gains in consilience by admitting these substantive theses about supervenience into our theory: namely, the now well-known scope of EEs, together with the apparent inability of any other science (e.g., physics) to account for the same phenomena. If, however, EEs do all the explanatory work that MEs do — plus some — then there seems no reason to add substantive theses about moral property-supervenience into our theory, given that we already have the theoretically simpler and more consilient EE. If the supervenience of evolutionary facts will do all the relevant explanatory work, why add the supervenience of moral facts to our best theory of the world?

Claims of identity or supervenience, then, will not — in isolation — save moral realism from the explanatory argument. The moral realist must earn his right to such claims by both (a) vindicating the identity/supervenience thesis on nonexplanatory grounds, and (b) vindicating the added theoretical complexity involved in that thesis by demonstrating that it produces a gain in consilience or some cognate epistemic virtue (e.g., explanatory unification).

B. The argument from explanatory loss

The moral realist, then, who would defend moral facts on explanatory grounds must claim that *without* moral facts we suffer an explanatory

---

[49] Perhaps this is not true of *all* identity claims: consider, for example, the identification of the morning star and the evening star. However, reductive identifications — reducing one class of things to a wholly different class of things — plainly require a substantial theoretical edifice to motivate them. It is, to put the matter gently, hardly obvious, for example, that "morally right" just picks out "maximizations of utility." Theoretical complexity, however, requires an epistemic payoff, such as consilience, at least when we are comparing explanations.

[50] By *physicalism*, I will just mean the doctrine that everything that exists is physical, that is, occupies some discrete points in space and time.

loss:[51] just as physics cannot do the same explanatory work as evolutionary biology, so too evolutionary biology (or psychology, sociology, etc.) cannot do the same explanatory work as moral facts. Can the moral realist sustain this central claim?

Unfortunately, there is no way to approach this question except on a case-by-case basis. No *a priori* considerations can demonstrate that eliminating moral facts from our best account of the world will never lead to explanatory loss. Two sorts of considerations, however, may make us skeptical of the moral realist's claim. First, if we go outside the contemporary philosophical debate and look to scholars in other disciplines actually concerned with explanatory questions, I think we will be hard-pressed to find anyone doing serious explanatory work with moral facts. Outside of informal ways of speaking and "folk explanations," moral facts appear to play no role in any developed explanatory theory. The moral realism literature often makes much of these folk explanatory theories, but, as the comparison with naturalistic theories suggests, it is doubtful that these folk theories will make it into our best account of the world. Philosophers would perhaps do well not to forget that while, for example, there are Marxist historians using broadly "economic" facts to explain historical events, there is no school of "Moral Historians" using moral facts to do any interesting or complex explanatory work.[52]

A second ground for skepticism about moral explanations is more specific: namely, that the actual candidates proffered in the literature are, by and large, not very promising. Some moral explanations are just patently vacuous,[53] but even the more promising candidates do not, I think, stand up to scrutiny. Let me conclude by considering some examples from the work of Sayre-McCord, Brink, and philosopher Joshua Cohen.

Nonreductive moral realists want to defend moral explanations in a way akin to philosopher Jerry Fodor's defense of the autonomy of the special sciences:[54] they want to claim that there are distinctive "groupings" and generalizations in moral explanations that cannot be captured by a more "basic" explanatory scheme or science. Just as nothing in physics captures the distinctive categories and generalizations of economics and psychology, they say, so too do biology and psychology miss the distinctive generalizations of moral theory.

---

[51] Supervenience claims are the most common in the moral realism literature, so I will largely focus on them in what follows.

[52] See, however, the discussion of Railton's program in note 81, below.

[53] This is true, I think, of almost all of Sturgeon's examples. My own feeling is that if I were seeking an explanation for Hitler's conduct and was offered the explanation "He was morally depraved," I would take such an answer to be a bit of a joke: a repetition of the datum rather than an explanation. Contrast Sturgeon's moral "explanation" of Hitler with a sophisticated, and not at all vacuous, account such as that provided in Erik H. Erikson, *Childhood and Society*, 2d ed. (New York: Norton, 1963), 326–58. Erikson's account makes no use of putative moral facts to explain Hitler's behavior.

[54] See Jerry A. Fodor, "Introduction," in Fodor, *The Language of Thought* (Cambridge, MA: Harvard University Press, 1975).

Part of the appeal of Fodor's argument, of course, is that psychology, economics, and biology really seem to be engaged in important explanatory work, so it would be a real loss if their distinctive facts had to be dropped in a physicalist ontology of the world. If the moral realist is to avail himself of a similar defense, then we must be similarly impressed by moral explanations. Both Sayre-McCord and Brink try to suggest that moral explanations are impressive in this way, but their accounts, I will argue, are not persuasive.

Here, for example, is Sayre-McCord pursuing the strategy just described:

> [C]ertain regularities—for instance, honesty's engendering trust or justice's commanding allegiance, or kindness' encouraging friendship—are real regularities that are unidentifiable and inexplicable except by appeal to moral properties.[55]

There is, of course, a double claim here: first, there must be "real [moral] regularities"; second, it must be the case that we cannot explain or even identify them without moral facts. Sayre-McCord's proposal falters with respect to each claim. Is "honesty's engendering trust" a "real regularity"? To the contrary, it seems honesty just as often engenders not trust, but annoyance, bitterness, or alienation; people, as is well-known, do not want those around them to be *too* honest.[56] Indeed, someone who is too honest may often be thought untrustworthy, precisely because he or she cannot be expected to guard one's secrets and keep one's counsel. Looking to Sayre-McCord's other examples, it seems that justice provokes opposition as often as it produces allegiance: many people have little interest in just arrangements, and so resist them at every step. Furthermore, do we necessarily befriend the kindly, or do we simply appreciate them—or perhaps take advantage of them? In sum, it is far from obvious that Sayre-McCord's folksy examples bear much scrutiny; there appears to be little that is "regular" about these putative regularities.[57]

---

[55] Sayre-McCord, "Moral Theory and Explanatory Impotence," 276.

[56] Trust, of course, also seems engendered by much else besides honesty: in the political realm, it is notorious that people trust their leaders notwithstanding a long and familiar history of deceit (consider Americans during the Persian Gulf War, trusting their leaders notwithstanding the experiences of Vietnam and Watergate). With respect to government, it seems more likely that it is what the anarchist Randolph Bourne called an attitude of "filial mysticism" toward the state rather than honesty that accounts for the willingness of the citizenry to "trust" the authorities. We might prefer an explanation of trust (if there were one) that would cover all these cases of trust-engendering.

[57] The moral realist might protest that moral explanations have ceteris paribus clauses, and so there will naturally be exceptions to the regularities. The skeptic might ask, however, for a specification of the parameters of both these claimed regularities and their exceptions. Appeal to ceteris paribus clauses without *any* account of what these parameters are simply permits the defender of folk moral explanations to discount any counterexample to his claims with some hand-waving about "ceteris paribus."

Sayre-McCord's proposal fails with respect to the second claim as well. Do we need moral facts to explain these putative regularities—or just the assumption that people who believe others are honest will trust them?[58] In fact, surely the latter is a *better* explanation, for if there is a regularity here, it requires only the perception of honesty, rather than its actual presence. Perceived honesty should, it seems, engender trust as readily as real honesty, while making real honesty the basis of the regularity will leave out of the regularity's explanatory scope those cases where people trust those who only seem honest, but really are not. Similarly, what people *believe* or *perceive* to be "just" probably does engender allegiance, whereas the regularity collapses when we talk about *real* justice, which is often a threat to privileged groups. What explanatory gain, then, would we get from assuming with Sayre-McCord that there are moral facts (e.g., about honesty or justice)?

Brink, with somewhat greater detail, pursues the same line as Sayre-McCord does; Brink claims that "moral explanans will generalize better than would explanans in terms of the lower-order facts that constitute these moral facts."[59] Brink gives the example of explaining "political instability and social protest in [apartheid] South Africa" in terms of racial oppression (an unjust practice), rather than in terms of the particular social, economic, and political conditions in which it happened to be realized in South Africa; surely, he says, "there would still have been racial oppression and instability and protest under somewhat different" conditions.[60] As a result, he claims, the "moral explanation"—appealing to the unjust practice of racial oppression—"will occupy a distinct and privileged explanatory role."[61]

Will it? Brink himself notes that "our interest in explanations is typically an interest in understanding past events or predicting future events."[62] During the heyday of the empiricist covering-law model of explanation during the 1940s and 1950s, there was supposed to be a strict symmetry between explanation and prediction.[63] However, philosopher Carl Hempel later relaxed this requirement as follows: "Any rationally acceptable answer to the question 'Why did X occur?' must offer information which shows that X was to be expected—if not definitely, as in the case of . . . explanation [by appeal to a covering law], then at least with reasonable

---

[58] This question is just a variation of the question posed by Harman's account of the flaming cat case in Harman, *The Nature of Morality*, chap. 1.

[59] Brink, *Moral Realism and the Foundations of Ethics*, 195.

[60] Ibid.

[61] Ibid.

[62] Ibid., 194.

[63] In their classic 1948 paper discussing the covering-law model, Hempel and Paul Oppenheim set out one of its central tenets: "an explanation of a particular event is not fully adequate unless its explanans, if taken account of in time, could have served as a basis for predicting the event in question." Carl Hempel and Paul Oppenheim, "Studies in the Logic of Explanation," reprinted in Joseph C. Pitt, ed., *Theories of Explanation* (New York: Oxford University Press, 1988), 12.

probability."[64] Thus, to think we have understood the past event, we must think that if we had known what we now take to explain that event, we would have been able to predict its occurrence—at least with reasonable probability.

We have to be careful, however, how stringent we make this demand, lest it start to label as pseudo-explanations seemingly sound and familiar explanations, such as the sort found in history. Yet Brink's example cannot even satisfy a very weak requirement of predictability. Racial oppression existed *for decades* in South Africa without the significant political unrest and social protest that finally marked the collapse of apartheid. Racial oppression in the American South was similar; it existed for nearly a hundred years after the Civil War with only episodic and ineffectual resistance. From the standpoint of the historian, then, what exactly is the "distinct and privileged explanatory role" of racial oppression? What predictions, if any, follow from knowing that a society is racially oppressive? Does it not seem, instead, that we have to turn precisely to the particular lower-order social, economic, and political facts to really explain why social protest arose against racial oppression at the times it actually did? Indeed, we look in vain for real historians explaining the end of American apartheid by reference to its injustice.[65]

Brink's moral explanation, like Sayre-McCord's, also faces the difficulty that it seems sufficient for his explanation (such as it is) that people *believe* racial oppression to be unjust, regardless of whether it really is unjust. That is, it seems sufficient to "explain" the social protest against racial oppression in terms of the protesters' belief that racial oppression is unjust; we need not assume that it really is unjust. To be entitled to the additional assumption that it really is unjust, we must know what explanatory gain is to be had by complicating our theory and ontology in this way.

We would have such an explanatory gain if two conditions were satisfied. First, injustice would have to produce certain regular effects (e.g.,

---

[64] Carl Hempel, "Aspects of Scientific Explanation," in Hempel, *"Aspects of Scientific Explanation" and Other Essays* (New York: Free Press, 1965), 369.

[65] One possible exception is found in Thomas Haskell's account of the demise of slavery in his contributions to Thomas Bender, ed., *The Antislavery Debate: Capitalism and Abolitionism as a Problem in Historical Interpretation* (Berkeley: University of California Press, 1992). It is unclear, however, whether Haskell's account depends on slavery being *really* wrong or simply on people *believing* it to be wrong (conjoined with the rise of national and international markets, which both altered people's sense of self and responsibility and made slavery more visible as an institution than ever before). In the case of the demise of segregation, the standard historical accounts emphasize three factors: (1) the migration of Southern blacks to the North (in the wake of the collapse of the Southern agricultural economy), which gave rise in the 1930s and 1940s to congressional districts in which blacks had real political power; (2) the frustration of black World War II GIs who faced segregationist impediments to seizing GI Bill opportunities, and who, in conjunction with newly empowered black labor-unionists, came to constitute much of the leadership of the civil rights movement at the local level; and, most importantly, (3) Cold War imperatives to do something about Jim Crow, which impeded efforts to win the hearts and minds of Africa and Asia.

social instability, revolution, etc.), either independently of what people believe about the justice of socioeconomic arrangements, or because of what people believe, where these beliefs are themselves best explained by the reality of injustice. Second, the injustice would have to be multiply realized in nonmoral states of affairs. Both conditions are essential. The first condition guarantees that it is injustice itself, and not simply people's beliefs, that does the explanatory work. The second condition guarantees that the regularity at issue correlates with the moral fact of injustice itself, and not with some nonmoral state of affairs to which injustice is (allegedly) reducible. If injustice is multiply realized in various kinds of nonmoral states of affairs, then only the fact of injustice will suffice for identifying the regularity.[66] Of course, as in the case of water, we might argue that even if injustice is not multiply realized, appreciating its microreduction base in some nonmoral states of affairs permits the unification of what were thought to be disparate macrophenomena, and thus the added theoretical and ontological complexity of the identity thesis at issue would still earn its place in our best picture of the world. However, this is a fragile thesis, for this kind of reduction might be thought to eliminate, rather than vindicate, the macroproperty; everything would turn on the details of the proposed reduction.

Cohen's recent argument that "the injustice of slavery contributed to its demise"[67] seems to offer an account that would satisfy both conditions above. Cohen explicitly rejects the view that "all that matters [in explaining the demise of slavery] . . . are beliefs about injustice" rather than the injustice of slavery itself.[68] He argues that "the injustice of a social arrangement limits its viability" and thus explains why such arrangements collapse or are overthrown.[69] It is, of course, hardly controversial that slaves, like all people, have interests in "material well-being, autonomy, and dignity"—"fundamental interests," as Cohen calls them[70]—that are violated by the institution of slavery, nor should it be controversial that the fact that "slavery conflicts with the interests of slaves" contributes to "the limited viability of slavery."[71] What is crucial, as Cohen recognizes, is that the "injustice" of violating fundamental interests "conveys infor-

---

[66] I am assuming here, with Fodor and others, that multiple realizability blocks reduction. In fact, this seems to me true only on contentious assumptions about reduction, but these issues would take us too far afield. For critical discussion of the multiple realizability argument, see Jaegwon Kim, "Multiple Realization and the Metaphysics of Reduction," reprinted in Kim, *Supervenience and Mind* (Cambridge: Cambridge University Press, 1993); and Brian Leiter and Alexander Miller, "Closet Dualism and Mental Causation," *Canadian Journal of Philosophy* 28, no. 2 (1998): 161–81, esp. 171–73.

[67] Joshua Cohen, "The Arc of the Moral Universe," *Philosophy and Public Affairs* 26, no. 2 (1997): 94.

[68] Ibid., 124. See also ibid., 95: "I am concerned with the consequences of slavery's injustice . . . and not simply the consequences of the fact that some people think of it as wrong."

[69] Ibid., 93.

[70] Ibid., 116.

[71] Ibid., 94.

mation relevant to explaining the demise of slavery that is not conveyed simply by noting that slavery conflicts with the interests of slaves."[72] Why, though, should we think this is true? Why isn't appeal to the brute conflicts of interests between slaves and masters enough?

One possibility is that the moral convictions of some people (e.g., abolitionists) that slavery was unjust contributed causally to the demise of slavery, and that these moral convictions are themselves best explained "by the injustice of slavery."[73] As Cohen writes:

> [P]art of the explanation for the moral belief [that slavery is unjust] is that slaves have interests in material well-being, autonomy, and dignity, and are recognized as having them; that slavery sharply conflicts with those interests, and is recognized as so conflicting; and that those interests are legitimate, and recognized as such. And why is this sequence of points not naturally captured by saying that people believe slavery to be unjust in part because it is unjust?[74]

The final and putatively rhetorical question, however, simply masks the fact that explanatory considerations are doing no work here. Even Thrasymachus and Callicles could agree that slaves have the "fundamental interests" Cohen ascribes to them, and that slavery "sharply conflicts with those interests," yet not agree that any of this has anything to do with injustice.[75] This additional theoretical claim depends on the viability of Cohen's substantive account of justice; this account, which, following John Rawls and T. M. Scanlon, is "based on an idealized notion of consensus—a free, reasonable, and informed agreement,"[76] is one that Thrasymachus and Callicles reject. We need, then, an independent argument—one having nothing to do with explanatory considerations—about why *this* is what justice *really* consists in.

What Cohen (and Brink) ultimately need to claim is that "injustice" identifies "features of the [socio-economic] system" that "are a source of instability."[77] However, they also need to claim that use of the moral term

---

[72] Ibid.

[73] Ibid., 123. Cohen fudges here, and says only that the moral convictions are "explained in part by the injustice of slavery" (ibid.). However, this claim would only suffice if it were shorthand for "[T]he injustice of slavery is part of the *best* explanation for the moral convictions." It is not clear that this is what Cohen claims, or what he is entitled to claim.

[74] Ibid., 128–29.

[75] It would have to be possible, of course, to define the relevant notion of "interest" without its being a fundamentally *normative* notion. However, we can surely equate "interest" with, for example, what agents would desire under appropriate conditions, and do this without endorsing such desires.

[76] Cohen, "The Arc of the Moral Universe," 120. For Rawls's and Scanlon's accounts, see John Rawls, *A Theory of Justice* (Cambridge, MA: Harvard University Press, 1971); and T. M. Scanlon, *What We Owe to Each Other* (Cambridge, MA: Harvard University Press, 1998).

[77] Cohen, "The Arc of the Moral Universe," 132.

"injustice" is a way of classifying causally relevant phenomena that identifies regularities we would miss if we only employed the classificatory
schema of some underlying domain of facts (e.g., psychosocial facts about
interests and their conflict). Sustaining this latter claim would make the
argument directly analogous to Fodor's argument that the special sciences give us classificatory schema (and resultant causal regularities) that
would be lost if we could avail ourselves only of physics. In the end,
though, Cohen never gives us an argument for this claim—essentially, for
the second condition above. He writes, for example, that one could explain the demise of slavery

> simply [by] stat[ing] the properties of slavery—the conflict between
> slavery and slave interests—. . . without taking a position on whether
> those properties indeed are what makes slavery unjust; in short . . .
> the fact that the properties *are* injustice-making is not itself a part of
> my argument. Still, they are, and can unobjectionably be presented
> via the moral classification. Moreover, that mode of presentation is
> morally important. For the world looks different if we think that
> injustice-making features limit the viability of systems that have
> them.[78]

This extraordinary passage, alas, confirms the worry that moral explanations are, as Cohen feared, "simply collages of empirical rumination and
reified hope, pasted together with rhetorical flourish."[79] The only reason
Cohen gives for employing the "moral" explanation—a classification, by
the way, that is only "unobjectionable" to moral realists of the contractarian variety that Cohen favors[80]—as distinct from the nonmoral account of *the same causal features* is that when we talk the language of
morality, "the world looks different." This is no doubt true, but it hardly
counts, on its face, as an epistemic virtue that a classificatory scheme
makes things "look different." Even our Spirit Realist could claim as
much: a world populated by good and evil spirits does indeed look
different from a world divested of illusions.
      The accounts of Sayre-McCord, Brink, and Cohen do not, of course,
exhaust the possibilities for the moral realist.[81] Yet given the absence of

---

[78] Ibid.
[79] Ibid., 93.
[80] That is, contractarian moral theorists such as Rawls and Scanlon; see note 76 above.
[81] In particular, I have said nothing about Railton's theory, the most detailed in the
literature. Railton presents us with a slightly different—and also more complex—case, since
he is alone among contemporary moral realists in regarding his program as reductionist by
way of reforming definitions of moral terms. See Railton, "Moral Realism"; and Railton,
"Naturalism and Prescriptivity." This still does not, however, relieve Railton of the explanatory burden: if our explanatory account of the world is to include reforming definitions of
moral terms in naturalistic terms, there must be some explanatory gain to justify doing so.
In rough summary, Railton's approach is this: Railton claims that "what is morally best" is

moral explanations in the disciplines actually concerned with explanatory questions, the difficulties confronting the actual examples of moral explanations considered above ought to encourage a healthy skepticism about whether the moral realist can carry the explanatory burdens his case requires.

VI. CONCLUSION

We have seen, then, that the argument from explanatory impotence does not *necessarily* rule out moral realism. The moral realist, however, must bear a double burden. If she is to show that moral facts will figure in the best explanatory picture of the world, she must either (a) defend an account of moral facts as being identical with or supervening upon explanatory nonmoral facts, or (b) argue that dropping moral facts from our ontology results in some explanatory (or cognate) loss. To do (a), however, the moral realist must also do (b); that is, a defense of admitting substantive theses about identity and supervenience into one's best theory of the world will inevitably depend on a showing of the explanatory or epistemic need for moral facts. Thus, if I am right that doing (b)—which both possible defenses of moral realism require—is probably not possible, then moral realism will have been refuted on explanatory grounds. Perhaps then we may, with greater confidence, join Nietzsche in saying that when it comes to ethics, "it is a swindle to talk of 'truth' in this field." [82]

Law and Philosophy, University of Texas, Austin

"what is instrumentally rational from a social point of view" (Railton, "Moral Realism," 200), but he also claims that we can explain certain historical developments in terms of "a mechanism whereby individuals whose interests are denied are led to form common values and make common cause along lines of shared interests, thereby placing pressure on social practices to approximate more closely to social rationality" (ibid., 199). Thus, in short, instrumental social rationality—or deviations therefrom—explains historical change, but instrumental social rationality also is just that to which "morally right" refers. Railton also seems to argue that we do get a gain in consilience from this moral explanation: on Railton's story, seeing the connection between the explanatory mechanism, social rationality, and morality allows us to appreciate certain general historical tendencies in the evolution of moral norms (ibid., 195–96). Note three points about Railton's proposal: (1) for it to work at all, Railton's quite specific reforming definition of "morally right" must be independently defended (Kantians and constructivists, among others, will dissent); (2) this reforming definition must really afford us some explanatory gain; and (3) the explanatory theory itself must be a good one if the explanatory considerations are to support moral realism. The refreshing amount of explanatory detail that Railton provides also makes his theory a clear target for critics of the explanatory paradigm: see, e.g., Alexander Rosenberg, "Moral Realism and Social Science," *Midwest Studies in Philosophy* 15 (1990): 150–66. Even supposing that Railton's theory could overcome the explanatory objections, it will still falter, I believe, because of its proposed reforming definition. Here, however, it will be considerations pertaining to the diversity of recognizably *moral* opinion, rather than explanatory impotence, that will prove fatal to the theory. I plan to address these issues elsewhere.

[82] Friedrich Nietzsche, *The Will to Power*, sec. 428.

TWO SOURCES OF MORALITY*

By Philip Pettit

I. Introduction

This essay emerges from consideration of a question in the epistemology of ethics or morality. This is not the common claim-centered question as to how moral claims are confirmed and whether their mode of confirmation gives us grounds to be confident about the prospects for ethical discourse. Instead, I am concerned with the less frequently posed concept-centered question of where in human experience moral terms or concepts are grounded—that is, where in experience the moral becomes salient to us. This question was central to moral epistemology in the form it took among thinkers such as Locke, Hume, and Kant, and it remains of the first importance today.[1]

The question calls for a naturalistic genealogy of moral terms and concepts. I assume that we are not possessed of an irreducibly moral sense whereby irreducibly moral properties might be revealed to us. I also assume that we human beings have no nonnaturalistic faculties of perception and cognition, and that in any case there is nothing nonnaturalistic that such faculties might register. The question, then, is what it is about naturalistic experience—what it is about experience of the kind that raises no particular worries for a scientific view of the world—that can occasion moral conceptualization and create an opportunity for the useful deployment of moral terms.

The analysis that one offers of moral terms or concepts will sometimes point to a genealogy in this sense. If one offers a noncognitivist

* In writing this essay, I benefited from exchanges with Allan Gibbard, Oswald Hanfling, Brad Hooker, Victoria McGeer, Susan Mendus, Michael Ridge, Michael Smith, and R. Jay Wallace, and from comments from this volume's contributors and editors. I was particularly influenced by conversations with Stephen Darwall and Geoffrey Sayre-McCord, and I owe a very considerable debt to each. The essay was also improved by helpful discussions when it was presented at the annual meeting of the British Society for Ethical Theory in July 2000, and at a university seminar at the University of Nebraska, Lincoln, in September 2000.

[1] For a recent influential discussion of the concept-centered problem, see Christine M. Korsgaard, *The Sources of Normativity* (New York: Cambridge University Press, 1996); and Christine M. Korsgaard, "Self-Constitution in the Ethics of Plato and Kant," *Journal of Ethics* 3, no. 1 (1999): 1–29. My approach is rather different from hers, as I trace ethical conceptualization to a more social, and less reflective, origin; in this respect it is closer to the approach found in Gerald J. Postema, "Morality in the First Person Plural," *Law and Philosophy* 14, no. 1 (1995): 35–64. For another different approach, one that involves many congenial themes despite supporting noncognitivism, see Allan Gibbard, *Wise Choices, Apt Feelings* (Cambridge, MA: Harvard University Press, 1990).

analysis in which moral evaluation is conceived of as a species of at-titudinal expression or projection, for example, then that will point to a distinctive story as to what it is about experience that occasions such evaluation.[2] Often, however, the analysis of moral terms will leave the genealogical question undischarged. Suppose that one postulates a net-work analysis of moral terms under which the meanings of these dif-ferent terms are established by the linkages that we recognize both among the terms themselves and between these terms and terms of a nonmoral kind; I favor this sort of approach myself.[3] Such a network analysis presupposes that there are some points at which the net-worked concepts make contact with experience; some moral concepts—some of the terms implicated in the web of moral discourse—must get pinned down for us in experience, however tentatively, by more direct semantic means. But while the analysis will recognize the need for such points of contact, it may say little on how they are established; it may leave the genealogical question effectively unanswered.

While I favor a cognitivist network analysis of moral terms, I try to pursue the genealogical question here in abstraction from issues of analy-sis. I do often speak in this essay in a way that presupposes that moral concepts serve to ascribe properties, so that, as cognitivists say, the eval-uations in which they figure are true or false. I presuppose such cogni-tivism, however, only at points where those who think that evaluations are merely expressions of noncognitive attitude will be able to recast the argument in a manner that is congenial to their views. For example, in Section VI, I will introduce an account of how sentiments give rise to moral conceptualization. While this account is cast in terms favorable to cognitivism, it will not be difficult to see how a corresponding noncog-nitivist story would go.

The remainder of this essay is organized into six sections. In Section II, I argue that *intentional subjects*—subjects who form and act on beliefs and desires—need not have any normative concepts whatsoever. In Sec-tion III, I argue that creatures who are *discursive* as well as intentional—that is, creatures who express their intentional states through the use of common, voluntary signs—do have to possess certain normative con-cepts: namely, those associated with reasoning. In Section IV, I point out that the normative concepts required for discourse fall short of being

[2] For a sketch of the cognitivist position I defend, see Frank Jackson and Philip Pettit, "Moral Functionalism and Moral Motivation," *Philosophical Quarterly* 45, no. 178 (1995): 20–40; and Philip Pettit, "Embracing Objectivity in Ethics," in Brian Leiter, ed., *Objectivity in Law and Morals* (Cambridge: Cambridge University Press, 2001). For a critique of expres-sivism and an indirect argument for cognitivism, see Frank Jackson and Philip Pettit, "A Question for Expressivism," *Analysis* 58, no. 4 (1998): 239–51.
[3] For examples of this sort of approach, see S. L. Hurley, *Natural Reasons* (New York: Oxford University Press, 1989); Jackson and Pettit, "Moral Functionalism and Moral Moti-vation"; and Ralph Wedgwood, "Conceptual Role Semantics for Moral Terms," *Philosophical Review*, forthcoming.

moral concepts proper. And then Sections V and VI focus on two ways in which moral considerations can become salient for discursive creatures. The first involves people privileging discourse as a form of interaction, and the second involves them extending such discourse to the realm of sentiment. Privileging discourse and using discourse to express sentiment are the two distinct sources of moral conceptualization that are signaled in the title of this essay, and I argue in a brief concluding section— Section VII—that the different concepts they provide represent rival possibilities in the construction of moral theory.

II. Intentional Subjects May Lack Normative Concepts

Human beings are intentional creatures who form and act on beliefs and desires in a more or less rational way. Is the experience of intentional creatures bound to make moral considerations salient, and bound therefore to provide an occasion for the formation of corresponding concepts? No, it is not. I argue in this section that, on the contrary, being an intentional subject is consistent with completely lacking normative concepts.

Any intentional subject has to be designed so that it performs well in representational and related respects, and being an intentional subject amounts to nothing more and nothing less than satisfying such design specifications.[4] This is, at any rate, what I shall assume. The intentional subject will represent things as they appear within the limits of its perceptual and cognitive organization, updating these representations appropriately in the light of new inputs. And it will act in ways that further its desires—presumptively, desires that reflect its overall needs and purposes—in the light of these representations or beliefs. The intentional subject may not perform these tasks perfectly, of course, but it will have to do them well—and perhaps do them well as a result of a certain history or organization—within what are thought to be feasible limits and favorable circumstances.

The rational achievements that the intentional subject has to display, according to this account, are quite impressive. Nevertheless, it turns out that even a relatively simple mechanical or organic system can be intentional in this sense. Without itself having any sort of control over the process, an animal or robot might be constituted so as to adjust to incoming information in a relatively faithful manner, forming beliefs that determine, in the presence of certain standing or situationally variable desires, what the creature does. A suitably preset design could function so as to update the creature's beliefs in response to changes in perceptual input,

[4] On design specifications, see Daniel C. Dennett, *The Intentional Stance* (Cambridge, MA: MIT Press, 1987); Philip Pettit, *The Common Mind: An Essay on Psychology, Society, and Politics* (New York: Oxford University Press, 1993), chap. 1; and Peter Railton, "On the Hypothetical and Non-Hypothetical in Reasoning about Belief and Action," in Garrett Cullity and Berys Gaut, eds., *Ethics and Practical Reason* (Oxford: Oxford University Press, 1997).

and these beliefs could then interact with the creature's desires in a similarly preset way so as to determine the creature's actions. Such a creature might not fulfill the criteria for being an intentional subject at all times, but at least might do so within intuitively feasible limits and under intuitively favorable circumstances.

The beliefs and desires of a simple subject like this will be constraint-bound or norm-bound so far as they have to follow the pattern described. The beliefs will meet certain entry and exit conditions; for example, they will tend to enter the scene as the subject is presented with evidence supporting them, and will tend to exit when the subject is presented with evidence opposing them. Furthermore, both the beliefs and the desires of the subject will meet a range of performance conditions. The desire that p will tend to interact with the belief that if p then q so as either to generate the desire that q or to weaken the desire that p. The belief that p will tend to interact with the belief that if p then q so as either to generate the belief that q or to weaken one of the other beliefs. The desire that p will tend to interact with the belief that one can bring about p by X-ing so as to generate the action of X-ing. And so on.

Even though simple intentional subjects will have to satisfy such constraints or norms of rationality—specifically, of inferential rationality— they will not do so with any awareness of the demands that those norms support. In forming a new belief in a manner dictated by perception, they will not register that the perception makes this belief the right one to uphold. In forming a desire dictated by amendments to their beliefs or by spontaneous inclination, they will not register that these beliefs or the goal to which they are spontaneously inclined make that desire more or less appropriate. In moving to action on the basis of their beliefs and desires, they will not register that the actions they perform are the things they are to do given the ends that attract them and the opportunities available. Normative notions of what it is right to believe, what it is appropriate to desire, or what it is correct to do will have no place in their psychology. Simple inferential subjects may conform to the demands of relevant norms, but they will not conceptualize them as demands with which they ought to conform.

Thus, for the creatures envisaged, perceiving things a certain way will be nothing short of believing that they are that way. Likewise, being inclined to make things a certain way will be nothing short of acting, where possible, to make them that way—nothing short of forming an unqualified desire or disposition to act in that manner. For subjects like us human beings, perceiving things a certain way—that is, having a fallible perception of them as being that way—gives us an inferential reason to believe that they are that way, though a reason that we can override. And for subjects like us, being inclined to make things a certain way gives us an inferential reason to desire without qualification to make them that way, though again we can ignore or inhibit this reason. Perception and inclination exist for us as states that we conceptualize as such, giving them presumptive but not necessarily conclusive authority in the determination of our final beliefs and our unqualified desires.

For the simple intentional creatures imagined here, however, perception and inclination will lack such visibility and have a drastically different role. In these creatures, perception and inclination will operate invisibly and ineluctably in the determination of how the world presents itself and how it elicits action. The creatures who are moved by certain perceptions and inclinations will be unable to see those states as we do, as presumptive but not compelling indicators of what is the case and what is to be done. Looking through their perceptions, simple intentional creatures will see the world as it is according to the beliefs that they unthinkingly form; looking through their inclinations, they will be moved to act according to the desires that they unthinkingly conceive. Such creatures will be the captive audiences of their perceptual representations and the captive executors of the ends to which they are inclined. They will be the slaves of perception and inclination.

The upshot of this discussion of simple inferential creatures is that we can hardly tell a story as to how the moral becomes salient for creatures like us merely on the basis that we are intentional subjects. There is nothing in intentionality as such that would explain why intentional subjects see things in a manner that might give rise to the introduction of normative terms and concepts. If we are to provide a naturalistic genealogy of such terms and concepts, then we must start from a richer image of human beings.

III. DISCURSIVE SUBJECTS WILL HAVE NORMATIVE, INFERENTIAL CONCEPTS

A. From intentionality to discourse

We human beings are not just intentional subjects who form and act on beliefs and desires in a more or less rational manner. One of the most striking features of our species is that we are also conversational or discursive creatures.[5] Like many nonhuman animals, we form beliefs and desires; unlike nonhuman animals, however, we also give voluntary or intentional expression to the ways that things present themselves as being in the light of our beliefs and desires. We have not just the ability to believe that p, but the ability to assert that p: we can use a "voluntary sign," in Locke's phrase, to represent how things present themselves as being, given this belief.[6] Similarly, we have not just the ability to desire

---

[5] On this point, see Terrence W. Deacon, *The Symbolic Species: The Co-Evolution of Language and the Human Brain* (New York: W. W. Norton, 1997).

[6] John Locke, *An Essay Concerning Human Understanding*, ed. P. H. Nidditch (Oxford: Oxford University Press, 1975), bk. III, chap. 2.

that q, but the ability to assert that the prospect that q is, say, attractive: we can thus also use a voluntary sign to represent how things present themselves as being, given this desire. We can express our beliefs in regular, content-specifying sentences, and we can express our desires in sentences that ascribe attractiveness or something similar to the items desired.

That we are discursive creatures means that we have access to voluntary signs of these kinds and that we employ these signs with a view to noncoercively and noncollusively reaching a common mind on certain matters. We use voluntary signs not just to bully, impress, or threaten one another—though we may obviously do these things, too—but to discourse or reason together about certain theoretical or practical issues. Our using signs for this sort of purpose is intimately associated with our nature as human beings. Indeed, one traditional view is that the discursive use of signs is constitutively required for human beings to be able to think.[7]

In order to practice discourse, we must have access to both the concept of a sign and the associated concepts of meaning and representation. If we are to use signs as signs and do so intentionally or voluntarily—that is, out of a desire to represent or misrepresent how things are, believing that the signs we use will achieve this representational function—then we must be able to conceive of the signs as having a meaning. I do nothing here to explain how naturalistic creatures can get to have the required concept of meaning.[8] I instead assume that the concept is accessible to creatures of our kind—our naturalistic kind—and I try on the basis of this assumption to develop a story as to how we come to think in moral terms. My reliance on this assumption means that from a naturalistic point of view, there is an important debt in this essay that remains undischarged.

Without explaining how we access the concept of meaning as such, however, it will be useful to say something in explanation of how we generally manage, as discursive creatures, to give our words and sentences the same meanings, and indeed, how we do so in such a way that we know we each mean the same things, know that we know this, and so on. I suggest that we achieve commonality of meaning, at least in the general run of cases, by putting three regulative assumptions to work in our dealings with one another. The assumptions are: first, that the world of common experience makes available candidates for the meanings of our sentences and words; second, that in any speech community we each intend for our sentences and words to have the same presumptively salient meanings; and third, that ordinarily we each have the ability to use

---

[7] For a qualified defense of this sort of view, see Pettit, *The Common Mind*. For further elaboration of its implications, see Philip Pettit and Michael Smith, "Freedom in Belief and Desire," *Journal of Philosophy* 93, no. 6 (1996): 429–49; and Philip Pettit, *A Theory of Freedom: From the Psychology to the Politics of Agency* (Cambridge: Polity Press, 2001).

[8] For an attempt to deal with some of the issues involved in this problem, see Pettit, *The Common Mind*.

our sentences and words according to such intended meanings. These assumptions of common experience, common intent, and common competence can be seen as guiding a practice such that if it is successful, then we will indeed be using our words and sentences to say corresponding things.

So far as things go smoothly, the assumptions will lead us to ascribe to others those beliefs and desires that we would ourselves avow if we were to use the words and sentences that others employ. Things will not always go smoothly, however. Someone may use a given, apparently belief-expressing sentence such as "p" in a situation where others say, or would say, "Not p." What are we to make of such a case?

As a matter of fact, what we make of it is something that the regulative assumptions reflect well. We balk at the sort of divergence in question and assume that something more or less contingent is amiss. We see whether the divergence may be explained away by the fact that one of the parties is expressing a desire rather than a belief, by the fact that the sentence "p" is vague at a relevant margin, by the fact that it is covertly indexical in the fashion of a sentence using "I" or "now," or by some other relatively simple fact. If any such easy explanation applies, then that means that our three regulative assumptions are unchallenged, and that the default setting under which different parties' words mean the same thing has been preserved. If, however, we fail to explain away the divergence through these simpler methods, we must search for a deeper explanation that will save the assumptions and enable us to preserve the default setting.

The ideal, multilateral way of preserving the default setting would be for the parties to air the considerations that lead them on their different ways—or to seek out further relevant considerations—and thereby find themselves able to agree that one of them, as they will say after the fact, did not fully understand the terms, was underinformed, or was misled as a result of certain limitations, obstacles, or blind spots; more on these in a moment. A somewhat less satisfactory, but still multilateral, way of saving the default setting would be for the parties to agree that they have such different beliefs on collateral matters that there is no practical prospect of resolving the issue at hand, even if it is resoluble in principle. And short of achieving a multilateral resolution of the divergence, the parties might still preserve the default setting, each doing so in its own way, by unilaterally postulating that the other party is unwittingly affected by destabilizing factors and so is not fully competent on this particular occasion or on this particular topic.

What do we do if we find that even this sort of unilateral explanation of the divergence is not available? At that point, and at that point only, we will have to accept that the default setting is mistaken. In such a case, the parties have different meanings for one or more of the words in question, or perhaps the words do not have any proper meaning at all—perhaps we were wrong to suppose that there was something real for the words to ascribe.[9]

As envisaged in the story just told, the regulation provided by our three assumptions does not proceed on the basis of prior agreement as to what constitute the limitations or obstacles or blind spots, or the collateral sources of discrepancy, that are likely to destabilize discursive performance. Such destabilizing factors will be identified in the process of mutual regulation, as the parties to the enterprise gradually converge on lists of factors that can serve in any area to disturb discursive competence. The factors that the parties ought to identify as destabilizing, given the enterprise at hand, are those factors such that by indicting them as destabilizers the parties can maximize noncoercive and noncollusive convergence between one another. We can think of the collaboration that the regulative assumptions sponsor as a search procedure whereby destabilizers are identified—rightly or, as it may be, wrongly—and the assumptions are vindicated.[10]

This point is worth illustrating. Consider the ways in which you and I might coordinate in the use of a color predicate such as "red." Assuming common experience, common intent, and common competence, we will expect convergence between us in the use of this predicate. If there is divergence that we cannot explain away through use of an aforementioned "simple" explanation—say, that one of us is using "red" in the indexical sense of "looks red to me"—then we must search around for a factor that is disrupting my color-recognition competence or yours. We can think of the factors actually recognized as destabilizers of such competence—wearing colored glasses, operating in sodium lighting, being partially color-blind—as factors that are identified in the course of precisely this sort of search.

The practice just described can be summed up in a flowchart that each of us can be represented as implementing; see Figure 1 below.

I noted above that the three regulative assumptions guide a practice that, if successful, ensures that we have common meanings in mind. This point is relatively straightforward. The assumptions will successfully drive the practice, so far as we manage in cases of discrepancy to identify the destabilizers whose presence the assumptions predict; we will have to do this by way of multilateral resolution in many cases, though sometimes we will only be able to engage in unilateral explanation of one another's failures. If the assumptions are successful in this way, then the practice will make it the case that what a sign denotes is that particular element that will reliably prompt the employment of the sign in those favorable circumstances where destabilizers are not at work. What "red" refers to,

---

[9] On this claim, however, see ibid., chap. 2.
[10] For more on this approach, see Philip Pettit, "A Theory of Normal and Ideal Conditions," *Philosophical Studies* 96, no. 1 (1999): 21–44.

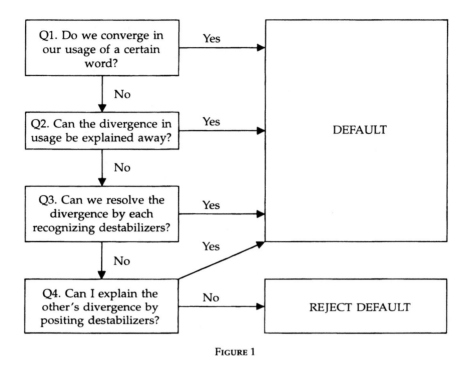

FIGURE 1

for example, is the property that makes things look red, and reliably prompts people to say "red," in circumstances where factors of the kind illustrated above are absent—that is, circumstances that are favorable for the perception of red.

Does the fact that we are discursive creatures in the sense envisaged here mean that our experience will make moral matters salient and will call for the introduction of moral terms? I go on to argue now that as discursive creatures, we must have experiences of certain responses as being normatively required, and normatively required in a way that is salient to us all. As I explain in Section IV, however, I think that these experiences leave us short of moral concepts proper.

B. The normative becomes salient

We saw above that beliefs and desires are constraint-bound or norm-bound in the sense that we only ascribe them to a subject so far as we find—at least in intuitively favorable circumstances and within feasible limits—that the states in that subject meet various design specifications (i.e., various entry, exit, and performance conditions). Given that beliefs and desires are bound to norms of inferential rationality in this way, however, the sentences in which any one of us voluntarily expresses how things present themselves in the light of our beliefs and desires must engage in a more intimate way with corresponding norms.

Consider some of the requirements of inferential rationality, conclusive or defeasible, to which intentional subjects must generally conform, however blindly. To revert to our earlier examples, the fact that perception provides evidence that p rationally requires an intentional subject to form the belief that p. The fact that a subject believes that p and that if p then q rationally requires the subject to believe that q. The fact that a subject desires that p and believes that he or she can bring p about by X-ing rationally requires the subject to X. And so on. If the beliefs and desires of intentional subjects have to satisfy these sorts of inferential norms, then the same is going to be true of the sentences in which discursive subjects like us express these beliefs and desires; otherwise, the use of these sentences will not amount to serious and sincere expression. Just as the belief that p has to be sensitive to evidence supporting or refuting p, for example, the serious and sincere assertoric use of the sentence "p" will have to be equally sensitive to such evidence. Furthermore, just as the desire that p has to be sensitive to the things the agent believes and the things toward which the agent is inclined, the serious and sincere expression of the desire that p through use of a sentence such as "The prospect of p is attractive" will also have to be sensitive to those matters—presumably, to those matters as they themselves are capable of being expressed in sentential usage.

We can imagine beliefs and desires evolving on an involuntary, mechanical basis so as to keep in step with the required demands of rationality. In such cases, a subject's beliefs and desires will be sensitive to the demands of inferential norms without this sensitivity being controlled by beliefs as to what these demands are. But we cannot envisage our human performance with voluntary signs as displaying sensitivity to norms in the same blind fashion. While beliefs and desires may materialize and mutate within intentional creatures in a norm-sensitive manner to which the creatures' beliefs are irrelevant, nothing of the kind can be true of the ways in which linguistic representations unfold.

The reason for this, at base, is that how these representations unfold will have to reflect our beliefs as to what they mean; this goes back to the undischarged assumption that we have access to the concept of meaning. These beliefs amount to nothing more or less than beliefs as to when we ought and ought not employ the signs. To know the meaning of a sign as such, after all, is precisely to be able to tell, with greater or lesser exactitude, when it is right to use the sign and when it is not. If our sentences unfold under the control of such beliefs as to what they mean, then this is to say that our employment of the representations is controlled by the relevant norms instead of merely being sensitive to them; it is guided by our beliefs as to the demands of the norms.

Consider the inferential norms mentioned earlier in this section, putting aside complications to do with their defeasibility. According to the first norm, the fact that perception provides evidence in support of p rationally requires an intentional subject to form the corresponding belief. Whereas merely intentional subjects will blindly conform to this requirement and form the belief that p, discursive subjects will go further by endorsing the corresponding voluntary representation under the control of a belief that the perception makes it right to say that p. According to the second norm, the fact that an intentional subject believes that p and that if p then q rationally requires the subject to believe that q. Merely intentional subjects will again blindly conform to this requirement and form the belief, whereas discursive subjects will endorse the corresponding voluntary representation under the control of a belief that the fact that p and that if p then q, as they are taken to be, make it right to say that q. Finally, according to the third norm, the fact that a subject desires that p and believes that he or she can bring p about by X-ing rationally requires the subject to X. Analogously with the other cases, merely intentional subjects will blindly conform to this requirement and adopt the required action, while discursive subjects will adopt that action under the control of a belief that the attractiveness of the prospect of p, combined with the linkage between X-ing and this prospect, makes X-ing the thing to do.

This discussion shows, then, that when we practice voluntary signing or expression, we must become aware of certain normative requirements — namely, the demands of inferential rationality on our performance. As well as being able to register what inferential norms demand, of course, we must be able to regulate our responses as the norms require; that is, we must be able to regulate suitably both our utterances and the beliefs, desires, and actions associated with them. Otherwise, we could not successfully practice discourse; there would be no point in anyone's talking to us. We must be able to think that this or that is what we ought to say and ought to believe, desire, or do, and we must be able to keep ourselves in line with such normative thoughts, saying what we think we ought to say, and believing, desiring, and doing what we think we ought to believe, desire, and do. In short, we must be able to ratiocinate or reason, or at any rate we must be able to do so under favorable circumstances and within feasible constraints, however they are identified.[11]

Let me offer one last word in qualification of this picture. Consistently with being governed by reason in this way, the signs that I utter may be deployed in a relatively habitual and unmonitored manner. All that is required is that even if habit or inertia rules the things I say in expression of my beliefs or desires, or the things I do on the basis of these representations, I will intentionally review and amend the things that I say or do

[11] On this point, see Victoria McGeer and Philip Pettit, "The Self-Regulating Mind," forthcoming in *Language and Communication*.

in the event of any inferential irrationality becoming apparent; in relations of discourse it may be assumed that such irrationalities can always become apparent. The governance exercised by reason may be virtual rather than active, in other words. It may be that habit explains many of the things that we say in discourse, with reason remaining on standby, ready to intervene as soon as there is a challenge to the inferential rationality of those utterances.[12]

IV. DISCURSIVE SUBJECTS MAY LACK MORAL CONCEPTS

Let us grant that discursive subjects will have to be aware of the demands made in different cases by shared norms of inferential rationality. Let us also grant that to this extent discursive subjects must be in possession of normative concepts. What we now have to notice, however, is that having access in this way to normative concepts does not involve having access to moral concepts.

What sorts of normative considerations will discursive subjects be able to access in the formation of their beliefs and desires, and in the actions they choose to perform? The facts that p and that if p then q, as they see them, may give them reason to believe that q. The fact that some prospect r is attractive and that r only if s may give them reason to desire that s. The fact that the r-prospect is attractive together with the fact that they can bring about r by X-ing may give them reason to perform the action of X-ing. Given that facts of this sort are admitted—and conceptualized in common terms—discursive subjects will generally be able to invoke common norms of inferential rationality to justify the moves they make to others. They may occasionally diverge from one another in such moves, but divergence of that kind will always cause them to balk and to try to explain or resolve the difference between them; the differences will not be regarded with insouciance, as if they were fault-free.[13] That the moves illustrated are subject to the rule of reason—in this case, the rule of inferential reason—means precisely that divergences in those moves must always raise the possibility that someone is at fault in the move they make.

It is important to note that all of the normative considerations available in this way to discursive subjects involve belief. They bear on what the subject should come to believe, period; or on what the subject, given an existing preference, should come to desire—or come to do—in virtue of a change of belief. Conspicuously, however, they do not include considerations that might support the formation or revision of any particular basic

---

[12] For discussion of this notion of virtual control, see Philip Pettit, "The Virtual Reality of *Homo Economicus*," *The Monist* 78, no. 3 (1995): 308–29.

[13] I borrow this notion of fault-freedom from Huw Price, *Facts and the Function of Truth* (Oxford: Blackwell, 1988).

desire: that is, any desire of the kind that is not explained by the agent's preexisting preferences together with his or her beliefs as to how those preferences are best satisfied.

This should not be surprising. While divergences among discursive parties with respect to the beliefs they form cannot be regarded as fault-free—at least not if the beliefs are determinate and nonindexical—divergences among them with respect to their basic desires certainly can be regarded in this way. As noted above, discursive subjects differ from intentional subjects in that discursive subjects express their beliefs and desires voluntarily. Given the function of belief in representing the ways things are, beliefs cannot rationally diverge, and therefore discursive subjects' expressions of belief cannot rationally diverge either. Because desire has a directive rather than a representational function, however, desires can rationally diverge, and discursive subjects can rationally support divergent expressions of desire. As a result of this difference between expressions of belief and desire, discursive subjects will be under pressure to provide reasons for holding beliefs that diverge from those of others, but will be under no pressure to provide reasons for holding desires that diverge from those of others.

For all that the story so far suggests, the divergence that is possible in desire may be so radical that there are cases in which we cannot see the desire evinced in another's actions and words as an intelligible desire to embrace. In such a case, not only may we not ourselves feel the desire in question, but we may not even be able to see how we could be moved by it if we were in the agent's position. The desire might be as silly as the basic, unintelligible inclination, in Elizabeth Anscombe's famous example, to possess a saucer of mud.[14]

The upshot of this analysis of desire is that while discursive creatures can express desires in a way that provides an inferential grounding for the formation of other desires and the performance of certain actions, they may lack a capacity to do anything about resolving differences between those whose basic desires diverge. This is because discursive creatures may lack the capacity to provide reasons in support of such desires. Discursive creatures may try to resolve practical as well as theoretical predicaments in a discursive way. However, they will resolve shared predicaments only so far as the relevant parties happen to have convergent desires, and they will resolve individual predicaments only so far as they take the desires of the individual in question—even the basic desire for a saucer of mud—as an unchallengable given. The considerations that express the desires of discursive creatures may be action-supporting in a distinctive way, but they will not themselves be reason-supported; there will be no question of justifying the desires these considerations express by invoking something that makes these desires the right ones for an agent to have.

---

[14] G. E. M. Anscombe, *Intention* (Oxford: Blackwell, 1957).

I sum up this result by saying that the discursive creatures envisaged so far will have normative, inferential concepts available to them, but they will not have access to moral concepts proper. A moral or ethical consideration is meant to be able to provide an inferential reason, conclusive or defeasible, for forming a certain desire and performing a corresponding action: it does this in the same way that the normative consideration that something is attractive—the sort of consideration that expresses a desire—may provide a similar inferential reason. However, a moral consideration is also supposed to be a sort of consideration such that divergence between certain parties in regard to whether it is endorsed—divergence on whether it is believed—is not a matter of indifference; it is not something that is necessarily fault-free. A moral consideration is meant to be not just an action-supporting consideration, but also a reason-supported one.

Moral considerations will satisfy this dual condition of being reason-supported as well as action-supporting as long as one of two things is assumed by all those invoking them: either that they are agent-neutral considerations that everyone has some reason to endorse, or that they are agent-relative considerations that anyone in the agent's position would have some reason to endorse.[15] Examples of agent-neutral considerations include "This is the kind thing to do," "This is the only just response," and "This is for the overall good." In contrast, examples of agent-relative considerations include "This will bring me pleasure," "This will help my children," and "This will be for the good of my friends."

It is not particularly contentious to say that divergence with respect to moral considerations is not treated as a fault-free matter of indifference among those who invoke them. The role played by moral considerations in supporting an appraisal of what people do, and the associated role they play in enabling people to justify their desires and actions to one another, require that divergence over such considerations suggest fault. In order to admit the point, we do not have to think that every moral divergence lends itself to mutually satisfactory resolution; as noncognitivists usually say, there may be some values with respect to which people will differ in a fault-free way. All that has to be allowed is that the considerations that people invoke in a moral key generally invite discussion, and that such discussion generally holds out a prospect of leading to noncoercive, noncollusive agreement. In other words, all that has to be accepted is that divergences over moral considerations generally allow of discursive resolution.

---

[15] An agent-neutral consideration is expressed in general terms, and can be fully understood independently of who the agent is for whom it is a consideration. An agent-relative consideration is expressed in indexical terms—terms like "me" or "my" or "mine"—and cannot be fully understood independently of who the agent in question is. If you overhear me say that I am moved by a concern for the general happiness, you can know all there is to know about which consideration is in question without knowing who is speaking. If you overhear me say that I am moved by a concern for the welfare of my children, you do not know all there is to know about which consideration is in question without knowing who is speaking, and in particular without knowing which children are to be favored.

The argument of this section has shown that considered in the abstract, discursive subjects are capable of having divergent desires without this divergence offending against any norms that they recognize; they may lack the moral concepts that would raise questions about it. The upshot is that we have to look beyond our status as discursive creatures in order to explain how the morally normative, as opposed to the merely inferentially normative, becomes salient to us; I do this in the next two sections. Before going on to those discussions, however, it is worth mentioning that the previous section does not leave us quite as badly off as might be thought. While the discussion of discursive subjects does not explain how moral terms or concepts materialize, it does take us well past the point at which the discussion of intentionality left us.

I argued in Section II that simple intentional subjects would have no awareness, as such, of their perceptions and inclinations. For such subjects, perceiving things a certain way would be nothing short of believing them to be that way; analogously, being inclined to make things a certain way would be nothing short of being decisively disposed—desiring, without qualification—to make them that way. Given these observations, it appeared that there would be no call in such creatures for an awareness of perception as providing a reason for belief, or of inclination as providing a reason for (unqualified) desire; perception and inclination would operate in these creatures with an invisible, ineluctable force, and would determine their beliefs and their desires.

The thing to notice about the discursive image of human beings, as distinct from the merely intentional image, is that just as the discursive image is not consistent with perception maintaining a silent, irresistible role in the determination of people's beliefs, it is also not consistent with inclination remaining in such a position with respect to people's desires. The discursive image requires that humans be able to become aware of inclinations as such, other people's as well as their own.

Assume that people use signs that express how the world presents itself in the light of their perceptions, saying on the basis of perception that this or that is how things are. It is inevitable that sooner or later others will differ from them, finding different claims perceptually compelling. This means that people are bound to become aware that their perceptions are not incontrovertible evidence that things are this or that way. Making sense of divergence with others under the regulative assumptions of discourse will force people to recognize their perceptions—and the perceptions of others—for what they really are: representations of how things are that may go wide of the mark. This recognition will not give people a perception of perception—it will not bring an extra experiential faculty into play—but it will force them to notice and conceptualize the perception that has always been there. The "glass" of perception will fog up, as it were, and cease to exist as a purely diaphanous, unnoticed medium.

As it is with perception, so it is with inclination. Discourse in which people give voice to their perceptions makes clear, according to the account just presented, that how things are in the world is not an immediate given; it is given only through perception. Likewise, discourse in which people give voice to their inclinations, speaking of what is attractive and what is unattractive, will make equally clear that the way the world inclines them to act is not an unquestioned given either; it is a product of what they will have to see as inclination. They will previously have looked through their inclinations, unaware of them as such, and seen the world as a single field for action. After engaging in discourse, they will be sensitized to the fact that the world presents itself as a different sort of field to different discursive participants. For people to make sense of this, they will have to recognize that the way the world elicits action from each of them is a function of the inclinations that each of them brings to the world, not just a reflection of what is available in common to all.

As I argued earlier in this section, there will be no pressure on people to avoid divergence in their basic desires, though there will be pressure to avoid divergence in ultimate beliefs. For all that we need suppose up to this point in our story, people may be generally reconciled to competition and conflict in the realm of desire; they may resolve practical predicaments only so far as they are led by agreed matters of belief, and their existing inclinations, to a common desire. The mere fact that people use signs to express how the world presents itself in light of their inclinations will be enough on its own to make inclination visible. This will reveal to people that the world is not an action-generating environment with which they are in immediate contact any more than it is a belief-generating environment with which they are in immediate contact. It will force them to see themselves and one another not just as centers of individually variable representation, but also as centers of individually variable inclination.

This observation establishes a negative element in the genealogy of moral concepts. It shows that discursive creatures, unlike merely intentional ones, are not slaves of unnoticed inclinations in a way that rules out the appearance or relevance of moral considerations. We must now turn from this negative argument, however, to an attempt to explain how, more positively, discursive creatures can get to be sensitized to moral considerations that are capable of regulating inclination and desire. I argue that there are two forms of experience that will serve discursive creatures in this respect.

V. Privileging Discourse Will Give Rise to Certain Moral Concepts

So far as people enter discourse with one another, so I have argued, they will have to become aware as such of their own inclinations and the rival inclinations of others. How can people take a further step and come to access action-guiding considerations that are capable of directing inclination in the distinctively moral or ethical manner? What experiences available to them in the discursive scenario sketched above could give rise to terms and concepts with the dual capacity, distinctive of the moral, to support action and be supported by reason? In this section, I describe one more or less obvious way in which certain experiences can perform this task, and in the next I move on to another.

Under the picture presented in Section IV, people are inevitably going to be involved at various times in discourse with one another. While many conversations serve nondiscursive purposes, conversation will often be devoted to the resolution of discursive questions as to how a certain theoretical puzzle or practical predicament should be resolved. Some of the questions may concern what one or another party to the conversation should think or do, while others may focus on what the group as a whole—be it a group of two, three, or more—should think or do collectively. When people take part in such a conversation, they will put their heads together and reason with one another about how the puzzle or predicament should be resolved.

This sort of discourse embodies the recognition of rational, inferential norms that describe when it is appropriate, in view of how things are perceptually presented, to endorse a given consideration; when it is appropriate to endorse two or more considerations at the same time; when it is appropriate to move from the endorsement of one or more considerations to the endorsement of a further consideration; and when it is appropriate to move from the endorsement of certain considerations to the performance of a particular action. We could not treat another person as a discursive partner if he or she were not generally able to recognize and respond to what such norms require. If he or she failed to internalize inferential discursive norms in this way, then we might as well be talking to the dog or the wall.[16]

Given that discursive conversation of this kind has to be governed by rational, *inferential* norms of discourse, it follows that those taking part in it will have to conform also to corresponding *interactive* norms of discourse. If I am reasoning together with you about something, then the discursive conversation in which we are involved requires by its very nature that all the overtures we make be consistent with the joint endeavor's being governed by rational, inferential norms in the manner envisaged. Thus, if I put forward a consideration that I know to be false, I am not behaving in line with this endeavor. Likewise, I am not behaving in line with the endeavor if I insincerely voice an intention as to what I will do in the future, or if I make a coercive threat to the effect that I will punish you unless you agree to something. Reasoning together, by its

---

[16] On this point, see Pettit and Smith, "Freedom in Belief and Desire."

very nature, is inconsistent with such modes of conduct among the parties involved. If any of them behave in these ways, then whatever transpires between them cannot be described as an instance of reasoning in common about a discursive question.

Not only will people have to conform to interactive norms of discursive conversation—that is, the norms that derive from the more basic inferential norms. People who take part in discursive conversation must also be aware of what these interactive norms require, at least on a case-by-case basis, and they must prove generally responsive to these requirements. Being able to take part in such conversation is a skill that people learn, not something that comes by way of automatism and reflex. In learning this skill, it is essential that people are enabled to recognize and reject the sorts of deceptive, manipulative, and coercive moves that are inconsistent with the exercise of reasoning with others about the resolution of a theoretical or practical issue. People will be free to deceive or not to deceive, to manipulate or not to manipulate, to coerce or not to coerce, but they must be able to see the deceptive, manipulative, or coercive option as being inconsistent with maintaining a discursive posture toward others. And of course, they must be able to respond to this perception and prove themselves capable of treating others in the manner of a fellow reasoner.

If, however, people are to be able to see certain types of options as being inconsistent with the discursive posture—the posture of mutual address, as Stephen Darwall calls it[17]—then they must be in a position to introduce terms with ethical force in order to describe the options in question. In what follows, these terms will be represented by the letter "O" (for "objectionable"). To the extent that discourse and address are practices in which people engage, the consideration that an option is O will have the profile, action-supporting and reason-supported, of a moral consideration.

The consideration that an option is O will serve to direct or support action to the extent that the consideration gives expression to an unquestioned, willing involvement in the discursive practice that makes the O-concept available in the first place. To think, situating oneself within discourse, that a certain sort of action is O will be to register a reason, conclusive or defeasible, for not performing that action. It will be like thinking, as one stands behind a certain inclination or desire, that things inconsistent with the satisfaction of that desire are unattractive.

However, the consideration that an option is O will also be capable of being supported by reason, unlike, say, the consideration that things inconsistent with possessing a saucer of mud are unattractive. There is nothing that a person can do to provide support for the basic desire for a saucer of mud. Nothing about that desire, so we have been supposing,

[17] Stephen Darwall, "Reciprocal Recognition: The Second-Person Standpoint in Moral Thought and Theory" (manuscript).

makes it something that it is in any sense right—right, by common lights—to embrace. Things are very different, however, when it comes to the desire for the sort of discursive involvement that is presupposed when one treats O-considerations as action-guiding. Such involvement is bound to recommend itself to people generally, given their discursive nature. Therefore, every individual will be in a position to justify their treating the fact that an option is O as a reason for not performing the corresponding action; every person can ground such treatment in the fact—however they express it—that such treatment is required for maintaining the discursive or addressive stance.

O-type predicates may be dependent on discourse and address in either of two ways, both of which are consistent with this observation. Someone who says that an option is O may be speaking from a neutral or outside perspective, in which case he or she is saying that the option is inconsistent with address—that is, the option is ruled out by the discursive practice of mutual address. Alternatively, one who says that an option is O might be speaking from within the perspective of mutual address, thus taking that perspective as given and putting its relevance beyond current question. In this case, one is saying that the option is ruled out, period, though perhaps only ruled out defeasibly rather than conclusively. The first construal would make O-type terms *relational* in character; the second would make them *perspectival* or *locational*.

I assume that O-type terms and concepts are going to be address-dependent in the locational way. This construal is more economical than is the relational, since it does not require people to have the explicit concept of discourse or address; it requires only that people be involved willingly and unquestioningly in discursive practice. In virtue of occupying the discursive stance, people will see certain types of actions as O, but they may not notice the relationship with discourse in virtue of which the actions present themselves as O. The discursive stance will cast a shadow on relevant action-types, as it were, and make them saliently available for conceptualization as O. Furthermore, it will do this without people necessarily being aware of the role that the stance plays in casting this shadow.

There is another advantage, apart from this economy, in taking O-type terms to be locational rather than relational in character. The locational construal makes sense of why people are spontaneously prepared to see actions performed outside the context of discursive address as O; it expands the domain in which O-type terms are naturally and nontendentiously applied. Taking up the discursive stance, I may think that my doing something to another person would be O, even if at the time I had no interest in addressing the person affected; in thinking this, I am spontaneously and understandably privileging the discursive stance I currently occupy. And in the same way that I may think this sort of thing about actions that I might myself perform outside of a context of address, so I may think it of actions that others are currently performing outside of such a context. Having no hesitation about privileging the context of address that I occupy myself, I may be quite happy to denounce those actions as O.

The elements of a genealogy of moral concepts are now in place. Discourse involves something that we may hope is naturalistically unobjectionable: the exchange of common signs in voluntary expression of intentional states. Those within the discursive stance will have to see the use of these signs as being subject to rational, inferential norms, as I argued in Section IV. And, as I have just argued in this section, these people will have to see activities that engage with the discursive exchange of such signs—activities that may or may not be consistent with practicing discourse and address—as being subject to interactive norms and corresponding moral considerations.

I think that this account should prove reasonably persuasive for anyone who accepts the discursive image sketched in Section III. However, even if the account is mistaken in some respects, it should still serve to render ethical conceptualization intelligible. The fact that people could become sensitized to moral considerations in the manner described here at least establishes that there is nothing inherently mysterious, even under broadly naturalistic assumptions, about their having access to moral terms and concepts. Let the account be entirely hypothetical in character, and it will still serve to render the appearance of ethical terms and concepts intelligible.[18] Donald Davidson has claimed to render our semantic competence with respect to an indefinite number of sentences intelligible by showing that it could have come about—though actually it certainly did not—through our mastering a certain sort of theory for the language in question.[19] We might claim that the account provided above, even if it is not true to the actual evolution of moral concepts, can render moral conceptualization intelligible in the same way.

Rather than end this discussion of address-dependent concepts on a weak note, however, I would like to emphasize how much discursive address distinguishes and enhances human life and how natural it is that it should provide the entrée to ethical talk and thought. It is possible for one person to exercise a substantive influence over another in a discursive exchange by proving to be better-informed, clearer-headed, more persuasive, or whatever. The influence thereby exercised is quite different from deceptive, manipulative, or coercive influence, or from any sort of influence found elsewhere in the sentient world. It is of a kind that must be welcomed by the person influenced, so far as he or she is genuinely concerned with the discursive issue under discussion. It is also of a kind

[18] It would be entirely hypothetical under the story told in Robert B. Brandom, *Making It Explicit* (Cambridge, MA: Harvard University Press, 1994).
[19] Donald Davidson, *Inquiries into Truth and Interpretation* (Oxford: Oxford University Press, 1984).

that in no way detracts from the fitness of the influenced person to be held responsible for whatever he or she does; it does not undermine or diminish his or her autonomy as an agent.[20] If discursive exchange is the locus at which ethical terms and concepts first gain life, it is as fitting a locus as we could ever imagine.

VI. Discursifying Sentiment Will Give Rise to Other Moral Concepts

In the account just provided, people take the practice of discourse as given and from the privileged perspective that it supplies they distinguish activities that are dissonant with discursive address from activities that are consonant with it, indicting the former as O. In other words, people privilege discourse and let the discursive stance partition activities into those that are O and those that are not.

Can we see how people might develop ethical terms and concepts apart from the address-dependent ones that this privileging of discourse will explain? Is there any other source of ethical conceptualization that we can identify on the basis of the account provided so far? I mentioned earlier that a person may see the attractiveness of an option as an inferential reason to choose it without that consideration being supported in the manner required for ethical force—that is, without there being any reason, accessible to the agent, for why he or she should endorse that consideration as a reason for action. The question now is whether people can be expected to develop concepts whereby some such considerations can be invested with reason-supported as well as action-supporting status, on the model of address-dependent considerations.

I think that we can expect people to develop such concepts. They will be given reason enough to do so by the fact that, having entered ethical space—having come to see the possibility of regulating inclination on the basis of mutually endorsed considerations—they are bound to be attracted by the possibility of the richer coordination of their activities that further ethical concepts would hold out. Moreover, as there is reason for people to try to develop further ethical concepts, so there is also going to be a resource available whereby they can achieve this goal.

For any option that an agent might see as attractive, people will be in a position to support the action-supporting reason in question—the presence of the inclination—so far as they converge on standards for when it is appropriate to form and act on the inclination. This means that people will be in a position to endorse the action-supporting reason provided by any inclination to the extent that their assessments converge with respect to a property that the inclination can be generally supposed to track. The possibility of finding standards for when embarrassment or fear is appropriate, for example, is just the possibility of finding a property—that of being truly embarrassing or truly frightening, as we may say—that feelings of embarrassment or fear are supposed to track.

This observation points us toward a search procedure whereby people might aspire to single out inclinations that can generate ethical considerations. People might work with the assumption that a given sentiment, such as embarrassment or fear, has the status of representing some property commonly available to all—the truly embarrassing or the truly frightening—and see how far this assumption proves workable. The assumption will prove workable if people generally find it possible to converge in their responses involving that sentiment and, where they diverge, to resolve or explain the divergence in a manner that is consistent with the sentiment's having representational status. The assumption will prove workable with fear, for example, so far as people tend to call the same scenarios "frightening" and find themselves able, in cases of divergence, to agree on which of the discrepant responses should be discounted.

The search procedure envisaged here can be more precisely characterized in abstract terms. Suppose that people tend to experience a sentiment S according to a relatively common pattern—that is, facing certain stimuli under certain conditions routinely leads people to experience S. People in such circumstances might wish to test S for its capacity to be supported by reason and to serve in an ethical role. They can do this by introducing a predicate "D" (for "desirable") as an expression of S in the same way that "frightening" is an expression of fear, and then seeing if they can subject "D" effectively to the three regulative assumptions involved in common discursive practice. They can try, that is, to determine whether they can "discursify" the predicate "D," enabling it to function in a way that parallels regular descriptive predicates. The question to be tested in the exercise will be whether people, while taking "D" as an expression of the sentiment S, can still successfully regulate their discursive practice by the assumptions (1) that there is an agent-neutral or agent-relative property, D, waiting to be tracked by "D"; (2) that each individual using "D" intends to track the same, presumptively salient property—whatever that is—in his or her use of "D"; and (3) that each individual is generally competent in his or her tracking attempts.

Let us think about how the process might go. People will use "D" in expression of S, intending thereby to mark the presence of a property that provides a reason for ascribing D and holding S. So far as people manage to converge in their usage of "D," all will go well. And so far as they diverge, all will still go well if they can sustain the regulative assumptions. They will be able to sustain these assumptions to the extent that they can come to agree, case by case, on the sorts of factors that destabilize discursive performance and give rise to divergence. In other words, they will be able to sustain these assumptions to the extent that they have a shared means of identifying certain conditions—call them C—that are free of such destabilizing influences and are favorable for detecting the presence of the property D, and hence for endorsing the sentiment S.

There will be a fact of the matter, under this picture, as to whether something is D or not, and this fact will be independent of whether the subject feels S or not. This is why the picture can make room for thinking that the consideration expressed by "D," which will provide an inferential reason for the agent to act as S prompts, may or may not be deserving of endorsement. To the extent that limitations, obstacles, blind spots, and the like are possible—to the extent that C-conditions may not obtain—it will be possible for a person to feel S when the sentiment is rationally ruled out and not to feel S when it is rationally ruled in. Thus, it will be possible for people to feel S when the object of their sentiment is not D—as they may themselves be able to see—and not to feel S when the object of their sentiment—again, as they may be able to see—is D. The connection between the sentiment S and the property D will not be that something has the property if and only if it produces S in a relevant person. Rather, it will be that something has the property if and only if it produces S in a relevant person under the C-conditions where the person's response is not in any way destabilized.

This story, it should be noticed, is quite consistent with people's thinking of the property D as a feature of the world in itself, or of the world in the way it impacts on the agent, without their registering its connection to a sentiment. Just as O-type terms can be dependent on address without being relational terms that express the relationship of being inconsistent with address, so D-type terms can be dependent on sentiments without being relational terms that express the relationship of occasioning sentiment. As in the case of address-dependent concepts, it is more economical to assume that these sentiment-dependent concepts are perspectival or locational, since this means that the registering and conceptualization of D-properties will not require a prior registering and conceptualization of the S-sentiments or the C-conditions. Those who use the D-type terms need not have distinguished C-conditions as a general type, they need not have identified or named the S-sentiments within themselves, and they need not be aware of the fact that the things they call "D" give rise to S under C-conditions.[21] As was the case with O-type terms, the assumption that D-type terms are locational also has the effect of expanding the potential domain in which these terms can be spontaneously applied. I may think that my doing something would be D, even were I not at the time to feel or endorse the sentiment S, and I may think that the same is true of others' currently acting in that way, even others who do not feel or endorse the sentiment.

[21] See Philip Pettit, "Realism and Response-Dependence," *Mind* 100, no. 4 (1991): 587–626; and Philip Pettit, "Terms, Things, and Response-Dependence," *European Review of Philosophy* 3 (1998): 61–72.

What might be examples of D-type terms? Some will be terms that answer determinately to recognizable sentiments, such as "frightening," "embarrassing," "thrilling," "nauseating," "humiliating," and "inspiring." Others will be similar to these except so far as they mark more explicitly the fact that you can have a sentiment without the relevant predicate being applicable—as, of course, you can be frightened without anything being truly frightening—and vice versa. In this second category are terms such as "admirable," "honorable," "desirable," and the like, as well as negative counterparts such as "abominable," "dishonorable," and "undesirable." Still other terms will focus not on the sentiment involved in the response, and not on the fact that this may or may not be rightly held, but on the sort of action, person, or state of affairs that attracts the positive or negative sentiment in question. In this third category are more descriptively laden terms such as "kind" and "cruel," "fair" and "biased," "courageous" and "cowardly," "prudent" and "imprudent," and so on.

Notice that among these examples of D-type terms we should expect to find terms that register aspects of experience and interaction that are dependent on the practice of discourse itself and the prior development of O-type terms. So far as O-ness becomes salient in the light of discursive practice, and so far as it is more or less bound to be motivating, it is bound to engage with our sentiments; plausibly, it will engage with the phenomenologically distinctive sentiments of resentment and indignation to which Peter Strawson draws attention.[22] To the extent that those actions that present themselves as O—deception, manipulation, coercion, and the like—inherit these features of O-ness, they are likely also to attract autonomous sentiments of disapproval. We should be ready to admit that there will inevitably be interactions of these kinds between address-dependent and sentiment-dependent ethical concepts.

We have seen why terms or concepts that fit with the D-schema should have the dual capacity that is distinctive of the ethical. D-considerations, being expressive of sentiments in the way in which "attractive" is expressive of inclination, will provide inferential reasons, conclusive or defeasible, for acting. D-considerations will also be supported by reasons, so far as there will be reason to endorse them in those cases where they truly obtain. Whereas O-considerations are likely to be agent-neutral in character, presenting reasons that all of us have reason to endorse, D-considerations are going to be agent-relative as often as they are agent-neutral. They will include considerations to do with the children or projects for which the agent has a special sentiment—that is, his or her own—as well as considerations to do with matters in respect of which we may all expect to feel roughly the same sentiments.

---

[22] Peter Strawson, "Freedom and Resentment," in Gary Watson, ed., *Free Will* (Oxford: Oxford University Press, 1982).

The account given of O-type terms in Section V explained how creatures like us, so far as we practice discourse and privilege the addressive stance, will experience certain activities as being morally objectionable or, of course, unobjectionable. The account just given of D-type terms plays a similar genealogical role. It explains how discursive creatures like us, already familiar with ethical concepts, can privilege certain sentiments—those that we find capable of being "discursified"—and can experience the objects of these sentiments as being morally desirable or undesirable. Under the account, an arbitrary X will be D if and only if X is disposed to produce S in conditions C. What this formula communicates is that concepts of the D-type will be available in canonical or nonparasitic mode only to those creatures who are capable of having the S-response and who discursify this response in the sense of standing by it just in those conditions that prove to be C.

Just as the earlier genealogy sheds light on the possibility of ethical conceptualization even if it is not accurate in its details, the same applies in this case as well. It is worth mentioning, however, that the genealogy provided in this section has a long history of support and may be regarded for this reason as having particularly telling claims. The genealogy conforms to a narrative of sentiment and training in sentiment that was common currency during the Enlightenment period, being best known today through the work of David Hume.[23] It also fits well with the work of those contemporary metaethical thinkers who remain faithful to the broadly Humean framework.[24]

VII. Conclusion

The epistemology of ethics needs to give some account of how ethical judgments are to be confirmed, but it also has to address the question of how ethical conceptualization can arise from experience. The experience of intentional subjects cannot give rise as such to moral conceptualization,

---

[23] David Hume, *"Of the Standard of Taste" and Other Essays*, ed. John W. Lenz (Indianapolis, IN: Bobbs-Merrill, 1965); David Hume, *A Treatise of Human Nature*, ed. L. A. Selby-Bigge, 2d ed. (Oxford: Oxford University Press, 1978); and David Hume, *An Inquiry Concerning the Principles of Morals*, ed. J. B. Schneewind (Indianapolis, IN: Hackett, 1983). See also Geoffrey Sayre-McCord, "On Why Hume's 'General Point of View' Isn't Ideal—and Shouldn't Be," *Social Philosophy and Policy* 11, no. 1 (1994): 202–28; Stephen Darwall, *The British Moralists and the Internal "Ought"* (Cambridge: Cambridge University Press, 1995); and J. B. Schneewind, *The Invention of Autonomy* (Cambridge: Cambridge University Press, 1998). Writers who emphasize the possibility of reading Hume on cognitivist lines, so that his approach would mirror that taken in this essay, include J. L. Mackie, *Hume's Moral Theory* (London: Routledge, 1980); R. M. Sainsbury, "Projections and Relations," *The Monist* 81, no. 1 (1998): 133–60; and Peter Railton, "Taste and Value," in Roger Crisp and Brad Hooker, eds., *Well-Being and Morality: Essays in Honour of James Griffin* (Oxford: Oxford University Press, 2000).

[24] For a modern development of the Humean approach, see, for example, Michael Smith, *The Moral Problem* (Oxford: Blackwell, 1994). Whereas Smith's approach gives prominence to the notion of an ideal point of view, however, it is arguable that Hume relied instead on the notion of a general point of view. For a fine case in support of this interpretation, see Sayre-McCord, "On Why Hume's 'General Point of View' Isn't Ideal."

but the experience of discursive creatures certainly can. The experience of discursive creatures will inevitably occasion the appearance of normative concepts, since these are required for reasoning. Such experience also has the capacity to give rise to properly moral conceptualization. It will do this first by making salient the demands presupposed by the practice of discursive address, and second by fostering the "discursification" of certain sentiments.

These two genealogical stories are both fairly persuasive to my eye, though each needs more detailed development. Distinguishing them is important, because the address-dependent and sentiment-dependent concepts that they respectively underpin are quite different in character. Any comprehensive moral theory has to recognize the place of each sort of concept, and has to tell a story about how the different demands in question should be reconciled. The relative priorities a moral theory assigns to each of these types of concepts will play a large role in determining the overall shape of the theory.

The address-dependent concepts are, broadly speaking, deontological in character. The question to which they relate bears on whether an action is in breach of discursive norms—whether it is *deon*, to use the Greek word, or owing to another—and it applies only to the actions that people take in relation to others. It may be possible to treat such action-centered, negative considerations in a consequentialist rather than a nonconsequentialist way: someone might think that right action requires the maximization of nonobjectionable behavior toward others, for example, even if this means that one must sometimes engage in objectionable behavior oneself. The normal response to such considerations, however, is going to be nonconsequentialist in character. It is going to recommend that people seek to instantiate nonobjectionable properties, even at a cost in the extent to which the properties are realized overall; such an approach is supported in traditional theories of obligations and rights, as well as in more recent versions of contractual theory.[25]

The sentiment-dependent concepts, in contrast, are axiological rather than deontological in nature. They relate to the question of what is for the best—what is *axios* or desirable—which applies in principle to almost any variety of item: not just to actions, for example, but also to people, motives, and situations. One sort of axiological approach that such concepts might prompt is virtue-ethical in character, focusing on the properties that virtuous agents ought to instantiate. However, the axiological approach is just as likely to assume a consequentialist form, directing our attention instead to the properties that people ought to promote, even if promoting them sometimes means not instantiating them in their own behavior, psychology, or relationships.

---

[25] On obligations and rights, see Ronald Dworkin, *Taking Rights Seriously* (London: Duckworth, 1978). On contractualism, see T. M. Scanlon, *What We Owe to Each Other* (Cambridge, MA: Harvard University Press, 1998).

The argument of this essay suggests that address-dependent, essentially deontological concepts have a certain primacy in moral thought, representing the ethical considerations that introduce us—and that may be uniquely capable of introducing us—to the space of ethical reasons. This suggestion is consistent, of course, with the view that issues of what it is right or wrong to do are ultimately determined by what is for the best overall—that is, by consequentialist considerations. I defend such a view myself, believing that however serious the demands associated with the requirements of address—however serious the demands of civility or comity, as we might call them—they will have to be overridden in circumstances where it is clear that honoring them is not for the best.[26]

I believe that the debate between different approaches to ethical theory, consequentialist and nonconsequentialist, should benefit from recognition of the very different currencies provided for ethical thought by address-dependent and sentiment-dependent concepts. It may be that a failure to recognize this divergence in conceptual currency explains attachments on either side of the divide over consequentialism, even if recognition of the divergence does not argue unambiguously in favor of any particular position. Once we see the divergent ways in which our species comes to conceptualize ethical considerations, we may be better placed to assess the different ethical positions to which reflection on these considerations can drive us.

*Philosophy, Research School of Social Sciences,
Australian National University*

---

[26] See Philip Pettit, "The Consequentialist Perspective," in Marcia Baron, Philip Pettit, and Michael Slote, *Three Methods of Ethics: A Debate* (Oxford: Blackwell, 1997). See also Philip Pettit and T. M. Scanlon, "Contractualism and Consequentialism," *Theoria* (2000): 228–45.

"BECAUSE I WANT IT"*

By Stephen Darwall

I. Introduction

How can an agent's desire or will give him reasons for acting? Not long ago, this might have seemed a silly question, since it was widely believed that all reasons for acting are based in the agent's desires.[1] The interesting question, it seemed, was not how what an agent wants could give him reasons, but how anything else could. In recent years, however, this earlier orthodoxy has increasingly appeared wrongheaded as a growing number of philosophers have come to stress the action-guiding role of reasons in deliberation from the agent's point of view.[2] What a deliberating agent has in view is rarely his own will or desires as such, even if taking something as a reason is intimately tied to desire.[3] Someone who wants to escape a burning building does not evaluate her options by considering which is likeliest to realize what she wants or wills. She is focused, rather, on her desire's object: getting out alive. The fact that a successful route would realize something she wants is apt to strike her as beside the point or, at best, as a trivial bonus.

This point is sometimes put by saying that desires are in the "background," rather than the foreground, of the practical scene a deliberating agent faces.[4] The metaphor is somewhat misleading, however, since an agent's desires are normally not so much in the background of her deliberative field as outside of it altogether.[5] If we must locate them spatially, a better place might be within or behind the standpoint from which

* An earlier draft of this paper was presented at a conference on practical reason at the University of Rome (La Sapienza). I am indebted to members of the audience, especially to Jonathan Dancy, Carla Bagnoli, Allan Gibbard, and Tito Magri. I also owe much to the other contributors to this volume. Finally, I am indebted to Nishiten Shah for very helpful discussion.
[1] Where 'desire' is understood in the broad sense, as any disposition an agent might have to bring something about. I shall generally follow this usage.
[2] For earlier criticisms of this view, see Thomas Nagel, *The Possibility of Altruism* (Oxford: Clarendon Press, 1970); E. J. Bond, *Reason and Value* (Cambridge: Cambridge University Press, 1983); and Stephen Darwall, *Impartial Reason* (Ithaca, NY: Cornell University Press, 1983). For more recent critiques, see Philip Pettit and Michael Smith, "Backgrounding Desire," *Philosophical Review* 99, no. 4 (1990): 565-92; Warren Quinn, "Putting Rationality in Its Place," in Quinn, *Morality and Action* (Cambridge: Cambridge University Press, 1993), 228-55; and T. M. Scanlon, *What We Owe to Each Other* (Cambridge, MA: Harvard University Press, 1998), 41-55.
[3] On this latter point, see Scanlon, *What We Owe to Each Other*, 39-41.
[4] Pettit and Smith, "Backgrounding Desire."
[5] I take the term "deliberative field" from Barbara Herman, *The Practice of Moral Judgment* (Cambridge, MA: Harvard University Press, 1993), 193-207.

the agent views her alternatives rather than toward the back of the scene she views. Sometimes desires shape the way an agent sees things, as in the burning building just mentioned. In other cases, desires seem shaped themselves by what the agent takes as reasons, as in Thomas Nagel's category of "motivated desires."[6] Here, that the agent has a certain desire may "simply *follow*" from the fact that she takes certain considerations as reason-giving.[7] In either case, it can seem puzzling why the fact that an agent desires or wills something (as opposed to facts about *what* she wants or wills) should give her a practical reason, that is, a consideration bearing intrinsically on what she should do.

Despite this, "Because I want it" can sometimes give one a reason for acting that is additional to the reasons for which one wants or wills. Consider, for example, what we might say to someone seeking advice about what to do. Although we might well begin by pointing to reasons for wanting to do this or that, we could suggest as well that what she (that is, the agent) wants in light of these reasons is also relevant, perhaps decisively so. Appreciating the backgrounding of desire from the agent's point of view makes it difficult, however, to see why this should be so. In what follows, I shall suggest what may seem a surprising explanation of why it is, namely, our standing as free and rational persons among others, able to address claims *to* others *as* free and rational. To make a claim is, necessarily, to express one's will. In claiming, therefore, we commit ourselves to the reason-giving character of the will. Ultimately, I shall argue, we can justify claims that we, as free and rational, make on others only by acknowledging an equal standing that all free and rational agents have to make such claims. Moreover, I shall argue, our epistemic access to this status comes through such "second-personal" claim-making. The point will not be that the reason-giving character of the will depends on any actual claim we make on others or that they make on us. Rather, the thought will be that in addressing such reasons to each other, second-personally, we commit ourselves *a priori* to the standing of free and rational persons to make such claims, and thereby commit ourselves to accepting the reason-giving character of the will. Ironically, it will turn out, what explains why an agent's own will can give *him* reasons is inextricably linked to why his will can also give them to others.

II. THEORETICAL AND PRACTICAL REASON: A PRELIMINARY COMPARISON

The basic idea can be glimpsed by reflecting on a disanalogy between theoretical and practical reason to which we shall return in Section V. Belief, by its very nature, aims to represent the world and so is appro-

[6] Nagel, *The Possibility of Altruism*, 29–30.
[7] Nagel argues that this is true, for example, of moral and prudential reasons. Ibid., 29.

priately regulated by it. Correct representation is belief's "constitutive aim," so it is guaranteed by what beliefs are that we ought to believe truths and disbelieve falsehoods.[8] The idea is not just that beliefs are mental states that picture the world as being some way, say, that p. That is as true of supposing or pretending that p as it is of believing that p. If p is not the case, a supposition that p is false no less than is a belief that p. Rather, the thought is that, unlike pretense and supposition, belief aims to represent the world *correctly*. Truth is regulative for any state of mind we will count as a belief. If a mental state represents the world as being that p, but is insufficiently responsive to evidence of p's truth, we will count it, not as a belief that p, but as some other kind of representative state.[9]

We might think of the set of a person's beliefs as defining her subjective theoretical standpoint, but this simply means her standpoint on the world — how the world seems to her or the world-as-she-believes-it-be. Suppose we ask how the fact that one person believes something can give another a reason to believe it. It follows from the nature of belief that it can do so only insofar as it can give the other person evidence. Even if someone's belief that p is reasonable, in the sense of being supported by evidence available to her, it may give us no reason to believe p whatsoever if our evidence explains away hers as misleading. A similar consequence follows concerning the relation of an individual's own subjective theoretical standpoint to what she has reason to believe herself. Only if her believing that p gives her some evidence that p is true, as it might, for example, if she has some evidence about the reliability of her beliefs, can it give her some reason to maintain her belief that p.

Compare now practical reason. What, if anything, plays the role in practical reasoning that the world does in theoretical reasoning? (We can ignore for the present the difference between desire and willing something as an end; I will use 'desire' here to refer to both.) It has become

---

[8] Or, at least, it is guaranteed that we ought to believe the truth on some matter if we have any beliefs on it at all. For discussion of the idea that belief has this "constitutive aim," and of whether desire does, see J. David Velleman, "The Possibility of Practical Reason," *Ethics* 106, no. 4 (1996): 707–26. A problem with the view in the text might be that even if belief's constitutive aim is correct representation, it cannot follow directly that we ought to believe truths (or not believe falsehoods), because such an 'ought' would have to be categorical, and for that to follow it would also have to be true that belief's aim is one we ought to have. An alternative picture might be to treat it as a conceptual truth that beliefs ought to be regulated by the truth (or the world), since, from the first-person point of view, deliberation about what to believe is no different from inquiry into what is true. Whatever the details, however, what seems clear is that it is of the nature of belief that it is regulated by something (truth, or the world) that is what it is independently of norms for belief. I am indebted here to some work by, and discussion with, Nishiten Shah.

[9] As David Velleman puts it, "When someone believes a proposition . . . his acceptance of it is regulated in ways designed to promote acceptance of the truth," whereas, for example, when "someone assumes a proposition, he or his cognitive faculties are disposed to regulate his acceptance of it in ways designed to promote the ends of argument or inquiry," and so on. J. David Velleman, "The Guise of the Good," *Noûs* 16, no. 1 (1992): 14.

common to treat desire and belief as having contrasting functions given by complementary "directions of fit."[10] In a slogan, beliefs aim to fit the world, whereas desires aim for the world to fit them. This difference between desire and belief need not entail the Humean thesis that, since desires lack the representative function of beliefs, they are regulated by nothing, so that, strictly speaking, there are no normative reasons for desire or action. Desires might be regulated by norms for desire and action, whatever these might be, and by normative practical reasons ultimately grounded in these norms. The point is that norms for desire and action must be given in some other way than they are for belief. We cannot discover them by considering some representative function, since desires have none.[11]

Suppose, however, that there were something to which desires aim to be responsive in some broader sense, if not to represent it. Call this "value." Desires would then be regulated by value, just as beliefs are regulated by the world. Ultimately, I will reject this analogy. At this point, however, I want to consider what would follow if the analogy held. Desires would not be regulated by value, of course, "*just* as" beliefs are, since the way beliefs are regulated follows from their representative function, and desires have none. Desires would not aim to *represent* value. Nonetheless, we might try out the idea that in some broader way, desires are mistaken when they are out of proportion to value. It will now follow from the nature of desire that we ought not desire what lacks value, we ought not desire one thing more than another when there is no difference in value, and so on.[12]

By analogy with what we said about belief and an individual's subjective theoretical standpoint, we can define an individual's subjective practical standpoint by the set of her desires.[13] Since, however, desire lacks a

[10] See, for example, Michael Smith, *The Moral Problem* (Oxford: Blackwell, 1995), 111–19. Smith cites Mark Platts, *Ways of Meaning* (London: Routledge and Kegan Paul, 1979), 256–57; Platts attributes the idea to G. E. M. Anscombe, *Intention* (Oxford: Basil Blackwell, 1957).

[11] See note 8 above.

[12] The "value" at issue here is not "agent-relative value" (that is, not value *to the agent*— either value-as-the-agent-sees-it, or value from the agent's point of view, *or* benefit to the agent [the agent's good]), but rather what is called "agent-neutral value" or value *period*. For the distinction between "agent-relative" and "agent-neutral" generally, see Thomas Nagel, "The Limits of Objectivity," in Sterling M. McMurrin, ed., *The Tanner Lectures on Human Values*, vol. 1 (Salt Lake City: University of Utah Press, 1980), 97–139; Thomas Nagel, *The View from Nowhere* (New York: Oxford University Press, 1986), 164–88; Derek Parfit, *Reasons and Persons* (Oxford: Clarendon Press, 1984), 3–14; Samuel Scheffler, *The Rejection of Consequentialism*, rev. ed. (Oxford: Clarendon Press, 1994); and David McNaughton and Piers Rawling, "Agent-Relativity and Terminological Inexactitudes," *Utilitas* 7, no. 2 (1995): 319–25. For the relevance of this distinction to value in particular, see Amartya Sen, "Evaluator Relativity and Consequential Evaluation," *Philosophy and Public Affairs* 12, no. 2 (1983): 113–32.

[13] Using 'desire' in the broad functionalist sense given by its direction of fit. So understood, desires will include many things that could usefully be distinguished in a more fine-grained analysis: intentions, instances of norm acceptance, emotions, and so on.

representative function, we should not say that a person's practical point of view is simply the way value seems to her. Her desires or will are not simply value-as-she-sees-it. Nonetheless, since we are taking desires to be, intrinsically, regulated by value, our tentative picture will have it that the relation of an individual's subjective practical standpoint to what others have reason to desire and do (and for what she has reason to desire and do herself) is the same as that we noted above concerning an individual's subjective theoretical standpoint. If an individual's desire does not track value, it will give another no reason for acting whatsoever, even if the person's desire is reasonable in the sense of responding to value-as-she-sees-it, or to value as it would be on her view of the (nonevaluative) world, or to value as it would be on a subjectively reasonable view of the world, and so on.[14] Similarly, the fact that she desires something will give *her* a reason for acting only if she has some reason for regarding her desires as reliable indicators of value.

In theoretical reasoning, an individual point of view is simply one perspective on the world—an appearance—and it can be discounted as mere appearance if we have some reason to think it is illusory. Similarly, on our tentative picture, an individual's practical perspective is, if not discountable as mere appearance, discountable all the same if it fails to track real value. If an agent's desires fail to track value, then they fail to give *anyone* reasons for acting, the agent *or* others, regardless of how strongly held or how rational the desires might be in subjective terms.[15] However much something matters *to* someone, unless its mattering to her is evidence that it matters *period*, the fact that it matters to her will give no reason to others *or* to her either to do, or to forbear doing, anything.[16] On the current picture, the only way a person's values can give *anyone* reasons is by reflecting, or providing evidence of, value.

To contemplate such a picture is, I think, to find it both questionable and repellent.[17] It is questionable because it assumes that desire and the will have, like belief, a constitutive aim that is *substantive* in the sense of being able to be formulated independently of norms for the relevant attitude.[18] Our concepts of the world (what is the case) and truth are

---

[14] Unless, of course, the satisfaction of desire has value in itself, but, as I discuss further in Section IV, this seems implausible when we reflect on desire's direction of fit.

By a "subjectively reasonable" view of the world, I mean whatever beliefs are supported by evidence available to the person.

[15] That is, they fail to give anyone what we might call *objective* reasons. They would still give anyone who reasonably thought they tracked real value *subjective* reasons (that is, evidence of objective reasons).

[16] Unless, of course, it matters period that it matters to her (or to someone else). I discuss this case four paragraphs below.

[17] For an important discussion of these matters in a more general context, see Nagel, *The View from Nowhere*.

[18] For discussion of this distinction between "substantive" and merely "formal" aims in relation to belief and desire, see Velleman, "The Possibility of Practical Reason," 714-15.

distinct concepts from the concept of what we ought to believe, so the constitutive aim of belief (truth) is substantive in this sense.[19] When we say that belief is regulated by truth, we are not simply making the tautologous claim that we ought to believe what we ought to believe. We are making a substantive claim, albeit one that is guaranteed by the nature of belief. It is constitutive of belief that it aims at, and is responsible to, something independent of compliance with norms for belief that is the source from which these norms can be derived. It is not obvious, however, that there exists a defensible concept of value, independent of the concept of what we ought to desire, esteem, and choose, that could serve as a substantive constitutive aim for desire and the will in the way that truth does for belief. It is not obvious, in other words, that desire is, in its nature, responsible to anything independent of norms for desire that is the source from which such norms can be derived (in the way they can for belief). If it were responsible to some such thing, we would be making a substantive, rather than merely formal, claim when we say that we ought to desire the desirable (or that value is desirable) or when we say that we ought to choose the choiceworthy (or that value is choiceworthy).

Now, one way we *could* think desire to be responsible to something in this way is if we were to accept a Moorean conception of intrinsic value. According to G. E. Moore, for something to have intrinsic value is for it to be the case that it "ought to exist for its own sake."[20] If we were to accept this meaning, we could claim something substantive by saying that we ought to desire what is intrinsically good, since it is a substantive claim that we ought to desire (choose, bring about) what ought to exist. As I shall discuss further in Section IV, moreover, this substantive claim might seem defensible in a way that is analogous to the way in which the normativity of truth is defensible in contexts of belief. Truth is normative for belief because, as it is sometimes said, belief is the "holding true" attitude.[21] If desire is, as it is also said, the "making true" attitude, then it might be natural to think that what we should *make* true (desire) is what should *be* true.[22]

---

[19] In "The Guise of the Good," Velleman suggests that the "attainable" might provide a substantive constitutive aim for desire; however, that would provide no help in this context.

[20] Since Moore can be read as giving special emphasis to the irreducible normativity of value (cf. his famous "open question" argument), it might seem odd that his views could underwrite the picture we are currently considering. The reason they might, as is now explained in the text, is that Moore's idea appears to be that value is normative, not for choice, desire, or action in the first instance, but for states of affairs. G. E. Moore, *Principia Ethica*, ed. Thomas Baldwin (Cambridge: Cambridge University Press, 1993), 34.

[21] Actually, this is insufficient, since assuming p also is a way of holding p true. What makes truth normative for belief is that belief is the kind of holding true that responds to truth (or evidence of it) in belief's distinctive way.

[22] As Velleman puts it, "desire takes its propositional object as representing *facienda* — things that aren't the case but are to be brought about," whereas "belief takes its propositional object as representing *facta* — things that are the case and in virtue of which the proposition is true." Velleman, "The Possibility of Practical Reason," 707.

To think this, however, we would have to think it possible for it to be true that a state of the world ought to exist (for its own sake) quite independently of any truths about what anyone should desire, feel, esteem, aim at, or do. I shall argue that we cannot defensibly think this. 'Oughts' gain their sense through their role in normative guidance, so only what can be normatively guided can be subject to a norm. If this is so, however, then we lack a defensible idea of what ought to *be* that is independent of the notions of what anyone, actual or hypothetical, ought to desire, esteem, feel, aim at, or do in the way required to provide a substantive rather than merely formal constitutive aim for desire (as truth does for belief). The practical realm seems different from the theoretical realm in that practical normative reasons are not grounded in any aim that is itself independent of practical norms. The aims of practical reason seem (practically) normative all the way down.

We will find the above picture repellent, moreover, because we are repelled by the thought that we should allow others to pursue projects to which they are passionately committed—or that one should further projects of one's own about which one cares deeply—only to the extent that these projects track genuine (agent-neutral) value. To the contrary, we are apt to believe that persons have some claim to pursue their own projects, so long as these do not pose threats to others. On this alternative picture, a person's desires create, within these limits, *agent-relative* reasons whether or not his desires reflect the (agent-neutral) value of any state of the world.[23] One's own desire or will can, within limits, create a reason for one to act, and those of others can create a reason for one not to interfere. These agent-relative reasons are not reducible to the (agent-neutral) value of people pursuing their own projects or of their being allowed to do so. An agent-relative reason not to interfere *oneself* differs from any (agent-neutral) reason to promote noninterference, since the agent-relative reason counsels not interfering oneself even when not interfering would bring it about that another person interferes in an exactly similar case. Rather, we find it natural to think that we have a reason to *respect* others' pursuits that is additional to and independent of any we might have to promote them. Here we take it that we have reasons that derive from an agent-relative *norm of action* (the norm of respect) that does not itself derive from the value of any state of the world. A similar logic applies for the agent-relative reason to do what *one* wants or wills.

Viewed this way, an individual's practical standpoint is not merely a perspective *on* some external thing called value; it is the perspective *of* a free and rational agent. Because of this, the standpoint can ground a claim to respect that cannot be reduced to any agent-neutral value it might have more or less adequately in view. The perspective of a free rational agent can never be discounted as mere appearance. Of course, to bring out this

Kantian aspect of the alternative picture is not yet to defend it. My present purpose is simply to point to how we might see practical reasons and reasoning as fundamentally different from reasoning about belief, and to suggest that we might find in this difference a way of grounding the reason-giving character of an agent's desire (and will) for herself that is similar to the way that it can ground its reason-giving character for others. What underlies both, I shall argue, is our standing in rational *inter*-action to make claims *as* free and rational agents on others—and what gives us epistemic access to this status is our participation in such second-personal rational activity.

First, however, I want to show how other attempts to ground the reason-giving character of desires fail, and to illustrate how puzzling desire's (or the will's) reason-giving character should seem if we view deliberation solely from within a single agent's first-person point of view, neglecting the second-personal character of certain forms of rational thought, deliberation, and discourse. I will begin with the common, but I believe mistaken, idea that instrumental reasoning entails or presupposes that an agent's desires or ends give him reasons for acting.

III. INSTRUMENTAL REASONING

There is an utterly uncontroversial form of instrumental reasoning that agents engage in from their desires or ends. Given this, don't agents, in reasoning instrumentally, take their desires as reasons for acting, specifically, as reasons to take the means necessary to achieving their desired ends?[24] Furthermore, since instrumental reasoning is uncontroversially rational, doesn't it also follow that an agent's desires actually *are* such reasons? It takes some care to see what is or should be uncontroversial here. To see this, however, is to see why neither consequence follows. Consider the two following patterns of reasoning, one theoretical, the other practical:

I.	p	II.	A is to (should) be done
	If p, then q		A will be done only if B is done
	Therefore, q		Therefore, B is to (should) be done

Suppose someone believes the premises of Argument I. There is then an obvious sense in which these beliefs will give him reason to believe q (support his believing that q). This obvious sense, however, is only that

---

[24] Again, we will be ignoring the difference between desiring something and adopting or willing it as an end. In doing this, we will be simplifying even more than we have to this point, since the instrumental reasoning we will be considering only holds, strictly speaking, for the case of willing something as an end, and not for the general case of desire. This will not affect the argument of this section, however. If we can show that the validity of instrumental reasoning does not entail that the fact that one wills an end is a reason to take the means to achieving it, we will be able to conclude *a fortiori* that it also does not entail that the fact that one desires something is a reason to take steps to realize what one desires.

what he believes (that is, p and if p, then q) gives him reason to believe q, not that his *believing* these propositions does. After all, he may have no reason to believe either of these premises, no reason to believe both, or, worse, reasons to disbelieve both or either of them. To take the worst case, suppose that he ought not (has reason not) to believe either premise. It will be hard to see in this case how the fact that he does have these beliefs can give him any reason whatsoever to believe q. This does not mean, of course, that nothing follows from his believing these premises concerning what he has reason to, or ought to, believe. It follows that he ought *either* to believe q *or* to give up one of his beliefs, that p or that if p, then q. This much is demanded by the requirement of consistency in belief. Only if he ought (has reason) to believe both p and if p, then q will it follow that he ought to believe q. By virtue of the validity of Argument I, reasons for believing its premises become reasons for believing the conclusion, and reasons for disbelieving its conclusion become reasons for disbelieving the conjunction of the premises.

The situation is exactly analogous in the practical case. To simplify, suppose that someone who wills A accepts that A is to be done and vice versa. Consider now someone who accepts both premises of Argument II: she wills that A (adopts A as an end) and believes that A will be done only if B is done. Here also, there is an obvious sense in which her belief and end give her reason to do B (accept that B is to be done). Again, though, the relevant sense is that *what she accepts* gives her these reasons. Correct reasoning from her belief and end, in this sense, leads to the conclusion that she should will B. Analogously, however, the facts that she has this belief and end may give her no reason at all to will B. Maybe she has no reason to have either or both of these commitments, or, worse, reasons not to have both or either of them. In the worst case, in which she has reason not to have A as an end and not to believe that A will be done only if B is, the fact that she has this desire and belief may give her no reason whatsoever to will B. If, however, she does have this end and belief, then something does follow about what she ought to do: she ought either to will B or to give up either her end of doing A or her belief that B is necessary to doing A. We might think of this requirement as a demand of *practical* consistency that is analogous to theoretical reasoning's requirement of consistency in belief. Finally, if she does have reasons for willing A and for believing that A will be achieved only if B is, then it will follow that she ought to will B. Reasons for accepting these premises of Argument II become reasons for accepting the conclusion, and reasons for rejecting the conclusion become reasons for rejecting one of the premises.[25]

It is a familiar thought that instrumental reasoning issues "hypothetical" rather than "categorical" imperatives. However, care is required in interpreting this idea. On the basis of the last two paragraphs, what we

---

[25] I discuss this point in Darwall, *Impartial Reason*, 15–17, 43–50. For more extensive discussion, see John Broome, "Normative Requirements," *Ratio* 12, no. 4 (1999): 398–419.

should say is that the imperatives or prescriptions that follow from in-strumental reasoning are imperatives of practical consistency. They tell the agent either to take the means or to give up the end or the belief that the means in question is the only means. They do *not* tell the agent, If A is your end, and B the only means, then you should do B. There is a sense in which they do recommend B *hypothetically*, but in this sense B is rec-ommended conditionally on a "hypothesis" that the agent assumes *in having* A as her end, namely, that A is to be done. The imperatives, then, do not recommend doing B simply on the condition that the agent *has* A as an end.[26] In this way, they are just like hypothetical theoretical rea-soning: *assuming* that p and that if p, then q, then q. Theoretical reasoning of this kind gives a person no reason to believe q simply on the condition that he believes p and if p, then q. It only gives him a reason to believe q on the hypotheses he accepts in having those beliefs. Likewise, instru-mental practical reasoning gives an agent no reason to take the means to his end simply on the condition that he has the end and the belief about the means to it. Rather, it gives him a reason to take the necessary means on the hypotheses he accepts in having the relevant end and belief.

An analogous line of thought applies to formal theories of decision, which assume some ranking of preferences (utilities) and subjective probabili-ties.[27] Here, too, the uncontroversial kernel of such theories can be seen in terms of hypothetical reasoning and the demand for practical consistency, extended now to the more complex case in which agents must deal with potentially conflicting ends and preferences. The rational force of the prin-ciple of maximizing expected utility (preference-satisfaction), like that of instrumental reasoning, is that of a consistency demand requiring that an agent *either* choose the utility-maximizing act *or* change her preferences or probability estimates. In particular, the formal theory of decision does *not* entail that an agent's preferences give her reasons for acting. As with in-strumental reasoning, it says which action is most highly recommended, conditionally or hypothetically—conditionally, however, not on the agent's having the preferences and beliefs she does, but on what she assumes in having those preferences and beliefs.

IV. DIRECTION OF FIT, STANDARDS, AND THE PHENOMENOLOGY OF DESIRE

If, however, the idea that an agent's desires give her reasons is unsup-ported by instrumental reasoning, it also finds no apparent support when we reflect on what it is to have a desire from the agent's point of view. Consider, again, the familiar view that belief and desire are functional

[26] On this point, see Patricia Greenspan, "Conditional Oughts and Hypothetical Imper-atives," *Journal of Philosophy* 72, no. 10 (1975): 259–76; and R. M. Hare, "Wanting: Some Pitfalls," in Robert Binkley, Richard Bronaugh, and Ausonio Marras, eds., *Agent, Action, and Reason* (Toronto: Toronto University Press, 1971).

[27] I discuss this at greater length in Darwall, *Impartial Reason*, chap. 6.

states that are defined by complementary directions of fit. It is intrinsic to belief that it must fit the world, and desire, as one influential writer puts it, is "a state with which the world must fit."[28] In neither case, of course, is the 'must' a logical 'must'. The point is not that it is logically impossible to believe what is false or for the world not to be as desired. Rather, the intended sense is that of a normative requirement or standard. The world provides a standard of correctness and regulation for beliefs. In complementary fashion, it is said, desires provide a standard of correctness and regulation for the world.

What can this talk mean, though, when it comes to desire? In the case of belief, the situation seems straightforward enough. It follows from the nature of belief that we ought to believe what is true. However, in what sense must the world fit or be regulated by desires? An obvious problem in interpreting this idea is that the world provides a single, consistent standard for beliefs, but desires provide no such standard for the world. If beliefs are in conflict, the world rules on which, if either, is correct. However, if desires exist for contradictory states, as they plainly can either intersubjectively or intrasubjectively, what can it mean to say that the world "must fit" these conflicting desires?

Now, ultimately our goal is to understand the relation between desire and normative reasons for acting, and a normative reason is something that can count in favor of an action in deliberation from the agent's point of view. Hence, we might consider whether there is a natural interpretation of desire's claimed direction of fit that is, as it were, phenomenological, from the agent's point of view. We have already seen problems inherent in the very idea that desires can provide standards to which the world must fit. This is false, moreover, to the phenomenology of desire. To the person who desires that *p*, it is not as if *her desire* somehow grounds or creates a standard that the world should be such that *p*. For instance, to the person who wants to escape a burning building, it is not as if she must find a way out because this is what she wants. It is more like she must escape because she must live. Therefore, we might try the following: to the person with a desire that *p*, it is *as if the world should be that* p. From the perspective of the desiring agent, it is as if there is this standard that the world should fit.[29] If I desire the relief of a child's suffering, then it is to me as if the world should be such that the child's suffering is relieved. Alternatively, if I spy a juicy apple and want to eat it, then it is to me as if the world should contain my eating the apple, as if that should be true of the world.

On this interpretation, the claim about desire's direction of fit would be a claim about how things seem from the perspective of the agent who has the desire, or perhaps better, how the agent sees things insofar as he has the desire.[30] If we interpret the claim about desire's direction of fit in this way, the claim would not be, again, that from the agent's perspective it is as if *his desires* provide standards (or "reasons") for the world. An observer explaining the agent's conduct by referring to his beliefs and desires (perhaps the agent himself as self-observer) might identify the agent's desiring that p with his *holding* the world to the standard that p be true. However, this would be a psychological rather than a normative hypothesis: a claim about how things are in the head rather than about how things should be, or what anyone should do, in the world. From the deliberative standpoint, an agent who desires that p will take it that p should be true *simpliciter*, not that p should be true *because he desires it*, or that the world should be as he desires it to be. The latter claims reflect the way things would seem to someone with the second-order desire for the satisfaction of his first-order desires *whatever they might be*.[31]

This way of projecting direction of fit into the phenomenology of desire is a further reflection of the thought that, from the agent's point of view, desire is "backgrounded." Just as a belief that p is an attitude toward p, and not toward any attitude toward p, so, similarly, is a desire. The desire that p is also an attitude toward p, and not toward an attitude toward p. However, it is a different attitude than belief. Whereas believing p is its being to one *as if* p *is true*, desiring p is its being to one *as if* p *is to be (or should be) true*. To appreciate the backgrounding phenomenon, consider unconscious desires. To someone with the unconscious desire for approval, it is not as if *his desire* for approval is a standard for the world, since he is not even aware of having this desire. It is to him as if things should be such that he is approved of by others. Alternatively, think of someone who consciously wants approval, but has low self-esteem. To suggest that it is to him as if the world should be such that others approve of him because this is what he wants would seem a cruel joke.

How do action and, ultimately, reasons for acting get into this picture? On the standard model, desires are for states of affairs, say, that the world be such that p. Such a state of affairs might include an action. If I desire to keep a promise, for example, then it is to me as if things should be such that I keep the promise. In other cases, the state of affairs might not itself

---

[30] Note that the agent might simultaneously have a conflicting desire, say, that not p, from which perspective it will seem that the world should be such that not p. It is also possible for him to have the desire that p, but regard it as entirely discreditable. In this case, although the desire presents him with a kind of "appearance" that the world ought to be such that p is true, like a knowledgeable viewer of the Müller-Lyer optical illusion, he gives this appearance no weight at all in his overall judgment of how the world should be. (The Müller-Lyer illusion is two lines of equal length that appear to be of different lengths because one is flanked by inward-pointing arrows and the other is flanked by outward-pointing arrows.)
[31] The italicized portion is important. The mere having of a second-order desire for the satisfaction of one's desire that p would not necessarily involve its being to one as if it ought to be that p because one desires that p.

include an action, but be something that will obtain only if action is taken. Suppose I want someone's pain to stop, and that will happen only if I can find her some pain-relieving medication. If I reason instrumentally from my desire that her pain stop (that is, from the "appearance" my desire gives me), I will be led to a state in which it is to me as if I should find her some medication (if this is possible). Now, perhaps I am not in a position to find any and you are. Instrumental reasoning with this premise will lead me from my original desire to a desire that you find the medication. It will then be to me as if the world should be such that you find the medication.

This brings out two important consequences of interpreting direction of fit phenomenologically. First, if desire involves an appearance of a standard for world-states, it involves an appearance of a standard of action only in an unusual sense, namely, as a constituent of some such states. In the first example, wanting to keep my promise is wanting that my promise be kept, and this involves its being to me as if the world should be such that I keep my promise. It is important to note that this, though, is different from its being to me *as if I should keep my promise*. The latter appearance involves a standard *for action* (and, perhaps derivatively, a standard for desire), not a standard for what actions the world should contain. On our current picture, however, to an agent with a desire, (apparent) standards for action only come into play via standards for world-states of which actions are constituents.

The second consequence is implicit in what we have just noted, since any standard for states of the world is, of necessity, agent-neutral. A standard according to which the world (intrinsically or nonderivatively) ought to be that p will not be sensitive to whether an act that would bring p about is done by the agent or by someone else. To the agent who desires that p, and to whom it is as if the world should be that p, it is, *so far* anyway, a matter of indifference whether p is brought about by her, by someone else, or by some nonagential cause. It will be to her as if the world should contain a bringing about of p period.[32] Of course, p might be something self-referential. An agent might desire, for instance, that she tie her own shoes. On the current picture, this would lead by instrumental reasoning to a desire that what is necessary to bring about her tying her shoes take place. The point is that, as a logical matter, the means that figure in the object of the derived desire could, in principle, as easily include acts by someone else as by the agent herself *and* that, just insofar as the agent desired the *state* of her tying her shoes, she would be indifferent between whether these means were taken by her or by someone else, assuming that they were equally effective in producing this state.[33]

---

[32] Unless, of course, she desires that p occur uncaused.

[33] Obviously, some means necessary for *this* state of affairs could not, as a logical matter, be taken by anyone other than her.

We have had two goals in reflecting on desire's direction of fit in this section. One has been to argue that, contrary to what formulations such as "Desire is a 'state with which the world must fit'" might suggest, it is actually quite puzzling how an agent's desires or will could give her practical reasons when we think about desire's direction of fit from the agent's point of view. To an agent with a desire that p, it will seem much more like the world should be that p than that the world should be as she desires, or that it should be that p because she desires it. A second goal, however, is to begin to debunk the view of practical reasons that the picture we have been considering suggests. If desire involves an appearance of a standard for a state of the world, then this standard can give us practical reasons only if we can credit this appearance. We give weight to our beliefs in considering what to believe because we take our beliefs to be formed with a view toward getting things right. We frequently take them, moreover, to be formed in response to an engagement with the very states of the world to which they aim to respond. For something similar to be true of desire, we would have to take our desires to bear some similar relation to the normative standards for world-states of which our desires seem to be appearances. Whatever practical reasons our desires would then give us would be owing to their more or less reliable responsiveness to independent facts about what states of the world ought to exist ("for their own sake," as Moore said).[34]

On reflection, however, such a picture is quite incredible. Even disregarding the problem of what processes might underlie epistemic access to such normative standards, the very idea that it could underivatively be the case that a state of affairs ought to exist, independently of any fact concerning what any person, actual or hypothetical, ought to desire, feel, or do, seems incoherent. If someone ought to believe, feel, or do something, then there is a valid norm that requires or recommends that action or attitude. For example, believers ought (must) not believe both of two contradictory propositions, since there is a norm of consistency of belief requiring this. Agents ought (must) not adopt something as an end, believe that something else is a means necessary to it, but fail to intend (or worse, intend not) to take the means; this is due to a valid norm of instrumental practical reasoning. And similarly, in general, for any truth about what someone ought to believe, feel, do, care about, fear, esteem, and so on. Any sensible 'ought' claim, it seems, must make implicit reference to some norm. How, though, could there be norms for states of affairs? By their very nature, norms can hold only where normative guidance is possible—only, that is, where it is possible that they be complied

---

[34] Such a view would be an instance of "substantive realism," as Christine Korsgaard calls it. For her discussion, see Christine Korsgaard, *The Sources of Normativity* (Cambridge: Cambridge University Press, 1996), 35–37.

with or violated, followed or flouted. A state of affairs cannot comply with or violate anything.[35]

V. Desire and Taking as a Reason

Alternatively, we might relate the phenomenology of desire, not to norms for states of the world, but more directly to normative reasons for action and attitudes.[36] To desire something, we might think, is to be disposed to take certain things *as* reasons for acting. To a person who wants to get out of a burning building, it is as if she has reason to flee. Her attention is "directed insistently," as Scanlon puts it, to the fact that she will burn to death if she remains inside, a fact that "presents" itself as a reason to get out.

On this picture, desire involves the appearance, not of a norm for a state of the world, but of a reason for acting. To someone with the desire to survive, the fact that survival can be achieved only by jumping out of a window presents itself as a reason to jump. The idea here is not that the appearance of this reason is its seeming as if one's survival is a state that ought to exist for its own sake, giving anyone equally a reason to promote it. The necessity of jumping to survival can present itself as a reason for *one* to jump without its appearing that others have reason to help one survive. (This does not mean, of course, that it appears that they do not have such a reason.)

The idea that an agent's desire or will can give him reasons for acting is nevertheless equally puzzling on this view. To have a desire is to be disposed to take certain facts about the desire's *object* as reasons, not the fact that one has the desire. On this picture, desire is more like a mode of access to practical reasons—that through which practical reasons appear— than it is a reason for acting itself, or a ground on which practical reasons might depend. In this respect, the current alternative is structurally analogous to the position we considered in Section IV. Whether desire involves appearances of standards for states of affairs or practical reasons directly, on either alternative its role seems to be epistemic rather than that of a practical reason or of a ground of practical reasons.

One advantage the current picture has over that discussed in Section IV is that it has no need of the Moorean notion of a state of affairs's oughting to exist for its own sake. Nonetheless, like the earlier alternative, it analogizes the epistemological structure of practical reason to that of theoret-

---

[35] Sometimes we say things like "It should not happen that children go to bed hungry," even when there is nothing we can do that could prevent it. However, such talk can be understood in terms of norms for attitudes, if not for actions (e.g., "It is lamentable [undesirable, shameful, etc.] that children go to bed hungry").

[36] Something like this is suggested by Scanlon's discussion of desire in the "directed-attention sense." Scanlon, *What We Owe to Each Other*, 39.

ical reason. If desire involves an appearance of practical reasons, as ordinary perceptual beliefs involve appearances of the world, then we should credit these practical reasons only if we should credit the appearances that desire provides us. Respectable empirical and philosophical theories support this on the theoretical side, since they warrant us in believing that beliefs involving world-appearances can be related to the world in some reliable way. Here we seem to have a metaphysically respectable conception of an independent reality to which our beliefs are responsible and to which our perceptual apparatus and other belief-forming mechanisms may become well tuned. It is far from obvious, however, that we have in the practical realm any comparably defensible picture of free-standing facts of practical reason to which desires (or practical experience of some other kind) respond and give us epistemic access.[37] All there is, one is inclined to say, are norms of practical reason, not an independent order of fact to which desire is in its nature responsible and from which norms for desire can be derived.[38]

VI. Giving Practical Reasons, Will, Freedom, and Authority

The moral of our story so far has been twofold. First, so long as we think of practical reason on the model of theoretical reason, it will be puzzling how an agent's will or desires could give her reasons to act (and, as well, how they might give others reasons to allow her to act on them). Second, however, we have found grounds for skepticism about this analogy between theoretical and practical reason. In this section, I want to consider a specific disanalogy between theoretical and practical reason with an eye toward locating desire- or will-based practical reasons in the standing of free and rational agents to make claims on one another as free and rational.

Consider, first, how one person can give another person a reason for belief. If someone says that p, that will give you a reason to think that p only to the extent that it gives you evidence of p. The clearest case is where what the person says is evidence. You want to know whether to believe the party is to be this Saturday or next, for example, and someone says that it is unlikely to be next Saturday because everyone will be leaving for vacation next Friday. It is also possible for someone to give you a reason to believe that p just by asserting p. Even in this case, however, although what the person says is not evidence, her saying it must be. If you have no reason to treat what someone says or her saying

[37] This is, of course, the problem that Gilbert Harman raised in Gilbert Harman, *The Nature of Morality* (New York: Oxford University Press, 1977), 3–10.
[38] I think Scanlon does not sufficiently appreciate this difficulty in Scanlon, *What We Owe to Each Other*, 55–72, and, in any case, that the considerations adduced in Section VI provide a better account of how considerations of "the reasonable" can provide reasons for acting.

it as evidence of the truth of what she says, she can give you no reason to believe it.[39]

Consider now the practical case. In particular, consider cases where one person attempts to give another a reason for acting, not by expressing his belief (even his beliefs about practical reasons), but by expressing his desire or will. Here we recognize a variety of cases where one person (or collective body) can give others reasons that are not similarly parasitic on the relation between the addresser's desire or will and something independent to which the addressees take the desires to be appropriately responsive and from which they take the reasons ultimately to emanate. Unlike the theoretical case, in these instances the reason seems to depend entirely on the relationship of addresser to addressee, specifically, on the *authority* the addresser has to give the addressee a reason in this way.

Think about orders, for example. When a sergeant tells her platoon to fall in, her charges do not take it that the reason she gives them derives from the value of a state of affairs, their falling in, that she has revealed to them by her order. The reason depends, rather, on the nature of the relationship between the sergeant and her charges—that is, on the sergeant's authority to demand that her platoon act in this way. Something similar holds for decrees, legislative acts, requests, demands, and claims more generally. When a legislature expresses its legislative will, it is understood to give citizens a reason to comply that derives, not from the independent value of some state that is the object of this legislative will (citizens paying a tax, say), but from the relative standing and authority that legislative bodies have with respect to citizens. (Of course, various conditions must be satisfied for this authority to exist in the first place, and neither a sergeant nor a legislature can require, or even request, that a person do just anything.) Similarly, if a subject makes a request of the king, or if one person simply asks another for the time of day, these requests are also thought to give their addressees reasons because of the standing the relevant individuals have to express their will to relevant others in these ways and thereby to give them, if not (in these cases) reasons for compliance, at least reasons to *consider* complying. Finally, if one person demands certain treatment from another as an equal no less

---

[39] It is consistent with this that in *telling* someone something, addressing him second-personally, the addresser may be able to give the addressee a reason for believing what the addresser says that that addressee would not have had if the addresser's saying it were considered only third-personally, as a mere assertion. A relation of trust between addresser and addressee might explain why telling something to someone could give the addressee reasons for belief that he would not have but for this second-personal address. Edward S. Hinchman, "Telling as Inviting to Trust," unpublished. Even if it is possible for one person to give another a distinctive "fiduciary" reason second-personally, however, this reason is ultimately parasitic on evidence in the usual way. If the addressee has no reason to think that the addresser's beliefs have *some* reliable relation to the truth, nothing the addresser could tell the addressee could give him reason to believe anything.

worthy than he, she attempts to give him a reason by presuming on their equal standing as one person among others.

Let us call expressions of will that purport to be reason-giving in this way *claims*. Claims have several important features that are worth noting. First, truistically, claims purport to give those to whom they are addressed reasons for acting. Second, these reasons are agent-relative. They are addressed to the agent himself, purporting to be a reason for compliance that cannot be reduced to the value of any state, even the state of agents' complying with this and equally worthy claims. When, for example, the sergeant orders her platoon to fall in, the platoon members do not thereby acquire a reason to most effectively promote some valuable state of affairs, say, that of military discipline; they simply have a reason to fall in themselves. Third, because the reason purports to be independent of the value of any state, including any such value to the addressee, it purports to be unconditional on the addressees' desires. A claim therefore advances a reason that is putatively *categorical*, that is, a reason that is not hypothetical *either* in the sense of depending on the desire of the addressee for any state *or* in the sense of depending on the truth of any appearance to which the addressee is subject (any "hypothesis" the addressee accepts) *in* having any such desire. Fourth, claims are implicitly presented as valid or, at least, as *reasonable* in the sense of warranting the consideration of those to whom they are addressed. Lastly, fifth, in addressing claims, addressers implicitly regard addressees as having the requisite authority and capacity to consider, recognize, and act on the reasons they purport thereby to give them.

This last feature is of particular importance. It is at the heart of Fichte's thesis that agents can acquire a conception of themselves as free and rational only when they entertain a claim or "summons" (*Aufforderung*) that is addressed to them by another agent.[40] Claims purport to give agents reasons that are independent of the agents' desires, and to do so, moreover, not by inducing a desire for any state of affairs, but through the agents' recognition of the addresser's authority to make the claim. To address a claim is, therefore, implicitly to address someone as free and rational in this sense. To see oneself as the addressee of a claim, consequently, is to *see oneself being seen as free and rational*, thereby gaining a second-personal perspective on oneself. One sees oneself, not as viewed "third-personally" in an "objectifying" way, but as summoned in a reciprocally recognizing rational interaction. In recognizing this view of oneself and responding, one implicitly identifies with and thereby recognizes the other by reflecting the other's view of oneself back to him or her. Even in hearing and seriously entertaining a claim, and gaining a second-personal perspective on that through reciprocal recognition with another,

---

[40] Johann Gottlieb Fichte, *Foundations of Natural Right*, ed. Frederick Neuhouser, trans. Michael Baur (Cambridge: Cambridge University Press, 2000), 29–52.

one gains an awareness of oneself as "self-active."[41] In the second-personal addressing and entertaining of claims, agents reciprocally recognize each other as free and rational.

To appreciate properly the point Fichte is trying to make, we need to think of a pure case of claim-making. Any actual case, of course, may involve a mixture of various "nonrational" elements like intimidation, coercion, manipulation, or seduction, or other rational elements such as trying to get the addressee to appreciate reasons in the neighborhood of the claim but distinct from it. A's foot, let us suppose, is squarely on B's gouty toe, causing B pain he wishes to be rid of. Suppose that B requests or demands that A remove his foot. B might do this in a variety of ways that mix other elements with a pure claim. B might look threateningly at A, attempting to induce either fright or a rational calculation of costs and benefits. Alternatively, B might try to induce a sympathetic desire in A so that A will take B's pain as a reason to remove his foot regardless of any claim B might have to A's doing so. Or, perhaps, B might look at A with his best Charlie Chaplin grin, hoping to charm A and curry favor.[42] In a pure case, however, B addresses a claim not to be hurt to A that purports to give A a reason to remove his foot from B's toe that is independent of any reason A might appreciate through sympathy or a desire for any state (say, the relief of B's pain), and, therefore, that is independent of the value of any state.[43] Moreover, B attempts to influence A rationally rather than by such nonrational influences as intimidation, charm, and fear.

Theological voluntarists, like Pufendorf, argued that moral reasons are created in this fashion by divine command. In commanding us not to harm each other, for example, God addresses us as free and rational agents and thereby gives us a reason not to harm that cannot be reduced to any good that complying with this command can achieve. Pufendorf believed, of course, that the validity of these reasons depends on an assumption of God's superior authority over us.[44] However, he also thought that the possibility of moral reasons being created in this way depends on the *internal* acceptance of this authority by those God addresses, so that ultimately they can hold themselves accountable second-personally by

[41] Ibid., 32. Christine Korsgaard makes a similar point in Korsgaard, *The Sources of Normativity*, 139–43.

[42] Compare here Adam Smith's contrast between the distinctively human capacity for independent, second-personal "exchange" as opposed to the attempts of animals to gain the goodwill of humans "by every servile and fawning attention." Adam Smith, *An Inquiry into the Nature and Causes of the Wealth of Nations* (Indianapolis, IN: Liberty Fund, 1981), 1:26.

[43] Although sympathy is not required, *empathy*, placing oneself in the other's shoes, is. Arguably, however, empathy is required for second-personal reciprocal recognition in the first place. For the differences between empathy and sympathy, see Stephen Darwall, "Empathy, Sympathy, Care," *Philosophical Studies* 89, no. 2 (1998): 261–82.

[44] Samuel Pufendorf, *De Jure Naturae et Gentium Libri Octo* (On the law of nature and nations), trans. C. H. Oldfather and W. A. Oldfather (Oxford: Clarendon Press, 1934), I.i, secs. 2–6, pp. 4–7; I.vi, sec. 4, p. 89. I discuss this aspect of Pufendorf's views in Stephen Darwall, "Autonomy in Modern Natural Law," unpublished.

making the same demands of themselves that God makes of them.[45] The problem that Pufendorf faced, however, was that although he believed that God's commands can create reasons for any free and rational agent to whom they are addressed *and* that His commands can create these reasons only through free and rational agents' recognition of God's superior authority, he had no good argument for why a free and rational agent would necessarily recognize this authority. He took this relationship for granted and assumed that any other free and rational being would do so as well.

What authority, however, is a free and rational agent bound to recognize? Only, it would seem, whatever authority one is committed to in making and considering claims in the first place. To make or entertain claims at all is to be in a second-personal relation in which each reciprocally recognizes the other as free and rational.[46] Even to consider a claim seriously is to reflect back to the addresser a recognition of the addresser's authority to submit claims for consideration (which is itself a kind of claim), and to make a claim is to put it forward as something it would be reasonable for the addressee to consider and accept. It seems implicit in the very idea of one free and rational will making a claim on another (as free and rational) that the former must take the latter to be capable of accepting this claim and being guided by it, thereby being accountable to

---

[45] This claim is implicit in Pufendorf's distinction between coercion and being under an obligation. Many things can "influence the will to turn to one side" or the other, but other evils "bear down the will as by some natural weight, and on their removal [the will] returns of itself to its former indifference." Obligation, however, "affects the will morally," so that it "is forced of itself to weigh its own actions, and to judge itself worthy of some censure, unless it conforms to a prescribed rule." In effect, Pufendorf here invokes a notion of *internal* blame or censure, that is, accepting blame as justified (blaming oneself in authorizing the view of the other who blames one). Pufendorf, *De Jure Naturae et Gentium Libri Octo*, I.vi, sec. 5, p. 91.

[46] There may seem to be many obvious counterexamples to this statement. Most vividly, what about orders to children or to slaves? It is important to distinguish, again, the pure claim from any attempt simply to cause a certain action or response. Claims are issued with the aim of getting a certain response *in virtue of a recognition that the validity of the claim* creates a reason so to respond. Thus, a pure order is issued to gain a response by virtue of a recognition that the validity of the order (one's authority to issue such an order) gives a reason. By their very nature, then, claims are issued to beings who are implicitly regarded as competent to recognize their valid, reason-giving character and to freely act on them. Of course, one can issue a claim even if one does not *believe* that the addressee is thus competent — the point is that one regards or treats him as though he were. Frequently, of course — for example, with children — this is done to insinuate proleptically the very recognition on the addressee's part that is necessary for the claim to "come off."
  Still, the suggestion that participants in any second-personal claim-making implicitly regard *each other* as (equally) free and rational may seem implausible. What, again, about masters and slaves? Here we should recall Hegel on "lordship and bondage." Hegel claims that there is a contradiction in the master's second-personal address since he asserts a superiority that is belied by the recognition he seeks from the slave. G. W. F. Hegel, *Phenomenology of Spirit*, trans. A. V. Miller (Oxford: Oxford University Press, 1977), 111–19. Any pure order presupposes a free recognition of the validity of the order. If, of course, the master can expect that the slave will freely respect the authority his order presupposes, then no contradiction need be involved. However, see the next paragraph.

the other by holding himself accountable. Further, the addresser of the claim must apparently also take the addressee to share (or to be capable of sharing) this understanding. The possibility of such a shared understanding seems a presupposition of any such claim.

What claims might one free and rational will make on another and reasonably expect reciprocation? The very logic of the question suggests a line of response that is developed in different ways in Kant and post-Kantian German idealism, especially in Fichte and Hegel (and before that, I would argue, in Adam Smith), and, in our own time, in, among others, Rawls and Scanlon. If we take no particular moral relationship for granted and simply ask what demands one free and rational will might make on another and reasonably expect reciprocation, a natural answer would seem to be: whatever demands *any* free and rational being would make on any other. This answer emerges because it will be reasonable to make a demand only if it would be reasonable to accept it, and it will be reasonable to accept it only if one would reasonably make it also oneself.

Our ultimate goal in considering claim-based reasons and their relation to reciprocally recognizing second-personal reason-giving is to find there some basis for the idea that an agent's will can be a source of reasons, both for herself and for others. To that end, consider the parable of A and B. A and B both contemplate the same juicy apple with the same desire. A desires that he have the apple and forms the end of getting it for himself. He sees the state of his having the apple as something to be brought about, and sees the juiciness of the apple as a reason for him to get it. For her part, B desires that she have the apple and adopts the end of getting it for herself. She sees the state of her having the apple as something to be brought about, and sees its juiciness as a reason for her to get it. Suppose that A and B each become aware of the other and the other's desire. To simplify, suppose also that neither is moved to sympathy and that their desires remain as before.

At this point, neither A nor B treats his or her desire for the apple as a source of reasons or value. Their desires are, from their respective practical perspectives, "backgrounded." Each sees his or her having the apple as a state that should be brought about. Similarly, each sees the other's having the apple as having no value, as not being a state to be brought about. From the practical perspective of each, the other's agency is simply a potential instrument or obstacle to a valuable state. Indeed, so far anyway, the same is true of A's and B's views of themselves. From the perspective of their respective desires for these states, *their own* rational activity (and will) figures practically only to the extent of its usefulness in bringing about this valuable state.

Suppose, however, that A turns to B and attempts to give her a reason to let him have the apple. We might imagine A to begin by expressing his desire, saying that his having the apple is a state of affairs that should be brought about, while B's having the apple is not. Of course, this cannot succeed, since from B's perspective, nothing is to be said for A's having the apple and everything is to be said for her having it. B has no reason to trust A's judgment that he should have the apple since, from B's perspective, A's judgment is illusory, a mere expression of his desire. Any such attempt by A to give B a reason would not differ structurally from theoretical reason-giving. It could succeed only to the extent that B has reason to think there exists some reliable relation between A's judgment and that of which it purports to be. It would not yet be an instance of claim-making.

At the same time, however, A's expression of his desire might give B pause in the credit she accords her own desires' appearances as evidence of reasons. From a first-person perspective, unchallenged by another's will and corrected only by further appearances that come with better-informed desires, B could comfortably credit the epistemological access she apparently got to reasons through her own desires. Now, though, here is A, and his desires appear to give him access to reasons no less than B's do for her. Moreover, and this is the critical point, B can provide no explanation of why her desires' appearances (or A's, for that matter) should be correct. Not only does she lack an account of the sort she could give of why she credits her experiential beliefs—namely, that she has reason to take her having them to be best explained by the facts that her experiences make apparent to her. In addition, seeing herself as a free and rational agent addressed by another puts her into a position to see why there could not be such an account. She sees herself as free to accept a source of categorical reasons that is utterly independent of anything of which desires could be an appearance.

Suppose now that A attempts to make a claim on B. "I would have the apple," A says, "so you, B, should let me have it." For the first time, B feels the force of A's will as an attempted claim, *as purporting to be reason-giving for her*. In response, she, for the first time, feels the force of *her* will as no less a reasonable basis for such a claim. "I, too, would have the apple," she might say, and say something further that could bear the following philosophical translation: "Neither of us can assume any antecedent authority over the other, so it would be unreasonable for you to expect me to just let you have the apple. Neither can I reasonably make such a claim of you." Suppose she continues, making use of philosophical materials we have recently surveyed: "We are already implicitly reciprocally recognizing each other's authority to propose and consider claims, by addressing these claims and considerations to each other as free and rational." "So," she concludes, quoting now a famous philosopher, "we are already implicitly recognizing each other as 'self-originating sources of valid claims'."[47] A and B might then agree, on that basis, that each could make

[47] John Rawls, "Kantian Constructivism in Moral Theory," *Journal of Philosophy* 77, no. 9 (1980): 543.

a reasonable claim, say, to half of the apple, and then divide the apple between them, with one cutting and the other choosing.

When an agent acts solely on desires represented within his own practical perspective, he takes the reasons his desires present him with for granted, that is, as reasons grounded, not in his desires, but in the desirable features of their objects, as he views them under his desires' influence. It is only when an agent is addressed in a way that makes him aware, simultaneously, of a potential source of reasons in the will of another rational and free agent *and* in his own rational will, that he becomes aware of reasons anchored in the rational authority of *a free rational agent*, himself or another. What enables the agent to authorize the reasons generated within his own practical standpoint—to say that what he cares about gives him reasons because, on reflection, *he* cares about it—simultaneously decenters his practical view. It makes him aware that he is one person, occupying one practical standpoint, among others; commits him to reasons that transcend his practical perspective; and commits him, as well, to his freedom to act on those reasons.

VII. A KANTIAN CONCLUSION

Christine Korsgaard has written recently that "the instrumental principle can only be normative if we take ourselves to be capable of giving laws to ourselves—or, in Kant's phrase, if we take our own wills to be legislative." [48] The normativity she has in mind is not simply the hypothetical, practical consistency of instrumental practical reasoning discussed in Section III, but the further claim that I there argued goes beyond this uncontroversial core, namely, that, as she puts it, "your willing [an] end gives it a normative status for you." [49] Although it may appear otherwise, there is ultimately no incompatibility between the sort of Kantian defense Korsgaard gives of a more substantial instrumental principle and the line of thought I have sketched here. [50] If there is a Fichtean lesson to be learned, however, it is that the idea of freedom cannot be taken for granted within the first-person deliberative standpoint. Our access to a conception of ourselves as able to act on reasons whose force we can appreciate independently of desire comes through second-personal rational interaction. Once we have this conception, we can enrich the first-person perspective into that of a free and rational agent. Only then can we hope to articulate a defensible conception of reasons for acting, having fully internalized that the first-person standpoint is the practical perspec-

---

[48] Christine Korsgaard, "The Normativity of Instrumental Reason," in Garrett Cullity and Berys Gaut, eds., *Ethics and Practical Reason* (Oxford: Clarendon Press, 1997), 246.

[49] Ibid.

[50] Although I agree with John Broome, and against Korsgaard, that, taken by itself, instrumental reasoning does not entail that the agent's desires or will provide reasons, as I argued in Section III. See Broome, "Normative Requirements," 417-19.

tive of a free and rational person, not just a point of view on some independent thing, value or objectively prescribed states of affairs.

It is notorious that Kant's own view of the source of our self-conception as free changes when one moves from the *Groundwork* to *The Critique of Practical Reason*. In the *Groundwork*, Kant held that action is impossible except under the idea of freedom.[51] However, although an agent must take herself to be free to act on reasons as she sees them and believe that her acceptance of rational norms is "independent of alien influences," this does not yet give us the "positive" idea of freedom Kant has in mind, namely, that the will is a law "to itself" in the sense that we must be able to regard practical reason-giving norms as "self-legislated." From a first-person perspective not yet enriched by second-personal interaction, the former assumptions could coexist with a "substantive realist" conception of practical reasons as anchored in independent facts concerning what states of affairs ought to exist for their own sake.[52] An agent deliberating about what to do in light of the appearances of reasons and norms provided by her desires could well assume that she is free to do whatever it will seem to her, on reflection, that she should do. Moreover, because desire is backgrounded, she might take it that the validity of the practical norms that are apparent to her through her desires does not itself depend on her desires, any more than the really circular shape of a cup one can see before one depends on one's visual experience of it. The only idea of freedom we cannot help but act under, therefore, is not what Kant means by positive freedom or autonomy: the will's being a "law to itself."[53]

In the *Critique of Practical Reason*, Kant moved to the view that our awareness of freedom comes through our awareness of being bound by the moral law (the "fact of reason").[54] However, what gives us this latter idea? Since Kant's best arguments for the existence of a law of equal dignity that binds any free and rational agent (in *Groundwork* III) already presuppose the idea of autonomy, it is hard to see how we can have earned the right to a conception of the moral law without also laying claim to the idea of freedom. On the Fichtean line of thought I have sketched, a conception of oneself as free comes simultaneously with a conception of the equal authority of free and rational agents and, consequently, a conception of oneself as bound by norms applying to one as such a being. The two conceptions come together, and neither can be taken for granted within the first-person deliberative standpoint. Rational interaction is the source both of our awareness of our own freedom and of our commitment to a law that enshrines the equal dignity of free and

[51] Immanuel Kant, *Groundwork of the Metaphysics of Morals*, in Immanuel Kant, *Practical Philosophy*, ed. and trans. Mary J. Gregor (Cambridge: Cambridge University Press, 1996), 95 (Ak. p. 448).
[52] See note 34 above.
[53] "Autonomy of the will is the property of the will by which it is a law to itself (independently of any property of the objects of volition)." Kant, *Groundwork*, 89 (Ak. p. 441).
[54] "Consciousness of this fundamental law may be called a fact of reason." Immanuel Kant, *Critique of Practical Reason*, in Kant, *Practical Philosophy*, 164 (Ak. p. 31).

rational persons. We might see Fichte, therefore, as filling in a lacuna in the Kantian framework. In rational interaction, we commit ourselves *a priori* to a conception of ourselves as free and rational that is necessary both to a conception of the moral law as well as to a philosophically adequate appreciation of a fundamental disanalogy between theoretical and practical reason.

The irony of the resulting position will not, perhaps, have been lost on the reader. According to the old orthodoxy, the practically normative force of the agent's own will is straightforward and by default, whereas whatever normativity morality might have is problematic and to be argued for from that starting point. According to the line of thought I have sketched here, however, this is almost the reverse of the truth. The ground of the reason-giving power of an agent's own will is also the basis of a moral conception of the equal authority of free and rational persons.

Philosophy, University of Michigan

REALISM, NATURALISM, AND MORAL SEMANTICS*

BY DAVID O. BRINK

I. INTRODUCTION

The prospects for moral realism and ethical naturalism have been important parts of recent debates within metaethics. As a first approximation, *moral realism* is the claim that there are facts or truths about moral matters that are objective in the sense that they obtain independently of the moral beliefs or attitudes of appraisers. *Ethical naturalism* is the claim that moral properties of people, actions, and institutions are natural, rather than occult or supernatural, features of the world.[1] Though these metaethical debates remain unsettled, several people, myself included, have tried to defend the plausibility of both moral realism and ethical naturalism.[2] I, among others, have appealed to recent work in the philosophy of language—in particular, to so-called theories of "direct reference"—to defend ethical naturalism against a variety of semantic worries, including G. E. Moore's "open question argument." In response to these arguments, critics have expressed doubts about the compatibility of moral realism and direct reference. In this essay, I explain these doubts, and then sketch the beginnings of an answer—but understanding both the doubts and my answer requires some intellectual background.

* For helpful discussion of issues addressed in this essay, I would like to thank Richard Arneson, Thomas Bontly, David Copp, Michael Moore, Russ Shafer-Landau, Evan Tiffany, Mark Timmons, Steven Yalowitz, the editors of this volume, and an audience at the University of British Columbia.
[1] This way of understanding ethical naturalism presupposes realism or at least cognitivism insofar as it presupposes that there are moral properties and that moral judgments ascribing moral properties to person, actions, and institutions can be true or false (with some being true). This, I think, is a traditional way of understanding ethical naturalism. It might be contrasted with a broader understanding, according to which the ethical naturalist simply tries to fit moral practices and judgments within a naturalistic worldview. Cf. Gilbert Harman, "Is There a Single True Morality?" in David Copp and David Zimmerman, eds., *Morality, Reason, and Truth* (Totowa, NJ: Rowman and Allanheld, 1984). Notice that, on this broad understanding, various forms of moral skepticism and noncognitivism might qualify as forms of ethical naturalism.
[2] David O. Brink, *Moral Realism and the Foundations of Ethics* (New York: Cambridge University Press, 1989). Cf. Richard Boyd, "How to Be a Moral Realist," in Geoffrey Sayre-McCord, ed., *Essays on Moral Realism* (Ithaca, NY: Cornell University Press, 1988); Peter Railton, "Moral Realism," *Philosophical Review* 95, no. 2 (1986): 163–207; and Nicholas Sturgeon, "Moral Explanations," in Copp and Zimmerman, eds., *Morality, Reason, and Truth*.

II. The Open Question Argument

In *Principia Ethica*, G. E. Moore used the open question argument (OQA) to deny that moral properties, such as rightness or goodness, are natural or metaphysical (that is, supernatural) properties.[3] Moral properties, on his view, are nonnatural and *sui generis*. The OQA attempts to establish this ontological or metaphysical thesis by semantic means.[4] The OQA assumes that if moral properties are natural properties, then moral predicates can be defined in terms of natural predicates, which Moore apparently understood as nonmoral predicates drawn from the natural and social sciences (broadly construed). In arguing this way, Moore assumed something like *the semantic test of properties*, according to which predicates pick out the same property just in case they are synonymous. The OQA is supposed to show that no moral predicate is synonymous with any natural or, more generally, nonmoral predicate. Consider any moral predicate 'M' and any nonmoral predicate 'N'. If 'M' and 'N' mean the same thing, then it ought to be an analytic truth that N-things are M, just as it is an analytic truth that M-things are M. We can see, though, that there are no such analytic truths. It is not possible to doubt that M-things are M—"Is this M-thing M?" is always a closed question. However, it is always possible to doubt that N-things are M—"Is this N-thing M?" is always an open question. The fact that the first question is closed but the second is open shows that they are not *epistemically equivalent*—that is, they differ in what can be believed about them. Epistemic inequivalence would establish semantic inequivalence if speakers were authoritative about the meaning of their words. Speakers would be authoritative about the meanings of their words if a *descriptional* theory of meaning—according to which the meaning of a word or phrase is the set of descriptions or properties that speakers conventionally associate with it—were true. For, on a descriptional theory, if two terms are synonymous (semantically equivalent), speakers competent with both terms must associate the same properties or descriptions with both terms and should be able to recognize that they do. The epistemic inequivalence of the sentences using 'M' and 'N' implies that speakers associate different descriptions with those terms and, hence, that those terms differ in meaning. The semantic test of

---

[3] G. E. Moore, *Principia Ethica* (Cambridge: Cambridge University Press, 1903), chap. 1, esp. pp. 7–17.

[4] A number of commentators have interpreted one strand in the OQA as reflecting Moore's concern with the normativity of ethics. On this internalist reading, the OQA claims that moral properties could not be natural or supernatural properties, because no natural or supernatural property has the requisite internal or conceptual connection with practical reason or motivation that moral properties have. See, for example, Stephen Darwall, Allan Gibbard, and Peter Railton, "Toward *Fin de Siècle* Ethics: Some Trends," *Philosophical Review* 101, no. 1 (1992): 115–89, esp. pp. 117–18. This may well be one strand in the OQA, but much of the OQA makes no appeal to internalist assumptions. Though much of my discussion carries over to the internalist reading, I focus on those parts of the OQA that do not presuppose internalism.

properties, then, implies that M and N are different properties. In this way, the OQA undermines ethical naturalism: the failure of synonymy implies that moral predicates are not naturalistically definable, and the semantic test of properties implies that, as a result, moral properties are not natural properties.

Moore and other intuitionists were *cognitivists*. According to cognitivism, moral predicates are used to ascribe moral properties to actions, people, and institutions; moral judgments ascribing moral properties to such things can be true or false; and moral judgments express the appraiser's beliefs about the moral properties that such things possess. Because Moore and other intuitionists rejected not just naturalistic ethics but any attempt to define moral terms in nonmoral terms (Moore rejected metaphysical ethics as well), they concluded that moral predicates pick out nonnatural *sui generis* properties. However, it is arguable that as a historical matter, noncognitivism rather than intuitionism was the real beneficiary of the OQA. *Noncognitivists* deny that moral judgments express the appraiser's beliefs about the moral properties of actions, institutions, and people; instead, they claim that moral judgments express the appraiser's noncognitive attitudes and commitments, such as her desires. The noncognitivists agreed that the OQA undermines ethical naturalism, but found the metaphysical and epistemological commitments of intuitionism mysterious and implausible. They reasoned that if ethics could not be fit into a naturalistic worldview, then it was better to give up the cognitivist presuppositions of ethical naturalism and intuitionism than to accept intuitionism's metaphysical and epistemological commitments.

III. NONNATURALISM

The moral realist has two main ways to avoid the noncognitivist legacy of the OQA. One option would be to defend nonnaturalism. Nonnaturalism would be problematic for many people if it posited properties that were in no way related to familiar natural properties. However, nonnaturalism, at least as Moore understood it, does not imply this. To commit the "naturalistic fallacy," which the OQA is supposed to expose, is to confuse two properties that are correlated with each other for each other.[5] Hence, the OQA is supposed only to block the *identification* of moral properties with natural properties—but the denial of property-identity is compatible with recognizing various other relations between moral and natural properties. For example, Moore believes that moral properties strongly *supervene* on natural properties, in the sense that the natural properties of a situation fix or determine its moral properties, such that two situations cannot differ in their moral properties without differing in their natural properties. In his reply to critics, he writes:

[5] Moore, *Principia Ethica*, 10, 13, 14, 16.

I should never have thought of suggesting that goodness was 'non-natural,' unless I had supposed that it was 'derivative' in the sense that, whenever a thing is good (in the sense in question) its goodness ... 'depends on the presence of certain non-ethical characteristics' possessed by the thing in question: I have always supposed that it did so 'depend,' in the sense that, if a thing is good (in my sense), then that it is so *follows* from the fact that it possesses certain natural intrinsic properties, which are such that from the fact that it is good it does *not follow* conversely that it has those properties.[6]

One explanation of why moral properties supervene on natural ones is that they are constituted by, but are not identical with, complex configurations of natural properties. On this view, moral properties stand to natural properties much as a statue stands to the bronze out of which it is constituted. If so, there is one sense in which moral properties are nothing over and above the natural properties on which they supervene: the natural properties of a situation fix or determine its moral properties; the moral properties of a situation do not have to be added separately to the natural properties of that situation. In another sense, though, the moral properties *are* something over and above the natural properties on which they supervene. The same moral properties could have been realized by somewhat different configurations of natural properties; this modal difference implies that the properties are different properties, and grounds the constitution claim rather than the identity claim. This constitution-relation is a common one. For instance, one could conceive of a lump of bronze with a particular shape as a statue, in the sense that the statue is constituted by, but is not identical with, the bronze. This is precisely because the statue could survive changes in the particular shape of the bronze or could have been realized by a somewhat different bronze shape. Insofar as this view about the relation between the moral and the natural appeals to the 'is' of constitution rather than the 'is' of identity, it even allows us to say that moral properties *are* natural properties. Moreover, this constitution-relation is thought by some to characterize the relation between various higher-level and lower-level categories and sciences. Indeed, it is in just such terms that nonreductive ethical naturalism is sometimes formulated.[7] But then Moore's nonnaturalism may be no less plausible than nonreductive ethical naturalism.

IV. Ethical Naturalism and Direct Reference

The second main response to the OQA is to reject it altogether. Even if nonnaturalism is a coherent—perhaps even plausible—position, Moore's

---

[6] G. E. Moore, "Reply to My Critics," in Paul Arthur Schilpp, ed., *The Philosophy of G. E. Moore* (La Salle, IL: Open Court, 1942), 588.

[7] See, for example, Brink, *Moral Realism and the Foundations of Ethics*, chaps. 6–7, esp. pp. 156–67, 172–80, 193–97.

argument for it is a bad one. In particular, the OQA is not a good argument against the ethical naturalist who identifies moral properties with natural properties. The OQA depends upon the *semantic thesis*, according to which moral predicates cannot be defined in naturalistic terms, and the aforementioned semantic test of properties, according to which terms pick out the same property if and only if they are synonymous. Both premises are questionable.

We might question the semantic thesis. The OQA rightly recognizes the epistemic inequivalence of moral and natural predicates, but it is not clear that epistemic inequivalence implies semantic inequivalence. As I said, the inference from epistemic to semantic inequivalence might be reasonable if a descriptional theory of meaning were true, because on this view, speakers could be expected to recognize whether they associate the same descriptions with different words and, hence, whether those words are synonymous. This view has some plausibility as an account of *nominal* or dictionary definition, but little plausibility as an account of *real* definition. A descriptional view of meaning will seem problematic if we combine it with the traditional view according to which meaning determines reference, for then the descriptional view implies that a term refers to all and only those things that satisfy descriptions conventionally associated with the term. This view of reference is problematic for names and natural-kind terms for a number of reasons. First, it does not allow us to use names and general terms to refer to individuals or properties about whom or which we could associate erroneous descriptions. Intuitively, it seems that speakers can use names and general terms to refer to things about which they associate erroneous descriptions; for example, we might wrongly associate the description 'teacher of Plato' with the name 'Aristotle'. To explain how it is that we might say falsely of Aristotle that he was Plato's teacher, the name 'Aristotle' must not refer via the satisfaction of an associated description (which might include 'student of Plato'). The problem here for the descriptional theory is that it does not distinguish properly between what speakers' words refer to and what speakers believe.

This problem manifests itself in another way: the descriptional theory has difficulty representing disagreement. Genuine disagreement requires univocal meaning or reference and incompatible beliefs about the nature of the things to which one's words refer. If the descriptional theory is true, then meaning just consists in the descriptions conventionally associated with terms. On this account, it becomes impossible to represent a familiar kind of disagreement. Whereas the descriptional theory can represent different speakers disagreeing about whether something in the world satisfies a given description associated with a given word or phrase, it cannot represent disagreement about which descriptions to associate with a given word or phrase.

Consider *synchronic disagreement*. At any one stage in an intellectual inquiry, there may well be a number of descriptions conventionally associated with the use of a general term. Suppose most speakers associate features X, Y, and Z with general term 'G'. It ought to be possible for a heretical inquirer to express disagreement with the prevailing view. A speaker ought to be able to say that the very thing that most speakers use 'G' to refer to is not X, Y, and Z, but rather is A, B, and C (where 'X, Y, and Z' and 'A, B, and C' have different extensions). However, this is ruled out by the traditional descriptional theory, for on this view the meaning and reference of 'G' is given by the description—X, Y, and Z—that is conventionally associated with 'G'. The heretic's claim would thus be analytically false. But certainly not all heretical claims are false—much less analytically false—as the progressive nature of various inquiries shows us.[8]

This leads naturally to the case of *diachronic disagreement*. As I mentioned, at any one stage in an intellectual inquiry, there may be a set of descriptions conventionally associated with the use of a general term. As inquiry progresses, the descriptions associated with these terms are likely to change. We would normally like to say that there is diachronic disagreement and progress, but both judgments presuppose univocal meaning and reference. According to the traditional descriptional theory, however, there is no such continuity. Under this theory, the two linguistic communities in the example above associate nonequivalent descriptions with their terms, and hence mean and refer to different things when using them. They no more disagree than do two interlocutors when one says "The bank [= financial institution] is a good place for your money" and the other says "The bank [= side of the river] is not a good place for my money." On this view, there can only be diachronic intellectual *change*; there can be no genuine intellectual disagreement, continuity, or progress.[9]

These problems arise from the descriptional theory because it allows reference to be determined by senses or descriptions. A natural alternative to this kind of *mediated reference* is a theory of *direct reference* that does not make reference depend upon speakers' associated descriptions or beliefs. One account of direct reference, the *causal theory of reference*, grew out of suggestions made by Keith Donnellan and was developed by Saul

[8] On an individualistic version of the descriptional theory, 'G' means different things in the mouths of the orthodox and the heterodox. On this view, the heterodox is not making analytically false claims, but neither is he disagreeing with the orthodox—he has simply changed the subject. Thus, this version of the descriptional theory is also incapable of allowing for genuine disagreement.

[9] These arguments are framed in terms of the traditional version of the descriptional theory and do not directly address other versions of the descriptional theory, like Searle's, that make the meaning of a term consist, not in a single (though perhaps complex) description, but rather in a cluster or family of descriptions, some but not all of which need to be satisfied in order for the term to refer. See John Searle, "Proper Names," *Mind* 67, no. 266 (1958): 166–73. However, like Kripke, I think that the arguments in the text apply, with only small modifications, to the cluster theories of descriptions. See Saul Kripke, *Naming and Necessity* (Cambridge, MA: Harvard University Press, 1980), 74–77.

Kripke and Hilary Putnam.[10] According to the causal theory, names and natural-kind terms refer to things in the world via complex causal histories. On this view, language-users introduce words (e.g., names and general terms) to pick out interesting features of their environment. In the idealized case, a group of speakers introduces a term such that what their term refers to is that bit of the environment (e.g., that object, property, or relation) that explains what they found interesting and intended to pick out. Subsequent speakers borrow this term with the intention of referring to the same thing; their use of the term inherits reference to the same features of the environment via a causal-historical chain extending from their use of the term, through the original "dubbing ceremony," to the relevant aspects of the environment. For example, the term 'water' was introduced to pick out the colorless, odorless stuff found in lakes, rivers, etc. that is suitable for drinking, bathing, supporting life, etc. This liquid is actually made of H_2O, and it is this chemical composition that allows it to serve these various functional roles. According to the causal theory, the reference of the term 'water' is determined by this causal-historical chain; past, subsequent, and present use of 'water' refers to H_2O, even as speakers' beliefs about water have been very different. Because people have not always realized that the chemical composition of water is H_2O or even that water has a chemical composition, the causal theory allows us to explain how speakers can use terms meaningfully while being quite ignorant, perhaps mistaken, about their extension, and how speakers can speak about the same thing while disagreeing significantly in their beliefs about the subject matter. On this view, determining what the term 'water' refers to involves reliance on scientific theorizing about the chemical structure that explains the liquid's properties. We appeal or defer to experts, not because their beliefs determine what our terms refer to, but because those beliefs provide us with the best available evidence about the real nature of the referents of our terms.

Friends of the causal theory who want to preserve the traditional connection between meaning and reference will accept a *referential view* about meaning, according to which the meaning of names and natural-kind terms just is (or at least involves) their reference.[11] On this view, ascriptions of meaning to natural-kind terms involve explicit or implicit theoretical commitments, and speakers cannot be assumed to be authoritative about the meaning of their words. This referential view about meaning

[10] See Keith Donnellan, "Reference and Definite Descriptions," reprinted in Stephen P. Schwartz, ed., *Naming, Necessity, and Natural Kinds* (Ithaca, NY: Cornell University Press, 1977); Kripke, *Naming and Necessity*; and Hilary Putnam, "The Meaning of 'Meaning'," reprinted in his *Mind, Language, and Reality*, vol. 2 of his *Philosophical Papers* (New York: Cambridge University Press, 1975).

[11] In "The Meaning of 'Meaning'," Putnam conceives of meaning as a "vector" consisting of (a) syntactic markers; (b) semantic markers; (c) stereotypes, which do not determine extension; and (d) modal extension. Thus, the meaning vector for 'water' would be (a) mass noun; (b) natural kind, liquid; (c) transparent, odorless, colorless, potable; and (d) H_2O.

leads to an account of real, as opposed to nominal, definition. The meaning of our terms is fixed by the nature of the world and can be known only through substantive investigation. On such a view of meaning, terms might have the same meaning yet differ in connotation or cognitive significance. If so, there is no reason to suppose that epistemic equivalence is a condition of semantic equivalence. 'M' and 'N' might have the same meaning or real definition even if 'Are N-things M?' is an open question. In this way, a referential account of meaning might lead us to question the semantic thesis.

Alternatively, we might question the semantic test of properties. If we accept a descriptional theory of meaning, or any other view of meaning on which competent speakers must be authoritative about the meaning of their words, then it is harder to separate semantic and epistemic equivalence, but it becomes very implausible that semantic or epistemic equivalence is a test of property-identity. We entertain and accept many synthetic identity claims whose truth is not ensured by the meanings of the words in which those claims are expressed. In doing so, we suppose that 'F' and 'G' might express the same property without being synonymous. Sometimes these claims involve intertheoretic identification; in these cases, we suppose that general terms from different disciplines express the same property, as when we suppose that water = H_2O or that heat = mean kinetic molecular energy. Terms and categories from different disciplines typically have different epistemic and semantic values, which explains why intertheoretic identifications were discoveries and might still be news to some competent speakers. It follows from this that neither epistemic nor semantic equivalence is required for property-identity. These and other claims of metaphysical equivalence are synthetic claims to be assessed by the same dialectical standards under which we assess all theoretical claims.

The implications for the OQA of these general worries about the semantic thesis and the semantic test of properties ought to be pretty straightforward. Ethical naturalism implies that moral properties are natural properties—that is, properties that can be picked out by means of predicates from the natural and social sciences (broadly understood). On one reading, this is to be understood as a constitution claim rather than an identity claim. It is not clear that the OQA is meant to challenge this sort of nonreductive ethical naturalism.[12] The main target of the OQA is the claim that moral and natural properties are identical, that is, that moral predicates and nonmoral predicates from the natural and social sciences can express the same property. The OQA appeals to the semantic thesis and the semantic test of properties to undermine this version of ethical

---

[12] However, the intuitionist's reasons for accepting the semantic test of properties—that all necessity is analytic—may also undermine the claim that moral properties, though not identical with natural properties, nonetheless strongly supervene on, and are constituted by, natural properties.

naturalism. However, the ethical naturalist can plausibly reject either the semantic thesis or the semantic test of properties.

The ethical naturalist might be a referentialist about the meaning of moral terms. If so, she will think that the meaning of a moral predicate is (or involves) the property it picks out. On this view, speakers cannot be assumed to be authoritative about the meaning of moral terms; what they mean is a matter of substantive moral theory that we articulate and defend by familiar dialectical methods. The (reductive) ethical naturalist supposes that moral terms can be given this sort of real—as opposed to nominal—definition, in naturalistic terms. The epistemic inequivalence of moral definienda and naturalistic definiens is no obstacle to the sort of real definition to which this sort of ethical naturalist might be committed. For instance, an ethical naturalist might put forward hedonistic utilitarianism as a real definition of moral duty, according to which an agent's duty is to perform the action, among the alternatives available, that would maximize overall pleasure. This real definition is not undermined by the epistemic inequivalence of the phrases 'maximizes pleasure' and 'is one's duty'. Rather, it is to be assessed (and I would suppose ultimately rejected) dialectically in terms of its fit with our other moral beliefs.

Alternatively, the ethical naturalist might accept, at least for the sake of argument, the sort of descriptive theory of meaning on which the semantic thesis seems to rest. She will then infer semantic inequivalence from epistemic inequivalence and so accept the semantic thesis, but then she can and should reject the semantic test of properties. Moral and nonmoral terms can pick out the same property even if those terms are not synonymous. These will be synthetic property-identity claims, which are to be justified by a dialectical moral inquiry. For example, hedonistic utilitarianism is not false just because 'is one's duty' and 'maximizes pleasure' are not synonymous. This particular property-identity claim is a synthetic claim, to be assessed on substantive moral grounds.

Hence, we might say, speaking somewhat loosely, that the probative force of the OQA is confined to analytical ethical naturalism and does not extend to synthetic or metaphysical ethical naturalism.[13] Insofar as synthetic or metaphysical ethical naturalism appeals to the theory of direct reference, it promises to explain how we can use moral terms meaningfully and to refer even when speakers have erroneous moral beliefs, and

---

[13] It is common to distinguish *analytic truths*, as those statements made true by virtue of the meanings of the words in which the statement is expressed, and *synthetic truths*, as those statements whose truth depends upon the way the world is and not simply the meanings of the words in which the statement is expressed. If analytic truths are simply statements made true by virtue of the meanings of the words in which the statement is expressed, then real definitions might express analytic truths, and so at least one way of defending ethical naturalism could be understood as a defense of analytical naturalism. It is common, however, to think that analytic truths ought to be comparatively obvious truths about which competent speakers ought to be authoritative. Insofar as this is part of analyticity, even the referentialist about meaning ought to reject analytical naturalism.

how speakers can use moral language univocally and succeed in dis-agreeing even when they have very different moral beliefs. This is be-cause on this view a moral appraiser's words refer to features of people, actions, and institutions via her participation in an extended causal-historical chain linking past and present speakers of her language to moral features of the world—not via speakers' associated descriptions or beliefs. Moral appraisers can thus use moral language, such as "right" and "wrong," meaningfully and to refer, provided that their use is part of this causal-historical chain—even if they have few beliefs or largely false beliefs about which actions are right and which are wrong, or about what makes right acts right and wrong ones wrong. Moreover, participation in the same causal-historical chain will ensure univocal meaning or refer-ence for the use of common moral terminology, such as "right" and "wrong," by different speakers at a time and by speakers at different times, regardless of differences in their moral beliefs and their criteria for applying these terms. This allows us to represent how both synchronic and diachronic disagreement are possible between speakers with very different moral codes. It also allows us to represent changes in moral attitude that have other relevant progressive aspects—for instance, when informed and reflective changes in moral attitude are unidirectional—as forms of moral progress.[14]

V. Doubts about Realism, Naturalism, and Direct Reference

I have come across two main kinds of worry about the moral realist's use of the theory of direct reference to defend synthetic ethical natural-ism. These worries share a common conception of how the ethical natu-ralist makes use of the theory of direct reference, consideration of which suggests an alternative conception that promises to resolve both worries. I will explain the two worries first and then discuss possible resolutions.

I begin with the worry that is easiest to state. Though it has echoes in published discussions,[15] I have come across it most clearly in conversa-tion.[16] Stated baldly, the worry is that substantive moral reasoning and theorizing become obsolete if we let the ethical naturalist respond to the OQA by appeal to the causal theory of reference. The causal theory of reference appears to make the reference of speakers' use of moral pred-icates a matter of empirical—specifically, historical—fact insofar as sub-sequent use of these predicates inherits reference, via speakers' intentions to use the predicates with the same reference as earlier speakers, from the original use of those predicates to name interesting features of the envi-

---

[14] See Brink, *Moral Realism and the Foundations of Ethics*, 204-9; cf. Michael Slote, "The Rationality of Aesthetic Value Judgments," *Journal of Philosophy* 68, no. 22 (1971): 821-39.
[15] See Eric H. Gampel, "A Defense of the Autonomy of Ethics: Why Value Is Not Like Water," *Canadian Journal of Philosophy* 26, no. 2 (1996): 191-209.
[16] Especially with John G. Bennett.

ronment of those original speakers. If so, it would seem that the causal theory implies that disputes about the meaning or reference of moral terms ought to be resolved not, as one would think, by moral reasoning, but by means of a historical inquiry about which features of actions, people, and institutions moral appraisers intended to pick out when those moral terms were introduced. If so, appeal to the causal theory of reference is not a good response to the OQA.

The first worry, then, assumes that determination of which properties causally regulate, in the relevant way, speakers' use of moral terms is a purely historical matter. The second worry concerns the possibility that some speakers have their use of moral terms causally regulated by different properties of the people, actions, and institutions that their moral judgments concern. This worry is set out most elaborately by Mark Timmons and Terence Horgan in a series of articles.[17] The upshot of their argument is that they see a tension between moral realism and ethical naturalism insofar as the defense of ethical naturalism against the OQA requires appeal to theories of direct reference, such as the causal theory, which they see as incompatible with moral realism. On their view, you can be a moral realist or an ethical naturalist, but not both.

Timmons and Horgan begin by noting that recent defenses of moral realism have tended to eschew the apparent mysteries of intuitionism in favor of some form of ethical naturalism, and have defended ethical naturalism against Moore's OQA by appealing to claims about meaning and reference that are part of the direct-reference tradition. They focus on Richard Boyd's account of the causal theory of reference, according to which

> *Roughly*, and for nondegenerate cases, a term t refers to a kind (property, relation, etc.) k just in case there exist causal mechanisms whose tendency is to bring it about, over time, that what is predicated of the term t will be approximately true of k. . . . Such mechanisms will typically include the existence of procedures which are approximately accurate for recognizing members or instances of k (at least for easy cases) and which relevantly govern the use of t, the social transmission of certain relevantly approximately true beliefs regarding k, formulated as claims about t . . . , a pattern of deference to experts on k with respect to the use of t, etc. . . . When relations of this sort obtain, we may think of the properties of k as regulating the use of t (via such causal relations), and we may think of what is said

[17] See Terence Horgan and Mark Timmons, "New Wave Moral Realism Meets Moral Twin Earth," *Journal of Philosophical Research* 16 (1990-91): 447-65; Terence Horgan and Mark Timmons, "Troubles for New Wave Moral Semantics: The Open Question Argument Revived," *Philosophical Papers* 21, no. 3 (1992): 153-75; and Terence Horgan and Mark Timmons, "Troubles on Moral Twin Earth: Moral Queerness Revived," *Synthese* 92, no. 2 (1992): 221-60. The first two of these articles are most directly relevant to my present concerns.

using *t* as providing us with socially coordinated *epistemic access* to *k*; *t* refers to *k* (in nondegenerate cases) just in case the socially coordinated use of *t* provides significant epistemic access to *k*, and not to other kinds (properties, etc.).[18]

Timmons and Horgan link a naturalistic approach to ethics, such as my own, with Boyd's version of the causal theory, thereby associating ethical naturalism with the following *causal semantic thesis*:

Each moral term t rigidly designates the natural property N that uniquely causally regulates the use of t by humans.[19]

They then ask us to consider a Twin Earth story of the sort Putnam used to motivate his referential account of meaning.[20] In Putnam's original version, Earth and Twin Earth are otherwise indistinguishable planets, but the stuff on Earth that causally regulates the use of 'water' is H_2O whereas the stuff on Twin Earth that causally regulates the use of 'water' is XYZ (where XYZ ≠ H_2O). Putnam used Twin Earth scenarios to argue that meaning and reference are a function of causal interaction with the speaker's environment, and concluded that natural-kind terms, such as 'water', would mean different things in different environments (on Earth and Twin Earth, for example). Timmons and Horgan ask us to imagine that Earth and Moral Twin Earth are otherwise indistinguishable, but that the same moral term 'M' is causally regulated by different natural properties on the two planets. We are to imagine that people, actions, and institutions on the two planets are qualitatively indistinguishable except for the standards for moral assessment that appraisers on each planet employ. For simplicity, they ask us to imagine that consequentialist considerations uniquely causally regulate use of moral language on Earth, whereas deontological considerations uniquely regulate the use of moral language on Moral Twin Earth.[21]

---

[18] Boyd, "How to Be a Moral Realist," 195. There is a puzzle here insofar as Boyd appears to commit the causal theory to successful reference, for I take fallibilism and the possibility of reference failure to be a defining feature of realism. However, perhaps Boyd would regard reference failure as a "degenerate" case.

[19] Horgan and Timmons, "Moral Realism Meets Moral Twin Earth," 455.

[20] See Putnam, "The Meaning of 'Meaning'."

[21] However, there is an important difference between Putnam's Twin Earth and Moral Twin Earth. The difference between Earth and Twin Earth appears to be merely compositional—the stuff on Earth is H_2O, whereas the stuff on Twin Earth is XYZ—and not to have wider functional significance. However, the difference between Earth and Moral Twin Earth appears not to be merely compositional. Presumably, different people, actions, and institutions will satisfy consequentialist and deontological standards. If people have the same commitments to morality on Earth and Moral Twin Earth, the differing standards will cause each planet's people to assess people, actions, and institutions differently; over the long run, this should affect the course of individual and social histories on Earth and Moral Twin Earth. Though the members of both planetary pairs—Earth and Twin Earth and Earth and

In these circumstances, would Earthlings and Moral Twin Earthlings use moral language with a common meaning and reference—and hence have disagreements in moral beliefs—or would moral language on Earth and Moral Twin Earth have different meaning and reference? The moral that Putnam draws from his Twin Earth scenarios would seem to suggest that the meaning and reference of moral language are different on Earth and Moral Twin Earth. This is also what the causal semantic thesis would seem to imply, inasmuch as the same 'M' is causally regulated by different N-properties on Earth and Moral Twin Earth. However, this would appear to imply interplanetary semantic relativism. Timmons and Horgan find this consequence unattractive, presumably because they want to interpret Earthlings and Moral Twin Earthlings as being involved in a genuine moral disagreement, which presupposes univocal meaning and reference. Indeed, they think that the moral realist must deny this sort of interplanetary relativism.

This claim may seem a bit puzzling. Whereas we often contrast realist and relativist claims, it may seem peculiar to require the moral realist to deny this sort of semantic relativism. After all, Putnam appeals to a semantic relativist interpretation of his Twin Earth story as part of an argument for direct reference, and direct reference is supposed to be part of—or at least compatible with—metaphysical realism. Putnam sees no tension between metaphysical realism and his brand of semantic relativism. Why should we see a tension between moral realism and this sort of semantic relativism? The answer, I think, lies in the kind of semantic relativism with which we are dealing. One reason metaphysical realism seems compatible with the kind of semantic relativism implicit in Putnam's version of direct reference is that both realism and direct reference want to distinguish between speakers' beliefs and the subject matter of those beliefs; this is what allows the realist to distinguish between how things are and how they appear to inquirers. Putnam's semantic relativism respects this condition; the meaning of the term 'water' is different on Earth and Twin Earth, but this is because of differences in physical composition on Earth and Twin Earth, not because of different beliefs of Earthlings and Twin Earthlings. However, the semantic relativism in Timmons and Horgan's case would make multiple reference a consequence of different moral beliefs on Earth and Moral Twin Earth, because speakers have different moral beliefs just insofar as they regulate their use of moral language by different N-properties. If so, it appears that the semantic relativist interpretation of Moral Twin Earth is inconsistent with moral realism.

Moral Twin Earth—are, as I said, *otherwise* indistinguishable, this caveat includes many more differences in the second pair than in the first. As it seemed important to Putnam's original arguments that differences between Earth and Twin Earth be minimized, the more extensive differences between Earth and Moral Twin Earth may complicate Timmons and Horgan's argument. In what follows, I ignore these complications, if only for the sake of argument.

Moreover, interplanetary relativism might seem problematic for the moral realist if it is just the first step toward intraplanetary relativism. Why shouldn't the use of moral language by different cultures and by different groups within a given culture here on Earth be causally regulated by different N-properties? Indeed, isn't this just what moral disagreement involves—that appraisers *do* have their use of moral language causally regulated by different N-properties? But then it looks as if all moral disagreements would involve multiple meaning and reference. Hence, the causal semantic theory to which the ethical naturalist is committed implies a rampant intraplanetary relativism, which it would be hard to square with moral realism.

It would be ironic if direct reference commits us to moral relativism, inasmuch as it was supposed to be a virtue of the theory of direct reference that it allowed us to represent common meaning and reference among inquirers with very different beliefs about a given subject matter. Be that as it may, the worry is that the Moral Twin Earth scenario exposes a tension between ethical naturalism and moral realism; the defense of ethical naturalism involves semantic commitments to direct reference that are inconsistent with moral realism. If so, we can be realists or naturalists about ethics, but not both; in particular, we cannot defend moral realism against Moore's OQA, as some (including me) have recently supposed, by understanding ethical naturalism in terms of the theory of direct reference.

We can now see how the first and second worries about the moral realist's use of the theory of direct reference to defend synthetic ethical naturalism depend on a common conception of the theory of direct reference. They both understand the theory of direct reference in terms of the causal semantic thesis that moral terms refer to whatever N-properties causally regulate their use. If so, ascertaining the meaning and reference of moral terms would appear to be a historical inquiry rather than a moral inquiry. Moreover, we should not expect appraisers' use of moral terms always or even usually to be causally regulated by the same N-properties—the causal semantic thesis thus appears to support relativism, not realism.

VI. Causal Regulation

It would be premature to accept these two worries about the moral realist's use of direct reference to defend ethical naturalism, for the common conception of direct reference underlying these two worries deserves rethinking. On Boyd's version of the causal theory, which Timmons and Horgan associate with ethical naturalism, a speaker's term refers to those features of the world that causally regulate her use of the term, including her use of it to communicate with others. One important issue for this view concerns the proper understanding of how features of the world causally regulate the use of moral-kind terms. Both of the worries discussed in the previous section are most plausible when regulation is understood in a narrowly extensional way. This *extensional interpretation* understands regulation in terms of the features of the world that causally regulate people's *actual* use of moral terms. Determining which N-properties regulate a speaker's actual use of moral-kind terms looks like a historical inquiry rather than a moral inquiry, and the existence of significant moral disagreement suggests that actual usage is regulated by different N-properties in different speakers. However, causal regulation can and should be understood in *counterfactual* terms. On this view, terms refer to properties that regulate not just actual usage, but also counterfactual or hypothetical usage—in particular, the way speakers would apply terms upon due reflection in imagined situations and thought experiments.

Any interpretation of regulation must also understand it in a way that is sensitive to various demands of consistency. To apply moral terms in virtue of N-properties is just to have a set of beliefs, however implicitly, about which N-properties are morally relevant. Presumably, even actual usage does not track any one set of morally relevant properties consistently. We therefore need an account of error. Any ascription of local error will ascribe to the speaker principles, however implicit, about which N-properties are morally relevant. In this way, we can see local errors as performance errors against the background of an underlying competence. We might decide which principle to ascribe to a speaker by seeing which one minimizes the ascription of error to her. As we seek consistency in the application of moral terms across imagined as well as actual situations, there is greater room for inconsistency and so a greater need to understand regulation in a way that will allow for principled correction to a speaker's usage. Demands of consistency arise not only from patterns in actual and counterfactual use of a given term, but also from the use of other terms, both moral and nonmoral. This is because the principles that implicitly regulate a speaker's use of any one moral term interact with a number of other moral and nonmoral views that she holds.

This leads to a picture of regulation that is *dialectical*. Our actual use of moral predicates is imperfectly guided by our (perhaps implicit) acceptance of moral principles that identify morally relevant factors. We identify principles by looking for patterns in our actual and counterfactual judgments that employ those predicates; we test these principles by drawing out their implications for real or imagined cases and comparing these implications with our own existing or reflective moral assessments of those cases. If a principle has counterintuitive implications, this counts against it. If the counterintuitive implications of the principle are fairly common, this is reason to abandon or modify the principle. However, if a counterintuitive implication is isolated and the principle explains our views—especially our common moral views—better than alternative principles, then this is reason to revise the particular judgment or precept that conflicts with the principle. Ideally, we make trade-offs among our principles, considered moral judgments, and other views in response to conflicts, making adjustments here at one point and there at another, as coherence seems to require, until our ethical views are in dialectical equilibrium.[22]

On this view, a natural property N causally regulates a speaker's use of moral term 'M' just in case his use of 'M' would be dependent on his belief that something is N, were his beliefs in dialectical equilibrium. Both worries about the use of the theory of direct reference to defend synthetic ethical naturalism — the worries that it makes moral reasoning obsolete and that it implies a form of semantic relativism that is incompatible with moral realism — are less compelling when we shift from the extensional to the counterfactual or dialectical understanding of causal regulation.

Determining the meaning and reference of moral terms might look like historical reasoning rather than moral reasoning if we are interested in the properties that extensionally regulate moral terms. Insofar as the relevant notion of regulation is counterfactual and dialectical, though, the process of ascertaining the meaning or reference of one's moral terms will involve just the sort of thought experiments and analogical reasoning that is characteristic of moral reasoning.

There is enough difference in people's actual beliefs about morally relevant factors to make it plausible, at least in the case of some speakers, that different properties extensionally regulate their use of the same moral terms. However, the problem of multiple reference and relativism is less compelling on the counterfactual conception of regulation. The issue here is really just the familiar one about whether extant moral disagreement undermines prospects for dialectical convergence. Although dialectical reasoning takes people's pretheoretical moral beliefs as input, these beliefs will be revised in the process of reaching dialectical equilibrium. Indeed, there is no guarantee that any of the beliefs with which one begins the dialectical process will be preserved unmodified. A proper dialectical equilibrium should be broad, representing a dialectical accommodation not simply among our moral beliefs, but among our moral beliefs and various philosophical and empirical beliefs.[23] Given the dependence of many of our moral beliefs on complex empirical and philosophical issues, there is every reason to expect any broad dialectical fit between various (moral and nonmoral) beliefs to be revisionary. Because a broad dialectical fit is an intellectual aim that we can at best hope to

---

[22] This account of dialectical methods and dialectical equilibrium is, of course, similar to Rawls's account of reflective equilibrium. See John Rawls, *A Theory of Justice* (Cambridge, MA: Harvard University Press, 1971), 19–21, 46–51, 578–81. See also David O. Brink, "Common Sense and First Principles in Sidgwick's *Methods*," *Social Philosophy and Policy* 11, no. 1 (1994): 179–201.

[23] See Brink, "Common Sense and First Principles in Sidgwick's *Methods*," 184–87, 200.

approximate, the existence of prereflective and even reflective moral disagreement is no sign that moral disagreement is in principle unresolvable.
Indeed, the claim that moral disagreements are in principle unresolvable
by dialectical methods is just one claim about what the results of a systematic dialectical inquiry among different interlocutors would be, and
enjoys no privileged *a priori* position in relation to its nonskeptical com-
petitors. This means that whereas there is in the nature of things no
guarantee of common reference, this provides no reason to doubt that our
terms do have common reference or that dialectical methods are our route
to moral knowledge.[24]

If this is right, the two aforementioned worries about the moral realist's
use of the theory of direct reference to defend synthetic ethical naturalism
rest on an inadequate understanding of the way in which features of the
world might regulate the use of language. If the moral realist understands
the meaning and reference of moral-kind terms, as Boyd does, in terms of
causal regulation, then regulation should be understood in counterfactual
and dialectical terms. When regulation is understood in this way, the
worries about the obsolescence of moral inquiry and about multiple reference become less compelling.

VII. Referential Intentions and the Moral Point of View

Perhaps the dialectical understanding of causal regulation gives us a
decent reply to the two worries about the moral realist's use of the theory
of direct reference to defend synthetic ethical naturalism, if we assume, as
Boyd and Timmons and Horgan do, that the ethical naturalist must embrace an account of direct reference that makes the meaning and reference
of moral-kind terms a function of the properties that causally regulate
their use. I am not sure, however, that we should understand direct
reference this way. We get a different semantic picture when we recognize
and emphasize the role, within the theory of direct reference, of speakers'
intentions in determining meaning and reference.[25] After explaining these
claims, I will briefly contrast this conception of direct reference with one
that invokes the causal regulation thesis.

One way in which referential intentions function in the theory of direct
reference is to provide continuity of reference among a community of
inquirers. It is sometimes said that participation in the causal-historical
chain linking words to the world allows later speakers to "borrow" reference from earlier ones. What allows later speakers to do this—what
makes them a link in the same chain—is their use of their predecessors'

---

[24] For a fuller discussion of the resources within a dialectical method for dealing with
moral disagreement, see Brink, *Moral Realism and the Foundations of Ethics*, 197–209.

[25] Donnellan, Kripke, and Putnam all recognize the importance of referential intentions in
fixing reference; their importance is also stressed in Alan Sidelle, *Necessity, Essence, and
Individuation: A Defense of Conventionalism* (Ithaca, NY: Cornell University Press, 1989).

words with the intention of talking about the same thing that they did. It is these shared referential intentions among synchronic and diachronic communities of inquirers that establish common meaning and reference. If so, shared referential intentions among communities of moral inquiry should also establish common meaning and reference. The intentions of moral inquirers to say and think things about the same features of people, actions, and institutions as each other will block ascription of different meanings or reference to fellow participants in a common moral inquiry, and will lead us to interpret such differences as there are as differences in belief about the extension of moral terms.

This may block the slide from interplanetary relativism to intraplanetary relativism, precisely because there is, at least typically, intellectual and linguistic interaction among moral inquirers here on Earth. However, where there is no such interaction—by hypothesis, there is none in the interplanetary case, and there might fail to be any in some intraplanetary cases—there apparently can be no such shared referential intentions. In these cases, we cannot appeal to such intentions to secure common reference.

Does this commit us to a more limited relativism? If so, we could ask whether this form of relativism is inconsistent with moral realism. I think that we can avoid answering this question, though, because the role of referential intentions within the theory of direct reference provides a more thoroughgoing response to the relativist worry. The relativist posits two or more lines of moral inquiry in which the same words have different meaning and reference. However, if these lines of inquiry are distinct—that is, they do not interact—and are counterfactually and dialectically regulated by different properties, what justifies us in interpreting each line of inquiry as a line of *moral* inquiry? It is true that both communities of inquirers use the same words—'right', 'wrong', 'virtuous', 'vicious', etc.—but these might be mere homonyms. If we are participants in one community, why should we assume that assertions using these words, if made by participants in a different community, should be interpreted as moral assertions?

One answer requires understanding the role of speakers' intentions in fixing the reference of a term at the time of its introduction. Consider again the nonmoral case. What makes it the case that the introduction of a term picks out one particular feature of the speaker's environment rather than another? It is the intentions of the speaker. To borrow from an example used by Donnellan, I use the description "the man holding the martini" to pick person A out of the foreground of a crowd at a party, of whom I correctly say something else, for instance, that he is wearing a nice suit.[26] I can successfully pick out A even if we discover that his glass contains water rather than a martini. What makes my description pick out

[26] Donnellan, "Reference and Definite Descriptions," 48.

A, rather than nobody or B, who was hidden from view but was drinking a martini, is my intention, which you recognize, to single out the fellow in the foreground who is drinking from a martini glass and wearing a suit. Similarly, those who introduced the term 'water' intended to refer to the structure, whatever it is, that explains the perceptible and functional features of the colorless, odorless stuff—found in lakes, rivers, etc.—that is suitable for drinking, bathing, and supporting life. It is this intention that fixes the reference of 'water'. As it turns out, it is the chemical microstructure H_2O that answers this explanatory description. Moreover, the role of referential intentions explains why ascertaining the meaning and reference of 'water' is a scientific inquiry, not a historical inquiry: the meaning and reference of 'water' depends upon the answer to the scientific or explanatory question about what features of the colorless, odorless liquid explain its observable and functional properties.[27]

To apply this account to the moral case, we need some parallel descriptive specification of the referential intentions of moral inquirers that would justify us in interpreting a community of inquirers as engaged in moral inquiry. This requires a descriptive formulation of the moral point of view, but it must be a description that is sufficiently abstract, so that a wide variety of views (some quite unorthodox) might be thought to satisfy this description. Moreover, what best satisfies this description must be a matter of substantive moral theory.[28] We might put these points in terms of the useful distinction between *concepts* and *conceptions*.[29] Often, we want to distinguish between an abstract concept and different substantive conceptions of that concept. For example, we distinguish between the concept of distributive justice, on the one hand, and utilitarian, egalitarian, and libertarian conceptions of distributive justice, on the other hand. To explain how different conceptions are all conceptions of the same concept, we need some abstract characterization of a given subject matter that allows us to see different conceptions as rival accounts of that subject matter. In this instance, we might explain the concept of distrib-

---

[27] Different speakers, or even the same speakers in different contexts, can employ different intentions with respect to the same word, though to do so they cannot have the intention to refer to whatever the other speakers are talking about. For instance, some speakers might use 'fish' to pick out a biological kind, in which case their use of 'fish' would not refer to whales. Other speakers or conversational contexts might not share this intention directly, or indirectly by way of an intention to refer to whatever the speakers with biological intentions were talking about. For instance, those who live by the sea might use 'fish' to pick out marine life, in which case their use of 'fish' would refer to whales. This kind of relativity of meaning or reference with respect to intention is perfectly compatible with the theory of direct reference.

[28] These claims suggest that direct reference and descriptional theories need not be antithetical, provided that the descriptional theory gives the meaning of natural-kind terms in sufficiently abstract descriptions, the satisfaction of which is a potentially controversial substantive matter.

[29] Cf. H. L. A. Hart, *The Concept of Law*, 2d ed. (Oxford: Clarendon Press, 1994), 159–60; Rawls, *A Theory of Justice*, 5, 10; and Ronald Dworkin, *Law's Empire* (Cambridge, MA: Harvard University Press, 1986), 70–72, 90.

utive justice as concerning the appropriate distribution of benefits and responsibilities among members of a society; utilitarian, egalitarian, and libertarian conceptions offer different substantive distributive principles. Analogously, to ascertain whether inquirers have referential intentions that would justify us in regarding them as moral inquirers, we need some abstract account of the concept of morality common to different conceptions of morality. Which conception is the best conception of the concept of morality—and hence determines the extension of moral terms—will be a substantive theoretical matter to be determined by dialectical methods.[30]

We can entertain different descriptive specifications of the concept of morality. Present purposes do not require settling on one specification in preference to all others; all we need is a plausible illustration of how such a specification can function to establish common meaning or reference. One possibility is that we adopt the moral point of view toward anything when we assess it as meriting praise or blame. However, this account of the concept of morality threatens to be too broad, forcing us to represent all evaluation as moral evaluation. Another familiar idea appeals to the contractualist idea that assuming the moral point of view involves assessing one's own conduct and that of others in terms of standards that admit of *interpersonal justification*.[31] Hume articulates this idea in *An Enquiry Concerning the Principles of Morals*:

> When a man denominates another his *enemy*, his *rival*, his *antagonist*, his *adversary*, he is understood to speak the language of self-love, and to express sentiments, peculiar to himself, and arising from his particular circumstances and situation. But when he bestows on any man the epithets of *vicious* or *odious* or *depraved*, he then speaks another language, and expresses sentiments, in which he expects all his audience are to concur with him. He must here, therefore, depart from his private and particular situation, and must choose a point of view, common to him with others; he must move some universal principle of the human frame, and touch a string to which all mankind have an accord and symphony.[32]

---

[30] There are dangers inherent in making any one description, however abstract, constitutive of the concept of morality, insofar as one ought to be quite liberal about what might count as a conception (however unorthodox) of morality. Another possible understanding of the concept of morality, which I will not explore further here, is that we count something as a moral code (however unorthodox) just in case its organizing principles make explanatory contact with some of our pretheoretical beliefs about morality.

[31] For a contemporary statement of contractualism, see T. M. Scanlon, "Utilitarianism and Contractualism," in Amartya Sen and Bernard Williams, eds., *Utilitarianism and Beyond* (Cambridge: Cambridge University Press, 1982).

[32] David Hume, *An Enquiry Concerning the Principles of Morals* [1751], ed. P. H. Nidditch, 3rd ed. (Oxford: Clarendon Press, 1975), sec. 9, pt. 1.

On this account of the concept of morality, what is distinctive of the moral point of view is that we assess people, actions, and institutions according to standards that others can and should accept.

This understanding of the concept of morality admits of many very different conceptions. It admits of a Kantian interpretation in terms of the universal law formulation of the Categorical Imperative, as well as a Humean interpretation in terms of affective responses from the general point of view. It does not settle important questions about how best to model interpersonal justification, such as what counts as reasonable agreement or rejection. Nor does it settle what principles or standards would be adopted under the right conception of interpersonal justification—whether they would be egoist, utilitarian, deontological, or something quite different. Working out answers to these and other questions about interpersonal justification involves forming and defending substantive conceptions of morality.

Appealing to this account of the moral point of view in terms of interpersonal justification allows us to elaborate further the way a moral realist can understand and invoke the theory of direct reference. On this view, we should understand perhaps all moral appraisers, and certainly those who introduced moral categories and terms, as using those categories and terms with the intention of picking out properties of people, actions, and institutions—whatever those properties are—that play an important role in the interpersonal justification of people's characters, their actions, and their institutions. Subsequent appraisers inherit this intention, if only because they use the same words as their predecessors and have the intention of continuing an inquiry into the same subject. This picture allows us to explain the conditions under which it is reasonable to interpret the judgments of distinct communities of inquirers as moral judgments. Even when appraisers from distinct communities use language in ways that are counterfactually regulated by different properties of their environments, we should interpret their language as moral language and the judgments that employ that language as moral judgments only if those judgments are based on standards that the appraisers endorse, if only implicitly, as interpersonally justifiable.

This account answers the puzzle for the relativist concerning the conditions under which we should interpret the judgments made on Moral Twin Earth as moral judgments. It does so, however, in a way that undermines the relativist interpretation of Moral Twin Earth. Recall that relativism appeared to be the commitment of the theory of direct reference insofar as this theory was unable to identify a common meaning and reference about which appraisers from Earth and Moral Twin Earth held different beliefs. But our account of the shared referential intention to pick out people, actions, and institutions that are interpersonally justifiable, in virtue of which the judgments of Earthlings and Moral Twin Earthlings are both moral judgments, identifies just such a common meaning or reference about which the two communities have a disagreement in be-lief. Their disagreement is one about which features of people, actions, and institutions make them interpersonally justifiable, with Earthlings holding consequentialist views and Moral Twin Earthlings holding de-ontological views.[33] Moral realism and the theory of direct reference, then, are compatible, and there is no reason to see a tension between ethical naturalism and moral realism.

Moreover, this picture of the role of referential intentions within the theory of direct reference also helps us answer worries about whether the theory of direct reference implies the obsolescence of moral reasoning. If it is part of the referential intentions of moral appraisers to use moral language to pick out the properties—whatever they are—of people, ac-tions, and institutions that make them interpersonally justifiable, then the process of ascertaining the meaning or reference of moral terms just *is* an inquiry into the properties of people, actions, and institutions that make them interpersonally justifiable. This inquiry can only be conducted by substantive moral reasoning.

Notice that this appeal to the role of referential intentions within the theory of direct reference in order to defend a semantics for moral realism makes no use of the causal regulation thesis, which Boyd embraces and Timmons and Horgan associate with ethical naturalism. On the present view, reference is fixed by an original intention to adopt the moral point of view—that is, to use moral language to pick out those properties, whatever they are, that make objects of assessment interpersonally justifiable—not by the properties that regulate, perhaps only implicitly and counterfactually, speakers' use of moral terms. Whereas the account of reference in terms of causal regulation must allow that the moral language of different speakers might be regulated by—and so refer to—different properties, the account of direct reference in terms of referential intentions does not imply that there is multiple reference whenever lan-guage use is regulated by different properties. This brings out a way in which an account of reference in terms of causal regulation cannot dis-tinguish between a speaker's beliefs and her subject matter. Under the causal regulation thesis, the properties that regulate, perhaps only dia-lectically, a speaker's use of moral terms just reflect the moral beliefs she does hold or perhaps would hold in dialectical equilibrium; this implies that the meaning and reference of a speaker's terms is fixed, perhaps in a very complicated way, by her beliefs. Hence, on this account, differences in belief of the right sort between speakers do imply that they are talking about different things. Of course, the emergence and appeal of direct

---

[33] Not surprisingly, this response to the relativist worry shares structural features with familiar responses to other relativist worries, in particular, the reply to relativist worries about moral disagreement that attempts to explain moral disagreement by finding shared or common principles that are applied in different empirical conditions, or at least in conjunc-tion with different empirical beliefs.

reference was due in significant part to its promise to distinguish between differences in belief and differences in subject matter and to explain how there could be genuine disagreement of belief. Furthermore, it is the commitment to fallibilism about our pretheoretical and reflective beliefs—characteristic of realism—that explains why this promise of direct reference is especially appealing to realists. However, the promise of direct reference, especially for the realist, is better realized by understanding reference in terms of referential intentions rather than in terms of causal regulation.[34]

VIII. Concluding Remarks

In conclusion, it may be worth noting that this account of moral semantics in terms of referential intentions to adopt the point of view of interpersonal justification is fiercely nonreductionist. To characterize the moral point of view in terms of interpersonal justification is to characterize it in ineliminably normative terms. This makes it a substantive question, which I have not addressed here, whether moral terms do refer and, if so, which properties they pick out. Thus, I have not argued directly on behalf of moral realism or ethical naturalism in this essay. In particular, I have not argued that there is a set of properties of people, actions, and institutions (presumably, in some sense, unique) in virtue of which characters, actions, and institutions are interpersonally justifiable, much less that those properties are natural properties. Those issues should not be settled by adopting a theory of reference. Rather, my primary aims have been to respond to doubts about the compatibility of moral realism and direct reference, and to make moral semantics safe for moral realism. The moral realist is free to use the theory of direct reference to defend ethical naturalism against the OQA.

Philosophy, University of California, San Diego

---

[34] If so, Boyd's semantic commitments turn out not to be robustly realistic.

INCOMPLETE ROUTES TO MORAL OBJECTIVITY: FOUR VARIANTS OF NATURALISM*

By David Sidorsky

I. Introduction

The search for moral objectivity has been constant throughout the history of philosophy, although interpretations of the nature and scope of objectivity have varied. One aim of the pursuit of moral objectivity has been the demonstration of what may be termed its *epistemological thesis*, that is, the claim that the truth of assertions of the goodness or rightness of moral acts is as legitimate, reliable, or valid as the truth of assertions involving other forms of human knowledge, such as common sense, practical expertise, science, or mathematics.[1] Another aim of the quest for moral objectivity may be termed its *pragmatic formulation*; this refers to the development of a method or procedure that will mediate among conflicting moral views in order to realize a convergence or justified agreement about warranted or true moral conclusions. In the ethical theories of Aristotle, David Hume, and John Dewey, theories that represent three of the four variants of *ethical naturalism* (defined below) that are surveyed in this essay, the epistemological thesis and the pragmatic formulation are integrated or combined. The distinction between these two elements is significant for the present essay, however, since I want to show that linguistic naturalism, the fourth variant I shall examine, has provided a demonstration of the epistemological thesis about moral knowledge, even if the pragmatic formulation has not been successfully realized.

There is a significant difference between the ways in which the search for moral objectivity has been carried out in the ancient and modern periods. In the ancient period, the degree of confidence ascribed to beliefs

---

* This is the concluding essay of a two-part series on moral objectivity. The first essay, "Incomplete Routes to Moral Objectivity: Rationalism and Pluralism," is scheduled for publication in the forthcoming volume of *The International Yearbook of Hermeneutics*, published for the Italian Academy.

[1] This formulation may bypass, but need not exclude, an interpretation of the ontological aspects of moral objectivity. Despite its origins in Platonic philosophy, moral objectivity can be interpreted so that it does not require an ontological realism, in the sense that the goodness or rightness of moral acts represents or embodies features of the universe that exist antecedent to or independent of human life on the planet. Yet it would be consistent with the epistemological thesis to hold that the rightness of an action is a real feature of the world, constituted by the existence of the reasons that justify the action. This is analogous, for example, to the claim that Gilbert Ryle did not deny the reality of mind in *The Concept of Mind* (London: Hutchinson, 1949) when he insisted that the Cartesian *res cogitans* had no separate existence and that all mental terms could be interpreted as modifications of human behavior.

in objective morality was at least as great as that ascribed to the results of investigations in astronomy, physics, or biology. Value-neutrality was not considered to be a necessary feature of scientific inquiry. In the classical thought of Plato and Aristotle, for example, proofs of the objective truth of moral claims were often continuous with or intrinsic parts of demonstrations in the mathematical, astronomical, physical, or biological sciences.

In the early modern period after the scientific achievements of the seventeenth century, the regions of paradigmatic confidence changed. As a result, the ideal of moral objectivity was viewed, in many cases, as with Hobbes and Spinoza, as the extension and projection of the truth of a value-neutral physics and geometry into the field of moral inquiry. Whether in the classical or modern world, however, the route to moral objectivity required that moral judgments be established as one of the domains of human knowledge.

Throughout the history of ethical inquiry, the diversity of ethical practices, relative to time and place, has represented a challenge to moral objectivity. As a philosophical thesis, moral relativism has received recurrent refutations ever since the confrontation between Socrates and the Sophists. Yet the recognition of the diversity of moral practices in different societies or different historical periods nevertheless remained a perennial motive for doubts about universal moral truths and for skepticism about the possibility of finding a procedure for determining valid norms in contexts of cultural conflict.

Ironically, Western religious traditions were skeptical of the rational derivation of moral norms even as they asserted moral obligations to be absolute. The logical demonstration that moral structures and fundamental moral imperatives are deducible from empirical features of the world was considered to be beyond the capacity of human reason. Such a philosophical ambition could only be based, in the phrase of Matthew Arnold, upon a perspective that placed excessive confidence in the possibilities of "Sweetness and Light" and avoided confronting the harsh realities of human culture. Contrary to such perspectives, Western religious traditions required that moral obligations be grounded in a nonrational, binding faith commitment to a covenant with a deity whose voice commanded or whose example defined moral behavior.

Skepticism about the possibility of rational demonstration of ethics has also coexisted with a belief in moral objectivity in the recurring forms of intuitionism. In ethics, intuitionism is the claim that fundamental moral assertions do not require or admit of rational demonstration but are universally true and objectively known. Accordingly, to the intuitionist, the redundancy of moral argument indicates the fruitlessness of any procedure of justification where the relevant primary intuition is lacking.

Against these enduring relativist and skeptical challenges, the philosophical tradition in ethical theory has developed a variety of routes to moral objectivity. These have ranged from Immanuel Kant's metaphysical derivation of a universalist and monistic ethics to Isaiah Berlin's argument that the existence of plural conceptual frameworks is compatible with moral objectivity. In its many variants throughout the history of philosophy, ethical naturalism has also provided a significant route to moral objectivity. Central to the thesis of ethical naturalism is the demonstration of a connection between statements of value and statements of fact. According to the ethical naturalist, the objective truth of a value judgment is assertable in light of the discovery of the truth of the factual claims to which it is connected.

The ways in which the program of ethical naturalism has been carried out can be differentiated. They include, in early Greek ethics, the grounding of the moral conventions of a society in *physis*, that is, in the nature of the universe and of human nature. A climactic result of this tradition is the systematic "biological" naturalism of Aristotelian ethics. On an interpretation of Hume that places him in the context of the Enlightenment, his ethical theory provides a second variant of ethical naturalism. Hume's derivation of a form of moral objectivity is based upon his location of the "original" of morals in the shared sentiments of universal human nature. A third, Deweyan version of ethical naturalism conceived of itself as an extension of Hume's theory of ethics. The distinctive characteristic of this pragmatic ethical naturalism is its attempt to interpret moral judgments as empirical hypotheses that can be confirmed in a manner analogous to the methodology of scientific verification.

In the twentieth century, the great tradition of ethical naturalism was confronted by the nonnaturalism formulated in various ways within major philosophical movements; figures such as G. E. Moore, Rudolph Carnap, A. J. Ayer, Martin Heidegger, and Jean-Paul Sartre were instrumental in the elaboration of nonnaturalism. The development of a fourth, linguistic ethical naturalism was a minimalist resurrection of the naturalist tradition in the face of the nonnaturalist challenge. Central to this form of ethical naturalism is its treatment of moral terms as being related intrinsically to relevant reasons, which are characteristically factual in their statement-type.

According to linguistic naturalism, the justification of particular moral claims can be carried out by an appeal to the truth of the relevant reasons that are constitutive of moral assertions. The thesis that moral assertions involve a reference to reasons is derived from an analysis of moral discourse, including the presuppositions or *significance conditions* of such discourse. Of special interest is linguistic naturalism's application in the defense of theories of natural rights. Seventeenth-century theories of natural rights represented a form of ethical naturalism, since they sought to derive moral rights from the hypothesized existence of a state of nature. A contemporary reformulation of this route to moral objectivity, such as that proposed by H. L. A. Hart, takes the linguistic turn and justifies "natural rights" by referring to the presuppositions of the use of rights-discourse.[2] When considered as a linguistic naturalist formulation, the claim for the existence of a natural right is connected with the role of reasons in the moral vocabulary.

The present examination of the use of the thesis of ethical naturalism as a route to ethical objectivity does not aim to provide a detailed historical reconstruction or specific interpretation of the views held by any particular figure in the history of philosophy. Rather, the aim is to exhibit the pattern of argument identified as a form of ethical naturalism that leads toward moral objectivity. In the retracing of the argument, the special focus of this essay is upon discovering its limits or incompleteness as a route to moral objectivity.

II. ARISTOTELIAN NATURALISM

For an Aristotelian, the nature of the human animal as a nutritive, reproductive, locomotive, sensing, appetitive, and rational being provides objective moral norms for the human species. The discovery of the norms, excellences, or virtues of the human species is, in principle, no different from the biological investigation of the norms and excellences of other species of plants and animals. If there is an objective identification of the functions that are constitutive of being human, then it follows that there can be objective evaluation of the degree of excellence that individuals achieve in the fulfillment of these functions. Accordingly, objective knowledge of the moral virtues or excellences of the human species, such as courage or prudence, is attainable.

This thesis has been contested on "foundational" grounds in two ways. First, Moore and other nonnaturalists challenged the possibility of the derivation of moral conclusions from premises that are descriptive facts, such as, in the Aristotelian case, the potentialities of human nature. For Moore, the demonstration that a human being has actualized his potentialities *qua* human leaves open the question of whether such an actualization is good or not. Consequently, the claim that objective knowledge of moral virtues has been demonstrated by Aristotelian naturalism is subject to the criticism that this demonstration conceals a fallacy.

In a second challenge to Aristotelian naturalism, Heidegger denied the Aristotelian assumption that a fixed and essential human nature is similar to the fixed and essential nature of other species with reference to goals, aims, or ends of life. In his view, the existential character of being human leads to the distinction between an essential nature, with its given ends and functional goals, and the existentially free person, who chooses his own commitments and objects of concern. Consequently, for Heidegger, the Aristotelian derivation of objective knowledge about human excel-

---

[2] H. L. A. Hart, "Are There Any Natural Rights?" *Philosophical Review* 64, no. 2 (1955): 175.

lences erroneously avoids the recognition of the necessarily arbitrary character of moral choice.

Bracketing Moorean nonnaturalism and Heideggerian existentialism for subsequent discussion, it is relevant to note that the Aristotelian confidence in the objective knowledge of human moral excellences is conjoined with the aim of setting standards for moral practices. Aristotle's epistemological thesis that morality admits of objective knowledge leads directly to his pragmatic formulation detailing the method for applying this knowledge in practice. This method involves distinguishing between behavioral dispositions that constitute a virtue when applied to specific contexts of action and those dispositions that are in some way excessive or defective. The Aristotelian approach to resolving a conflict over the drawing of such lines in the identification of moral excellences can be interpreted as a search for the convergence of the opinion of "moral connoisseurs." Aristotle appeals to the judgment of men of practical reason (*phronêsis*) who could determine in some objective fashion what behavior should be characterized as an excellent fulfillment of human function. There is a body of experiential evidence throughout human history and culture that persons of practical reason are capable, for example, of deciding which actions ought to be considered courageous, as distinct from cowardly or foolhardy, and which ought to be considered courteous, as opposed to rude or condescending.

Both skeptics and relativists can object to Aristotelian naturalism on the ground that the convergence of the judgments of connoisseurs, particularly in areas such as morality, is not equivalent to a process of objective verification of hypotheses by a universal community of inquiry. For the skeptical critic, the specter of trendiness is perennial in human culture. There is no guarantee that convergence represents the discovery of a universal moral norm rather than the emergence and dominance of a trend that reflects custom, fashion, style, or taste.

The Aristotelian naturalist may wish to resist the skeptic's argument by stressing the significance that the possibility of convergence holds for objectivity; the naturalist might, for example, note the role that convergence plays with respect to judgments in fields as diverse as the evaluation of wine, the setting of standards of design in crafts, and the critical appraisal of great works of art and literature. In these fields, where convergence takes place over historical periods and across lines of class or culture, the naturalist may argue that the judgments resulting from the convergence are objective. The cultural relativist, however, can claim that without the demonstration of an actual physiological basis for these judgments, such convergence still includes an element of relativity to cultural conventions, and hence is not simply rooted in universal human norms.

Furthermore, the relativist may point to the evidence of continued divergence by men of practical reason on any number of normative questions. Where there is a convergence of the community toward some norm, the relativist can argue that such convergence characteristically takes place within the closed circle of a particular society and therefore exhibits not the objectivity of human norms, but rather the hypostatization of parochial and provincial practices as universal. Despite the Aristotelian attempt to ground moral virtues by reference to the biological facts of human nature, a retrospective reflection upon the virtues that Aristotelian ethics justified reveals that at least some of the putatively universal norms generated by that ethical view represent the values of the Greek city-state of Aristotle's time. If ethical naturalism is to provide a route to moral objectivity, it must be demonstrated that the normative moral claims ethical naturalism generates are free of this kind of cultural bias.

A significant criticism of the Aristotelian argument is that it involves circularity. The criteria for selection of the moral connoisseur are related to the outcome of the process by which moral judgments converge. Aristotelian persons of practical reason are precisely the constituency that would converge toward viewing prudence and courage as virtues. Characters like Falstaff, Iago, the picaresque hero of Donleavy's *The Ginger Man,* and the resentful Dostoyevskian "underground man"—characters whose rankings of moral claims might converge toward cowardice, imprudence, or malice—would be excluded from being moral connoisseurs. The Aristotelian argument requires a demonstration that the standards that would be arrived at by these kinds of persons would either move toward the norms determined by men of *phronêsis* or deteriorate into nonstandards that would themselves exhibit internal incoherence or represent a departure from empirical characteristics of human nature.

This criticism of Aristotelian naturalism reflects a general problem with setting objective moral standards, for it parallels a familiar argument that has been directed against rationalism in Kantian or Rawlsian ethical theory. According to this argument, the Rawlsian priority of the values of liberty and equality for human society is justified by the consensus or convergence of reasonable persons. Yet otherwise reasonable persons such as Hobbes or Plato, both of whom would choose the value of order over liberty and the value of hierarchy over equality, could be judged under the Rawlsian account to be unreasonable because of these choices. While Rawls's commitment to pluralism may avoid the charge of circularity, the Rawlsian appeal to the justification of values by a consensus of reasonable persons is flawed if the criterion for being a reasonable person involves a circular reference to these values.

The ideal of objectivity in standards of appraisal seems to be approached when there is cross-cultural and transhistorical convergence of opinion on these standards by persons who are recognized as having achieved mastery of the relevant subject matter. Even if the Aristotelian naturalist could avoid this general problem by providing a noncircular method of convergent agreement on moral virtues, however, there remains a gap between the identification of these virtues and the application of moral norms in practical situations. The challenge to moral objectivity in contexts of practice is not met when a virtue like courage or prudence is validated; rather, what is required is some criterion for the application of these virtues to specific situations. Kant asserted one formulation of this difficulty at the outset of the *Groundwork of the Metaphysics of Morals*, where he recognized that the virtue of courage could be harmful in its application in particular social contexts. The extraordinary courage of German soldiers in defending the approaches to Nazi Germany in the winter of 1944 is a recent historical illustration of the Kantian view of the limitation of an Aristotelian ethics of virtue. The moral imperative for those soldiers was in conflict with their pursuit of virtues like courage and loyalty. Cowardice and desertion would have been preferable moral responses for the fulfillment of their humanity in such circumstances. One response to this Kantian line of criticism is to point to the multiplicity of casuistic reasoning that has been employed in the Aristotelian tradition to bridge the gap between the cardinal moral virtues and the practical application of ethical imperatives. These casuistries, however, tend to demonstrate the potentiality for disagreement on practical moral decisions that exists when there is no consensus about other values or no shared interpretations of the moral situation.

The Aristotelian route to moral objectivity is naturalist because it derives objective norms for human behavior from the empirical properties of human nature. Furthermore, Aristotle argues that empirical facts about human rationality can provide a sufficient basis for the application of moral knowledge in social contexts. These two features of Aristotelian naturalism have remained a continuous element in the historical development of other variants of ethical naturalism. Yet from the perspective of the history of philosophy, the Aristotelian route to moral objectivity appears to be incomplete, for the legitimacy of any derivation of values from empirical facts has been contested. In addition, the objectivity of Aristotelian judgments of value on practical issues has been challenged by the pluralist recognition of the role of historical culture in the shaping of these judgments. In some measure, subsequent variants of naturalism can be interpreted as ways of resolving the issues that mark these problems with the Aristotelian route to moral objectivity.

III. HUMEAN NATURALISM

The Humean formulation of an ethical naturalist thesis would appear to be immune from the criticism that it derives moral conclusions from premises that contain only descriptive facts about human nature, a criticism later identified by Moore as "the naturalistic fallacy." This immunity, it has been claimed, should lead to the categorization of Hume's ethical theory as nonnaturalist, especially since Hume argued explicitly that the "original" of virtue and vice could not be derived from matters of fact. The development of the competing interpretations of Hume's moral theory is a topic that goes beyond the scope of this essay. In this context, the concern is the delineation of Hume's argument as a possible route to moral objectivity. Furthermore, the focus is placed upon the difficulties that mark the incompleteness of the Humean argument as a route to moral objectivity.

Hume can be interpreted as an ethical naturalist in the sense that he traces the distinction between vice and virtue back to the capacity and disposition of individual human nature to express and assert sentiments of approval or disapproval when its desires, interests, and utilities are, respectively, furthered or impeded. The domain for the assertion of moral sentiment is extended beyond the individual egoist by the existence within human nature of a capacity for sympathy. Since individual human beings, during the inevitable socialization of their human nature, come to feel sympathy for various other persons, the benefits or harms that are done to these persons also give rise to expressions of approval or disapproval, respectively.

In this Humean account of how the origin of the distinction between vice and virtue lies in the human passions, logical positivists such as A. J. Ayer saw a skepticism of the possibility of moral universalism and moral objectivity, a skepticism that foreshadowed the logical positivists' own ethical theory. Positivist theory can be characterized as *noncognitivist* because it denies that moral statements can be either true or false, and as *emotivist* because it interprets moral statements as expressions of emotive attitude. While Hume's argument provides a basis for its extension in the direction of nonnaturalism and logical positivism, such interpretations do not adequately reflect the ways in which Hume, as a figure of the European Enlightenment, appeals to universal human nature as a source of moral sentiment.

Hume's methodology exhibits a constant pattern in several areas of philosophical analysis, in that it consistently combines reductive skepticism with a commonsense "conservatizing" realism. Thus, Hume's various skeptical critiques—of the existence of material objects and of the mind, of the nature of causality, and of the status of moral judgments—are conjoined with a recognition of the enduring features of their reality. After Hume has reduced the "material object" to a class of impressions, he is prepared to accept the class of possible impressions of a counterfactual hypothetical observer; this lets Hume allow for the continuity and objective characteristics of material things. Similarly, after Hume has reduced "personal identity" to a collection of memories, he is prepared to infer the hypothetical extrapolation and interpolation of memories in order to preserve the continuity of personal identity.

In the case of ethics, Hume begins by skeptically reducing moral assertions, arguing that they are merely the sentiments of approbation extended by the empirical capacity of sympathy. Significantly, however,

Hume proceeds to show that an actual moral assertion could only come from an impartial or disinterested hypothetical observer who, knowing all the relevant facts, feels a sentiment of approbation "upon the general view or survey" of the moral situation. Hume concludes that moral judgments based upon subjective impressions or sentiments can be transformed into objective judgments when they are not limited to individuals' desires, special interests, or idiosyncratic emotional tendencies, but instead represent what an enlightened hypothetical human nature would feel or approve upon the general survey.

With reference to developing a method for arriving at objective moral judgments, the hypothesis of an impartial observer expressing approbation after a general survey operates in Humean naturalism in a manner similar to the way in which the convergence of persons of practical judgment functions in Aristotelian naturalism. The relativist challenges faced by each sort of naturalism are also analogous. The outcome of a general survey of human approbations does not meet the criterion of objectivity if the requirements for this criterion are set by comparison with the empirical ability of a community of inquiry to confirm a scientific hypothesis, or on an analogy with the universality of practical agreement with respect to ordinary commonplace observations about the familiar objects of daily experience.

A moral claim that is based upon a general survey by a person with no specific vested interest in the outcome may still reflect a particular perspective or bias in framing the issue and may represent a rationalization of other nonneutral interests. The difficulty of characterizing Humean moral assertions as satisfying the requirement for objectivity and universality has been recognized in the analysis of the ambiguity of the Humean general survey. C. D. Broad, for example, interpreted the general survey as being a kind of poll of the opinions of the public, and concluded that Hume consequently failed to satisfy the objectivity and universality requirements.[3] A survey of human preferences might lead to a consensus of human sentiment, but this would fall short of representing moral objectivity. A majoritarian sentiment for a political institution (one obvious example being the acceptance of the practice of slavery in the ancient world) is not sufficient ground for its justification. A Humean moralist can defend Hume's theory by arguing that Broad has misunderstood Hume's conception of the general survey. If one understands the general survey to reflect a viewpoint in which one is free from special interests, then one could coherently argue that a hypothetical observer adopting the general survey would arrive at a disapprobation of the institution of slavery even in a society in which slavery was acceptable to the majority.

---

[3] C. D. Broad, *Five Types of Ethical Theory* (1930; reprint, London: Routledge and Kegan Paul, 1971).

In practical contexts, then, the more relevant analogy for Humean naturalism is not the convergence of a moral opinion poll, but rather the concept of "impartial arbitration." In a characteristic arbitration procedure, for example, the two interested parties opposing each other in a given dispute are each represented by a separate arbitrator. If both arbitrators select a third person whose impartiality each of them trusts, the resulting decision may be considered an approximation of the Humean idea of the sentiment of a hypothetically impartial observer upon the general survey. As a result, the Humean moralist would argue, the decision gains a certain measure of objectivity.

Yet even this approximation indicates how difficult it is to realize universality and objectivity under the Humean model. Impartial arbitration, whatever its significant practical value in dispute resolution, does not satisfy the criterion for objectivity indicated above, that is, it does not provide the sort of corrigible confirmation that is present in scientific inquiry or the kind of consensus that is uncontested in the recognized commonplaces of longstanding observation and human practice. As a matter of empirical experience, impartial arbitrators at times may hold a structured perception or interpretation of the issues relevant to the given dispute, a perception or interpretation that remains immune from revision on the basis of the evidence unearthed during the process of decision-making. In such cases, the requirement of neutrality has not been met by the procedures of impartial arbitration. Moreover, as a resolver of a practical dispute, the function of an arbitrator may become identified with that of a mediator between the parties in conflict. In such cases, the arbitrator-as-mediator arrives at a decision that reflects the relative power positions of the contending parties rather than satisfying the Humean criterion of impartiality that reflects the general survey.

Even if it is conceded that the procedures of impartial arbitration do demonstrate an approximation of the Humean model, examples of political conflict show the difficulty in applying the concept of the approbation felt by a disinterested party "upon the general view or survey." The conflict over Kosovo in the late 1990s offers a good example of the strengths and weaknesses of the application of the Humean criterion for moral objectivity. After examining the situation in Kosovo, the great majority of members of the United Nations, almost all of whom had no national or special interest in the region, arrived at a consensus regarding the governing interpretation of the situation. This interpretation, based on manifestly verifiable evidence, reflected the view that great numbers of innocent Kosovar residents were being chased from their homes by the Yugoslav army. These circumstances gave rise to a sentiment of disapprobation toward the Yugoslav activity, which was characterized as "ethnic cleansing"; this eventually led to an intervention against the Yugoslav army by the forces of NATO.

The support for this action, however, was not unanimous and may not constitute the results of a Humean general survey. Apart from Yugoslavia and its historical ally, Russia—states whose opposition to NATO's action may have represented their national interests—the People's Republic of China and a number of other disinterested parties also sided against the NATO intervention. This opposition's interpretation of the situation, which was also based on verifiable evidence, differed crucially from the interpretation held by the passive majority of the UN. Under the opposition interpretation, NATO, a military alliance that had been founded solely for defensive purposes to resist aggression from a potentially hostile sovereign state, was carrying out an armed incursion against the territory of another sovereign state. That sovereign state, Yugoslavia, was not a threat to NATO and had committed no act of international aggression, but rather was responding to a secessionist insurrection led by the Kosovo Liberation Army within Yugoslavia's historical and internationally recognized boundaries. The governing judgment that emerged from this opposing interpretation was that such acts of intervention against sovereign states should, under an impartial general survey, meet with a universal sentiment of disapprobation.[4]

Both of these conflicting interpretations provide a measure of support for the Humean model of moral objectivity, for both sides agree that, ceteris paribus, the spectacle of an army chasing residents from their homes and the spectacle of a military force bombing the territory of a nonbelligerent sovereign state should both give rise to a sentiment of disapprobation in an impartial spectator. The truth of the moral judgments regarding the specified actions, if those actions are considered in isolation, is not inferior to the truth of many other conclusions of reliable knowledge that are arrived at by a survey of the relevant evidence by an impartial community of inquiry. To this degree, the epistemological thesis of moral objectivity obtains under the Humean model.

Yet real-world actions are not isolated; rather, they occur in a historical context. This context characteristically gives rise to competing interpretations of the relevant circumstances; these contrasting interpretations

---

[4] This discussion of the Kosovo situation has been developed to illustrate various aspects of the Humean method of arriving at moral agreement. In actual historical situations, there are many disputed ancillary issues that are relevant in the process of decision-making. For example, in the Kosovo situation, the Yugoslav government had agreed to allow unarmed observers from the Organization for Security and Cooperation in Europe (OSCE) to monitor human rights violations in the territory. These observers did not succeed in preventing small-scale outbreaks of violence, but did represent a bar to large-scale warfare or ethnic cleansing. The conflict-resolution option these observers represented was eliminated in order to pursue a more comprehensive solution to the Yugoslav conflict. The OSCE observers were withdrawn in order to make possible the bombing of Yugoslavia. The U.S. secretary of state had apparently assumed that this bombing would achieve its intended goal within a few days and that a more robust force of observers would then be reintroduced. In fact, it did achieve its goal, but only after a long period of armed activity and the flight of half a million people. To arrive at a moral evaluation of decisions made in a situation like this, a hypothetical impartial observer would have to reconstruct the complexities of the situation at particular moments in time; the resultant evaluation would probably contain equivocal elements.

generate different governing moral principles. Consequently, there are usually unresolved differences in the moral evaluations of concrete historical actions. If a route to moral objectivity must meet the pragmatic requirement that it provide a method for resolving such differences in moral evaluation, then the Humean route to moral objectivity is incomplete.

In some accounts of Hume's ethical theory, as previously noted, his work is considered to be a precursor of the emotivist and noncognitivist interpretation of moral judgments. Some historians of analytical philosophy, such as J. O. Urmson, have suggested that Hume's position is a form of ethical emotivism, with the distinction that Hume's theory has its basis in his philosophical interpretation of human nature, while the emotivism of the logical positivists has its basis in the analysis of the language of moral statements.[5]

The contrary interpretation of Hume as a proponent of the thesis of moral objectivity is evidenced dramatically in his discussion of the analogy between moral predication and the predication of the colors of objects. For Hume, colors are secondary qualities of an object. Thus, they are "subjective" in the sense that they depend upon the perceptions of the experiential world by a subject (i.e., an observer). This form of *subjectivism* is compatible with human competence in asserting true statements of color predication regarding the objects of the world. Moreover, where there is color-blindness or distortion of color, there is sufficient knowledge to explain these phenomena as defects or departures from the norms of standard color observation for the species. Consequently, the "subjectivity" of secondary qualities such as colors is no bar to satisfying the epistemological criterion of objectivity with respect to color predicates: knowledge of the colors of objects is not inferior to other kinds of reliable knowledge.

Accordingly, Hume's argument that moral qualities are subjective or similar to secondary qualities, in that they presuppose the interaction of human agents with their experiencing of the world, satisfies a thesis of moral objectivity. The explication of moral objectivity in epistemological or pragmatic terms does not require that the ontological status of moral predicates be that of primary qualities that exist independently of human agency or human interaction. It is an objectivist consummation, devoutly to be wished for, that the perception of the wrongness of theft or murder would generate as well-founded and universal an agreement cross-culturally as do perceptions of color. Those philosophers, such as George Santayana and C. I. Lewis, among others, who have made use of the vocabulary of "qualities" in their arguments for moral objectivity have not aspired to a standard in which the moral properties of an object are as demonstrable as secondary qualities, such as color. Their objectivist claim has been that the moral properties can be considered to inhere in objects

[5] J. O. Urmson, *Philosophical Analysis: Its Development Between the Two World Wars* (London: Oxford University Press, 1971).

or states of affairs as a kind of "tertiary" quality that is open to appre-
hension or verification by the human observer or agent. Hume's analogy
between color properties and moral properties is evidence for a view that
the sentiments of universal human nature could arrive at a hypothetical
ideal of objective or impartial moral predication. Yet the difficulties noted
above remain; it is not clear how one can apply the Humean conception
of an impartial observer or a universal human nature to the resolution of
specific moral controversies.

Both utilitarians and pragmatists have contended that they can extend
Hume's method of empirical analysis of human nature into ways of arriving at objective decision-making between competing moral hypotheses. By focusing on the twin motives of pleasure and pain, the utilitarians
pressed Hume's reductionist search for the origin of morals even further
than Humean sentiment did. They escalated his standard of objectivity
beyond that of an impartial observer on the general survey to that of a
quantifiable calculus of the balance of pleasures and pains among all
members of the community. Among the American pragmatists, Dewey
cited the continuity between his own arguments for moral objectivity and
Hume's doctrines.[6] From this perspective, the Humean account of an
objective knowledge of the moral sentiments of universal human nature
leads toward a Deweyan formulation of a generalized "scientific method"
verifying moral judgments about human conduct.

IV. DEWEYAN NATURALISM

The Deweyan variant of ethical naturalism is directly related to the
view that there exists a generalized scientific method that is derivable
from an understanding of the practices of the empirical sciences. Dewey
places himself within the tradition of ethical naturalism, exemplified by
Spinoza and Bentham, in which moral truths can be realized through
scientific method. Dewey insists, however, that his scientific methodology
is genuinely empirical, in contrast to those of his predecessors.

Dewey's empiricist interpretation of scientific method is based upon
the Peircean analysis of the nature of scientific inquiry. For C. S. Peirce, a
community of scientific inquirers—no matter how diverse their cultural
starting points, their initial selections of facts, or even their bents of
mind—is fated to converge upon the true statements about the subject
matter of their inquiry. The objectivity of these true statements does not
derive from a demonstration of the real properties of the antecedent
objects of the world. Rather, the real properties of the world are discovered because they are what will be asserted to exist in the true statements
toward which a community of inquiry converges; this is analogous to the

⁶ John Dewey, "Introduction," in Dewey, *Human Nature and Conduct* (New York: Modern
Library, 1957), 3–13.

Quinian ontology in which to be is to be the value of a variable. For Peirce, the ground for this convergence is the adoption by the community of inquiry of the scientific method. This method requires the community of inquiry to admit all verifiable hypotheses and decide among them by appealing to their consequences in observation and experiment. This methodology guarantees, according to Peirce, that however fallible the results of scientific inquiry are at any particular time, they are both corrigible and progressive. Accordingly, the community of inquiry can have confidence that it is embarked on a process that leads (albeit asymptotically) to true conclusions regarding the objective properties of the world.

In American pragmatism, Peircean scientific method was considered to be applicable to any field of inquiry, and not restricted to the natural or positive sciences. Dewey argued that the Peircean model of scientific method could be applied to inquiries into values or ethics. The adoption of this procedure for ethics presupposes ethical naturalism, in the sense that judgments of value must be related to judgments of fact. This is because the process of decision-making between competing moral hypotheses that is dictated by the Peircean model requires the confirmation or refutation of those hypotheses through appeals to predicted factual consequences.

Dewey's argument for ethical naturalism crucially involves his rejection of any naturalistic fallacy in the definition or "construction" of good.[7] Thus, Dewey argues that there is no slippage between fact and value terms in the Millian thesis (sometimes cited as "Mill's howler") that just as the ultimate proof that something is visible is that it is seen and that something is audible is that it is heard, so the ultimate proof that something is desirable is that it is desired.[8] A veritable host of critics of Mill and Dewey have noted that "desirable" differs from "visible" or "audible" in ordinary language because the criterion for desirability is not only that something *can* be desired, as in the case of "visible" and "audible," but that it *ought* to be desired.

The Deweyan response to such criticism is to consider the class of dispositional terms, particularly those that he singles out as "ble" predicates. Thus, to say that a play is "enjoyable" or that a person is "likeable" can suggest more than the idea that the play could be enjoyed or that the person could be liked. In these cases, as in the case of "desirable," Dewey argues that there is a prescriptive or commendatory component in the "ble" term. Thus, Dewey seeks to establish the continuity between the "is" statement as factual and the "ought" statement as prescriptive. If I recommend a play as enjoyable, I am asserting that it would be enjoyed by persons of a certain quality of perception or taste. Indeed, even the cases of audibility or visibility can receive a similar analysis. The playing

---

[7] John Dewey, "The Construction of Good," in Dewey, *The Quest for Certainty: A Study of the Relation of Knowledge and Action* (London: G. Allen and Unwin Ltd., 1930), 242–72.

[8] This thesis is presented in John Stuart Mill, "Of What Sort of Proof the Principle of Utility is Susceptible," chap. 4 of Mill, *Utilitarianism* (New York: Liberal Arts Press, 1948), 37–44.

of a violinist cannot be faulted as inaudible if the listeners have defective hearing or if his playing is drowned out by a series of unexpected noises, even though he is not or cannot be heard in those circumstances. Audibility implies that the playing could be heard by a community of normal listeners under some set of normal environing conditions. Generalizing, Dewey would claim that to say that an act is desirable, enjoyable, or likeable means that it would be desired, enjoyed, or liked by persons who understood their desires, joys, or likes and knew the consequences of the relevant act. Accordingly, this type of assertion bears within it both a factual or predictive component and a prescriptive or commendatory component. Deweyan ethical naturalism concludes from this analysis that moral statements asserting that some action is "good" are to be understood as hypotheses claiming that this action would be desired over the long run by persons who understood the nature of their desires and the consequences of the action.

In *Theory of Valuation*, Dewey provides another formulation of his ethical naturalism. This volume was published as part of *The International Encyclopedia of Unified Science*, which represented an authoritative statement of the positions of the logical positivist movement. In the book, Dewey confronts the logical positivists' thesis that ethical statements, as expressions of emotive attitude, are neither true nor false with his own pragmatic formulation that moral statements are cognitive and can be verified as either true or false. For this purpose, Dewey draws the distinction between "prizing" and "appraising." While prizings are subjective and may be expressions of emotive attitude, judgments of appraisal are determined to be true or false by reference to evidence. Thus, in the moral context, an appraisal of an action as good or right involves both the claim that such an action has been prized by human agents and a predictive claim regarding the action's consequences, including its being prized in the future. Statements of appraisal, accordingly, can function as admissible hypotheses to be confirmed or refuted through application of the scientific method. Moral hypotheses that are verified are true—in Dewey's preferred vocabulary for true statements, they are "warrantedly assertible"—in a manner parallel to other probabilistically confirmed hypotheses of the sciences. Consequently, the classification of moral judgments as statements of appraisal represents a naturalistic interpretation of ethics in which moral judgments can be rendered as true or false by reference to statements of fact.

In the Deweyan route to moral objectivity, the epistemological thesis holds that moral knowledge that is arrived at through confirmation of empirical hypotheses about human desires and prizings does not differ essentially from other kinds of knowledge that are attained by the methods of science. Dewey's scientific naturalism also projects a way of satisfying the pragmatic requirement of moral objectivity, that is, a way of developing a procedure for the practical resolution of conflicting moral assertions. Competing moral claims are to be considered as empirical hypotheses. The consequences of these hypotheses are to be evaluated by a community of inquiry committed to the scientific method. Dewey argues that the ideological conflicts of his time could be replaced by an experimental social science that would (as in the Peircean model of science) mediate conflicting opinions by an appeal to consequences.

Deweyan ethical naturalism must confront the difficulties posed by an interpretation of moral judgments as experimental hypotheses of the empirical sciences. Where moral assertions can be presented as proposals for policy or legislation, such as raising the minimum wage or criminalizing hate speech, there appears to be a basis for a formal analogy between such judgments and empirical hypotheses about future consequences. Where moral assertions seem to represent fundamental intuitions of right or wrong, like an imperative against the torture of innocent children or against the hacking off of human limbs, presenting such assertions as if they were merely empirical hypotheses seems forced and misleading. The affirmation or negation of such imperatives does not seem analogous to the confirmation or refutation of the consequences of competing hypotheses about human practice.

For a Deweyan analysis, however, all moral assertions can be represented as empirical hypotheses about future consequences. In the case of moral claims that take the form of policy proposals, justification of these claims depends upon whether there is a realization of their envisaged beneficial results or whether the claims have unanticipated harmful consequences. Furthermore, the judgment of the evaluation of the consequences as beneficial or harmful is itself an empirical hypothesis open to revision and correction in light of the evidence. In the case of seemingly absolute moral intuitions, Deweyans, while accepting these intuitions' status as prima facie moral imperatives, recognize the ways in which such imperatives are embedded and applied in contexts of practice. When prima facie moral imperatives conflict in particular historical circumstances, moral options emerge as competing hypotheses that are tested by examining their consequences. The justification of engaging in warfare, for example, brings with it a necessity to overrule prima facie moral imperatives against the killing of fellow human beings; this can only be justified by an appeal to the consequences of such an overruling for the future of the human condition.

Even if moral judgments were to be interpreted on the model of competing hypotheses about policy options, the Deweyan belief that scientific method can verify or falsify these hypotheses does not appear to have been vindicated, given the historical persistence of many issues of moral disagreement. This persistence of moral disagreement indicates a difficulty with any thesis under which conflicting moral opinions are subject to reversal, correction, or convergence in the light of experimental evidence.

The Deweyan vision is that the future development of the social sciences will provide a basis for determining the objective truth of competing moral claims. The achievements of the social sciences in the twentieth century have fallen short of this projection. In retrospect, Dewey's faith that scientific method can resolve moral disagreement takes on some of the characteristics of the illusory ambitions of "scientism" that were prevalent in different types of philosophy before the Second World War. The logical positivist movement's confidence that it could resolve all philosophical problems by an analysis of the language and methods of science reflects this feature of European and American historical culture. Similarly, the widespread and cross-cultural acceptance of Marxism as the realization of a *science* of history that could predict and guide future social transformation was a phenomenon of this cultural period. In social or cultural terms, this faith in scientism experienced a shock when its adherents became aware of the genocidal actions that took place before and during World War II. These actions showed that there could be a moral regression in societies that were achieving and enshrining scientific progress. This fact, together with the intensity of ideological rivalry after the war, overtook the Deweyan belief in the ability of inquiry in the social sciences to resolve social conflict.

Dewey integrates his pragmatic thesis that competing moral hypotheses can be mediated by a convergent process of scientific inquiry with the epistemological thesis that the conclusions of such a process are objectively true or warrantedly assertable. This linkage between moral objectivity and the method of scientific inquiry was confronted with three different kinds of philosophical criticism. First, even in the 1930s, the heyday of Dewey's philosophical influence, C. L. Stevenson argued that moral disagreement was often a "disagreement-in-attitude."[9] "Disagreement-in-attitude," for Stevenson, was not resolvable by an appeal to factual consequences, because on his account, agents' attitudinal commitments structure their views on the selection and acceptability of the evidential data. The Deweyan response, while disagreeing with many aspects of Stevenson's thesis, concedes the elements of disanalogy between the resolution of moral disagreement and the resolution of a scientific dispute.

Second, the Deweyan conception of scientific inquiry is, as noted above, based upon a Peircean interpretation of a generalized scientific method by which any conceivable factual hypothesis could be probabilistically confirmed or refuted by reference to its experimental consequences. Since statements of value are interpreted as factual hypotheses in Deweyan ethical naturalism, the Peircean methodology becomes applicable. Thomas Kuhn, however, developed a celebrated interpretation of the history of science that challenged the Peircean account. For Kuhn, the process of scientific confirmation through an appeal to predictive consequences op-

---

[9] Stevenson developed various models of ethical disagreement in C. L. Stevenson, *Ethics and Language* (New Haven, CT: Yale University Press, 1940). Some of these corresponded to the Deweyan model, and others represented a "disagreement-in-attitude."

erates under given individual paradigms of science. In contrast, a shift from one paradigm to another does not take place through a similar process of predictive confirmation of consequences, but rather through a pattern that is similar to a "conversion." Accordingly, the model of scientific inquiry that Dewey uses for realizing objective moral justification is vulnerable because of competing interpretations of scientific method generated by research in the history of science.

Third, more narrowly, in the development of the philosophical school of "ordinary language" analysis, the vocabulary of morals was investigated in a way that revealed the unique and special characteristics of different moral terms such as "good," "right," and "obligatory." This analysis was naturalistic in that it connected statements of value or moral predication with the reasons that supported or constituted these claims. The contours of moral discourse, however, are distinctively different from those of the language and procedures of science. Consequently, linguistic naturalism has adopted a different route to moral objectivity than has Deweyan scientific naturalism.

The justification of linguistic naturalism involves the defense of that thesis against the criticisms of ethical naturalism that derive from Stevenson's analysis of disagreement and Kuhn's theory of scientific revolutions. Linguistic naturalism did not emerge historically from an effort to reformulate the Deweyan variant of ethical naturalism, but was instead generated by those who were confronting various phases of nonnaturalist ethical theory.

V. Linguistic Naturalism

A. Moral statements and the truth of reasons

The major claim of linguistic analysis in its interpretation of the moral vocabulary is that moral assertions are to be understood by reference to the reasons that are given or may be provided for their support. This claim of linguistic naturalism, according to which the reasons for the ascription of a moral predicate are constitutive of relevant moral assertions involving that predicate, indicates a path to moral objectivity: if those reasons can be determined to be true or false, then the truth or falsity of the moral assertions can be justified. Linguistic naturalism thus provides a justification for moral objectivity in the epistemological sense — that is, it justifies the claim that moral knowledge is as legitimate as knowledge in other areas of human experience, inquiry, and disputation.

The linguistic naturalist claim that the moral vocabulary exhibits an intrinsic reference to reasons seems straightforwardly derivable from analysis of the ordinary usage of moral terms such as "good." Yet the justification of linguistic naturalism in the twentieth century involved a series of confrontations with nonnaturalist philosophical theories. These theories sought to show that there is an inexpugnable gap between statements of fact or descriptive knowledge and assertions of values or moral knowledge.

The primary point of departure for the exposition of this gap between fact and value was Moore's *Principia Ethica*. As I will discuss below, Moore's analysis reverberated in England both among philosophical exponents of moral intuitionism and the literary and artistic figures of the Bloomsbury circle.

A radically different philosophical approach was the source for a complementary interpretation of ethical nonnaturalism. Logical positivism involved the generalization that cognitive languages were exhaustively comprised of only two forms of language: analytic statements that were true or false by virtue of rules of language, and empirical statements that were true or false by virtue of verification. This classification of all possible languages led to the conclusion that moral language was not cognitive, so that its statements were neither true nor false. Accordingly, logical positivism provided a different basis for the nonnaturalist assertion of a gap between the domain of empirical fact or descriptive statement and the domain of emotive expression or prescriptive injunction.

The nonnaturalist thesis was also implicit in philosophical existentialism. Since moral conclusions represented arbitrary and free choices by human agents, these conclusions could not be directly connected to factual assertions. Without any intention of justifying Moore or logical positivism, existentialist thought shared the nonnaturalistic thesis in morals.

Accordingly, the justification of linguistic naturalism involves the demonstration of its adequacy in the rejection of the nonnaturalist thesis from each of these diverse points of view.

B. Nonnaturalism

While ethical naturalism has received a number of classical formulations in the history of philosophy (the preceding references to Aristotle, Hume, and Dewey represent a partial sample of the list), the contrary thesis of nonnaturalism, despite its several variants, has its *locus classicus* in Moore's *Principia Ethica*. Moore's nonnaturalist views involved the claim that all variants of naturalism commit a "naturalistic fallacy" in their attempts to define "good" by means of natural or descriptive properties.

In the context of the review of routes to moral objectivity, it is significant that Moore did not seek to undermine the objective status of normative ethical statements. Consequently, one route to objectivity posited by those philosophers who accepted the existence of the naturalistic fallacy was to use Moore's thesis that "good" is knowable but indefinable as an argument in favor of moral intuitionism. Perhaps moral intuitionism gained further credibility at that time because its development coincided with the formulation of mathematical intuitionism, a position involving the claim that the unavoidability of belief in primary unprovable intuitions is a prerequisite for mathematical demonstration and truth. Moral intuitionists argued that naturalism in ethics does not do justice to the immediate sense of revulsion, almost instinctive, that is present in the observation of extreme moral atrocities and arbitrary cruelty. In the intuitionists' view, intuitions like this are prerequisites for any further moral assertions. The linguistic naturalist is required to either provide an adequate explanation for this role of intuition in moral experience or develop an effective substitute for that role. This requirement currently appears more urgent, since the contemporary period has been characterized by public awareness and viewing of acts of massive horror.

The Bloomsbury intellectuals of the early twentieth century, a group that included E. M. Forster, Roger Fry, and Lytton Strachey, adopted Moore as their visionary thinker and *Principia Ethica* as their canonic text. After reading *Principia Ethica*, Strachey wrote to Moore, "I think your book has not only wrecked and shattered all writers on Ethics from Aristotle and Christ to Herbert Spencer and Mr. Bradley, it has not only laid the true foundations of Ethics . . . I date from Oct. 1903 the beginning of the Age of Reason." [10] Under the Bloomsbury interpretation of Moore, moral objectivity is realizable in the same manner in which aesthetic objectivity can be achieved. According to the Bloomsbury account of aesthetics, the cultivation of visual sensibility enabled a person to see and appreciate what was objectively to be seen in a modernist painting, and the cultivation of a person's sensitivity to music enabled him to hear and appreciate what was objectively to be listened for in modernist music. This cultivation of sensibility or development of a sensitive taste was not arbitrary or relative to attributes of class or birth. The fact that the majority of people at the time did not appreciate modernist art or music was not considered to be evidence for the relativity of aesthetic judgment or a refutation of the objective value of the work. The Bloomsbury account of morality, derived from the circle's reading of Moore, is analogous to this account of aesthetics: under the Bloomsbury account of morality, it is held that the cultivation of both moral sensibility and sensitivity to human relations would result in more insightful and reliable moral judgments.

As noted above, the philosophical debate that ensued over Moore's nonnaturalism resulted, after a series of confrontations, in the emergence of linguistic naturalism. In this debate, nonnaturalism can be identified as the insistence upon a measure of discontinuity between the moral vocabulary, including such terms as "right" or "good," and the vocabulary of an empirical language. Moore's formulation of nonnaturalism was but one way to argue for the existence of this sort of discontinuity; two other important nonnaturalist alternatives also emerged. The nonnaturalism that

[10] Lytton Strachey to G. E. Moore, reprinted in Michael Holroyd, *Lytton Strachey* (London: Random House, 1994), 89–90.

derived from logical positivism, for example, is similar to Moore's non-naturalism, but also differs from it in important ways. The logical positivists' nonnaturalism stressed the gap between the terms of an empirical language, which are verifiable, and the predicates of moral judgment, which the logical positivists argued are not verifiable but are expressive of emotive attitude. Many logical positivists agreed with A. J. Ayer's argument, representative of the movement's doctrines, that "X is good" is simply a way of saying "Hurrah for X." It is ironic but correct that virtually all of the main figures of the logical positivist movement who went into exile from continental Europe in the 1930s held both the moral belief "Nazism is wrong" and the further philosophical belief that it was not possible to say "'Nazism is wrong' is true." This result occurred, in part, because the logical positivists treated the analysis of ethical terms as a corollary of the more general interpretation of the nature of cognitive languages. Cognitive languages, they posited, are built upon two central pillars, analyticity and verifiability (subsequently referred to by W. V. O. Quine as the "Two Dogmas"). Allegedly being neither analytic nor verifiable, the language of morals was placed in the general class of noncognitive language, alongside metaphysical constructions and theological formulations. In the light of the positivist clarifying vision of the domains of cognitive and noncognitive languages, the specific characteristics of the language of morals were bypassed. Thus, nonnaturalism as the claim of a gulf between moral terms and descriptive terms was supported by an argument from a very different starting point than that of Moorean analysis.

A third support for nonnaturalism is found in the tradition of existentialist philosophy in the 1930s and 1940s. This tradition's critique of naturalism as a connection between facts and values is characteristically directed against an Aristotelian or Spinozistic version of such a connection, in which the good or the end of any being is derivable from the nature or essence of that being. The Heideggerian formulation of the argument that "Man alone exists," for example, represents an explicit counter to an Aristotelian *scala naturae* in which all things—whether mineral, vegetable, capable of sensation, appetitive, or rational—are actualizations of potentiality and have an essence that defines their end or good.[11] Heidegger argues that while there *are* rocks, trees, horses, angels, and God, none of these things *exist*. Only man exists, since only human

---

[11] This review of Heidegger's criticism of Aristotelian ethics focuses on the issue of naturalism versus nonnaturalism. The Heideggerian critique can be construed as involving an ontological dimension. The Aristotelian schema of the actualization of potentialities throughout nature is structured, in Heideggerian terms, by a highest region of Eternal Actuality or Being and a lowest region of Potentiality that is not Non-Being. A Heideggerian would assert that just as Plato did not abandon Pythagoreanism in his idealization of justice as modeled on the harmony of the spheres, so Aristotle never eliminated the traces of Parmenideanism in both the affirmation of the necessary existence of Actuality and the negation of Non-Being or Nothingness. The Parmenidean fragment that Aristotle confirms but Heidegger rejects is "Non-Being cannot be."

beings possess self-consciousness and choose their own ends. This freedom of choice is incompatible, Heidegger argues, with the assumption of an essential human nature. Consequently, there is a discontinuity between the empirical facts of human nature and the values of human existence. As noted in Section II, then, for Heidegger, human existence is radically contingent, making any human choice or commitment unavoidably arbitrary. Accordingly, moral activity is identified with the actions of agents who are engaged in or committed to exercising free choice in the conditions of human existence. This sketch of moral activity provides a contrast to some traditional naturalistic conceptions of human beings under which human beings are viewed as deciding rationally how to fulfill given ends, realize their conative properties, or maximize empirical utilities.

In existentialist ethics, a human action is a moral act if it is an expression of an authentically free choice by a human being. In confronting the difficulties of a morality that would equate the rightness of an act with the authenticity of the agent's choice, some existentialist theorists, such as Jean-Paul Sartre, have recognized additional criteria for the determination of an authentically free choice, and hence for the attribution of a moral property to a human action. Yet these theorists exclude the consequences of the action from its moral evaluation. This interpretation of the moral vocabulary provides a contrast to ethical naturalism. Ethical naturalists consider the empirical properties and consequences of a human action to be relevant aspects of its moral evaluation. The relevant issue is that the existentialists affirm that there is a gap or gulf between the ascription of moral properties to actions and the description of the empirical properties of those actions; ethical naturalists, in contrast, deny this. Despite the general absence of dialogue between Continental existentialism and analytical philosophy, the evolution of linguistic naturalism involves a rejection of existentialist theory with respect to the analysis of ethical language.

Linguistic naturalism thus provides, in an indirect way, a basis for the rejection of the nonnaturalism that is intrinsic to the existentialist account of moral action. It also includes a direct rebuttal of the Moorean thesis of a naturalistic fallacy as well as an explicit refutation of the nonnaturalist ethical theory that has been derived within logical positivism. The naturalistic rejoinders to these positions did not originate in a defense of the various philosophical structures of ethical naturalism from Aristotle to Dewey. Rather, they emerged in the context of the criticism, by logical positivists themselves, of logical positivism's interpretation of the domains of language.

This internal criticism was carried out by Ludwig Wittgenstein and the "Oxford school" of ordinary language analysis. The work of these philosophers led to a change in the focus of language analysis. This change led away from both the construction of formal artificial languages (such

as logic or mathematics) and a concern with the properties of the empirical languages of science; it moved instead toward the clarification of
concepts in ordinary language. This change brought about an overturn of
the systemically driven trichotomous classification of language into the
categories of analytic, empirical, and noncognitive; it was this classification that had led to ethical judgments being placed in the category of
noncognitivist expressions. The positivist identification of "good" as primarily a term that is expressive of emotive attitude could not withstand
the successive series of analyses of the ways in which "good" is used in
ordinary language. The distinction between saying "X is good" and "Hurrah for X" becomes obvious and transparent in the contexts of their usage.
In the context of opting to cheer for one team or another, the decision can
be derived from prior commitments or a choice of loyalties without any
evaluation of the properties or merits of the team. In the context of deciding that the team is a good one—that is, when ascribing a value
predicate—there is a required reference to the characteristics or properties
that serve as reasons for this evaluation.

In a similar way, the method of linguistic analysis served to rebut
significant features of Moore's nonnaturalist argument. Moore's view,
that the meaning of "good" as "the idea or object for which 'good' stands"
is unrealizable, is subverted by the general thesis that the meaning of a
term is identified with the ways in which the term is used in "language
games." Along these lines, *contra* Moore's quest for an intentionalist synonymy with his explicit rejection of "dictionary definitions," it is appropriate to make use of the dictionary's compilation of usage as a tool for
the clarification of ordinary language terms. A dictionary definition of
"good" as an adjective of commendation recognizes Moore's insistence
on the nondescriptive properties or function of that term. Yet the linguistic function of commending an action, person, or thing presupposes, in
many or most contexts, the naturalistic thesis that reasons are required for
such commendation. "Good" has been shown to have diverse functions,
including prescribing, commending, grading, guiding, goading, praising,
and appraising. Characteristic functions of "good" include its use as a
description of empirical properties of desired objects (e.g., "The straw-
berries are good, as opposed to being sour or rotten") and as a delineation
of appropriate means to a desired end (e.g., "Cleopatra tested various
poisons for their speed and painlessness in inducing death before deciding that the bite of an asp provided a good means toward her end").

The relationship between the relevant reasons for a prescription and
the prescription itself as a moral judgment is not arbitrary. In some forms
of existentialism, it is permissible to accept the premises of a logical
argument and yet freely choose not to be compelled by those premises to
accept the logical conclusion. (Dostoyevsky's "underground man," for
example, chooses to refuse to believe that two plus two is four.) Similarly,
in another extreme version of existentialism, the existential agent is free to

acknowledge all the evidence available for an empirical hypothesis, yet is not compelled to accept that hypothesis even if it is deducible from the evidence. More relevant to ethical theory is the existentialist argument that an agent can recognize the entire set of factual claims or reasons that support a prescriptive conclusion and still be free to reject any prescription supported by these facts or reasons. Without entering into the question of an agent's freedom to accept or reject logical theorems or empirical conclusions, there remains, according to this argument, a gap between the facticity of the premises in a moral argument and the act of commitment engaged in by a moral agent. (It is significant to note that despite the great difference in philosophical idiom, this existentialist argument parallels Stevenson's contention with respect to Deweyan naturalism that moral agents could agree on all the facts in a moral dispute, yet maintain conflicting attitudes.)

The naturalist rejoinder to this argument makes use of the analysis of ordinary language, and seeks to show that there is no ineliminable gap between a judgment of ascription, prescription, imperative, or commendation and the reasons advanced for the judgment. The route to moral objectivity for linguistic naturalism emerges in the recognition of the connection between moral judgments and the reasons that are advanced to support them. The connection at issue here is the claim that the truth of a moral judgment is assertable on the basis of the truth of the relevant reasons that serve to support it.

C. Reasons in contexts of moral practice

The adequacy of the linguistic naturalist thesis is open to challenge by those who argue that 'relevant reasons' is an ambiguous concept and by those who see the interpretation of relevant reasons in practical contexts as "essentially contested." Accordingly, the following survey of several proposed ambiguities in the interpretation of relevant reasons in contexts of moral practice will probe the completeness of the linguistic naturalist route to moral objectivity.

1. *Contested reasons.* The concept of relevant reasons has been contested, to take one example, in its application to the delivery of health care and analogous human welfare needs. Bernard Williams has argued that the only relevant reason for providing medical treatment is the illness of the patient.[12] Ability to pay is identified by Williams as an enabling circumstance within a society, but not as a relevant reason for treatment. Accordingly, on pain of irrationality, medical treatment ought to be provided for the ill rather than for those who possess both health and wealth.

---

[12] Bernard Williams, "The Idea of Equality," in Peter Laslett and W. G. Runciman, eds., *Philosophy, Politics, and Society,* 2d ser. (Oxford: Basil Blackwell, 1962).

There is a logical plausibility to the claim that, ceteris paribus, illness is the only relevant reason for medical treatment. (It would be absurd for a highly skilled surgeon to devote his time to the manicuring of a wealthy patient, even if that patient were prepared to outbid all other claims for the doctor's services.) Yet disputes over what constitutes a sufficient or relevant reason for providing medical treatment or distributing health care are part of complex contexts of historical experience and institutional practice. Any system of health care in a world of finite resources finds itself compelled to consider the cost of a treatment as a relevant reason for not delivering it. Thus, it might be considered irrational to exclude cost as a relevant reason affecting judgments involving medical treatment.

The indeterminateness of the criteria for relevant reasons is evident in the generalization that advocates of the egalitarian political tradition tend to adopt a perspective, like that of Williams, according to which need is the primary relevant reason for distribution of several kinds of welfare (such as food, health, and shelter), while advocates of the nonegalitarian tradition tend to frame the issue so that other factors are included as relevant reasons. If the determination of relevant reasons is dependent upon ideological or political frames of reference, then linguistic naturalism does not satisfy the criteria for moral objectivity. In support of moral objectivity, however, it remains significant that both parties to disputes over medical treatment often justify their claims by an appeal to relevant reasons. These claims admit of being judged as true or false inasmuch as it is possible to demonstrate the relevance and truth, or irrelevance and falsity, of the given reasons.

2. *Internal and external reasons.* In another context, Williams has pointed to an ambiguity in the concept of reasons itself that casts some doubt on its use as a grounding of moral objectivity. Williams draws a distinction between "internal" and "external" reasons according to which internalization of reasons is required if they are to be interpreted as motives for human action.[13] In the naturalistic pattern of moral objectivity, the justification of an action by an appeal to the relevant reasons that support it may not require that those reasons are internalized or function as motives.

A hypothetical case involving the Marquis de Sade is a useful illustration of the significance of Williams's distinction. De Sade may be informed by reasonable persons that the pursuit of his sexual fulfillment is not a good enough reason to justify his giving poisoned candy to pre-teenaged girls. The marquis may counter, in this hypothetical development of the issue, that this may not be a reason in another person's experience, but that it has been a very good reason in his own experience. De Sade could then argue that the denial of his right to pursue his own

---

[13] Bernard Williams, "Internal and External Reasons," in Williams, *Moral Luck* (Cambridge: Cambridge University Press, 1981), 101–13.

path to fulfillment represents the intrusion of a hostile power or authority citing relevant reasons that are alien to his being. In order for the moral objectivist to condemn de Sade for the attempted murder of the girls, it must be shown that the reasons or motives he provides in support of his behavior do not satisfy the criteria of "good reasons."[14]

One possibility for the moral objectivist is to pursue the internalization model and argue that de Sade himself might come to believe that his stated motives are not justifying reasons for his action. It is not difficult to imagine that de Sade might agree that the sexual pleasure derivable from an act of killing another would not be a good reason to carry out such an action against persons whom he loves or wishes to protect. Similarly, he might be brought to oppose the argument that, for example, the idiosyncratic pleasure that a puritanical bully might realize in sadistically torturing him constitutes a good reason to sanction that action. Thus, in those cases where the human agent is concerned with consistency and realizes that what motivates him is not universalizable, it is feasible to suggest that the agent might condemn his own aberrational behavior.

Yet the moral objectivist need not base his position upon the requirement that de Sade will agree that he does not have good reasons for his action. There is evidence to support the claim that during episodes of mental illness, persons have rationalized extreme behavior and been impervious to evidence that would dissuade them. Significantly, after recovery, the insight that illness provides an excusing motivation for aberrant behavior can be joined with the recognition that this behavior was not justified by good reasons. If de Sade's behavior can be explained as a compulsion based upon physiological flaws or an emotional illness, then his motivation to poison the girls does not constitute a justifying reason. In such a case, an explanation of de Sade's behavior, which would have been external to his own set of beliefs, would not beg the question if it

---

[14] In a forum sponsored by the *Journal of Philosophy* as a Festschrift for Bernard Williams, this example was raised by Allan Gibbard as a probe of Williams's insistence on internal reasons for ethical justification. In his response, Williams cited the statement of Oscar Wilde: "Blasphemy is not a word in my vocabulary." (Williams's point is missed in the pedantic riposte that Wilde, as the author of *Salomè*, a text that was influenced by Flobere's *Herodius*, was aware of the distinctions among such concepts as apostasy, heresy, and blasphemy.) Williams's point is that it would be a conceptual and moral error to hold that a person is responsible for a supposed moral breach if the elements of that breach have no place within his own conceptual moral framework. This response is problematic, however, for it is important to guard against those who commit wrong acts and then claim to lack an understanding of the moral vocabulary. Perpetrators of genocide, for instance, have argued that they did not consider their human victims to be members of the species *Homo sapiens*.

In the case of blasphemy, virtually all secular cultures have some concept of courtesy or rudeness as well as some notion of prized or cherished objects. Consequently, the idea of blasphemy as the desecration of objects that are held sacred by another person can be understood in secular languages. On this analysis, the conceptual divide between moral judgments and the reasons supporting them is crossed or bridged. The moral question thus becomes whether there are good reasons for not desecrating the objects that others hold sacred or whether there are countervailing reasons that make it permissible, justified, or even mandatory to commit such acts.

rejected his stated reasons for his act. The ability of de Sade to understand the nature of his illness is not a necessary condition for the condemnation of his action. The condemnation is justified by relevant reasons that presuppose empirical facts about the norms of human physiology and sexuality as well as evidence of the degree of rigor or flexibility permissible in the rules that a society must adopt to protect its members against unwanted violations of their bodies or persons.

In summary, the route to moral objectivity may involve the legitimacy of using external reasons to judge an agent with subjective attitudes and beliefs. The bar to illegitimate invasiveness in another person's life rests upon the demonstrability of the relevance and truth of such reasons.[15]

3. *Reasons as internal to language and culture.* In the context of cultural pluralism, moral relativists have argued that what constitutes a relevant reason in a given society is internal to that society's language and culture. The value of toleration for religious and cultural differences has been a basis for the recognition of the legitimacy of different ways of life with their differing patterns of morality.

Montesquieu was supporting the value of religious toleration when he suggested that just as the religion of Christianity was the best one for the conquistadores, so the Aztec religion might be the best one for the Aztecs. Isaiah Berlin has cited Montesquieu's view with approval, presumably as being consistent with his own advocacy of pluralism. Yet this illustration of Aztec religion provides one of the more direct ways of countering a moral relativism based on the argument that relevant reasons are internal to a particular culture. The Aztec religion is said to have justified human sacrifice for a relevant reason, namely, that the blood of the victims was needed to move the chariot of the sun across the sky. The counterclaim, formulable in the language of the Aztecs, is that this reason is false. Even if the Aztecs would not have agreed to undertake an experiment that might have refuted their own religious hypothesis, the fact that the sun's motion is independent of the spilling of human blood is not internal to

---

[15] In this discussion of the Marquis de Sade, the issue with Williams's thesis of the internality of reasons is not squarely joined. Throughout the discussion of linguistic naturalism in this essay, the model of usage for the term "reason" is that of the tradition of the "Good Reasons" school of Oxford ordinary language analysis. Uses of the term "reason" are hence given an objectivist cast. An example is provided by statements of the form "The reason that the New York Yankees are a good baseball team is that they have three hitters with a .300 average in the middle of their batting lineup as well as three relief pitchers whose earned run average is below 2.50." This pattern is also used in statements that concern human agency and the moral vocabulary: the reason that it is wrong to act aggressively against members of one's family in a dispute is that one makes a fool of oneself and causes pain to persons whom one loves. Williams's analysis, however, takes its point of departure from an analysis of usage of the term "reason" in statements of the form "A has a reason to ϕ . . . where 'ϕ' stands in for some verb of action. . . ." An analysis that justifies the universalizability of reasons while delineating such a position's points of agreement or disagreement with Williams's account is found in T. M. Scanlon, "Appendix: Williams on Internal and External Reasons," in Scanlon, *What We Owe to Each Other* (Cambridge, MA: Belknap Press, 1998), 363–73.

the set of categories and modes of perception used by the Aztecs. Thus, in some cases at least, clashes of cultures over moral issues appear to be resolvable by appeals to the truth of the relevant reasons.

The thesis of the moral relativist, which appears to be incompatible with the thesis of moral objectivity, is that in some cultures, the moral vocabulary as well as the terms in which the relevant reasons are formulated are, in a sense, untranslatable. Accordingly, *contra* the universalism of the moral objectivist, moral pluralists or relativists claim that the values ascribed to some practices and institutions in these cultures are not commensurable with those ascribed to apparently similar practices and institutions in other societies. Along these lines, Alasdair MacIntyre once suggested that "suttee" is not translatable as "widow burning." On this view, the banning of suttee by British colonial administrators reflected their adoption of a Benthamite utilitarianism as a guide for public policy and their inability to comprehend the relevant reasons for actions that are internal to the culture of India.

The moral objectivist counter to this claim is that there exists sufficient translatability of concepts and commensurability of human physiology and psychology to justify the cross-cultural comparison of suttee with the voluntary immolation of widows. Apart from the fact that humans share a biological similarity in their reactions to fire, intense grief and an impulse to commit suicide after the loss of one's husband or wife are discoverable in cultures of both the East and the West. The title of a Welsh widow's lament, *Leftover Life to Kill* (written by Caitlin Thomas after the death of her husband Dylan),[16] suggests that the reasons that may have inspired suttee are not alien to other cultures. Furthermore, the widows of India, even within the framework of their traditional culture and historical language, could recognize that suttee was not reciprocal for widowers. The framework of the language does not exclude the possibility of formulating skepticism or criticism of the culture's dominant practices. The reasons that are cited to justify the immediate death of a woman who survives her husband are also part of a cultural pattern that includes grounds for the rejection of suttee; this cultural pattern, for example, provides relevant reasons for parents to nurture the growth and fulfillment of their daughters. Analogously, the relevant reasons for legalizing suicide by widows in the West or for banning suttee in the East are formulable within the languages of each culture and are translatable between them.

Even if the moral relativist accepts the translatability of moral vocabulary, the argument against the moral objectivist is that the concepts of this vocabulary are embedded in frameworks of discourse that generate incommensurable evaluations of cultural practices. In several historic religious cultures, the idea of rights ascribable to an individual is not found in the culture's terminology and does not have an identifiable function, even though the idea itself may be translatable by paraphrase in the

---

[16] Caitlin Thomas, *Leftover Life to Kill* (Boston: Little, Brown, 1957).

culture's language. Thus, in these societies, there is no formulation of the value of granting men and women equal rights. The status of both men and women is prescribed within a conceptual framework that formulates the duties that persons of each gender have to God. Without any assertion of explicit gender favoritism or discrimination, men are required by an ultimately divine law to fulfill their particular kinds of duties, just as women must fulfill their own appropriately prescribed duties. It is conceded as part of the foundational narratives of religious cultures that the duties of men often assume a role or burden of responsibility that is greater and possibly more difficult than that of the duties of women. Within such a social pattern, moral agents do not consider themselves cruel or indifferent to the needs of women; one example of this pattern of behavior is the willingness of the patriarchs and matriarchs of cultures in which women are not granted equal rights to sacrifice and zealously protect the honor, status, and privileges of daughters. The willingness of the moral agents of such societies to punish actions of gender discrimination that violate the prescribed structure of duties suggests that the conceptual framework of these societies' cultures cannot be interpreted as examples of the "false consciousness" of an antiegalitarian society.

The issue for the moral objectivist as linguistic naturalist is whether the justification of the moral framework of an alternative society presents an appeal to relevant reasons that are internal to that society and immune from criticism by outsiders. In the specific case of the traditionalist religious society that justifies gender differences by appealing to the relevant reason of genders having different duties toward God, it is not difficult to show that there are other values that are internal to that religious culture that could be used to justify equal treatment for the sexes. Even if an external observer lacks a basis for internal criticism of such a culture, however, he is not excluded from challenging the truth of the culture's religious foundations. If these foundational claims can be determined to be false in some objective way, then the moral prescriptions that are related to them can be denied on objective grounds. Although the duties to God derived from a foundational religious narrative offer a more complex framework for relevant reasons than does the reference in Aztec religion to the physical nature of the sun's motion, the naturalist thesis is that the practices derived from the narrative can nevertheless be criticized in a similar fashion by an appeal to the truth of the reasons that are asserted in its support.[17]

[17] The theoretical issue of moral objectivism is independent of different ways of approaching practical solutions for the problem of gender inequality in traditional cultures. In practical contexts, the principles of religious toleration and self-determination, which suggest that each society should find its own path to safeguarding the values that it justifies, may be outweighed by the effective results achievable through intervention, coercion, or sanction in the pursuit of universal human rights. In striking a balance, when cultural practices appear to violate universally accepted standards, it may be significant to recognize that every cultural pattern involves plural values and that these may provide a basis for each culture's own internal method of reform of abuses and wrongs.

Even if the moral relativist concedes the universalist thesis in its affirmation of the translatability of the moral vocabulary, the commensurability of cultural practices, and the bridgeability of alternative conceptual frameworks, there remains a significant defense against the application of universal standards to the values of a historical culture. This defense recognizes that specified cultural institutions or practices may be shown to be wrong for universally valid reasons, but asserts that in many cases, such institutions or practices have, over a long historical period, become part of a way of life. The abolition of these institutions or practices may have deleterious consequences for the continuation of these ways of life, in which other social values have been advanced, protected, or stabilized. Though it grants the wrongness of the institutions or practices when they are considered as isolated particulars, this argument may justify their continuation as parts of cultural wholes, since the new ways of life that will result from changes in these cultural wholes are not predictable and may bring with them equal or greater evils.

There are diverse examples of institutions or practices that are recognized as wrong but have been sustained on the ground that they are considered integral to a way of life. Many elders of a native Canadian tribe were prepared to agree with the Canadian police authorities that an initiation ordeal that was a test of courage could be considered excessive since it resulted in serious bodily harm for a majority of the initiates. Yet the elders opposed the banning of this historic rite by the authorities, who had proposed outlawing the practice as a form of voluntary torture. The express concern of the elders was the impact of the loss of this rite upon the tribe's morale and way of life. In another context, many supporters of the American Confederacy recognized the evil of the continuation of slavery. However, they were willing to consider the cluster of values and way of life associated with the secession and independence of the Southern states as justifying the acceptance of a constitution that did not lead to the abolition of slavery in the Confederacy.

The thesis of the moral objectivist, however, is not negated by this defense of moral relativism, since the defense explicitly recognizes the wrongness, for relevant reasons, of a particular institution, even if it argues for sustaining that institution as part of a way of life. The justification of the other values that are embedded in that way of life also requires the demonstration of the truth of the reasons that support them. It is not sufficient that the way of life be defended as that of the historical tradition of the tribe, nation, religion, or culture, since the continuation or abolition of these traditions must be justified by relevant reasons.[18] The

---

[18] Conservative thinkers from Edmund Burke to Michael Oakeshott have argued that the existence of a tradition is itself a reason for its justification, since the tradition would not have come into existence unless it had been an adequate response to human needs and desires over a long stretch of time. Yet even if this conservative argument on behalf of traditionalism is conceded, it does not rebut the claims that reasons are required to justify the continuation of a tradition and that there can be sufficient reason to terminate a particular tradition.

linguistic naturalist claim is that moral judgment can be passed upon a particular institution or upon a set of practices by referring to reasons that can be evaluated as true or false. Accordingly, linguistic naturalism represents a validation of the epistemological thesis of moral objectivity that the truth or falsity of value statements is not necessarily inferior to the truth or falsity of other kinds of empirical assertions. Neither linguistic naturalism nor the epistemological thesis of moral objectivity entails a claim to knowledge of the consequences of large-scale social change or of the perils and possibilities of social engineering.

4. *Reasons and moral evil.* The relationship between moral predication and reasons has received a seemingly paradoxical test in the moral catastrophes that punctuated the history of the twentieth century. So horrendous were some of these actions that they seemed to call for an explanation of the moral phenomena either in terms of religious doctrines involving "original sin" and a "postreligious" deterioration of the moral conscience, or in terms of a breakdown of fundamental moral intuitions.

Yet the analysis of moral language reveals that those who performed these actions attempted to justify them by appealing to sets of relevant reasons. Those performing genocidal actions, for instance, often tried to justify them by appealing to an ideology and idealistic rhetoric of national regeneration. This ideology mandated programs of genetic purification that themselves found purported justification in reasons that formed part of a theory of racial anthropology. In other contexts, individuals tried to justify the liquidation of large populations by referring to an ideology of revolutionary transformation that appealed to reasons that were part of a theory of historical inevitability. The need of the governing political authorities to assert these various sorts of reasons, even if they functioned as rationalizations for prejudice and the drive for unlimited power, indicates that these authorities believed that actions can only be justified if they are supported by relevant reasons that are true. If these reasons are demonstrably false, however, such justifications are refuted. Accordingly, the linguistic naturalist thesis that moral predication is constituted by relevant reasons is not challenged by the evidence of large-scale actions of moral evil, for like other forms of ethical naturalism, linguistic naturalism makes no claim about the efficacy of rationality in history or about the power of good reasons to overcome the deep sources of perverse violence in human nature and society.

5. *Reasons and malicious acts.* In contrast to those systematically instituted immoral actions that were justified by an appeal to a complex ideological structure of reasons, the defense of ethical naturalism appears to be more difficult in confronting acts of extreme malice or perversity that are carried out without any reference to justification, ground, or reason. The pattern of behavior in these contexts does not exhibit dialogic discourse over relevant reasons that may be discovered to be true or false. Such acts as arbitrary murder or torture, which appear to be carried out as expressions of malice or of the pleasure that it is possible to achieve

through causing the suffering of others, are often characterized by indifference or moral incomprehension. Like horrendous actions based on reasons, this extreme type of behavior has given rise to explanations in terms of religious theories and in terms of rationalist theories of the breakdown of fundamental moral intuitions.

Ethical naturalists interpret these malicious or perverse acts as representing the absence or avoidance of moral discourse. Without the introduction of ontological theses about the nature, existence, and formation of human conscience and moral intuition, the claim of the linguistic naturalist is that agents committing such acts have not met a condition for moral discourse, namely, an appeal to reasons. Such agents do not offer reasons or rationalizations in their justifications of their actions, but rather ignore any reference to moral language and reject the admissibility of any grounds for evaluating their acts. This poses a problem for the linguistic naturalist, for if these agents avoid all moral discourse, then it will be difficult to draw the connection that the linguistic naturalist posits between moral predication and values.

The rejoinder of the linguistic naturalist here is to point to the existence of forms of moral discourse in the language of these agents. It is significant that those anthropological accounts (such as Montaigne's well-known essay, "On Cannibalism") in which indifference to any norm of moral behavior is exhibited often suggest that there are cultures, languages, and human agents that lack any form of moral discourse. Yet historical records in which behavior of extreme malice and perversity is exhibited always document as well the existence of moral discourse in the culture and in the language of its human agents. Characteristically, the agents who carry out moral atrocities do understand, in other contexts, the nature of moral discourse and the linguistic pattern of justification by appeal to reasons.

There is a degree of parallelism between the moral intuitionist thesis that some acts (like the documented cases of the playful firing of a gun in the mouth of an innocent child) are intrinsically abhorrent and the linguistic naturalist claim that persons who indifferently or maliciously commit such acts without any attempt at justification are violating the significance conditions of any moral discourse. In both cases, condemnation of the action can be justified without the agreement of the agent.

Agents who perform arbitrary, malicious actions are able to use a language whose significance conditions include the conception that there are reasons for human action, as opposed to a conception under which human actions are the random behavior of beings who lack agency. (This language may even presuppose the knowledge that these agents' human victims are human beings rather than members of another species of animal.) Thus, the linguistic naturalist interpretation of the nature of ethical language as involving an appeal to reasons is not rendered false or inadequate by the recognition that some immoral acts are carried out by persons who refuse to engage in or accept moral discourse in selective contexts.

6. Reasons and rights-discourse. The response of ethical naturalism to arbitrary or malicious actions, which characteristically involve the taking of life, the inflicting of bodily abuse, or the infringement of the liberty of others, has been reinforced by the linguistic naturalist analysis of rights-discourse. Linguistic naturalists have extended their interpretation of moral language from a focus on moral predicates such as "good" and "right" to develop an argument involving the linguistic presuppositions of claims of fundamental natural rights, such as the rights to life and liberty. Significantly for the linguistic naturalist thesis that there is an intrinsic relationship between moral vocabulary and reasons, this argument, derived from an analysis of the functions of the language of rights in its various social contexts, states that this use of language presupposes that reasons must be given for human action.

H. L. A. Hart's essay "Are There Any Natural Rights?" puts forth this argument. In the essay, Hart seeks to demonstrate that any language in which the concept of moral or legal rights is used involves the presupposition that some reason must be given in order to interfere with another person's freedom.[19] The legal right of an employee to the payment of his salary, for example, presupposes interference with the freedom of the employer to make use of his own funds. Hart extends the logic of the discourse of legal rights to develop a general interpretation of natural rights. The denial of a natural right to liberty is, in this view, equivalent to the claim that *no reason* must be given to justify interference with a person's freedom.

If the agents within a society make use of the concept of rights in diverse contexts, then the presuppositions of the usage of that concept can be invoked in the evaluation of their moral behavior. Consequently, it would be contradictory for an agent in a society to claim his moral or legal rights in one context and also assert that no reasons need be given for his violent acts against other persons. The agents who have carried out the most egregious violations of human rights to life and liberty in the recent past have been persons who understand and apply the concept of rights in their own lives. Consequently, the justification of their actions cannot rely upon the claim that they need provide no reasons for their

---

[19] Hart, "Are There Any Natural Rights?" There are obviously significant differences between Hart's linguistic interpretation of natural rights and the doctrine as it was present in seventeenth- and eighteenth-century philosophical theories. It is also significant, however, to note the similarities. Jefferson's rhetorical statement that "all men are created equal" may not be too distant from the claim that a significance condition of rights-discourse is the recognition of the difference between human beings and other species of animals. More pointedly, Jefferson's doctrine of the "self-evidence" of the truths of natural rights can be interpreted to mean that no rational person who understands the meaning of the terms in the proposition "all men are created equal" can deny the proposition itself. On this view, the "self-evidence" of rights is not too distant from the presuppositions implicit in rights-discourse.

actions; their understanding that natural rights exist is, in practical terms, a recognition that an appeal to reasons is required. This interpretation of rights-discourse may not constrain the undesirable behavior of violators of human rights, since their defenses may rest upon the invocation of reasons that reflect xenophobic or racialist beliefs. Yet as noted above, these proffered reasons become subject to a test of their truth or falsity.

Interpreting fundamental natural rights as presupposing a claim that reasons must be given in order to interfere with another person serves to clarify the compatibility of natural rights with the inevitable limitation of rights in social contexts. While such rights as those to life, liberty, and property are generally held to be absolute and inalienable, it is recognized that these rights are compatible with acts of capital punishment, imprisonment, and taxation. The limitation of such universal natural rights in any particular situation depends, therefore, upon the reasons that can be supplied for these acts.

According to the linguistic naturalist, each of the contending parties to a moral dispute—for example, a dispute involving the limits on the right to freedom of expression—is required to appeal to relevant reasons to justify its position. The linguistic naturalist argument for the epistemological thesis of moral objectivity is that such reasons admit of truth or falsity. The language of rights, in shifting a moral dispute into a dispute over the truth or falsity of the supporting reasons for either position, strengthens the thesis of moral objectivity. Yet while the shift to reasons frames the structure of the dispute, it does not specify a procedure that would necessarily lead to resolution of the underlying moral disagreement.

D. Linguistic naturalism and moral objectivity

The preceding review of linguistic naturalism has indicated its use as a route to moral objectivity and has also suggested the obstacles that exist for the completion of that route. Linguistic naturalism requires that there exist a language in which moral discourse takes place. Moral objectivity would clearly not be attainable if there were societies that had no form of moral discourse or languages that had no moral vocabulary. This obstacle may be empirically insignificant, for it is difficult to imagine any human society with a structured way of life that lacks some pattern of moral discourse.

It is more readily imaginable that societies could have patterns of moral discourse that are embedded in forms of cultural expression that reject a justification by an appeal to reasons. A pattern of moral discourse in which there is no appeal to justification by reasons would represent an obstacle to moral objectivity. Moral objectivity, for the linguistic naturalist, requires that the involvement of moral assertions with appeals to reasons must, by nature of the linguistic form of such assertions, be cross-cultural and transhistorical.

Some forms of cultural expression provide a challenge to the thesis that reasons are presupposed in moral assertions. One such form of cultural expression is represented by those taboos in which a feature of their status as taboos is that no rationale for them is required or admitted. Similarly, there are religious commands that call for obedience or submission on grounds of faith without requiring any appeal to supporting reasons. Some forms of political authority have insisted that the edicts of the rulers should be obeyed even when no reason is supplied for them. Presented with these examples, the linguistic naturalist may maintain that these forms of cultural expression do not represent domains of moral discourse. In this view, it is only in contexts where identifiably moral terms form part of the vocabulary that the presupposition of reasons obtains.

Yet taboos, religious commands, and political edicts impinge upon the moral life of the community and have consequences for social morality. An investigation of some of the texts of these forms of religious or political authority suggests that the justification of these sorts of imperatives may depend upon their organic relationship to the existence of the community or to its accepted values. In the case of political edicts, the demand for submission is related to the claim of the legitimacy of the political authority. Accordingly, the linguistic naturalist could argue that reasons really *are* being given for obedience to these problematic sorts of imperatives. These reasons may be that these taboos or commands form part of a justified or accepted way of life, or that these edicts are expressions of legitimate authority. Seen this way, these reasons form a pattern of justification for persons who choose to be loyal or faithful members of the society.

The argument that reasons are being given in support of these forms of cultural expression can be strengthened by the recognition that there are grounds available for rejecting taboos, imperatives, and edicts within those societies that have them. Critics who are inside the society can pursue the claim that there is no organic connection between these imperatives and the existence or values of the community. Similarly, the option of denying the legitimacy of the source of such imperatives has often been carried out within closed communities. The demand for the reason why a reigning authority is legitimate is often asserted within authoritarian societies, even at the price of a break with the dominant social pattern. Accordingly, even in these "extreme" cases where the language of morality appears to be intermeshed with a culture of taboos or of religious or political authority, the possibility of raising the question of justificatory reasons emerges.

The discussion of these "extreme" cases serves to indicate the requirement of linguistic naturalism that the term "reason" have a univocal meaning. The preceding survey has probed the possibility of the denial of the univocality of reasons. This is an important topic, for to the degree that the concept of reasons can be demonstrated to be univocal, linguistic naturalism provides a basis for moral objectivity.

VI. Conclusion

A. Ethical naturalism and moral objectivity

A central theme of ethical naturalism, common to the four variants examined in this essay, has been the connection between the values that human beings wish to assert, defend, or justify and natural structures, including particularly the nature of human nature. In each of these variants, the demonstration of such a connection has generated the claim that knowledge of such values is as legitimate or valid as those kinds of reliable knowledge that have usually been considered intersubjective or objective.

In significantly different ways, each of the four variants has included arguments for the possibility of asserting the truth of ethical statements by referring to the truth of statements about empirical experience. Thus, in a classical formulation of ethical naturalism, Aristotle justifies standards for human conduct by considering human excellences as norms in the actualization of the distinctive potentialities of the human species.

In contrast, Hume, who declares his skepticism about the possibility of any logical derivation of human values from the facts of nature, is able to locate the source of these values in the capacity of human nature to express approval and disapproval of human action. Accordingly, for Hume, as an ethical naturalist, if a hypothetically impartial human nature can express universally shared sentiments, then value claims can be justified on the ground that they represent judgments that are as universally valid as those that Hume, as an enlightened skeptic, is prepared to grant to other properties of the objects of the world.

In the Deweyan variant of naturalism, the ambitious project is the demonstration that value statements as judgments of practice can be considered warrantedly assertable if they pass through a process of scientific inquiry. For Dewey, moral judgments can be arrived at in the same way that scientific inquiry arrives at other judgments, including judgments of fact; this process involves mediating conflicting opinions through appeals to their consequences in experience.

Finally, in the less expansionary mode that has characterized philosophy's self-imposed limitation to the analysis of language, the naturalistic thesis emerges as the claim that the truth of a value statement is justified by the truth of the reasons that can be provided for its support and that, in a significant way, constitute its meaning. Thus, this minimalist form of ethical naturalism allows for a significant parallel between the truth claims of ethical statements and truth claims involving statements in other areas of knowledge. Just as truth claims in many areas of knowledge are vindicated by appeals to the evidence or grounds for their assertion, under linguistic ethical naturalism the truth of a moral assertion is justified by the truth of the reasons that support it.

B. Nonnaturalism

In the course of the above survey of the variants of naturalism, particularly the elucidation of linguistic naturalism, it was requisite to carry out some examination of the arguments for nonnaturalism in ethics. Emotivism, existentialism, and intuitionism have, each in their own way, asserted that there is a gap between ethical expressions and descriptive reasons. Each of these theories has been able to illuminate some aspect of the phenomenology of morals. Thus, emotivists, from the analysis of G. E. Moore to the models of ethical disagreement of C. L. Stevenson, focused upon the nature of moral predication as prescriptive and expressive of attitudes. Existentialists laid special emphasis upon the recognition that moral action represents the outcome of free choice rather than the characteristics of what is given in the world independently of human existence. Intuitionists stressed the ways in which violations of fundamental moral imperatives appear to be so abhorrent as to be considered beyond the possibility of or need for factual support or argument.

The contention of the linguistic naturalist is that each of these views fails to adequately consider the nature and function of moral discourse. In cases of violations of fundamental moral claims where the agent performing the actions asserts no reasons for them, the conditions for moral discourse have been avoided. Where any form of moral discourse is present, there is an appeal to relevant reasons in the justifications of moral claims. Accordingly, the linguistic naturalist thesis that moral vocabulary is intrinsically connected with justificatory reasons emerges from a confrontation with variants of ethical nonnaturalism.

C. Moral disagreement and objectivity

Each of the four variants of ethical naturalism reviewed in this essay has involved some methodology for the resolution of moral disagreement. Yet as noted during the consideration of each of the variants, no methodology has emerged that can resolve many of the more formidable ethical disagreements that arise in human societies. The Aristotelian appeal to the potential for convergences of judgment by persons of practical reason appears to fall short of arriving at universal truths in moral decision-making. The Humean invocation of a hypothetically impartial observer who approves or disapproves of actions in reference to a general survey provides no secure basis for the impartiality of the verdict or the generality of the survey. The Deweyan belief in the possibility of the resolution of moral disagreement by a generalized scientific method does not appear to have been vindicated in the operations of the social sciences. The linguistic naturalist points to the truth of justificatory reasons as providing a procedure for arriving at the truth of moral assertions. Yet this identification of the nature and function of the moral vocabulary does not entail that the linguistic naturalist procedure will lead to universally accepted conclusions.

This kind of incompleteness in the resolution of moral disagreement does not demonstrate the incompletability of the route to moral truth and cannot be interpreted as a denial of moral objectivity. The continuation of unresolved disagreement is commonplace within various fields of reliable or objective knowledge. Historians, for example, appeal to evidence to justify the truth of statements in their narratives. Their reliance upon evidence, which is open to confirmation or refutation, is generally considered sufficient reason to think of the field of history as providing objective knowledge, even if historians are incapable of resolving disagreements over such continually contested topics as the causes for the decline of Rome or the inevitability of the American Civil War. Meteorological science is not viewed as lacking objectivity simply because it is unable to achieve consensus on such a central issue as global warming. Clinical practice in medicine is rife with long-term unresolved disagreements over how to treat major illnesses. The continuation of these sorts of disagreements is compatible with the identification and classification of history, meteorology, and medical practice as fields involving objective knowledge, since opinions in these fields are justified in a process of inquiry on the basis of empirical evidence.

The different patterns of human experience appear to generate different points of view that are not readily abandoned in moral disputes over such normative issues as abortion, capital punishment, economic redistribution, and other topics. The continuing occurrence of disagreement on major moral questions has been viewed by some as representing a denial of moral objectivity. Yet as the preceding illustrations indicate, other fields contain such disagreements and are nevertheless considered objective. Consequently, a consistent standard for application of the term "objectivity" would allow for the moral objectivist claim that knowledge in the area of ethics is not necessarily inferior to knowledge in other domains of empirical inquiry.

D. Completability and incompleteness

The fact that there is continuing and pervasive moral disagreement does not justify the denial of moral objectivity in its epistemological sense. Such a denial would further require that the procedures for the resolution of moral disagreement could never be completed. This sort of "incompleteness theorem," which would be analogous to the incompleteness theorems of mathematics, would show that it is not possible to have objective knowledge in ethics. Linguistic naturalism provides a justification of the possibility of reliable knowledge in ethics. Though it does not provide a demonstration that the process of achieving such knowledge could ever be completed, it would deny any incompleteness theorem for ethics that would foreclose the possibility of arriving at objective moral judgments. Accordingly, it is relevant to consider some of the formulations of "incompleteness" that have been suggested in contemporary discussions of ethical theory. The demonstration of an ineliminable ambiguity in the concept of "reasons" discussed in the preceding section would provide a basis for such a claim of incompleteness. Ethical inquiry would also be unable to arrive at moral objectivity if reasons were relative to historical cultures.

From a different direction, Continental philosophers like Michel Foucault and Jacques Derrida have concluded that all ethical norms are arbitrary. Although the patterns of their arguments are complex and in some ways dependent upon an alternative conception of philosophical method, they can serve, in this context, to clarify the general issue of the incompleteness of moral objectivity.

In the case of Foucault, the arbitrariness of moral norms is based upon the claim that all knowledge of human affairs in a culture reflects that culture's *episteme*. This *episteme*, which is unearthed by an archaeology of knowledge, is a mixture of the facts of power in a culture as these impinge upon the paradigms of knowledge. Consequently, Foucault argues, a society's moral norms inevitably reflect, to some degree, the bias of those who hold power. Therefore, any moral inquiry that aims at arriving at an objectively true conclusion can never complete its goal.

From Derrida's perspective, any construction of language about human affairs admits of its own deconstruction in a way that excludes the assertion of univocal meanings. Accordingly, for Derrida, any structure of knowledge in the human sciences has been "decentered" so that its truth claims cannot be justified. No inquiry into a moral issue, then, can ever overcome the inherent limitation to its objectivity that is implicit in its formulation in human language.

If we consider moral objectivity with respect to its epistemological thesis that the status of ethical knowledge is comparable to that of knowledge in other fields, then the criticisms of both Foucault and Derrida fall short of denying such objectivity, since they reach too far against other forms of knowledge. The criticisms of Foucault and Derrida apply to many fields of inquiry, including archaeology, anthropology, history, and literary criticism. Accordingly, they do not constitute refutations, in particular, of moral objectivity.

These criticisms can serve, however, to illuminate the underlying argument regarding the incompleteness of the route to moral objectivity. This general argument is that the selection and admissibility of the reasons that constitute and justify moral assertions are themselves determined by prior structures. These prior structures have been variously identified as attitudes, conceptual frameworks, structures of perception, *epistemes*, or paradigms. If these prior structures that determine relevant reasons are not subject to revision in the light of empirical evidence, then any appeal to reasons in the justification of morals will be limited or rendered necessarily incomplete. On this general question, then, the ethical naturalist view is that these sorts of prior structures are not immune from revision in the light of evidence.

As Stevenson showed, deeply held attitudes function to select perceptual data in a way that reinforces the original attitudinal commitment. Yet attitudes, and even prejudices, are not entirely immune to erosion or change when confronted by evidence. Analogously, Kuhn documented how conceptual frameworks or paradigms can also govern the interpretation or discovery of perceptual data. Yet the history of inquiry also exhibits evidence that conceptual frameworks or paradigms that are historically embedded have not been able to withstand the impact of experience that continually confounds their expectations. To the degree to which prior structures are open to revision in light of evidence, the possibility of arriving at justified judgments in inquiry cannot be excluded.[20] Accordingly, the completability of the route to moral objectivity is compatible with the reality of disagreement between competing moral assertions, when these assertions appeal to reasons.

In summary, then, linguistic naturalism is a minimalist variant of ethical naturalism. Like all variants of ethical naturalism, it asserts a connection between statements of value and statements of fact. The linguistic naturalist account of this connection does not entail the empirical beliefs about the norms of human nature that were asserted in classic Aristotelianism. It also abstains from taking a position on the recognition of the sentiments of a universal human nature; such a recognition characterized the Enlightenment, even under Humean skepticism. The linguistic naturalist shares with Dewey the claim that he referred to as "the primacy of method"—that a naturalist ethical theory need not assume or assert any substantive moral judgments. Linguistic naturalism does not, however, share in the Deweyan vision of the scientific method as a procedure that can arrive at true judgments in morals when facing conflicting moral hypotheses.

The linguistic naturalist explication of the connection between fact and value is that in all forms of moral discourse, reasons are given in support of values and decisions. Even as a minimalist theory, linguistic naturalism requires that there be constraints on the term "reason"; these constraints are elucidated in the analysis of moral disagreement or discourse. Yet

[20] The thesis that these structures are subject to revision in light of evidence is closely argued in Israel Scheffler's criticism of the immunity of Kuhnian paradigms from a process of empirical refutation; see Israel Scheffler, *Science and Subjectivity* (Indianapolis, IN: Bobbs-Merrill, 1967).

these constraints would not exclude the assertion of any differing view for which some reason could be given. Accordingly, linguistic naturalism is neutral on substantive moral claims. This neutrality is not trivial, however, since the requirement that any moral view must be justified by reasons opens the door to the examination of the truth or falsity of the relevant reasons. This opening of the door does not guarantee moral agreement, since two common features of our society are the development of individual attitudes or group loyalties with different points of view and the proffering of diverse reasons in the face of moral disputes. Yet the linguistic naturalist requirement that moral terms relate to reasons excludes various kinds of arbitrariness and makes possible moral judgments that can be justified.

Linguistic naturalism is a true heir of the philosophical quest for moral objectivity that was pursued by all variants of ethical naturalism. Its distinctive linguistic affirmation is that the analysis of the use of human language reveals that embedded within its practice is a route to moral objectivity.

Philosophy, Columbia University

EXPLANATION, INTERNALISM, AND REASONS FOR ACTION*

By David Sobel

I. Introduction

These days, just about every philosophical debate seems to generate a position labeled *internalism*. The debate I will be joining in this essay concerns reasons for action and their connection, or lack of connection, to motivation. The internalist position in this debate posits a certain essential connection between reasons and motivation, while the externalist position denies such a connection. This debate about internalism overlaps an older debate between Humeans and Kantians about the exclusive reason-giving power of desires. As we will see, however, while these debates overlap, the new debate is importantly different from the old debate.

Bernard Williams inaugurated the new debate about internalism. He argued that genuine reasons must be *internal*, that is, they must have a certain specified connection to the motivations of the agent whose reasons they are purported to be. Williams tells us that the most fundamental arguments for internalism stem from what I will call his *explanation condition*. Before we get bogged down in the attempt to formulate precisely what the explanation condition and internalism amount to, however, let me offer a quick road map of this essay. In this essay, I will try to reach a better understanding of (1) the thesis that Williams has labeled internalism, (2) the "interrelation of explanatory and normative reasons" that Williams claims exists, and (3) how Williams thinks (2) helps establish (1). I will argue that Williams's claim that reasons must be interrelated with explanation in a particular way, that is, his explanation condition, does not support internalism as he supposes. Furthermore, I will argue that Williams's explanation condition is false. Finally, I will argue that internalism is false.

The essay will have two major parts. In Section II, I try to understand the explanation condition and argue that it cannot be the key underpinning of internalism. I will argue that plausible interpretations of the explanation condition are either too weak to rule out externalism or so strong that they amount to the thesis of internalism itself. I also take issue

* I am grateful to David Copp, Janice Dowell, and Mike Weber for valuable comments on this essay. I am also grateful for helpful comments from the other contributors to this volume, Ellen Frankel Paul, and Carrie-Ann Biondi.

in this section with the way in which Williams argues to the conclusion that sound deliberation involves knowing the facts of the matter but not being motivated toward prudence or morality.

In Section III, I argue that the explanation condition and internalism are both false. The explanation condition and internalism posit a particular relationship between motivation and reasons for action. I offer arguments for resisting this particular understanding of the relationship. As I shall show, however, resisting this particular understanding of the relationship is compatible with maintaining that there is nonetheless a fundamental connection between motivation and reasons. The arguments I offer against the explanation condition and internalism do not tell generally against *subjectivism about reasons for action* — the view that it is the agent's subjective motivational set that makes it the case that an agent does or does not have a reason to ϕ. Rather, I argue that the best version of subjectivism must reject the explanation condition and internalism.

II. Williams and Internalism

A. The explanation condition as a motivation for internalism

Williams understands internalism to be the view that "A has a reason to ϕ only if he could reach the conclusion to ϕ by a sound deliberative route from the motivations he already has. The externalist view is that this is not a necessary condition, and that it can be true of A that he has a reason to ϕ even though A has no motivation in his motivational set that could, either directly or by some extension through sound deliberation, lead him to ϕ."[1] Williams argues in favor of internalism by trying to show us how only internal reasons can properly capture and respond to the force of the explanation condition.

Williams tells us that there are "two fundamental motivations for the internalist account" of reasons for action.[2] The first is what I have been calling the explanation condition. The second fundamental motivation turns out to be "another application of the same point" insisted upon by the explanation condition.[3] Thus, understanding and assessing the explanation condition is, Williams strongly insists, pivotal to understanding his case for internalism.

But how should we understand Williams's explanation condition? Here are the two most helpful passages in which Williams discusses it:

> [A fundamental motivation of the internalist account] is the inter-relation of explanatory and normative reasons. It must be a mistake

[1] Bernard Williams, "Internal Reasons and the Obscurity of Blame," in Williams, *Making Sense of Humanity* (Cambridge: Cambridge University Press, 1995), 35.
[2] Ibid., 38.
[3] Ibid., 39.

simply to separate explanatory and normative reasons. If it is true
that A has a reason to ϕ, then it must be possible that he should ϕ for
that reason; and if he does act for that reason, then that reason will
be the explanation of his acting. So the claim that he has a reason to
ϕ—that is, the normative statement 'He has a reason to ϕ'—introduces
the possibility of that reason being an explanation. . . .[4]

In considering what an external reason statement might mean, we
have to remember . . . the dimension of possible explanation, a consideration which applies to any reason for action. If something can be
a reason for action, then it could be someone's reason for acting on a
particular occasion, and it would then figure in an explanation of that
action. Now no external reason statement could by itself offer an
explanation of anyone's action. Even if it were true (whatever that
might turn out to mean) that there was a reason for Owen to join the
army, that fact by itself would never explain anything that Owen did,
not even his joining the army. For if it was true at all, it was true
when Owen was not motivated to join the army. The whole point of
external reason statements is that they can be true independently of
the agent's motivations. But nothing can explain an agent's (intentional) actions except something that motivates him so to act.[5]

Williams takes it that there is at least a necessary condition on a consideration providing a normative reason for action—namely, that that
consideration has a special kind of explanatory power. This claim is what
I am calling the explanation condition. What exactly is the explanatory
power that a consideration must have if it is to be able to generate a
normative reason? One thing is obvious: the consideration need not be
able to explain an actual action. To suppose otherwise is to suppose that
a person could not fail to act as her normative reason instructed. Williams
is clear that he rejects such a view. Rather, the consideration must be in
some sense capable of explaining action. Capable, however, in what sense?

Let us focus on Williams's claim that "If it is true that A has a reason to
ϕ, then it must be possible that he should ϕ for that reason." We could,
somewhat dimly, understand this merely to mean that it is a necessary
condition of A having a reason to ϕ that there be a possible world in
which A ϕs. I will call this thesis *Explanation I*. This is independently
plausible and is ensured by the principle that "ought implies can," but it
is not what Williams is after. The Explanation I formulation fails to distinguish, in the way Williams means to distinguish, considerations that
can ground the truth of the claim that A has a reason to ϕ from considerations that cannot do so. Williams wants to be able to say that even if

[4] Ibid., 38–39.
[5] Bernard Williams, "Internal and External Reasons," in Williams, *Moral Luck* (Cambridge:
Cambridge University Press, 1981), 107.

Owen does have some sort of reason to join the army, a consideration (e.g., of family honor) that does not appeal to anything in Owen's subjective motivational set cannot ground this reason.

What does Williams mean to add to Explanation I with the thought that for consideration C to support a reason for A to ϕ, A must not only be able to ϕ, but must be able to ϕ "for that reason"? It seems to be A's ϕ-ing "for that reason" that brings in the special explanatory element Williams is looking for. Claiming that A has a reason to ϕ does not yet give a potential ground of the normative justifiability of ϕ-ing. Thus, when Williams says that "If it is true that A has a reason to ϕ, then it must be possible that he should ϕ for that reason," it is not immediately clear what the "for that reason" is meant to refer to. The antecedent of the conditional does not appear to specify the right kind of thing such that it makes sense to say that one could do anything "for that reason."

I think we do best to understand Williams to be saying this: if a consideration C truly provides A with a normative reason (hereafter, reason) to ϕ, then it must be possible that A could ϕ and that at least part of the explanation for his doing so involves his contemplation of and subsequent motivation by C. If we so understand Williams, the possibly explanatory reason in the consequent of Williams's original claim does refer to the sort of thing that could potentially justify A's ϕ-ing. Williams's point seems to be that if ϕ has the status of being something that A has a reason to do, then it must be the case that A can ϕ for the same reasons that give ϕ-ing that status.[6]

Understanding Williams in this way would help us understand the other crucial passage in which he deploys the explanation condition. In the second extract above, Williams writes, "If something can be a reason for action, then it could be someone's reason for action on a particular occasion, and it would then figure in an explanation of that action." The consequent of this conditional invokes an "it" that is supposed both to refer us to the "something" in the antecedent and to be capable of serving as an agent's subjective ground for action. Thus, if the "it" is to be able to play the latter role, the "something" in the antecedent must be understood to be the sort of thing that could stand in the justifying relation. Furthermore, since the conditional has the form of "If it is true that . . . , it must be the case that it can seem to the agent that . . . ," we need to understand the "something" in the conditional's antecedent as something that is truly a reason for action. Therefore, we must again understand Williams as saying that if some consideration C can objectively ground a claim that A has a reason to ϕ, it must be the case that A could ϕ in response to the subjective ground provided by C.

---

[6] Notice that this formulation anticipates a discussion below to the effect that what Williams seems to really be after is not internalism but *subjectivism*. I conceive of the latter as an account of what makes it true that one has a reason to ϕ rather than merely an account of how to determine if one has a reason to ϕ.

Given this understanding of Williams, we might amend Explanation I
so that it expresses the following claim: if consideration C gives A a
reason to ϕ, it must be the case that A can ϕ *and* that in some possible
world in which A does ϕ, his doing so is explained by his being motivated
by C. Let us call this thesis *Explanation II*. This formulation avoids the
problem that confronts Explanation I, because it tells us when a consideration lacks the power to provide A with a reason to ϕ. A consideration
lacks this power when there is no possible world in which (1) A ϕ's, and
(2) her ϕ-ing can be explained by the consideration.

Yet the Explanation II formulation cannot be exactly what Williams
means, either, for this version of the explanation condition does not help
support internalism. Recall that Williams's version of internalism claims
that "A has a reason to ϕ only if he could reach the conclusion to ϕ by a
sound deliberative route from the motivations he already has." Explanation II, however, makes no distinction between a consideration motivating via a sound deliberative route and motivating via some other means.
For example, this version of the explanation condition would be satisfied
if an agent who has no interest in counting blades of grass comes to have
such an interest only in those possible worlds in which she undergoes
radical brain surgery. According to Explanation II, the possibility of such
surgery, and of the subsequent motivation to count blades of grass, means
that the considerations in favor of counting blades of grass can provide
reasons for A even if he does not actually undergo such surgery, and even
though without the surgery he has no interest in his subjective motivational set that counting blades of grass would further. Because of this,
Explanation II is a rather weak thesis (although I will find grounds for
resisting it in Section III of this essay). Only considerations that could not,
in any possible world (even including brain surgery scenarios or the like),
motivate A to ϕ would be shown to not provide A with a reason to ϕ.

The version of internalism that Williams wants to argue for claims that
consideration C only gives one a reason to ϕ if one could reach the
conclusion to ϕ for the reason that C via a sound deliberative route. Yet
as we have seen, Explanation II is insensitive to the distinction between
A's being motivated by C to ϕ via a sound deliberative route and A's
being so motivated in other ways (such as radical brain surgery). Because
of this, it is possible to accept Explanation II but reject Williams's internalism. Indeed, this combination of accepting Explanation II and rejecting
internalism seems to be John McDowell's view.[7]

Thus, it is unclear how Explanation II could provide the fundamental
motivation for internalism and against externalism. One could accept
Explanation II but reject internalism by holding Explanation II while
denying that it is a necessary condition on consideration C providing A a

[7] John McDowell, "Might There Be External Reasons?" in J. E. J. Altham and Ross Harrison, eds., *World, Mind, and Ethics: Essays on the Ethical Philosophy of Bernard Williams* (Cambridge: Cambridge University Press, 1995).

reason to ϕ that A would be motivated by C to ϕ after sound deliberation. That is, one could hold that a consideration that provides a reason must be able to motivate, but need not necessarily do so after sound deliberation. Because of the availability of this position, it is unclear how Explanation II could be thought to be the key to a defense of internalism against externalism.

As a final option, we could understand the explanation condition to express the claim that a jointly necessary condition of consideration C providing A a reason to ϕ is that (1) A could ϕ; (2) in some possible world in which A ϕs, his ϕ-ing can be explained by means of his contemplation of, and subsequent motivation by, C; and (3) in some possible world in which (1) and (2) are the case, A is deliberating soundly from his actual subjective motivational set. Let us call this thesis *Explanation III*.

Before considering the merits of Explanation III, let us pause to wonder what intuitive basis there could be for resisting Explanation III in favor of Explanation II. The only reason for doing so would have to be that one thinks it is a constraint on good reasons that they motivate after bad deliberation. After all, Explanation II posits a connection between reasons and what can motivate, while Explanation III posits a connection between reasons and what can motivate after sound deliberation. Thus, those who embrace Explanation II but resist Explanation III must champion a connection between good reasons and bad deliberation. I see no intuitive support for such a connection.

Let us turn now to Explanation III. Understood as I define it above, Explanation III just *is* the thesis of internalism, and thus is not a possible motivation for embracing that thesis. (The reader may want to go back and compare Explanation III with Williams's definition of internalism, which I quote at the beginning of this section.) The addition that we saw we needed to add to Explanation II to make it incompatible with externalism (namely, the bit about sound deliberation) was the only difference between Explanation II and internalism. Thus, Williams's explanation condition, which he took to be the centerpiece of his case for internalism, turns out to be, depending on how one interprets it, either too weak to support internalism or to be the thesis of internalism. In either case, Williams's claim that the explanation condition provides crucial support for internalism is misguided.

B. Sound deliberation: why does it involve knowing the facts?

There is another way in which Williams's argument for internalism is misguided. Consider how he argues that "sound deliberation" necessarily involves knowing the facts, but not necessarily being motivated to comply with prudence or morality:

> [I]f we are licensed to vary the agent's reasoning and assumptions of fact, it will be asked why we should not vary (for instance, insert)

prudential and moral considerations as well. . . . The internalist proposal sticks with its Humean origins to the extent of making correction of fact and reasoning part of the notion of 'a sound deliberative
route to this act' but not, from outside, prudential and moral considerations. . . . The grounds for making this general point about fact
and reasoning, as distinct from prudential and moral considerations,
are quite simple: any rational deliberative agent has in his S [i.e., his
subjective motivational set] a general interest in being factually and
rationally correctly informed.[8]

There are two problems with Williams's argument here. First, Williams warns against those who claim that "every rational deliberator is
committed to constraints of morality." He rightfully tells us that "there
has to be an argument for this conclusion. Someone who claims the
constraints of morality are themselves built into the notion of what it is
to be a rational deliberator cannot get that conclusion for nothing."[9]
But Williams offers no argument for the claim that each rational agent
has in his S "a general interest in being factually and rationally correctly informed." Williams, then, seems to be trying to get this claim
for nothing. Williams may have in mind here some form of the thought
that belief necessarily aims at truth and that believers therefore necessarily have an interest in having true beliefs. Such a line could perhaps
be made persuasive. But surely Williams expects a champion of the
claim that prudential and moral concerns are requirements of rational
deliberation to do more than vaguely gesture toward promising argumentative strategies for establishing such a conclusion.

Second, even if the above claim that all rational agents want to be
correctly informed could be established, this would not support Williams's conclusion that sound deliberation involves knowing the facts.
Note that my argument here is that Williams's premise seems irrelevant
to his conclusion; I am not claiming that his conclusion is false. That is, I
am not disputing that sound deliberation involves knowing the facts.
Rather, I am taking issue with how Williams hopes to argue for that claim.

Williams has championed a connection between what is in our S and
our reasons for action. Thus, if Williams could establish that in each
agent's S there is necessarily a motivation to be correctly informed, this
might help him reach the conclusion that each agent has a reason to
become correctly informed. However, this does nothing to make compelling the thought that being correctly informed is a requirement of sound
deliberation.

There is a difference between claiming that one's motivations determine one's reasons and claiming that one's motivations determine what

[8] Williams, "Internal Reasons and the Obscurity of Blame," 36–37.
[9] Ibid., 37.

counts as sound deliberation. Williams seems to confuse these things. At least we can say that such a confusion is suggested by Williams's treating the claim that any rational agent has in his S a motivation to be factually informed as if it helped establish the claim that being so informed counts as part of sound deliberation. Consider that even if it could be established that all rational deliberators have an interest in viewing great works of art rather than schlocky knockoffs, this would not show that sound deliberation is deliberation done while viewing great works of art. There is no general reason that Williams offers (or that I can think of) for supposing that if all rational agents want something, then having that thing is necessary for sound deliberation. Surely, then, we might be convinced that Williams's internalism is correct—that our reasons are constrained by what we could be motivated to pursue after sound deliberation—without supposing that the content of sound deliberation is also determined by the agent's motivations.

There is a more plausible variant of the kind of position that Williams seems to be advocating here. Connie Rosati has recently proposed a version of internalism (in her case, internalism about a person's good) that she calls *two-tier internalism*. The central thought behind two-tier internalism is that for ϕ-ing to be good for an agent, not only must the agent be able to care about ϕ in some set of counterfactual conditions, but those counterfactual conditions themselves must answer to her concerns. That is, the appropriate counterfactual conditions in which an agent's reactions determine her good themselves must be such that the agent finds that her reactions in those counterfactual conditions are authoritative. Put most simply, Rosati's proposal has it that an agent's concerns not only determine her good, but that they also determine the appropriate way for the agent to be idealized such that her reactions from that idealized vantage point determine her good. She writes:

> [C]ounterfactual conditions C are appropriate only if the fact that a person would come to care about something X for her actual self when under C is itself something that she would care about while under ordinary optimal conditions. [We achieve "ordinary optimal conditions," Rosati says, when we are in "whatever normally attainable conditions are optimal for reflecting on questions about what to care about. . . ."] A person need not care about X itself while under ordinary optimal conditions in order for X to be good for her. But if her good is not to be alienated, the fact that she would care about X for her actual self under a particular set of counterfactual conditions had better be something that would prompt her concern under ordinary optimal conditions.[10]

[10] Connie Rosati, "Internalism and the Good for a Person," *Ethics* 106, no. 2 (1996): 307.

Rosati explicitly attempts to argue that the same thoughts that led internalists to internalism should lead them to two-tier internalism, and thus that we should allow an agent's concerns to shape what counts as a sound deliberative route for her. I cannot adequately explore Rosati's fascinating proposal here, but notice that she does not allow just any aspect of an agent's concerns to shape what counts as sound deliberation for that agent. Rosati specifically assigns this role to the agent's concerns about what forms of deliberation she finds authoritative.

If Williams or internalists generally want to argue that we can look to an agent's subjective motivational set to help shape what counts as sound deliberation, I think they would do better to follow Rosati's proposal rather than Williams's tacit suggestion. My own hunch, however, is that the internalist is best advised to sever the connection between what counts as sound deliberation and an agent's subjective motivational set. In my opinion, subjectivists like myself should argue that sound deliberation necessarily involves correct factual premises but not prudence or morality; however, I think we should do so on other grounds. That is, we should be subjectivists about reasons for action, but not about the vantage point from which an agent's reactions determine her reasons for action.

The subjectivist, at least by my lights, needs a defense of the thought that sound deliberation involves knowing the facts, a defense that (1) does not depend on finding certain elements in an agent's subjective motivational set, (2) does not also justify counting prudential or moral motivation as a necessary part of sound deliberation, and (3) is continuous with the general subjectivist framework rather than being ad hoc or incorporating objectivist elements. I believe that such a defense can be given, but this is not the place to attempt to make good on this claim.

III. AGAINST THE EXPLANATION CONDITION AND INTERNALISM

In the previous section, I claimed that Williams's argumentative strategy for vindicating internalism is flawed in two ways. Of course, this by itself does not show that the explanation condition or internalism is itself false. In this section, however, I will argue for the falsity of both of those theses. I will argue that they are inadequate not because of their connection to neo-Humean subjectivism, but rather as a result of not being compatible with the best versions of such. Seeing the grounds for rejecting the explanation condition and internalism will lead us toward, rather than away from, an adequate subjectivism about reasons for action.

Before we examine these objections to the explanation condition and internalism, we will need to take a brief detour through some literature on well-being. In that literature, one finds an account of well-being that is importantly similar to Williams's internalism about reasons for action. I will call this the *full information account of well-being*. John Stuart Mill's competent-judges test offered an early model of the account, Henry Sidgwick offered perhaps its first explicit formulation, and Richard Brandt, R. M. Hare, John Rawls, David Gauthier, James Griffin, Stephen Darwall, David Lewis, Peter Railton, and John Harsanyi have each developed and/or endorsed the view.[11] Roughly, the picture is this: an agent's life goes best if she gets those things that she would want if she had full knowledge of the options available.[12]

Sidgwick's formulation of the account went like this:

> [A] man's future good on the whole is what he would now desire and seek on the whole if all the consequences of all the different lines of conduct open to him were accurately foreseen and adequately realized in imagination at the present point in time.[13]

This formulation quickly runs into difficulties. For example, consider that even though our fully informed self would never want more information for itself, we are firmly convinced that sometimes it can be intrinsically in our interest to gain information. The fact that the fully informed agent lacks a desire for information clearly does not threaten the thought that it would be good for a noninformed agent to get information. Furthermore, our fully informed selves no doubt have a refined palate, and may well highly value expensive complex wines that taste just like the cheaper stuff to us. Yet it is implausible that one wine is much better for

---

[11] John Stuart Mill, *Utilitarianism* (Indianapolis, IN: Hackett, 1979), chap. 2; Henry Sidgwick, *The Methods of Ethics*, 7th ed. (Indianapolis, IN: Hackett, 1981), 111–12; Richard Brandt, *A Theory of the Good and the Right* (Oxford: Clarendon Press, 1979), 10, 113, 329; R. M. Hare, *Moral Thinking* (Oxford: Clarendon Press, 1981), 101–5, 214–16; R. M. Hare, "Replies," in Douglas Seanor and N. Fotion, eds., *Hare and Critics: Essays on "Moral Thinking"* (Oxford: Clarendon Press, 1990), 217–18; James Griffin, *Well-Being* (Oxford: Oxford University Press, 1986), 11–17; John Rawls, *A Theory of Justice* (Cambridge, MA: Harvard University Press, 1971), 407–24; David Gauthier, *Morals by Agreement* (Oxford: Clarendon Press, 1986), chap. 2; Stephen Darwall, *Impartial Reason* (Ithaca, NY:'Cornell University Press, 1983), pt. 2; Peter Railton, "Facts and Values," *Philosophical Topics* 14, no. 2 (1986): 5–31; David Lewis, "Dispositional Theories of Value," *Proceedings of the Aristotelian Society*, n.s., 63 (1989): 113–37; John Harsanyi, "Morality and the Theory of Rational Behavior," in Amartya Sen and Bernard Williams, eds., *Utilitarianism and Beyond* (Cambridge: Cambridge University Press, 1973), 55. Several important caveats apply to some of the above authors' commitments to subjectivism, and some would decline the label. Robert Shaver raises some of these caveats in the case of Sidgwick. See Robert Shaver, "Sidgwick's False Friends," *Ethics* 107, no. 2 (1997): 314–20; see also David Sobel, "Reply to Shaver," published in 1997 in the e-journal BEARS, available at http://www.brown.edu/Departments/Philosophy/bears/9707sobel. html [posted on July 7, 1997].

[12] In David Sobel, "Well-Being as the Object of Moral Consideration," *Economics and Philosophy* 14, no. 2 (1998): 249–83, I consider ways that such a theory could try to respond to the fact that some of our concerns are moral or quasi-moral and hence not perfectly correlated with our well-being. I conclude that any such method will reveal that well-being is not the appropriate object of moral concern. I defend instead the *autonomy principle*, which would allow agents to throw the weight they are granted in moral reflection where they informedly see fit. For a different take on similar issues, see Stephen Darwall's "Self-Interest and Self-Concern," *Social Philosophy and Policy* 14, no. 1 (1997): 158–78.

[13] Sidgwick, *The Methods of Ethics*, 111–12.

me than another when I cannot tell the difference (assuming that it is only the taste of the expensive wine that causes our idealized self to prefer it over the cheaper stuff).[14] Hence, the presence of this desire in the informed agent does not give us grounds to suppose that satisfying this desire would be good for the nonidealized agent. In both of these examples, we are presented with a major problem in Sidgwick's formulation: the idealization process he postulates turns us into such different creatures that it would be surprising if the well-being of one's informed self and one's ordinary self consisted in the same things.[15]

In response to problems such as these, Railton has revised the full information account, proposing that

> an individual's good consists in what he would want himself to want, or to pursue, were he to contemplate his present situation from a standpoint fully and vividly informed about himself and his circumstances, and entirely free of cognitive error or lapses of instrumental rationality.[16]

The adoption of a "wanting to want" framework neatly eschews the implausible identification of interests between informed and ordinary selves, while retaining the insight that "the advice of someone who has this fuller information, and also has the deepest sort of identification with one's fate, is bound to have some commending force." [17]

Railton's move here with respect to discussions of well-being has been duplicated to some extent by Michael Smith in the sphere of reasons for action. Smith claims:

---

[14] I take this example from Griffin, *Well-Being*, 11.

[15] I have presented these reasons for moving from a Sidgwickian view (and to a Railtonian view—see below) in David Sobel, "Full Information Accounts of Well-Being," *Ethics* 104, no. 4 (1994): 784–810.

[16] Railton offers this account in "Facts and Values," 16. But see ibid., 25 and Peter Railton, "Moral Realism," *Philosophical Review* 96, no. 2 (1986): 175–76 n. 17, for the claim that this account merely "tracks" one's good, that is, while the account shows what an agent's good is, it is not the case that an agent's good is her good because it fulfills the account's criterion. (I discuss this distinction in more detail later in this section.) Notice that Railton's compelling claim that it would be "an intolerably alienated conception of someone's good to imagine that it might fail in any way to engage him" (Railton, "Facts and Values," 9), is compatible with the claim that the full information account merely tracks one's good. In his more recent work, Railton claims that the subjective reactions from the approved vantage point are indicators of the presence of a fit between an individual and an end. See Peter Railton, "Aesthetic Value, Moral Value, and the Ambitions of Naturalism," in Jerrold Levinson, ed., *Aesthetics and Ethics: Essays at the Intersection* (Cambridge: Cambridge University Press, 1998).

[17] Railton, "Facts and Values," 14. Consider, however, that our idealized self could want our ordinary self to want X because the idealized agent knows that our ordinary self's doing so will be instrumentally effective in bringing about, albeit unintentionally, Y, something that the idealized agent finds to be best for our ordinary self. If we say that what is good for our ordinary self is what our idealized self wants our ordinary self to want, we seem to misdescribe these cases of indirection. Perhaps it would be better to focus on the kind of life that the idealized agent wants the ordinary self to have.

[W]hat it is desirable for us to do in certain circumstances—let's call these circumstances the 'evaluated possible world'—is what we, not as we actually are, but as we would be in a possible world in which we are fully rational—let's call this the 'evaluating possible world'—would want ourselves to do in those circumstances. That is, it tells us that facts about the desirability of acting in certain ways in the evaluated world are constituted by facts about the desires we have about the evaluated world in the evaluating world.[18]

Let us, following a convention Railton uses in his essay quoted above, call the actual person whose reasons we are investigating A, and the idealized version of A, who engages in ideally sound deliberation, A+. Railton and Smith argue that to determine A's good or reasons for action, we should consult A+'s advice for A rather than what A+ himself finds motivating. Railton and Smith have fairly definite ideas about what ideally sound deliberation looks like. However, we need not agree with them on these matters to take the point that the ideally sound deliberator is best viewed as an advisor rather than as someone who will himself be motivated toward that which A has a reason to get. Sidgwick and Brandt, notably among others, do conceive of the idealized agent as someone who would himself be motivated to ϕ if and only if it is good for A to ϕ, and this can be seen to be a mistake even if we disagree with Railton and Smith about the contours of ideally sound deliberation.

The process of becoming an ideally sound deliberator can turn an agent into someone whose reasons for action differ from those of the agent's nonidealized self.[19] That is, the process of changing A into A+ can alter the reasons for action that this person has. If we are to look to A+ to determine A's reasons for action, we must take care, lest A's reasons that are present because he is a nonidealized agent get lost or altered. We are not interested in what reasons for action A+ has. This is why it is best to think of the idealized agent as an advisor. Partially as a result of these considerations, I think the move to *ideal advisor accounts* is a clear improvement over views such as Sidgwick's, Brandt's, and Williams's, each of which grants normative status to what A+ himself is motivated to do.[20]

[18] Michael Smith, *The Moral Problem* (Oxford: Blackwell Publishers, 1994), 151.
[19] This highlights a rather general problem for conditional theories. See Robert K. Shope, "The Conditional Fallacy in Contemporary Philosophy," *Journal of Philosophy* 75, no. 8 (1978): 397–413; and Robert K. Shope, "Rawls, Brandt, and the Definition of Rational Desires," *Canadian Journal of Philosophy* 8, no. 2 (1978): 329–40. I am grateful to Steve Darwall for these references.
[20] I take the useful term "ideal advisor account" from Connie Rosati, "Persons, Perspectives, and Full Information Accounts of the Good," *Ethics* 105, no. 2 (1995): 296–325. Rosati goes on in that paper to critique such accounts. I critique such accounts in "Full Information Accounts of Well-Being." Although both of these papers are critical of such accounts, both agree that the move from the simpler accounts (we might call them *direct motivational accounts*) to ideal advisor accounts is a step in the right direction. Although both papers' critiques are offered against full information accounts of well-being, they are equally effective against full information accounts of reasons for action.

If we are persuaded by these sorts of considerations to look to A+ as an advisor to A, then Williams's explanation condition and his formulation of internalism are both threatened. Let us start with the explanation condition. As noted in Section II, Williams claims that "If it is true that A has a reason to ϕ, then it must be possible that he should ϕ for that reason," and that "If something can be a reason for action, then it could be someone's reason for acting on a particular occasion, and it would then figure in an explanation of that action." In Section II, we had some difficulty generating a precise formulation of these thoughts such that they could play the role that Williams wanted them to play. But now we are in a position to see that it is the central idea here, not just a particular formulation, that is false. The central idea of Williams's claims, I take it, is that if consideration C provides A a reason to ϕ, then it must be the case that A could ϕ because C motivated him to ϕ.

If I have a reason to ϕ, then I have a reason to ϕ in the actual world. Thus, Williams's explanation condition might be thought to express the claim that the consideration that makes it true that I have a reason to ϕ in the actual world must be able to explain my ϕ-ing in the actual world. But counterfactual sound deliberation by A+ in some other possible world, and A+'s subsequent motivation to recommend to A that he should ϕ, cannot explain A's ϕ-ing in the actual world. A might, for example, lack epistemic access to the information that A+ has, with the result being that A could not act for the considerations that the information makes available to A+.

It will rightly be objected that this by itself does not threaten the explanation condition, since that condition need not specify that it is A's actions in the actual world that must be able to be explained. But if these are not the actions that the condition requires be explicable, to what actions does the condition refer? Perhaps the thought is that if consideration C truly provides A with a reason to ϕ, then C must be able to explain A's action after A has deliberated soundly. However, the above analysis of ideal advisor views makes clear that A+—who *is* A after ideally sound deliberation—need not himself be motivated or take action toward that which A has a reason to do. The fact that for C to provide A with a reason to ϕ, A+ must in some sense recommend to A that he ϕ on the ground provided by C does not support the claim that C could explain A's or A+'s ϕ-ing. Thus, on ideal advisor views, it can be true that consideration C provides A with a reason to ϕ without it being the case that C could explain A's or A+'s ϕ-ing. Therefore, adherents to the most plausible versions of subjectivism about reasons for action must reject Williams's explanation condition.

Put in a different way, the problem with the explanation condition is that it cannot accommodate the existence of what I will call *fragile reasons*. One has a reason to ϕ, at least according to ideal advisor views, if one's ideally informed self would in some sense recommend ϕ-ing to one's actual self. One's reason to ϕ is fragile if the process of becoming ideally informed results in the ideally informed agent lacking a reason to ϕ. I call such reasons fragile because the process of becoming an ideally sound deliberator destroys them. To put this in terms of A and A+, we can say that A's reason to ϕ is fragile if and only if A has it but A+ lacks it.[21] For example, suppose there is a distinctive taste that, once one has tasted it, one is glad to have done so but has no desire to do so again. After one has tasted it, one would recommend to versions of oneself that have not tasted it to try it, but considering the taste itself could never motivate one, whether informed or not, to try it.

There are likely to be fragile reasons when the considerations that ground the reasons for A to ϕ involve the fact that A is not ideally epistemically situated to determine his reasons. The fact that extreme alterations are needed to make a person an ideal advisor suggests that it will frequently be the case that the reasons of A will differ from the reasons of A+. Thus, I suspect that fragile reasons are common.

Reasons can be so fragile that the only vantage points from which one could appreciate the way in which ϕ-ing furthers something in the actual agent's subjective motivational set are vantage points in which one lacks a reason to ϕ. These are what I will call *superfragile reasons*. Superfragile reasons are reasons that one cannot have and be motivated by simultaneously. The case of the singular taste offered above might be an example. We should expect superfragile reasons when appreciating the considerations that make it true that ϕ-ing would further something in A's subjective motivational set itself makes it the case that the agent who so appreciates these considerations himself lacks a reason to ϕ. If there are superfragile reasons, then there are cases in which no vantage point that a person could take up would be such that from that vantage point a person would both have the reason to ϕ and be motivated by the consideration that gives rise to that reason.

Fragile reasons are the key to my rejection of Explanation III and internalism. Superfragile reasons are the key to my rejection of Explanation II. Because the existence of superfragile reasons is more contentious than the existence of fragile reasons, my case against Explanation II is weaker than my case against Explanation III and internalism. However, as I argued in the previous section, I see no intuitive basis for Explanation II except that which is better captured by Explanation III.

The existence of fragile and superfragile reasons shows us that it is a mistake to insist that the same consideration that provides one with a reason must also be able to explain action in accord with that reason. This, it seems to me, strikes at the heart of the explanation condition and

---

[21] There will, of course, also be cases in which A lacks a reason to ϕ but A+ has one. However, the example of fragile reasons as I define them in the text is sufficient to make my case.

internalism, and shows us that both are just wrong. Yet giving up the claim that reasons and motivations are connected in this way does not force us to give up the thought that one's reasons are determined by one's subjective motivational set.

It might be that there cannot be fragile considerations that ground the fact that it would be rational for A to ϕ. Considerations that ground rationality claims cannot so radically exceed the ken of the agent as can the considerations that ground his reasons. Rationality is a matter of making good use of the information that one has or could reasonably be expected to get. Thus, considerations that it was reasonable for one to be unaware of cannot undermine the claim that one was rational to ϕ. Claims about rationality, then, should be relativized to take into account the agent's predicament and epistemic situation.

Williams's project does not engage in this sort of relativization. On the contrary, the deliberation that Williams claims can close the gap between our current motivations and our genuine reasons is deliberation that, in many cases, we are unable to carry out. Often, for example, the relevant facts that one would need in ideal deliberation have not yet been discovered. Additionally, the deliberation that Williams thinks can close the gap will in many cases be deliberation that it would be impractical for actual people to pursue.

Whatever the merits of his proposal, Williams is hoping to capture the sense of having a reason to ϕ in which one might retrospectively say of oneself, "I had a reason all along to ϕ and did not realize it or have any reason to suspect it until now." In everyday parlance, we do speak as if we could have had a reason to ϕ "all along" even if we had never had any information that would have made ϕ-ing a rational choice at the time. This shows that reason claims, unlike rationality claims, need not be relativized to the agent's epistemic predicament. Therefore, reason claims are significantly more likely to be fragile than are rationality claims. It is thus important to my case that Williams is offering an account of reasons, not an account of rationality.[22]

Let us turn now from considering how the move to ideal advisor views undermines the explanation condition to the issue of how it undermines internalism. As noted above, internalism is the claim that "A has a reason to ϕ only if he could reach the conclusion to ϕ by a sound deliberative route from the motivations he already has. The externalist view is that this is not a necessary condition, and that it can

[22] I make this case much more fully in David Sobel, "Subjective Accounts of Reasons for Action," *Ethics* 111, no. 3 (2001): 461–92. I also argue in that essay that attention to the distinction between an account of reasons and an account of rationality undermines Christine Korsgaard's case against the instrumentalism of Hume and Williams that she offers in Christine Korsgaard, "Skepticism About Practical Reason," in Korsgaard, *Creating the Kingdom of Ends* (Cambridge: Cambridge University Press, 1996); and Christine Korsgaard, "The Normativity of Instrumental Reason," in Garret Cullity and Berys Gaut, eds., *Ethics and Practical Reason* (Oxford: Oxford University Press, 1997).

be true of A that he has a reason to ϕ even though A has no motivation in his motivational set that could, either directly or by some extension through sound deliberation, lead him to ϕ." Thus, as an internalist, Williams supposes that if A has a reason to ϕ, it must be the case that, via sound deliberation, A could reach the conclusion that he himself ought to ϕ. The problem again is that there need not be, at least according to ideal advisor views, a single version of A who both (1) has a reason to ϕ, and (2) is himself motivated to ϕ or would conclude that he ought to ϕ after sound deliberation. According to ideal advisor views, the crucial motivation that we should fix on is what A+ recommends to A. The normatively special motivation is, on such views, not a motivation or conclusion for A himself to take action toward ϕ.

Thus, it will sometimes be true that even though A "has no motivation in his motivational set that could, either directly or by some extension through sound deliberation, lead him to ϕ," the best subjectivist accounts of reasons for action will nonetheless claim that A has a reason to ϕ. Fragile reasons work like this. Therefore, fragile reasons are, according to Williams, external reasons. As a result, the best subjectivist accounts of reasons for action must tolerate external reasons as Williams defines them.

Again, the arguments offered here to reject internalism emerge from an acceptance of subjectivism about reasons for action. The thought is that the most plausible version of subjectivism must follow the path of ideal advisor views. When we follow this path, we recognize that it is not a necessary condition on consideration C providing A a reason to ϕ that there be any particular version of A that can conclude via a sound deliberative route that he ought to ϕ.

Williams is arguing for internalism rather than subjectivism. Williams's internalism is compatible with either a "tracking" or a "truth-making" interpretation.[23] To understand this distinction, consider the American holiday of Groundhog Day. On February 2 of each year, groundhogs are observed as they emerge from their holes; if, rather than venturing outside, the groundhogs return to their holes (upon being scared by their shadow, as I hear it), it is said to mean that there will be six more weeks of winter. Now, it is reasonably clear that the groundhogs' behavior is not thought to make the winter linger. We cannot blame the cold on them, for this would be to blame the messenger. Rather, the groundhogs' behavior is claimed to be a reliable guide to the weather.

[23] Stephen Darwall's formulations of *existence internalism* (Darwall, *Impartial Reason*, 55) and *metaphysical internalism* (Stephen Darwall, "Reasons, Motives, and the Demands of Morality: An Introduction," in Stephen Darwall, Allan Gibbard, and Peter Railton, eds., *Moral Discourse and Practice* [New York: Oxford University Press, 1997], 308–9) are both, like Williams's formulation of internalism, put in terms of necessary conditions for being a reason. Thus, these versions of internalism that Darwall describes are also subject to the importantly different interpretations mentioned in the text. Darwall briefly notes this ambiguity in the latter discussion.

Tracking internalism holds that one's informed pro-attitude toward ϕ-ing is similarly just a reliable guide to one's reasons, not what makes it the case that one has a reason to ϕ.[24] It is thus compatible with objectivism rather than subjectivism about reasons for action. Objectivism and subjectivism, in this context, are theses about what makes it the case that one has a reason to ϕ. If an account claims that the answer to this question is not to be found in the agent's contingent pro-attitudes, then it counts as a version of objectivism. On the other hand, *truth-making internalism* embraces the subjectivist's claim that what makes it the case that one has a reason to ϕ is that one has the relevant informed pro-attitude toward ϕ-ing. Although Williams's defense of internalism is compatible with either the subjectivist or objectivist interpretation, the spirit of his discussion makes clear that he is more inclined to embrace the subjectivist account.

Because of this, I am not inclined to investigate whether or not a successor notion of internalism that avoids the problems discussed above can be found. It seems to me that the interesting philosophical debate here centers on the acceptability of subjectivism rather than the acceptability of internalism. The most philosophically interesting aspect about the debate over internalism has been the debate over what makes it the case that one has a reason to ϕ. Christine Korsgaard, for example, argues that Kantian accounts (and indeed, any philosophically respectable accounts) of practical reason should embrace internalism. She writes, "Practical reason claims, if they are really to present us with reasons for action, must be capable of motivating rational persons. I will call this the internalism requirement."[25] I actually think that this version of internalism is mistaken for reasons completely different from those I have presented in this essay.[26] Yet the point to notice for the moment is that leading proponents of the two fundamentally different accounts of practical reason do not take themselves to differ over the thesis of internalism. The interesting dispute between neo-Humeans like Williams and neo-Kantians like Korsgaard is over what makes it the case that one has a reason for action. The interesting question is hence not whether to embrace internalism or externalism, but whether to embrace objectivism or subjectivism—a debate that may boil down to a dispute about the powers of practical reason to

[24] Michael Smith's account of reasons for action in *The Moral Problem* is best understood as a version of tracking internalism. He thinks that the desires of all ideally rational agents converging on certain things is necessary and sufficient for our having reasons, and in particular reasons to do what our desires converge on. According to Smith, the best explanation for such a convergence, if it occurred, would be that there are "extremely unobvious a priori moral truths" (Smith, *The Moral Problem*, 187). On his view, it is these truths that make it the case that we have reasons to do certain things; our ideally informed deliberations simply get our motivations to track these truths. I critique Smith's arguments for convergence in David Sobel, "Do the Desires of Rational Agents Converge?" *Analysis* 59, no. 3 (1999): 137–47.
[25] Korsgaard, "Skepticism About Practical Reason," 11.
[26] See Sobel, "Subjective Accounts of Reasons for Action."

bring about consensus in the motivations of people who start out with radically different motivations.

IV. Conclusion

Williams writes, "The whole point of external reason statements is that they can be true independently of the agent's motivations." That is, Williams thinks that external reasons would not be essentially relative to the agent's subjective motivational set. But Williams's claim here about externalism is not a necessary consequence of rejecting the explanation condition and internalism. There is room in logical space for resisting the thought that a true reason for A to ϕ must motivate A to ϕ after sound deliberation while accepting that what makes it the case that A has a reason to ϕ is that A "has some motive that will be served or furthered by his ϕ-ing."[27]

It is clear enough why it would seem natural, if one were positing a connection between motivations and reasons, to think that it is a constraint on having a reason to ϕ that one be motivated to ϕ after sound deliberation. After all, should it instead be a constraint on having a reason to ϕ that one be motivated to do something else, say X, after sound deliberation? Yet as we have seen, ideal advisor views better capture the wanted relationship between the sound deliberator and the reasons of nonidealized agents than do views that look to what the sound deliberator is motivated to do or concludes that she has reason to do. When, as a consequence, we embrace an ideal advisor account, we leave behind the thought that if consideration C grounds a reason for A to ϕ, it must be that C could motivate A to ϕ.[28] Thus, in searching for the best understanding of the pro-attitudes that have a fundamental connection to our reasons, we are forced to leave the explanation condition and internalism behind.[29]

Philosophy, Bowling Green State University

---

[27] Williams, "Internal and External Reasons," 101. This is Williams's casual and "very rough" characterization of internalism in the earlier paper. The formulation of internalism offered in the later "Internal Reasons and the Obscurity of Blame," which I cite at the beginning of Section II of this essay, is clearly intended to be his official "nonrough" characterization of internalism. This formulation is also the sort Williams invokes in Bernard Williams, "Replies," in Altham and Harrison, eds., *World, Mind, and Ethics*, 186–94. Furthermore, the later characterization is the one that has been picked up by subsequent writers on internalism such as Darwall and Korsgaard.

[28] Throughout this essay I have been treating the concepts of 'motivation' and 'desire' as unproblematic so as to focus on other issues. In fact, I find these concepts not yet satisfactorily analyzed. For some initial misgivings, see David Sobel and David Copp, "Against Direction of Fit Accounts of Belief and Desire," *Analysis* 61, no. 1 (2001): 44–53.

[29] Unfortunately, I did not read Robert Johnson's excellent "Internal Reasons and the Conditional Fallacy," *Philosophical Quarterly* 49, no. 194 (1999): 53–71, until it was too late to take it into account here. Johnson offers compelling arguments for some of the central conclusions that I urge in the second half of this essay.

MORAL KNOWLEDGE AS PRACTICAL KNOWLEDGE*

By Julia Annas

I. Different Perspectives

In the area of moral epistemology, there is an interesting problem facing the person in my area, ancient philosophy, who hopes to write a historical paper which will engage with our current philosophical concerns. Not only are ancient ethical theories very different in structure and concerns from modern ones (though with the rapid growth of virtue ethics this is becoming less true), but the concerns and emphases of ancient epistemology are very different from those of modern theories of knowledge. Some may think that they are so different that they are useful to our own discussions only by way of contrast. I am more sanguine, but I am quite aware that this essay's contribution to modern debates does not fall within the established modern traditions of discussing moral epistemology.

Because ancient moral epistemology is rather different from modern kinds, two kinds of danger arise when we try to compare them. On the one hand, we may produce a historical account which fails to engage with modern concerns. On the other hand, we can pose a philosophical question in terms of modern assumptions about knowledge, and then find that the ancients' answer to it appears naive or off the point.

While both can be unhelpful, the second is likely to be more so than the first. In what follows, I shall begin with a passage from a modern author which displays a dramatic misunderstanding of a famous ancient position. I shall then try to isolate the assumptions which prevent a better understanding. However, I will also, and mainly, be concerned to bring out one aspect of the ancient position which I think marks not just a significant difference between ancient and modern approaches to moral epistemology, but also a weakness in the modern approaches, and a point where we might actually learn from the ancients.

II. Examining Assumptions

In his influential book *Ethics: Inventing Right and Wrong*,[1] John L. Mackie argues that our intuitive confidence that there are what he calls "objective values" is misplaced; a very simple argument shows that there can be no

* I am very grateful to David Brink, David Owen, Mark van Roojen, and the other contributors to this volume for their comments on an earlier draft of this essay.
[1] J. L. Mackie, *Ethics: Inventing Right and Wrong* (Harmondsworth, NY: Penguin, 1977).

such things.[2] For, if there were any objective values, they would be extremely "queer" things:

> If there were objective values, then they would be entities or qualities or relations of a very strange sort, utterly different from anything else in the universe. Correspondingly, if we were aware of them, it would have to be by some special faculty of moral perception or intuition, utterly different from our ordinary ways of knowing everything else.[3]

Since, it is assumed, this is unacceptable, we conclude that there are no objective values—that is, there is nothing which is both a value, directing our actions, and objective.

At once we can see that most moral philosophers of the past have been in error on this point, with an especially spectacular form of the error to be found in Plato.

> [T]he main tradition of European moral philosophy from Plato onwards has combined the view that moral values are objective with the recognition that moral judgements are partly prescriptive or directive or action-guiding. Values themselves have been seen as at once prescriptive and objective. In Plato's theory the Forms, and in particular the Form of the Good, are eternal, extra-mental, realities. They are a very central structural element in the fabric of the world. But it is held also that just knowing them or 'seeing' them will not merely tell men [sic] what to do but will ensure that they do it, overruling any contrary inclinations. . . . Being acquainted with the Forms of the Good and Justice and Beauty and the rest [the rulers of the *Republic*] will, by this knowledge alone, without any further motivation, be impelled to pursue and promote these ideals.[4]

And later on:

---

[2] I am aware that discussion of moral realism has moved on since Mackie, but there has been surprisingly little change on the point I wish to examine. It is often assumed that the realist options are either a kind of minimalist realism, making only the internal commitments of moral discourse (for an example of this kind of realism, see Ronald Dworkin, "Objectivity and Truth: You'd Better Believe It," *Philosophy and Public Affairs* 25, no. 2 [1996]: 87–139), or a more substantial realism, making metaphysical commitments external to moral discourse, and this option is readily labelled "Platonism."

[3] Mackie, *Ethics*, 38. Mackie frequently makes disparaging references to "intuition," which he gives no account of. He assumes that we know what intuition is from "the intuitionists," but this is not a great deal of help, since theories calling themselves intuitionist have diverged widely over what they take intuition to be and what kind of items (e.g., principles, kinds of value, individual features of situations) they take to be the objects of intuition.

[4] Ibid., 23–24.

Plato's Forms give a dramatic picture of what objective values would have to be. The Form of the Good is such that knowledge of it provides the knower with both a direction and an overriding motive; something's being good both tells the person who knows this to pursue it and makes him pursue it.[5]

Mackie allows that,

It may be thought that the argument from queerness is given an unfair start if we thus relate it to what are admittedly among the wilder products of philosophical fancy—Platonic Forms, non-natural qualities, self-evident relations of fitness, faculties of intuition, and the like.[6]

This hostile portrayal of the Forms of moral qualities as bizarre entities picked out by an equally peculiar faculty of intuition is clearly a coarse and imperceptive interpretation of Plato.[7] What is of interest here, however, is not just for specialists to complain that Mackie's interpretation of Plato is terrible, but to try to isolate the assumptions that lead to it, or at least help to produce it. For what Mackie is missing is very important— and not just Mackie, of course; I have focused on him as being representative of (and also, to a certain extent, responsible for) a widespread view of the available options in moral epistemology. I think that this view is impoverished, and that one significant indication of this impoverishment is precisely its peculiar view of what is going on in the case of Plato and the moral Forms.

A number of the assumptions that Mackie makes are rather obvious. (In what follows, I shall concentrate on the epistemological rather than the metaphysical side of the queerness argument.) A crucial assumption is that our epistemological access to values is "utterly different from our ordinary ways of knowing everything else." On this view, values are not part of the world that we have access to either empirically or by reasoning.[8] First, the brisk exclusion of values from the area to which we have empirical access, in turn, presupposes that our access to that area is epistemologically unproblematic and that there are no serious problems in

---

[5] Ibid., 40.

[6] Ibid., 41.

[7] This harsh verdict is reasonable in that Mackie did, after all, read Plato in the original and was not dependent on possibly misleading translations. Mackie is also insensitive to Plato's uses of argument, reading the dialogues crudely as ways of putting forward positive ideas of Plato's own. Mackie regards the arguments of the *Protagoras*, for example, as Plato's own attempts to put forward a positive position, and deals with the obvious resulting problems by cheerfully ascribing to Plato "a lot of sophistry" (Mackie, *Ethics*, 187).

[8] More expansively, we cannot access them by "sensory perception or introspection or the framing and confirming of explanatory hypotheses or inference or logical construction or conceptual analysis, or any combination of these" (ibid., 39).

demarcating what that area contains. Second, the exclusion of values from the area to which we have access through reasoning also presupposes a highly determinate philosophical account of what reason and reasoning are, one in which reason itself is assumed to have no motivating force. On such an account, reasoning can lead to conclusions, for example, but a completely different kind of factor is required to get those conclusions to lead to action. A third assumption is that values motivate by "prescribing"; ethics is envisaged as telling others (and presumably also yourself) what to do. Mackie thus assumes that ethics is primarily about action, and about getting others and yourself to act in certain ways.

Mackie cites A. J. Ayer and C. L. Stevenson as influences on his thinking, although he rejects logical positivism as a characterization of his position, preferring to call it empiricist.[9] It can also, more broadly but defensibly, be called scientistic, for it assumes that we have a clear notion of observation and explanation which excludes values without the need for any argument. Such a notion relies on the idea that the sciences (envisaged as a unified "science" in a way that Mackie seems not to regard as controversial) will demarcate such a notion for us, and that this demarcation will be deferentially accepted by people outside the sciences.[10]

In any case, whatever we call the position, Mackie's assumptions are widely shared in contemporary philosophy (though in the broader culture they cannot be taken for granted, and the idea in particular is widely rejected that we defer to science in defining value-excluding notions of experience and observation). Someone who shared these assumptions but was a more sympathetic interpreter than Mackie might come out with a less absurd interpretation of Plato's moral Forms; nonetheless, it would be hard for such a person to do justice to what I shall now try to present as a leading point about moral epistemology in Plato's arguments for Forms. This will take up Sections III through V, and I will return to the empirical assumptions in Section VI.

---

[9] In his notes to chapter 1 of *Ethics*, Mackie says that his views were first written down in 1941, and cites Ayer's *Language, Truth, and Logic* and Stevenson's *Ethics and Language* as helping to determine the main outlines of his position (ibid., 241). He rejects characterization as a logical positivist on the grounds that he rejects both the verifiability principle as a criterion for descriptive meaning and the idea that moral judgments lack descriptive meaning (ibid., 39–40). Mackie's characterization of his position as empiricist can be faulted on the ground that many positions describing themselves as empiricist start from much less restrictive assumptions. Also, although in *Ethics* he holds that morality has to be "made" and that we "have to decide" what moral views to "adopt" (ibid., 106), he writes a whole book on ethics, thus insulating his practice from his theoretical view. I have made some remarks on this issue in my "Doing without Objective Values: Ancient and Modern Strategies," in Stephen Everson, ed., *Ethics*, vol. 4 of *Companions to Ancient Thought* (Cambridge: Cambridge University Press, 1998), 193–220, esp. 216.

[10] For a valuable discussion of these claims, see Tom Sorell, *Scientism* (London: Routledge, 1991). Scientism takes many forms; here I am concerned only with assumptions made by philosophers who give science primacy in defining our epistemological concepts. These assumptions are not shared in the wider culture, even where that culture contains other kinds of deference toward science.

III. Searching for Moral Knowledge

I will start by giving a straightforward (and probably embarrassingly simple) account of the argument, which appears more than once in Plato's Socratic dialogues, to get us to recognize what Plato (sometimes) calls Forms.[11] Then I will bring out the important feature of this and similar arguments; this is the feature on which I want to focus. I should emphasize at the start that this account is not idiosyncratic or presented as in any way original; it could reasonably be regarded as a standard account among philosophers in the area of ancient philosophy.

In the *Laches*, two generals, who are both unquestionably brave, have gotten into a discussion about bravery. Will a fashionable new course of training help to make young men brave or not? Disconcertingly, the brave generals disagree, and Socrates, in his usual annoying way, gets them to examine the question of what bravery is and try to come up with a satisfactory account of it. (We know, of course, since this is a Socratic dialogue, that they will not succeed; part of the point of the dialogue is to get the reader engaged in that task.) It is not surprising that the value term that is under discussion is a virtue term, since virtue is a central notion in all of ancient ethics.

Laches, one of the generals, tries to give an account of bravery by pointing out that people are brave who stand up to the enemy in battle and do not break the ranks by running away (190e). Socrates points out that while this is true, courage can also be shown by people who do what looks like the opposite—namely, strategic retreat (191b–c). He then sets out his conditions for an adequate understanding of courage:

> I wanted to learn from you not only what it is to be brave as an infantryman [i.e., standing firm], but also as a cavalryman [i.e., strategic retreat] and in general as anyone fighting in an army; and to learn about the brave not just in a war but in dangers at sea and when facing illness or poverty, and in public life; and, further, not just the brave in face of pains or fears, but those who are intelligent at battling with desires and pleasures, whether by standing firm or by strategic retreat.... All these people are brave, but some possess courage in pleasures, others in pains, some in desires and others in fears, while others again possess cowardice in these circumstances.... What each of these is—that's what I wanted to find out. (191c–e)

It is clear enough that we do not understand what courage is, and that we cannot give an adequate account of what courage is just by having

---

[11] Actually the terms *eidos* and *idea* do not occur very often; Plato is not so much arguing for a new notion to which he will give a new technical name, as drawing out the implications of ways of thinking which have appeal anyway, and rendering these more precisely.

some moral beliefs, that is, some beliefs about courage and courageous people. It is worth pointing out that Socrates does not suggest that these beliefs are *false*. Soldiers who stand firm in the ranks and fight are indeed brave. However, if we rely on these beliefs, we are let down, and this is because, while they are true, they are unsatisfactory in being ungrounded and disunified. These two defects are connected. If we look at the various ways in which Socrates indicates that people are brave, we find a ragbag. What does standing firm in the ranks have to do with firmly facing financial ruin? Nothing obvious. Why, then, do we think that in both these situations someone can be *brave*? The reason is, again, not obvious. We would reasonably think that unless the concept is confused, there would be something common to brave ways of fighting in battle and brave ways of facing poverty. What this is, however, cannot be read off from the contexts of bravery themselves. Beliefs about bravery are formed and picked up from our experience, but our experience itself does not tell us how to unify them, nor, hence, how to understand what their basis is. Until we understand what it is that we understand bravery to be, we will not understand why we recognize the examples of bravery that we do. We will also be unable to improve on our present understanding of bravery by extending our use of the term, for how could we be sure that a new example was an example of bravery or not?

Hence, to understand what bravery is, we must use our minds rather than relying on our experience. (Note that here and in what follows, "experience" is used in the everyday sense, not in a restricted philosophical sense restricting it to what empiricism or some other theory decrees — the input of the sense organs, for example.) We pick up, just from looking or from having others tell us, that certain types of action are brave.[12] But, although we are not wrong, we lack understanding of bravery until we have used our minds to think through what bravery is in a way which goes beyond what we can learn from experience. Hence what bravery is, the nature of bravery — or, if you prefer, the Form of bravery — is something that can be grasped only by the mind. But, whether you call this a Form or not, the performance involved is quite ordinary. We have found nothing so far to justify talk of bizarre intuitions of mysterious objects. We simply have the rather straightforward thought that to find what fighting in battle bravely and facing cancer bravely have in common, we need to use our minds to think about the matter rather than just relying on our experiences or reports from others about theirs. The beliefs we acquire from these experiences need to be thought through for us to be able to unify and hence understand them.

The difference between moral belief and moral knowledge, then, is that a moral belief is an isolated grasp of a particular fact or set of facts, while

---

[12] Note that it is types of action which are in play from the start. The argument has nothing to do with supposed deficiencies of particular actions.

moral knowledge is understanding of what underlies and unifies our bringing different types of fact together as examples of bravery or whatever. Knowledge is not thought of here, as it is in some modern theories, as being an improved state with respect to the very same particular fact about which the person previously had a belief. Such a conception of knowledge is familiar to ancient philosophers, and even occurs elsewhere in Plato. What is operative here, however, is something different: knowledge as understanding. Rather than focusing on individual beliefs, concern with understanding focuses on what unifies a number of possibly disparate-looking beliefs so that they can be grasped as examples of the subject in question. Understanding is achieved over an area or subject matter when you can grasp what relates the different beliefs to make them understandable as a unified subject matter. This is the more dominant notion of knowledge in Plato, and indeed in ancient epistemology more generally.[13]

In the *Laches*, then, we see an ordinary brave but unreflective person coming to see that he has true beliefs about bravery but lacks knowledge—that is, lacks understanding of what unifies his beliefs as beliefs about bravery. A person who comes to have this understanding (Socrates does not, for all the attempts in the dialogue to find this knowledge fail) would have moral knowledge. As I have stressed, this is a mundane enough accomplishment in principle, even though the dialogue's failure to come up with any moral knowledge indicates that the task is difficult.[14]

Some may complain that what we have just seen is too mundane to be what Plato means by coming to grasp a Form. It is true that in some other dialogues Plato says much less mundane things about Forms; they are sometimes characterized as the objects of intellectual aspiration and said (in the *Phaedo* and the *Republic*, for example) to be eternal and unchanging.[15] Furthermore, Plato in some dialogues raises the level of under-

---

[13] Knowledge as understanding and knowledge as improved true belief are both prominent in ancient epistemology. As noted, Plato is mostly concerned with the former, though the latter is in question in the *Meno* and at the end of the *Theaetetus*. For a good introduction to these different strands in ancient epistemology, see Stephen Everson, ed., *Epistemology*, vol. 1 of *Companions to Ancient Thought* (Cambridge: Cambridge University Press, 1990), particularly Everson's introduction.

[14] The *Laches* is particularly interesting in that Socrates's actual demand seems controversial: do we really show courage in resisting pleasures and temptations, as well as in resisting pains and discouraging factors? The claim that we do comes from thinking of courage as involving the idea of endurance more centrally than the idea of resisting unpleasant or dangerous circumstances. This is something on which people may reasonably disagree.

[15] We should remember, however, that in the first part of the *Parmenides* Plato has Socrates put forward an account of Forms much as they are found in the *Phaedo* and the *Republic*, and then has the account subjected to the same kind of relentless criticism that Socrates elsewhere directs at the positions of others. Furthermore, as in these other cases, the objections are nowhere met. Plato was obviously aware of intellectual difficulties in his account of Forms, and he continued to work toward more satisfactory characterizations. What we rather misleadingly call "the theory" of Forms is a cluster of ideas which Plato engaged with in different ways at different times.

standing that is required for someone to have a grasp of Forms; I shall return to this point later. Even where Forms are thought of in more metaphysically elevated ways, however, there is still nothing to justify talk of strange intuitions. To have grasp of a Form always requires you to use your mind by thinking: in some dialogues, thinking at great length and with great complexity and formality. Nothing could be further from the idea of effortlessness and passivity suggested by the idea of intuition.[16] The notion of a peculiar intuition is a construct of the empiricist assumptions we saw at work in Mackie's interpretation, and does not correspond to anything in Plato.

IV. Expertise as a Model

Why does Plato think it so obvious that what we should do, faced by piecemeal moral beliefs, is to try to understand them by thinking through their unifying basis? Why does our search for moral knowledge take this form?

We cannot miss the way that Socrates, in the shorter Socratic dialogues, constantly appeals, in his search for moral knowledge, to examples of various types of skill. Flute-players, shoemakers, launderers, doctors, and navigators regularly crop up as relevant comparisons in the search to understand the moral terms we use. Indeed, the interlocutor in one dialogue complains about this, on the elitist ground that these occupations are socially beneath the kind of thing he wants to talk about.[17]

"Skill" here is technê, which is also sometimes translated as "art" or, more recently, as "expertise"; someone who is skilled is an expert in some area. The appeals to technê knowledge are appeals to the knowledge of the expert—more precisely, to the knowledge of the expert in a practical field. (In other dialogues Plato appeals to the knowledge of experts in fields like mathematics, but I am concerned here only with his appeal to expert knowledge as a kind of practical knowledge.[18]) When Socrates is trying to understand what courage or piety is, the kind of knowledge—that is, understanding—that he is looking for is illuminated by the knowledge of

---

[16] When Plato uses language that suggests insight or grasp, this is not as an alternative to hard and effortful thinking, but suggestive of what it is to come to understand something by thinking hard about it. Perception is a misleading metaphor for moral thinking if it is used (as it sometimes has been) to suggest that no effort is required, or that getting it right is easy and obvious. Such ideas could scarcely be further from Plato's insistence that moral thinking is hard and requires effort which many people are too lazy, or too focused on material success, to make.

[17] Callicles, at Plato, Gorgias, 490e–491a.

[18] The appeal to mathematics in particular goes with a greatly raised standard for what is to count as having understanding of the kind which is sought.

the practical expert, because practical expertise is, at least in these dialogues, Plato's model for knowledge.[19]

What is so appealing about practical expertise as a model for knowledge? It brings together a number of features which further specify the kind of unified understanding of piecemeal beliefs already mentioned. First, skill or expertise is teachable; there is conveyable intellectual content which a learner can learn from a teacher.[20] A skill is intellectually complex and requires thought to acquire; it is not just something which can be picked up casually from experience. Hence, it is contrasted with a "knack" (*empeiria*, literally "experience"), which you can pick up just by copying other people without thinking much about it.

Second, a skill or expertise demands a complete understanding of the relevant field. For example, to be an expert in French requires that you have a grasp of everything relevant to the understanding of French, such as grammar, syntax, vocabulary, and so on. The field is defined by what is relevant; understanding modern French does not require understanding medieval French, for example, or modern Italian (though these might be useful). Hence, this requirement can be seen to be an expansion of the demand, already seen, that our understanding of a subject matter should unify the various beliefs that we have about that subject matter. Learning French involves acquiring numerous beliefs about vocabulary, word order, and so on; understanding French is achieved only when all of these beliefs are brought together in a way which gives the learner control of French, the whole subject matter, in a unified way.[21] (This example also brings out a further point, namely, that when this point is achieved, you are no longer dependent on the books, etc. from which you originally learned; the understanding is now yours in a way which is no longer dependent on its sources.)

Finally, skill or expertise requires that the expert, unlike the mere muddler or the person with the unintellectual knack, be able to "give an account" (*logon didonai*) of what it is that she is expert in.[22] The expert, but not the dabbler, can explain why she is doing what she is doing; instead of being stuck with inarticulacy, or being reduced to saying that "it feels right this way," she can explain why this is, here and now, the appropriate thing to do in these circumstances. What such an explanation will look like will of course vary with the skill in question: "You have to use the

---

[19] This point has been recognized in the secondary literature for some time now. See Paul Woodruff, "Plato's Early Theory of Knowledge," in Everson, ed., *Epistemology*, 60–84, for a very useful discussion of the many issues involved.

[20] See Plato, *Meno*, 89e ff. and Plato, *Protagoras*, 319e ff. The obvious and agreed teachability of kinds of expertise comes in when these discussions center on the teachability or otherwise of virtue.

[21] In the case of the productive skills, exercise of the skill produces a unified object whose organization reflects the expert's unified grasp of her skill and its requirements; see Plato, *Gorgias*, 503d–504b.

[22] On this point, see ibid., 465a, 501a.

subjunctive here because . . . ," "You can't have the electricity line going there because . . . ," and "You need to steer the boat to the right here because . . ." all appeal to different kinds of considerations, but what is being appealed to is the understanding which the expert has of French, electricity, or navigation.

This demand for articulate explanation is what would be expected given the point about teachability; the teacher gets the expertise across to the apprentice first by example and then by explanation of what has been done. And what the expert teaches and explains is the understanding of what unifies the relevant subject matter. The different requirements are themselves comprehensibly unified. Moreover, they give, together, a reasonable picture of what it is to have a practical expertise. There is nothing particularly time-bound about this idea, although of course Plato's examples belong to the ancient world.[23]

When Socrates seeks moral knowledge, then, it is only to be expected that this will be seen on the model of practical expertise, since this is the model for knowledge in general. We should note that it is particularly appropriate for the specific kind of moral knowledge that is being sought, knowledge of various virtues, since the virtues themselves have the intellectual structure of skills. Plato in fact thinks of virtue as a special kind of skill, an idea which had a continuing appeal in ancient ethics. Aristotle, for example, holds that virtues are *like* skills, while the Stoics revert to the more straightforward thesis that virtue is itself a skill. Coming to understand what courage is, is thus the same kind of performance as coming to understand any subject matter which is an area of expertise.[24] But, although the attraction of the idea that virtue is like skill may explain the enthusiasm of Plato and other philosophers for the idea, it does not itself account for the use of practical expertise as a model for knowledge. The model is sufficiently attractive in itself as a model for the kind of knowledge expressed in living well for it not to be dependent on virtue in particular as its application in the moral case.

---

[23] A common objection is that we are in fact prepared (even if the ancients were not) to call someone an expert if she can reliably come out with a certain performance, whether or not she displays articulate understanding. Thus we are (allegedly) prepared to call someone an expert gardener even if they are stubbornly unwilling to say anything about the basis of their success, and to call someone an expert who knows lots of facts about, say, ranches in the Southwest between 1880 and 1885, despite never relating this to any wider context. There is more than one response to this alleged problem. First, we might be misusing the term "expert" in using it of these people, since they lack articulate understanding of what they are doing. It might also be the case that we are assuming that the people in question do have a unified understanding of what they do, but for some reason cannot, or are unwilling to, articulate it. If we thought the gardener really unable to relate frosts to early plantings, or the history buff completely ignorant of other contemporary facts, I doubt that we would call them experts.

[24] My "Virtue as a Skill," *International Journal of Philosophical Studies* 3, no. 2 (1995): 227–43, traces some of the implications of this idea for virtue as a concept in a theory of morality.

There is one important disanalogy between particular skills and moral knowledge conceived of as a skill. Particular skills have an aim—mastery of French, fixing the car—which is local; it is an aim which you might well in other circumstances not have, and from which you can readily become motivationally detached, since the aim is one you have conditionally on your having certain broader interests and needs. When moral knowledge is thought of as a skill, however, its object is global—namely, your life as a whole. The Stoics make this point by calling virtue the "skill in living." When you start reflecting morally, you already have a life; you have a particular family, country, job, and the results of some moral education. If you are not content to drift along and wish to live your own life, you come to think of these circumstances as raw material which can be formed by understanding into a result which is the product of reflection, which is *your* life and what you have made of it, rather than just being what circumstances have left you with. The object of the "skill of living" is thus not optional, as are the objects of local skills. The options are between drifting along and trying to live your life on the basis of overall understanding of it, since you are going to live your life whether you think about it or not; this is not something from which you can become motivationally detached by a shift in interests.[25]

Moral knowledge, then, is thought of as explicated on the model of expertise, because both are cases of practical knowledge, and expertise appears as illustrative of the kind of understanding that the moral person has. The moral person who lives well and does the right thing is thought of as being relevantly like the skilled worker who does a good job and knows the appropriate thing to do. There are two relevant points here. One is the thought of skill as the specific model for moral understanding. There are many factors tending to make this seem alien and even peculiar to us, some deriving from the different roles of skill in the ancient and modern worlds, some from modern misapprehensions about skills.[26] In the present context I shall pass these over, since they are not relevant to my particular point in this essay, which concerns moral knowledge rather than the particular application of the idea of skill. The point I shall pursue here is the more general one, that practical expertise serves as a useful model for moral knowledge because both are examples of *practical knowledge*, knowledge expressed in action.

One reason, then—perhaps the main one—why Mackie's interpretation of Plato is so grotesque is that the ancients do not worry about moral knowledge within assumptions that make it problematic how there can

---

[25] Hence, it is ineffective to object that moral knowledge cannot be thought of as a skill because the aims of local skills are obviously optional. Nor does the analogy import the claim that the object of moral thinking is already fixed, as with local skills. Clearly, living your life in a good way is not an aim which can be clearly defined in advance, unlike, say, the aims of plumbing or car repair.

[26] For discussion of these various factors, see Annas, "Virtue as a Skill."

be any such thing. For it is a kind of practical knowledge—like expertise, in fact, a kind of practical knowledge that we are already familiar with and good at identifying.[27] Different philosophers diverge on just how similar moral knowledge is to expertise. But they do not doubt that it is a kind of practical knowledge, and that our familiarity with expertise helps us to understand it.

V. PRACTICAL KNOWLEDGE

When it comes to practical expertise, we are in an advantageous position: we have some! In fact, we have quite a lot. You or I may not individually have much, but nobody can sensibly deny that there is some. When I mess up the computer, find a leak under the sink, or find that the car will not start, I take my problems to the relevant experts. They are practical experts; I want not a theoretical computer whiz, but someone to fix the software, not a Ph.D. in engineering, but someone who can stop the leak, fix the oil gauge, and so on. Serious skepticism about the existence of practical experts of this kind does not get off the ground. (This is a major reason why discussions of moral knowledge in ancient ethics are not structured by skeptical concerns.) I may wonder whether my plumber is really an expert, but there is something deeply wrong about the idea that I might hesitate to call *anyone* listed under "Plumbers" in the Yellow Pages to fix my leaking pipe, on the grounds of doubt as to whether there was such a thing as *knowledge* of plumbing.

Nowadays, few philosophers think that this point about the obvious existence of practical knowledge as manifested in plumbers and car mechanics has much bearing on issues of moral epistemology. Coming from study of a moral tradition where practical expertise is standardly found very relevant to discussions of moral knowledge, I find this noteworthy, and suspect that it is explained more by the persistence of assumptions that come from outside the subject than by serious reflection on the nature of moral knowledge itself. Moral knowledge is, after all, practical knowledge, whatever account we give of this; it is knowledge of what to do, and results, often, in doing something. An obvious starting-point for understanding what moral knowledge is would appear to be some practical knowledge where there actually is agreement that such a thing exists, that

---

[27] When we first begin to acquire moral knowledge, how can we be sure that we have identified the right moral experts? We can't; the person whom we take as an expert and follow initially might turn out to be a fraud, or flawed. We can identify the expert confidently only to the extent that we ourselves are progressing toward the relevant understanding. This does not make the account circular, though it does indicate that it requires a "boot-strapping" progress whereby you become surer that you have got the aim correctly specified as you progress in the skill of acquiring the aim. This is true of some local skills as well. If this is found objectionable with respect to moral knowledge, this must depend on an assumption such that moral considerations must be available equally to all, however much (or little) effort they make to understand them.

we have it, and that we can say some useful things about its structure, how it is acquired, and how it demands that we reflect on our experience. The kind of practical knowledge displayed in plumbing may be mundane, but it offers us just this kind of advantage. For we can then go on to ask what makes moral knowledge similar to, and different from, the easier case—a task developed by ancient moral theorists from Plato onwards.

Perhaps this advantage is not apparent because homely performances like fixing the computer are not thought of as amounting to *knowledge*. Here we can only ask why. Prephilosophically, we have no problems in saying that the mechanic knows how to mend the car—*if*, that is, he is an expert; that is how we distinguish experts at car repair from mechanics who are not experts.

It is possible, of course, to introduce a special philosophical category of "knowing how" and oppose it to "knowing that," where it is the "knowing that" category that brings in familiar epistemological issues, and "knowing how" is supposed to be different in kind. Labeling the issue, however, does not much further us. Either "knowing how" involves "knowing that" or it does not. If it does not, then what we think of as practical knowledge is being construed as a kind of inarticulate practical knack, an ability to manipulate the world which is not at a sufficiently rational level to be judged epistemically. This, however, would amount to saying that there is no such thing as practical expertise, only knacks—that there is no significant difference between the inarticulate practitioner and the expert in the field. This is ridiculous. However, if "knowing how" does involve "knowing that" in some way, then we have not evaded any of the issues that arise when we speak of practical knowledge.

We do (some of us) have practical knowledge—namely, expertise. The significance of this for moral epistemology has been insufficiently appreciated in modern discussions.

VI. Practical Knowledge and Values

This brings me back to Mackie and the assumptions which drive his interpretation of Plato's moral Forms as peculiar entities which are supposed to exert a peculiar force making people act in accordance with their intuitions of them. Mackie failed to see that there is nothing in the least peculiar about coming to understand a moral Form, any more than there is about coming to understand French or computer languages. They are all examples of practical knowledge. They all involve using your mind to get understanding of a subject matter about which (especially in learning which) we have beliefs which on their own are piecemeal; coming to understand them, we unify our understanding of the subject matter and come to be able not only to act accordingly but also to explain why our decisions and actions are as they are. Coming to understand a moral

Form is harder than the other cases, because morality is harder than French or electronics; but this in itself is no reason to deny that both are examples of practical knowledge.

I suggested earlier that Mackie's caricature Forms were constructs of his assumptions, particularly the assumption that values are, unproblematically, not accessible to experience and not accessible to reasoning. These in turn rested on very strong and narrow assumptions about experience and reasoning. It is worth asking what happens if we approach practical expertise in a way structured by these assumptions. For the argument is not presented as being directed at specific features of values that make them *moral* values, but just at *values*.[28] It is "objective values" which are supposed to be so mysterious, since we need them to explain how the "authoritative prescriptivity" of the pattern of reasoning is to be made available to the agent.

Take the expert plumber. Faced by a leak, he exercises his expertise by working out what the problem is which he has to solve, and then figures out the best solution to it in the circumstances. Working through this problem he comes to the banal conclusion, say, that he should turn off the water near the leak. This is a response to his expert appraisal of the problem, and it appeals to him with the "authoritative prescriptivity" of being the best immediate step in solving the problem; he turns off the water there (and not somewhere else). On Mackie's view, there is a deep mystery in the view that the plumber is motivated to do something (i.e., turn off the water here rather than there) because it is (part of) the best way of mending the leak. There is, of course, a "natural fact," accessible through the normal workings of the senses and low-level reasoning, consisting of the fact that turning off the water here bears such and such causal relations to the leak and further actions involving it. The plumber, however, is motivated not just by this natural fact, but by the further fact of its being what he, here and now, ought to do (given that it is the best immediate step in solving the problem of fixing the leak). What is the connection between this natural fact and the "practical fact" that he ought to do it? It must somehow be the case that he ought to do it *because* it bears such and such causal relations to the leak. This is the conclusion of his practical deliberations. "But just what *in the world* is signified by this 'because'?"[29]

In his eagerness to show that there are no objective values "in the world," Mackie has produced an argument which (if it is regarded as successful) not only debunks the objects of moral knowledge, as intended, but subjects ordinary practical expertise to the same objections. This is not surprising if moral knowledge and practical expertise are both

---

[28] The inconclusive "argument from relativity" is directed at "moral codes," while the "argument from queerness" is directed at objective values.

[29] Mackie, *Ethics*, 41.

kinds of practical knowledge, as we prephilosophically assume and as appears obvious to philosophers who, like the ancients, are not working within the framework of Mackie's assumptions.

This point may have passed unremarked because of the apparent implausibility, to philosophers, of the point that moral reasoning could be relevantly like anything as ordinary as practical expertise. (I shall return to this in Section VIII.) It may also be at least in part due to another assumption, Mackie's second, which is very common in much modern discussion of practical reasoning. This assumption is that there is a prima facie problem as to any kind of reasoning's motivating us to act. Since we do act, we must be motivated by something different, and this is assumed to be desire. It is accordingly thought simpler to interpret any presumed case of reason's being practical as a case where what provides the practical force is really a desire, and reason is limited to the means-end task of figuring out how to fulfill the desire.[30] If we have good reason to make this assumption, then practical reasoning like the plumber's will be no exception.

This approach, however, fails, because it simply misrepresents the reasoning of the practical expert. The expert's deliberations are typically exercised in problem-solving, figuring out what to do in providing a solution. Faced by the leak, the expert plumber, regarding it as a problem to be solved, deliberates as to the best way to do it; having worked this out, he then acts accordingly, since this is what he ought to do. Nothing in this story requires us to bring in the plumber's *desires*. The plumber shuts off the water where he does because this is what he ought to do as part of the expert way of fixing the leak; he does not shut off the water as a means to satisfying a desire. The suggestion is grotesque—for one thing, desires usually signal their presence by pain and frustration until they are fulfilled, something we have no reason to ascribe to the plumber. Experts deliberate about the objects of their expertise, not about how to fulfill their desires (of course they might do the latter, but not in a way relevant to the exercise of their expertise).

The standard response to this is to appeal to the common orthodoxy that there *must* be a desire, or the plumber would not have shut off the water; for the action must have been brought about by a combination of belief and desire, and here the items we need are a desire to fix the leak and a belief that shutting off the water here is a means to fixing the leak and hence to satisfying that desire.

However, this case makes three points about the response uncomfortably clear. First, it obviously trivializes the notion of desire, since a desire is invoked mechanically to account for action, with no independent grounds

---

[30] This idea is often associated with "Humean" theories of reasoning, but I shall not go into the question of whether any of this relates to Hume, or into the larger matter of exactly which modern theories are held to be Humean.

whatever.[31] Second, it is not adequate to say (perhaps by way of response to the first point) that the notion of desire in question is a theoretical one. If we take desire just to be what the theory invokes to bring about action in every case, it is completely unclear how it is to fulfill this function, if not by way of having at least some of the characteristics of a real desire— for example, pressuring us to fulfill it by way of getting rid of the pain and frustration it produces until fulfilled. Standard invocations of a desire in order to provide the needed motivation to bring about action often blur together two ideas: of a real desire, something that can reasonably be seen as actually getting the person to do something, and of a theoretical item posited *a priori* to meet the demands of a theory regardless of whether the conditions for there being a real desire are met or not.

Finally, a third problem with the response is that the case of the practical expert is one in which it is particularly unconvincing that what the person does is brought about by desires—either real desires or the fictitious desires postulated by a theory that demands a desire for every action. It just is not plausible that either kind of desire is had by the expert translator who uses the Italian subjunctive to translate an English expression containing no subjunctive, the expert papyrologist who conjectures the presence of Greek letters from marks on a papyrus, or the forensic expert who detects blood on the murder weapon. They have all solved problems; it is not plausible that they have devoted their energies to fulfilling their desires.[32]

The idea that practical expertise is to be accounted for in terms of purely means-end reasoning requires us to misdescribe how experts actually think, and to posit fictitious and irrelevant desires. Of course the plumber has some desires: to take on the job in the first place, for example. But no desires that can convincingly be ascribed to the plumber figure in his expert practical reasoning as to how to fix the leak.

---

[31] In this part of the discussion, I have tried to use the notion of a desire as that figures in the recent literature. I cannot resist, however, pointing out that in ancient discussions, desire is understood in a more restricted way (one which in fact answers to our modern folk psychology better than the modern philosophical concept). In ancient ethics, a desire is not just any goal-directed, forward-looking, or "mind to world" motivation, but a subset of these which also have a significant backward-looking element, since *a desire signals a perceived lack or need*. (It is because of this fact, indeed, that desires typically have the phenomenology they do, namely, that of producing frustration until satisfied.) For example, when the world produces the irritating state of me that consists in hunger, I will (normally) have a desire to eat, indicated by certain feelings of pain and frustration, and the satisfaction of this desire will remove those feelings. As sources of motivation, desires will typically be reactive and short-term. Given this picture, there is little temptation to represent all forward-looking motivation as brought about by desire. I think, though, that it is of interest to show that even the broad modern concept of desire, incorporating no reference to need and with no explanation of desire's phenomenology, is not well-suited to account for the plumber's practical motivation.

[32] I am not under the illusion of having made a contribution to the vast modern secondary literature devoted to the discussion of Humean versus non-Humean theories of motivation. I have simply tried to indicate what the major issues are for the kind of position I am sketching, and to make some comments from outside the modern orthodoxy.

A defender of the orthodoxy will object that it is, in fact, the plumber's desire to take on the job which sets the end that his deliberations achieve. The reasoning he employs results in the achievement of the end set by that original desire (even if we allow that we do not need *further* desires once that is granted, such as the desire to turn off the water). This, however, misconceives the expert's end. His end as an expert is established by his response to the problem. His desire to take on the job, if he has it, gives him an end he has as somebody with bills to pay. The translator, papyrologist, and forensic expert all no doubt have desires to make money, get a reputation, or the like. As experts their ends are set by their responses to the problems to be solved: the English to be made comprehensible to Italians, the holes in the papyrus text to be filled in, and so on. This is in part what distinguishes the expert's reasoning, for the desire to make money can be fulfilled perfectly well by amateur, nonexpert deliberation. If what is done is done expertly, it is done to achieve the expert's end of responding to the problem by solving it; desires do not form a part of this and do not set it going.

"Objective values" are in play in ordinary practical expertise as well as in moral and aesthetic reasoning. We cannot avoid this conclusion by regarding the former as not grand enough to be brought into comparison with the latter. Nor can we avoid it by claiming that practical expertise is merely a matter of purely means-end reasoning. Any gains aimed at in making this move are vastly outweighed by the costs of inventing implausible, fictitious desires for the purely means-end reasoning to be the means to fulfill. If we honestly recognize ordinary practical expertise for what it is, we will see that the kind of argument so familiar from Mackie and others is an attack on the whole idea of practical knowledge, not just moral knowledge in particular: the problem is that of how objective values can motivate, and it is the practicality of practical knowledge that is in question, not the specific demands of morality.

VII. Skepticism and Practical Knowledge

I have already mentioned that Plato and other ancient philosophers are not motivated by skepticism when they discuss moral knowledge, even though they are alert to it elsewhere. It is already clear why this is the case. We are not normally skeptical that there is such a thing as the expertise that gets a battery replaced, restores a crashed hard drive, or builds a house. It is clear by now that widespread modern assumptions about values imply that we ought to be. I am suggesting, obviously, that this might well make us more critical of those assumptions.

There are plenty of places where skepticism about moral knowledge in particular might reasonably arise. We might not be sure that we adequately understand the moral beliefs that we have; they might contain unresolved problems and conflicts.[33] And there are ways, stressed by Aristotle, in which moral knowledge looks different from expertise. Perhaps the special features of morality limit the usefulness of using expertise to illuminate it. (This particular issue was explored in depth in ancient debates.) These problems get going, however, on the basis of a generally unskeptical acceptance of the existence of expertise. This surely reflects something important about our everyday reasonings about morality. Our everyday moral discourse takes for granted that we have a lot of true moral beliefs. The problem comes when we try to give an articulate account of what we have these beliefs about. We have the model of practical expertise; the problems come with morality, because coming to understand morality is harder than it is with electronics or engineering. But this is just what we would expect if moral knowledge is a kind of practical knowledge; other forms of practical knowledge, then, are still a useful beginning for understanding the moral kind.

A point of contrast between ancient and modern approaches to moral knowledge can be seen if we consider the role often played in modern discussions by the figure of the amoralist. This is the person who, in all other respects normal, is fully aware of and appreciates moral considerations, but is motivationally indifferent to them. The amoralist has often been used to undermine different forms of internalism,[34] but whatever the use to which the amoralist is put in the argument, the assumption is that there is nothing conceptually incoherent or confused about the idea of a person who is fully aware of all the relevant moral considerations, perfectly conscious of which is the most salient, and ready to accept that as a result of this she ought to make a moral response (acting, responding, intervening, and so on), and who yet fails to make this response, not as a result of ignorance, stupidity, misinformation, or failures of reasoning, but simply because all these conditions leave open the possibility of the failure of the relevant motivation.

Could there be such a person as the "apracticalist"? This would be the expert who responds to the problem of the crashed computer, fully realizes that the best way to solve the problem of fixing the computer involves reinstalling the software, is fully cognizant of all the factors pointing to this, yet remains aloof and motivationally detached from actually reinstalling the software, but not as a result of ignorance, failure of reasoning, and so on. How do we make sense of this? In the case of the expert, failure to actually reinstall the software implies either imperfect understanding of what was the right way to proceed or a rethinking of what the

[33] Cf. note 14 above, concerning the understanding of courage.
[34] "Internalism" has been used for a variety of different positions; here I take it to be the position that fully to understand a moral requirement is to be (to some degree) motivated by it. See David O. Brink, *Moral Realism and the Foundations of Ethics* (Cambridge: Cambridge University Press, 1989), 45 ff.

best way to fix the computer is. This is just a corollary of the point that expertise is expressed in the problem-solving kind of deliberation.

Faced by an actual expert who knows what to do but fails actually to do it, we are not generally puzzled, because we take it that the aims of local skills and kinds of expertise are likewise local. You can become detached motivationally from one or more of them if your interests shift (i.e., you are no longer concerned to achieve the aim) or your other interests become more pressing (i.e., you want to complete the job but are distracted by other matters). Failure to act on a local kind of practical knowledge shows only that the expertise in question is local.

But this is, of course, the respect in which local skills differ from moral knowledge where that is thought of as a skill. Its aim is not local, nor is it conditional on your other interests and concerns; hence, it is not similarly unproblematic for you to become motivationally detached from that aim. Living your life well is not an aim from which you can become detached by boredom or the prospect of better pay elsewhere. So if the apracticalist is not, while the amoralist is, a coherent and threatening idea, this must rest on some *other* difference between moral knowledge and other forms of practical knowledge. Such a difference could of course be established, but to avoid begging the question it should not rest on the postulation of the kind of assumption that we saw at the beginning.

VIII. CONCLUSION

I am quite aware that the conclusions of this essay will not recommend themselves to philosophers who share Mackie's framework of assumptions or related ones. It might also be argued that to think of moral knowledge as primarily practical knowledge may commend itself to the ancients, but does not fit modern ways of thinking of morality. Indeed, I stressed at the beginning of this essay that ancient and modern ways of thinking of epistemology are rather different. It would be a mistake, however, to think that the only results of this inquiry are archaeological. To think of moral knowledge as a kind of practical knowledge is not just intuitive to the ancients; it is intuitive for us also, and the right contrast is between this prephilosophically appealing view and a view of moral knowledge which depends on very specific philosophical assumptions about things other than morality.

Moral knowledge is knowledge which is, among other things, about how to act; it is also knowledge that is put into practice. This is a simple enough thought, and it is significant that so many modern positions in moral epistemology not only refuse to start here, as we prephilosophically do, but make the practicality of moral knowledge mysterious, or even regard it as forcing us to accept debunking conclusions about value.

One assumption of Mackie's which has not yet much figured in this essay is the third one, that morality is basically a matter of telling others (and yourself) what to do. Mackie acknowledges the influence of Stevenson's emotive theory of ethical terms, and it is familiar that theories which conclude that there is something deeply faulty about our everyday assumptions that people and actions really are good or bad also tend to conclude that part or all of the function of ethical terms is nondescriptive: they express attitudes, or "prescribe" what to do, and so on. There is a model here of moral discourse as fundamentally focused on pressuring people (others and oneself) to act in certain ways. The more emphasis is put on the supposed nondescriptive element in moral terms, the more moral discourse is presented as a matter of influencing people to act in certain ways, ways that might have a contingent and possibly remote connection to whatever descriptive content moral terms are allowed. This way of thinking, a descendant of logical positivism, is eerily postmodern in the way it represents moral discourse as really being a power struggle.

By contrast, to think of moral knowledge as being, like expertise, a kind of practical knowledge is to think of it as a humbler, more cooperative kind of activity. When Aristotle says that learning to be just is like learning to be a builder, this may strike us not only as insufficiently grand, but as missing the combative element so familiar from modern analyses. The apprentice builder is learning something from teachers or role models who are better at it than she is; she is learning to think for herself about what she has learned from others. She does not start off pressuring others to think differently; if she does think that she and others should think in a way different from the one she has learned, this comes later, when she has learned something to disagree with. Similarly, the moral learner is coming to think for himself about what he has learned from others. When he has done this, of course, he will be in a position to tell others what to do, and to try to get them to do it if they disagree; but on the expertise model, conflict, or pressuring people to act, comes later, and presupposes that the critic has already learned something from others.

Perhaps this humbler model has little appeal to philosophers because it is simply assumed that moral discourse is fundamentally a matter of conflict, what matters being winning, getting others to accept your view. Perhaps, on the other hand, the expertise model has advantages in reminding us that we do all, in fact, learn to be moral before we get to the point of criticizing what we have learned and telling others what to do. Perhaps there is something to be said for respecting this idea of becoming moral as a process of learning in which we all start as pupils or apprentices, and where it is up to us to become experts.[35]

If we start with something like Mackie's assumptions, then moral discourse will indeed seem to be a set of pressures brought to bear by some people on other people, and the moral learning we have done, before we

---

[35] For discussion of respect for the idea of moral learning, see the excellent comments in Rosalind Hursthouse, *On Virtue Ethics* (Oxford: Oxford University Press, 1999), 12–16.

started to reflect about the nature of moral knowledge, will appear to be nothing but the acquisition of error, something to be wiped out rather than respected. Perhaps it should even be by-passed for future enlightened generations, if this could be done, as in Neurath's chilling proposal that moral education should be done in terms that do not even allow the learner to formulate "incorrect" concepts.[36]

I have argued in this essay that if we go back to ancient views of moral epistemology we will see the attractions of an alternative view. We do not, in principle, need to go back to the ancients to discover this, but it is helpful to enable us to see both that the hold of a common modern set of assumptions is not inescapable, and that an alternative model is not only possible but was actual for quite some time. This is one way in which, I hope, paying attention to past philosophers, rather than patronizing them, can help us to understand where we are coming from, to ask whether we might find a starting-point other than the ones familiarized by tradition, and to enrich our view of the options that are open to us.

Philosophy, University of Arizona

---

[36] "Must everyone in turn go through metaphysics as through a childhood disease? . . . No. . . . *Every child can in principle learn to apply the language of physicalism correctly from the outset.* . . . A new generation educated according to unified science will not understand the difference between the 'mental' and the 'physical' sciences, or between 'philosophy of nature' and of 'culture.' " Otto Neurath, "Unified Science and Psychology," in Brian McGuinness, ed., *Unified Science: The Vienna Circle Monograph Series* (Dordrecht, The Netherlands: Reidel, 1987), 1–23. On page 8 Neurath says, without apparent irony, that he himself has long employed "an *index verborum prohibitorum*" such as "norm," "categorical imperative," and "intuition." Such is the world without Mackie's "errors."

PRACTICAL REASON AND MORAL PSYCHOLOGY IN ARISTOTLE AND KANT*

By James Bernard Murphy

I. Aristotle and Kant in Dialogue

For a long time, it seemed that Aristotelians and Kantians had little to say to each other. When Kant the moralist was known in the English-speaking world primarily from his *Groundwork* and his *Critique of Practical Reason*, Kant's conceptual vocabulary of "duty," "law," "maxim," and "morality" appeared quite foreign to Aristotle's "virtue," "end," "good," and "character." Yet ever since philosopher Mary Gregor's *Laws of Freedom*,[1] published in 1963, made Kant's *The Metaphysics of Morals* central to the interpretation of his ethical thought, it has become clear that such "Aristotelian" terms as virtue, end, good, happiness, and character are also central to Kant.[2] Aristotelians and Kantians now see that they have plenty to say to each other, and they have gone from being adversaries to

* I wish to acknowledge my gratitude for the enormously helpful comments, criticisms, and suggestions I received from Ellen Frankel Paul, David O. Brink, Michael Moore, David Luban, Fred D. Miller, Jr., Walter Sinnott-Armstrong, Mark S. Stein, Susan D. Collins, Marcus Fischer, Steven B. Smith, Louis Dupré, David Peritz, and Susan Shell. I am especially grateful to Allen Wood for his very detailed, searching, and helpful criticisms and suggestions. I am also most appreciative for the support that the Earhart Foundation and the Pew Charitable Trusts provided me during the writing of this essay. Finally, I wish to acknowledge the indispensable help of my research assistants, Conor Dugan and Angela Russo.

[1] Mary Gregor, *Laws of Freedom* (Oxford: Blackwell, 1963).

[2] Listed below are the abbreviations I use for references to Kant's works and translations of those works. Throughout this essay, bare numbers refer to the page numbers of the standard Prussian Academy edition of *Kants gesammelte Schriften* (Berlin: de Gruyter, 1902-). For the *Lectures on Ethics*, which takes up more than one volume of the Academy edition, I provide the Academy volume number with the page references. I use "p." with page numbers if the translation I use does not contain the Academy page numbers; this occurs for several works that are not yet included in Paul Guyer and Allen Wood's ongoing *Cambridge Edition of the Works of Immanuel Kant*. Finally, I refer to the *Critique of Pure Reason* in the standard fashion, by the Academy page numbering of the first (A) and second (B) editions.

> *Anth.* *Anthropology from a Pragmatic Point of View* [1798], trans. Mary Gregor (The Hague, The Netherlands: Nijhoff, 1974), Ak. vol. 7
>
> *I* *Idea for a Universal History with a Cosmopolitan Purpose* [1784], in Hans Reiss, ed., and H. B. Nisbet, trans., *Kant: Political Writings* (Cambridge: Cambridge University Press, 1991), Ak. vol. 8
>
> *G* *Groundwork of the Metaphysics of Morals* [1785], in Mary Gregor, ed., *Cambridge Edition of the Works of Immanuel Kant: Practical Philosophy* (Cambridge: Cambridge University Press, 1996), 37–108, Ak. vol. 4
>
> *KpV* *Critique of Practical Reason* [1788], in Gregor, ed., *Practical Philosophy*, 133–272, Ak. vol. 5

sharing a sometimes unprincipled urge to merge central aspects of Aristotle's and Kant's ethical thought.

I think the current dialogue between Aristotelians and Kantians can powerfully illuminate not just the interpretation of Aristotle's and Kant's texts, but also key questions in contemporary ethical theory. What implications do human nature and psychology have for practical reason? Are the moral virtues perfective of our nature or at odds with it? What is or ought to be the relation of the desires and the passions to reason in moral deliberation? To what extent can moral agents transcend their natural and acquired dispositions? This dialogue is most illuminating when its participants resist the temptations to perform either a summary execution or a hasty rapprochement. That Aristotle and Kant deploy many seemingly similar concepts does not mean that they share similar conceptions of these concepts, or that the shared concepts play similar roles in their overall ethical theories.[3] Rather, Aristotle and Kant have just enough in common to make for some really profound and important disagreements. Like the English and the Americans, they are divided by a largely common language.

We are most likely to overlook the deep divide between Aristotle and Kant when we interpret their ethical treatises in isolation from the other dimensions of their thought. Yet what most strikingly unites Aristotle and Kant is that, in sharp contrast to contemporary moral philosophers, they ground their ethical thought in an epistemology, metaphysics, psychology, philosophical anthropology, and politics. In Kant's case, his philosophy of history is also relevant. Although Kant has frequently been accused

KrV   *Critique of Pure Reason*, 2d ed. [1787], trans. Norman Kemp Smith (New York: St. Martin's, 1975)

KU   *Critique of Judgement*, 2d ed. [1793], trans. James Meredith (Oxford: Clarendon Press, 1952), Ak. vol. 5

MS   *Metaphysics of Morals* [1797], in Gregor, ed., *Practical Philosophy*, 353–604, Ak. vol. 6

Rel. *Religion within the Boundaries of Mere Reason* [1793], in Allen W. Wood and George Di Giovanni, eds. and trans., *Cambridge Edition of the Works of Immanuel Kant: Religion and Rational Theology* (Cambridge: Cambridge University Press, 1996), 39–216, Ak. vol. 6

TP   *On the Common Saying: That May Be Correct in Theory, But It Is of No Use in Practice* [1793], in Gregor, ed., *Practical Philosophy*, 273–310, Ak. vol. 8

VE   *Lectures on Ethics*, in Peter Heath, ed. and trans., and J. B. Schneewind, ed., *Cambridge Edition of the Works of Immanuel Kant: Lectures on Ethics* (Cambridge: Cambridge University Press, 1997), Ak. vols. 27, 29

VP   *Education* [1803], trans. Annette Churton (Ann Arbor: University of Michigan Press, 1960), Ak. vol. 9

[3] Thus, Nancy Sherman rightly warns: "Rapprochement can be dangerous, however, especially when it obscures important demarcating lines. To a certain extent this has happened in the present debate, with the rush to mutual accommodation eclipsing the structural and foundational integrity of each theory." See her *Making a Necessity of Virtue: Aristotle and Kant on Virtue* (Cambridge: Cambridge University Press, 1997), 2.

of divorcing his philosophical ethics from an account of human nature, it is only in relation to his very distinctive and disturbing account of human nature that Kant's ethics actually makes sense. As we shall see, although both Kant and Aristotle talk about happiness, virtue, self-love, prudence, and character, what they each mean by these shared concepts, in light of their respective views on moral psychology and anthropology, contrasts so sharply that the similarities between the two often seem merely verbal.[4]

On the relation of practical reason to moral psychology, Aristotle and Kant represent fundamental alternatives: never the twain shall meet. They diverge radically on the question of how deeply human nature can be oriented to moral virtue, a question that is inseparable from that of the extent to which moral agency can transcend our natural and acquired dispositions. I do not attempt to adjudicate this debate in this essay; rather, I seek to locate precisely the points of agreement and disagreement. I will also sometimes speculate about what each philosopher might say to the other. What we shall discover is that Aristotle's and Kant's strikingly different accounts of practical reason are driven largely by their strikingly different understandings of human nature and psychology. Indeed, when we reflect on how sensitive ethical theories are to the views of moral psychology that underlie them, we might become sympathetic to philosopher G. E. M. Anscombe's famous plea that we cease doing moral philosophy "until we have an adequate philosophy of psychology."[5]

II. THE PRUDENTIAL AND THE MORAL

Perhaps the most obvious contrast between Aristotle and Kant concerns the unity of practical reason. Aristotle's practical wisdom (*phronêsis*) is the intellectual virtue ordering all practical reasoning toward the fullest realization of happiness over a complete life. Practical wisdom governs deliberation and choice about conduct that shapes the character of the agent, whether it is, as we would say, prudential or moral, self-regarding or other-regarding. Aristotle contrasts *phronêsis* with technical skill (*technê*), which is the virtue guiding deliberation and choice about conduct that shapes external matter. He also contrasts *phronêsis* with shrewdness (*deinotês*), which is instrumental cunning in the realm of practical conduct. According to Aristotle, practical wisdom governs de-

---

[4] Robert Louden, in his recent book *Kant's Impure Ethics* (New York: Oxford University Press, 2000) and Allen Wood, in his recent *Kant's Ethical Thought* (Cambridge: Cambridge University Press, 1999), have shown the deep grounding of Kant's ethics in his moral psychology, anthropology, and philosophy of history. Perhaps this helps to explain why these interpretations of Kant so strongly underscore the contrasts, rather than the similarities, between Kant and Aristotle. In this regard, compare Wood's contribution to the other Kantian perspectives in the excellent collection edited by Stephen Engstrom and Jennifer Whiting, *Aristotle, Kant, and the Stoics: Rethinking Happiness and Duty* (Cambridge: Cambridge University Press, 1996).

[5] See G. E. M. Anscombe, "Modern Moral Philosophy," reprinted in Roger Crisp and Michael Slote, eds., *Virtue Ethics* (Oxford: Oxford University Press, 1998), 26.

liberation about both the ends and the means of practical conduct; by
contrast, technical skill and practical shrewdness merely guide the calculation of means toward ends that are already given. Aristotle famously
says that a doctor does not deliberate about whether to treat a patient, but
only about how to treat. But, on his account, it would be more precise to
say that a doctor, *qua* technician (that is, one making use of his *technê*),
does not deliberate about whether to treat a patient, but only about the
right course of treatment; *qua* practically wise man (that is, one making
use of his *phronêsis*), however, a doctor must sometimes deliberate about
whether to treat a patient, as in triage. Thus, while practical wisdom is, in
one sense, just one kind of practical reasoning, along with technical skill
and practical shrewdness, in a deeper sense, practical wisdom includes
and transcends these other kinds of practical reason by orienting them to
the lasting good and happiness of an agent.

Similarly, the merely shrewd man does not deliberate about his ends,
but whatever his ends happen to be, he pursues them shrewdly: "If the
end is noble, then shrewdness is praiseworthy; but if the end is base, then
shrewdness is unscrupulousness; hence both practically wise men and
unscrupulous men are called shrewd [*deinos*]" (*NE* 1144a26).[6] There is
something frightening about the merely shrewd man who is capable of
anything (*panourgos*). Notice that in Aristotle's account, practical wisdom
can be distinguished, but not separated, from mere shrewdness. Indeed,
practical wisdom includes shrewdness: "Practical wisdom is not the same
capacity [as shrewdness] but it [practical wisdom] requires this capacity
[of shrewdness]" (*NE* 1144a28). Shrewdness is a mere power or capacity
(*dynamis*) for a kind of instrumental practical reasoning; if it is to play its

---

[6] I will use the abbreviations below in my references to Aristotle's works; except for
Irwin's translation of the *Nicomachean Ethics*, all of these translations have been reprinted in
Jonathan Barnes, ed., *The Complete Works of Aristotle*, 2 vol. (Princeton, NJ: Princeton University Press, 1984). Barnes's edition reprints, with some modifications, translations that
previously appeared in W. D. Ross, ed., *The Works of Aristotle*, 12 vol. (Oxford: Clarendon
Press, 1908–52). For these works, the dates in the listings below give the year of the translation's publication in the Ross series.

DA   *De Anima*, trans. J. A. Smith (1931), reprinted in Barnes, *Complete Works of
      Aristotle*, 1:641–92

EE   *Eudemian Ethics*, trans. J. Solomon (1915), reprinted in Barnes, *Complete Works of
      Aristotle*, 2:1922–81

Met. *Metaphysics*, trans. W. D. Ross (1908), reprinted in Barnes, *Complete Works of
      Aristotle*, 2:1552–728

MM   *Magna Moralia*, trans. St. George Stock (1925), reprinted in Barnes, *Complete
      Works of Aristotle*, 2:1868–921

NE   *Nicomachean Ethics*, trans. Terence Irwin (Indianapolis, IN: Hackett, 1985)

Pol. *Politics*, trans. Benjamin Jowett (1921), reprinted in Barnes, *Complete Works of
      Aristotle*, 2:1986–2129

Rhet. *Rhetoric*, trans. W. Rhys Roberts (1924), reprinted in Barnes, *Complete Works of
      Aristotle*, 2:2152–269

I have occasionally modified Irwin's excellent translation of the *NE* and Stock's translation
of the *MM*.

proper role in excellent practical reasoning, shrewdness must be trained into a stable disposition (*hexis*) and integrated into the unified intellectual and moral excellence of practical wisdom.

To see how practical wisdom includes but transcends mere shrewdness, we must consider the relation of practical wisdom to moral virtue. The practically wise man is shrewd as well as good. Does this simply mean that practical wisdom is a compound of moral virtue (so that we can perceive the right ends) and instrumental shrewdness (so that we can select the right means)? Actually, moral goodness and instrumental shrewdness are much more intimately intertwined in Aristotle's view. Aristotle says that "[w]e cannot be fully good without practical wisdom or practically wise without virtue of character" (*NE* 1144a36, 1144b17, 1144b31). Practical wisdom is a virtue of intellect, that is, a developed rational state capable of both identification of genuine goods and calculation in pursuit of them. At the same time, practical wisdom is also the perfection of the virtues of character, which are developed states of desires and passions dynamically oriented toward the pursuit and enjoyment of goods. In short, the practically wise man is not only more virtuous than the merely shrewd man, he is also shrewder. Why? Because the merely shrewd man, lacking insight into the deepest goods of a complete life, exercises retail wisdom but wholesale foolishness.

On Aristotle's account, just as practical wisdom realizes fully what is only potential in mere shrewdness, so true authoritative (*kuria*) virtue realizes fully what is only potential in mere natural virtue (*NE* 1144b1–3). He tells us that by natural virtue, our desires and passions are already dynamically oriented toward goodness and virtue even from birth, though that natural orientation often suffers from poor "eyesight," so to speak, and hence poor aim. The fullness of true virtue requires that understanding (*nous*) sharpen the aim of our immature desires so that they become accurately and reliably oriented toward goodness (*NE* 1144b4–13). As a result of this maturation, the practically wise man is not only able to rationally identify genuine goods, he is also emotionally motivated to pursue them. Just as all moral virtues involve rational insight into the good, so also does rational insight depend on moral virtue: the best good is apparent only to the good person (*NE* 1144a34). Thus, in practical wisdom, states of intellect and states of character are inseparably interwoven.[7]

Aristotelian practical wisdom is excellence in deliberation and choice of thought, word, or deed. Through this excellence, a person directly shapes,

[7] As John Cooper says, "Aristotle holds that moral virtue, which is a certain condition of the desires, and practical intelligence [*phronêsis*], a condition of the mind, are in every way parallel to, and indeed interfused with, one another: one does not have *either* the moral virtues *or* practical intelligence unless (a) one desires a certain ultimate end *and* judges that it is the correct one to pursue; (b) one judges that certain things—states of affairs, actions, and so forth—will serve to achieve this end, *and* desires to produce them; and (c) one recognizes occasions for action as they arise *and* desires to act and, in consequence, does act on those occasions." John Cooper, *Reason and Human Good in Aristotle* (Indianapolis, IN: Hackett, 1986), 63.

in the first place, his own intellect and character, and indirectly shapes, in the second place, those of others. Contemplation of what is necessary (*theoria*), and therefore not subject to deliberation and voluntary action, falls outside of practical wisdom, as does the fabrication of external matter into artifacts. However, practical wisdom *is* involved in deciding whether or not to become the kind of person who contemplates or fabricates. Practical wisdom thus ranges over matters little and great, over matters of my own well-being and the well-being of others, and over matters that are merely instrumentally valuable (e.g., disposal of property) and matters intrinsically valuable (e.g., enjoyment of friendship or of beauty). Since practical wisdom is oriented to happiness (*eudaimonia*), and happiness requires a range of goods—external goods, goods of the body, and goods of the soul—practical wisdom is required to ensure, in myriad quotidian ways, that our acquisition and enjoyment of lower-order goods is always properly ordered to, and limited by, the higher-order goods. It requires a great deal of knowledge and skill in managing one's possessions and affairs to ensure that we acquire those external goods—and only those external goods—necessary to support the higher goods of body and soul, and to ensure that we properly order our cultivation of bodily health and vigor to the exercise of the virtues of intellect and character. In all these decisions, we both express and shape ourselves as persons who, in contemporary parlance, "have their priorities straight"; as persons who, in even the most seemingly trivial of matters, act in relation to the supreme and complete good of human life; as persons focused on the deepest and most lasting sources of happiness; as persons aiming to make the best of the short time allotted to us by avoiding dispersion and distraction. Aristotle thus does not contrast "merely prudential" reasoning, motives, and deeds with "truly moral" reasoning, motives, and deeds; practical wisdom is not displayed on special "moral" occasions, like piety on Sunday. The Aristotelian virtue of practical wisdom means simply that everything we think, say, and do is ordered to our pursuit of our highest good over a complete life.

According to Aristotle, "[w]hat is most desirable for each and every man is the highest he is capable of attaining" (*Pol.* 1333a29). What are we to make of this aspiration to a complete ordering of all aspects of our lives toward the highest realization of excellence in character and intellect? Although we admire the unity, focus, and integrity of such a life, we might also be troubled by its terrible demands. In this relentless pursuit of perfection—in which every thought, word, and deed either contributes to or detracts from the highest perfection we might attain—there seems to be little or no room for what the Stoics would later call "things indifferent." As Thomas Aquinas will say, many matters might be indifferent in the abstract (whether or not to take a walk, for example), but in the concrete circumstances of my choice, every possible action will either promote or fail to promote my good, meaning that no deliberate thought, word, or deed is genuinely indifferent.[8] In an ethics of aspiration, we cannot fulfill our duties and then relax and enjoy life; in an ethics of aspiration, our work is never done. True, Aristotle certainly allows for recreation, but our use of recreation must be ordered to a more perfect realization of excellence in occupation and in leisure. In short, recreation is a serious matter. Does this relentless pursuit of perfection in every detail of life represent, as Kant charges, a kind of moral fanaticism?[9] Aristotle might reply that a practically wise person must know how to set priorities in order to avoid being bogged down in minor details; he may, for example, use a steward to manage his household affairs (*Pol.* 1255b35). Moreover, the acquisition of good habits enables a virtuous person to make many minor decisions excellently and with dispatch. Deeper concerns with the relentless pursuit of perfection will arise in Christian thought with Augustine and perhaps sooner—concerns that will be echoed by Kant. These thinkers see in Aristotle's ideal a dark temptation to prideful arrogance; indeed, pride in one's own quest for perfection might be the deepest and most dangerous kind of pride, since it is disguised so effectively as our noblest aspiration. What this means is that the pursuit of perfection in a post-Augustinian world is additionally burdened with a duty to the careful examination of conscience to insure that our aspirations to moral and intellectual perfection are not vitiated by pride.[10]

In contrast to Aristotle's ideal of a perfect integrity of practical reason across all dimensions of human conduct, Kant sharply divides practical reasoning into technical reasoning, prudential reasoning, and moral reasoning. Kant says that all practical reason by human beings involves imperatives, that is, rational requirements that ground actions independently of our transient wants or desires (*G* 413). Technical reason involves imperatives of skill: "Whether the end is rational and good is not at all the question here, but only what one must do in order to attain it" (*G* 415). For whatever end we desire, technical reason tells us what we must do in order to attain it. Given that the ends a child will face in the future are unknown, parents seek to educate their children by equipping them with various sorts of technical knowledge and skills that will help the child pursue his future ends no matter what they may turn out to be (*G* 415). The ends made achievable by the development of technical reasoning need not be praiseworthy, however: as Kant notes, the same technical skill that enables a doctor to help a patient also enables a poisoner to kill his

[8] Thomas Aquinas, *Summa Theologiae*, I–II, q. 18, a. 8–9. Aristotle recognizes "things indifferent" mainly in a legal context; see *NE* 1134b20.

[9] Kant calls this "fantastic virtue" because it is concerned with every detail: "the human being can be called fantastically virtuous who allows *nothing to be morally indifferent*" (*MS* 409).

[10] Thus Kant, just when he pronounces the duty of self-perfection, reminds us that we can never know the goodness of our motives (*MS* 393).

victim. In his later discussion of one's duties to one's own perfection, Kant mentions the duty to cultivate one's technical skills (*Kunstfähigkeit*) and other powers "so that they are fit to realize any ends you might encounter" (*MS* 392). On this view, then, technical reason is merely an amoral power or capacity whose good use depends upon moral reason.

Although Aristotle also says that the medical art can produce both health and disease (*Met.* 1046b7), he sees a closer relation between virtue and technical skill than does Kant. Aristotle himself appears to have been of two minds about technical reason: in some places, he defines it as a mere power or capacity that can be used for good or evil, yet in other places, he defines it as a stable disposition whereby the soul possesses true knowledge, making technical reason a virtue (*NE* 1139b15). Is the medical art a mere capacity or a virtue? Certainly, as an inert body of information and a collection of skills, medicine is a capacity that can be, and has been, used for torture, mutilation, and murder. Yet the aim of medical education has never been to impart amoral capacities for good or ill; rather, the aim of medical education has always been to integrate these powerful capacities into a virtuous love of human life and health. Students acquire medical information and skills not in the abstract, but in the deeply moral context of saving lives and restoring health; medical education aims beyond mere capacities to medical virtue, which combines a love for health and life with the skills conducive to promoting them.

On Kant's model, we equip our students with morally neutral skills and knowledge so that they are capable of anything; we then instruct them to use these powers only in ways that are morally permissible. On Aristotle's model, by contrast, we teach our students skills already oriented toward various moral and intellectual goods (namely, the moral and intellectual virtues), so that they acquire, in one unified state of excellence, both the skills and the motivation needed to achieve good ends. Kant says that we have a moral duty to cultivate our natural powers so we can be capable of anything (*G* 423; *MS* 392, 444–45), but Aristotle says that being capable of anything (*panourgia*) is mere villainy (*NE* 1144a27). Kant says that parents want their children to acquire a wide range of skills for a wide range of ends. Aristotle would say that parents want more than this, that they want their children to acquire moral and intellectual virtues, which unite instrumental efficacy with a motivation toward what is good.

On Kant's view, moral goodness resides in the will of the agent, who uses his own skills as if they were external instruments. On Aristotle's view (but put in Kant's language), moral goodness resides neither in the will alone, nor in skill alone, but rather in the unity of a good will and skill that is known as a virtue. The difference may seem subtle, but it reflects a deep divergence between the two accounts with respect to the self-conception of agents. The Kantian identifies himself primarily with the goodness of his will and tends to regard his own skills (and his passions, as we shall see) at a distance, as instruments. The Aristotelian, by contrast, identifies himself primarily with his virtues, which unite skills to a good motivation. Thus, he regards his own skills (and passions) not at a distance, but as part of his very self. Here we should note a pattern: Aristotle says that practical wisdom is the full realization of instrumental reason, while Kant says that moral reasoning filters or regulates technical reasoning. Similarly, as we shall see in Section V, Aristotle describes virtue as the rational realization of our desires and passions, while Kant describes virtue as what filters or regulates our desires and feelings.

Just as Kant's account of technical reason is less inherently oriented to moral goodness than is Aristotle's, so too is Kant's characterization of prudential reason. Kant and Aristotle agree that every person, by nature, seeks his own happiness and that "prudence" reasons to our best judgment as to what conduces to happiness over a complete life. Yet here the similarities end, for despite the fact that *Klugheit* ("prudence") is used to translate Aristotle's *phronêsis*, *Klugheit* has strong connotations of an amoral cleverness and cunning that make it closer to the Aristotelian shrewdness than to practical wisdom. Still, Kant means more by "prudence" than indiscriminate cunning. Though Kant often describes prudence as "skill in the choice of means to one's own greatest well-being" (*G* 416; cf. *KpV* 20, 36–37; *VE* 27:246; *MS* 216), his prudence is not only about means. It is also about ends: prudence must select an optimal set of compossible desires whose satisfaction constitutes happiness over the long run (*G* 405; *Anth.* 266).

Kant distinguishes "worldly prudence" (*Weltklugheit*), skill in the manipulation of others for one's own ends, from "personal prudence" (*Privatklugheit*), sagacity in setting priorities among one's desires to promote happiness in the long run. A person who is merely cunning in the short run might display worldly prudence, but lack personal prudence (*G* 416n); he would be, as we say, "too clever by half." Does this distinction between mere cunning and long-term prudence correspond to Aristotle's distinction between shrewdness and practical wisdom? It might seem so, but Kant sees prudential reason as deeply amoral and unprincipled. Indeed, although he begins his account of practical reason by saying that all practical reason involves imperatives (*G* 413), when we get to prudence, we discover that there are no imperatives or precepts of prudence, but only contingent "counsels" (*G* 416). As we shall see in Section III, prudence lacks precepts because happiness lacks objective or universal determination.[11]

Kant asks "whether it is prudent or whether it is in conformity with duty to make a false promise"; he answers "the first can undoubtedly often be the case" (*G* 402; cf. *G* 422). In short, says Kant, lying can often be the best way to promote your own long-term happiness. Prudential

---

[11] See Wood, *Kant's Ethical Thought*, 68–69, for an argument why the counsels of prudence do not constitute imperatives.

reason, like technical reason, is amoral, and the maxims of prudential reason must be filtered by moral reason if we are to act aright. Aristotle, by contrast, would say that prudential reason is not amoral, because happiness requires the acquisition and exercise of the moral and intellectual virtues. He would insist that there is an objective structure to human flourishing that is undermined by the making of false promises. We might feel an initial attraction to lying because manipulating other people gives us a feeling of superiority, but from experience we usually learn that such a feeling of superiority is not deeply or lastingly rewarding. We discover that deeper and more lasting happiness stems from our own achievements rather than from our position vis-à-vis others. Furthermore, when we lie, we divide ourselves so that what we say does not correspond with what we think; experience shows us that by being honest, we find a happiness in the harmony of our thoughts, words, and deeds that is deeper than the happiness we would achieve through lying. In short, as we shall see in Section III, Aristotle thinks that our crude conceptions of happiness, in which immorality is often the best policy, can be transformed by education into more refined conceptions that rule out immorality. For him, our pursuit of happiness is not filtered or regulated by an external capacity of moral reasoning, but rather is internally transformed by the demands of moral goodness. This does not necessarily mean that our best judgment of what conduces to our own happiness would never lead us to tell a lie; it means only that, contrary to Kant's claim, lying is not often conducive to our long-term happiness.

Aristotle and Kant agree that to act prudentially, that is, to act according to our best judgment of what conduces to our own happiness, is to act from self-love. Unlike Aristotle, however, Kant thinks that self-love is compatible with fairly radical attacks on one's own self-respect and integrity. Thus in several places he says that prudence and self-love are likely to condone suicide; the prudential man may say that "from self-love I make it my principle to shorten my life when its longer duration threatens more troubles than it promises agreeableness" (G 422). According to Kant, however, morality absolutely forbids suicide (VE 27:1427, 27:343; G 422). Kant also says that a merely prudential man may favor sheer idleness over the cultivation of his own talents (G 422–23), that he might well give false testimony and steal other people's goods and money (KpV 25–26), and that he quite possibly would refuse to help anyone in hardship, preferring instead his selfish complacence (G 423). Thus, given Kant's own rigorous conception of moral duty, he clearly sees the prudential quest for happiness as compatible with profound immorality. Indeed, he says that the principle of one's own happiness is the direct opposite of the principle of morality (KpV 35). Kant and Aristotle agree that the quest for happiness is central to human nature, and their sharply opposed views of the relation of morality to happiness reflect not only radically different views of happiness, but radically different views of human nature as well.

Whereas Kantian prudential reason aims lower than Aristotelian practical wisdom, Kantian moral reason seems to aim higher. Whereas Aristotle's ethics takes its starting point from human nature and human acts, Kant's conception of moral philosophy has two components: a purely *a priori* metaphysics of morals and a partly empirical pragmatic anthropology. The pure metaphysics of morals develops practical principles for any community of rational wills, be they divine, angelic, or human; a pragmatic anthropology enables us to apply these general principles to the specific requirements of human nature.[12] Kant is emphatic that in establishing the foundational moral laws we should not take human nature into account: "Moral laws must never be laid down in accordance with human weakness, but must be presented as holy, pure, and morally perfect, be the nature of man what it may" (*VE* 27:294; cf. *VE* 27:301; *G* 425). Where ancient ethics went wrong, Kant states, was in accommodating moral law to the capacity of human nature (*VE* 27:294). Kant repeatedly says that *all* rational wills stand under the moral law; that divine and other holy wills are already subjectively in conformity with moral law; and that because of the imperfections of the human will, the moral law must for us take imperative force (*G* 414; cf. *G* 425, 426, 431, 438, 447, 448, etc.). Kant puts it directly: "The moral law is holy (inviolable)" (*KpV* 87; cf. *VE* 27:302). Yet for imperfect human beings ("a human being is certainly unholy enough" [*KpV* 87]), the moral law is also a law of duty and of reverence for duty; this holy law governs the kingdom of morals in which men are both lawgivers and subjects (*KpV* 82).[13]

Kant's extravagant supernatural language for describing the moral law reveals its origins in the Christian theology of the heavenly kingdom of God. He often compares the purity and holiness of the moral law to the purity and holiness of the Gospel (*VE* 27:301; *KpV* 83). He even describes the community of moral agents as a *corpus mysticum* (*KrV* B836). Furthermore, Kant's moral law is suprahuman in precisely the same way as the law of the Gospel is: just as the Gospel teaches us that human beings cannot expect to fulfill its law without the aid of grace, so Kant says that human beings cannot expect to fulfill the moral law without divine assistance (*VE* 27:294; *Rel.* 52).

The radical disparity between human nature and moral law on Kant's account is evident not only in the quasi-religious respect and reverence he thinks we owe the moral law, but also—and even more compellingly—in the humiliation he says we feel when we compare our conduct to the moral law: "the moral law unavoidably humiliates every human being

---

[12] In ibid., 193–95, Wood shows how Kant's understanding of the relation of these two parts of moral philosophy shifted from the position of the *Groundwork* (*G* 388–89) to that of the *Metaphysics of Morals* (*MS* 217).

[13] The religious language employed by Kant in his discussion of the moral law reveals its suprahuman character: "The moral law is, in other words, for the will of a perfect being a law of *holiness*, but for the will of every finite rational being a law of *duty*, of moral necessitation and of the determination of his actions through *respect* for this law and *reverence* for his duty" (*KpV* 82).

when he compares it with the sensible propensity of his nature" (*KpV* 74; cf. *KpV* 75–78, 85, 155). Indeed, Kant repeatedly insists that we are able to respect the moral law only after we feel humiliated by it (*KpV* 74, 78, 79); to feel humiliated by the moral law is to have a rationally founded respect for it (*KpV* 79). Perhaps all of us would indeed benefit from having our self-conceit deflated a bit, but Kant goes further than this. He describes the humiliation we feel when our conduct is compared to the moral law as a feeling of worthlessness (*KpV* 77, 78, 161; cf. *G* 426). In short, reverence for the moral law leads us to holiness, but only after we have felt our natural worthlessness—as Kant says, in explicitly theological terms, "[o]nly the descent into the hell of self-knowledge can pave the way to godliness" (*MS* 441). We cannot begin the journey to holiness until we grasp that every human being deserves infinite punishment and exclusion from the kingdom of God (*Rel.* 72). Thus on Kant's account, the gap between human nature and moral duty is, in a sense, the gap between hell and heaven. Of course, Aristotle's ethics also transcends the bounds of human nature when he tells us to take as our measure of perfection not human or mortal life, but divine being; he says we must immortalize ourselves (*NE* 1177b30–33). Therefore, Kant and Aristotle agree that ethics depends upon an understanding of the relation between the divine perfection and human frailty; they agree that "God or pure reason," to use Aristotle's terms, is the ultimate measure of man. Yet they understand our moral relation to the divine differently: Aristotle begins with the human quest for happiness, which finds its completion by ascending to the divine; Kant begins with a pure rational law among all wills—one to which divine entities, by definition, conform—and then translates it down into specifically human duties of virtue.

The suprahuman demands of Kantian morality are especially evident in his view that we ought to strive for moral purity. Kant reminds us frequently that we can never fully fathom our own motives, and hence there cannot be a *perfect duty* to moral purity. However, he also insists that we strive for moral purity in our motives as an *imperfect duty*—we do, therefore, have a duty to act (only) from duty. Now, Kant's discussion of moral purity is complex and exceedingly subtle, in part because Kant sometimes means by purity that we must strive never to allow nonmoral motives to confuse the "determination of duty" (*TP* 279); here, "purity" refers to the purity of the motive of duty itself. Yet Kant also says at times that we must strive to eliminate cooperating nonmoral motives (*TP* 285); in this context, "purity" seems to refer to the purity of the rational will as a whole.[14] Thus, in his discussion of our duty to our own moral perfection, Kant says "this perfection consists subjectively in the *purity* (*puritas moralis*) of one's disposition to duty, namely in the law being by itself alone the incentive" (*MS* 446). Just as moral perfection requires purity of

[14] In many passages, one cannot be sure whether Kant is referring to a pure motive or a pure will (*VE* 27:258; *Rel.* 48).

will, so moral evil involves impurity: in discussing human beings' various levels of propensity to evil, Kant calls one such level "impurity," in which the human heart has not "adopted the law *alone* as its *sufficient incentive*" (*Rel.* 30; cf. *Rel.* 46).

Kant is driven to this aspiration for moral purity by a number of considerations, one being his claim that the principle of happiness (that is, self-love) is the direct opposite of the principle of morality (*KpV* 35). Where respect for moral duty is a sufficient motive for my deed, Kant does not say there is anything wrong or immoral with the presence of nonmoral cooperating motives, but says that "we give the most perfect esteem to compliance with it [moral law] at the sacrifice of everything that could ever have value for our dearest inclinations" (*KpV* 158). In short, Kant rejects the common view of *motivational overdetermination*, in which moral motives and cooperating nonmoral motives pile on their additive force in deliberation. Kant insists, by contrast, that moral and nonmoral motives cannot be compared in force "any more than a mile can be compared to a year." They are simply not commensurate: "If we combine pragmatic and moral motives, are they homogeneous? No more than honesty, if a person lacks it, can be replaced by his having money, or than an ugly person acquires beauty if he possesses ample funds, can pragmatic motives be inserted into a series of moral motives and compared with them" (*VE* 27:259).

Kant's concern with purity of motive simply has no counterpart in the thought of Plato or Aristotle. In the *Republic*, Plato says that justice belongs to the noblest class of goods, those goods we love both in themselves and for what they produce, such as understanding, sight, and health (*Republic* II 357–58). Throughout the *Nicomachean Ethics*, Aristotle lists three objects of choice: the fine or noble (*kalon*), the expedient, and the pleasant (*NE* 1104b31). He identifies a virtuous person as one who acts "for the sake of the fine" (*NE* 1115b12, 1116a28, 1116b2–3, 1117b9, 1119a18, etc.). Does he mean that a virtuous person acts *only* "for the sake of the fine," a motive corresponding in purity to Kant's acting from duty? Some very distinguished scholars claim that Aristotle insists on the same purity of motive as Kant does, though they assert this without any direct textual evidence.[15]

I think Aristotle differs from Kant on this issue in a way that is quite instructive for understanding the deepest issues between them. Aristotle, says

---

[15] Both Christine Korsgaard and Julia Annas compare Aristotle's "acting for the sake of the fine" to Kant's "acting from duty." About Aristotle's conception of acting "for the sake of the noble," Korsgaard says: "This isn't a judgment about whether doing this action will serve some further purpose, about whether it is useful." True, but Aristotle, unlike Kant, sees no problem with doing the noble also because it is useful and pleasant. Annas says of Aristotle: "Doing the virtuous action for its own sake excludes doing it for some ulterior motive; insofar as the action is a virtuous action, the action is then done for the sake not of what is useful or pleasant, but what is fine." In her note to this astonishing claim, Annas cites no textual evidence and weakly says: "Although this connection is not spelled out, it is, I think, fairly obvious." Christine Korsgaard, "From Duty and for the Sake of the Noble," in Engstrom and Whiting, eds., *Aristotle, Kant, and the Stoics*, 217; Julia Annas, "Morality and Practical Reasoning," in Engstrom and Whiting, eds., *Aristotle, Kant, and the Stoics*, 242.

Terence Irwin, clearly contrasts "acting for the sake of the fine" with acting "only for some further end to which the fine action is merely instrumental."[16] However, he seems to suggest that we ought to act for the pleasant and expedient as well as for the fine, if they are all compatible. For example, Aristotle distinguishes between three kinds of friendship, basing them, respectively, on virtue, expedience, and pleasure. However, he is quite emphatic that the noble friendship based on virtue is also expedient and pleasurable (NE 1156b12–17, 1157a1–3). Indeed, Aristotle believes, contrary to, say, Machiavelli, that what is fine is also likely to be expedient; in some cases, he thinks, we may have to choose the fine at the cost of the expedient, but this will be unusual.[17] As for what is pleasant, for a virtuous man, what is fine is also, necessarily, pleasant (NE 1099a7–21, 1104b3, 1117a35–b16, etc.). Given these views, we have lots of indirect evidence that Aristotle is not at all concerned with the purity of the motives behind virtuous acts. Indeed, there are reasons to believe that he welcomes a mixture of motives: when we act for the fine as well as for the expedient and the pleasant, our motives begin to converge by their habitual association—just like the motives of people who regularly associate.

Kant, as we shall see in Section V, has a dark view of human nature: he is worried that the motive to duty will be dragged down and corrupted by base inclinations. Aristotle, I will suggest, has more confidence in human nature and believes that our passions can be educated by reason. On Aristotle's account, pursuing the expedient and the pleasant in the context of pursuing the fine is likely to have an edifying effect on the lower motives. One can easily imagine a developmental process in which we begin by doing fine actions only for reasons of expedience. Over time, we begin to value the fine actions in and of themselves, even when they are not expedient. Eventually, the fine becomes so pleasant to us that we learn to love to act for the fine, and perhaps even to think of it as expedient also. Many people have this experience in regard to political participation. We may well enter politics merely to promote our own interests, but come to value the political process for its own sake, even when that process fails to promote our own interests. Eventually, we may find politics at once ennobling, pleasant, and even expedient (once we think of our interests more broadly). In this Aristotelian process, acting for the fine or noble, far from being incompatible with lower motives, has the potential to elevate these lower motives.

III. Happiness

Kant clearly has little faith that prudential concern for happiness will lead us to do our moral duty, let alone to do it out of duty. Aristotle, by

---

[16] This is how Irwin puts it in his edition of the NE, at 401.

[17] For example, Aristotle argues that for a tyrant, to govern like a king is to choose what is fine as well as expedient: "For then his rule will of necessity be nobler and happier. . . . His power too will be more lasting" (Pol. 1315b5–9).

contrast, thinks that the pursuit of happiness, rightly understood, can and will lead us not only to do what is right, but also to do it for the right reasons—that is, to do it "for its own sake" or "for the noble." Here the contrast between Aristotle and Kant rests not so much on what right reason demands, but on what relation virtuous conduct has to our natural quest for happiness. This relation, in turn, rests on a deep contrast in their underlying views of happiness.

Kant's description of happiness (*Glückseligkeit*) often revolves around the subrational psychological states of pleasure, desire-satisfaction, and contentment. Kant can even sound quite Benthamite; consider, for example, Kant's statement that "[h]appiness is the satisfaction of all our desires, *extensively*, in respect of their manifoldness, *intensively*, in respect of their degree, and *protensively*, in respect of their duration" (*KrV* B834; cf. *G* 399, 405).[18] On Kant's account, in seeking happiness, we select our activities and ends purely on the basis of the sum of expected pleasure: "The only thing that concerns him, in order to decide upon a choice, is how intense, how long, how easily acquired, and how often repeated this agreeableness is . . . [that is,] *how much* and *how great* satisfaction [the objects of choice] will furnish him for the longest time" (*KpV* 23). The pleasures that constitute happiness differ from each other only in degree (*KpV* 23). When Kant is not describing happiness in terms of quanta of pleasure, he often describes it in the similar terms of subjective wish fulfillment and contentment. At various places, he characterizes happiness as the condition "that *everything* should *always* go the way you would like it to" (*MS* 480), as the enjoyment of the gratification of desire when "everything goes according to [a person's] wish and will" (*KpV* 124), and as contentment or a lasting satisfaction with one's state (*MS* 387; *G* 393). Given this reduction of happiness to pleasure, it is not surprising that Kant sometimes often refers to the quest for happiness as bestial and animalistic (*VE* 27:275; *Anth.* 325).

We all know that our desires are not all mutually compatible, and that not every pleasure can be maximized. Hence, we need a rational idea of happiness that frames a subset of compossible desires for us to pursue; prudential reason thus frames such a subset, which Kant calls "an idea in which all inclinations are summed up" (*G* 399; *KU* 208; *KpV* 73). Whereas animals satisfy their desires one by one, only human beings possessing prudential reason can frame an idea of a coherent set of desires in which reason constrains immediate pleasure for the sake of contentment over a complete life.[19] Kant does not ascribe to prudence the capacity to trans-

---

[18] Bentham lists intensity, duration, certainty, propinquity, fecundity, purity, and extent as the dimensions of pleasure. See Jeremy Bentham, *An Introduction to the Principles of Morals and Legislation* (London: Athlone Press, 1970), 39.

[19] This is the case, Allen Wood says, because "the pursuit of happiness could not possibly arise from mechanical self-love, or from natural inclinations by themselves. Happiness is an *idea* we make for ourselves through imagination and reason. Put otherwise, the desire for it is a second-order desire for the satisfaction of a certain rationally selected set of first-order inclinations." Wood, "Self-Love, Self-Benevolence, and Self-Conceit," in Engstrom and Whiting, eds., *Aristotle, Kant, and the Stoics*, 145.

form our desires, but rather the capacity to show us a way to satisfy them selectively. Prudence looks to overall satisfaction of desire and to general maximization of pleasure. Kant thinks the fanatical pursuit of one pleasure is folly (*Anth.* 266).

What counsels does prudence offer for guidance in the overall satisfaction of our desires? As we have seen, Kant believes that our prudential concern for our own happiness offers very little normative constraint on our motives: all manner of villainy is compatible, he thinks, with a prudentially rational quest for happiness. This thought finds its root in Kant's claim that the objects of desire or aversion and the pleasure or displeasure we take in relation to them are radically subjective, idiosyncratic, and unstable over time. Given this, we can form no universal or necessary laws about what contributes to happiness, because the causes of happiness are radically contingent on empirical circumstances (*G* 417–18; *KpV* 23–25, 28); that you and I or even all of us agree about what makes for happiness is pure coincidence (*KpV* 26, 28). "Only experience can teach what brings us joy. Only the natural drives for food, sex, rest, movement, and (as our natural predispositions develop) for honor, for enlarging our cognition and so forth, can tell each of us, and each only in his particular way, in what he will *find* these joys; and, in the same way, only experience can teach him the means by which to *seek* them" (*MS* 215). Even inductive generalities based on long observance of the human quest for happiness are so tenuous as to offer little or no guidance to the challenges every person faces in finding what makes him or her happy (*MS* 216). Thus, for some people, immorality and evil are what best conduce to happiness, while for others, perhaps, upright and saintly conduct fills this role. It is for this reason that Kant denies that happiness is unconditionally good, for, as philosopher Allen Wood puts it, no one can approve of "the happiness a villain might derive from his villainy." [20]

Prudential reason cannot exercise any real constraint over the content of the pursuit of happiness because the very idea of happiness, says Kant, is a chimera. Since we cannot know the future in advance, any plan we might frame for future happiness is likely to go astray: Kant tells us to be careful what we wish for, we might get it (*G* 418)! Kant says that the idea of happiness is an ever-changing figment of our imagination: "We can never produce a complete whole with which we could be wholly satisfied; hence this is an imagining to which no concept corresponds." [21] No doubt, if we conceive of happiness as the product of blind fortune and the vagaries of subjective contentment, then Kant is no doubt right that any determinate conception of my own happiness is a chimera, for I have no idea whether I will be pleased in the future with what pleases me now,

---

[20] Wood, *Kant's Ethical Thought*, 24; here, Wood is paraphrasing *G* 393.
[21] Immanuel Kant, "Lectures on Anthropology," in Kant, *Kants gesammelte Schriften*, 25:1081, cited in Allen Wood, "Kant vs. Eudaimonism," unpublished manuscript.

nor how changes in fortune will make a mockery of my plans. Kant suggests that we might "consider the happiness of this life, which consists only in illusion, and where often the beggar at the gate is happier than the king on his throne" (*VE* 27:367).

Since prudential reason cannot generate any reliable standard for us to judge our own happiness, we seek the next best thing: to reassure ourselves that we are at least happier than others. If there is no way to measure my absolute level of happiness, then I naturally look for my relative happiness; as Kant says, "only in comparison to others does one judge oneself to be happy" (*Rel.* 27).[22] Unfortunately, however, this urge to compare our happiness to that of others backfires and only undermines our hopes for happiness. By seeking comparative advantage, we are led to jealousy and rivalry, upon which are grafted what Kant calls the "diabolical vices" of envy, ingratitude, and spitefulness (*Rel.* 27). Thus, paradoxically, as Wood argues, happiness for Kant consists mainly in contentment, but our pursuit of happiness leads us to comparisons with others that undermine our contentment. Still, what is bad for the individual turns out to be good for the species: in Kant's unique historical theodicy, our competitive rivalry, which he calls our "unsocial sociability" (*I* p. 44; cf. *Anth.* 324–30), is essential as a spur for the development of our talents and culture.[23] Man's original nature leads him to prefer indolent contentment to industrious self-development; without the spur of honor and competitive rivalry, none of our talents would be cultivated: "Without this honour, nobody would trouble to devote himself to the sciences. If he were on a desert island, he would throw away all his books, and prefer to hunt for roots" (*VE* 27:410).[24]

Aristotle obviously has quite a different understanding of happiness, which he defines as "an activity of the soul in accordance with the most complete virtue in a complete life."[25] Aristotle's understanding contrasts sharply with Kant's on several dimensions. First, happiness for Aristotle is not to be identified with pleasure, desire-satisfaction, or contentment; rather, these states are valuable if and only if they are a by-product of the completion of excellent activities (*NE* 1153a9, 1176a24–29, 1174a2–4). Thus, says Aristotle, we would pursue many activities, such as acquiring knowledge and the virtues, even if they did not cause us to experience such states of pleasure (*NE* 1174a4). Second, happiness for Aristotle is not a state at all, but an activity of self-realization, the actualization of our

---

[22] "For if everyone alike in the town is eating rotten cheese, I eat it too, with satisfaction and a cheerful mind, whereas if everyone else were well-fed, and I alone in sorry circumstances, I would deem it a misfortune" (*VE* 27:367).

[23] On the whole question of "unsocial sociability" in Kant, see Wood, "Self-Love, Self-Benevolence, and Self-Conceit," 147.

[24] "Without these asocial qualities . . . all human talents would remain hidden for ever in a dormant state, and men . . . would scarcely render their existence more valuable than that of their animals" (*I* p. 45).

[25] This is how Terence Irwin summarizes *NE* 1098a16–18 in his "Kant's Criticisms of Eudaemonism," in Engstrom and Whiting, eds., *Aristotle, Kant, and the Stoics*, 72.

potential for moral and intellectual excellence. Such activities of self-actualization (for example, learning mathematics, how to play chess, or how to be a good spouse) often require that we submit to the arduous discipline of developing new skills by meeting the challenges of over-coming obstacles and solving problems. On this account, then, happiness in the sense of human flourishing is an objective perfection of human potential that does not rest on the subjective feelings and opinions of an agent: we flourish by the acquisition and exercise of the moral and intel-lectual virtues, whether or not such activities always make us pleased or contented.

Aristotle and Kant differ so radically on the meaning of happiness that they do not seem to be talking about the same thing. Happiness for Ar-istotle is primarily an objective fact about the level of moral and intellec-tual excellence achieved by a person; Aristotle says little about a happy person's subjective contentment, except to note that while a happy person may not always be blessed, he is never miserable (NE 1100b33–35, 1101a6–8). Kant, by contrast, makes happiness primarily about subjective psycholog-ical states. When Aristotle says that no child could be described as happy (NE 1100a1), we sense the distance between his objective conception of hap-piness and Kant's—and our—more subjective understanding.

Aristotle offers a normative account of happiness and provides criteria for judging the degree of happiness one might attain; Kant offers a more descriptive and psychological account of happiness. Thus, where Kant sees happiness as a gift of fortune (G 393), Aristotle sees happiness as an achievement of the self. If we think of happiness, with Kant, as mainly a gift of fortune, then we might well be dismayed by the happiness of vicious people, just as we would be dismayed by their prosperity or longevity.[26] If, however, we think of happiness mainly as a moral and intellectual achievement, then we may be confident that vicious people cannot enjoy true happiness. The Kantian and Aristotelian accounts also differ in how they connect happiness and virtue. Though they each mean quite different things by the terms, both Kant and Aristotle agree that virtue and happiness ought to go together. But whereas Kant thinks vir-tue is often positively inimical to happiness,[27] and that in this world, virtue is only at best accidentally linked to happiness, Aristotle sees a deep internal relation between the two concepts, even while he recog-nizes that virtue can lead to the sacrifice of goods upon which full hap-piness depends. Aristotle would find Kant's worries about undeserved happiness to be misplaced because he thinks that, for the most part, people enjoy the happiness they deserve; Kant would argue that Aristotle

[26] As Kant says: "The Stoic believes that inner worth is already happiness. But in that case the wicked man would have to be always unhappy, and yet he is not. He is often in full enjoyment of happiness" (VE 29:623).

[27] "Virtue . . . contributes much to human unhappiness" (VE 29:623); "For virtue . . . also involves sacrificing many of the joys of life" (MS 484).

is too complacent about the fact that the achievement of happiness depends to a significant degree on accidents of native intelligence, temperament, and upbringing.

Nowhere does Kant break more decisively from Aristotle than in his argument that our prudential concern for our own happiness might well lead us to eschew self-perfection: "the basis on which man should develop his capacities (for all sorts of ends) is not regard for the *advantages* that their cultivation can provide; for the advantage might . . . turn out on the side of his crude natural needs" (*MS* 444–45). Indeed, Kant goes so far as to say that practical reason itself undermines our happiness, that human beings would be better off if the ends and means of our conduct were left to instinct: "we find that the more a cultivated reason purposely occupies itself with enjoyment of life and with happiness, so much the further does one get away from true satisfaction" (*G* 395). Not only is the acquisition and exercise of skill in practical reasoning destructive of one's own happiness, Kant says, but even the development of the arts and sciences has produced more discontent than happiness (*G* 396).

Aristotle's account, in contrast, links happiness and practical reason tightly together. According to Aristotle, to suppose that brute instinct or illiterate savagery is more conducive to human happiness than is rational self-direction or literate civility betrays an extremely degraded understanding of what constitutes happiness. For an Aristotelian view, discontent hardly excludes the possibility of happiness: some degree of discontent is *necessary* to encourage us to engage in the activities of self-realization through which we flourish. Aristotle tells us that when an activity becomes habitual, it also becomes pleasurable (*Rhet.* 1370a3–7); however, learning a new activity involves "acts of concentration, strong effort, and strain" that "are necessarily painful" (*Rhet.* 1370a13). As Leibniz said, "l'inquiétude est essentielle à la félicité des créatures": the acquisition and exercise of skills requires the suspension of contentment in order to meet the challenges of solving puzzles and overcoming obstacles.[28] If contentment were essential, we would never embark upon a project of self-realization because, as Jon Elster reminds us, "Aller Anfang ist schwer"— every beginning is difficult.[29]

Recall that Kant thinks that without our asocial vices of enviously competitive vanity and the insatiable urge for superiority, human beings would never develop their natural capacities. Since without these asocial vices, our natural desire for happiness would lead us to "throw away our books," Kant says that the proper motive to self-cultivation should be respect for our moral duty to be worthy of the humanity that dwells

[28] G. W. Leibniz, *Nouveau Essais sur l'Entendement Humain*, in Leibniz, *Die Philosophischen Schriften*, ed. C. I. Gerhardt (Hildesheim, Germany: Olms, 1966), 6:175, quoted in Jon Elster, "Self-Realization in Work and Politics: The Marxist Conception of the Good Life," *Social Philosophy and Policy* 3, no. 2 (Spring 1986): 103.
[29] Elster, "Self-Realization in Work and Politics," 104.

276 JAMES BERNARD MURPHY

within us (*MS* 386–87; cf. *G* 441–42).[30] Indeed, says Kant, we may well need to set aside our natural desire for happiness and accept that "it is a command of morally practical reason and a *duty* of man himself to cultivate his capacities" (*MS* 445). Aristotle would agree that competition for honor can be a useful spur to excellence in the arts and sciences, but he has much more confidence that human beings are by nature inquisitive and that we thrive by acquiring and exercising complex skills. In short, Kant sees happiness as the fulfillment of a desiring self, while Aristotle sees happiness as the fulfillment of right desire and as the actualization of capacities into skilled performance. This contrast reflects a deeper underlying contrast between Kant and Aristotle on the self-conception of agents in relation to their pursuit of happiness: Am I a bundle of desires to be optimally satisfied, or am I a bundle of trained desires to be satisfied combined with a set of capacities to be realized? How central are my capacities and their realization in skills to my self-conception?

Aristotle and Kant thus diverge radically in their understanding of the relation of self-development to happiness. Aristotle would agree, however, that if happiness were essentially about subjective contentment, then Kant would be right to place it in opposition to moral and intellectual development. Benjamin Constant follows Kant in saying:

> [I]s it so evident that happiness, of whatever kind, is the only aim of mankind? If it were so, our course would be narrow indeed, and our destination far from elevated. There is not one single one of us who, if he wished to abase himself, restrain his moral faculties, abjure activity, glory, deep and generous emotions, could not demean himself and be happy.... It is not to happiness alone, it is to self-development that our destiny calls us.[31]

IV. DESIRE, INCLINATION, AND PASSION

Other scholars have pointed out that given Kant's views on happiness and virtue, his critique of ethical eudaimonism has little bearing on non-hedonist kinds of eudaimonism, such as Aristotle's.[32] Kant's many radical denunciations of eudaimonism, such as his frequent claim that acting for happiness is the opposite of acting from morality,[33] simply do not

---

[30] Kant on the duty of self-perfection: "This duty can therefore consist only in *cultivating one's capacities* (or natural predispositions), the highest of which is *understanding*, the capacity for concepts and so too for those concepts that have to do with duty. At the same time this duty includes the cultivation of one's *will* (moral cast of mind), so as to satisfy all the requirements of duty" (*MS* 387).

[31] Benjamin Constant, "The Liberty of the Ancients Compared with That of the Moderns" [1819], in Constant, *Political Writings*, ed. and trans. Biancamaria Fontana (Cambridge: Cambridge University Press, 1988), 327.

[32] As Irwin argues in "Kant's Criticisms of Eudaemonism."

[33] "The direct opposite of the principle of morality is the principle of *one's own* happiness" (*KpV* 35).

apply to the Aristotelian version. Since Kant's hedonist conception of happiness is so distant from Aristotle's, perhaps it makes more sense to briefly compare Kant's understanding of the relation of virtue to happiness with Aristotle's understanding of the relation of virtue to pleasure. Kant is no more against happiness than Aristotle is against pleasure; both philosophers deny that happiness or pleasure, respectively, is the supreme good, but both see it as part of the complete good (*KpV* 110; *NE* 1153b14). Just as Aristotle sees pleasure as a good by-product of virtuous activity—as the completion and perfection of virtuous activity—so Kant sees happiness as the rightful corollary to the attainment of virtue.[34]

Once we have achieved self-perfection in virtue, says Kant, we feel happy (satisfied or contented) with the sheer consciousness of our rectitude. Indeed, Kant later adds, the awareness of our own respect for duty can surpass mere contentment and lead to a positively blissful moral pleasure—though this bliss, of course, cannot be the motive for our self-perfection (*MS* 387–88, 391). For Aristotle, not only can the virtuous person hope for pleasure, but what it is to be a virtuous person is precisely to take pleasure in performing virtuous actions (*NE* 1099a7–21, 1104b3, 1117a35, 1170a8); furthermore, like Kant, he thinks that the virtuous person also takes pleasure in the consciousness of his or her own rectitude (*NE* 1166a23). Neither Kant nor Aristotle see happiness or pleasure, respectively, as the highest good, because we can often err if we aim at happiness or pleasure rather than the virtuous activities completed by happiness or pleasure. For Kant, as we have seen, aiming for happiness by no means leads us reliably to virtue; indeed, Kant even describes the quest for happiness as the opposite of the quest for virtue (*KpV* 35; cf. *KpV* 111). Aristotle says that it is appropriate for a virtuous man to also aim at the pleasure that completes a virtuous action (*NE* 1175a16), but that while we are on the road to complete virtue, we ought to aim at what is good and noble rather than at what is merely pleasant. This is because pleasure in itself is not an accurate marker of virtuous activity. For instance, there are some things we should do even if they bring no pleasure (*NE* 1174a4), and some things (e.g., acts of bravery) we should do even if they are inseparable from great pain (*NE* 1117a32). Furthermore, because of the intensity of physical pleasure, we are often tempted to pursue lower pleasures at the expense of higher and better pleasures. Hence, pleasure can mislead us about the good (*NE* 1104b30, 1109b7, 1113a33, 1154b3) or even destroy our conception of the good (*NE* 1140b13, 1144a34).

Given Kant's reduction of happiness to pleasure, it makes sense that his account of the relation of virtue to happiness ought to be in some ways analogous to Aristotle's view of the relation of virtue to pleasure. Nonetheless, the two philosophers ultimately part company in their accounts of these relations because of their strongly contrasting views of whether the desires that move us to seek pleasure/happiness are educable by

---

[34] On Aristotle, see *NE* 1174b24–25, 1174b33, 1175a16. On Kant, see *KpV* 110–11; *VE* 27:247.

JAMES BERNARD MURPHY

reason or not. Aristotle sees desire as educable in the sense that we can learn to desire higher and finer things so that the virtuous man takes pleasure only in the higher and finer things. Thus, the challenge of moral development is not so much to repress one's desires: a virtuous person, Aristotle says, is not without desires (*NE* 1104b24). The real challenge is to develop these desires properly. In this vein, Aristotle states that the difficulty with the young is not only that they are often dominated by their passions, but that their passions are not yet sufficiently rational.[35]

Although Aristotle often employs the political metaphor of the ruler and the ruled to discuss the relation of reason to the passions (*ta pathê*) and the desires (*orexeis*), this device in no way completely captures his understanding of the interrelations of the various rational faculties to the various nonrational faculties.[36] In what follows, I will attempt to unpack some of the richness of this account; in the process, I will point to those features of Aristotle's understanding that underpin his confidence that in a virtuous person, the prudential quest for happiness will lead us to moral and intellectual excellence.

Aristotle's terminology for the nonrational faculties is not consistent across his writings. Under the broad rubric of desires he seems to include both passions and appetite (*epithumia*). Aristotle's discussion of the passions, especially in Book II of the *Rhetoric*, focuses on their cognitive powers: passions embody evaluations or judgments about the world. Pity and indignation, for example, rest on judgments of justice (*Rhet.* 1386b10); anger involves a judgment of something as insulting (*Rhet.* 1379a30).[37] Passions are thus intentional attitudes that embody perceptions and evaluations of our relation to the world; changes in passions are in part changes in those perceptions and evaluations.[38]

We experience some passions, however, less as modes of cognition than as physiological "drives" pushing us. Aristotle seems to recognize this distinction: he says that one kind of desire, appetite, is more concerned with pleasure and pain than about making judgments, and that it is a craving that is often a wild beast (*Pol.* 1287a31) and contrary to choice (*NE* 1111b16).[39] Aristotle says that passions are open to reason in a way that

[35] Aristotle thus says that the young are not suitable students of political science because they tend to be guided by their desires. As we mature, however, we learn "to be guided by reason in forming our desires and in acting" (*NE* 1095a10; cf. *NE* 1128b17).

[36] For examples of the ruling metaphor, see *Pol.* 1254b6–9, 1260a5–6, 1254a28. Aristotle's full account of the relations between the rational faculties (including *nous, logismos, aisthêsis, phronêsis, prohairêsis*, etc.) and the nonrational faculties (*hormê, thumos, pathos, epithumia, orexis*, etc.) is very subtle and complex, and it shifts throughout his various treatises. (I omit from my list here *boulêsis*—rational desire—which bridges the rational and nonrational parts of the soul and hence becomes the basis for deliberation and decision.)

[37] "It is not that being angry makes us view the object of emotion as insulting, but being angry involves viewing the object as insulting." Stephen Leighton, "Aristotle and the Emotions," *Phronesis* 25, no. 2 (1980): 147.

[38] On passions and judgments, see *Rhet.* 1378a20–23; on passions and perceptions, see *NE* 1149a24–31; *DA* 460b1–16.

[39] For an argument that Aristotle strongly distinguishes appetite from the passions, see Leighton, "Aristotle and the Emotions."

appetites are not (*NE* 1149b1–4, 1119b7); in other words, you might talk someone out of his fear, but not out of his hunger. However, even though you cannot talk someone out of an appetite, you may be able to talk him out of acting on that appetite (*NE* 1113b27). Appetites lead us without attempting to persuade us; they are devoid of reason (*EE* 1224b2). Passions have grounds in the beliefs and judgments of agents (*Rhet.* 1378a28), appetites only have causes.[40] Because appetites are not grounded in the beliefs of agents, we cannot conquer them with arguments, as we can passions. Thus, when Aristotle speaks of "ruling and mastering" the non-rational part of the soul, this harsh language seems appropriate only in the case of the appetites.

Despite the special challenge the appetites pose, Aristotle thinks that the whole of the nonrational soul is responsive to reason—not to cold rational proof, but to rational chastening, reproof, and exhortation (*NE* 1102b28–1103a1). Training in virtue means that our passions are not merely controlled or ruled by reason, but that they become internally transformed so as to converge with the demands of reason. The virtuous person will thus experience fear in proportion to real threats, pity in proportion to real misfortune, and indignation in proportion to real injustice. Once a person's passions are grounded in his rational judgments, he will respond, interpret, and engage the world in a manner responsive both to reason and the passions. In our experience of moral life, just as in our experience of tragic drama, Aristotle insists upon a unity of rational thought and feeling, "since to feel in the right way toward the right things, just *is* one integral dimension of understanding their human sense and meaning."[41] After all, we expect people to respond to us and engage us not merely at a cerebral level, but also at an affective level. Thus, we should aspire to engage our world with our whole selves—reason and passion. No doubt the integration of appetites with reason poses special obstacles, but Aristotle thinks that the virtuous person has such integrity.

Our appetites are initially oriented toward their objects in a rather crude and scattershot way: children, for example, like dogs, thirst for anything liquid. On Aristotle's account, over time our appetites are internally transformed by our rational beliefs about what properly satisfies thirst, so that, to continue our example, we no longer desire mere liquid, but potable liquids that do not belong to other people.[42] But Aristotle's account of the interrelations of reason and desire cannot be captured by a model of education whereby reason simply teaches the passions and desires to straighten up and fly right; rather, Aristotle sketches a "polit-

---

[40] As Leighton puts it in ibid., 164.

[41] Stephen Halliwell, "Pleasure, Understanding, and Emotion in Aristotle's *Poetics*," in A. O. Rorty, ed., *Essays on Aristotle's Poetics* (Princeton, NJ: Princeton University Press, 1992), 254.

[42] Here I borrow from Barbara Herman's "Making Room for Character," in Engstrom and Whiting, eds., *Aristotle, Kant, and the Stoics*, 36–60.

ical" model in which reason and the desires converge through a process of debate and deliberation. A decision, he says, is a deliberative desire (*bouleutikê orexis*) to do an action within our power, for "when we have judged [that it is right] as a result of deliberation, our desire to do it expresses our wish" (*NE* 1113a10). The proper basis of decision and action is neither a reason alone nor a desire alone, but the convergence of reason and desire. When understanding becomes desiderative (*orektikos nous*) and desire becomes thoughtful (*orexis dianoêtikê*), then we will make proper decisions (*NE* 1139b4).

Aristotle's clearest account of this convergence of reason and the passions is found in a passage in the *Magna Moralia* (1206a36 ff.). Aristotle begins by observing that when reason rules the passions, we have mere self-control or continence; when the passions rule reason, we have incontinence. Taken to extremes—when the passions simply override the protests of reason, or when reason simply overrides the protests of the passions—moral immaturity is evident.[43] What virtue requires, by contrast, is reason becoming commensurate with the passions and the passions becoming commensurate with reason.[44] Under Aristotle's political model of deliberation, passions often propose objects of choice, and, after sufficient debate, practical wisdom decides how the individual should proceed by putting prospective courses of action to the "vote" of the assembled passions and types of reason.[45]

The proposal for a course of action, then, seems to originate in the desires, both natural and habituated;[46] practical wisdom, employing the insight of understanding (*nous*), sharpens the aim of natural desire to make it a truly deliberative desire. Aristotle says that we have a dynamic natural orientation (*aretê physikê*) to perform just, brave, and temperate actions. However, without the understanding cultivated by practical wisdom, the inchoate natural virtues lack focus: we stumble around in the

---

[43] "One may see this from the case of children and those who live without reason. For in these, apart from reason, there spring up, first, impulses of the passions towards right, and reason supervening later and giving its vote the same way is the cause of right action. But if they have received from reason the principle that leads to right, the passions do not necessarily follow and consent thereto, but often oppose it" (*MM* 1206b21).

[44] "For we assert that there is excellence when reason being in a good condition is commensurate with the passions, these possessing their proper excellence, and the passions with the reason; for in such condition they will accord with one another, so that reason should always ordain what is best, and the passions being well disposed find it easy to carry out what reason ordains" (*MM* 1206b17). Aristotle's authorship of the *Magna Moralia* is disputed, but the passages I cite here and in the text explicate the notion of a "deliberative desire" found in the *Nicomachean Ethics*.

[45] "Speaking generally, it is not the case, as others think, that reason is the principle and guide to excellence, but rather the passions. For there must first be produced in us (as indeed is the case) an irrational impulse to the right, and then later on reason must put the question to the vote and decide it" (*MM* 1206b17).

[46] "Reason does not teach the origins either in mathematics or in actions; [with actions] it is virtue, either natural or habituated, that teaches correct belief about the origin" (*NE* 1151a17).

dark and are a danger to ourselves and others.[47] The desires are thus potentially rational and reason is potentially desiderative; these potentialities are actualized in the deliberations of the virtuous person.

How might we understand the dialogue between the desires and reason? Philosopher Nancy Sherman describes the cognitive role of desires (what she calls "emotions") in deliberation by calling them "modes of attention": the emotions powerfully fix our attention on what is most salient in ourselves and our world; they reveal to us what we most value.[48] By forcefully drawing our attention to various aspects of the world, the emotions furnish indispensable information for practical deliberation. Often, for example, we do not realize how important a person or object is to us until we fear or grieve his or its loss. Moreover, many of our practical decisions are between goods that are rationally incommensurate—not just between chocolate or vanilla ice cream, but also between becoming a scholar or a lawyer. Without hearing from the passions, our reason might well be paralyzed, unable to choose between the two options. If our desires and other emotions are well integrated into practical reason, then the guidance they give will not be arbitrary, but will lead us to what is most perfective of our unique nature. Of course, our passional evaluations are often overstated, misleading, biased, contradictory, and otherwise inadequate. This is why our desires must deliberate with our reason. In short, for Aristotle, virtue is not so much the triumph of reason over desire, but rather the collaboration of desire and reason in pursuit of genuine goods.

Kant's understanding of the role of desires in moral life is radically different from Aristotle's; this difference will help us to see why, unlike Aristotle, he tends to place the prudential quest for happiness in opposition to the moral quest for virtue. Within the overall faculty of desire, Kant distinguishes a capacity for taking pleasure or displeasure in a representation. This capacity, which he calls feeling (Gefühl), includes affects, desires (in the narrow sense), inclinations, and passions (MS 211). Kant sometimes ranks these according to the threat that they pose to reason and morality. The first major threat to rational morality is when an impulse (Trieb, Antrieb), affect (Affekt), or desire (Begierde) becomes habitual; it is then an inclination (Neigung). The other major threat to morality that Kant discusses is the passions (Leidenschaft), those inclinations that reason either cannot control or can control only minimally (Anth. 251, 265). None of these components of feeling directly determines our will, but when incorporated into maxims of action they can become incentives to free choice. Kant thinks, however, that because of self-love, we are

---

[47] "For each of us seems to possess his type of character to some extent by nature, since we are just, brave, prone to temperance, or have [other features], immediately from birth. . . . [T]hese natural states belong to children and to beasts as well [as adults], but without understanding they are evidently harmful" (NE 1144b4–10).

[48] Sherman, Making a Necessity of Virtue, 39–52.

often tempted to prefer to act on maxims grounded on passion even when they are contrary to moral and even prudential maxims. Discussing the affects and passions, Kant repeatedly describes them as kinds of mental illness: "A mind that is subject to affects and passions is always *ill*. . . . [A]n affect is a rash. . . . For pure practical reason, the passions are cancerous sores" (*Anth.* 251, 252, 266).[49]

In sharp contrast to Aristotle's view that the desires embody cognitive evaluations of ourselves and the world, Kant resolutely denies that the capacity for feeling plays any cognitive role whatever. He argues that unlike sensation (*Empfindung*), which can be an element of our knowledge of objects, feeling is purely subjective and contains no relation to an object of possible knowledge (*MS* 211; *KU* 189, 206). Our feelings give us no information about the world or even about ourselves (*MS* 211; *KU* 206). For this reason, pleasure, like the tendency to pursue happiness, is simply a given datum of subjective experience that is not susceptible of normative justification or rankings: "Any feeling has a private validity only, and is not accessible to anyone else . . . once anyone appeals to a feeling he is giving up all grounds of reason" (*VE* 27:276).[50]

If we were aware that our feelings lack any cognitive power, then we would not confuse our emotional imaginings with truth about ourselves or the world. However, we are typically duped by our feelings into all manner of delusion (*Wahn*), including fantasies, wishful thinking, and superstition. Thus, Kant calls the inclinations "the deceiver within ourselves" (*Anth.* 151) because the passions subject us to delusion: "the inner practical illusion of mistaking a subjective element in the grounds of action for something objective" (*Anth.* 274). Our feelings and other desires are deeply unreliable as guides to moral duty because they cause us systematically to confuse our subjective projections with objective knowledge of ourselves and of others.

Kant's stance toward the varieties of these feelings and desires is complex. He says that they are good and that it would be futile and contrary to duty to try to extirpate them (*Rel.* 26, 57–58); rather, we must attempt to escape from the power of some of our feelings, strengthen our capacity for others, and even at times seek to seduce our feelings into becoming unwitting allies of virtue. Kant proposes several ways to do these things. He says, for instance, that we have a moral duty to cultivate apathy—the absence of affects—in order to counter the affects' influence; as we shall see, he also suggests that acquiring the social graces can be instrumental in molding the passions so that they are more receptive to proper conduct. Yet even with these methods of dealing with the feelings, we can

[49] On Kant's understanding of the affects and passions, I have relied on Wood, *Kant's Ethical Thought*, 250–53.
[50] Despite Kant's repeated insistence that feeling cannot have a cognitive role, Nancy Sherman thinks that emotions might play a cognitive role for Kant in presenting information about both the world and ourselves. See Sherman, *Making a Necessity of Virtue*, 145–46.

never aspire to a condition in which our feelings are grounded in reliably rational judgments of what is valuable to us, because on Kant's view our feelings have no cognitive capacity. However we attempt to deal with the power of our feelings, we will always relate to them at a distance, never achieving a unity of feeling and reason in a virtuous will. Our emotions will always be a counterweight to our duty (G 405).

Virtue, Kant thinks, is moral strength in obeying the moral law. This moral strength makes use of certain natural powers of mind, body, and soul that are means to all possible ends. Sherman plausibly reads Kant as saying that among these natural powers whose development will support virtue are some natural emotional powers, such as sympathy, sorrow, and joy. It by no means follows, however, that "we are to develop our talents and emotional capacities as part of virtue.[51] As we saw above in our discussion of technical reason, Kant sees all of our natural powers and skills as amoral capacities for all possible ends, good or ill. In other words, we have a duty to cultivate benevolent feelings as all-purpose powers that are good when deployed by a good will and bad when deployed by a bad will. Aristotle, by contrast, thinks that our intellectual and emotional powers are not mere capacities to be deployed for good or ill, but become stable states of virtue or vice.[52] There is no evidence that Kant thinks that emotional powers can be reliably oriented toward goodness anymore than can any other natural human power. Indeed, Kant would point out, no doubt, that even such emotional states as sympathy and affability—states we may think of as paradigmatically supportive of the good—are as valuable to the con man as they are to the saint.

We can see that Kant makes benevolent feelings mere instruments in the hands of virtue, rather than a part of virtue, by how he describes their role in moral life. Speaking of sympathetic joy and sadness, Kant says that until reason develops the strength of moral virtue, we must use these feelings "as a means to promoting active and rational benevolence" (MS 456, 457). Yet once reason acquires the strength of moral virtue, we have no need for sympathy: "it was . . . wisdom on nature's part to implant in us the predisposition to sympathy, so that it could handle the reins *provisionally*, until reason has achieved the necessary strength. . . . [Sympathy is] a temporary substitute for reason" (*Anth.* 253). As mere emotional props, Kant argues, the benevolent feelings have no intrinsic moral value apart from encouraging those good people who have not yet achieved the full rational strength of virtue to do their duty. Kant goes even further in dismissing the benevolent feelings by strongly denying that there is any value in a merely emotional response to suffering. For example, in cases where I learn of the suffering of someone whom I cannot help, I must not

[51] Ibid., 143; cf. 150, 157.
[52] Throughout her discussion of Kant, Sherman speaks of "cultivating" the emotions without ever distinguishing between the mere cultivating of a power (for whatever end) and cultivating a power into a state (either a virtue or vice).

be compassionate, for compassion is a useless multiplication of suffering and ought to be avoided (*MS* 457).

Although he thinks benevolent feelings have no intrinsic moral value, Kant says that they do have intrinsic value of an aesthetic sort. He calls benevolence a "great moral adornment" that makes the world "a beautiful moral whole in its full perfection" (*MS* 458). Since beauty is for Kant a symbol of moral goodness, perhaps the primary way in which emotions support virtue is by their attractiveness as social graces. Emotion, says Kant, is a "garment that dresses virtue to advantage" (*Anth.* 282). Kant concedes that a life of virtue "involves sacrificing many of the joys of life," which might cause us to become "gloomy and sullen." These emotions might make us resent our duty and hence fail to practice virtue. Thus, we have a duty to do our duty with a "cheerful heart," lest virtue itself become hated and drive adherents away (*MS* 485).

Why does Kant insist that acquiring the capacity to express the feelings known as the social graces is a duty of virtue? Why does Kant care about whether virtue is fashionably dressed? Recall Kant's view about the need to seduce our feelings; one way he thinks we can do this is by creating "a beautiful illusion resembling virtue" (*MS* 473). "Affability, sociability, courtesy, hospitality, and gentleness ... are, indeed, only tokens, yet they promote the feeling for virtue itself by a striving to bring this illusion as near as possible to the truth" (*MS* 473). Through these rituals of social courtesy, our passions become attracted to the symbol or illusion of virtue, thus helping to neutralize the passions as counterweights to virtue. Kant is clear, however, that the feelings associated with social grace, agreeableness, tolerance, mutual love, and respect are by no means a part of virtue, but are merely a good form of advertising: they "promote a virtuous disposition by at least making virtue fashionable" (*MS* 474).

It should be clear that Kant's account of playing at virtue in the hopes of becoming virtuous has little relation to Aristotle's.[53] Aristotle thinks that by imitating the external deeds of a virtuous person, we can come to associate those deeds with the appropriate reasons, passions, and desires; we can thereby discover what virtue feels like "on the inside." Eventually, we will make the harmony of right reason and right passion into a stable state of virtue. Kant thinks, by contrast, that by imitating the rituals of courtesy, we aim to seduce our feelings into mistaking the social graces for true virtue—true virtue being much less attractive—and thus enlist the unwitting cooperation of our feelings in pursuit of virtue. In short, for Aristotle we become virtuous only by actually doing the deeds of a virtuous person; for Kant, by contrast, we might seduce our feelings into a love of virtue by playing at the simulacra of virtue called the social graces.

[53] For Sherman to treat Kant's account of social imitation as similar to Aristotle's is misleading because she cites Kant's discussion of the need to seduce our emotions as evidence that Kant is speaking of the need to "cultivate emotions." See Sherman, *Making a Necessity of Virtue*, 170.

In short, on the Kantian view, our feelings, like our skills, are mere powers to be deployed as instruments—but always at a distance—by a good will. There is no evidence that Kant thinks that feelings can be cultivated into steady states reliably oriented toward goodness: how could they become precise or reliable modes of responding to moral circumstances when Kant tells us that they convey no knowledge of ourselves or the world?[54] Kant thinks that moral agents will always be at odds with their feelings and desires, and that the Aristotelian ideal of the integration of reason and passion neglects the rationally intractable nature of our feelings and desires. This difference between Kant and Aristotle has further implications, for as with our relation to our own talents, our relation to our feelings will deeply shape our self-conception as persons: Are we constituted in part by our feelings and desires, or are they external supports for our deeper self, like our property? Who am I, a desiderative or a rational creature—or both?

V. Self-Love

According to the *Oxford English Dictionary*, the term "egoism" was used in the eighteenth century only to refer to the metaphysical doctrine known today as "solipsism." At the very end of that century, however, this meaning quickly became supplanted by our more familiar use of egoism to refer to theories of human conduct that assign self-regarding motives paramount importance.[55] This transition from metaphysical egoism to moral egoism is evident in Kant, and I think it is illuminating. When, for example, Kant contrasts egoism with "pluralism," he says that this contrast can be made in a metaphysical as well as in an anthropological perspective (*Anth.* 130). Yet even when he restricts himself to an anthropological perspective, his notion of egoism is still quite broad. He distinguishes between logical, aesthetic, and moral egoism. In each case the egoist presumes the adequacy of his own logical, aesthetic, and moral judgments, respectively, while the "pluralist," by contrast, tests his own judgments against those of others (*Anth.* 128–29). Kant's egoism, that is, the attitude of "being occupied with oneself as the whole world," sounds like solipsism;[56] yet whether an individual is an egoist in the logical, aesthetic, or moral sense, his failure is ultimately a moral one, namely, he does not recognize himself "as a citizen of the world" (*Anth.* 130). Though

---

[54] Sherman says that Kant's view of emotions as mere "psychic sensations" is implausible and "undercuts the very roles he assigns emotions in moral practice." See ibid., 183. But for emotions to play an important supporting role in moral practice is quite consistent with Kant's claim that they lack cognitive value, so long as we do not suppose that the emotions are a *part* of virtue.

[55] *Oxford English Dictionary*, 2d ed., s.v. "egoism." According to the *OED*, Thomas Jefferson was the first to use egoism in a moral sense in English; he did so in 1795.

[56] Indeed, Kant gives *"solipsismus"* as the Latin equivalent of his "egoism" (*MS* 433).

they can reflect such a moral failure, egoism and self-love are virtually
metaphysical necessities on Kant's account, so deeply rooted are they in
human nature. Kant notes that when children first begin to speak, they
refer to themselves in the third person, but that "from the day a human
being begins to speak in terms of 'I,' [that is, about age 3] he brings forth
his beloved self wherever he can, and egoism progresses incessantly"
(*Anth.* 128).

This first-person egoism is so deep-seated and so insidious that it poses
a profound obstacle to respect for moral law. According to Kant, the love
of self is the main enemy of morality (*KpV* 26, 36); it is the source and
expression of the radical evil in human nature. The natural inclinations
are not intrinsically the enemy of moral duty; in fact, they are intrinsically
good (*Rel.* 27, 35). Evil comes from the free decision of practical reason,
under the influence of self-love, to prefer our own happiness to moral
duty—from the choice, that is, to subordinate moral duty to self-love (*Rel.*
36).[57] Bound up with our human nature, we have a brute predisposition
to pleasure as well as a suprahuman (that is, purely rational) moral predisposition to duty; our specifically human predisposition to self-love is
the source of our evil subordination of moral duty to the quest for happiness (*Rel.* 27). Since happiness is defined in terms of pleasure, and since
pleasure is truly solipsistic, Kant sees the prudential quest for happiness
as intrinsically bound up with self-love. Ultimately, the drama of free will
lies in the choice between pursuing my own private happiness out of
self-love and respecting a universally valid moral law.

Love, as Kant often says, means both "good will" (*Wohlwollen* or *be-
nevolentia*) and "delight" or "good pleasure" (*Wohlgefallen* or *complacien-
tia*) (*VE* 27:417; *Rel.* 45n). The love of good will consists in the inclination
to promote the happiness of others; the love of good pleasure consists in
the satisfaction that we derive from appreciating the perfections of others.
What is crucial here is that for Kant the love of good pleasure is the basis
of the love of good will. Only if we happen to be pleased with someone
are we inclined to promote their good. Recall that pleasure is blind and
idiosyncratic for Kant; given this, there is no predicting who will please
us, and consequently we cannot have any duty to love another person.
Our moral duty of beneficence is thus not based in love. Nevertheless,
practicing beneficence out of duty could lead one to eventually practice it
out of love.

In self-love Kant also distinguishes good will toward oneself as "self-
love" (*Eigenliebe* or *philautia*) from delight or pleasure in oneself called
"self-conceit" (*Eigendünkel* or *arrogantia*) (*KpV* 73). Both kinds of self-love,
taken together, are "selfishness" (*Selbstsucht*) or "practical solipsism."

---

[57] "Now a rational being's consciousness of the agreeableness of life uninterruptedly
accompanying his whole existence is *happiness*, and the principle of making this the supreme
determining ground of choice is the principle of self-love" (*KpV* 22).

Since self-conceit is the basis of self-love, we can see why Kant so radically denigrates self-love, seeing it, indeed, as the root of all evil. For if our good will toward ourselves, that is, our love for our well-being and happiness, rests merely upon the pleasure we happen to take in ourselves, then Kant is right that this self-love is appallingly blind and degraded. For given how blind, stupid, and invincibly ignorant our pleasures are on Kant's account, we might well take delight in our most bestial and satanic vices, meaning that what we would count as the pursuit of our own well-being and happiness would be equally immoral.

Love of what pleases us—in others or in ourselves—is the key notion here, for this love is the basis of the benevolent love of others and the pursuit of one's own happiness. If this love of what is pleasant is not demanding, has no internal standards of what ought to please us, or is indiscriminate, then Kant is right that this kind of self-love is the enemy of morality. Kant strongly contrasts this blind love with the morally discriminating attitudes of esteem (*Hochschätzung*) and respect (*Achtung*): we esteem and respect that which has intrinsic value, but we merely love that which happens to please us (*VE* 27:407). Thus, in relation to others, we can love a bad man without in the least respecting him (*VE* 27:358), just as we can be esteemed by others without being loved by them. Indeed, Kant even sees love and esteem as opposed: we are not likely to love a person whom we esteem, because such a dutiful person will not ingratiate himself to us (*VE* 27:358). Even in friendship, says Kant, it is difficult to combine love with respect, "[f]or love can be regarded as attraction and respect as repulsion, and if the principle of love bids friends to draw closer, the principle of respect requires them to stay at a proper distance from each other" (*MS* 470).

In relation to ourselves, love and respect are even more at odds since self-respect depends upon conformity to moral law, but as soon as I compare my inclinations and conduct to that moral law, my self-conceit is humiliated (*KpV* 73, 74). The humiliation of our self-conceit makes possible the elevation of respect for moral law and, thus, the development of true self-esteem. Respect is a tribute we pay, willingly or not, to virtue, but paying it gives us so little pleasure—that is, paying respect is so unlovable—that we do so only reluctantly (*KpV* 77). Here the contrast with Aristotle is obvious, for Aristotle thinks that virtuous love is internally oriented toward what is most to be respected and esteemed. On the Aristotelian view, the virtuous man loves himself for his own good character, and he loves in others what he most loves and respects in himself. Aristotle would agree with Kant that spontaneous, natural, innocent love might well be blind, but Aristotle is confident that love trained by experience and insight can discern what is worthy of its affections.

That Kant thinks love is inherently morally blind is evident from his descriptions of the attitudes and conduct that he takes to be illustrative of self-love. While the form of self-love is a rational maxim to take one's own subjective inclinations as the determining objective ground of the will, the content of self-love is merely those subrational inclinations (*KpV* 74). Self-love is directed not at the noble, but at "one's own comfort" (*Rel.* 3n; cf. *VE* 27:357). As we saw in Section III, Kant says that self-love could lead us to turn our backs on those in need, let our talents lie fallow, lie, steal money, and even commit suicide (*G* 422–23). As we shall see below, these are precisely the kinds of actions that Aristotle would associate not with self-love, but with contempt for self.

The rational structure for the pursuit of self-love or one's own happiness is prudence. Kant says that the basis of the maxims of prudence is the desire to dominate other people—we seek our own happiness mainly by manipulating other people for our own ends of honor, domination, and money (*Anth.* 271). Recall that Kant distinguishes worldly prudence (skill in manipulating others for one's own purposes) from private prudence (skill in making judgments as to one's long-term happiness). We can now see the relation between these senses of prudence, for generally we pursue our own long-term happiness most effectively when we manipulate other people for our own selfish ends. Revealingly, in discussing this, Kant adds that by pursuing our own happiness as a result of holding self-love as our supreme maxim, we are deceived by our own desires, and by manipulating others for our own selfish purposes, we miss our highest end, which is not happiness, but virtue (*Anth.* 271). So our self-love turns out to be intrinsically self-destructive, and our "prudence" seems highly imprudent.

Given Kant's view of happiness and his view of the dark abyss of self-love, it is not surprising that he should so strongly reject ethical eudaimonism. One of Kant's friends said of his conversations: "[H]ow often he lifted our minds and feelings from the fetters of selfish eudaemonism to the high consciousness of freedom, to unconditional obedience to the law of reason, to the exaltation of unselfish duty!"[58] Kant himself put the same point more bluntly, noting that "all eudaemonists are practical egoists" (*Anth.* 130). Kant is right that eudaimonism is committed to the psychological, metaphysical, and practical priority of self-love; Aristotle insists, though, that if love need not be a blind passion—if love may be trained and educated by reason to take delight in what is noble—then self-love need not be selfish.

Kant and Aristotle obviously disagree about the psychology of self-love. Kant thinks that self-love is an inescapable feature of human nature and the chief obstacle to morality (*MS* 451); Aristotle sees the cultivation of self-love as a central requirement of practical wisdom. To put it in Kantian terms, Aristotle thinks that self-love is a duty, whereas Kant believes that we cannot have a duty to what is unavoidable in human nature. The debased selfishness that Kant sees as excessive self-love is for

[58] See Kant, *Lectures on Ethics*, trans. Louis Infield (New York: Harper Torchbook, 1963), ix.

Aristotle more akin to self-hatred. Aristotle argues that the vicious person is full of psychic conflict, regret, and self-hatred because of his self-destructive vices: "Hence the base person appears not to have a friendly attitude even toward himself, because he has nothing lovable about him" (*NE* 1166b17, 1166b26). As evidence of this self-loathing, Aristotle says that base people shun their own selves and seek distraction in the company of others (*NE* 1166b13); only by developing the virtues, he argues, can we learn to love ourselves and then to love others (*NE* 1166b28). The virtues create a pleasing integrity of word, thought, and deed; make doing what is right pleasant; express love of life and of living; unify reason and passion; and safeguard us from regret. In all these ways, and more, they make us lovable to ourselves and to others (*NE* 1166a10 ff.).

Aristotle uses terms such as love and friendship (both referred to by the Greek *philia*) in both a *focal* or *central* sense and in a *derivative* or *analogous* sense. For example, when referring to friendship in the focal sense, we refer to a friendship based on virtue: this is the fullest and most complete expression of friendship. However, we can also speak of friendships that are based on pleasure or utility; these are friendships in the derivative or analogous sense. Similarly, self-love also has a focal sense, evident in the love that a virtuous person has for what is most precious in himself, and a derivative sense, observed in the love a person has for what in himself gives him pleasure. Discussing these two senses of self-love, Aristotle rejects the common view that those whom we call selfish because they hoard money, honors, and bodily pleasures (*NE* 1168b16) are the people who love themselves most. On this common view, the virtuous, because they do not hoard these things, are not called self-lovers (*NE* 1168b25). The Aristotelian account turns the common view on its head: Aristotle argues that the vicious person, in gratifying only his lower appetites — making his reason a slave to his passions — loves himself only in the lesser, derivative sense. By identifying himself only with his passions, he alienates himself from what is most truly him, his reason (*NE* 1168b34). Far from being a friend to himself, he is his own worst enemy. The virtuous person, whose choices bring reason and passion into harmony, and who thus affirms and identifies with what is both best and most pleasant in himself, turns out to be his own best friend and to love himself most of all.

VI. Temperament and Character

Aristotle says that "to become good and wise [*agathos kai spoudaios*] requires three things; these are nature, habit, and reason [*physis, ethos, logos*]" (*Pol.* 1332a38).[59] This triad forms both a temporal and a logical

---

[59] Similarly, at *NE* 1179b20: "Now some think that we are good by nature, others by habit, others by being taught [*didakê*]."

progression: we begin with our natural powers and dispositions, then we cultivate some of these natural powers and dispositions into right habits of character, and finally, we reflectively adjust our habits in light of right reason. In this model of human self-realization, our habits presuppose human nature but cannot be reduced to it, just as our reflective rationality presupposes our habits but cannot be reduced to them. Corresponding to these three dimensions of human development are three kinds of human faculties (*dynameis*): "those that are innate [*suggenês*], those that come by practice [*ethos*], and those that come from teaching [*mathêsis*]" (*Met.* 1047b31). These form a hierarchy: "The contribution of nature clearly does not depend on us but results from some divine cause in those who have it, who are the truly fortunate ones. Argument [*logos*] and teaching [*didakê*] surely do not influence everyone, but the soul of the student must have been prepared by habit [*ethos*]" (*NE* 1179b21).

On Aristotle's account, then, our ability to achieve moral or intellectual excellence is only partially within our voluntary power. Without the right natural gifts and the proper upbringing, we simply cannot become good and excellent. Aristotle seems to include in human nature much of what we would call temperamental and intellectual dispositions. He says, for example, that compared to the Europeans and the Asians, the Greeks uniquely combine both high-spiritedness (*thumos*) and intelligence (*Pol.* 1327b19 ff.). These are the natural gifts that are most easily molded by legislators into a virtuous polity. Ideally, education, both by habit and by reason, will work in harmony with our natural dispositions, but "men do many things against habit and nature, if reason persuades them that they ought" (*Pol.* 1332b8). He says that anger, wishing, and desire are present from birth, but reason and understanding are developed as one grows older, so the training of the nonrational passions must precede the development of reason (*Pol.* 1334b21).

In Aristotle's view, our voluntary control over our natural dispositions is fairly extensive, meaning that we must take responsibility for not just our habits, but also for some aspects of our nature. For example, he says that those who are incontinent by habit are more easily cured than those who are incontinent by nature, "for habit is easier to change than nature"; indeed, "habit is longtime training . . . and in the end training is nature for human beings" (*NE* 1152a25). But some natural dispositions are beyond the reach of training in virtue or vice, such as the bestial states; for example, if someone has a natural fear of everything (a kind of panphobia), then he has bestial cowardice, not vicious cowardice (*NE* 1149a1).

Aristotle frequently associates moral virtue not with the gifts of human nature, but with the acquired excellences of habituation. At *NE* 1103a16, for example, he says that virtue of character (*êthos*) comes from habit (*ethos*). Since habit can direct our natural powers either to virtue or to vice, Aristotle sometimes seems to suggest that our nature is morally neutral: "Thus the virtues arise in us neither by nature nor against nature.

Rather, we are by nature able to acquire them, and reach our complete perfection through habit" (*NE* 1103a24). In the end, however, Aristotle does not believe our nature is morally neutral. Recall that Aristotle says that at birth we possess natural virtues, which become full virtues when perfected by practical wisdom. We therefore possess our moral character, to some extent, by nature (*NE* 1144b4). Instead of sharp divisions between human nature, moral character, and reason, then, we see that on Aristotle's account our nature is potentially virtuous, just as our virtuous habits are potentially rational. Virtue is a state of excellence with natural, habituated, and rational dimensions.

Kant also has a triadic hierarchy of human nature, which both parallels and diverges from Aristotle's in profoundly revealing ways. Kant says that we can "divide what belongs to man's appetitive power (what is practical) into what is characteristic [a)] *in his nature*, his natural tendency, b) *in his temperament* or way of sensing, c) *in his character* simply, or his way of thinking [*Denkungsart*]—The first two tendencies indicate what can be made of a man; the last (moral) tendency shows what man is prepared to make of himself" (*Anth.* 285). We find roughly the same triad in Kant's discussion of the predispositions to animality, to humanity, and to personality (*Rel.* 26–28). Here, Kant says that the power of choice constituted by respect for the moral law is "character," which just is "personality" or "the idea of humanity considered wholly intellectually." The contrasts with Aristotle are clear. Whereas Aristotle sees moral virtue as the perfection of the whole person—nature, habit, and reason—Kant sees moral virtue as involving only reason. Whereas Aristotle thinks we have the voluntary power to shape aspects of our nature, our habits, and our reason, Kant says that we can only change our rational character (*Anth.* 292).

Aristotle says that we might have a virtuous or a vicious character, depending upon how we are brought up and educated. Kant says, by contrast, that to have a rational character at all is to have a good one, for character means "the property of will by which [a person] binds himself to definite practical principles that he has prescribed to himself irrevocably by his own reason" (*Anth.* 292). A vicious person, Kant says, has no character (*VP* p. 99), because there is no evil from principle—evil comes only from abandoning principles (*Anth.* 293–94). In short, character means virtue. Virtue is strength of the rational will, and in no way involves feeling. Kindliness that has its source in temperament is not a trait of character (*Anth.* 293); sympathy, as a matter of temperament (*VP* p. 97), is also not a character trait.[60] Aristotle would say that natural and habituated sympathy ought to be perfected by practical wisdom. According to

---

[60] "Virtue is needed, in fact, precisely to the extent that good conduct is hard for us, since it consists in the strength we need to perform a difficult task. A person whose temperament is happily constituted so that virtue is less often necessary, may still be virtuous, but virtue is a quality of *character*, not of temperament." Wood, *Kant's Ethical Thought*, 331.

Kant, moral character or virtue cannot educate our emotional temperament; rather, it must deploy, suppress, and dupe various aspects of that
temperament: "by character we can get the better of our ill-natured temperamental disposition" (*Anth.* 293).

Aristotle's triad is a developmental view of education: early childhood
training develops our natural powers into stable habits while, later, rational instruction imbues our habits with the reflective rationality necessary
for true virtue. Children might well act in conformity with reason, but only
adults can act from reason. Similarly, Kant's triad is at work in his quite
different view of education: "man is in succession infant (requiring nurs-
ing), child (requiring discipline), and scholar (requiring teaching)" (*VP* p. 1).
Since Kant identifies character with reason, the only positive part of education, on his account, is instruction; the disciplining of the temperament, he says, is purely negative (*VP* p. 3). In other words, according to
Kant the discipline of the desires can only remove obstacles to rational morality, whereas for Aristotle the discipline of the desires is an essential part
of moral education. Where Aristotle says that moral education begins with
the training of the desires by habit, and that the soul of a student is not
receptive to rational argument until it acquires the right habits, Kant says
that moral education begins with rational maxims (*VP* p. 84; *Rel.* 48).

We cannot begin to grasp Kant's doctrine of virtue except against his
distinction between character and temperament.[61] As noted above, Kant
says that nature and temperament show what can be made of a person,
while character shows what a person is prepared to make of himself
(*Anth.* 285) If temperament shows "what can be made of us," then might
it be the result of social custom as well as nature? Perhaps, though Kant
goes on to say that "[w]hat nature makes of [a person] belongs to temperament (where the subject is for the most part passive); only by what
man makes of himself can we recognize that he has character" (*Anth.*
292). Kant is clearly not very interested in sorting out what belongs to
innate nature and what belongs to nurture. His focus, rather, is on individual passivity or agency: character involves what an individual, in and
of himself, chooses to do; temperament, in contrast, is largely a "gift of
nature." What this means is that temperament and character are divided
by the gulf that divides our empirical nature from our moral nature, our
feeling from our reason, our passivity from our activity, our being causally determined from our being morally free—and even our prudence
from our morality.[62]

---

[61] Allen Wood strongly emphasizes the connection of Kant's doctrine of virtue to his
understanding of character and temperament; it is surprising that in *Making a Necessity of
Virtue*, Nancy Sherman entirely neglects this connection, since she wrote a book about virtue
and character in Aristotle. See her *The Fabric of Character: Aristotle's Theory of Virtue* (New
York: Oxford University Press, 1989).

[62] "*Klugheit* [prudence] is a matter of temperament. Morality is a matter of character" (*VP*
p. 96).

PRACTICAL REASON AND MORAL PSYCHOLOGY

Kant distinguishes physiological temperament, including physical constitution and physical complexion, from psychological temperament, which is constituted by the emotional and appetitive capacities; Kant thinks the psychological temperament is rooted in the physiological (*Anth.* 286). If "character" refers to the rational capacity for adopting moral principles, then why does Kant speak of the "character" of faces, sexes, and nations? This is simply because he distinguishes two senses of "character": one is physical character, which includes differences in nature and temperament, and the other is moral character, which does not vary and is the structure of the rational will (*Anth.* 285).[63]

Among the "gifts of nature," Kant lists "talents of mind," such as understanding, wit, and judgment, as well as "qualities of temperament," including courage, resolution, and perseverance (*G* 393). Aristotle, of course, denies that any of these are gifts of nature; he calls understanding and courage, for example, intellectual and moral virtues, meaning that they involve nature, habit, and reason. On Kant's account, however, we might be praised for our good temperament—just as we might be praised for our other gifts of nature—but we are esteemed only for our good character. Conversely, we cannot justly be blamed for an unattractive temperament any more than we can justly be blamed for being ugly or stupid: since one's temperament is mainly a gift of nature, one is not responsible for it.

Kant says that the qualities of temperament, like the other gifts of nature, can be harmful if not deployed by a good will or character. Furthermore, not only is acting from a benevolent will or character different from acting in ways encouraged by a sympathetic temperament, he argues, but a good character is especially manifest when it must overcome a cold and indifferent temperament (*G* 398). In this vein, Kant says that we might not be so judgmental of others if we were to consider the obstacles their temperaments pose for their moral virtue: we might think that were we given others' temperaments, we might do the same things they do (*VE* 27:418). Kant's views, of course, depend on his claim that we are not morally responsible for our temperaments.

We can now see why Kant's notion of virtue differs so profoundly from Aristotle's. Where Aristotle sees virtue as the harmony of desire and reason, or what Kant calls the temperament and character, Kant sees virtue as the strength we acquire from the battle between our character and our temperament—the strength of character we acquire by constantly resisting our temperament (*VE* 27:571). Aristotelian virtue (*aretê*) means

---

[63] Allen Wood curiously neglects Kant's distinction in senses of character and simply says that Kant "regards gender, national, and racial differences as matters of *character*—that is, as the results of free agency." See Wood, *Kant's Ethical Thought*, 205–6. But Kant clearly distinguishes the study of physical (including psychological) character (i.e., physical characteristics) from that of man's (moral) character. Indeed, these two senses of "character" derive from the two Greek words for "character": *charaktêr* and *êthos*.

not strength,[64] but excellence, which is proper, harmonious, and complete functioning (*Met.* 1021b15). Kant's notion of virtue as strength of self-mastery thus seems to resemble not what Aristotle means by virtue, but rather what Aristotle calls strength of self-control (*enkrateia*). Kant says that at first, virtue is very difficult, but as we gain in strength, virtue becomes easier and even pleasurable (*VE* 27:655–56). However, this greater ease does not necessarily mean that character is in greater harmony with temperament—it just means that it is easier for the individual to lift the counterweight to duty that the temperament poses. For Kant, virtue is always in progress: if we are not gaining in strength, we are getting weaker, because the struggle between our character and our temperament cannot ever end in peace—virtue can never become the stable state of Aristotle's *hexis* (*MS* 409). Indeed, harmony between character and temperament would not be virtue at all, but suprahuman holiness. Kant says that in the war between a man's moral character and "the monsters he has to fight," the greatest and only true honor he can win is moral courage (*MS* 405).

It is tempting to interpret Kant as saying that while perfect harmony between character and temperament is not possible for human beings, self-perfection in virtue is a gradual development from mere self-control to the cultivation of the temperament toward greater and greater harmony with the demands of character.[65] This reading, I think, ignores Kant's strong distinction between temperament and character, which is at the center of his account of virtue. For example, Kant carefully distinguishes between physical courage and moral courage: physical or temperamental courage refers to a resolve to withstand a strong but unjust external opponent, whereas moral courage, or virtue, is what one uses to withstand internal opponents of character (*MS* 380). In his lectures on the *Metaphysics of Morals*, he explains why moral courage is not temperamental courage. Recall that Kant lists this temperamental courage as one of the gifts of nature, which have value only when deployed by a good will (*G* 393). Temperamental courage, then, is a given fact about our physical nature, and belongs to what nature has made of us. As a result, we cannot cultivate temperamental courage—we can only train our habits to compensate for our temperamental timidity. "[Temperamental courage] is

---

[64] Kant says that the word "virtue" designates "courage and valor (in Greek as well as in Latin) and hence presupposes the presence of an enemy" (*Rel.* 57). While this is true of the Latin *virtus*, it is not true of the Greek *aretê*, except in its Homeric usage.

[65] As Sherman argues of Kant: "To take the perfection of oneself as an end is to cultivate one's agency *and* the supportive structure of one's agency in one's nature." Sherman, *Making a Necessity of Virtue*, 346. Sherman simply neglects Kant's fundamental distinction between our active relation to our character and our essentially passive relation to our nature and temperaments. As Robert Louden observes, "Still, the strong dichotomy between natural temperament and moral character that Kant often defends in the *Anthropology* lectures is hard to swallow. Among other things, it would seem to follow from this position that agents are not ultimately responsible for many of their most basic moods and emotions." Louden, *Kant's Impure Ethics*, 81.

physically inbuilt, and belongs, like all talents, to a man's natural endowments. A naturally diffident man will never acquire courage, though by exerting his powers of resistance he may habituate himself to overcoming dangers" (*VE* 27:653–54). In contrast, moral courage, or virtue alone, is something we *can* make of ourselves—it is a facet of our character.

The temperament/character distinction plays an important part in Kant's strong distinction between the worth of one's condition and the worth of one's person (*KpV* 60). The worth of one's condition depends on all the gifts of nature or *merita fortunae* (rewards of fortune), including congenial temperament, wealth, health, and happiness (*G* 393, 398; *Anth.* 285), while the worth of one's person depends on one's character, what we make of ourselves (*G* 392; *MS* 223; *Anth.* 291–92). Kant argues that "[v]irtue has to do solely with the worth of our person, and not with our condition" (*VE* 29:623). Our condition matters to our person inasmuch as our condition might pose temptations to violate duty. Thus Kant says that "adversity, pain, and want are great temptations to violate one's duty" (*MS* 388). He might well have added to this list "a cold-blooded temperament," which could tempt us to violate duties of beneficence. Kant says that if these conditions are temptations to vice, then perhaps we have a duty to promote our own "prosperity, strength, health, and well-being in general" (*MS* 388). Again, he might have added a duty to develop a congenial temperament. Kant also says, though, that since these external gifts of nature are only a means for removing temptations to moral goodness, our real end is the worth of our person. Thus, to seek prosperity might be, at best, indirectly a duty, insofar as poverty is a great temptation to vice (*MS* 388). Similarly, we might have an indirect duty to strengthen our capacity to sympathize actively for the fate of others (*MS* 457), if a cold-blooded temperament tempts us to violate our duty.

Kant's comments from the *Metaphysics of Morals* are one-sided, and can easily mislead us into thinking that Kant asserts a strong relation between one's condition and one's worth, or between one's temperament and one's character. The suggestion that we have indirect moral duties to promote various aspects of our temperament or condition seems to be the most obvious sign of this relation. Yet we know from the opening of the *Groundwork* that Kant believes that even the good gifts of nature can be temptations to vice: power, riches, honor, health, and happiness, he says, "produce boldness and thereby often arrogance." Does this imply that we have an indirect duty to seek impotence, poverty, dishonor, illness, and misery in order to avoid the temptation to arrogance? Furthermore, Kant notes that good qualities of temperament, such as courage, resolution, and perseverance, will make a bad man even worse. Given these factors, Kant thinks, it is clear that the relation of my condition to my person, or of my temperament to my character, is so contingent and idiosyncratic that there can be no general moral duties to cultivate any particular temperamental quality. Thus Kant says that a cold-blooded temperament, though it makes a bad man worse, makes a good man better than does a congenial temperament, because cold-bloodedness is more constant (*VE* 27:420).

Kant distinguishes between sympathy and compassion in a manner analogous to his distinction between moral courage and temperamental courage: sympathy is a reflective, active moral response to others' plight, whereas compassion is merely a passive emotional response to others' suffering. Kant says that we have a direct duty only to sympathy (*MS* 456–57), but that we also have an indirect duty to cultivate the strength of our temperamental compassion as a support to our moral sympathy (*MS* 457). However, even this sort of indirect duty would seem to be contingent on the distinctive qualities of our own given temperament, for if our temperament were already strongly disposed toward compassion, then developing further temperamental compassion would be an obstacle to duty rather than a support. This is because compassion in itself, when not guided by active principles of beneficence—that is, when one merely passively shares the suffering of others whom one cannot help—is a vice. Thus, even this indirect duty to cultivate temperamental compassion is really no more than a counsel of prudence that is contingent on individual circumstances; Kant's other mentions of "indirect duties" to develop aspects of our temperaments or increase our material comforts are best seen in the same way. In short, for Kant there is no such thing as a virtuous temperament, or even a temperament reliably supportive of virtue; any temperamental quality has the potential to be either a support or an obstacle to moral duty, depending on the circumstances.

Kant's understanding of temperament can be illuminated by contemporary discussions of personality traits. Some psychologists and philosophers distinguish personality traits, such as being introverted or extroverted, from character traits, such as being honest or dishonest; one way of putting the distinction is to say that people are responsible for their character traits in a way in which they are not responsible for their personality traits. Many personality traits emerge in infancy, whereas character traits are acquired later. A two-year old, for example, may well have a very strong personality but cannot have an acquired character; he might clearly be extroverted, but could hardly be described as honest. Philosopher Bernard Gert says that personality traits are dispositions to certain feelings rather than dispositions to certain actions. He says that shyness, for example, is a disposition to feel anxiety when meeting new people, not the disposition to avoid them; irascibility is the disposition to feel angry whenever one's plans are disrupted.[66] In considering the personality/character trait distinction, it seems that cer-

---

[66] Bernard Gert, *Morality* (New York: Oxford University Press, 1988), 181–83. Gert sounds very Aristotelian in his confidence that even personality traits can be shaped by education: he advocates that "children be raised so as to develop a personality such that they come to enjoy acting morally." Ibid., 183.

tain personality traits might pose obstacles to the acquisition of certain character traits. If I were extremely introverted, I might find it hard to respond to the needs of others with spontaneous compassion. In such a case, I would not attempt to cultivate my personality (which I am stuck with), but instead try to compensate for my personality by learning how to be attentive to others and how to express compassion appropriately. An introverted person will never really enjoy meeting new people, but he may learn how not to avoid meeting new people and even how to reduce his anxiety in such encounters. The distinction between personality and character traits is, of course, reminiscent of Kant's distinction between temperament and character.

Kant evidently thought that a great deal of our emotional and desiderative lives was essentially fixed in our inherited personality or temperament. He was also quite aware of the importance of this temperament to the acquisition of virtue. However, he decisively rejected the Aristotelian confidence that habit could become our second nature, that our moral character could become our temperament.[67] Kant discusses temperaments of feeling and temperaments of activity in terms of the four humors (*Anth.* 287–92). Following the ancients, Kant classifies temperaments into the sanguine temperament of the volatile man, the melancholy temperament of the grave man, the choleric temperament of the hot-blooded man, and the phlegmatic temperament of the cold-blooded man. These four humors much more closely resemble what we would call personality traits than they resemble character traits: they are brute givens in our innate constitution, and the affective expressions of essentially physiological forces.

As we saw above, Kant thinks that our faculty of feeling has no cognitive power; on his account, our affects and desires are largely brute facts that are rationally intractable. Indeed, if we thought that most of our affects and desires were linked to personality traits—for example, being introverted or extroverted—we would agree with Kant. For example, the anxiety experienced by an introverted person when encountering strangers is a brute fact that does not seem to be grounded on any (cognitively accessible) belief; rather, this anxiety is more like an automatic, rationally intractable reaction to certain triggering cues. We might well be able to argue an introverted person out of many of his other fears and anxieties by challenging the beliefs that they embody, but we are not likely to be able to argue him out of his anxiety as an introvert. Instead of these direct Aristotelian or cognitive strategies, it seems the introvert has to resort to oblique Kantian attempts to cope with, overcome, compensate for, avoid, or dupe his anxiety. Thus, the extent to which we think that our passions

---

[67] True, Kant does say that a virtuous person will act from duty with a "cheerfulness of mind" (*VE* 27:656) which he calls the "*aesthetic* constitution, the *temperament* so to speak, of virtue" (*Rel.* 24). But Kant speaks here only of one aspect of temperament, and he appeals to temperament by analogy.

are grounded on fixed personality traits—as opposed to corrigible habits
of thought—goes a long way toward determining whether we consider
Kant's views on moral education more reasonable than those of Aristotle.

VII. Conclusion: Character as Integrity and Destiny

It has long been observed that Aristotle's virtuous person is a model of
integrity in which reason and desire, deliberation and habit, mind and
heart, and body and soul are all internally oriented toward moral and
intellectual excellence. Kant's virtuous person, by contrast, never achieves
this kind of integrity; instead, his spontaneous—and even his trained—
affects and desires must always be filtered and scrutinized in light of the
moral law. Aristotle's virtuous person thus sees himself very differently
from how Kant's virtuous person sees himself. In this conclusion, I want
to explore briefly how Kant's and Aristotle's contrasting understandings
of the psychology of moral character affect their perspectives on the
integrity and freedom of moral agents.

According to Aristotle, practical wisdom includes and perfects instrumental shrewdness, meaning that my self-conception as a virtuous person combines my good motivation and my intellectual and moral skills.
Aristotelian virtues are "success" terms: they combine a good will with
the effective skills for reliably attaining the relevant good. The Kantian
good will or virtue does not include any skills, and reliable success neither adds nor detracts from the worth of a good will (G 394). Of course,
a virtuous Kantian will acquire whatever skills he thinks will be helpful
in pursuing moral ends, but those skills are not a part of his virtue; Kant
says that whereas prudence requires good technical skills, morality requires only good will (VE 27:259). Thus, the Aristotelian values himself as
much for his intellectual and moral skills as for his good will, and as
much for his reliable success as for his good intentions. The Kantian, in
contrast, values himself (in the sense of "finds himself worthy") strictly
for the goodness of his will, whatever bad may result from it.

What this means is that the Kantian is to some extent alienated from his
own intelligence and skills; he sees them as quite distinct from his deepest
self, moral character, or good will. Kant says that we have a duty to
acquire skills and knowledge just as we have a duty to acquire strength,
health, and money—namely, as necessary means to any possible end.
Because the Aristotelian identifies himself largely with the unity of good
skill and good will, he thinks that we would not acquire a skill except
insofar as it is conducive, not to any possible future end, but to a good
end that is in view. The Aristotelian would sharply distinguish his skills
from his money, since his skills are incorporated into his self-identity as
a virtuous man, while his money really is external to him. Kant, by
contrast, goes so far as to say that our intellectual skills and talents are no
more valuable to us than money, for they are all merely means to an end

(*VE* 27:665). The Kantian thus relates to his own intellectual and moral skills at a distance, as instruments that are quite distinct from his own worthiness.

By integrating moral character so closely with our natural powers and our acquired habits, the moral goodness of Aristotle's virtuous man is, to a considerable degree, held hostage to the accidents of birth, upbringing, and education. In fact, Aristotle says that one cannot have a rational commitment to virtue unless the proper natural gifts and childhood habits are already successfully in place.[68] Aristotle argues that the necessary harmony of nature, habit, and reason is possible only for the fortunate few (*NE* 1180a4). By the very nature of the deep integrity of both a vicious and a virtuous character, our character, on Aristotle's account, is virtually our destiny. True, in one place he does say that although nature, habit, and reason ought to be consonant, men can act by reason contrary to their nature and their habits (*Pol.* 1332b5–7). Despite this opening to moral freedom, however, Aristotle never discusses the possibility that someone vicious from childhood could transcend his bad character and resolve to become virtuous. Yet we all know that, by some inexplicable miracle, a few people manage to at least partially extricate themselves from their own vicious and even addictive habits—I say partially, because "reformed" addicts usually remain temperamentally disposed to addiction.

Curiously, character is a kind of destiny for Kant as well, but by identifying character purely with the strength of one's commitment to rational principles, Kant largely liberates moral character from the accidents of natural dispositions and acquired habits. Because we are, on the Kantian account, largely alienated from our own inherited gifts, powers, acquired skills, passions, desires, and temperaments, we are also thereby liberated from them to act from rational principle alone. Kant's ethics is a profound reflection upon the deeply mysterious capacity of some mature adults to deliberately set aside their bad Aristotelian character and take on a good Kantian character. Thus, whereas a reformed alcoholic is virtually inconceivable on Aristotle's moral psychology, he is central to Kant's. At the same time, as a "reformed" alcoholic is first to admit, rational transcendence of our nature and temperament is always only partial: we never wholly escape our character.

Government, Dartmouth College

---

[68] "It is not unimportant, then, to acquire one sort of habit or another, right from our youth; rather, it is very important, indeed, all-important" (*NE* 1103b23; cf. *NE* 1104b12, 1105a1, 1180a15).

HYPOTHETICAL CONSENT IN KANTIAN CONSTRUCTIVISM*

By Thomas E. Hill, Jr.

I. Prologue: Kantian Constructivism and Moral Epistemology

Epistemology, as I understand it, is a branch of philosophy especially concerned with general questions about how we can know various things or at least justify our beliefs about them. It questions what counts as evidence and what are reasonable sources of doubt. Traditionally, epistemology focuses on pervasive and apparently basic assumptions covering a wide range of claims to knowledge or justified belief rather than very specific, practical puzzles. For example, traditional epistemologists ask "How do we know there are material objects?" and not "How do you know which are the female beetles?" Similarly, *moral* epistemology, as I understand it, is concerned with general questions about how we can know or justify our beliefs about moral matters. Its focus, again, is on quite general, pervasive, and apparently basic assumptions about what counts as evidence, what are reasonable sources of doubt, and what are the appropriate procedures for justifying particular moral claims.

If we were to assume that moral beliefs are substantially like beliefs about the empirical features of the world, then moral epistemology would face the task of explaining the apparent disanalogies between the procedures of giving evidence for empirical propositions and providing reasons for moral claims. If, instead, we supposed that fundamental moral propositions are about nonempirical objects in the same way that fundamental propositions of mathematics are (on some interpretations), then moral epistemology would face a different set of problems. The special problems raised by moral *realism* of both kinds, and by skeptical doubts about the underlying assumptions of each kind, are so frequently discussed that they may seem to exhaust the field of moral epistemology. However, there are other questions about justification that should count as belonging to moral epistemology. For example, although Kantian constructivists typically try to avoid realist/antirealist epistemological disputes, they still need to face general questions regarding moral knowledge or justified belief as understood in their constructivist theories. What do they count, most generally, as grounds for substantive moral claims? If

* I am grateful to Andrews Reath, Shelly Kagan, Philip Pettit, Thomas Pogge, David Copp, Geoffrey Sayre-McCord, and David Brink for helpful comments on earlier drafts of this essay.

moral principles are "constructed," what are the building materials and what is the procedure of construction?

"Kantian constructivism," unfortunately, is a broad label that has been used to characterize significantly different views.[1] A common theme in these views is that moral principles are to be seen as the outcome ("constructions") of certain procedures of thought (or will) rather than as facts about the world (empirical or nonempirical). Ideas about what these procedures are vary, but Kantian varieties of constructivism require us to consider what universal principles all persons "could" or "would" endorse if they were thinking rationally and in a position specified as appropriate.[2] Some Kantian constructivists hold that the moral truth or justification of substantive moral claims *consists* in their being the product of the appropriate procedure of construction; others affirm only that the procedure and outcomes are valid or useful for "practical" or "political" purposes. Some take an agnostic position on the metaphysical and epistemological issues in debates about moral realism, while others take a negative (antirealist) stance; generally, however, constructivists have been disinclined to engage in these debates. One theme that is quite common among these diverse Kantian constructivist positions is that moral philosophy is itself "practical," a claim usually understood as implying that moral philosophy's results are not derived from (or refutable by) science and metaphysics.

To simplify, I will restrict my discussion, for the most part, to one version of Kantian constructivism: namely, Kant's moral theory as I interpret and partially reconstruct it.[3] Kant holds that knowledge and jus-

---

[1] Ideas of Kantian constructivism can be found in the work of Immanuel Kant (on some interpretations), John Rawls, Onora O'Neill, and others who comment on their work. See, for example, Immanuel Kant, *Groundwork of the Metaphysics of Morals*, ed. and trans. Mary Gregor (Cambridge: Cambridge University Press, 1998); John Rawls, "Kantian Constructivism in Moral Theory," *Journal of Philosophy* 77, no. 9 (1980): 515-72; John Rawls, *A Theory of Justice* (Cambridge, MA: Harvard University Press, 1971); John Rawls, *Political Liberalism* (New York: Columbia University Press, 1993); Onora O'Neill, *Constructions of Reason* (Cambridge: Cambridge University Press, 1989), esp. chap. 11; Onora O'Neill, *Towards Justice and Virtue: A Constructive Account of Practical Reasoning* (New York: Cambridge University Press, 1996); Brian Barry, *Theories of Justice* (Berkeley: University of California Press, 1989), vol. 1 of *A Treatise on Social Justice*; David O. Brink, *Moral Realism and the Foundations of Ethics* (Cambridge: Cambridge University Press, 1989); Thomas E. Hill, Jr., *Dignity and Practical Reason in Kant's Moral Theory* (Ithaca, NY: Cornell University Press, 1992), chap. 11; and Thomas E. Hill, Jr., *Respect, Pluralism, and Justice: Kantian Perspectives* (Oxford: Oxford University Press, 2000), chaps. 2, 4, 8.

[2] Onora O'Neill's views might seem to be an exception here because she criticizes Rawls for arguing from a hypothetical idealized choice situation (see O'Neill, *Constructions of Reason*, 207-13; and O'Neill, *Towards Justice and Virtue*, 44-48), but her arguments from the thought that everyone "cannot share" certain principles presuppose at least some modest rationality conditions (as well as other background conditions) in her procedure of construction. Thus, my broad characterization of Kantian constructivism includes O'Neill's position, but nothing substantive in my discussion depends on fine points about how we use this broad term of classification.

[3] In this essay, I will only describe aspects of Kant's moral theory when they are immediately relevant to my questions about the justificatory roles of actual, possible, and hypothetical consent. Fuller discussions of Kant's moral theory are contained in Hill, *Dignity and*

THOMAS E. HILL, JR.

tified belief about moral matters are based not on theoretical (or "speculative") reason but on practical reason. Both are forms of rational reflection, but theoretical reason is concerned with what exists whereas practical reason is concerned with what ought to exist. The distinction, as Kant interprets it, is important, for it is incompatible with the realist idea that moral values and imperatives are objects in the world to be discovered empirically, by intuition, or through speculative metaphysical thinking. For Kant, morality is, in a sense, the *product* of practical reason, not merely some independent thing that reason discovers.

This controversial feature of Kantian constructivism, however, is not essential to my main concerns in this essay. The important feature for present purposes is that Kant offers, in several forms, practical constructivist procedures for determining what moral principles to accept. That is, he proposes, at least as workable heuristic devices, several kinds of reflection that draw conclusions about what we ought to do from premises about what rational, free, and appropriately situated persons could or would willingly accept. In this way, like John Rawls's theory of justice, Kant's moral theory is constructivist even if certain ultimate premises (about rationality and the appropriate deliberative perspective) are not themselves "constructed." The Kantian procedures, in contrast to Rawls's, are to be found in the various formulas of the Categorical Imperative (Kant's supreme moral principle) and in Kant's idea of an original contract.

My main question, then, is this: *within Kantian constructivist procedures,* what are the roles of actual consent, possible consent, and hypothetical consent in guiding and justifying particular moral beliefs? This is one question of moral epistemology about the commitments of Kantian constructivism. There are other such questions, of course, that moral epistemologists may want to raise. For example, they may reasonably question whether Kantian constructivists are warranted in the stance they take on the moral realism debates. If the constructivists' position (like Kant's, in my view) is not realist, what justifies this? If their position (like Rawls's) is agnostic, what justifies its claim to be independent of the realist/antirealist issues? Another legitimate epistemological question would be to ask how the basic procedures of construction endorsed by Kantian constructivism can themselves be justified. These further questions, however, will not be my concern here.

II. Outline and Preview of Conclusions

In everyday life we often argue that acts or practices are wrong because appropriately placed persons *do* not, *could* not, or *would* not consent to having them take place. Moral philosophers commonly use all of these

---

Practical Reason in Kant's Moral Theory, esp. chap. 11, and Hill, *Respect, Pluralism, and Justice,* esp. chaps. 1, 2, 4, 8.

forms of argument, but they often privilege one or another form as basic, treating the others as derivative and constrained. Kant and contemporary Kantians are no exceptions. Any moral theory that is Kantian in spirit will specify ways that we must not treat others without their actual consent, but regarding basic principles Kantians generally acknowledge that the crucial question is either "Is the principle *possible* for all to accept and follow?" or "What principles *would be* agreed on by ideally free and rational agents?" The first question is primary for Onora O'Neill, for example, while the second is primary for Rawls. It is a matter of controversy which question *should* be primary in our efforts to interpret and extend Kant's ethics.

Within Kantian theory, then, how are we to understand attempts to justify moral claims by appeals to actual consent, possible consent, or agreement under hypothetical conditions?[4] What are the relations among these types of claims? Are the differences between them fundamentally important? Are familiar objections decisive against the idea that whether moral and political principles are justified is determined by what ideal rational agents would agree to in specified hypothetical conditions?

I begin with some remarks about the role of different forms of consent and agreement in the *Groundwork of the Metaphysics of Morals* (hereinafter *Groundwork*), and then I turn to Kant's political philosophy, especially his use of the idea of an original contract.[5] In both contexts, what Kant treats as fundamental is not what people *actually* consent to, but what is *possible* for them to will. Though important, appeals to actual consent presuppose a background of practices and principles that must be justified by asking what (rational) agents could or would agree to as standards for everyone. In the *Groundwork*, which I focus on in Section III, Kant's basic standard usually refers to possible willing rather than hypothetical agreement. For example, Kant's *universal law formula* of the Categorical Imperative says: Act only on maxims that you *can will* as universal law.[6] What it is possible to will, in the relevant sense, is that which can be willed in a presupposed context of choice without contravening certain presupposed standards of rationality. These standards can be interpreted as minimum standards

---

[4] Although for some purposes it might be important to distinguish "consent," "agreement," and "will," I use them more or less interchangeably here. It may be more natural to speak of the "consent" of actual persons to particular proposals and the "agreement" of ideal rational agents on general principles, but using the terms more flexibly helps to highlight the comparisons I want to make.

[5] For Kant's references to an original contract, see Hans Reiss, ed., *Kant: Political Writings*, 2d ed. (Cambridge: Cambridge University Press, 1991), 77, 79, 80–83, 85, 91 (from Immanuel Kant, "On the Common Saying: 'This May Be True in Theory, but It Does Not Apply in Practice'" [hereinafter "Theory and Practice"]), 94, 99–100 (from Immanuel Kant, "Perpetual Peace"), 140, 158, 162–64 (from Immanuel Kant, *The Metaphysics of Morals*).

[6] The universal law formula is one of several ways that Kant expresses the Categorical Imperative. Kant, *Groundwork*, 15 [4:402], 31 [4:421]. Numbers in brackets refer to volume and page numbers in the standard Prussian Academy edition of Kant's works. A fuller discussion of the universal law formula follows in Section III.

(e.g., logical consistency) or as more robust standards (e.g., treating humanity as an end in itself). In the *kingdom of ends formula* of the Categorical Imperative, the formula on which my essays often rely, Kant suggests that the basic moral test is to ask what rational agents *would* agree to, rather than what they *could* agree to. I suggest, however, that this formal difference is not in itself deeply significant.[7] The rational standards on which the "could will" test relies can (though they need not) be expressed in terms of what rational agents necessarily "would will if rational." Moreover, under the kingdom of ends formula, the prohibitions that hypothetical rational agents would will are just those that are rationally necessary for them to will, given their situation.[8] Both formulas, then, presuppose as background some general standards of rational willing. Furthermore, whatever substantive permissions and prohibitions, if any, would be legislated for our condition by perfectly rational legislators must constrain what we can (rationally) will as universal law. Thus, what we *could* will under Kant's universal law formula may depend on what we *would* will under his kingdom of ends formula. Treating Kant's ethics as primarily concerned with *possible* willing, then, is not in itself a way of avoiding the apparent problems in reconstructions that express his basic ethical test in terms of what it is to which rational agents *would* agree.[9] The merits of either approach for further developments of Kantian ethics depend, in the end, on the details of how the standards of rationality and other features of the imagined choice problem are spelled out.

Review of Kant's use of the idea of an original contract as a test for constitutions seems to confirm these general points; I will engage in such a review in Section IV. The basic standard of assessment is not whether all or most citizens actually consent to the constitution, or did so in a historical contract. The test is whether it is logically possible for citizens to have a united will on a proposed constitution if they are rational and in an appropriate position to choose. Again, the relevant standards of rationality may be interpreted thinly or thickly, and the merits of the test for different purposes will vary accordingly. Whether the test is expressed in terms of hypothetical agreement or possible agreement does not seem deeply significant.

In Section V, I conclude the essay by suggesting that several common objections to arguments that appeal to hypothetical agreement for justi-

---

[7] Kant sets forth the kingdom of ends formula at Kant, *Groundwork*, 41–44 [4:433–37]. A fuller discussion of this formula follows in Section III.

[8] The kingdom of ends formula invites us to ask what laws rational agents would will. As I reconstruct the idea, it is assumed that the hypothetical agents are fully rational, and the question is what they would necessarily will *qua rational* (and properly informed) agents regarding all the possible general permissions and prohibitions that we might want to assess. Thus, they would (necessarily) will a prohibitive law if and only if it is rationally necessary for them to will it in the context in question. See Hill, *Dignity and Practical Reason*, chaps. 3, 11.

[9] For an example of this sort of reconstruction, see O'Neill, *Constructions of Reason*, 206–18.

ficatory purposes do not undermine the force of such arguments, at least as used in Kant's ethics as I reconstruct it. For example, hypothetical consent is not merely a weak practical substitute for actual consent in particular cases where actual consent should be the standard. Also, Kantian theory does not attempt to reduce values to empirical facts about what everyone with certain descriptive characteristics would agree to. The theory makes explicit use of idealizations, but I argue that these idealizations are not of a kind that should alienate us from conclusions drawn from the theory. Next, I respond to an apparent dilemma that confronts any theory that purports to draw moral principles from the thought that everyone would agree to those principles under certain (ideal) conditions. The objection is that either the theory presupposes independent standards of rationality or it does not; in the first case, reference to hypothetical agreement may be unnecessary, and in the second case, hypothetical agreement would be arbitrary and so its results would have no moral force. The best Kantian response, I suggest, is to embrace the first horn of the dilemma, admitting that Kantian hypothetical agreement presupposes independent rational standards, but argue that this does not necessarily undermine the value of using the Kantian constructivist model. Finally, I note that, although Kantian hypothetical-agreement arguments will not necessarily convince extreme rational egoists, they were not designed for that purpose.

III. Actual Consent, Possible Willing, and Hypothetical Rational Agreement in the *Groundwork*

A. Possible consent, not actual consent, is basic under Kant's formulas

In various ways the *Groundwork* affirms the importance of obtaining the actual consent of those affected by our actions; this is a moral consideration prominent in appeals to "autonomy" in contemporary applied ethics. We expect Kantian ethics, more perhaps than any other, to place severe limits on what we can do to others without their consent. Yet although actual consent is important, Kant's fundamental ethical principle is not a requirement to respect the actual consent of those affected by our actions. The sphere of actions that are "up to the individual," such that others may not interfere with them without the individual's consent, is determined by principles and practices that lie in the background of our everyday encounters. Normally we take for granted that we may not use others' property or touch them intimately without explicit or implicit consent. Usually we do not stop to think deeply about general principles regarding property and bodily integrity, but when questions arise about what requires consent and why, we need to address the more general issues.

Consider an example of Kant's in which disregard of the right of another to consent or dissent seems especially prominent. In taking money from another through a false promise to repay the loan, a person tries to escape difficulties in a way that leaves his victim no choice of whether or not to consent to giving up his property with no prospect of repayment.[10] Moral assessment of this case does not start from the absurdly impractical assumption that we may do something that affects another person if and only if the other person actually consents. Kant condemns the lying promisor's disregard for another's consent in the context of a particular set of practices—namely, promises and property. These practices include shared understandings relevant to the case. For example, it is part of the practice of promising that saying "I promise to do X" alleges an intention to do X. One should not say "I promise to do X" if one lacks the intention, although for good reasons, saying this in the appropriate context creates a binding promise even when (secretly) one has no intention to do what one says. Practices governing property authorize the man who needs money to take funds if they are given or loaned, but not if the gift or loan is obtained on false pretenses, especially deception regarding the parties' understanding of the nature of the transaction. Under these practices, consent has justificatory force only under certain complex conditions. For example, the mere fact that the deceived party *accepted* the promise as genuine and *consented* to the loan does not justify by itself the lying promisor's taking money from him.

Kant's arguments against the lying promisor, if sound, would show that given our practices, what he does is wrong.[11] Thus, the arguments presuppose practices that define when actual consent is necessary, but they are not arguments that appeal to actual consent. Kant condemns the lying promisor on the grounds that (a) the agent's maxim of profiting from lying promises *cannot* be willed as universal law, and (b) the victim *cannot* share the agent's end.[12] The first argument, if sound, would show that the lying promisor in Kant's example is wrong because one cannot rationally will as a universal law maxims that reflect disregard for certain requirements inherent in our practices of promising and property— namely, the requirement not to say "I promise" with apparent sincerity unless one has the requisite intention, and the requirement not to seek a

[10] Kant, *Groundwork*, 32 [4:423].

[11] My remarks here are not meant as a literal interpretation of Kant's arguments. To provide such an interpretation, much more preparatory work would be needed, including identifying the relevant maxim. (A maxim is a subjective principle, or personal policy statement, that summarizes, in a way relevant for moral assessment, one's understanding of what one intends to do, one's purpose, and one's underlying reasons.) My suggestion is that, Kant aside, practices of various kinds typically determine when consent is (and is not) needed, and so justifications of the form "He consented and so it is permissible" require moral evaluation of the practice to which one is implicitly appealing. When the issue is what practices are justifiable in the way they demand consent (or not), Kant's formulas of the Categorical Imperative move us to another level. The universal law formula, for example, asks whether we can will our maxim as universal law, but "the maxim" needs to be described in a way that appropriately reflects our practice-laden understandings.

[12] Kant, *Groundwork*, 32 [4:422], 38 [4:429-30].

loan under false pretenses. Respect for the (appropriately informed) lender's consent is required by these practices. These practices themselves, however, may ultimately need to be tested by asking whether the agent who uses them *could (rationally) consent* to a maxim to support and conform to them as universal practices. How, more specifically, the test posed by the universal law formula should be interpreted and whether it is ultimately tenable are, of course, disputed questions that I set aside for present purposes.

Kant's second argument, which derives from his *humanity formula* of the Categorical Imperative, focuses not on whether the lender actually consented to the loan but on whether he *could* agree with the borrower's end in making the false promise.[13] It is assumed that the lender consented to make the loan but did not consent to lending money that the recipient had no intent to repay. The problem, Kant implies, is that the lying promisor took what the lender had an antecedent right to (as a result of the background practices), and did so for ends that the lender "could not share." The point, surely, is not that it would be *impossible* for the lender to want the borrower to use the money for the borrower's own purposes, for the lender might be so generous that he would have given the borrower the money had he asked. The problem, it seems, stems from the fact that the borrower had an aim that is crucially relevant, under our practices, to the transfer of property—namely, the aim to bring about a transfer of the lender's property to the borrower without the borrower giving anything (now or later) in return. This is an end that the deceived lender cannot share *when he makes the loan* because, necessarily, lending is transferring one's property to another with the understanding that the other party means to return it or repay the lender.[14] Under the practice of loaning, it is logically impossible for both parties to share the crucial

---

[13] Kant expresses the humanity formula of the Categorical Imperative at ibid., 38 [4:429]: *"So act that you use humanity, whether in your own person or in the person of any other, always at the same time as an end [in itself], never merely as a means."* He then, almost immediately, applies this principle to the example of someone who tries to borrow money without intending to repay. Arguably there is more to the argument from the humanity formula, at least implicitly, than is captured in the idea that we must treat persons as those who can share (or "contain in themselves") the end of the action, but the further ideas are not important for present purposes.

[14] A complication I ignore here: Suppose the would-be borrower pretends that he intends to repay and the would-be lender does not believe him but pretends that he does. Has a loan been made? I suppose so, for the lender could complain afterward when the borrower does not repay, and the borrower could not defend his not paying, when he learns that the lender did not believe him, by saying, "I do not owe you anything because you never believed that I would give the money back." Therefore, the "understanding" the lender needs, perhaps, for a loan to exist is not strictly that the borrower intends to return the money, but just that the borrower intends (in borrowing) to cause the lender to believe that he intends to return the money. The lender in Kant's example, we may suppose, has this understanding. In fact, it is natural to suppose that the lender will transfer the funds only because he thinks that the borrower intends to give them back, and with this understanding the lender, in making what he understands is a *loan*, cannot share the borrower's end, that is, that the borrower get money cost-free (i.e., without repaying it).

intention of the borrower while engaging in the mutual act that constitutes the making (and receiving) of a loan. Whether or not we think that
this argument is morally decisive, its implication, as before, is that one's
treatment of another is justified only if the other party *could* consent in
appropriate conditions (e.g., if not deceived about the first party's intention). The treatment does not become legitimate just because the person
actually consents to the act as he or she (mistakenly) understands it.[15]

B. Appeals to possible consent presuppose further normative standards

Though I have only presented one so far, Kant actually develops two
universal law formulas of the Categorical Imperative; each of these invokes a standard that refers to what an agent *can* will. As noted above,
Kant's universal law formula says that we must act only on "that maxim"
which we can "at the same time" will as a universal law; that this formula
involves possible willing is relatively straightforward. The *universal law of
nature formula*, which Kant puts forth soon after he states the universal
law formula, says that we must act as if our maxims were to become,
through our will, universal laws of nature.[16] Examples Kant provides
make clear that this test is really about whether we can, or could if we had
the power, will our maxim as such. Hence, this formula seems to involve
possible willing, not ideal willing in hypothetical conditions.

Both textual considerations and charity, however, give us reasons to
understand that the tests proposed under the universal law formulas ask
whether an agent can *reasonably* will her maxim as universal law (i.e.,
reasonably will her maxim and at the same time will that all may, or do,
adopt and follow it). Kant's concern is with what we can will *as rational
beings*, even if the full idea of pure practical reason has not yet been
invoked.[17] What someone who is crazy, inconsistent, or even very stupid
can will is not what matters. Likewise, one's inability to will that everyone adopt a particular maxim is not morally relevant if the reason one
cannot will this is that one suffers from some psychological quirk (e.g., "I
could not will for anyone to eat *that*") or some rationally indefensible

[15] There are other ways to interpret Kant's humanity formula, but under any plausible
interpretation, it places limits on what actual consent can justify and helps to explain why
actual consent, though important, is not always decisive.
[16] The universal law of nature formula is expressed at Kant, *Groundwork*, 31 [4:421].
Scholars differ on whether the difference between the universal law formula and the universal law of nature formula is significant, but for my present purposes it is not. Because of
their structural similarity, the two formulas are often referred to collectively as "the universal law formulas."
[17] That is, the universal law formulas do not themselves specify the underlying standards
that determine what we can will reasonably and what we cannot. There are many different
ideas about what these specific standards count as irrational willing: for example, willing
what proves to be logically impossible, having an incoherent set of intentions, willing that
everyone adopt one's maxim even though this would defeat one's initial purpose in adopting it, willing contrary to the rationally necessary value of humanity in a person, and so on.

individual bias (e.g., "I would be revolted if those people were allowed to eat with us"). Furthermore, maxims that one cannot will for everyone to act on merely because contingent circumstances make it in fact impossible for everyone to act on them are surely not to be condemned just for that reason.[18] Each of these points underscores that for Kant, the test of one's being able to "possibly consent" to maxims becoming universal law is really a matter of the *absence of any relevant rational bar to consent*. This raises a question: what are the further relevant standards of rational willing beyond what has already been formally given (namely, that rational wills act only on maxims that they can, as rational, will as universal laws)?

Defenders of Kant's universal law formulas suggest different answers to this question, and none, I suspect, are entirely satisfactory. A few points seem clear. For example, when we try to decide what we can will as universal law, we can assume that the set of principles that we will must meet rational standards of logical consistency and coherence. No doubt we would also take for granted what I call *the Hypothetical Imperative*, a general principle stating that we must take the necessary means to our ends or else revise or abandon those ends. We might assume that other formal principles of rational choice are applicable as well.[19] Since the other forms of the Categorical Imperative (i.e., the kingdom of ends formula and the humanity formula) are supposed to involve tests of rational necessity, they should impose some constraints on what we can rationally will as universal law.[20] For example, the humanity formula suggests that

[18] Consider a policy under which individuals drink a certain kind of wine on their birthdays. One can imagine a case in which, because of scarcity, it would be impossible for everyone to follow this policy. If in fact only a few people want to act on the policy, however, the scarcity of the wine should not be taken as any reason to condemn the policy for those few who want to adopt and act on it. The general point here has been noted often. For example, Kurt Baier presents a "universalizability" requirement analogous to Kant's (though different), and he qualifies his principle "doing X should be forbidden by the morality of the group if it would be harmful for everyone to do X" by adding, along with other stipulations, "provided doing X is an indulgence and not a sacrifice." Kurt Baier, *The Moral Point of View* (Ithaca, NY: Cornell University Press, 1958), 211. If we interpret the universal law to say that maxims are wrong to act on unless we can will them as *permissible* for everyone to act on, then, in cases where only a few want to act on a maxim, the maxim could turn out to meet the formula's test even though it is not possible in fact for everyone on Earth to act on it. See Thomas Pogge, "The Categorical Imperative," in Paul Guyer, ed., *Kant's "Groundwork of the Metaphysics of Morals": Critical Essays* (Lanham, MD: Rowman and Littlefield, 1998), 189–213. Whether or not maxims can be as specific as the policy in my example above remains a controversy.

[19] For more on the Hypothetical Imperative, see Hill, *Dignity and Practical Reason*, chaps. 1, 7. Other principles of rational choice that might well be taken for granted are, for example, those that Rawls calls "counting principles"; see Rawls, *A Theory of Justice*, 411–16.

[20] Some may argue that these later formulas cannot add significantly to the universal law formulas on the ground that the later formulas are derivative, but this is debatable. In any case, a reconstructed Kantian moral perspective can make use of ideas of autonomy and humanity as an end in itself in attempts to apply the universal law formulas. Doing so may help to deflect some familiar arguments against the universal law formulas, though problems with those formulas will remain.

we cannot rationally will any maxim as universal law if it treats humanity in any person as a mere means and not at the same time as an end in itself. However, to introduce further substantive moral principles as intuitive rational standards for what can be willed as universal law seems at odds with Kant's aims in presenting and illustrating the universal law formulas, even if introducing such principles would provide some practical advantages.[21] For example, we may think that it is intuitively irrational to prefer superficial popularity to deep personal relationships, but Kant apparently aims to provide a rational test for moral decisions that does not rely on particular intuitive beliefs of this sort.

If we accept that general standards of rational willing are presupposed in assessing what we can and cannot will as universal law, then asking what we *could* rationally will no longer appears to be deeply different from asking what we *would* rationally will. Of course, "could" and "would" are not identical in meaning, but the relevant Kantian tests, it seems, are inseparable. We could will a maxim (rationally) as a universal law if doing so is consistent with all principles that we would necessarily will *qua* rational. Furthermore, as rational legislators in a kingdom of ends, we would necessarily will prohibitions of acts the maxims of which could not be (rationally) willed as universal law.[22] Rational standards do not have to be expressed by reference to what rational agents would necessarily will; one can use the apparently simpler form, "It is rationally necessary to X." Yet expressing the standards by reference to what rational agents would necessarily will may make us less tempted to picture the standards as self-standing objects of intuition rather than as procedures inherent in practical reasoning.[23]

---

[21] If, as it seems, in using Kant's decision-guiding procedures we are supposed not to rely on further, substantial intuitive assumptions about what we have "reasons" to do and prefer, then this is a way in which Kant's procedures for justifying our decisions to others differs significantly from the procedures proposed by T. M. Scanlon in his recent book, *What We Owe to Each Other* (Cambridge, MA: Harvard University Press, 1998).

[22] In general, it does not follow from "We could not rationally will X" that "We would rationally will not-X," for in some contexts it is possible that we neither rationally will X nor rationally will not-X. My point, however, does not depend on this false inference. Kant's universal law formula and kingdom of ends formula provide the context here. The kingdom of ends is a highly idealized model. We assume that its legislators are perfectly rational, appropriately informed, and have a will in favor of or against all the possible permissions and prohibitions that we might put to them. The analogy with a divine will is obvious. In calling the formula of universal law a Categorical Imperative, Kant claims that fully rational persons, as such, will that they not act according to a maxim if it is impossible to will that maxim as a universal law. Therefore, if acting as described in a given maxim cannot be (rationally) willed as universal law, then rational legislators in the kingdom of ends must will that they, and anyone relevantly like them, not act in that way. This is just what "legislating" in this context amounts to, for the ideal kingdom of ends is not a legal system in which public offenses are defined and sanctions are imposed. Without any sanctions, necessary rational willing of the Kantian "legislators" against an act is supposed to make not acting that way imperative for us as imperfectly rational beings.

[23] Such "objects of intuition" would be, for example, nonnatural intrinsic values as conceived of by G. E. Moore, or Platonic Forms as they are often interpreted. See G. E. Moore,

C. The role of actual, possible, and hypothetical rational agreement under the kingdom of ends formula

Kant's idea of a kingdom of ends has been a source of inspiration to many, but its interpretation remains controversial. Here I can only comment on a few points. The first few remarks are needed, for the sake of historical accuracy, to supplement my previous discussions of the kingdom of ends. Those earlier discussions deliberately emphasized certain features of Kant's idea of a kingdom of ends in order to highlight its similarities to Rawls's constructivism and its differences from Kant's universal law formulas. In the process, however, I may have suggested a somewhat exaggerated picture of the centrality of the idea of a kingdom of ends in Kant's ethics, its similarities with Rawls's idea of hypothetical agreement, its advantages over the universal law formulas, and the closeness of the analogy between the kingdom of ends and political communities. So I begin with some brief cautions on these points.

In the past I have proposed possible reconstructions of the kingdom of ends formula that make it look like a moral analogue to Rawls's appeal to an original position (with important differences).[24] As I have noted, there are problems with trying to square this kind of reconstruction with all that Kant actually says, and with trying to make the kingdom of ends formula the centerpiece of Kantian ethics.[25] For example, Kant himself does not think of the formula as a better practical guide to moral decisions than are the universal law formulas. In the *Groundwork* he says that the universal law formula is a better practical guide, and in *The Metaphysics of Morals* he writes as if the humanity formula is also more useful for practical purposes.[26] In discussing the kingdom of ends, Kant seems less concerned to offer yet another guide to practical decision-making than to highlight his ideal of moral motivation independent of contingent interests.

In an earlier paper I suggested that the kingdom of ends formula avoids the problem of maxim description that plagues the universal law formulas.[27] The problem of maxim description is this: there is no definitive way to decide what the relevant maxim of our proposed act is, and yet whether or not we can will our "maxim" as universal, and hence whether or not the act is right or wrong, depends on how the maxim is described. The

Principia Ethica (Cambridge: Cambridge University Press, 1903), chap. 1. Julia Annas's paper in this volume criticizes the common view that Platonic Forms are intuited independent objects or properties like Moore's intrinsic values.

[24] Hill, *Dignity and Practical Reason*, 58–66, 243–50; Hill, *Respect, Pluralism, and Justice*, 33–56, 220–30.

[25] Hill, *Dignity and Practical Reason*, 65–66; Hill, *Respect, Pluralism, and Justice*, 36, 51–55.

[26] Kant, *Groundwork*, 44 [4:437]. It is the humanity formula that Kant appeals to most frequently in later moral arguments, especially in the second part of *The Metaphysics of Morals*. See Immanuel Kant, *The Metaphysics of Morals*, trans. Mary Gregor (Cambridge: Cambridge University Press, 1996), 173–218 [6:418–74].

[27] Thomas E. Hill, Jr., "The Kingdom of Ends," in Hill, *Dignity and Practical Reason*, 58–66.

kingdom of ends formula avoids this problem, I suggested, because un-like the universal law formulas, it does not make essential use of the idea of a maxim. This suggestion, however, goes beyond, and probably against, Kant's own view because (a) he did not seem to acknowledge the prob-lems regarding maxim descriptions, and (b) there is some evidence that he thought that the way we "legislate" in the kingdom of ends is by acting only on maxims that we can will as universal laws.

Although Kant describes the kingdom of ends in political metaphors that suggest an ideal community in which members jointly make the laws of the community (as authors) and obey them (as subjects), he also ex-plicitly draws an analogy between the kingdom of ends and a harmoni-ous order or realm of nature.[28] The "laws" that we conceive of agents giving to themselves in the kingdom of ends differ from the laws of states (even a possible world state) because they are moral requirements that, as such, do not impose coercive external sanctions (e.g., legal punishment) and are not limited to our "external acts."[29] Kant alludes to the "sover-eign" of the kingdom of ends, but this is just a "holy will" that wills essentially the same as all the members do.[30] The only difference between the sovereign and the kingdom's members is that, because it lacks a liability to temptation, the sovereign is not properly said to be "subject" to the laws, which are willed by everyone in the kingdom. This picture is very different from that of a secular head of state, whose authority de-pends on his power and who can make and enforce corrupt laws.

These cautions are important for purposes of historical accuracy, but they are compatible with the basic point that the kingdom of ends for-mula puts before us an ideal that treats moral requirements as the nor-mative "laws" that agents, as lawgivers, *would* give themselves (as subjects) if they were rational and autonomous. The kingdom of ends is not actual, but possible and ideal; it is conceived abstractly as how things would be if everyone did his or her duty and if God were cooperative in making nature allow the ends of the virtuous to be satisfied. We are supposed to act by the laws of a possible kingdom of ends even if others do not.[31] The members are not merely abstractly conceived, but idealized, for they make laws rationally in a way that makes possible a harmonious system of ends and their law-giving is not improperly influenced by particular interests. The political metaphors of "law-giving," being "subject" to laws, a "sovereign," "the union of different rational beings under common

[28] Kant, *Groundwork*, 44 [4:436], 45–46 [4:438–39].
[29] See Kant, *The Metaphysics of Morals*, 20–22 [4:218–21].
[30] Kant refers to a possible "sovereign" of a kingdom of ends that is also head of the realm of nature, implying a power to harmonize the two, presumably in a way that allows the natural end (happiness) of the virtuous to be realized. Kant, *Groundwork*, 41 [4:433], 46 [4:439]. This power, so used, would give us additional motive to follow the laws of the kingdom, but is not necessary for its authority (or even for adequate motivation).
[31] Ibid., 45 [4:438].

laws," "validity" of laws, and the like invoke the model of (idealized) secular legislation.

Some passages in Kant's work, however, suggest that we give ourselves laws in the kingdom of ends by following the principle "never to perform an action except on a maxim such as can also be a universal law."[32] The idea suggested here is that we must find the normative rules of the kingdom by generalizing from our reflections on whether various particular maxims can be willed as universal laws. This would mean that the universal law formula is the primary working decision-making guide (as Kant suggests after his review of the formulas).[33] Kant's texts, I think, are ambiguous about this. Nevertheless, the suggestion here is about just *how* the members of the kingdom legislate. It does not deny that, with the kingdom of ends formula, Kant endorses a model of morality in which justified moral principles are those principles to which idealized agents would rationally agree. What remains to be seen, however, is whether or not the suggestion that members of the kingdom legislate by using the universal law formula is useful for extensions of Kantian moral theory. This depends on whether the universal law formula's possible-will standard can fulfill the hopes that Kant, and some contemporary Kantians, have for it without falling back on implicit appeals to things that would or would not be agreed to by idealized rational agents. I doubt that the standard can do this, but I will not pursue the issue here.

Although there are different views about the interpretation and importance of the kingdom of ends formula, the views seem compatible with the following main points that I have wanted to emphasize. Under this formula, the fundamental Kantian standard judges principles and practices by considering what, as rational, persons necessarily would agree to from a certain perspective; this process, however, is inseparable from the consideration of what we could and could not rationally will. When and why actual consent is required must be judged by considering what we could and would will if we were rational in a presupposed sense.

IV. Kant's Idea of an Original Contract: Conditions, Purpose, Content

Kant uses arguments that call for thought experiments about what agents could or would consent to (or rationally agree upon) in many places besides the *Groundwork*. In the political works, Kant sometimes refers to a possible "general will" behind laws or policies. For example, the test that the supreme authority should use to determine the rightness or justice of legislation, he says, is to ask whether the laws *could* have been

---

[32] Ibid., 42 [4:434], 45 [4:434].
[33] Ibid., 43–44 [4:436].

produced by the united will of the people.[34] Now, however, let us focus not on this test for particular legislation but on the idea of an original contract that lies behind the authority of a legislator to make laws. Kant mentions the idea, but all too briefly, in many works, primarily "On the Common Saying: 'This May Be True in Theory, but It Does Not Apply in Practice'" (hereinafter "Theory and Practice"), "Perpetual Peace," and *The Metaphysics of Morals*.[35]

Kant uses the idea of an original contract for purposes quite different from those of other philosophers who invoke the idea. In contrast to Locke, Kant does not use the idea of an original contract to argue that we ought to obey just governments because we, or our ancestors, actually promised or contracted to obey. Nor is his purpose to argue, with Hobbes, that obedience is rational because submission to a particular kind of constitution would be the only possible point of agreement among rational self-interested persons in a very dangerous state of nature.[36] Kant's idea of an original contract is incompatible with some putative constitutions, but does not yield a particular one as the only rational alternative to a state of nature. Kant argues that only a republican form of government captures fully the spirit of an original contract, but he allows that, given limited options, rational persons in a state of nature could endorse a less-than-ideal constitution. Finally, Kant does not use the idea of an original contract, as Rousseau initially did, to argue that existing governments have no moral claim on our obedience because their supposed authority rests on a grossly unfair, and hence void, social contract.[37]

Instead, Kant invokes the idea of an original contract to test whether constitutions are compatible with the idea of right (*Recht*) and whether they conform fully to the requirements of practical reason.[38] Any provi-

---

[34] See Reiss, ed., *Kant: Political Writings*, 79 (from Kant, "Theory and Practice").

[35] See, for example, ibid., 77, 79, 80, 83, 91 (from Kant, "Theory and Practice"), 99, 100 (from Kant, "Perpetual Peace"), 143, 158, 162, 163, 164 (from Kant, *The Metaphysics of Morals*).

[36] A Hobbesian state would not have separation of powers of the sort that Kant's ideal constitution would have, and there would be no grounds of justice on which enlightened critics could criticize the legislation of the sovereign. States that meet Hobbes's stipulations could differ in various other ways (e.g., they need not be a hereditary monarchy), and so my reference to "a particular kind of constitution" is relative.

[37] See Jean-Jacques Rousseau, *Discourse on the Origin of Inequality*, in Rousseau, *The First and Second Discourses together with the Replies to Critics*, ed. and trans. Victor Gourevitch (New York: Harper and Row, 1986).

[38] Note that I include here two aims that I distinguish later. I leave aside whether there are other uses, though it seems that there are. In particular, Kant seems to appeal to the idea of an original contract, along with argument that it would be a duty in a state of nature to enter a civil order, to support a claim that we are *morally*, as well as legally, bound to obey the ruler of our state. What I have in mind here is the claim that under any legal constitution, no matter how badly designed and executed, we must see the ruler as the representative of the united will of the people, for the alternatives are a state of nature or a lack of final legal authority. The language of "united will" in both Rousseau and Kant strongly suggests an attempt at moral justification. This raises many problems, and so for present purposes I am limiting my discussion to the use of the idea of a possible original contract for arguments that purport to say what cannot (for conceptual or moral reasons) be in a constitution.

sion in a constitution, real or imagined, is supposed to be rationally indefensible if that provision could not be endorsed in an original contract expressing the united will of the people. Unfortunately, Kant suggests narrower and broader ways of understanding the necessary conditions for an original contract.[39] On the narrower understanding, all that is required for the possibility of an original contract on a constitution is that the constitution must outline a genuine system of law. In asking whether there could be an original contract on a constitution of some kind, then, we are checking whether the constitution provides for what is essential to a *juridical condition*. To determine this, we would not need to rely on special Kantian moral assumptions, but only on the idea of rule of law. For example, in Kant's view, some alleged constitutional systems (e.g., those with gaps in sovereignty) are objectionable because they fail to meet fully the logically necessary conditions for a legal order. These flawed constitutions, in effect, do not completely remove us from a state of nature.

On a broader understanding, Kant aims to determine higher standards for constitutions, namely, standards for judging whether they are fully compatible with what is right and just. The question to ask now is not "What is necessary and sufficient for a system of enforced rules to constitute a civil order with a *legal* right to my obedience?"[40] Rather, it is "What is *morally* defensible, given some basic *moral* assumptions, as the sort of constitution that we should hope and work for through whatever means are appropriate to our station?"[41] The latter question places the emphasis not so much on what is essential to law, but on what is essential to

[39] The evidence for this is complex and ambiguous, involving a significant controversy about the interpretation of the *Rechtslehre* that Thomas Pogge describes in his paper, "Is Kant's *Rechtslehre* Comprehensive?" *Southern Journal of Philosophy* 36, supplement (1997): 161–87. Here I will only attempt to characterize some possible alternative readings in a general way, to show their relevance to the discussion of types of consent, without undertaking the detailed review of passages needed for a definitive account. Among the problems here is that Kant uses the idea of an original contract in several different works, and it is doubtful that we should assume that remarks in one context automatically carry over to the other contexts.

[40] Note that even though this is not a moral question, it has a proper (though limited) place in Kant's overall project to lay out the basic moral limits and requirements on political and legal institutions and conduct. This is so at least insofar as Kant has moral arguments that legal systems ought to be maintained and respected. Thus, even if, as some suggest, the doctrine of law in *The Metaphysics of Morals* is a module setting out the necessary conditions of a juridical condition independent of the moral principles in Kant's moral theory, it still has an appropriate place in *The Metaphysics of Morals* when this is viewed as a work the primary purpose of which is to lay out moral conditions on law, political institutions, and personal choices.

[41] The qualification regarding appropriate means is needed because Kant believes that the means by which different people may work for constitutional reform are strictly limited. Philosophers can use public reason to criticize a constitution, but active resistance and revolution are forbidden. (We employ "public reason" when, as citizens, we participate in reasonable critical assessment of governmental laws and policies through newspapers, books, public speeches, etc., as opposed to what we may say privately or as representatives of special nonpublic institutions, such as a church or a club.) Rulers under nonrepublican constitutions may (and should) gradually work for reform, but even they are restricted in what they may do. The reason for the reference to "hoping" is that Kant's ideal constitution

legal orders that meet certain basic moral principles applicable to coercive systems that satisfy those conditions established by the first question. Kant apparently aims to answer each of these questions. Sometimes the narrower understanding makes the most sense of his arguments, but at other times the broader reading is needed. I shall return to this distinction shortly.

Kant uses the idea of an original contract in arguments for a variety of conclusions. These include the following:

(1) There can be no original contract endorsing a constitution that allows the state to be bought, inherited, or given away (as, it seems, some monarchs in eighteenth-century Europe wanted to allow).[42]

(2) There cannot be united will on a constitution that incorporates a right of revolution[43] or a right of the people to abrogate the original constitution.[44]

(3) There can be no united will on a constitution that allows permanent hereditary political privilege.[45]

(4) There can be no united will on a religious constitution that permanently prohibits questioning the officially sanctioned religious beliefs.[46]

(5) Any original contract, whatever the "letter" of its provisions regarding the mode of government, must be presumed to be made in the "spirit" that nonrepublican forms of government should gradually and continually be reformed, in legal ways, until they in effect conform to the ideal of a republic.[47]

(6) An original contract must be presupposed to account for the authority needed to make definite and secure property rights, which would be only "provisional" in a state of nature.[48]

(7) Generally, the idea of an original contract obliges the head of state to avoid acts of tyranny, to make only laws that could come from the united will of the people, and to respect the people's innate rights to equal freedom of external action under universal laws.[49]

serves not only as a practical action guide, but also as a point of reference when we look hopefully (as we should) for progress in history.
[42] Reiss, ed., Kant: Political Writings, 94 (from Kant, "Perpetual Peace").
[43] See ibid., 80–83 (from Kant, "Theory and Practice"), 127 (from Kant, "Perpetual Peace"), 162 (from Kant, The Metaphysics of Morals).
[44] Ibid., 83 (from Kant, "Theory and Practice").
[45] Ibid., 79 (from Kant, "Theory and Practice"), 99 (from Kant, "Perpetual Peace"), 153 (from Kant, The Metaphysics of Morals).
[46] Ibid., 58 (from Immanuel Kant, "An Answer to the Question: 'What is Enlightenment?'").
[47] Ibid., 163 (from Kant, The Metaphysics of Morals).
[48] Kant, The Metaphysics of Morals, 53.
[49] Reiss, ed., Kant: Political Writings, 73, 79–81 (from Kant, "Theory and Practice"), 99 (from Kant, "Perpetual Peace").

Kant also argues, contrary to Cesare Beccaria, that an original contract does *not* rule out capital punishment, for the parties to the contract, as such, have a will only regarding what is permissible in general, as opposed to a will regarding particular outcomes for their individual situations.[50] At another point, echoing Rousseau's language, Kant says that an original contract involves giving up natural (lawless) freedom for civil liberty backed by one's own law-giving.[51] An original contract is not a historical event, but an *a priori* standard. It is the foundation of all actual public contracts, and in fact all public rights.[52] It cannot do anyone an injustice, presumably because it is supposed to represent each person's will.[53]

Who are the supposed parties to the original contract? Kant's implicit answer is that these are all the people, across time, who are in a state under common laws.[54] However, since the arguments from the idea of an original contract are not supposed to rely on variable contingent circumstances, the differences among individuals and even cultures should not affect whether a united will on a certain constitution is possible in the relevant sense. If we like, we can think of the parties as a mix of malicious and kindhearted folk, the naturally greedy and the naturally generous, but the acceptability of constitutional provisions should not turn on the parties' individual temperaments and preferences.[55]

This brings us to a crucial question: what sorts of factors does Kant envision as rendering an original contract impossible? It seems clear that Kant is not thinking of contingent obstacles. The empirical fact that some people, for subjective psychological reasons, would refuse to consent to a given contract does not mean that such a contract is "impossible" in the relevant sense. For example, an original contract on a republican form of

---

[50] Kant, *The Metaphysics of Morals*, 108 [4:335]. Kant refers to Beccaria's influential work, Cesare Bonesana, Marchese di Beccaria, *On Crimes and Punishments* (New York: Bobbs-Merrill, 1963).

[51] Kant, *The Metaphysics of Morals*, 92–93.

[52] Reiss, ed., *Kant: Political Writings*, 164 (from Kant, *The Metaphysics of Morals*); see also ibid., 79 (from Kant, "Theory and Practice").

[53] Ibid., 79 (from Kant, "Theory and Practice").

[54] It can be questioned whether Kant means to include women in this category, because he assumes women are merely "passive citizens" without sufficient independence to be allowed the vote. If, as it should be, women were meant to be included as parties to the hypothetical original contract, then women could be treated as "passive citizens" only if enlightened women and men alike would accept a constitution with this provision when they take up an appropriate genderless point of view. Assigning women second-class citizenship would surely fail this test, despite what Kant himself apparently thinks.

[55] Presumably, at least for some uses of the idea of an original contract, this does not mean that tests of the acceptability of provisions completely abstract from empirical facts about human nature and the human condition in general; rather, it suggests that such tests only abstract from the specific preferences and temperaments that vary from person to person, culture to culture. Some more strictly *a priori* arguments about the acceptability of provisions may proceed just through analysis of the idea of law, but there is no way that Kant could reasonably suppose that he could spin out all the conclusions listed above—that is, (1)–(7)—without presupposing general facts about human nature.

government does not count as impossible, for Kant's theoretical purposes, just because some individuals' superstitions, pathological distrust
of authority, or ideological dogmas would block any effort actually to
achieve unanimous agreement on it. What is relevant, Kant implies, is
logical impossibility (assuming, no doubt, certain general background
conditions). The idea of an original contract, Kant says, provides an "in-
fallible *a priori* standard." [56] To apply the standard to proposed laws,
checking whether they are compatible with the idea of an original contract, we are supposed to ask whether or not it is "self-contradictory" to
suppose that the people unanimously agree. "For so long as it is not
self-contradictory to say that an entire people could agree to such a law,
however painful it might seem, then the law is in harmony with right." [57]
Presumably, Kant has at least two reasons for discounting disagreements
based on various subjective psychological factors. On the one hand, if a
constitution were rendered objectionable just because these factors would
prevent unanimous agreement on it, then probably no constitution would
be justified. On the other hand, even if there were a de facto agreement on
a constitution despite these obstacles, this by itself would not, in Kant's
view, justify the constitution. What matters is whether the agreement or
disagreement is appropriately grounded in rational considerations. Regarding law and politics, as with morality in general, actual consent
cannot justify basic principles but, to have force, must presuppose them.
    The factors anticipated as the sort that might render an original contract
on a proposed constitution impossible, I suggest, depend on whether in
the context Kant's aim is narrower or broader in the ways previously
mentioned. Suppose first that the aim is simply to determine *a priori* the
essential conditions for establishing a legal system that maintains a juridical condition as opposed to a state of nature. In this case, the only
barrier to an original contract on a proposed constitution would be that it
is incompatible with the very idea of a legal order. Rational parties seeking to establish a legal order could not agree to such an arrangement
because, unlike many options, it would fail to serve their end. The minimum standards of rationality presupposed here as what all rational persons *would* agree to need be nothing more than the Hypothetical Imperative
and the ability to understand the idea of a juridical condition and its
implications. It is this standard that might show that a constitution cannot
contain a (legal) right to revolution.
    Now suppose that the aim of invoking the idea of an original contract
is to argue that certain constitutions fall short of broader standards of
justice. That is, suppose the aim in invoking the idea of an original contract is to show that only constitutions that meet certain more demanding
standards count as morally defensible and fully "just" (as we might use

---

[56] Reiss, ed., *Kant: Political Writings*, 80–81 (from Kant, "Theory and Practice").
[57] Ibid., 81 (from Kant, "Theory and Practice").

the term).[58] The aim here is not to distinguish constitutions that require loyalty from those that do not, but rather to identify the basic features constitutions must have to be (morally) worth working and hoping for. Given this aim, what would be the factors that might, in a relevant way, prevent an unqualified agreement on a constitution?[59] Any reasonable reconstruction of Kant's answer will need to bring in at least Kant's basic ideas of the innate rights to freedom and equality, which he affirms throughout his political writings. Constitutions fall short of the ideal if they could not be the result of an original contract among rational agents who affirm these fundamental rights, their own as well as those of others. Hence, the rational standards presupposed in arguments that an original contract on a given constitution is impossible are moral standards, broadly conceived. To say more exactly what Kant presupposes in his all-too-brief arguments from the original contract is difficult, but it seems clear that he does not mean to presuppose his whole moral theory, nor even all its basic principles. For example, if we were to invoke all the implications of treating humanity as an end in itself when we evaluate constitutions, we would strike out far more provisions than those that are ruled out by the seven conclusions listed above. However, to show that those provisions incompatible with the listed conclusions could not themselves be part of an unqualified contract, it seems clear that at least Kant's moral assumptions about the basic freedom and equality of persons are needed. For example, these assumptions are needed to rule out hereditary political privilege and permanent religious requirements. Similarly, without those assumptions it is hard to make sense of Kant's claim that only a republican form of government satisfies fully the spirit of the original contract. All the more, the assumptions must be at work when, in "Theory and Practice," Kant tells us that the idea of an original contract obliges every legislator to frame his laws such that they could have been produced by the united will of the whole nation.[60]

On both the narrower and broader understandings of the appeal to an original contract, the basic pattern of argument seems the same. That is,

---

[58] I add the qualification because our common practice is to use "just" as a more general term of moral assessment than Kant did. Many traditional moral philosophers did use our broader sense; Hobbes and others narrowed the term's use such that its application was limited to those realms of activity that can be enforced by secular authorities.

[59] I add "unqualified" because Kant holds that there could be, and we must assume that there is, a united will in an original contract on any constitution that establishes the existing juridical order, no matter how far from ideal that constitution might be. What the higher standards prevent is rational agreement on such a constitution as a permanent arrangement. With no other viable options in certain periods of history, we can and should endorse whatever de facto government gives us rule of law, but we can form a united will on imperfect constitutions only with the understanding that these will be gradually, continually, and legally reformed to resemble a republican constitution. This, I take it, is the spirit of the original contract. See Reiss, ed., *Kant: Political Writings*, 163 (from Kant, *The Metaphysics of Morals*).

[60] Ibid., 79 (from Kant, "Theory and Practice").

on both understandings, constitutions are condemned if it is *impossible* for those taking an appropriate perspective to have a rational agreement on them, and determination of what is impossible in the relevant sense presupposes standards on which all rational persons *would* (*qua* rational) agree.

V. SOME OBJECTIONS CONSIDERED: IS KANT'S APPEAL TO HYPOTHETICAL AGREEMENT MISGUIDED?

Many objections have been raised against philosophers' use of the idea of agreement under hypothetical conditions. Kant uses this idea, I have suggested, in several different contexts—for example, in his discussions of both the kingdom of ends formula and the idea of an original contract. Let us consider briefly some of these objections.

A. Is hypothetical agreement merely a proxy for actual agreement?

One reason for initial skepticism about arguments that turn on claims about hypothetical agreement is that they can be used to make highly dubious moral claims in particular contexts. For example, a distant cousin of a homeowner might try to justify his trespass onto the owner's property by saying "They would not mind my using their house while they are away and cannot be reached." When someone dies without a specific will, family members sometimes just help themselves to favorite items in the estate, appealing to the thought "I am sure she would want me to have this." People who, for personal reasons, refuse to consent to life-prolonging medical treatments may be forced to undergo them because, it is said, "they would consent if they were thinking rationally." In the background of these cases are practices regarding property, wills, and medicine that, for good reasons, insist on actual consent as the norm for using another's property, establishing an inheritance claim, and authorizing invasive treatment of another's body. These practices typically allow that sometimes we can appeal to evidence of what a person would have consented to as a substitute for the person's actual consent. Such appeals, however, are in a shady area relevant only when it is clear that it is impossible to get the actual informed and competent consent of the person whose presumptive rights are being set aside. Actual consent is taken to be the norm; hypothetical consent is a poor substitute, worth considering only because, unfortunately, we do not have the express and competent consent of those affected by a decision. The worry about relying on hypothetical consent in this context is that the more crucial factor in justifying our treatment of others—that is, their actual consent—will be ignored or bypassed just because someone can argue, abstractly, that the relevant parties *would* consent if properly informed. The worry about using hypothetical consent to justify moral and political principles, then, would be the suspicion that such arguments will be used illegitimately to bypass or override the actual consent of the people who must live under the principles.

How seriously must we take this worry as an objection to Kant's use of the idea of hypothetical agreement in his abstract discussions of the kingdom of ends and the original contract? Are his appeals to hypothetical agreement simply a dangerous substitute for what primarily justifies institutions, namely, actual consent? I think not. Regarding particular questions such as "When is one entitled to enter another's house?" the normal standard is "When the owner actually consents." We allow hypothetical consent to serve as the second-best alternative in special circumstances where there is no opportunity to ask for actual consent, as when a genuine friend justifies entering my house without actual consent (e.g., to police patrolling the neighborhood) by saying, "He would have consented, had he been available, for I am sure he would want me to check on the cat." The background here is an ongoing set of complex conventions regarding trespassing on personal property that, for good reasons, make actual consent the norm but allow exceptions for cases in which the purposes of the conventions are not well served by rigid insistence on actual consent. This, however, is not the context when our question concerns standards for the basic social institutions themselves. When we ask whether these conventions themselves are justified, we cannot take for granted that the norms that are familiar and intuitive for particular cases are the relevant ones. Simply to apply those familiar norms in the assessment of basic institutions would be to suppose that, except in rare cases where actual consent cannot be consulted, moral practices (such as promising) and political institutions (such as constitutions) are justified when and only when people actually consent to them. As Kant recognized, however, even universal agreement does not make something right, nor is universal agreement required. Far from being necessary and sufficient for justification, actual readiness to consent to background institutions in fact often depends on ignorance, prejudices, and uncritical acceptance of whatever norms are familiar.

Kant invokes the idea of hypothetical agreement for very general abstract purposes. The kingdom of ends formula is supposed to express a combination of the basic normative ideas present in other formulas of the Categorical Imperative, and the idea of an original contract is supposed to express basic standards of practical reason for any constitution. Given that his aim is to articulate and apply these ideas as standards for our actual moral practices and political institutions, Kant cannot presuppose the requirements for actual consent that are defined by those practices and institutions. When we are trying to determine some general features of any justifiable practice, many of the specific, historically conditioned reasons for and against consenting to actual particular practices are irrelevant. Kant's ideas of a kingdom of ends and an original contract, then,

are not merely a second-best proxy for a universal actual consent that
would better serve his purposes if only it were possible to achieve.[61]

B. Does the appeal to hypothetical rational agreement
reduce values to facts?

A second source of worry about Kant's use of the idea of hypothetical
agreement might be the suspicion that such a use commits the same sort
of error—the *naturalistic fallacy*—as do certain contemporary reductive
theories of value. These theories equate value judgments with judgments
about what we would prefer or choose in specified hypothetical situations. Such theories commit the naturalistic fallacy because they treat
normative claims as if they were empirical or metaphysical claims. An
example would be a theory stating that what is *good* for a person to choose
is what that person *would in fact choose* if fully informed, reflective, and
put through a course of "cognitive psychotherapy."[62] The arguments
against such reductive analyses are familiar, and it is not necessary to
review them here. I mention them only to note that they reflect a concern
about some hypothetical-agreement arguments that does not apply to
Kant. Kant's basic commitments are incompatible with any attempted
reduction of claims about duty and justice to empirical or even metaphysical facts. A Kantian claim that rational contractors would agree
regarding a constitution cannot be tested by rounding up and questioning
people who meet purely descriptive criteria of rationality. Moral ideals of
freedom and equality are presupposed on the broader interpretation of
the conditions necessary for an original contract, and even the narrower
interpretation of these conditions presupposes norms of coherence in
willing. It should be obvious, too, that Kant's ideal of a kingdom of ends
invokes normative ideas of rationality, autonomy, humanity as an end in
itself, and abstraction from morally irrelevant differences. We cannot determine simply by empirical investigation or metaphysical argument what
such members of the kingdom of ends would agree upon.

Even if it seems at times that Kant wants to project his normative claims
about what practical reason can and cannot will as if they can be thought

---

[61] It must be admitted that any pattern of argument used to justify political institutions,
whether it appeals to hypothetical agreement or not, can be abused; one must also concede
that the conditions stipulated as appropriate idealizations that must be realized for a hypothetical agreement to count can always be challenged. Furthermore, I am not claiming
that Kant's own use of possible and hypothetical agreement, for example, in appeals to the
idea of an original contract, are altogether satisfactory. My more modest aim is to argue that
the appeal to hypothetical agreement in itself is not to be dismissed on the several grounds
reviewed in this section. The devil, and maybe the angels, are in the details.

[62] See Richard Brandt, *A Theory of the Good and the Right* (Oxford: Clarendon Press, 1979),
113–29. Cognitive psychotherapy is a "process for confronting desires with relevant information, by repeatedly representing it, in an ideally vivid way, and at an appropriate time."
Ibid., 113.

of as metaphysical facts about a nonempirical (*noumenal*) world, this still would not be the disturbing reduction of value to fact that most philosophers have worried about. Their concern is primarily about identifying values with natural or metaphysical properties that can be specified independently of the values in question.[63] Thus, on their view, goodness cannot be reduced to promoting the survival of the species or to obeying orders of a powerful Creator because these concepts are definable without any reference to evaluative notions. When Kant tries to square his ethical thought with his earlier work in epistemology and metaphysics, he suggests that we should think of the source of moral commands, a pure rational will, as something *noumenal* or, in other words, beyond what can be located in space and time and comprehended empirically. Kant grants, however, that our moral consciousness is our only ground for supposing that we are subject to the demands of a pure rational will, and moral reflection is our only basis for saying what a pure rational will would endorse. Since everything we can say about such a will derives from ethics, not from intuition or value-neutral metaphysical theory, it is no reduction of value to fact to claim that moral principles are those that pure rational wills would agree upon. The claim asserts a connection between certain related value concepts, not a derivation of value concepts from merely descriptive ones.

C. Are the parties to hypothetical agreement so idealized that their conclusions are irrelevant to us?

A third source of problems with Kant's use of hypothetical agreement might be that hypothetical points of view could be so alien to us that we have no reason to care about principles that would be agreed upon from those perspectives. More specifically, a perspective may "idealize" the parties to a hypothetical agreement in ways that render their vastly simplified choices irrelevant to ours.[64] For example, although it may be entertaining to read utopian fantasies about altruists in a world of unlimited abundance, these provide no grounds for us to adopt the moral and legal

---

[63] G. E. Moore famously objected to identifying normative concepts with descriptive ones. Such identification is prominent among the errors he called "the naturalistic fallacy." See Moore, *Principia Ethica*, chap. 1. Moore held that "intrinsic value" is a nonnatural, nonrelational, unanalyzable property that we can know by intuition. This identifies intrinsic value as a real metaphysical property that certain states of affairs have, and so it might seem at first to reduce values to descriptive facts. However, unlike typical metaphysical accounts of goodness, Moore's theory leaves no way to discover or even make sense of the property in question except by using the terms "good," "valuable for its own sake," and so on. What he calls "intuition" is, for all practical purposes, just evaluation without appeal to argument. Hence, despite initial appearances, his seemingly "metaphysical" account of intrinsic value does not reduce it to descriptive (nonevaluative) facts. In this one respect, I suggest, Moore's view is like Kant's, though Kant and Moore differ very substantially in other ways.

[64] See, for example, O'Neill, *Towards Justice and Virtue*, 44–48.

codes that would be workable in such situations. Even Rawls's more realistic "original position" is idealized in ways that have raised doubts about whether *we* have any reason to respect the principles that *they*, the hypothetical persons in that position, would adopt. In general, even if it is established that ideal legislators would agree that everyone should act on a certain principle, it does not follow, without further argument, that we ought to follow that principle when it conflicts with actual practices. Sticking with the less optimal actual practices may be justified, all things considered, especially if the actual practices are quite good, underlie existing legitimate expectations, and would be very costly to change. Determining the ideal solution for idealized conditions may be helpful as a background for reflection on what should be done under real conditions. Theorists use idealizations in an objectionable way, however, if they draw conclusions about what should be done in imperfect conditions directly from what they judge appropriate for ideal conditions.

These are concerns that must be taken seriously, but whether they amount to a decisive objection to the use of hypothetical agreement must be assessed in the context of each particular theory. The fact that a theory uses idealizations is not in itself a problem. In science as well as in moral philosophy, when our theories assume conditions unlike (and perhaps better or neater) than the situation to which they are to be applied, we must be sensitive to the differences between the theoretical assumptions and the actual conditions at hand. The question is whether the idealizations adequately serve a good purpose. They can be helpful in different ways. Idealizing theories may simplify problems in a harmless way if the ideal conditions are a fairly close approximation of actual conditions. Another way idealizations can be helpful is that in applying a theory, we can often find satisfactory ways to adjust our judgments about actual situations by taking into account the differences between the idealized conditions and the actual conditions. Practical scientists, for example, modify the equations appropriate for objects falling in a hypothetical perfect vacuum in order to take into account the air resistance encountered by actual falling objects.

A third way that idealizations can serve a good purpose is by deliberately forcing us to consider a worthwhile perspective. Some moral theories, for example, articulate a conception of the best possible perspective to try to adopt when evaluating imperfect real-world conditions. It is appropriate, given their aim, that such theories characterize ideal moral deliberators as better in some ways than we actually are in practice. To simplify with an imaginary example, suppose moral theorists specify that ideal deliberators about the real problem of racial conflict should be intelligent, well informed about the problem, and free from racial prejudice; these theorists may then argue that from this perspective certain affirmative action programs would be adopted. Many questions and doubts could be raised about such an argument, but it would be bizarre to object that the theorists have unduly idealized the deliberative perspective.[65] This would suggest that, in thinking about the problem, it is better to be more stupid, ignorant, and prejudiced.

Whether Kantian ethics employs troublesome idealizations is a large and important issue. Kant attributes to the legislating members of a kingdom of ends autonomy, a kind of rationality, and the ability to see things in abstraction from personal differences. These idealizations, or some modified version of them, can be seen as useful and harmless extensions of widely shared ideals for deliberation about general moral principles. When seen this way—as I have argued elsewhere that they should be[66]— their use need not be alienating. However, this issue is obviously too complex and controversial to pursue here.

Instead, let us briefly consider Kant's use of the idea of an original contract. Does this employ a reasonable and helpful idealization? Whether it does depends, of course, on the purpose for which the idea is used. Kant's purpose, I take it, is to set out at least minimal conditions for the rational and moral justification for thinking that no state constitution should contain certain provisions (e.g., those establishing permanent hereditary political privileges). Recall that Kant apparently has at least two different sets of working assumptions about what is necessary for there to be a united will on a constitution. His first, narrower view is that what is necessary is merely that the constitution structure a logically possible system of law. Here there is no worrisome idealization unless one has crept in under the idea of "law." We may question Kant's ideas about what is essential to a legal order and his assumption that such a system is the only alternative to lawlessness, but objections on these points alone are not charges that Kant is engaging in the troublesome kind of idealization that I have described. Kant does not assume, for example, that everything in the real world that is called a legal order actually satisfies his conditions; for example, he does not claim that all real-world legal orders lack gaps in authority. Articulating a certain conception of a legal order by laying out its necessary conditions can be of use for theoretical purposes, for the conception can provide a model relevant to deliberations about real-world conditions without decisively determining what should be done. In merely doing this, a theorist is not guilty of the alienating kind of idealization. Whether a theorist is in fact guilty of this charge depends on whether, *without adequate further argument*, the theorist

---

[65] Practically minded critics would naturally focus on the specific reasons offered to show that such ideal deliberators would adopt the programs in question, but philosophers would probably also question whether it serves any useful purpose to characterize ideal deliberators first rather than turning immediately to moral arguments for the programs. This latter concern seems a natural one to raise about the simple argument in my example because its account of ideal deliberators is so thin, but whether it is an important worry about more subtle and complex arguments of the same structure is less obvious. My discussion of the fourth objection to hypothetical-agreement theories returns to this issue briefly.

[66] See Hill, *Respect, Pluralism, and Justice*, chap. 2.

draws from his idealization conclusions about how actual social systems *should* be structured. Since Kant does not hesitate to make prescriptions for real-world conditions, whether we conclude that he is guilty of the troublesome kind of idealization will depend in the end on how we understand and assess the strength of his reasons for applying his model.

Consider briefly Kant's broader view of the necessary conditions for a united will on an original contract. This view employed idealizations, but arguably not the troublesome kind that render the possibility of ideal agreement irrelevant to our concerns. Unless we reject the rights of freedom and equality presupposed by Kant's broader view, we should not be indifferent to arguments that hypothetical constitution-makers who, among other things, accept these as basic rights could not endorse, in an original contract, any constitution with certain provisions.[67] Such arguments do not purport to ground these basic rights in the idea of an original contract, for the rights at this stage are presupposed, not "constructed." Whether such arguments are rationally compelling depends, of course, on whether the presupposed rights are independently well grounded. The arguments, we may say, take for granted certain ideals, but again, this is not to concede that they indulge in the troublesome sort of idealization we have been considering. They do not assume falsely that in the real world everyone accepts the basic rights; rather, they only assume that as a normative matter, persons *should* be guaranteed those rights. The conclusions of such arguments (e.g., that permanent hereditary political privileges are unjust) are not based on a failure to understand the differences between our imperfect world and a more ideal one. Some aristocrats, Nietzscheans, and postmodernists may reject the presupposed rights, but that would call for a separate debate. For most of us, it would be quite bizarre to complain that what the hypothetical parties to an original contract could agree on is irrelevant to us because they, given their commitment to basic rights of freedom and equality, are more ideal than we are.

D. Is hypothetical agreement a standard that is either arbitrary or useless?

My reply to the previous objection invites another objection commonly raised to theories that try to justify principles by arguing that they are, or would be, prescribed by ideal legislators. The objection can be put in the form of a dilemma: either the ideal legislators are guided by substantial reasons, or else their prescriptions are arbitrary. Both options have objectionable implications.[68] On the one hand, if there are substantial reasons

[67] Kantian arguments of this sort are analogous to arguments at what Rawls calls "the constitutional stage" of applying the Rawlsian basic principles of justice. See Rawls, *A Theory of Justice*, 95–101.
[68] Andrews Reath, Shelly Kagan, and Philip Pettit convinced me of the need to respond to this apparent dilemma.

why the ideal legislators prescribe the principles in question, then those reasons—not the fact that ideal legislators prescribed the principles—are what give the principles force. Reference to legislators' "legislative" choices seems irrelevant if the same principles could be justified directly by appeal to the substantial reasons that supposedly guide the legislators' choices. On the other hand, if the ideal legislators make arbitrary choices that are not based on good reasons, then the fact that they prescribe a principle seems to give us no reason to respect it.[69]

Kantian ethics, as I understand it, is clear about which horn of this dilemma it must avoid at all costs, and so the important question is whether there is any devastating force in the other horn. What seems obvious is that Kant does not think that what members of a kingdom of ends would legislate and what would be rationally excluded from an original contract are arbitrary choices. If we can find no adequate reasons why the hypothetical legislators or original contractors would accept or reject proposals, then Kantian theory has no grounds for attributing choices to these legislators or contractors. As noted already, however, Kant's thought experiments about what would or would not be agreed to in a kingdom of ends and in an original contract *presuppose* standards of rational choice that are not themselves products of choice or construction in the hypothetical-choice situations. Thus, Kantian constructivism is not subject to the complaint that it renders moral principles arbitrary.

How damaging, then, is the other horn of the dilemma? Kantian theory, I think, should concede that principles justified by reference to the hypothetical choices of members of the kingdom of ends might in principle be justified by more direct appeal to the rational standards presupposed by their alleged legislative choices. For similar reasons, it should not be denied that reference to the idea of an original contract could in principle be replaced by direct invocations of the rational standards presupposed in arguments that there could be no original contract on constitutions with certain provisions. In principle we might, for example, argue against such constitutions directly from the presupposed innate rights to freedom and equality. Whether these concessions pose a serious problem, however, depends on at least two questions. First, need Kantian constructivism claim to offer hypothetical-agreement arguments that are free from all presuppositions about rational and moral choice beyond what these arguments themselves can establish? The proper response, in my opinion, is that so long as the aims and limits of the constructivism are clear, there is nothing in itself objectionable about starting with assumptions that are not them-

---

[69] The dilemma posed here is analogous to the "Euthyphro problem," which is a dilemma that Socrates poses in Plato's dialogue, *Euthyphro*. Either what is pious (or righteous) is so because it pleases the gods or else what is pious (or righteous) pleases the gods because it is pious (or righteous). If the former is true, piety (or righteousness) seems to be arbitrary; if the latter is true, then the gods do not determine what is pious (or righteous), but merely respond to an independent truth about piety (or righteousness).

THOMAS E. HILL, JR.

selves the products of construction.[70] Kantians should not hesitate to admit that their thought experiments presuppose certain standards, nor should they hesitate to try to clarify what those standards are. Kantians need not contend that their constructivist procedures can justify substantive moral principles without making any initial assumptions about rationality and morality. The assumptions they do make, like those in any theory, may be questioned and debated, but unless constructivists claim to derive moral principles without any potentially disputable assumptions, there is no problem in principle with the constructivists' procedure. Constructivist arguments are not undermined by the mere fact that they are built with some equipment and tools that constructivists cannot claim to have constructed.

The second question is this: even if direct appeals to the rational presuppositions of hypothetical-agreement arguments could in principle achieve the same results that the arguments themselves yield, is there any theoretical or heuristic value in arguing by reference to hypothetical agreement? To answer this question, we need to work out more of the details of the Kantian appeals to hypothetical agreement. The constructivist question "What would be agreed upon in such-and-such a hypothetical ideal situation?" may bring together several evaluative assumptions, explicit and presupposed, to bear on a particular topic in a way that is more convenient and fruitful than treating those assumptions as so many separate premises in a direct argument. In addition, expressing standards as rational guides and constraints on hypothetical choices may discourage attempts to reify those standards as self-standing natural or supernatural facts. In any case, it is not a fatal objection to a proposal that the same job could be done another way.

E. Will arguments from hypothetical agreement convince egoistic amoralists?

Finally, another source of suspicion about Kantian appeals to hypothetical agreement might be the thought that such agreement does not provide arguments adequate to convince a "rational egoist" who has little regard for others. The short-term response to this claim must be that the point of hypothetical-agreement arguments in Kantian constructivism is to work out and defend certain principles as being morally justified, not to convince egoists lacking any moral commitment that they have purely self-interested reasons for accepting these principles. What we can say to such persons, if they exist, is another matter. Despite his insistence on the rationality of moral conduct, Kant in fact does not develop an answer that

---

[70] Onora O'Neill's constructivism is more ambitious in this regard than is the general account of constructivism that I am discussing here (which is closer to Rawls's position), for she aims to build her arguments from only thin, formal assumptions. See Onora O'Neill, "Constructivism in Kant and Rawls," in Samuel Freeman, ed., *The Cambridge Companion to Rawls* (forthcoming).

one could give to the utterly uncommitted egoist. He assumes that all moral agents have legislative reason (*Wille*), which forces on us, as it were, recognition of the authority of the moral law even when we violate it. He is even committed to the idea that, in a sense, we *actually will* for ourselves (at least as a standard) conformity to whatever rational agents with the most basic Kantian moral commitments *would agree* upon. Yet this presupposition of a deep "actual consent" to moral law is far from the everyday idea of actual consent with which I began this essay. The sort of "actual consent" presupposed by Kant, reflected in his discussion of the inescapable "fact of reason," is clearly not an actual readiness, or even public commitment, always to be fully governed by moral standards. It is an acceptance of the authority of the moral law, but, as we know, this is not always accompanied by a wholehearted resolve or commitment to obey.

VI. CONCLUSION

The primary question in this essay has been how to understand the justificatory role of actual, possible, and hypothetical consent within Kant's ethics. Kant's theory has been treated as one among several possible versions of Kantian constructivism. A brief review of the Categorical Imperative's various formulations and of Kant's idea of an original contract provides the basis for several conclusions. Contrary to what discussions of applied ethics often assume, Kant regards *actual* consent as having only a derivative and qualified relevance to how we may be treated. For Kant, a more basic standard is that practices are justified only if we *can*, as rational agents, consent to them being universal practices. To apply this standard, however, we must make assumptions about the context of choice and the rational principles that determine what it is possible, in the relevant sense, for us to will. When the assumptions necessary to make the standard plausible are made explicit, it turns out that, in effect, the possible-consent standard can be expressed as a hypothetical-consent standard. Hypothetical-consent standards condemn practices that are contrary to principles that any rational agent *would* will *under specified conditions*. The apparent simplicity, then, of the possible-consent test that asks "What can we will as universal law?" is deceptive. This test is not a way of avoiding the hard, controversial questions raised by hypothetical-consent standards. What are the principles and conditions of rational choice that are being presupposed when one applies these standards? Are these presuppositions defensible? Furthermore, when these presuppositions are made explicit, do the presupposed standards support intuitively plausible moral judgments? Particular versions of hypothetical-consent standards (such as that presented by Rawls's original position) raise special problems, but arguably the several objections to hypothetical consent that I consider in this essay are not decisive objections to the Kantian version of such a standard.

Philosophy, University of North Carolina, Chapel Hill

MILL'S "PROOF" OF THE PRINCIPLE OF UTILITY: A MORE THAN HALF-HEARTED DEFENSE*

By Geoffrey Sayre-McCord

I. Introduction

How many serious mistakes can a brilliant philosopher make in a single paragraph? Many think that Mill answers this question by example—in the third paragraph of Chapter IV of *Utilitarianism*. Here is the notorious paragraph:

The only proof capable of being given that an object is visible, is that people actually see it. The only proof that a sound is audible, is that people hear it: and so of the other sources of our experience. In like manner, I apprehend, the sole evidence it is possible to produce that anything is desirable, is that people do actually desire it. If the end which the utilitarian doctrine proposes to itself were not, in theory and in practice, acknowledged to be an end, nothing could ever convince any person that it was so. No reason can be given why the general happiness is desirable, except that each person, so far as he believes it to be attainable, desires his own happiness. This, however, being a fact, we have not only all the proof which the case admits of, but all which it is possible to require, that happiness is a good: that each person's happiness is a good to that person, and the general happiness, therefore, a good to the aggregate of all persons. Happiness has made out its title as one of the ends of conduct, and consequently one of the criteria of morality.[1]

The supposed mistakes in this paragraph are well known and seem to come at every step. (I will rehearse them in Section III.) Yet the idea that

---

* Earlier versions of this essay were presented at the March 2000 meeting of the International Society for Utilitarian Studies, the University of California at Riverside, the Australian National University, Tulane University, and to an informal group at the University of California at Irvine. I am grateful for the helpful comments people have offered on these occasions. I have especially benefited from conversations with and comments from Marc Baer, David Brink, Stephen Darwall, Gerald Gaus, Shelly Kagan, Dale Miller, Michael Ridge, Harriet Sayre-McCord, and John Skorupski.

[1] John Stuart Mill, *Utilitarianism*, ed. Roger Crisp (New York: Oxford University Press, 1998), IV, 3. Throughout this essay, passages from *Utilitarianism* will be identified using the chapter, paragraph, and line numbers from this edition.

someone so smart should make the glaring mistakes people find in Mill's "proof" seems beyond belief. Rightly so, for Mill did not make them. The appearance of rampant fallacies, I will argue, is due to rampant misunderstandings of the argument. Indeed, once the real structure of the argument is brought out, I maintain, not one of the (in)famous fallacies is to be found. Moreover, the general strategy underlying the argument is, I believe, the only strategy available to those who think moral knowledge cannot be justified solely by appeal to nonevaluative truths. To bring this out, I will—in a bizarre move—be defending Mill by stressing the structure his own notorious argument shares with another one of dubious repute: Kant's defense of the Categorical Imperative (in its second formulation).[2]

As this essay's title suggests, though, while I will be giving a more than half-hearted defense of Mill's "proof," it will be less than full-scale. I will be defending the structure of the argument, but not the content Mill ends up putting into the structure. Along the way, I will similarly be defending Kant's argument, though also only its structure and not the content Kant ends up putting into the structure. In any case, I will argue that an appreciation of this shared structure reveals Mill's proof to be much more plausible than it otherwise seems. Where his proof remains weak, the problems are found not in the reasoning offered, but in (as I see it) mistakes of fact concerning human psychology—concerning, for instance, what people value and why. Hence I share with Mill the view that, with the proof in hand, "all that remains is to consult practised self-consciousness and self-observation, assisted by observation of others."[3] Where I differ substantially and crucially with Mill is in my thinking that these sources reveal that the specific claims he relies on as premises—the content of his structure—are false. Similarly, as it happens, I think the claims Kant ends up putting into the same structure are false as well. Mill and Kant alike, it seems to me, attribute commitments to people—in Mill's case on psychological grounds, in Kant's on *a priori* grounds—that people do not actually have.

II. THE "PROOF"

A full proof of utilitarianism requires defending two things: its standard of conduct, or right action, and its theory of value. According to the standard of conduct, an agent has performed the right act if and only if that act is among the agent's best available options. To have taken any less than the best available option is, Mill thinks, to have performed the

---

[2] Immanuel Kant, *Grounding for the Metaphysics of Morals*, trans. James W. Ellington (Indianapolis, IN: Hackett, 1981), 36 (Ak. p. 429).
[3] Mill, *Utilitarianism*, IV, 10.5.

wrong act.[4] (Although, of course, failing to take the right action may not
reflect badly on the agent, depending upon why she failed to do what, as
a matter of fact, was right.) Just which options count as best depends
upon what is valuable and, in particular, on what is valuable as an end
(since, according to Mill, everything else of value is valuable, ultimately,
because it is a means to, or a part of, something valuable as an end). And
according to the theory of value, happiness is the only thing valuable as
an end.[5]

Mill pretty much just takes the consequentialist theory of right action
for granted (as did Henry Sidgwick and G. E. Moore after him), though
he is at pains, in Chapter V, to show that it is compatible with a proper
understanding and appreciation of justice. In taking it for granted, Mill
assumes that whatever turns out to be of value is such that we ought to
maximize it, and assumes too that the value to be maximized is additive.
A defense of both assumptions would be crucial to establishing utilitarianism, and Mill's failure to examine them means that the proof he does
offer, of his theory of value, does not settle the issue in favor of utilitarianism, even if it is successful.[6] Nonetheless, Mill does take the consequentialist theory of right action as given, and thinks that what needs
defending is the theory of value. Indeed, he claims: "That the morality of
actions depends on the consequences which they tend to produce, is the
doctrine of rational persons of all schools; that the good or evil of those
consequences is measured solely by pleasure or pain, is all of the doctrine
of the school of utility, which is peculiar to it."[7] Thus, as he sees it, the
controversial heart of the doctrine—and so what he tries to defend—is
"that happiness is desirable, and the only thing desirable, as an end. . . ."[8]

The third paragraph of Chapter IV is given over to defending the first
claim, that happiness is desirable as an end, while the rest of the chapter
is devoted to defending the second, that happiness is the only thing

[4] Mill distinguishes between the standard of conduct and "the criterion of morality,"
treating the latter as determined by the former (ibid., IV, 9.5). In addition, Mill suggests, at
least sometimes, that the morality of an action turns not directly on its effects, but on
whether it accords with "the rules and precepts for human conduct, by the observance of
which" the best results are secured (see, e.g., ibid., II, 10.10). Presumably, particular actions
that are among the agent's best available options might not be in accord with the relevant
rules and precepts, and particular actions that do satisfy the rules and precepts may be
among the options that are less than the best.
[5] More precisely, Mill sees happiness as a *measure* of the balance of pleasure and pain, and
holds "that pleasure, and freedom from pain, are the only things desirable as ends" (because
pleasure is good in itself and pain is bad in itself) and "that all desirable things (which are
as numerous in the utilitarian as in any other scheme) are desirable either for the pleasure
inherent in themselves, or as means to the promotion of pleasure and the prevention of
pain." Ibid., II, 2.10.
[6] Among other things, it would leave completely unaddressed the suggestion that distributive considerations are (nonderivatively) relevant to what ought to be done.
[7] John Stuart Mill, *Bentham*, in Mill, *Collected Works of John Stuart Mill*, ed. J. M. Robson
(Toronto: University of Toronto Press, 1969), 10:111.
[8] Mill, *Utilitarianism*, IV, 2.

desirable as an end. In both cases, the argument turns on a crucial principle of evidence, according to which "the sole evidence it is possible to produce that anything is desirable, is that people do actually desire it." In light of this principle, what Mill needs to show is that people do actually desire happiness as an end and that it is the only thing they desire as an end. Otherwise, given the principle, he would have no evidence for thinking, first, that happiness is desirable as an end, or, second, that it is the only thing desirable as an end. This is all pretty straightforward, though the principle of evidence is, of course, highly contentious.

In any case, the straightforward becomes much less so once it is appreciated that, as Mill would have it, what is desirable as an end is "the general happiness"—that is, happiness no matter whose and so the happiness of each and every person, not just that of the agent. This complicates things immediately since, first of all, it seems obvious that many people do not desire the general happiness as an end and that, whether they do or not, they often desire also their own happiness as an end, so the general happiness is not the only thing they desire as an end. The premises Mill apparently thinks he needs, to have evidence for his doctrine, seem simply not to be available.

Mill, of course, is aware of this difficulty and never claims that people do actually desire the general happiness, let alone that it is the only thing they desire.[9] Instead, he takes it that people do at least desire their own happiness, and relies on this as establishing "that happiness is a good: that each person's happiness is a good to that person" and that the general happiness is "a good to the aggregate of all persons."[10] Similarly, after the third paragraph, he sets out to show that what people desire as ends they always desire as a part of their own, and not the general, happiness. Presumably, following the parallel, this is supposed to establish that happiness is the only thing that is good (as an end): that each person's happiness is the only thing that is a good to that person, and that the general happiness is the only thing that is good (as an end) to the aggregate of all persons.

---

[9] Nonetheless, some have criticized Mill for implicitly assuming that people, either individually or collectively, do desire the general happiness. For instance, F. H. Bradley suggests that "[e]ither Mill meant to argue, 'Because everybody desires his own pleasure, therefore everybody desires his own pleasure"; or "Because everybody desires his own pleasure, therefore everybody desires the pleasure of everybody else.' Disciples may take their choice." Of course, the first claim is trivial and of no help and the second is obviously fallacious. Fortunately, it is pretty clear that Mill, whatever he meant, did not mean to offer either of these arguments. See F. H. Bradley, Ethical Studies, 2d ed. (Oxford: Clarendon Press, 1927), 113–14 n. 3. Along the same lines, C. D. Broad sees Mill as committed to thinking that something being desired is one and the same with it being desirable, so that when Mill holds that the general happiness is a good that is desirable to the aggregate of all people, he is, according to Broad, committed to holding (falsely) that the aggregate desires something— that is, the general happiness. Fortunately, again, it is pretty clear that Mill neither equated being desired and being desirable nor meant to hold that the aggregate desires anything at all. See C. D. Broad, Five Types of Ethical Theory (Paterson, NJ: Littlefield, Adams, 1959).

[10] Mill, Utilitarianism, IV, 3.10.

In the post–third paragraph discussion, the main effort is given over to acknowledging and accommodating two facts. First, people often "desire things which, in common language, are decidedly distinguished from happiness."[11] Second, desire aside, a person can willingly pursue ends "without any thought of the pleasure he has in contemplating them, or expects to derive from their fulfillment," and can even knowingly act in ways where the benefits expected "are outweighed by the pains which the pursuit of the purposes may bring upon him."[12]

The first fact, Mill argues, raises no difficulty for his view, once properly understood. There are, he acknowledges, a number of things originally distinct from happiness that people can come to desire for their own sake. Yet when this change happens, when someone actually does come to desire money, say, or virtue, for its own sake, she has simultaneously become someone for whom acquiring money or acting virtuously is a pleasure. "Whatever is desired otherwise than as a means to some end beyond itself, and ultimately to happiness, is desired as itself a part of happiness, and is not desired for itself until it has become so."[13] Admittedly, there are interesting and significant difficulties here surrounding Mill's psychological thesis. Specifically, he seems to run together the idea that people get pleasure from securing what they value for its own sake with the idea of their valuing it for the pleasure that securing it brings.[14] However, since my concern is to defend the structure of Mill's argument, not the truth of its premises, I will leave the psychological claim unchallenged.[15]

The second fact, Mill argues, likewise raises no difficulty for his view, since what matters to his argument is what people *desire*, not merely what they might be motivated to do. According to Mill, "Will, the active phenomenon, is a different thing from desire, the state of passive sensibility, and though originally an offshoot from it, may in time take root and detach itself from the parent stock."[16] It is desire—the passive sensibility—that is supposed by Mill to afford evidence of value, not the will nor particular motives that serve as the springs of action. Mill is here marking an important difference between what people desire and what they are

[11] Ibid., IV, 4.4.

[12] Ibid., IV, 11.5.

[13] Ibid., IV, 8.2. In this, Mill is largely following Aristotle, who identifies valuing something for its own sake with taking pleasure in it directly, rather than thanks to what it produces.

[14] T. H. Green seems to be picking up on this point when he writes, "It is the realization of those objects in which we are mainly interested, *not the succession of enjoyments which we shall experience in realizing them*, that forms the definite content of our idea of true happiness, so far as it has such content at all" (emphasis added). I think, though, that Green goes astray in equating happiness with the realization of what is valued. See T. H. Green, *Prolegomena to Ethics* (Oxford: Clarendon Press, 1890), bk. III, chap. iv, sec. 228, p. 244.

[15] As I have said, the source of my less than full-hearted support of Mill's proof is largely found in my unwillingness to embrace the psychological claims upon which the proof turns.

[16] Mill, *Utilitarianism*, IV, 10.

merely motivated to pursue. The difference will turn out to be crucial to understanding Mill's argument, and especially to understanding the way in which desire is supposed to be analogous to the senses.

These two facts taken account of, Mill thinks that the "practised self-consciousness and self-observation, assisted by observation of others" that I mentioned above will reveal that people do desire, as ends, all and only what constitute parts of their own happiness. This fact, he holds, provides the evidence, both necessary and sufficient, to establish that happiness, no matter whose, is desirable, and the only thing desirable, as an end. Before turning to the (more than half-hearted) defense of Mill's argument, let me briefly rehearse the familiar objections to it.

III. The Familiar Problems

Problems come up at the very beginning of the third paragraph, when Mill sets to defending the principle of evidence upon which the rest of the argument turns. According to Mill, "The only proof capable of being given that an object is visible, is that people actually see it. The only proof that a sound is audible, is that people hear it: and so of the other sources of our experience. In like manner," he famously maintains, "the sole evidence it is possible to produce that anything is desirable, is that people do actually desire it."

Right away there is reason to think this principle of evidence is exaggerated, even as applied to visibility and audibility. After all, we often have evidence that some particular thing is visible (or audible) even though we have never seen (or heard) it. Mill's actual view, though, and in any case all that he needs to rely upon, is the more modest empiricist one that the ultimate source of all our evidence that something is visible (or audible) is found in what people see (or hear), whether or not the particular thing is itself seen (or heard).

Regardless, it has seemed to many that the argument for extending the principle of evidence from visibility to desirability utterly collapses once one notes that "desirable" may have either of two meanings: it might mean "capable of being desired" as "visible" means "capable of being seen," or it might mean "worth desiring" in a way that makes plausible an identification of it with "good" or "valuable." Read in the first way, the analogy with vision, hearing, and the other senses is apt and well supports the principle of evidence, but is irrelevant to the question of what is actually worth desiring. Yet the claim to be defended concerns what is worth desiring. Read in the second way, the principle of evidence, if true, would be relevant, but the analogy with our senses seems totally beside the point. Moreover, when read in the second way, the principle looks pretty clearly to be false. The mere fact that someone or other desires something seemingly provides us with no reason at all to think that what is desired is good. Thus, either the principle is well-supported but irrelevant, or relevant but totally unsupported—and implausible as well. As Moore points out, "Mill has, then, smuggled in, under cover of the word 'desirable,' the very notion about which he ought to be quite clear. 'Desirable' does indeed mean 'what it is good to desire'; but when this is understood, it is no longer plausible to say that our only test of *that*, is what is actually desired." [17]

Putting aside the apparently irrelevant analogy with vision and the other senses, many (influenced by Moore) have thought the principle of evidence itself requires supposing that an evaluative concept can be defined in naturalistic terms, and so embodies the "naturalistic fallacy." Moore himself claims that Mill's reliance on the principle reveals "as naïve and artless a use of the naturalistic fallacy as anybody could desire." The fallacy comes, Moore urges, when Mill "pretends to prove that 'good' means 'desired'." [18] Why Moore believes Mill makes any such pretensions, however, is a mystery. What Mill says is that "the *sole evidence* that anything is desirable is that it is desired" [emphasis added]. While that might be overstating the case—there might be other sorts of evidence—it is not at all to hold that being desirable and being desired are one and the same property, nor is it to hold that "desirable" and "desired" have the same meaning. Still, one might think, the idea that what people actually desire is the sole evidence we might have as to what is in fact valuable may seem to borrow all its plausibility from the assumption that being desired and being desirable are one and the same. If its plausibility does depend on that assumption, then the principle would seem to require identifying an evaluative property with a natural one. Whether this would be genuinely fallacious, of course, depends upon whether the identification on offer, if there is one, is correct. As I will argue, however, Mill is making no such assumption, and has, instead, a different conception of the relation between desire and value. [19]

In any case, suppose that one accepts the principle of evidence, at least for the sake of the argument. Even then, the third paragraph invites complaints and even ridicule. This is because Mill moves blithely from the observation that people desire their own happiness as an end, which (in light of the principle of evidence) provides grounds for thinking that their own happiness is desirable as an end, to the required—but still completely unsupported—conclusion that *the general happiness* is desirable as an end. Given the principle of evidence, this conclusion would of course follow from the observation that people desire the general happi-

[17] G. E. Moore, *Principia Ethica* (Cambridge: Cambridge University Press, 1903), 67.
[18] Ibid., 66. Broad similarly claims that Mill "starts by assuming that 'desirable' means 'desired by someone'," in Broad, *Five Types of Ethical Theory*, 183.
[19] Specifically, on Mill's account, our concept of value and our evidence that the concept is satisfied are traceable to our capacity to desire, just as our concept of color and our evidence that the concept is satisfied are traceable to our capacity to see. Yet the concepts of value and of color are not concepts of the experiences that the capacities make possible.

ness as an end. Yet Mill does not rely on this (optimistic) observation.[20] Mill instead apparently tries to move from the claim that each person's happiness is desirable as an end, to that person, to the conclusion that the general happiness (which is just the happiness of all) is "a good to the aggregate of all persons." As Sidgwick points out, though, "an aggregate of actual desires, each directed towards different parts of the general happiness, does not constitute an actual desire for the general happiness, existing in any individual."[21] Thus, Mill could not in this way try to establish that the general happiness is the object of some individual's desire. Moreover, if Mill thought he only needed to show that someone or other desires the general happiness, his own case would have been enough. After all, he does desire the general happiness. However, Mill is clearly not trying to establish any such thing.

What is not so clear is why he thinks the value, to each, of his or her own happiness in any way goes to establish the value of the general happiness. Indeed, the reasoning seems to require one or both of the following: either an unjustified inference from the value (to someone) of each part of the general happiness to the value of the whole (which risks a fallacy of composition), or an unjustified inference from the value of the general happiness to all taken together (since each piece of the general happiness is valuable to someone) to the value of it to each, taken singly.[22]

The worries multiply if we move on beyond the third paragraph. The remainder of the chapter inherits the above problems because it simply redeploys the third-paragraph argument to show that happiness is the *only* thing desirable as an end on the grounds that it is the *only* thing desired as an end. It then adds to the difficulties quickly by embracing, apparently, either a simple-minded version of psychological hedonism or a question-begging assumption concerning the connection between desiring something as an end and desiring it as a part of happiness (or both).[23]

---

[20] Elijah Millgram argues that Mill is relying on the optimistic prospect that people in the future will desire the general happiness, and using this to support the claim that the majority of people (past, present, and future) give a decided preference to the general happiness even if people of his day do not. The success of the proof, on this view, turns on whether what is being "proven" ends up ultimately being accepted, and does not itself constitute any sort of argument for accepting it. See Elijah Millgram, "Mill's Proof of the Principle of Utility," *Ethics* 110, no. 2 (2000): 282–310.

[21] Henry Sidgwick, *The Methods of Ethics*, 7th ed. (London: Macmillan, 1907), 388. Broad presses the same point at Broad, *Five Types of Ethical Theory*, 184.

[22] Thus, to say that the general happiness is "a good to the aggregate of all persons," on the ground that each person's happiness is a good to that person, trades on ignoring the difference between "all" being used collectively (i.e., for all of us, taken together, all of it, taken together, is good) and its being used distributively (i.e., for each of us, considered individually, all of it, taken together, is good). See Alan Ryan, *John Stuart Mill* (New York: Pantheon Books, 1970), 200–201.

[23] These problems circulate around Mill's claim that "to desire anything, except in proportion as the idea of it is pleasant, is a physical and metaphysical impossibility" (Mill, *Utilitarianism*, IV, 10). I think it is pretty clear that Mill does not intend this claim to be true by definition, but it is hard to see why he thinks the empirical evidence would support it.

I propose to leave these additional difficulties to one side, though, because they are raised by Mill's attempt to establish the truth of one of his premises—that people desire only happiness as an end—and not by the argument's structure. It will be enough of a job to try to make sense of the overarching argument that gives point to Mill's trying to determine what people in fact desire.

IV. THE "PROOF" AGAIN—DESIRABILITY AND VISIBILITY

How is the argument supposed to go, if not by way of these multiple fallacies? Let us start with the principle of evidence and the analogy Mill draws between visibility and desirability. What is the analogy supposed to be if not one that commits Mill to interpreting "desirable" as "capable of being desired"?

When it comes to visibility, no less than desirability, Mill explicitly denies that a "proof" in the "ordinary acceptation of the term" can be offered.[24] As he notes, "To be incapable of proof by reasoning is common to all first principles; to the first premises of our knowledge, as well as to those of our conduct." Nonetheless, support—that is, evidence, though not proof—for the first premises of our knowledge is provided by "our senses, and our internal consciousness."[25] Mill's suggestion is that, when it comes to the first principles of conduct, desires play the same epistemic role that the senses play when it comes to the first principles of knowledge.

To understand this role, it is important to distinguish the fact that someone is sensing something from what is sensed, which is a distinction mirrored in the contrast between the fact that someone is desiring something and what is desired. In the case of our senses, the evidence we have for our judgments concerning sensible qualities traces back to what is sensed, to the content of our sense-experience. Likewise, Mill is suggesting, in the case of value, the evidence we have for our judgments concerning value traces back to what is desired, to the content of our desires. Ultimately, the grounds we have for holding the principles we do must,

---

[24] Some, hoping to defend Mill, have jumped on this disclaimer to excuse Mill for arguments that appear invalid. If no proof is to be had, they note, then Mill must not be offering the considerations he does as deductively valid grounds for his conclusion. Still, the argument he offers had better be reasonable, and so far the argument under discussion seems to violate even that requirement by turning on ambiguities, implausible definitions, confusions between an individual and the group to which she may belong, and so on. Complicating matters, Mill (at least in *A System of Logic*) advances a distinctive view of what counts as a genuine proof, according to which deductively valid "proofs" are not proofs at all, since anything to be found in the conclusion of such a "proof" must already be present in its premises, and so is assumed rather than proven. Rather, he supposes, genuine proofs need to establish conclusions that go beyond their premises—a proof establishes something new. John Stuart Mill, *A System of Logic*, in Mill, *Collected Works*, bk. II, chap. 1, sec. 2, 7:158–62. Whether Mill thinks the "ordinary acceptation of the term" "proof" includes deductively valid arguments is unclear. See Millgram, "Mill's Proof."

[25] Mill, *Utilitarianism*, IV, 1.

he thinks, be traced back to our experience, to our senses and desires. Yet the evidence we have is not that we are sensing or desiring something, but what it is that is sensed or desired.[26]

When we are having sensations of red, when what we are looking at appears red to us, we have evidence (albeit overrideable and defeasible evidence) that the thing is red. Moreover, if things never looked red to us, we could never get evidence that things were red, and would indeed never have developed the concept of redness. Similarly, when we are desiring things, when what we are considering appears good to us, we have evidence (albeit overrideable and defeasible evidence) that the thing is good. Moreover, if we never desired things, we could never get evidence that things were good, and would indeed never have developed the concept of value.[27]

Recall that desire, for Mill, like taste, touch, sight, and smell, is a "passive sensibility." All of these, he holds, provide us with both the content that makes thought possible and the evidence we have for the conclusions that thought leads us to embrace. "Desiring a thing" and "thinking of it as desirable (unless for the sake of its consequences)" are treated by Mill as one and the same, just as seeing a thing as red and thinking of it as red are one and the same.[28] Accordingly, a person who desires x is a

---

[26] The interpretation I am advocating thus differs from those that suggest that Mill is appealing to the fact that people desire happiness as an end as establishing that it is *possible* to desire happiness as an end. According to these accounts, the appeal to what people desire plays out against the assumption that what we ought to desire is constrained by what we can desire, and is meant to show that happiness can be desired and is the only thing that can be desired as an end. On this interpretation, happiness emerges as the only candidate for being what ought to be desired. Mill's own observation that "[i]f the end which the utilitarian doctrine proposes to itself were not, in theory and practice, acknowledged to be an end, nothing could ever convince any person that it was so" is often taken as supporting this interpretation. This interpretation, though, leaves Mill with no positive argument for thinking happiness is good—it would simply have survived as the only candidate. Moreover, the argument has not established even this much by the end of the third paragraph, where Mill infers that happiness has been shown to be at least among the things that are desirable as an end. Thus, this interpretation has trouble both with finding Mill a positive argument for thinking happiness is valuable and with making sense of the structure of the text. For discussions of this interpretation, see James Seth, "The Alleged Fallacies in Mill's *Utilitarianism*," *Philosophical Review* 17, no. 5 (1908): 469–88; R. F. Atkinson, "J. S. Mill's 'Proof' of the Principle of Utility," *Philosophy* 32, no. 121 (1957): 158–67; Norman Kretzman, "Desire as Proof of Desirability," *Philosophical Quarterly* 8, no. 32 (1958): 246–58; and George Clark, "Mill's Notorious Analogy," *Journal of Philosophy* 56, no. 15 (1959): 652–56. In contrast, on my reading, Mill's point here is not guided by 'ought' implies 'can', but instead, as I will suggest, by an appreciation of the fact that evaluative conclusions require evaluative premises (i.e., no 'ought' from only 'is's).

[27] Whether the experience is of something as red, or of it as good, the evidence we have is constituted by the content of our experience, not the fact that we had the experience.

[28] Mill, *Utilitarianism*, IV, 10.10. Here Mill first equates desiring something with thinking it pleasant, and then he equates thinking of it as pleasant with thinking of it as desirable. (He actually writes "finding it pleasant" rather than "thinking it pleasant," but goes on immediately to equate aversion to a thing with "thinking of it as painful," not "finding it painful," so in this passage he seems clearly to be using "finding it" and "thinking of it" interchangeably.)

person who *ipso facto* sees x as desirable.[29] Desiring something, for Mill, is a matter of seeing it under the guise of the good.[30] This means that it is important, in the context of Mill's argument, that one not think of desires as mere preferences or as just any sort of motive. They constitute, according to Mill, a distinctive subclass of our motivational states, and are distinguished (at least in part) by their evaluative content.[31] Thus, Mill is neither assuming nor arguing that something is good because we desire it; rather, he is depending on our desiring it as establishing that we see it as good.

At the same time, while desiring something is a matter of seeing it as good, one could, on Mill's view, believe that something is good without desiring it, just as one can believe something is red without seeing it as red. While desire is supposed to be the fundamental source of our concept of, and evidence for, desirability, once the concept is in place there are contexts in which we will have reason to think it applies even when the corresponding sensible experience is lacking. Indeed, in Chapter IV, Mill is concerned not with generating a desire, but with justifying the belief that happiness is desirable, and the only thing desirable, as an end, and so concerned with defending the standard for determining what should be desired.[32]

Mill's aim is to take what people already, and he thinks inevitably, see as desirable and argue that those views commit them to the value of the general happiness (whether or not their desires follow the deliverances of their reason). Those who, like Mill, desire the general happiness already hold the view that the general happiness is desirable. They accept the claim that Mill is trying to defend. As Mill knows, however, there are

---

[29] Within this broadly empiricist approach to concepts and evidence, there is an important question of how to understand the original experiences that give rise to concepts and provide evidence for their application. These experiences are often characterized not only by using the concepts they are supposed to explain, but in a way that seems to suppose the concepts are already available to the person having the experience. This obviously needs to be avoided on pain of circularity. In the case of desire and value, then, Mill needs to suppose that while desiring x is something like seeing x as desirable or good, the experience of desiring x does not require already possessing the concepts of desirability or value.

[30] Views similar to Mill's in this respect (though not others) have recently been defended in Dennis Stampe, "The Authority of Desire," *Philosophical Review* 96, no. 3 (1987): 335–81; Warren Quinn, "Putting Rationality in Its Place," in Quinn, *Morality and Action* (Cambridge: Cambridge University Press, 1993); and T. M. Scanlon, *What We Owe to Each Other* (Cambridge, MA: Harvard University Press, 1998).

[31] While he believes that "[i]n what we call Desire there is . . . always included a positive stimulation to action," he also thinks there is always included (to use his father's phrase) "the idea of something good to have." See James Mill, *Analysis of the Phenomena of the Human Mind*, 2d ed., ed. J. S. Mill (London: Longman, Green, Reader, and Dyer, 1869), chap. 19; and John Stuart Mill's notes to that edition, ibid., 194–95. The notes can also be found in Mill, *Collected Works*, 31:215.

[32] In some cases, of course, Mill thinks that the correct standard will recommend desiring something other than the general happiness. At the same time, there is, on Mill's view, an important difference between justifying a belief—giving evidence of its truth—and showing that it would be good to adopt it.

many who do not have this desire—many who desire only their own happiness, and some who even desire that others suffer. These are the people he sets out to persuade, along with others who are more generous and benevolent, but who nonetheless do not see happiness as desirable, and the only thing desirable, as an end. Mill's argument is directed at convincing them all—whether their desires follow or not—that they have grounds for, and are in fact already committed to, regarding the happiness of others as valuable as an end.

Mill recognizes that whatever argument he might hope to offer will need to appeal to evaluative claims people already accept (since he takes to heart Hume's caution concerning inferring an 'ought' from an 'is').[33] The claim Mill thinks he can appeal to—that one's own happiness is a good (i.e., desirable)—is something licensed as available by people desiring their own happiness. Yet he is not supposing here that the fact that they desire their own happiness, or anything else, is proof that it is desirable, just as he would not suppose that the fact that someone sees something as red is proof that it is. Rather, he is supposing that if people desire their own happiness, or see something as red, one can rely on them having available, *as a premise for further argument*, the claim that their own happiness is desirable, or that the thing is red (at least absent contrary evidence).[34] As he puts it in the third paragraph, "If the end which the utilitarian doctrine proposes to itself were not, in theory and in practice, acknowledged to be an end, nothing could ever convince any person that it was so."

Thus, in appealing to the analogy between judgments of sensible qualities and judgments of value, Mill is not trading on an ambiguity, nor does his argument here involve identifying being desirable with being desired or assuming that "desirable" means "desired." He is instead relying consistently on an empiricist account of concepts and their application—on a view according to which we have the concepts, evidence, and knowledge we do only thanks to our having experiences of a certain sort. In the absence of the relevant experiences, he holds (with other empiricists), we would not only lack the required evidence for our judgments, we would lack the capacity to make the judgments in the first place. In the presence of the relevant experiences, though, we have both the concepts and the required evidence—"not only all the proof which the case admits of, but all which it is possible to require."[35]

---

[33] As is made clear by his discussion of it in Mill, *A System of Logic*, bk. VI, chap. 12, sec. 6, 8:949–52.

[34] Note that even in the presence of contrary evidence, the content of one's desires or visual experiences will be on board as potential counterevidence.

[35] When he writes this in the third paragraph, Mill is just summarizing the case for thinking that happiness is good, not yet that it is also the only thing good, as an end. However, the stronger conclusion is supposed to rest simply on a redeployment of the same argument form. See Mill, *Utilitarianism*, IV, 9.5.

V. The "Proof" Again — From Each to All,
with Kant in Tow

Needless to say, even if Mill can legitimately invoke the analogy between vision and desire, and so appeal to desire in establishing desirability, he is a long way from having given any argument at all for thinking
that the *general* happiness is desirable. Mill's first step in offering such an
argument, of course, is his claim that, as a matter of fact, people desire
their own happiness—and so see their own happiness as good. This fact
(assuming it is one) means that we can rely on this view being available
to people when one offers them an argument for thinking that the general
happiness is desirable. In the same way, the fact that someone has a
certain sort of visual experience means that she sees her car as red, and
we can rely on this view being available to her in offering her arguments
about the color of other things, or of the car, should it turn out to be
someone else's.

Significantly, beginning with the claim that each person desires her
own happiness, Mill infers that *each person's* happiness is a good *to that
person*, and that the general happiness is a good *to the aggregate of all
persons*. Thus, as Mill presents the case, there are two proprietary aspects
of the situation: first, the happiness in question is supposed to be someone's; second, the value it is supposed to have is a value to someone. As
it turns out, though, the conclusion Mill ultimately wants to establish is
proprietary along neither dimension: he wants to show that happiness, *no
matter whose*, is valuable *simpliciter*, not just valuable *to* one person or
another or even *to* everyone.

That Mill is out to show that happiness, no matter whose, is valuable,
is clear; "the happiness which forms the utilitarian standard of what is
right in conduct, is not," Mill notes, "the agent's own happiness, but that
of all concerned."[36] That he also is trying to show that it is valuable
simpliciter, as opposed to valuable to each and every person, is much less
clear. Indeed, it is tempting to think that he has not successfully re-
sponded to egoists, and so not defended the general happiness as valuable as an end in the relevant way, until he has shown that it is a good to
each person, egoists included.

So it is worth noting that Mill explicitly denies that the general happiness is, in fact, a good *to each person*. Then it is worth trying to figure out
why he denies this. The denial is clear and comes up when, in a letter to
Henry Jones, Mill writes:

> [W]hen I said the general happiness is a good to the aggregate of all
> persons *I did not mean that every human being's happiness is a good to
> every other human being*, though I think, in a good state of society and

---

[36] Ibid., II, 18.2.

education it would be so. I merely meant in this particular sentence to argue that since A's happiness is a good, B's a good, C's a good, &c., the sum of all these goods must be a good. [emphasis added][37]

Here Mill is doing three things: (i) saying that he was not trying to show that the general happiness is a good to each and every human being, (ii) expressing his view that things would be better if the happiness of others were a good to each, and (iii) claiming that if each person's happiness is a good (note: a good *simpliciter*, not a good *to that person*), then the happiness of each, taken together, must be a good as well. Appreciating all three points is important to understanding Mill's view, but for now I will focus on the first claim.

What is it for something to be a good *to a person*? Why does Mill think that his defense of utilitarianism can succeed without showing that the general happiness is a good to each person? The answer to the first question is, in broad outlines at least, pretty simple. On Mill's view, and plausibly, for something to be good *to a* person is for it to be a good that the person gets, a benefit she receives, enjoys, or secures. Thus, if happiness is a good, for it to be a good *to a* person is for that person to get it, that is, be happy. If she is concerned about the welfare of another, and that other person's happiness is (as Mill supposes) a good, then when the other person is happy, that is a good to the person who is happy, and a good to her as well, insofar as she too is made happy. If, alternatively, she is unconcerned about the welfare of another, but (again as Mill supposes) that other person's happiness is nonetheless a good, then when the other person is happy, that is a good to the person who is happy, even as it is not a good to the one who is unconcerned.[38]

There is more than a little difficulty in the offing, though, when it comes to making sense of what it is for someone to receive, enjoy, or secure a benefit. It is not merely a matter of a person getting something that is

---

[37] John Stuart Mill to Henry Jones, June 13, 1868, reprinted in Mill, *Collected Works*, 16:1414.

[38] Roger Crisp appeals to the passage just quoted from Mill's letter to Henry Jones to argue that Mill does not mean to show that the general happiness is an appropriate end for each individual. According to the interpretation I am offering, however, Mill *is* trying to give each of us an argument for accepting the view that the general happiness is valuable as an end. That the letter does not deny this becomes clear once attention is paid to the difference between showing that something is a good and showing that it is a good *to* someone. To do the latter is, on Mill's view, to show that it will contribute to *that person's happiness*. In a better world, Mill notes, people's concerns would be structured so that they would take pleasure in the well-being of others. Until that happens, though, we need to acknowledge that while the well-being of others is in fact good, it does not always contribute to the well-being of an agent in the way that would underwrite saying that the well-being of another is a good *to that agent*. Mill wants to offer an argument that shows that when something makes someone happy, we are all constrained to admit that something good has been produced, whether or not we take it to be good and whether or not we ourselves are benefited by it (which we will be if we care for the other person's welfare, but may not be otherwise). See Roger Crisp, *Mill On Utilitarianism* (London: Routledge, 1997), 77–78.

good, since that might happen in a way that leaves the person herself no better off, even as, perhaps, she is as a result surrounded by more that is good. For her to benefit, for what she receives to be a good to her, it seems she must herself be better off thanks to its presence. Mill's view, I think, is that this happens exactly when the good either partially constitutes, or brings, happiness (or pleasure) to the person in question.[39] In any case, that something is a good *to* someone presupposes (on Mill's view) that it is good *simpliciter*—so if, say, happiness is a good to someone who has it, that presupposes the value of what it is she gets.

Needless to say, if happiness is a good, then the value of one person being happy can be compounded by others caring about her. That way, when she thrives, they do too.[40] That is one reason why Mill thinks that, in light of the value of happiness, things would be better if society and education worked so that one person's happiness was "a good to every other human being." Another is that to the extent people are motivated by what they value as ends (and so as parts of their own happiness), if one person's happiness is a good to another, the second person will more likely be motivated to promote the happiness of the first.

In point of fact, of course, some people are made unhappy when others do well. Even such people (assuming they desire their own happiness) are, according to Mill, committed to the value of other people's happiness, despite the other people's happiness not being a good to them. Yet, for all Mill argues, it is in principle possible that things would be best if one person's happiness were not always a good to another. Competition for goods may well be advantageous when it comes to the production of value. Hence, while Mill believes overall value would be advanced by people caring about one another's happiness, that belief assumes not only that happiness is valuable, but also that mutual concern would promote happiness. If mutual concern did not, in fact, promote overall happiness, Mill would oppose it on exactly the same utilitarian grounds he relies on in its defense. His central concern is not with whether people should care about each other's happiness, but with whether happiness is a good in itself, and so desirable as an end.

The last of the three claims Mill makes in the letter—that if A's happiness is a good, and B's is, and C's is, then their happiness taken together is a good as well—is, as I have mentioned, generally thought to turn on a fallacy of composition. Clearly, if the initial claims were that A's hap-

---

[39] Given Mill's views, everything that contributes to the happiness of the person in question will thereby count as good (either in itself or as a means), but not everything that is good will contribute to the happiness of that person. At the same time, what a person values (what is good according to that person) may or may not, on Mill's account, actually be good; whether it is depends upon whether it contributes to someone's happiness—either to the happiness of that person or someone else's. Also, what might otherwise not be good may be made so by the person valuing it (though only if, in fact, it brings her happiness).

[40] At the very least, they benefit. Of course, if unhappiness is bad, then the costs of one person being unhappy will be compounded by others caring about her.

piness is a good to A, B's a good to B, and C's a good to C, there would be no grounds for thinking that A's happiness, combined with B's, combined with C's, would be good to anyone, yet it would still be plausible to think it good to the group, which is all that Mill claims in giving the proof. Whether there would be grounds for thinking that the fact that each person's happiness is good *simpliciter* (as opposed to good to someone) shows that "the sum of all these goods must be a good" depends upon what sort of feature the value of happiness is supposed to be.

Commonly, worries about the move from the value of each person's happiness to the value of the general happiness—happiness, no matter whose—focus on Mill's claim that the general happiness is a good to the aggregate of all people. This claim, many assume, is what Mill sets out to establish in order to defend utilitarianism. Yet given Mill's understanding of what it is for something to be a *good to* someone, this claim turns on his already having established what is at issue: that the general happiness is a good in itself. Thus, when Mill writes that "happiness is a good: that each person's happiness is a good to that person, and the general happiness, therefore, a good to the aggregate of persons," the key claim is what precedes the colon: that "happiness is a good." What follows the colon are corollaries of the key claim, not what is primarily at issue.

The key claim, in Mill's eyes, is established, in light of the principle of evidence, by each person desiring her own happiness. Redeploying the same argument form in the rest of the chapter, the claim that happiness (no matter whose) is the only thing desirable as an end is supposed to be established, in light of the same principle, by each person desiring only her own happiness as an end. Analogous corollaries follow: that each person's happiness is the only thing good, as an end, to that person, and that the general happiness is the only thing good, as an end, to the aggregate of all persons.

In thinking about the value of happiness, it is important to mark the difference between what a person might have reason to do and what she might have reason to think is good. Mill seems prepared to acknowledge that a person has reason to do only what contributes to her own happiness—what is a good to her. That is, at least in part, why morality calls for sanctions and why it recommends working to make it so that people value the welfare of others (so that when others do well, one benefits also).

Recognizing the difference between what people have reason to do and what they have reason to think is especially important when it comes to understanding what Mill is trying to prove, and what he is not trying to prove, in Chapter IV. On the one hand, he is trying to convince someone who thinks of her own happiness as being the only thing that is valuable that she is mistaken. He is arguing, using that person's own commitments, that happiness, no matter whose, is valuable. That is, he is offering her reason to think that other people's happiness is good. On the other hand, he is not trying to convince people that they are *rationally* required to sacrifice their own happiness for the happiness of others—only that they are sometimes *morally* required to do so. He is addressing those who wonder whether other people's happiness matters, and arguing that it is valuable, even as he never tries to convince them that it matters to them, that is, that the happiness of others is a good to them.

Focusing on the claim that happiness (no matter whose) is a good, rather than that the general happiness is a good to each or a good to the aggregate of all persons, does not, of course, remove the central puzzle concerning the move from the desire for one's own happiness to the desirability of happiness (no matter whose). After all, it sure seems as if a person's desire for her own happiness commits her, at most, to the value of her own happiness, not to the value of happiness *per se*, just as seeing one's own car as red commits one to its redness, but not to the redness of anyone else's car. Still, focusing on the claim that the general happiness is a good does help to bring out that Mill is not trying to argue that the general happiness is a good to each and every person.

If this is the case, however, how is the move from the desire for one's own happiness to the desirability of happiness (no matter whose), supposed to go? A parallel question arises, to bring Kant in now, when Kant turns to defending the principle that people ought to treat not just themselves, but all other rational beings as well, as ends and not merely as means. According to Kant,

> The ground of such a principle is this: rational nature exists as an end in itself. In this way man necessarily thinks of his own existence; thus far is it a subjective principle of human actions. But in this way also does every other rational being think of his existence on the same rational ground that holds also for me; hence it is at the same time an objective principle, from which, as a supreme practical ground, all laws of the will must be able to be derived.[41]

Kant here is assuming that people all see themselves as valuable as ends, and assuming too that this view is (rationally) grounded by their thinking that "rational nature exists as an end in itself." With these assumptions in place, he is then arguing that the very reason people have for valuing themselves as ends—that the rational nature they possess exists as an end in itself—commits them to the value, as ends, of all who possess a rational nature.[42] Similarly, I believe, Mill is assuming that

---

[41] Kant, *Grounding*, 36 (Ak. p. 429).

[42] Needless to say, one might doubt that all people see themselves as Kant supposes they do, or doubt that those who do are relying on the grounds he supposes. Still, if he is right about these commitments, his argument kicks in directly.

people all see their own happiness as valuable as an end, and assuming too that this view is (rationally) grounded on their seeing happiness as valuable in itself. With these assumptions in place, he is then arguing that the very reason people have for valuing their own happiness—that the happiness they would enjoy is good in itself—commits them to the value of happiness no matter who happens to enjoy it.[43]

In both cases, the argument turns on the rational ground people (supposedly) have for their commitments. So it is worth trying to bring out what is distinctive about the sort of grounds Kant and Mill each attribute to people as underwriting their valuing, as they do, either their own happiness or their rational nature (or whatever). To bring out what is distinctive, imagine a rich, luscious, moist chocolate cake (which, I will be assuming, is a lot like happiness, at least in its being desirable). The cake may be predivided into proprietary slices—one is mine or mine to have, another is yours, etc.—or the pieces of cake may not be anyone's in particular, even if one person's getting some slice means that no one else can get that slice (and even if some may end up with none).

In the first case, in desiring a piece of cake I might specifically be desiring only my own piece and not someone else's (though of course I might also be desiring yours). In the second case, while I might selfishly desire certain pieces for myself, those pieces are not originally mine and may end up being someone else's. In the first case, but not the second, *that the piece is mine (or mine to have)* may be my reason for desiring it, and I may, in desiring it, be seeing *my* piece (or my having my piece) as valuable without additionally having, or being committed to, any views about other people's pieces. In the second case, in contrast, that the piece is mine will (by hypothesis) not be in play. Instead, whatever it is about the cake that I am desiring, and so desiring for myself, is something the cake may still have if someone else were to get it.[44] In seeing the cake as valuable (and so worth getting for myself), I therefore seem to be committed to thinking that if you should get it rather than me, you have gotten something good. Of course, I am not committed to desiring that you get it, nor to thinking that your getting it is a good to me. However, the grounds I have for thinking it would be a good to me, were I to get it, appear to

---

[43] Needless to say, one might doubt that all people see their own happiness as Mill supposes they do, or doubt that those who do are relying on the grounds he supposes. Still, if he is right about these commitments, the argument kicks in directly.

[44] In this second case there may well be two desires in play, one depending on the other, with the first being, in effect, a matter of seeing the cake as good, and the second being a matter of seeing getting the cake as good because it is the getting of something good. The second desire, of course, does not always follow upon the first, for a number of reasons. For instance, it may be that what one sees as good about the cake is something one cannot get, or it may be that one could get it, but only at the expense of someone else's not getting the cake, where that other person's getting the cake would be better. Note also that the second desire might be present without the first, since all the second requires is that one accept (perhaps as the content of a belief) the value of what it is that one desires for oneself.

commit me to thinking that you would be getting something good were you to get it.

It is important here to keep in mind the contrast between my desiring the pleasure I might get from the cake and my desiring the cake.[45] If it is the pleasure I desire (for myself), then my commitment vis-à-vis you would be to seeing your getting a similar pleasure as your getting something good. If the cake does not bring you that pleasure, then in getting a piece of the cake you would not be getting what I take to be good about it, and the difference could consistently be seen by me as making all the difference. What I cannot consistently do is see as valuable some feature of the cake, value getting the cake for myself on those grounds, and then deny that when you get it (with that feature), you get something good.

Analogously, if each of us is, in desiring happiness, desiring not merely *our own* happiness, but desiring happiness (for some nonproprietary feature of it) for ourselves, we cannot consistently then deny that when someone else gets happiness (with that feature), they get something good. Of course, again, we are not committed to desiring that someone else get it, nor to thinking that their getting it is a good to us. Nevertheless, the grounds we each have for thinking it would be a good to us, were we to get it, appear to commit us each to thinking that in getting it, someone else would be getting something good. Analogously too, if the grounds I have for thinking of my rational nature as an end are not originally proprietary, if the features they appeal to are features that your rational nature has no less than does mine, then in seeing my own as valuable as an end on those grounds, I am committed likewise to the value of your rational nature on exactly the same grounds.

Needless to say, so far nothing has been said in defense of the view that we desire our own happiness on grounds that are nonproprietary in the relevant sense, nor has any case been made for thinking that we view ourselves as ends on grounds that are appropriately nonproprietary. Although I will say something on Mill and Kant's behalf in defense of the nonproprietary character of the grounds of our evaluative commitments, my concern is not to defend either Mill's or Kant's substantive premise concerning our fundamental (and in Kant's case, necessary) evaluative commitments. Rather, my concern is to bring out the general force of the argument form they are offering, not the specific applications they present.

In thinking through Mill's version of the argument, and keeping the cake example in mind, we need to distinguish between two ways people might be thinking of happiness—one proprietary, the other not—when they are desiring their own happiness. It might be that they desire their

---

[45] It is also important here to keep in mind the contrast between my desiring *my own* pleasure, which I might get from the cake, and my desiring the pleasure (conceived of in nonproprietary terms) for myself. The former puts us back in the first case, where the relevant objects of desire come in proprietary packets, whereas the latter simply shifts from a case where it is the cake that is seen as valuable to one in which the pleasure is.

own happiness, where the happiness is being conceived of *as theirs*, as coming already divided up into proprietary packets that either belong to them or are something they will get. Alternatively, it might be that they desire happiness for themselves, where the happiness is being conceived of originally in terms of what it is like independent of who has it. In a similar way, in thinking through Kant's version of the argument, we need to distinguish between two ways people might be thinking of their own rational nature. It might be that they think of their own rational nature as existing as an end, where the rational nature is being conceived of *as theirs*, as coming already divided up into proprietary packets. Alternatively, it might be that the rational nature they think of as existing as an end is being conceived of originally in terms of what it is like independent of whose it is.

These differences make a big difference to the content of the evaluative position one is, from the start of each argument, supposed to have concerning the value of one's own happiness or rational nature. These initial evaluative positions are what Mill and Kant, each in their own way, set out to leverage into a commitment concerning the value of other people's happiness or rational nature. Predictably, how their arguments might go depends a great deal on what the initial evaluative position is supposed to be and whether what is valued is conceived of in proprietary terms or not. With this in mind, three distinct arguments are apparently in the offing, any of which might be attributed either to Mill or to Kant. The first two take the evaluative starting point to be proprietary, whereas the third does not. For ease of exposition, I focus primarily on Mill's suggestion that the commitments in question would concern happiness (either one's own, or *simpliciter*); the same arguments could, on Kant's behalf, be made substituting in a commitment to the value of rational nature (either one's own, or *simpliciter*), as I will note along the way.

According to one argument, the evaluative starting point is that each thinks "My own happiness is valuable," and so each has reason to think of others—given that others are in a parallel situation with respect to their own happiness—that they similarly think that their own happiness is valuable. Our positions, with respect to our own happiness, appear to be perfectly symmetrical. This, it might seem, puts pressure on anyone who would presume to think that he, and his happiness, stand out from the crowd. The symmetry, assuming it is in place, does establish that each person has as much reason as any other to think of her own happiness as valuable.[46] However, this does not translate into a reason for each to think of the happiness of others as valuable. Indeed, the argument does not even begin to give someone reason to believe that anyone else's happiness is valuable. The argument relies on our being symmetrically situated

---

[46] That is, as much reason as any other if the only reason anyone has is found in her own happiness appearing to her to be good.

with respect to our thinking *as we do*, and not with respect to *what we are thinking*—we are each seeing our own happiness, and not each other's, as valuable. Thus, the argument depends not at all on the content of the original evaluative premise, and so does not move to a conclusion informed by that content. Rather, it shows that we have to admit that, if others bear the same relation to their happiness that we bear to our own (that of "thinking it valuable"), then they, like us, will have grounds for thinking that their own happiness is valuable that parallel those we have for thinking our own is. Yet granting this is perfectly compatible with denying the value of others' happiness. Therefore, the symmetry considerations do not establish that people are committed to acknowledging the value of other people's happiness. As a result, it is pretty clearly not the argument Mill has in mind. For a similar reason, it is pretty clearly not the sort of argument Kant has in mind either. At most it would establish, with suitable adjustments to the supposed initial evaluative position, that we each have reason to think of others—given that others are in a parallel situation with respect to their own rational natures—that they similarly *think of* their own rational natures as ends, whereas the principle Kant is trying to establish would have it that rational nature, no matter whose, *is* an end.[47]

According to the second argument, the evaluative starting point is again each thinking "My own happiness is valuable," but this fact about each person is taken *as evidence*, with respect to each bit of happiness that is valued, that that bit is valuable. Each person is then seen as having reason to think that the happiness she enjoys is valuable, and reason to think of others—given that the others are in a parallel situation with respect to the happiness that they enjoy—that their happiness is such that there is the same evidence available to each for the value of the happiness that he or she enjoys as there is for the value of one's own happiness. If happiness is such that every piece of it is desired by someone, then it seems as if, in taking ourselves to have reason to see the bit we value as valuable, we are committed to acknowledging the value of all the rest. Analogously, the argument in Kant's hands would use as an evaluative starting point each person thinking "My own rational nature is valuable as an end," and take this fact about each as evidence, with respect to each person's rational nature that is valued, that it is valuable as an end. Each person is then seen as having reason to think of her own rational nature as an end, and reason to think of others—given that the others are in a parallel situation with respect to their own rational natures—that their rational natures are such that there is the same evidence available to each for the value of his or her rational nature as there is for the value of one's

---

[47] If the rational ground we each have for thinking of our own rational nature as an end has this standing turn, in each case, on the rational nature being *one's own*, then we would each only be committed to holding that for each person, his or her rational nature is an end for him or her.

own. If every rational being is such that her rational nature is thought of by her as an end, then it seems as if, in taking ourselves to have reason to see our own rational nature as an end, we are committed to acknowledging that other people's rational natures are likewise to be seen as ends. Unlike the first argument, this one does, if successful, move to an appropriate conclusion. Of course, its success depends on each person having reason to think of her own happiness, or rational nature, as valuable, as an end.

A structurally similar argument might be offered in response to someone who sees part of an elephant and wonders whether there is a whole visible elephant before her. If someone or other stands in relation to each part of the elephant in the same way that she stands to the part she takes herself as having reason to think is visible—because she seems to see it—then, if she knows of the others' situation, she has reason to think that they have an equally good reason to think of each part they (seem to) see as being visible. If each and every part of the elephant is such that someone (seems to) see it, then she has reason to think the whole elephant is visible even though she herself only sees a part of it.

We can use this elephant example to see the weakness of the second argument. The others do, I think, each have a reason as good as hers (because the same) for thinking that what appears visible to them is visible. This does not mean, however, that the reason they each individually have is equally a reason for her. After all, the force of the reason is supposed to depend, in the elephant case, on the person having a visual experience of the appropriate kind. Each has the same sort of visual experience with respect to some part or other of the elephant, but the person in question does not have that experience with respect to the parts she does not (seem to) see—thus, whatever evidence *she* has of those parts is not itself visual evidence of the kind in question.

In a similar way, when it comes to happiness, each person may have a reason as good as another's (because the same) for thinking that what appears valuable is valuable. This does not mean, however, that the reason they each individually have is equally a reason for others. While we might grant that we each have evidence concerning the value of our own happiness (thanks to it being such that we each find our own happiness to be good), there is room to worry that the fact that someone else sees something as good (that is, desires it) neither constitutes nor provides evidence for me that it is. In the case of happiness, the force of one's reason for thinking that the general happiness is valuable is supposed to depend on the person addressed by the argument having a desiderative experience of the appropriate kind. Each person has the same sort of desiderative experience with respect to some part or other of the general happiness, but people will not be having that experience with respect to the parts they do not desire—thus, whatever evidence one has concerning another's happiness is not itself desiderative evidence of the kind in question. The same point carries over to the grounds one might have for viewing one's own rational nature as an end.

Across the board, the argument brings out that, if others stand in the same relation to their own view of the elephant, or their own happiness, or their rational nature, as one stands to one's own, then one is committed to acknowledging that they have the same kind of reason to think as they do as one has for one's own view. However, this argument leaves those to whom it is addressed with no reason, so far, to think that other people's happiness is valuable, nor any reason to think that their rational natures are ends, even when one does have reason to think that of one's own happiness or rational nature. Moreover, even if we assume that other people's experiences can provide us with the appropriate evidence concerning the value of what appears good to them (by assumption, their own happiness), we would have evidence that happiness, no matter whose, is valuable only if everyone actually values (i.e., desires) his or her own happiness. Furthermore, we would somehow have to take account of the fact that some people desire that others not be happy, which, on this argument, would seem to count as evidence that other people's happiness is not good after all.

According to the third argument, the one I think Mill is actually offering, the evaluative starting point is that people (in desiring happiness) are thinking "Happiness is valuable" and, on that basis, wanting it for themselves. It takes this fact not as new evidence that might be added to or balanced against other evidence, but as reflecting an evaluative commitment each person already has on board. Then, in light of that commitment, the argument points out to each person that if what is valuable (on one's own view) is the happiness one wants to enjoy, then when someone else happens to get happiness, one is committed already to the value of what that other person gets. The argument thus appeals to something each person shows herself to accept in her desiring happiness for herself, and plays out what this implies—namely, that whether or not one happens to desire that other people be happy, if they have some share of happiness, then they have something of value. Analogously, again with suitable adjustments, this third argument, in Kant's hands, starts with people valuing their own rational natures as ends on the grounds that "Rational nature *per se* is an end." It takes this fact not as new evidence, but as reflecting an evaluative commitment each person already (and, according to Kant, necessarily) has on board. Then, in light of that commitment, the argument points out to each that if others similarly possess a rational nature, one is committed already to their standing as ends.

Significantly, this argument (whether in Kant's hands or Mill's) is directed at a broad audience: (i) those who are selfish and act as though they are the only thing of value; (ii) those who are skeptical and wonder why they should think someone else matters, given that they do not happen to care; and (iii) those who are committed to morality, but are unclear what is of value. At the same time, while the argument does rely on appealing to people's already-present commitment either to the value of the happiness they hope for or to their standing as ends insofar as they are rational, these suppositions concerning people's commitments are each widely accepted and not at all implausible.

As Sidgwick pointed out, however, this third argument, in depending on the idea that people have such nonproprietary commitments, leaves unaddressed those who hold that at bottom what is of value is *their own* happiness, not happiness *per se*, or that it is *their own* rational nature, not rational nature *per se*, that is an end.[48] Such people do not have the sort of initial commitment that the argument needs in order to extend beyond the case of the person to whom it is being addressed. Thus, a person with the appropriately proprietary fundamental desire for happiness, or conviction concerning her own rational nature, can perfectly consistently deny the value of other people's happiness and their standing, in virtue of their rational natures, as ends.

Mill and Kant might just have overlooked this possibility. However, I suspect that they thought there was something evidently untenable about having a proprietary evaluative commitment that is not underwritten by an evaluative commitment that is not proprietary. In any case, neither Mill nor Kant takes the possibility seriously, and it is not very difficult to find an argument that might back up their casual neglect of this view.

In valuing something (my happiness or my rational nature, say), there must be something I see as good about it. Whatever that feature is, it cannot be simply it being mine or my getting it, since obviously plenty of things that are mine, or that I do get, are not valuable at all. However, whatever other feature it might be will be a property potentially possessed by things that are not mine. For instance, if what is good about my happiness (according to me) is how it feels, then I am committed to thinking that this same feeling, if enjoyed by someone else, is good as well; likewise, if what is good about my rational nature (according to me) is the autonomy that it makes possible, then I am committed to thinking that same autonomy, if enjoyed by someone else, is good as well. Of course, this leaves room for the person who thinks that the crucial property is not simply *x being mine* but *x being my happiness* or *my rational nature*. If someone holds such a view, though, it is natural to ask her, What is special about your happiness or your rational nature if it is not merely that it is yours (which we have ruled out) and not some general feature of it that might be shared by someone else's? The point is not that someone could not hold this view, but that in holding it one would have no account of what is special about one's happiness or rational nature that distinguishes it alone as being of value. Needless to say, that one lacks such an account is not by itself a reductio of one's view, since any account

[48] Sidgwick, *The Methods of Ethics*, 420.

of value has to stop somewhere, with some feature or other that is supposed to account for the value of what has it. Nonetheless, it seems that
stopping one's account of value with an irredeemably proprietary property is not at all plausible.

Alternatively, of course, someone might reject altogether the idea that
happiness (or anything else) is good *simpliciter*, and hold that the important evaluative notion is "good to someone or other." Neither Kant nor
Mill ever explicitly considers this option; I suspect Mill, at least, supposed
it was not an option precisely because he assumed that for something to
be a good to someone requires that it be good *simpliciter*. Interestingly,
Moore later does explicitly consider—if only to reject out of hand—the
suggestion that something might be good to me, or "my own good,"
without being good *simpliciter* (or, as Moore puts it, "absolutely"). Moore
claims:

> When . . . I talk of anything I get as 'my own good,' I must mean
> either that the thing I get is good, or that my possessing it is good. In
> both cases it is only the thing or the possession of it which is *mine*,
> and not *the goodness* of that thing or that possession. . . . The *good* of
> it can in no possible sense be 'private' or belong to me; any more than
> a thing can exist privately or *for* one person only. The only reason I
> can have for aiming at 'my own good,' is that it is *good absolutely* that
> what I so call should belong to me—*good absolutely* that I should *have*
> something, which, if I have it, others cannot have. But if it is *good*
> *absolutely* that I should have it, then everyone else has as much reason
> for aiming at my having it, as I have myself. If, therefore, it is true
> of any single man's 'interest' or 'happiness' that it ought to be his
> sole ultimate end, this can only mean that *that* man's 'interest' or
> 'happiness' is the *sole good*. . . . What Egoism holds, therefore, is that
> *each* man's happiness is the sole good—that a number of different
> things are each of them the only good thing there is—an absolute
> contradiction.[49]

No such argument can be found in Kant or Mill, and it has its own
problems. Nevertheless, it expresses an intuitively attractive view, and I
suspect that it captures the sort of considerations that Kant and Mill
would have for not taking seriously the thought that, in seeing *x* as good
to me, I am doing anything other than seeing *x* as good and hoping to get
some of it (or seeing my getting it as good *simpliciter*). So natural is this
understanding of people's values, even of the values of those who are
obviously selfish, that I think Kant and Mill would understandably (even

[49] G. E. Moore, *Principia Ethica*, 98-99. I am not here recommending this as a sound
argument, only as one that gives voice, as if they are obvious, to the sort of assumptions I
am supposing Mill made without comment.

if, perhaps, not justifiably) treat the alternative as not borne out by the facts of human psychology.[50]

In any case, when it comes to appreciating the structure of Mill's argument, the important point is that he takes it that people come to the argument, so to speak, already committed to thinking of happiness *per se* as worth getting. Such a commitment is revealed, he thinks, by people's desires, and specifically by what they desire as ends and not merely as a means to something else. Happiness is at least among the things we desire in this way, according to Mill, and it is also all that we desire in this way. Were he right, then all the evidence, and the only evidence, one could use in determining what is worthwhile would end up appealing to happiness as the final arbitrator—so his argument goes.

Bradley, I think, comes close to seeing the point of Mill's argument when he notes that "[i]f many pigs are fed at one trough, each desires his own food, and somehow as a consequence does seem to desire the food of all; and by parity of reasoning it should follow that each pig, desiring his own pleasure, desires also the pleasure of all."[51] Mill, of course, never claims that people do desire the general happiness. He is trying to argue from the fact that people desire their own happiness to their being committed to acknowledging the value of the happiness of others. So there is no move in the argument from "people desire their own happiness" to "people 'somehow as a consequence' desire the happiness of all." Rather, from the fact that people desire their own happiness, Mill takes it that they think of their happiness as desirable, that is, as good. A proper understanding of their state, he assumes, is as one of desiring some happiness, because it is good, for themselves. The happiness desired does not, on Mill's view, come prepackaged in proprietary bundles. Instead, it is a kind of thing different people can enjoy in different degrees and hope to get for themselves or others. Thus, the idea is that in desiring happiness for myself, I am thinking of the happiness as good, and (selfishly) wanting it for myself. Should someone else get what I am after, I am committed (by considerations of consistency) to acknowledge that they got something good.

Even if Mill is wrong about what people in fact desire as an end—if, say, they value honesty, or respect, or freedom as ends—the strategy underlying the argument remains in place, although it would presumably recommend a different conclusion. For the underlying strategy is to rely on the initial evaluative commitments people find themselves with and show that considerations of consistency based on the content of these commitments carry further, and perhaps unexpected, commitments in their wake.

---

[50] That is not to say that they would be right. It would be a tricky and interesting challenge to try to settle whether people might ever have the sort of proprietary desire that Moore explicitly rejects as incoherent and Mill implicitly rejects as something we do not have.

[51] Bradley, *Ethical Studies*, 113.

The very same strategy is in place in Kant's argument, though of course the initial evaluative commitment he relies on differs significantly from Mill's in both its content and its standing as a necessary rather than contingent commitment. According to Kant, recall, "man *necessarily* thinks of his own existence" as "an end in itself" [emphasis added], and in so thinking, Kant holds, the very same rational ground is in play for each person: that "rational nature exists as an end in itself." That is, we all (supposedly necessarily) take it that rational nature, as opposed to *our own* rational nature only, is an end, and it is this commitment we each have that carries with it a commitment (often not acknowledged in action) that all others who have rational natures are likewise ends, and not merely means.

Why should one believe that each person (necessarily or not) thinks of her own existence as an end in itself? Furthermore, even if each person does, why should one believe that the ground each person has is not, in the respects relevant for the argument, proprietary? Mightn't each person think of her own rational nature as an end in itself without thinking that rational nature *simpliciter* shares that status? Needless to say, some argument—and presumably a pretty hefty one—is needed here to underwrite attributing to people the initial commitment upon which Kant relies. Nonetheless, with that commitment in place, Kant's argument, just like Mill's, supposes that a proprietary commitment must be grounded on a nonproprietary one, and moves on to show that the content of the latter sort of commitment inevitably extends to a like commitment concerning the value (in this case, as an end) of others. If the argument's premises are allowed, what the argument shows is that even someone who acts as if others are valuable as means only is committed to holding that, in fact, those others are valuable as ends in themselves—committed by the very view she relies on in holding that she herself is valuable as an end in herself.

Kant's claim that people *necessarily* think of rational nature as an end in itself puts an interesting twist on the argument. Mill, in contrast, apparently thinks of people's commitment to the value of their own happiness as merely a contingent commitment; if Mill is right, then it seems as if one could back out of the commitment to the value of other people's happiness by giving up the initial commitment to the value of the happiness one secures for oneself.[52] Whereas, if the commitment is necessarily had, then there is no room to back off of the initial commitment in light of its implications.

Interestingly, while this difference matters substantially to how one might respond in the face of the respective arguments, the necessity in

---

[52] Just how contingent the commitment is on Mill's view is a little unclear. He does, after all, claim that "to desire anything, except in proportion as the idea of it is pleasant, is a physical and metaphysical impossibility" (Mill, *Utilitarianism*, IV, 10). However, his grounds for this strong claim are less than clear, to say the least.

Kant's argument does not in itself augment its strength. What Kant claims to be necessary is not the truth of the commitment—that rational nature exists as an end in itself—but rather the thinking of it as true. Were the commitment necessarily true, of course, that would, assuming the validity of the argument that extends the commitment from the first-person case to that of others, make the argument as strong as can be. However, to discover (if it is a discovery) that people necessarily think of themselves in a certain way appears no more grounds for thinking that the implications of what they think are true than would exist if they thought as they did only contingently.

Nonetheless, if it is true that people necessarily think of themselves in a certain way, then from the point of view of each person, the content of that thought is available, and indeed inevitably available, as grounds for them to reach the conclusion it supports. Hence, while the necessity of the belief does not constitute extra evidence for what the content of the belief entails, the necessity of the believing does ensure the availability of the evidence (so thought of from the first-person point of view) needed to establish the conclusion. Each person considering the argument will, in the relevant sense, have the evidence needed for the conclusion of the argument—and necessarily so—even though the fact that each person necessarily has the belief the content of which is her evidence is not itself additional evidence. More accurately, it is not additional evidence absent some special account in light of which the fact that we necessarily think as we do is, in the case at hand, grounds for believing we are right. There are suggestions of such a special account in Kant's work, but pursuing them would take us away from considering the central form of argument that Kant and Mill share.[53]

This central form of argument starts with an evaluative commitment, to the effect either that happiness is good or that rational nature exists as an end in itself. It then extends this commitment from its initial role—underwriting the value we each place either on our own happiness or on our own rational nature—to a new role: underwriting as valuable the happiness of others or the standing of others as ends. The extension, as I have been emphasizing, turns on the initial commitment not being essentially proprietary, on its scope not being in the first instance limited in its application to the person who holds it. Whether Mill was right to assume, and Kant to maintain, that the relevant commitment satisfies this constraint is, of course, highly contentious. If one or the other is right, however, then his argument goes through fallacy-free.

Acknowledging that other people's happiness is valuable, or that other people are ends in themselves, is not yet to accept that one has reason to

---

[53] In offering the argument I am focusing on, Kant takes the claim concerning people's initial (and supposedly necessary) commitment as a postulate. It is defended in Kant, *Grounding*, sec. 3, 49–61 (Ak. pp. 446–63).

promote their happiness, or to respond to their standing as ends in them-selves. As a result, there seems to be room to accept either Mill's argu-ment or Kant's argument and yet still hold that one has no reason oneself to promote the admittedly valuable happiness of others or to respond to the recognized standing of others as ends in themselves.

There are, I think, two sides to Mill's position here. On the one hand, he apparently thinks, or at least is allowing the possibility, that one has reason to do only what is or will provide a good to oneself. Thus, in *Utilitarianism's* chapter on the sanctions of morality, Mill emphasizes the importance of arranging things so that people find themselves with rea-son to do as morality demands. On the other hand, he also seems simply to assume that the right thing for a person to do is always whatever is among the best of her options, where the value of the options is seen as not a matter of what is a good to the agent. He therefore seems to share with Sidgwick and Moore the assumption, to use Sidgwick's words, that "as a rational being I am bound to aim at good generally—so far as it is attainable by my efforts—not merely at a particular part of it."[54]

Put this way, Mill seems simply inconsistent. I think the inconsistency disappears, however, once Sidgwick's view that it is a requirement *of rationality* that one "aim at good generally" is distinguished from Mill's view that the standard of behavior—though *not* specifically the standard of rationality—is found in the requirement that one take (but, by the way, not necessarily aim at) one of the best available options, where the quality of options is determined by their contributions to the overall good.[55] Thus, I think, Mill is assuming that he and his opponents, and indeed everyone, accept the view that the right thing to do—what one should do—is whatever is best. All the contentious issues, he thinks, have to do with the nature of value, with egoists thinking myopically that only their own happiness is valuable, and others arguing that something distinct from happiness is valuable. Mill's main aim is to argue that those who embrace egoism do so (at least implicitly) on grounds that commit them to acknowledging the value of the happiness of others, and that those who embrace the value of something that appears different from happi-ness are always (at least implicitly) relying on the very same grounds as their standard, and so are likewise committed to acknowledging the value

[54] Sidgwick, *The Methods of Ethics*, 382. This is just the assumption Broad takes on, arguing that someone might acknowledge the equal value of others' happiness, but hold that each person "has an obligation to produce good experiences and dispositions in himself, and no such direct obligation to produce them in . . . anyone else." C. D. Broad, "Moore's Ethical Doctrines," in Paul Schilpp, ed., *The Philosophy of G. E. Moore* (La Salle, IL: Open Court, 1968), 45.

[55] As I understand Mill's position here, he is defending happiness as being the "sole end of human action, and the promotion of it the test by which to judge of all human conduct," but seeing morality and rationality as each "parts included in the whole," with neither being identical to the fundamental test of conduct, and each being different from the other. On his view, rationality is concerned specifically with what is good to the agent in a way that morality is not. Mill, *Utilitarianism*, IV, 9.

of the happiness of others (and themselves). Still, Mill consciously makes room for holding, and holds himself, that only what contributes to the happiness of a person is a good to that person, and that what a person has reason to pursue may be limited to what might be good to that person. Of course, when a person successfully does what she has reason to do, it is still open to others to criticize her for not acting morally.[56]

VI. CONCLUSION

My concern from the start has been to figure out how someone as smart as Mill could have offered an argument that looks as bad as his "proof" does. I have argued that his proof looks so bad—looks, to tell the truth, as if it is composed of a relentless series of fallacies—because the real argument of the proof is not what it appears to be. In fact, I maintain, the actual argument Mill offers contains not a single fallacy and, if only the initial premises were true, would be compelling.

In broadest terms, and so the most plausible terms, the argument's strategy is to identify a commitment people are all supposed to share (either as a matter of fact, in Mill's case, or necessarily, in Kant's) and then show that considerations of consistency alone bring further, and often contested (or at least not acknowledged), commitments in the wake of the initial one. It thus begins not by defending the truth of the initial commitment—an undertaking that would lead to an infinite regress—but instead by defending the claim that the commitment is available as a premise thanks to what people already accept. As a result, the argument is designed to accommodate well the fact that no evaluative conclusion will follow from purely nonevaluative premises.

In slightly less broad terms, and so a little more contentiously, the argument's strategy turns on the initial commitment being to the value or importance of some consideration that is generic rather than proprietary—to the value or importance of happiness *per se* or of rational nature considered as such, as opposed to the value or importance of only one's own happiness or one's own rational nature. If, in fact, people only had proprietary commitments, then considerations of consistency would never move people beyond what they are already assumed to acknowledge. However, if the commitment is, as arguments of this form suppose, to the significance of some generic feature, then the argument on hand gets the leverage required to establish that the significance of that feature carries implications for the significance of others. Given the right sort of initial commitment, arguments of this form can provide a person with

---

[56] In at least some cases, the criticism will also involve the claim that she is failing to care about what is of value. In such a case, the criticism will run, she has reason to value what she does not value, and in failing to value it finds herself without reason to do what she should.

reason to think that other people's happiness is of value (whether or not the person ends up valuing it), or with reason to think that other people are ends in themselves (whether or not the person ends up treating others as ends). The point of such arguments is to provide each person with reason to accept a certain claim as justified.[57]

In still less broad terms, and so even more contentiously, the argument's strategy turns on the particular initial commitment being to the value of happiness *simpliciter* (in Mill's version of the argument) or to the standing of rational nature considered in itself as an end (in Kant's version of the argument). Of course, even among those who share the view (perhaps because of the sort of argument that Moore offers) that people are committed to the significance of some generic feature or other, differences concerning just what features might play this role make a huge difference to the conclusions that could be established by the sort of argument used by Mill and Kant. My own hunch—and a source of my half-heartedness in defending Mill's "proof"—is that Moore is right that in valuing things, people are inevitably committed to the significance of some generic feature or other, but that Mill and Kant are both wrong in thinking that there is one single such commitment. Perhaps some people are committed to thinking of happiness *per se* as valuable in itself, and other people are committed to thinking of rational nature, considered in itself, as an end. I suspect, however, that plenty of other people have significantly different commitments—each of which would invite application of the sort of argument Mill and Kant offer, but not in a way that would lead everyone to a shared commitment.

Philosophy, University of North Carolina, Chapel Hill

---

[57] Such arguments thus leave open, in an interesting way, what the implications of the defended standard might be when it comes to what people should value. For all such an argument shows, it might be that the standard defended turns around and requires of people that they value something different than what has been defended as valuable. Indeed, it is a familiar fact about some versions of utilitarianism that they might require rejecting utilitarianism on utilitarian grounds.

INDEX

Action, 68, 76, 120, 122, 132, 140–41, 152, 181, 198, 201, 208–9, 213, 220, 239, 241 n. 12, 251, 334; right, 280, 332
Aesthetics, 196
Agency, 122, 149, 203 n. 15, 259, 294 n. 65, 312
Agent-neutrality, 115, 123, 125, 132 n. 12, 141
Agent-relativity, 115, 123, 125, 132 n. 12
Agreement, 303–4, 318; hypothetical, 304, 311, 320–24, 328. *See also* Consent; Will
Altruism, 86–87
Amoralism, 12–13, 25, 35–36, 253–54, 265–66
Annas, Julia, 269 n. 15
Anscombe, G. E. M., 114, 259
Anthropology, 267, 285
Antirealism, 2–3, 50 n. 4, 85, 90–91
Antirealist-expressivism, 1–8, 37–38, 40–41. *See also* Expressivism
Appetites, 278–79
Aquinas, Thomas, 262
Aristotle, 177–78, 181–82, 197 n. 11, 198, 212, 245, 253, 255, 257–71, 273–85, 287–94, 298–99, 334 n. 13
Assertions, 8, 10, 16
Augustine, 263
Authority, 146–48, 150–53, 312, 313–14, 316, 329; of moral judgments, 68–70, 72, 74; political, 211
Autonomy, 122, 152, 227 n. 12, 305, 309 n. 20, 312, 322, 324, 353
Ayer, A. J., 8, 179, 184, 197, 239

Bach, Kent, 19 n. 34, 22 n. 39, 25
Baier, Kurt, 309 n. 18
Barker, Stephen, 40 n. 69
Beccaria, Cesare, 317
Belief, 40 n. 69, 45 n. 1, 92 n. 48, 96–98, 130–31, 134, 142, 224, 242, 244, 357; commitment to, 10 n. 16; and desire, 104–8, 110–14, 116–17, 132, 136–37, 139–40, 250, 279; empirical, 66–67, 72 n. 10, 144, 169, 300; and justification, 300, 301–2, 340; moral, 1–3, 7–14, 29–32, 34–35, 37–39, 40 n. 69, 41–43, 62, 64–69, 72, 76, 83, 87, 92, 99, 154, 162–63, 166, 169, 175, 241, 243, 252–53, 300, 302; and reasons, 137–38

Benevolence, 283–84
Bentham, Jeremy, 189, 271 n. 18
Berlin, Isaiah, 179, 203
Biology, 86–87, 94–95, 180
Blackburn, Simon, 3, 8–9, 38–39, 85–86, 92 n. 48
Boghossian, Paul, 91
Bourne, Randolph, 95 n. 56
Boyd, Richard, 164–65, 167, 170, 175
Bradley, F. H., 333 n. 9, 355
Brandt, Richard, 227, 229
Bratman, Michael, 30
Bravery, 240–42
Brink, David, 82, 94–97, 99–100
Broad, C. D., 185, 333 n. 9, 336 n. 18, 358 n. 54
Broome, John, 151 n. 50
Burke, Edmund, 206 n. 18

Carnap, Rudolph, 179
Categorical Imperative, 302, 306 n. 11, 321, 329, 331; and humanity formula, 307, 308 n. 15, 309, 311; and kingdom of ends formula, 304, 309, 310 n. 22, 311–13, 320–22; and universal law formula, 303–4, 307–13; and universal law of nature formula, 308
Causation, 9–10
Character, 261–62, 290–95, 297–99
Choice, 181, 195, 213, 259, 281, 291, 304, 306; freedom of, 198; hypothetical, 327; rational, 309, 327, 329
Citizens, 145, 304, 317 n. 54
Coercion, 148 n. 45
Cognitivism, 1, 4, 85 n. 30, 103, 154 n. 1, 156
Cohen, Joshua, 94, 98–100
Commitment, 77, 200, 237 n. 2, 331, 347, 355, 359–60; to belief, 10 n. 16; ethical, 9, 38, 43, 92 n. 48, 328–29; evaluative, 348–49, 352–53, 356–57
Communication, 21–24, 26
Community, 312; language, 107, 159; political, 311
Compassion, 296–97
Conativism, 1–2, 5–11 passim, 13–14, 21, 40
Concept of Mind, The (Ryle), 177 n. 1
Concepts, 133–34, 341
Conscience, 84, 207–8, 263

Consent, 317; actual, 302–8, 313, 318, 320–
22, 329; hypothetical, 302–5, 320, 329;
possible, 302–4, 309, 329. *See also* Agree-
ment; Will
Consequentialism, 127–28, 192, 332
Consilience, 81–82, 88, 93, 101 n. 81
Consistency, 137–38, 142
Constant, Benjamin, 276
Constitutions, 304, 314–20, 322, 325–27
Constructivism: Kantian, 300–302, 305,
327–29; Rawlsian, 302, 311
Contract: original, 302–4, 314–22, 325–27,
329; social, 314
Conventions, 321; linguistic, 16–17, 19–22,
24, 26, 30–31, 34–35, 37, 42–43; moral,
179. *See also* Practices
Cooper, John, 261 n. 7
Cooperation, 85 n. 30
Coordination, 85, 91 n. 46, 122
Copp, David, 89
Courage, 183, 240–41, 242 n. 14, 294–96
Crisp, Roger, 343 n. 38
Critique of Practical Reason, The (Kant), 152,
257
Culture, 181, 183, 193, 203–6, 208, 215

Darwall, Stephen, 2 n. 2, 119, 227, 233 n.
23
Darwin, Charles, 86
Davidson, Donald, 121
Decision, 32–34, 76–77, 138, 280
Deflationism, 2–5, 7, 9, 37, 46
Deigh, John, 84, 85 n. 28
Deliberation, 129, 131 n. 8, 136, 219, 222–
26, 229–30, 233, 235, 259–61, 269, 280;
moral, 64, 258, 324–25; practical, 66, 68,
249–50, 252, 254, 281
Deontology, 127–28
Derrida, Jacques, 215
Desires, 115, 119–20, 131, 135, 141, 191,
228, 234 n. 24, 251–52, 261, 265, 272,
282, 285, 292, 297, 339, 347; and
belief, 104–8, 110–14, 116–17, 132,
136–37, 139–40, 250, 279; and the
good, 134, 335–36, 340, 351–52; and
happiness, 270, 276, 330, 332–38, 339
n. 26, 340–42, 345–46, 348–49, 353,
355; and reason, 258, 277–78, 280–81,
293, 298; and reasons, 129–30, 132–33,
136, 138–40, 142–47, 149–52, 218; and
value, 132–34, 336, 340 n. 29. *See also*
Passions
Devitt, Michael, 4 n. 7
Dewey, John, 177, 189–94, 198, 216
Dialectical equilibrium, 169, 175
Disagreement, 55–57, 64, 66, 69, 72, 74–75,
77, 166–67, 170, 175, 192–94, 210, 213–
14, 216; diachronic, 159, 163; synchronic, 158–59, 163

Discursive subjects, 103–4, 106–7, 109–11,
113–23, 127
Dispositions, 45 n. 1, 290, 296, 299
Donnellan, Keith, 159, 171
Dreier, James, 25 n. 45
Dummett, Michael, 16 n. 29
Duties, 66 n. 4, 162, 205, 263–64, 276–77,
283–84, 288, 298, 314 n. 38; moral, 264,
266, 268–70, 282, 286, 295–96. *See also*
Obligation

Education, 263–64, 266, 279, 290, 344;
moral, 256, 292, 298
Egoism, 184, 285–86, 328–29, 342, 354, 358
Emotions, 281, 282 n. 50, 283–84, 285 n. 54
Emotivism, 59 n. 11, 184, 188, 213, 255
Empathy, 147 n. 43
Empiricism, 96, 189, 239, 241, 243, 335, 340
n. 29, 341
Endorsement, 30, 41–42, 118, 124
Enlightenment, the, 126, 179, 184, 216
*Enquiry Concerning the Principles of Morals,
An* (Hume), 173
Epistemology, 89–90, 93, 143–44, 155, 193–
94, 207, 242, 300; and intuitions, 46;
moral, 81, 102, 126, 177, 236, 238–39,
247–48, 254, 256, 300, 302. *See also*
Knowledge
Equality, 182, 319, 322, 326
Error theory, 54–59, 62
Ethics, 45 n. 1, 80 n. 9, 101, 102, 126, 156,
178, 214–15, 239; ancient *vs.* modern,
177–79, 236, 242, 246–48, 251 n. 31,
252–54, 256, 267–70; Aristotelian, 179,
182–83, 197 n. 11, 267–68; of aspiration,
263; existentialist, 198; Humean, 183–
85, 188; Kantian, 182, 259, 268, 299,
304–5, 311, 324, 327, 329; virtue, 183,
236, 240, 245. *See also* Morality
Ethics: Inventing Right and Wrong (Mackie),
236, 239 n. 9
Ethics and Language (Stevenson), 239 n. 9
Eudaimonism, 276, 288
Euthyphro (Plato), 327 n. 69
Euthyphro problem, 327 n. 69
Existentialism, 180–81, 195, 197–200, 213
Experience, 212, 241, 244, 249, 272, 339, 340
n. 29, 341–42, 351
Expertise, 243–55
Explanation, 51–54, 57, 99, 218–23, 226,
230–32, 235, 239; evolutionary, 85, 87 n.
38, 88, 93; inference to the best, 79–80,
90; moral, 79–83, 87–88, 91, 93–97, 100–
101; naturalistic, 87–88, 91–92; psycho-
analytic, 85, 87 n. 38
Expressivism, 1–2, 6, 8–11, 25, 27, 29–31,
38–41, 59 n. 11. *See also* Antirealist-
expressivism; Realist-expressivism
Externalism, 3, 14, 218–19, 222–23, 234

Feelings, 282–85
Fichte, Johann, 146–47, 149, 153
Field, Hartry, 4 n. 7
Fine, Arthur, 80 n. 7
Flourishing, human, 266, 274
Fodor, Jerry, 94–95, 98 n. 66, 100
Forms, 237–43, 248–49, 310–11 n. 23
Foucault, Michel, 215
Fraassen, Bas van, 80 n. 7
Free will, 286
Freedom, 130, 146, 148–53 passim, 198, 200, 209, 298–99, 317, 319, 322, 326
Frege, Gotlob, 14–17, 19, 21, 35
Freud, Sigmund, 83–85
Friendship, 289

Gauthier, David, 227
Gert, Bernard, 296
Gibbard, Allan, 6, 8–9, 11, 27, 29–30, 41–42, 85–86, 91 n. 46, 202 n. 14
Good, the, 190, 195, 197, 199, 225, 228–29, 262, 289, 330; and desires, 134, 335–36, 340, 351–52; and happiness, 277, 333, 337, 341–48, 352, 354–55, 357, 359; and value, 339, 353, 358
Goods, 261–62, 264, 269, 281
Government, 95 n. 56, 314, 319
Green, T. H., 334 n. 14
Gregor, Mary, 257
Grice, Paul, 18–20, 22, 24, 35
Griffin, James, 227
Groundwork of the Metaphysics of Morals (Kant), 152, 183, 257, 295, 303, 305, 311, 313

Habituation, 289–92, 295, 297–99
Hamilton, W. D., 87
Happiness, 259, 262, 265, 269, 270–78, 282, 286–88; and desire, 271, 276, 330, 332–38, 339 n. 26, 340–42, 345–46, 348–49, 353, 355; and the good, 277, 333, 337, 341–48, 352, 354–55, 357, 359; and value, 337, 342, 344–47, 349–53, 355–60; and virtue, 266, 268, 273–74, 277, 281
Hare, R. M., 8, 13–14, 29, 38, 39–40, 227
Harman, Gilbert, 79, 83
Harsanyi, John, 227
Hart, H. L. A., 179, 209
Haskell, Thomas, 97 n. 65
Hedonism, 337
Hegel, G. W. F., 148 n. 46, 149
Heidegger, Martin, 179–80, 197–98
Hempel, Carl, 96
Hobbes, Thomas, 178, 182, 314, 319 n. 58
Honesty, 95–96
Horgan, Terence, 164–67, 170, 175
Human nature, 83, 107, 179–80, 182–85, 188–89, 198, 212, 216, 258–59, 266–68, 270, 273, 276, 286, 288, 290–91, 317 n. 55

Hume, David, 68, 126, 173, 177, 179, 183–86, 189, 212, 250 n. 30, 341
Hypothetical Imperative, 309, 318
Hypothetical observer, 184–86, 187 n. 4, 213

Impartial spectator, 187, 189
Impartiality, 185–87, 212–13
Imperatives, 137–38, 263, 265. *See also* Categorical Imperative; Hypothetical Imperative
Inclinations, 106, 116–18, 122–23, 270–71, 281–82, 286
Injustice, 96–100
Institutions, 204, 206–7, 321
Integrity, 266, 279, 289, 298
Intention, 7–8, 10, 12, 26, 29–31, 34, 38, 43, 118, 163, 170–76, 298, 306, 308
Intentional subjects, 103–6, 111–12, 114, 117, 126
Intentionality, 106, 116, 121
Interests, 98–99, 101 n. 81, 185, 254, 270, 311, 312
Internalism, 2–3, 7, 37–38, 42–43, 155 n. 4, 218–19, 221 n. 6, 222–26, 230–35, 253; and judgment, 2 n. 2; two-tier, 225–26
International Encyclopedia of Unified Science, The, 191
Intuitionism, 156, 161 n. 12, 164, 178, 195–96, 213
Intuitions, 192, 207–8, 237–38, 241, 243, 248, 310, 311 n. 23, 323 n. 63; case specific moral, 44–47, 52–63
Irrationality, 200–201, 308 n. 17
Irwin, Terence, 270
Is/ought distinction, 42, 190, 341

Jackson, Frank, 25
Jefferson, Thomas, 209 n. 19, 285 n. 55
Judgment, 150, 213, 266, 278–79, 283; internalism, 2 n. 2; and intuition, 45, 47, 48–49; moral, 1, 3, 5–10, 12–14, 21, 24–25, 27–30, 33, 38–39, 40 n. 69, 64–65, 68–78, 83–85, 87, 126, 154 n. 1, 156, 169, 174, 178–79, 181–82, 185, 187–92, 196–97, 199–200, 207, 212, 215–17, 237, 239 n. 9; normative, 86, 91 n. 46; practical, 76–77; value, 179, 190, 322, 338, 341
Justice, 65, 95–96, 98–99, 269, 302, 314 n. 36, 318, 332
Justification, 192, 201–2, 206–8, 210–11, 213–14, 221, 301–2, 321, 329; and belief, 300, 301–2, 340; interpersonal, 173–76; and intuitions, 44, 46, 49–51, 54–56, 62, 178; moral, 179, 194, 314 n. 38, 325; and moral judgment, 70–71, 76; of values, 182

Kant, Immanuel, 149, 151–52, 178, 183, 257–59, 263–77, 281–88, 291–99, 301–23, 325–29, 331, 346–50, 352–54, 356–58, 360
Knowledge, 178, 188, 212, 227, 236, 244, 264, 282, 300, 338; moral, 43, 170, 177, 183, 191, 194–95, 215, 241–43, 245–49, 252–56, 331; objective, 180–81, 189, 214–15; practical, 243, 246–50, 252–55. *See also* Epistemology
Korsgaard, Christine, 151, 232 n. 22, 234, 269 n. 15
Kosovo, 186–87
Kripke, Saul, 159–60
Kuhn, Thomas, 193–94, 216

Laches (Plato), 240, 242
Language, 85 n. 30, 196–97, 204–5, 212, 215, 217; moral, 188, 195, 197, 207–11; ordinary, 194, 198–200, 203 n. 15; philosophy of, 154, 193
Language, Truth, and Logic (Ayer), 239 n. 9
Law, 317 n. 55, 325; moral, 152–53, 267–68, 283, 286–87, 291, 298, 329; rule of, 315, 319 n. 59; universal, 303–4, 306, 309–10
Laws, 312–14, 318
Laws of Freedom (Gregor), 257
Legitimacy, 211
Leibniz, G. W., 275 n. 28
Lewis, C. I., 188
Lewis, David, 227
Liberalism, 64–65
Liberty, 182, 209, 317
Locke, John, 106, 314
Logical positivism, 184, 188, 191, 193, 195, 197–99, 239, 255
Louden, Robert, 259 n. 4, 294 n. 65
Love, 286–87, 289

MacIntyre, Alasdair, 204
Mackie, John, 236, 237 nn. 2 and 3, 238–39, 243, 246, 248–50, 252, 254–55
Magna Moralia (Aristotle), 280
Making a Necessity of Virtue (Sherman), 292 n. 61
Marxism, 193
Maxims, 281–82, 288, 292, 306 n. 11, 308–13
McDowell, John, 90 n. 44, 222
Meaning, 13–17, 27, 39–40, 107–9, 111, 164, 166–67, 169–75; descriptive theory of, 155, 158–59, 161–62; referential account of, 160–62, 165
Meno (Plato), 242 n. 13
Metaethics, 79, 154
Metaphysics, 4–6, 90, 267, 285. *See also* Ontology
Metaphysics of Morals, The (Kant), 257, 294–95, 311, 314, 315 n. 40
Mill, John Stuart, 64–65, 73, 190, 226, 330–50, 352–60

Millgram, Elijah, 337 n. 20
Montaigne, 208
Montesquieu, 203
Moore, G. E., 134, 142, 154–57, 179–80, 183, 195–97, 199, 213, 310–11 n. 23, 323 n. 63, 332, 336, 354, 355 n. 50, 360
Moral blindness, 57
Moral conviction, 30, 32, 42–43, 65, 68, 73, 99
Moral education, 256
Moral epistemology, 81, 102, 126, 177, 236, 238–39, 247–48, 254, 256, 302. *See also* Moral knowledge
Moral facts, 79, 81–83, 85–86, 88–96, 98, 101
Moral goodness, 264–66, 284, 299
Moral knowledge, 43, 170, 177, 183, 191, 194–95, 215, 241–43, 245–49, 331. *See also* Moral epistemology
Moral outlook, 69–78
Moral philosophy, 49, 259, 267, 301, 324
Moral point of view, 172–75
Moral Problem, The (M. Smith), 234 n. 24
Moral purity, 268–70
Moral realism, 1–2, 4, 6–7, 9, 14, 27–28, 37, 39, 41, 43, 51, 68, 79–83, 88–95, 100–101, 154, 156, 163–64, 166–67, 169–71, 174–76, 237 n. 2, 300–302
Moral sense, 48–49, 51, 56–58, 60–61
Moral terms, 100 n. 81, 156, 164, 168–71, 173, 175–76, 179, 194, 197, 211, 217, 255; genealogy of, 102–3, 107, 110, 116–26
Moral theory, 44–45, 47–48, 51–54, 58, 60, 89, 94, 104, 127, 162, 172, 200, 215, 324; Kant's, 301–5, 313, 315 n. 40
Morality, 42, 66 n. 4, 85–86, 153, 173–74, 223–24, 226, 239 n. 9, 249, 252–54, 266, 269, 276, 286–87, 298, 302, 313, 328, 332, 345, 358; and altruism, 86 n. 32; criterion of, 330, 332 n. 4; and naturalism, 28, 41, 85, 87, 91–92, 102, 121; and objectivity, 177–80, 182–84, 186–89, 191, 193–96, 200–207, 210, 212, 214–17; rational, 281, 292; and upbringing, 64–74, 77, 290. *See also* Ethics
Morality, Normativity, and Society (Copp), 28 n. 51
Motivation, 2–3, 6, 8–9, 11–13, 23, 25–26, 29–30, 37–38, 42, 155 n. 4, 201–2, 218–25, 229–35, 239, 250–54, 264–65, 298, 312 n. 30, 334–35, 344; and duty, 268–70, 277; moral, 84, 226, 269, 311
Multiple realizability, 98

Nagel, Thomas, 89–90, 130
NATO, 186–87
Natural-kind terms, 158, 160, 165, 172 n. 28
Natural selection, 86–87
Naturalism, 89–90, 94, 107, 199, 336; Aristotelian, 180–83, 185; Deweyan, 189–94,

Lightning Source UK Ltd.
Milton Keynes UK
UKOW05f0040230514

232124UK00001B/84/P